The Incas

The Peoples of America

General Editors: Alan Kolata and Dean Snow

This series is about the native peoples and civilizations of the Americas, from their origins in ancient times to the present day. Drawing on archaeological, historical, and anthropological evidence, each volume presents a fresh and absorbing account of a group's culture, society, and history.

Accessible and scholarly, and well illustrated with maps and photographs, the volumes of *The Peoples of America* will together provide a comprehensive and vivid picture of the character and variety of the societies of the American past.

Already published:

The Tiwanaku: A Portrait of an Andean Civilization
Alan Kolata

The Timucua
Jerald T. Milanich

The Aztecs, Third Edition
Michael E. Smith

The Cheyenne
John Moore

The Iroquois
Dean Snow

The Moche
Garth Bowden

The Nasca
Helaine Silverman and Donald A. Proulx

The Incas, Second Edition
Terence N. D'Altroy

The Sioux
Guy Gibbon

Mixtecs, Zapotecs and Chations: Ancient Peoples of Southern Mexico
Arthur A. Joyce

The Incas

Second Edition

Terence N. D'Altroy

WILEY Blackwell

This second edition first published 2015
© 2015 Terence N. D'Altroy

Edition History: Blackwell Publishing Ltd (1e, 2002)

Registered Office
John Wiley & Sons Ltd, The Atrium, Southern Gate, Chichester, West Sussex, PO19 8SQ, UK

Editorial Offices
350 Main Street, Malden, MA 02148–5020, USA
9600 Garsington Road, Oxford, OX4 2DQ, UK
The Atrium, Southern Gate, Chichester, West Sussex, PO19 8SQ, UK

For details of our global editorial offices, for customer services, and for information about how to apply for permission to reuse the copyright material in this book please see our website at www.wiley.com/wiley-blackwell.

Library of Congress Cataloging-in-Publication Data
D'Altroy, Terence N.
  The Incas / Terence N. D'Altroy. – Second edition.
     pages cm
  Includes bibliographical references and index.
  ISBN 978-1-4443-3115-8 (pbk.)
1. Incas – History. 2. Incas – Social life and customs. I. Title.
  F3429.D35 2014
  985′.019 – dc23

                                        2013047979

Paperback 9781444331158

A catalogue record for this book is available from the British Library.

Cover image: Photo of Machu Picchu ©Terence N. D'Altroy.
Cover design by Nicki Averill

Set in 10.5/13pt Minion by Laserwords Private Limited, Chennai, India
Printed and bound in Singapore by C.O.S. Printers Pte Ltd

1 2015

*To Mateo, Nicole, and Mariela, with all my love
and thanks for the patience*

Contents

Preface to the Second Edition   ix
Preface to the First Edition   xv

1   Introduction   1

2   The Land and Its People   33

3   The Incas before the Empire   68

4   The History of the Empire: Narrative Visions   91

5   Thinking Inca   119

6   The Politics of Blood in Cuzco   174

7   The Heartland of the Empire   198

8   Inca Ideology: Powers of the Sky and Earth, Past and Present   247

9   Family, Community, and Class   290

10   Militarism   321

11   Provincial Rule   351

12   Farmers, Herders, and Storehouses   392

13   Things and Their Masters   418

14   Invasion and Aftermath   449

References   476

Glossary of Foreign Terms   520

Index   527

Preface to the Second Edition

A second edition – why bother? Anyone who has seen books go through multiple editions has good reason to raise an eyebrow when a new one appears, so the reader may feel that some justification is in order. I can distill out my rationale for writing this book to three major points. The first is that we know far more about the Incas today than we did a dozen years ago when I was finishing the first edition. Both the documentary and archaeological databases that inform our understanding have grown significantly. On the written side, no great new chronicles have appeared, but archival work by historians has brought many important new documents to light. Archaeologists have also been vigorously conducting field studies throughout the entire Inca domain, sometimes at elevations that defy human existence. Work by scholars in the Cuzco heartland has been especially valuable, because it has vastly enriched our discussions of the Incas' rise to local power, and thus the origins of the empire itself. Scores of projects in the provinces are also enlightening us as to how the Incas put their rule into practice and how their subjects reacted in the face of Cuzco's imposed dominion. Overall, hundreds of new studies have been conducted or published in the last decade, more than enough to draw from to update our account of the Inca realm.

A second reason for a revised edition is that researchers today are asking different kinds of questions, and are using new methods to answer them, which is a sign of a vibrant research community. In the process, they often turn a critical eye to ideas that were broadly accepted in the past. They can also draw on theoretical premises that challenge our understanding of the nature of humanity, its self-perception or self-presentation, and the past. Some of the new answers are forcing us to revisit issues about the Incas' own notions about existence, time, causality, and power. They also invite us to rethink the relationships between the information contained in written sources or archaeological remains, or that never took a substantial material form (speech, for example). In the process, Andean research has increasingly become a laboratory for thinking about humanity's past in general.

In thinking about such topics, I have become increasingly convinced that the available documents and material remains do not provide two windows into precisely the same kinds of knowledge. Instead, they are partial complements, affording overlapping insights into different parts of the Inca world. That idea, which will pop up at various places in this book, leads us to ask questions about how the Incas classified things in their world and how they thought those things interacted. To provide one example, we know that the Incas apparently made almost no physical representations of their rulers or their actions that we can recognize today. They created no statues of them, no grand friezes, murals, or portraits, except for some illustrations sequestered in the main temple in Cuzco. Why not? Was there something about rendering things human in a material form that was dangerous, blasphemous, or even impossible? We know that many other pre-modern societies mastered representation of humans and their endeavors, including some Andean predecessors, such as the Moche. So why not the Incas?

Third, my own interests in the Incas have shifted over time. Most importantly, I have become drawn to the intellectual history that paralleled the physical and organizational projects that created the empire. As we will see in the text to follow, prehispanic Andean societies enjoyed a vibrant intellectual life, including the invention of an array of philosophical notions justifying the Incas' right to rule. It is a tremendous challenge to identify and make sense of those ideas, but if we can make some headway, we will be in a better position to understand how the Incas saw the world and what options lay before them during their run of power.

A note is also in order on a few of the sources cited in this edition of the book. Since the first version appeared, several important early texts have appeared in reliable English translation. The most significant are Sarmiento's (2007) chronicle of 1572, which was an official version of Inca history written for Viceroy Toledo to meet crown interests, and the hospice priest Molina's (2011) exposition on Inca religion. Another key document is the treatise of the neo-Inca ruler, Titu Kusi Yupanki (Titu Cusi 2005), presented to the same viceroy in 1570. That document was intended as an Inca counter-chronicle of the Colonial era, written in the hopes of legitimizing Inca rule and thus allowing the kings to retain status and resources as co-equals with the Spanish crown. I have chosen to cite those publications where possible in preference to the best regarded Spanish texts, because this book has been written for an English-speaking audience.

I warn readers away from some other translations, notably the appallingly inexact works of Sir Clements Markham, which are still reprinted or cited today. Readers of von Hagen and de Onis's edited translation of Cieza's work

(Cieza 1959) also need to be aware that the translation, while rendered reliably, conflates two separate books into one running text without systematic acknowledgment of the sources of the passages. For the quotations in the present book in which another translator is not explicitly cited, the translation is mine. Readers may also note that the names of the some of the early Spanish authors have been updated to conform to current understandings of their names. For example, Betanzos is now cited as Diez de Betanzos, Sancho de la Hoz is Sancho, and Polo de Ondegardo is now Polo Ondegardo (see Pillsbury 2008).

It is also worth emphasizing that the other sources cited in this text are largely in English, not because they are the most important available, but because I anticipate that many people reading the book will not be conversant in Spanish and other languages. The writings and insights of Spanish-language authors have been especially valuable to my own understanding, but my goal in the References is primarily to cite works that would be accessible to English-only readers, while giving proper credit to the sources of ideas and information. I have drawn on several times as many works as are listed in the current References in preparing the text, and will cite literature weighted toward the appropriate language in any future translation.

For this edition, I also draw more extensively from the often brilliant studies by modern ethnographers who have been working among both Quechua and Aymara speakers. In the first edition, I resisted using much ethnography for reasons that seem a little less persuasive to me now. One concern was that any discussion of today's Andean peoples treats societies that have been tinged by half a millennium of Christian and Spanish cultural influences, not to mention modern transportation and communication technologies. No matter how deep the traditions, modern peasant communities are in many ways a world apart from their ancestral kin. Recognizing the elements that provide sound insights into prehispanic societies is therefore fraught with all sorts of problems. Not least of those is any researcher's (perhaps unconscious) bias in the choice of the features that can be used as trustworthy analogies for pre-European social order, belief, and practice. It is sometimes easy to decide that an anomalous feature seen in today's communities has to be a post-contact introduction because of an idealized, relatively static notion we often have of life in the past or because of a particular stance we want to defend.

The converse, of course, is assuming that something described in the early Colonial era was not a new introduction. The practices of people forming social groups around an occupation, for example, or bartering or using money, or constantly re-sorting membership in kin groups or the hierarchies among them, or strategically moving about the social landscape and declaring a new history to justify it, are well represented in modern traditional communities. In contrast, they only occasionally figure in discussions of prehistory. A second reason for de-emphasizing studies of societies more than a few decades removed from independent Andean life is the sheer weight of the history and ethnography that has been produced. Its comprehensive inclusion in this work would make it unmanageable for my purposes. That said, so many kinds of insights can be found into prehistory from contemporary peoples that I thought it wise to expand judiciously on my use of ethnography in this edition. My apologies to those for whom this has just made the text a little more unwieldy.

I would like to repeat my thanks to the vast number of people whose hard work and generosity has made this book possible. Among them are many who I recognized in the first edition (see below), and who continued to provide comments, publications, and insight. It is hard to single out particular scholars whose work has made a major difference in my own thinking, but Gary Urton's and Frank Salomon's studies of the *khipu* knot-records have been a revelation; their work, of course, has been complemented by that of many other scholars. Similarly, the surveys and extensive publications by Brian Bauer, Alan Covey, Steven Kosiba, and others have rewritten the history of the heartland. The work of Peruvian scholars specializing in the archaeology of the Cuzco region has been vital to my understanding; among them are Arminda Gibaja, the late Alfredo Valencia Zegarra, and Ernesto García Calderón.

Other colleagues who helped me with friendship, guidance, and access to unpublished information include Carlo Socuayala Dávila, Joanne Pillsbury, and Gordon McEwan. Kenneth Wright provided access to his work on Inca hydraulic engineering; he also provided a walk-through of the waterworks at Saqsawaman. Chris Small and Yuri Gorokovich provided insights into the physical landscape during a shared trip through the heartland. Gary Urton, Darryl Wilkinson, Kevin Lane, Steven Kosiba, Kathryn Burns, and several anonymous reviewers have read sections of the text, offering advice that has improved it. Rodolfo Cerrón-Palomino graciously clarified a range of issues on Andean languages. Brian Bauer, Alejandro Beltrán-Caballero, David Beresford-Jones, Larry Coben, Kevin Floerke, Chad Gifford, Donato Amado Gonzales, Paul Heggarty, Vincent Lee, Ricardo Mar, John Reinhard, Vicente Revilla, Stuart and Sandy Schueler, Alexei Vranich, Darryl Wilkinson, the American Museum of

Natural History, and Dumbarton Oaks Research Library and Collection have made graphics available, which I much appreciate. I would also like to express a heartfelt word of gratitude to the delightful people who brought us electronic journals on line. My life has been much easier for it and this work much better informed as a result.

A special thanks goes to the people at Wiley-Blackwell, who solicited this edition of the book and then patiently encouraged me during its glacial emergence: Rosalie Robertson, Julia Kirk, Mark Graney, and Ben Thatcher. Most particularly, I would like to thank Annie Jackson for her close attention to detail, professionalism, and good cheer during the compacted copy-editing process. As always, the contributors are many, and the errors are mine (as much as I might wish it otherwise).

Preface to the First Edition

The Inca empire, called *Tawantinsuyu* ("The Four Parts Together"), was the grandest civilization ever created in the Andes and perhaps in the entire prehispanic Americas. Spanning over 4,000 km of western South America and encompassing more than ten million inhabitants, Tawantinsuyu was a century-long latecomer to Andean civilization, built on more than three millennia of complex societies. It was a land in which the lines were blurred between the past and the present, and between the quick and the dead, where living and mummified rulers vied for authority with one another and with the deities of the landscape and the cosmos. Inca power, as with so many of their predecessors, arose from a blend of genealogy, myth, mutual obligation, and coercion, all legitimized by a cultural vision that was constantly being reinvented, even after the empire had collapsed.

For all practical purposes, resistance by subject groups within the known world had been quashed, yet this most powerful of Andean societies fell to a relatively small brigade of Spanish invaders in 1532–3. How could that have happened? The Europeans certainly had some technological advantages in horses and armaments, but those alone were insufficient to account for the empire's demise. Instead, we need to look for Tawantinsuyu's fragility in its internal makeup, its political history, and the rifts that existed among its royalty and extraordinarily diverse peoples. This book is an exploration of that society, its history, strengths, and divisions, drawn from both historical and archaeological sources compiled over hundreds of years by eyewitnesses, travelers, and scholars.

I was drawn into research on the Incas almost against my will. Having spent a number of years doing archaeology on simpler societies in the United States, Mexico, and Peru, I was not ready to take up study of such a vast empire, especially one that hundreds of scholars had already been studying for well over a century. Even more daunting was the fact that overviews of the Incas and interpretation of particular archaeological remains were based on a large corpus of historical documents, many of them written in sixteenth-century Spanish peppered with Quechua, the native language of the Incas. I was well versed in anthropological archaeology, but not documentary analysis. When I set out to do fieldwork for my doctoral dissertation, I had intended to study the societies of central Peru in the epoch just before the advent of Inca rule, but my doctoral adviser gently pushed me forward in time, largely because we didn't understand the late pre-Inca chronology very well.

My background meant that I came into the field with a different perspective than that which prevailed in Inca studies, but it also meant that I had an enormous amount of catching up to do and came to rely on the goodwill and support of scores of friends and colleagues. I therefore owe an enormous debt of gratitude to the people who assisted by providing information, reading drafts, and preparing illustrations. Although it would be convenient to blame them for the mistakes that are found here, they probably would not let me get away with it. Brian Bauer has been a great help in a variety of ways. He read the entire manuscript and provided a number of the photos and other illustrations found here. His trenchant comments helped me recognize both the wheat and the chaff and persuaded me to remove most of the latter. Elena Phipps, Luis Jaime Castillo, and Tim Earle read sections of the book and convinced me to set aside as many of the professional debates as I could bear to part with. Special mention must go to the late John Hyslop, who was the first scholar to produce comprehensive archaeological overviews of Inca settlements and the road system, based on fieldwork throughout the empire. John first drew my attention to the southern part of the empire and generously shared his information and ideas with me, as he did with all of his colleagues. Similarly, Craig Morris has been more than gracious in sharing ideas and information, and access to the resources of the American Museum of Natural History. My discussions with Ana María Lorandi pointed me in directions with the historical literature and Andean societies that I would never have considered otherwise. Ramiro Matos and Jeff Parsons also deserve particular thanks for having introduced me to the archaeology of the Andes and for having shared their unpublished data on central Peru.

Many people generously provided information, unpublished manuscripts, references, and publications. Among them are Félix Acuto, Juan Albarracín-Jordan, Sonia Alconini, Roberto Bárcena, Monica Barnes, Brian Bauer, Robert Bradley, M. Constanza Ceruti, Ricardo Céspedes Paz, Antonio Coello, Miguel Cornejo, Beatriz Cremonte, Pío Pablo Díaz, Ian Farrington, Antonio Fresco, Alberto Rex González, Pedro Guibovich, Andrés Gyarmati, Frances Hayashida, Lee Hollowell, Flor de María Huaycochea, Jaime Idrovo,

Catherine Julien, Ann Kendall, Miguel León, Ana María Lorandi, Albert Meyers, Eleanora Mulvany de Peñaloza, Patricia Netherly, Axel Nielsen, Susan Ramírez, Glenn Russell, Dan Sandweiss, Juan Schobinger, Katharina Schreiber, Izumi Shimada, Chip Stanish, Rubén Stehberg, Steve Tomka, Debbie Truhan, and Verónica Williams. Christine Flaherty and Sumru Aricanli both assisted with the illustrations, Christine by preparing many of the maps and Sumru by facilitating access to the wonderful collection of images at the American Museum of Natural History. Scott Kremkau helped with a close reading of the text for citations. Thanks also go to the various sources of funding that have supported my research in the upper Mantaro valley, Peru, and the Calchaquí valley, Argentina, where I have studied the effects of Inca rule on provincial societies for more than twenty years. Those sources include the National Science Foundation, Columbia University, UCLA, the UCLA Friends of Archaeology, and the H. John Heinz III Charitable Trust. I would also like to extend a special thanks to Ken Provencher of Blackwell, who showed enormous patience and support in seeing this manuscript through a prolonged period of writing and editing. In addition, I am most grateful to Margaret Aherne, who paid close editorial attention to the text and lent wise counsel in bringing the book to its final form.

Finally, I owe a special debt to my family, first to my parents for exciting my initial interest in archaeology through trips to the Egyptian wing of the Metropolitan Museum of Art in New York. And most of all to my wife and daughter, who put up with me patiently while I finished this book.

Chapter One

Introduction

On Friday, November 15, 1532, Francisco Pizarro brazenly led a force of 168 frightened Spaniards into the maw of the most powerful empire ever seen in the Americas. Late that afternoon, the brigade entered the plaza at Cajamarca, an imperial Inca center in the Peruvian highlands. They had every reason to be dismayed by the sight that lay before them, since the Inca prince Atawallpa was savoring his recent victory in a dynastic war in the midst of an 80,000-man army camped just outside town. Because he was completing a fast at the hot springs of Kónoj, Atawallpa declined an invitation to disrupt his solemn duties. He would not meet his unwanted guests in the city that afternoon, but agreed to receive them after a night's rest. Astonishingly, he was Pizarro's prisoner by the next evening, captured during a surprise strike that was underpinned by equal parts of bravado, armaments, and faith.

Over the next eight months, the Spaniards extracted a ransom fit for an earthly deity in exchange for a promise of Atawallpa's freedom. An enormous amount of treasure was melted down from the empire's architectural dressings, personal jewelry, idols, and service ware hauled off from temples, aristocratic households, and perhaps even graves. By today's standards, the value would have been an astonishing US$335 million in gold and US$11 million in silver.[1] Once the ransom had been paid, Pizarro ordered Atawallpa to be tried and then executed on July 26, 1533, overriding the grave misgivings voiced by some members of his party. The power that the Inca had wielded over his vast domain even while captive had apparently convinced the Spaniard that decapitating the state was his best hope of staying alive and asserting his own control. In light of the divisions that had already riven the empire, his decision touched off the collapse of Tawantinsuyu, or "The Four Parts Together," as the Incas called their realm.

Fittingly, the Incas already had a word for such a cataclysmic change. They called it a *pachakuti*, a "turning over/around of time/space" – a moment

The Incas, Second Edition. Terence N. D'Altroy.
© 2015 John Wiley & Sons, Ltd. Published 2015 by John Wiley & Sons, Ltd.

when history ended and then began again. In their eyes, it was not the first time that the world had been destroyed, nor might it be the last. The mestizo chronicler Guaman Poma (1980) explained that all of creation had been wiped out four times in the ancient past, each time after a cycle of a thousand years (Urton 1999: 41). The first age was a time of darkness when the world was inhabited by a race of wild men. In each successive epoch, humans progressed, as they learned to farm, to make crafts, and to organize themselves for war and peace. The fifth "sun" was the age of the Incas. In their self-promoted vision, it was a glorious era during which they brought civilization and enlightened rule to a chaotic world. And under the circumstances, it was only right that the man who had created the empire took *Pachakuti* as his title. After all, he was the son of the Sun, a living divinity who remade the world.

Less than a century after Pachakuti died and ascended to join his celestial father, Atawallpa's forces closed the war with his half-brother Waskhar. According to one native account, his generals declared that it was time for another *pachakuti* (Callapiña *et al.* 1974). To help move the process along, they massacred Waskhar's extensive family and several other royal kin groups who had cast their lot with him. They also killed all the historians they could find and destroyed the knot-records called *khipu* (see chapter 5) on which history was recorded, so that the era could begin unburdened by its past. But before he could properly launch the new epoch, Atawallpa fell into Spanish hands and a century of rule by gods on earth came to an end.

The Spanish encounter with the Incas, despite its impact, was not a complete surprise to either people. In 1519, Hernán Cortés had overthrown the Aztec empire of central Mexico through a similar attack on the ruler with the aid of allies made in the new land. The descriptions of Mexico's cities and riches that made their way back to Spain fired enthusiasm for more adventures in the Indies. Many of the men who accompanied Pizarro to the Andes had already seen action in Central America and the Caribbean, while others had just come over to seek their fortunes. Pizarro himself had been in the Americas for thirty years and was hungry to make his mark in an uncharted land called *Pirú*. In the 1520s, a few Spaniards or Portuguese had actually penetrated the Inca domain, but left no significant impression on the Andes or reported back to the Europeans. A tangible glimmer of what the Spaniards were to find reached them in 1527, when an expedition captured a boat off Ecuador filled with cloth, metal ornaments, and other riches. Even so, they were not prepared for the grandeur of Peru.

In 1532, Tawantinsuyu was the largest polity the native Americas had ever seen (figure 1.1). Its ruler was a hereditary king who the Incas claimed had descended in an unbroken string from a creation separate from the rest of humanity. Though a powerful monarch, the *Sapa Inca* ("Unique Lord") did not rule alone. He was counseled by mummies of his immortal ancestors and their other descendants, who all joined him in Cuzco's most solemn ceremonies and drunken revelry. Totally unpersuaded by the Incas' assertions of divinity and appalled at their heresies, the Spaniards were

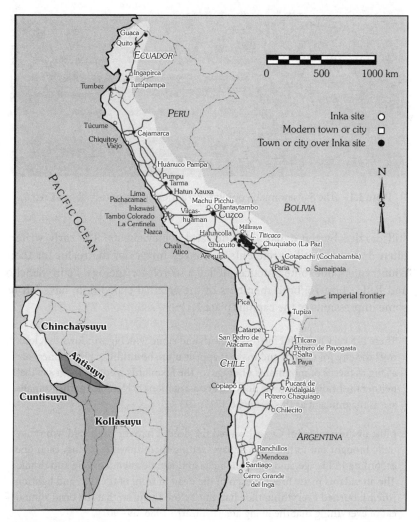

Figure 1.1   The Inca road and provincial installation (*tampu*) system, after Hyslop (1984): frontispiece; the four parts of the Inca realm are shown in the inset map.   •

Plate 1.1 The Saqsawaman complex, on a rocky promontory above Cuzco.

still dazzled by the dynasty's riches and achievements. The early writers often drew on familiar referents to convey images of the realm for their countrymen, but some practices defied a search for analogy. Pedro Sancho and Pedro Pizarro, both members of the original expedition, have left us some impressions of the capital (plate 1.1):

> There is a very beautiful fortress of earth and stone with big windows that look over the city [of Cuzco] and make it appear more beautiful … [The stones] are as big as pieces of mountains or crags … The Spaniards who see them say that neither the bridge of Segovia nor other constructions of Hercules or the Romans are as magnificent as this. (Sancho 1917: 193–4)

> Most of the people [of Cuzco] served the dead, I have heard it said, who they daily brought out to the main square, setting them down in a ring, each one according to his age, and there the male and female attendants ate and drank. The attendants made fires for each of the dead in front of them … and lighting [them], burned everything they had put before them, so that the dead should eat of everything that the living ate. (P. Pizarro 1986: 89–90)

Everywhere they traveled, the invaders saw the imperial imprint, whether it was in Cuzco's spare but grand architecture, the roads that traversed 40,000 km of rugged terrain, thousands of provincial installations, stocks of every supply imaginable, works of artistry in precious metal, stone, and cloth, or the government designed to manage the whole affair. About twenty years after the conquest, the soldier Pedro Cieza de León (1967: 213–14; translation from Hyslop 1984: 343) expressed his admiration for the empire's order:

> In human memory, I believe that there is no account of a road as great as this, running through deep valleys, high mountains, banks of snow, torrents of water, living rock, and wild rivers … In all places it was clean and swept free of refuse, with lodgings, storehouses, Sun temples, and posts along the route. Oh! Can anything similar be claimed for Alexander or any of the powerful kings who ruled the world?

The Incas' feats seemed all the more fabulous when the conquistadores heard that the realm was only about four generations old. As the Incas explained it, the empire was launched when Pachakuti usurped the throne from his father Wiraqocha Inka and began to annex the peoples around Cuzco. His successes and organizational genius were followed only by those of his son Thupa Inka Yupanki and grandson Wayna Qhapaq, and then by the final dynastic war (table 1.1).

For their part, the Incas were taken aback by the Spanish invasion, although they would later recount legends that had predicted the return of white, bearded strangers from the sea. Even so, their initial response was less one of awe than of anger and disbelief at the invaders' arrogance. Who were these men who dared to kill the Sapa Inca's subjects and seize the holy women for their carnal pleasures? Rather than wipe them out directly as they so richly deserved, the Incas let their curiosity get the better of them and allowed the interlopers to ascend the Andes to be examined first-hand. To Atawallpa's fatal regret, the Spanish incursion could not have been more propitiously timed. The prince, contemplating his recent victory and anticipating reunification of the empire, seemingly had nothing to fear from a small band of foreigners, as outrageous as their conduct may have been. He couldn't have been more wrong.

My goal in this book is to describe the Incas, their emergence as rulers of an empire, and the nature of their domain. That sounds straightforward

Table 1.1 The conventional Inca king list.

	Name as ruler	Gloss	Given name
1	Manqo Qhapaq	Powerful [Ancestor]	–
2	Zinchi Roq'a	Warlord Roq'a	–
3	Lloq'e Yupanki	Honored Left-handed	–
4	Mayta Qhapaq	Royal Mayta	–
5	Qhapaq Yupanki	Powerful Honored	–
6	Inka Roq'a	Inka Roq'a	–
7	Yawar Waqaq	He Who Cries Bloody Tears	Inka Yupanki, Mayta Yupanki
8	Wiraqocha Inka	Creator God Inca	Hatun Thupa Inka
9	Pachakuti Inka Yupanki	Cataclysm Honored Inca	Inka Yupanki, Kusi Yupanki
10	Thupa Inka Yupanki	Royal Honored Inca	–
11	Wayna Qhapaq	Powerful Youth	Titu Kusi Wallpa
12	Waskhar Inka	Golden Chain Ruler	Thupa Kusi Wallpa
13	Atawallpa	–	–

enough, but the Incas have proved to be remarkably malleable in the hands of historians and archaeologists. Let a social theorist or two get involved and things become even more baffling. Depending on the author, Tawantinsuyu has been held up as an exemplar of almost every form of political society except representative democracy. The Inca Garcilaso de la Vega (1966), son of an Inca princess, immortalized Tawantinsuyu in 1609 as a supremely well-run, homogeneous monarchy ruled by an omnipotent and benevolent king. Although he was writing to exalt the glories of his ancestors to a Spanish audience, Garcilaso's vision is still popular today. His efforts aside, other commentators have seen the realm in radically different lights – as a type of primitive communism, a feudal society, a despotic Asiatic state, and a territorial empire. Some modern scholars even doubt that an empire existed and instead see a patchwork of ethnic groups that were never truly unified.

How could one polity inspire such contradictory views? Part of the answer lies in the fact that no one who grew up in an independent Tawantinsuyu ever wrote about it.[2] Although they had the tools to record information precisely, the Incas had no writing system that we have been able to recognize and decipher. Instead, history was kept as oral tradition, supplemented by mnemonic registers. In Cuzco, poet-historians called *amauta*[3] and knot-record masters called *khipu kamayuq* (figure 1.2) recited sagas of the royal past at the bidding of the court. The *khipu* themselves seem to have encoded information about the past in ways that had as much to do with cultural visions of hierarchy, power, and space as with sequences of events. Aristocrats also memorized epic poems, some of which they recited to the Spaniards. Not surprisingly, the descendants of different rulers called up versions of the past that favored their own ancestors, while public recitations by the *amauta* were tailored to please the audience (Rostworowski 1999: vii–ix). Cieza (1967: 32) explained things this way:

> and if among the kings one turned out indolent, a coward, given to vices and a homebody without enlarging the domain of his empire, it was ordered that of such [kings] there be little remembrance or almost none at all; and they attended to this so closely that if one [king] was found [in the histories] it was so as not to forget his name and the succession; but in the rest they remained silent, without singing the songs [as they did] of the others who were good and valiant.

Early Spanish writers thus had to choose among a variety of stories in composing their chronicles. Many resolved the problem by favoring information provided by their oldest and most aristocratic witnesses and by dismissing reports by common Indians. Those circumstances mean that the documentary history of the Incas has been filtered through competing native views, translators, scribes, conflicting mores, and differing notions of the nature of the past. Conversion of Andean narratives into a European-style history is therefore an uncertain task; similar obstacles face us when we try to understand Andean social order, economics, or world views. Fortunately, archaeological research into the Incas has been active in recent years, along with art historical studies, so that the material residues of Tawantinsuyu and documentary accounts written down after its demise can be viewed as complementary sources of information in ways that were thought impossible a short time back. Even so, we still have less direct information to work with than do scholars who have studied many of the great empires of the Old World. In this introduction, then, I would like to sketch out how we can come to an understanding of the Incas, beginning by outlining how scholars have thought about empires and then by describing the information that we have for the Incas themselves.

CŌTADOR·MAIOR·ÍTEZORERO
ÏAVANTÏNSVÍOOVÍPOC
CVRACA·CON DOR·CHAVA

Figure 1.2 *Khipu kamayuq* with his *khipu, yupana* (counting tray, see pp. 160–1) in lower left corner; Guaman Poma's (1936) chronicle.

Investigating Empires[4]

Empires like Tawantinsuyu were the largest and most heterogeneous of the pre-modern societies, which makes studying them confoundedly difficult. By the term empire, I am referring to an extensive polity – often containing millions of subjects and covering hundreds of thousands of square kilometers – in which a core polity gains control over a range of other societies. The dominion may be political, military, or economic, and it may be remote or immediate, but the essence of an empire is that the core society is able to assert its will over the other peoples brought under its aegis. In the pre-industrial world, only a relative handful of such polities can be named. In the Old World, the Qin and Han Chinese and their successors, Middle and New Kingdom Egypt, the Macedonians maybe, the Assyrians, Neo-Assyrians, Romans, Parthians, Sassanians, Persians, Mongols, Mughals, Mauryas, and Vijayanagara, among others, can fairly be considered to have been empires. In the Americas, the Aztecs, Tarascans, Incas, and Wari qualify, although scholars occasionally dispute the status of each of them. The scale and diversity of those polities make their analysis an enormous challenge. Anyone studying the Romans, for example, might have to consider evidence drawn from more than forty modern countries, written in dozens of archaic, medieval, and modern languages. Even the Inca empire took in lands that now fall within six countries, whose native inhabitants spoke scores of languages.

Scholars have devised several ways to reduce this kind of research to manageable concepts that foster informed comparison (Sinopoli 1994; Alcock *et al.* 2001). Over the last few decades, the most widely used approach in anthropology and history divides empires into their *core* and *periphery*. The core is envisioned as the political, economic, and cultural heartland of the empire, while the periphery consists of the societies that are ruled and exploited by the core. Frequently, the relationship between the core and the periphery has been seen in terms of both power and space. The societies of a centrally located core were visualized as having been more complex politically and economically and more sophisticated culturally than the often barbaric peripheral societies. As the power of one core waned, it would be replaced by another center, often at the margins of the previous heartland. This view owed much to the nature and histories of the Roman and Chinese empires, in which heartland areas were periodically beset by troublesome borderlands peoples (e.g., Lattimore 1988).

As historians became more discerning in their analysis of empires as complex systems, they focused less on the layout of empires and more on the relations of inequality between the heartland and surrounding areas. Immanuel Wallerstein's (1974) world-systems model has been widely applied to early empires, even though the scholars who use his concepts often think that he downplayed the complexities of pre-modern empires. Wallerstein observed that macro-regions are often organized by economic relations that exceed political boundaries. Labor organization, resource extraction, accrual of wealth, and market relations, for example, result from relationships that integrate vast areas and, frequently, many politically independent states and even continents. Archaeologists have adapted this general idea to study relations between the heartlands of ancient states and neighboring regions (e.g., Chase-Dunn and Hall 1991; Algaze 2005).

An alternative conception focuses on strategies of imperial rule according to their intensity and mix of different kinds of power. The sociologist Michael Mann has proposed an influential model, in which he views an empire as being constituted by "multiple overlapping and intersecting sociospatial networks" of military, economic, political, and ideological power (Mann 1986: 1). Alternatively, strategies of rule have been portrayed as lying along a continuum from low to high intensity (Luttwak 1976; Hassig 1985: 100–1; D'Altroy 1992: 18–24). At the low end of the continuum is a *hegemonic* strategy, which produces a fairly loose, indirect kind of imperial rule. A hegemonic polity is built by a core state society that comes to dominate a series of client polities through diplomacy or conquest. An overriding goal of a hegemonic approach is to keep the costs of rule low. The downside is that a low investment in administration and physical facilities is offset by a relatively low extraction of resources and by limited control over subject peoples. The Aztecs provide a classic case of this kind of empire (Hassig 1985; Smith 2012).

At the other end of the continuum is a *territorial* strategy, which is an intense, direct kind of rule. That approach to governance is costly, since it requires a heavy investment in administration, security against external threats, and the physical infrastructure of imperial rule, such as roads, provincial centers, and frontier defense. The costs may be necessary to ensure the empire's continued existence, however, or to satisfy the demands of the upper classes. Rome of the first century AD and the Han Chinese provide good examples of territorial empires. Those two poles grade into each other, of course, and may be applied selectively in different regions or at different times as the situation warrants. Numerous factors may contribute to a particular choice of strategy: the organizations of the central polity and its various subject societies, historical relations between the central society and subjects, political negotiation, the distribution of resources, transport technology, and the goals of the imperial leadership.

A widely cited political science approach, described initially by Doyle (1986), organizes theories of empire into three categories, based on where the stimulus for development arose and on the motivations driving the core polity. The first of those categories, called *metrocentric* theories, argues that the central polities were driven by their own economic, military, or political interests in self-aggrandizement. As applied to pre-modern empires, the Romans of the Republican era (Harris 1979) and the Aztecs of central Mexico would stand out. In *pericentric* theories, the expansion of the core polity is catalyzed by the difficulties of maintaining stable relationships with surrounding societies. From this perspective, imperial expansion can be seen as a defensive effort to protect the core. The Roman annexation of Greece through transformation of client polities into provinces can be cited as an example here. The last kind of model, the *systemic*, tends to be focused on more modern cases. It suggests that great powers engage in imperial ventures in an effort to dominate and contain their rivals. Interventions by European powers through their colonialist ventures during the nineteenth and twentieth centuries are often seen in this light.

Recent network modeling builds more formally and quantitatively on some of the same ideas that fueled Mann's (1986) sociological approach. Network theorists argue that imperial relationships may be arrayed generally along economic, political, social, military, or ideological lines, or may be structured more narrowly around technologies like transport and communication (e.g., Smith 2005; Glatz 2009; Brughmans 2013). The approach emphasizes that such relationships were never static. They changed constantly, targeting links between key people or places, and leaping over intermediary spaces or societies, as conditions demanded. In this light, treating polities as neatly bounded territories misleads us as to how they actually worked. Even in the most intensively occupied lands, the hand of rule could be applied unevenly. The flows of ideas, people, and materials moved in both directions, from the central powers to subjects and back.

If we take the Inca case, the location of any place looks different in relation to Cuzco if we analyze relationships along the system of roads and provincial facilities or as spaces falling within geographic expanses (Jenkins 2001). Similarly, lines of communication (e.g., for military needs) may have been built on differing networks than lines along which valuable commodities flowed or foodstuffs were supplied locally. Moreover, the hundreds of radial arrays of sacred places on the landscape that lay at the heart of Andean societies' self-images may have had essentially nothing to do with imperial political networks or the movement of commodities. John Hyslop (1984) made this point explicit some time ago in his book on the Inca road system, when he argued that Inca rule really consisted of a series of overlapping networks, rather than a single integrated system. Where the new analyses often prove most valuable is in their quantitative and graphical formalities of spatial data. Approaches applied through geographic information systems (GIS), for example, can provide startling insights into how affairs ranging from daily practice to imperial strategy played out (Kosiba and Bauer 2012).

A final influential set of ideas about how to think about empires has arisen from post-colonial theory, which appeared as a kind of intellectual resistance to the Western domination of much of the world (e.g., Said 1978). The literature on this subject is too vast to do justice here, but a couple of guiding ideas can be highlighted. One is that people or social groups in positions of power often get to decide what constitutes knowledge and how it can be legitimated (Estermann 2009). Since elites determine what history is told publicly (Dietler 2005), they often cast it in a way that makes themselves the inevitable – and desirable – outcome of natural progress. Spencer (1974), Tylor (1958), and other nineteenth-century British social philosophers, for example, saw their nation's supremacy as a natural consequence of the progress of history. Britain's role as an imperial power was therefore entirely justified.

From the vantage point of the post-colonial critique, the study of the past and of non-Western societies by Western intellectuals may itself be part of the process of political domination. So the present book could be treated as part of an intellectual imperialism. It seeks to impose a particular analytical perspective on the world, one that prefers comparative study to explanation that makes sense exclusively within a particular society.[5] By analogy, archaeology as a professional discipline can be cast historically as a Euro-American project that helped to pillage the world's patrimony in the name of saving it. In this light, justifications for modern archaeological practice are little better than the sense of rectitude that the Spaniards brought to bear in overthrowing Inca claims to legitimate rule.

A second important idea that underpins post-colonial thought is that colonial or imperial leaders often apply derogatory concepts of "the other" to their subjects or peoples beyond their reach.[6] Societies outside the core can be safely dismissed as inferior in their intellectual capacities and accomplishments. As a logical consequence, those peoples would surely benefit from being civilized by more advanced societies. That kind of thinking underpinned the Christian imperative in the conquest of the Americas, for example, and Kipling's notion of "the white man's burden." Sweeping terms like Latin America, the Oriental, and the Third World are examples of western colonialist categories that post-colonial theory attempts to counter. The simplifications and caricatures inherent in colonial rule, it is argued, have been used to justify vast damage and exploitation in the name of superior humanity. As we will see, the Incas were no strangers to such ideas. They readily dismissed people outside the empire as barbarians, while the societies of the north coast were dog-eaters and sexual deviants, and the Uru people of the Lake Titicaca area were worthless vagrants.

As useful as they are, all of the broad approaches described here have some weaknesses. One common concern is that the conceptual division of an empire into a complex, cosmopolitan core and a less developed periphery is simply wrong on empirical grounds in several cases. Some imperial societies dominated peoples who surpassed them in urbanization, urbanity, population, social hierarchy, and economic specialization. The Incas are among the most prominent of the counter-examples, which also include the Mongols, Mughals, and Macedonians. A second concern is an unwarranted overemphasis on the power of the core society. Historical records indicate that many empires rose to power through coercive means – often conquest coupled with diplomacy that was backed by not so latent force. Even so, relations between imperial elites and peripheral societies were far more negotiated and dynamic than often thought not too long ago. To take just one counter-intuitive example, Barfield (2001) points out that, rather than extracting resources, Chinese rulers at times paid tribute to the steppe nomads to keep them at bay. They didn't call it that, of course, but the flow of wealth was often from the empire to the exterior.

Another concern is that general models often heavily focus our attention on the imperial elite or on interactions between them and subject elites. As research in provincial regions has advanced, especially within local communities, it has become increasingly clear that many important activities in ancient empires occurred without the intervention, interest, or awareness of the central authorities. Historians have long recognized that the grandiose claims of ancient emperors were often exaggerated. Imperial histories, whether inscribed on monumental architecture or written in texts, often attributed all decisions and power to the ruler. In part, that was a literary convention or imperial propaganda, but modern authors still commonly describe the functioning of empires in terms of individual rulers. I feel that this perspective attributes too much power to individual leaders, who were often at odds with factions made up of their closest associates, and emphasizes a top-down vision that misleads us about household and community life. Moreover, as Luttwak (1976) points out for the Romans, the tactical and strategic actions of the leadership were frequently at odds when analyzed over the long haul. The decisions of individual rulers could be designed to work for short-term political or tactical ends, while the long-term strategic development of the imperial system could smooth out the occasionally disastrous eccentricities of particular rulers.

Those concerns lead me to the approach taken in this book. My view is that an adequate analysis of an early empire must take into account the perceptions, actions, and interests of the dominant society and those of the highly varied subject peoples, if we wish to make sense of life at the grand and small scale. The overarching goal is to meld information drawn from historical, ethnographic, and archaeological sources, with an occasional dash of art history and linguistics. This approach differs from most other books on the Incas, which often rely on early documents, because they provide many details about history, social life, and rationales for behavior that are not available through archaeological sources (Rowe 1946; Davies 1995; Rostworowski 1999). When archaeology is brought into play, authors often use it to illustrate the elegance of architecture or objects or to describe the road system or provincial administrative settlements. The early written record, however, is heavily weighted toward the life and times of the royalty and other elites, especially in and around Cuzco. More troublesome is that vast areas of the empire, especially in the south, are largely blanks in the written record (D'Altroy *et al.* 2007). Conversely, until recently, treatments of Inca archaeology have generally been descriptive and draw on documents to explain sites' functions or place in the empire's historical development. Some works, especially John Hyslop's (1984, 1990) exceptional studies of the Inca roads and settlement planning, consciously weave the two lines of evidence together. Even so, history and archaeology are seldom systematically integrated. Because they provide different information and sometimes lead us to incompatible conclusions, I will try to highlight where variations arise and how we might resolve the conflicts.

Studying the Incas

Readers familiar with non-Western societies will not be surprised that the organization of this book does not correspond well to the ways that the Incas thought about their world. Andean peoples did not order things and relationships according to the same categories that we use to structure Western accounts – politics, economics, religion, and the grand chronological sweep of events, for example. In Tawantinsuyu, history served power, and the past was open to change if it furthered political ends. The Incas did not distinguish neatly between ideological and political leadership, since the ruler was both a deity and the head of government. Military power arose from a tangled mix of supernatural forces and human endeavor, while economic productivity resulted from the gifts of the earth, labor shared through social ties, and the favor of deities. In their world, priests could be generals and the dead could contribute to state policy.

So an Inca would have written a different book from mine. Or actually he would have given an oral exposition that featured give-and-take with the audience, since the Incas did not have a writing system in the sense that language was represented by inscribed symbols. Significantly, an Inca from another family would probably have recited an alternative narrative, because the telling of history depended heavily on who the speakers and listeners were. The multiple visions of the past that existed among the Incas themselves contributed mightily to the plenitude of Spanish-authored accounts that we have to work with today. Any explanation of life in Tawantinsuyu must therefore balance Western analytical categories with the ways that the Incas might have viewed any situation and what options may have arisen within their social logic, at least to the degree possible. We must also take care not to freeze Andean life into a single homogeneous instant, exemplified by the way things were in 1532 – but described half a century or more later. As we learn more, it has become increasingly clear that life and culture in the prehispanic Andes were creative, dynamic, and contested.

In an effort to bridge the chasm between Andean and European modes of thought for the reader, I have added a new chapter to this edition, called "Thinking Inca" (chapter 5). In it, I try to provide some perspective on Inca notions of the nature of existence, time, space, knowledge, information recording, and causality. My hope is that, by having some background on Andean reasoning, the reader may better understand how social order, power, and history played out in Tawantinsuyu. For those readers so inclined, it might help to read chapter 5 after this one, as some of the discussion in it could enrich a reading of chapters 2–4.

In the modern era, scholars have relied heavily on Colonial-era documents for their insights into the nature of life and power in the Inca realm. A wealth of detail and insight can be plumbed from eyewitness diaries, chronicles, letters, inspections, court depositions, church papers, and the other materials preserved in public and private archives. They provide both particular data and culturally based explanations that will never be accessible through archaeology. Over the last half century, the agenda for discussion of the documents has been set largely by such luminaries as John Rowe, John Murra, María Rostworowski de Diez Canseco, Franklin Pease, and Tom Zuidema. They have brought radically different assumptions to the table, but they all rely on close analyses of a wide range of documents.[7] In many of those historically based works, the role of archaeology has often been limited to providing illustrative material. Sites and objects are frequently interpreted through the lens of written information, and archaeological fieldwork is seen as a context within which ideas derived from historical study can be assessed. Even so, many scholars have worked to integrate historical and archaeological information on the Incas, and visions of the relationships among different sources have undergone radical changes in the process (e.g., Rowe 1946; Hyslop 1984, 1990; Malpass 1993; Burger *et al.* 2007; Malpass and Alconini 2010). Paradoxically, a significant impetus to that change arose from historiographic research, which began to assess more closely the genesis, character, biases, and lacunae of the historical record (e.g., Adorno 1986, 2001; Julien 2000).

The last couple of decades have seen a shift in the balance, so that archaeological interpretation of Inca-era material remains stands as a more independent source of knowledge of the past (e.g., Malpass and Alconini 2010). At the same time, ethnographers, archaeologists, and art historians began to introduce new approaches. Their work has relied more heavily on comparative theory drawn from such diverse sources as gender studies, visual theory, processual and post-processual archaeology, landscape studies, and mathematics (e.g., Classen 1993; Urton 1997; Abercrombie 1998; van de Guchte 1999; González and Bray 2008). In the last few years, post-colonial theory, semiotics, linguistics, bioanthropology, phenomenology, and performance studies have also begun to have an impact (e.g., Verano 2003; Coben 2006; Cummins 2007; Salomon and Hyland 2010). Those theories are generally beyond what I will treat in this book, but the scope of new thought on the Incas is both exciting and at times bewildering.

The new approaches suggest that we are in the process of reframing Inca studies, even if early documents and the archaeological record still provide most information. One idea that has nudged my own view of things in different directions recently is the recognition that documents and material remains do not provide two windows into precisely the same domains of knowledge. Instead, they are partial complements. By this I mean that the Incas themselves seem to have organized their own knowledge, ideas, and forms of communication into overlapping formats. They gave some a material form (e.g., textiles, architecture, *khipu* knot-records); they left some crucial things like the grand histories in the realm of the immaterial (e.g., oral narratives); and they linked the two through performances (e.g., daily rituals, state ceremonies, readings of *khipu*). The fact that no physical representations of Inca rulers or their exploits are known is especially telling. Information of that nature appears to have been almost exclusively reserved for oral presentations, assisted by mnemonic tools. As a result, to understand the Incas, we have to read the different sources with an eye as to why a particular kind of evidence is found in that place.

The Written Sources

Of the thousands of known documents that describe life under the Incas, no more than about fifty contain accounts of Inca history per se. The earliest eyewitness accounts were written by official scribes and soldiers in the heat of a military invasion of an alien land. Their comments were impressions written without time for reflection or understanding of the civilization they were observing. As the Spaniards learned Quechua and began to understand the Andes better, the indigenous peoples found more reason to conceal their activities and beliefs. The situation came to a head in 1559, when the Spaniards were stunned to discover that the Incas around Cuzco were still venerating the mummies of their past kings and queens. In Spanish eyes, the native peoples – far from having assimilated the word of the true church – were still inebriated with their heretical beliefs in living ancestors and a landscape filled with conscious beings.

The simultaneous clash and syncretism of cultures, combined with a gradual increase in mutual knowledge, meant that descriptions of the empire are never both immediate and informed. The eyewitnesses who wrote reflectively were few – Pedro Pizarro and Diego de Trujillo stand out among them, and they did not put quill to parchment until almost forty years had elapsed. They were paralleled by an array of soldier-entrepreneurs, administrators, and priests, who prepared their manuscripts as part of their duties, from personal interest, or for financial gain through publication. Some of them spoke good Quechua and they were often better informed than the earliest authors, but their reports drew from the memories of informants, rather than from first-hand knowledge of the empire. By the time that the Spaniards took a real interest in the Inca realm, their witnesses provided memories colored by time, political and economic objectives, and wariness of Spanish repression. Some of the authors of the first fifty years conducted or drew from the official inquiries that were periodically undertaken to assess the state of affairs in the Viceroyalty. The questions posed were often slanted by Crown interests in denying Inca legitimacy, rooting out heresies, or discovering effective ways to exploit the rapidly declining population.

In contrast, the native peoples did not begin to set down their visions of Tawantinsuyu until the end of the century, a long lifetime after the collapse of Inca power. Those authors were all of mixed ancestry, writing from the perspective of Christians with a foot in two cultures. The only native author to set down an account from the vantage point of an independent Inca polity was the Inca Titu Kusi Yupanki, who ruled the neo-Inca state in Vilcabamba from 1561 to 1571. In 1570, he sent a lengthy missive to the newly installed Viceroy Toledo, in a vain effort to validate his position as an independent and legitimate sovereign worthy of interacting with the Spanish ruler as a client king. For our interests here, it is regrettable that he picked up the story at the point of the Spanish invasion of 1532, but his text is still valuable for its insights into Inca political thought.

Historians have paid close attention to the lives of such authors, since the context in which the documents were produced heavily affected their content. The first few decades of Spanish rule were a tumultuous era, marked by Inca resistance, Spanish internecine wars, and conflicts among clerical, administrative, and private interests, as well as by personal feuds. In the practice of the day, authors freely borrowed from one another without citation and could reinforce errors simply by repeating them. For readers interested in more detail on the subject, I recommend a number of works that are devoted to critical examinations of those documents and potential sources of bias and cross-use.[8] What I present here simply highlights some of the major sources of information and how they were composed.

Eyewitnesses to the Spanish Invasion

Among the earliest writers were Hernando Pizarro, Francisco de Xerez, Pedro Sancho, Miguel de Estete, Cristóbal de Mena, and Juan Ruiz de Arce.

All of those men were part of the invading force that captured and killed Atawallpa at Cajamarca and then seized Cuzco. Xerez and his successor Sancho were secretaries to Francisco Pizarro, charged with keeping official records for the Crown. Their journals provide a virtual day-by-day timeline of the initial Spanish experience, without the understanding or revisionism that hindsight can bring. De Mena, on the other hand, was a soldier who returned to Spain and quickly published an account of his experiences in the new land, with the intent of profiting from the work. Pedro Pizarro, younger cousin to the expedition's leader, did not finish his memoirs until 1571. As a result, he could provide a perspective on the Incas that included a feel of immediacy, tempered by knowledge gained and memory lost over decades of life in Peru. Diego de Trujillo similarly wrote a soldier's account four decades later, providing a richly detailed – and embellished – memory of the first days of the Spaniards in the new land.

The Major Sixteenth-Century Spanish Authors

The Spanish authors of the mid-sixteenth century provide our greatest source of information on the Inca empire. Pedro de Cieza de León, a common soldier with an uncommon eye for detail, wrote one of the great early accounts. After spending a number of years in the Indies, he arrived in the northern Andes in April of 1547, at the age of 29. For the next three years, he traveled through the north half of the realm, making observations and inquiring about climate, constructions, daily life, local customs, myths, and sexual practices. When in Cuzco, Cieza interviewed Inca aristocrats about their past and the nature of their government. He wrote copiously on what he had seen – four volumes of his writings have now been published, but only one appeared in his lifetime (Cieza 1967). Cieza's accounts are filled with admiration for the Inca achievements, blunted by horror at the diabolically inspired religions and sexual customs that he learned about. Many of the best descriptions of Inca rule, the roads, the provinces, and Cuzco itself, come from his pen.

Juan Diez de Betanzos's *Narrative of the Incas* (1996) describes Inca history in a form that comes as close as any known source to a version told by a single royal family. Born in Spain, Diez de Betanzos lived in Peru during his adult life, becoming the most respected Quechua – Spanish translator in the Viceroyalty. In 1542, he may have served as an interpreter at an inquest held in Cuzco and soon thereafter was commissioned to prepare a bilingual doctrinal volume. He married Doña Angelina Yupanque (Cuxirimay Ocllo), an Inca princess who experienced a remarkable life. Niece to the emperor Wayna Qhapaq, she was betrothed to his son Atawallpa at 1 year of age; she married him in 1532 when she was 10, near the end of his war to unseat Waskhar. About 1538, Francisco Pizarro took her as his mistress and she bore him two sons. After Pizarro met his own death in 1541, she married Diez de Betanzos, bringing him enormous wealth and status. So adept at the language and so close to a royal family, Diez de Betanzos was uniquely suited to write the account of the Incas that Viceroy Mendoza commissioned in 1551 and that was completed in 1557. He apparently drew a great deal of his information from his in-laws, who were members of Pachakuti's descendant kin group (Hamilton 1996: xi). The first part of the account is thus largely a heroic biography of Pachakuti, while the second describes the Colonial era. The Incas' own rationales for proper behavior are visible in his narrative, which is only moderately filtered through European eyes. For all its richness, Diez de Betanzos's account is notable for its partisanship in favor of Pachakuti and the legitimacy of Atawallpa's cause.

The Licenciado (jurist) Juan Polo Ondegardo was one of the best informed of all the administrators of the first fifty years of Colonial rule. A mine and *encomienda* owner, he served two terms as the magistrate of Cuzco and one at Potosí. Polo undertook a variety of inquiries in Peru and Bolivia both for the Crown and to satisfy his own curiosity. His concern – as with much of the Spanish attention paid to native institutions – arose from his interest in using existing practices for more effective administration and not from preserving them for their own sake. His view was that the people could best be managed for Spain's interests if its officials understood how indigenous institutions worked. His many treatises on Inca religion, economics, politics, social relations, and other elements of native life were used by the Spanish authorities in setting policy, although not as widely as he wished. One of his great successes occurred in 1559, when he discovered the whereabouts of five royal mummies that had been spirited from one hiding place to another around Cuzco since the conquest. He was widely respected and quoted by some contemporary Colonial writers (e.g., Acosta), but was heavily criticized by the mestizo Jesuit Blas Valera for his alleged ignorance of Quechua and native customs (Hyland 2011: 35–7). Valera's (partial) texts are one of the few existing criticisms of Polo's views, but a number of other writers, such as the lawyer Falcón (1918), shared his interest in countering Polo's arguments on levels of taxation and the character of Inca rule (Hyland 2003: 89–90).

The arrival of the Viceroy Francisco de Toledo in Peru in 1569 irrevocably changed Andean life. A controversial figure then as today, Toledo undertook extensive reforms that included forced resettlement of natives to communities near Spanish centers, where they could be more easily controlled. He subdued the neo-Inca state in Vilcabamba in 1572 and supervised the execution of its Inca ruler Thupa Amaru over the strenuous objections of many of his compatriots. When he returned to Spain almost ten years later, he was called on the carpet by King Philip II and upbraided for killing a king (Bauer and Decoster 2007: 2). Three volumes of papers produced by Toledo, which include ostensibly verbatim interviews with Inca and other elites in 1570–2, as well as petitions brought to his attention, provide useful detail on life in Cuzco and the provinces (Levillier 1940).

Toledo gave one of his assistants, the well-educated Captain Pedro Sarmiento de Gamboa, the responsibility of compiling an official history of the Incas (Sarmiento 2007). Sarmiento had recently been appointed royal cosmographer and enjoyed a colorful but controversial career as mariner, geographer, administrator, and explorer (Bauer and Decoster 2007; Pease 2008b). Sarmiento interviewed more than a hundred record-keepers and royal historians in Cuzco for the project. Once he had completed his history in 1572, he took the unprecedented step of having the work's veracity confirmed through a public reading before forty-two Inca nobles. Although his history is one of the major sources on the Incas, the content is clouded by Toledo's express interest in demonstrating the illegitimacy of Inca rule. Perhaps more than some other chronicles, Sarmiento's treatise was a synthetic vision that was influenced as much by the interests and composition of his mentor as his informants. The absence of Atawallpa's kin among the witnesses may have had a significant effect on the content. On a more morbid note, the descendants of Thupa Inka Yupanki and Waskhar had been largely wiped out, so the views of those families carried little weight. Despite his efforts to produce an account that suited official interests, Sarmiento's text is salted with examples of unresolved differences among Cuzco's factionalized aristocracy.

Sarmiento's document was written in part to engage in a long-standing controversy in Spain over the nature and rights of the indigenous peoples of the Americas. By 1550, a debate had been ongoing for half a century over the legitimacy of Spanish conquest of the Americas and subjugation of its peoples. It reached a high point in Valladolid in that year, where Juan Ginés de Sepúlveda and the Dominican priest Bartolomé de las Casas argued for and against Spain's right to pursue its military ventures (Covey 2006a: 175; Decoster 2008). A series of papal bulls issued as early as 1493 had given Spain and Portugal the right, and even the obligation, to discover new lands and evangelize the peoples they encountered, but it wasn't entirely clear what kinds of actions were acceptable in those pursuits. Long an apologist for the protection of indigenous peoples, Las Casas (e.g., 1967) took a strong pro-native viewpoint. He argued that the American peoples had been members of civilized society before the Spanish arrival. Because they were inherently neither intellectually nor morally inferior to the Spaniards, their conquest could not be justified. Las Casas carried the day in Valladolid, but the debate would go on for decades to come.

For the Crown to continue its ventures legitimately, the Lascasian position needed to be refuted legally and morally. In light of this ongoing controversy, Sarmiento's history was compiled with an eye to providing ammunition for those who wished to demonstrate that the Incas themselves were usurpers and therefore could lawfully be displaced. Its repeated use of terms such as Inca tyranny and usurpation were intended to bolster Crown claims to rightful conquest. The debates about the standing of native Andean thought and values ran on for many more decades, with clerics taking both sides of the issue. The Andean-born Jesuit Blas Valera was an apologist, at considerable personal cost, for the integrity of native culture and its compatibility with Christianity (Hyland 2003). He suffered years of imprisonment, apparently for perceived misuse of Quechua and Aymara in religious contexts. In contrast, the Spaniard Fernando de Montesinos argued vituperatively and contemptuously against native religion and those who saw value in it (Hyland 2007).

Several more important documents were written by other priests either as an official charge or from their own interest.[9] Bartolomé de Segovia (1968), for example, wrote an eyewitness description of the last major Inca solstice ceremony in 1535. Cristóbal de Molina, a hospice priest in Cuzco for most of his life and exceptionally well informed about Inca religion, wrote several manuscripts on the subject. One of his treatises, completed in 1575 (Molina 2011), described Inca rituals in detail. He worked closely with another cleric, Cristóbal de Albornoz (1989), who crusaded against heretical religion from 1568 until 1586. Albornoz helped put down the millenarian *Taki Onqoy* ("dancing sickness") movement and claimed to have personally demolished over 2,000 native shrines in the Huamanga region. Miguel de Cabello Valboa (1951) completed a lengthy opus in 1586, which probably borrowed from Diez de Betanzos and Sarmiento, that interweaves Inca history with a love story. Cabello Valboa is notable for proposing the imperial-era chronology that is most widely used today. Fray Martín de Murúa (1986) also borrowed heavily from earlier authors in writing two overlapping manuscripts, but provides quite a few details about Inca life and times that appear to be independently derived.

Among a host of other authors who provide crucial information were the clerics José de Acosta, Francisco de Ávila, and José de Arriaga, who wrote or commissioned important works. Other valuable manuscripts were prepared by Falcón, Santillán, Zárate, Bibar, Matienzo, Lizárraga, and Valdivia. The last four constitute the few major works that we have by authors who visited the southern Andes in person. Two Quechua lexicons, by Domingo de Santo Tomás and González Holguín, and one in Aymara by Fray Bertonio, are also useful for their clues to social structure and conceptual linkages.

Authors with Andean Ancestry

The earliest native source on the prehispanic era may be part of a disputed account known as the *Quipucamayos de Vaca de Castro* (Callapiña *et al.* 1974). The document surfaced in 1608, but a section of it was ostensibly recorded at an inquest conducted in Cuzco in 1542 by the Licenciado Vaca de Castro. Two of the four witnesses said that they had been record keepers from the descendant kin group of the emperor Wiraqocha Inka. Scholars concur that the 1608 document manipulated accounts of the past to sustain a fraudulent royal genealogy, but disagree about the authenticity of the 1542 segment, despite considerable historical sleuthing (Duviols 1979a; Urton 1990; Pease 1995: 23; Julien 2000). The document emphasized the exploits of Wiraqocha Inka and earlier kings, attributing to them many of the conquests that are often assigned to the conventional founder of the empire, Pachakuti. The *Quipucamayos* claimed that Diez de Betanzos participated in the inquest but, as just observed, the pertinent parts of the latter's *Narrative* sustained the vision of Inca history told by Pachakuti's descendants. It conflicted outright with many elements of the *Quipucamayos'* version.

Both the *Quipucamayos* and Diez de Betanzos accounts differ crucially from another native source, known as the *Probanza de Qhapaq Ayllu* (Rowe 1985b). In 1569, the survivors of a massacre in Cuzco at the end of the final Inca civil war filed a claim to regain their lost estates. The *Probanza* listed the conquests of the emperor Thupa Inka Yupanki, apparently dictated from *khipu* records. It claimed for him alone many of the conquests that are elsewhere attributed to his father Pachakuti as monarch, but Thupa Inka Yupanki as general. The conflicted and flexible views of the Inca past seen in those three sources, each told from the perspective of a particular royal kin group, highlight some of the problems in making sense of Inca history in a European framework.

In 1570, the sitting Inca ruler of the neo-Inca state in forested Vilcabamba, Titu Kusi Yupanki, sent a remarkable document to Viceroy Toledo in Cuzco (Titu Cusi 2005; Regalado de Hurtado 2008). Written as a legal argument, it consisted in large part of a history of the era from the first Spanish entry into Peru in 1532 until the death of the first Vilcabamba king, Manco Capac, in 1545. The treatise is the only existing account of the indigenous view of the proceedings and thus provides an invaluable perspective on the early Colonial era. As in the *Quipucamayos* document, Titu Kusi Yupanki attempted to marshal prehispanic royal genealogy to sustain the idea that he was the rightful heir to the throne. In his account, Atawallpa had displaced Titu Kusi Yupanki's father (Manco Capac) as legitimate ruler, rather than Waskhar. Titu Kusi Yupanki received clerics into his otherwise defended domain, hoping to enlist favorably inclined Spaniards in his efforts to be recognized as a client king allied with the Spanish ruler. He could thus retain the right to rule within his own land and to regain extensive resources (Legnani 2005; Salomon 2005). He apparently died before any action could be taken and his successor, Tupac Amaru, was captured and executed soon after, in 1572.

Over the last four centuries, the Inca Garcilaso de la Vega has easily been the most influential Inca chronicler. His portrayal of benevolent and omnipresent Inca rule, in a land in which no one ever went hungry, is in many ways a rose-colored apology rather than a portrait of reality. Scholars nevertheless relied heavily on his writings because of his genealogy, and thus presumed access to Cuzqueñan accounts of Inca history. Today, his work remains the dominant image of the Incas in the popular press. Born in 1539 to a Spanish soldier and an Inca princess, Garcilaso was baptized Gómez Suárez de Figueroa. The youth lived in Cuzco until 1560, when he moved permanently to Spain in a vain effort to be compensated for his late father's service to the throne (Mazzotti 2008: 239). Educated under the patronage of his Spanish relatives, Garcilaso had brief military and lengthy literary careers, writing a variety of philosophical and historical treatises. Late in life, he adopted his father's name and wrote the *Royal Commentaries of the Incas*, which he completed in 1609 (Garcilaso de la Vega 1966). Garcilaso wrote from the perspective of a Christian educated in a Renaissance mode, with a passion for redeeming his Andean ancestors' reputation. His status as the pre-eminent authority on the Incas stood for centuries and the *Royal Commentaries* are still cited as the earliest literary masterpiece written by a native American. Beginning with Rowe's (1946) critical assessment, however, the historian Garcilaso has fallen mightily in the eyes of many scholars. He is most often valued today for his depictions of Inca society, government, and customs and not for the accuracy of his historical account.

Garcilaso drew enthusiastically from another mestizo author, the Jesuit Blas Valera, who finished his writings about a decade earlier. Valera's lengthy manuscript, *Historia Occidentalis* (History of the West), is now lost, like so many important sixteenth-century documents. In his writings that have survived to the present, Valera provided a lengthy list of ninety-three Inca kings, among them nine who took the name Pachakuti for their title as ruler. That list is not reproduced by any other author, and its veracity and relationship to past societies are a matter of open debate. Both Garcilaso's citations and other sources show that the two men sought to validate the values and stature of native Andean civilization in European eyes. Valera's vigorously expressed opinions – e.g., that Quechua and Aymara were as well suited as Latin to expression of doctrinal matters – were viewed as heresy by his fellow Jesuits (Hyland 2003, 2011). The result was that he spent the last fourteen years of his life in imprisonment and then exile. He died in 1597 from wounds received during the English assault on Cadíz, during which much of his writing was consumed by fire.

Four years after Garcilaso completed his great work, Felipe Guaman Poma de Ayala sent a document of more than a thousand pages to King Felipe III that is a fount of information on life in the Inca realm (Guaman Poma 1980, 2006). A son of ethnically mixed ancestry like Garcilaso and Valera, Guaman Poma found himself caught between two cultures. He assisted the Colonial administration in varied capacities for decades, including efforts to stamp out idolatrous practices. Even so, he was conflicted in his loyalty to things Christian and Spanish and to traditional Andean ways of life. In 1613, he completed his epic work, which included hundreds of drawings of Inca personages, history, religion, and customs, as well as an illustrated litany of Spanish abuses. His drawings are an irreplaceable source of visual detail, while the text – an often incoherent mélange of Spanish and Quechua – contains many useful particulars. Like Garcilaso and Valera, Guaman Poma wrote about expansive imperial Inca conquests earlier than many Colonial Spaniards or modern scholars have been willing to accept. In recent decades, Guaman Poma has excited renewed interest as a resistance author (see Adorno 1986; Pease 1995: 261–310). Along with his mestizo compatriots, he is viewed as an early spokesman for the importance of protecting native rights and culture for their own value, rather than for Crown interests, as Polo Ondegardo argued (1965a).

The Later Spanish Chroniclers

As the seventeenth century moved along, the pace of writing on the Incas subsided, but some important documents were still produced. The most prominent is the multi-volume work on Inca history, religion, and customs written by the Jesuit priest Bernabé Cobo. Born in Andalusia, Father Cobo traveled widely in his lifetime. He visited Mexico, but spent most of his adult life in Peru, where he completed his great work in 1653 (Cobo 1979, 1990; see Rowe 1979b). His writing is lucid and well organized, but Cobo was a naturalist and historian whose descriptions of the Incas were drawn from earlier manuscripts. Since he had access to several papers that are now lost, such as the full account of Cuzco's shrine system, his work is an invaluable source. Modern authors also rely on Cobo for his descriptions of daily life, even though the Jesuit applied his own seventeenth-century observations to the prehispanic past a century after the empire's fall (Rowe 1990a).

Spanish Inspections, Church Documents, and Court Records

In the latter half of the twentieth century, historians turned their eyes from the classic chronicles to the Andean and Spanish archives. During the early Colonial era, representatives of the Spanish Crown and the Church produced a blizzard of documents about the people, customs, and resources of their new holdings. Many of those documents were intended to provide information to the Crown that would facilitate administration of the new land and extraction of its wealth. In 1549, for example, the Crown ordered detailed inspections (*visitas*) of its holdings. The inspectors used a standardized series of questions about life before and under the Incas and recorded information about the natural resources of each region. In part because conditions were changing so rapidly with the decline of the native population and administrative reforms, new inspections were ordered in the 1560s. More inquests were held with Viceroy Toledo's vast restructuring program in 1570–2. Many of the inspections recorded from 1557 through 1585 have been published in the *Relaciones Geográficas de Indias* (1965; hereafter *RGI*). The Toledan and *RGI* sources are useful as regional snapshots of the realm that drew from interviews with local native elites.

A final set of archival documents comes from litigation. About two decades after the fall of the Incas, Andean peoples began to use the Spanish courts (*Audiencia Real*) to make claims for services that they had provided the Spaniards and to settle grievances with their neighbors. Many of their complaints arose when local societies tried to regain lands or other resources that had been taken by the Incas and given to colonists resettled by the state. Since several million people moved under Inca rule, the flood of paperwork that fell upon the court system has provided a great deal of useful information on ethnic groups, land tenure, inheritance customs, and land use practices, among many other things. Still other cases stemmed from competition over the inheritance of privileged positions, as local elites learned to make claims based on pre-Inca rights, offices granted by the state, and Spanish laws that favored primogeniture over other traditional customs.

Inca Archaeology

1860–1960

The study of Inca archaeology has a long and often distinguished career, dating back to the nineteenth century. The main figures of the early days were more adventurers than scientists, but some of their contributions to archaeology are still valuable. Among the outstanding figures were Ephraim George Squier, Charles Wiener, and Antonio Raimondi, who traveled throughout the central part of the empire by horse with a pack train. They described or mapped many Inca settlements along the main road system and paid special attention to a number of sites in the Urubamba river valley now recognized as royal family estates. The engravings that were featured in their volumes provide indispensable information, even if they were often romanticized, since quite a few of the sites have suffered considerable damage since then.

Just before 1900, a major figure appeared on the Andean archaeological scene – Max Uhle. A remarkably energetic researcher and prolific writer, Uhle set about developing a pan-Andean chronology using the innovative combination of comparisons of ceramic types and analysis of stratigraphic deposits. Uhle took a considerable interest in Inca archaeology, investigating ruins, for example, at the northern Inca capital at Tumipampa (Ecuador), at coastal Pachacamac, and in the highland Urubamba valley (Peru), thus spanning the coastal desert, the mountains, and the eastern Andean slopes. His studies have proved to be so valuable that some of them are periodically reprinted, not simply out of historical interest, but for the information they contain (Uhle 1903; 1909; 1917; 1923). In the northern Andes, the works of Jijón y Caamaño (e.g., 1919; Jijón y Caamaño and Larrea 1918) also stand out for Ecuador.

About the same time that Uhle was at work, other major scholars were advancing our knowledge of what was the southeastern quarter of the Inca empire. Adolph Bandelier, who is also known for his work in the North American Southwest and in Mesoamerica, conducted investigations at a series of Inca sites both on the Peruvian coast and at the sacred islands in Lake Titicaca (1910). Stig Rydén's (1947) work in Bolivia built upon and complemented Bandelier's explorations. In the southernmost part of the empire, Juan de Ambrosetti was working at Inca sites in northwest Argentina. His multi-volume publications from that region describe a variety of sites, notably Puerta de La Paya, where his excavations recovered the most elaborate set of Inca materials yet found in the south Andes. Debenedetti (1908) and Difrieri (1948), among others, also conducted important investigations on Inca installations such as Potrero de Payogasta.

Inca archaeology did not really catch the public's attention until 1912, however, when Hiram Bingham announced his discovery of Machu Picchu, one of the world's most spectacular archaeological sites. His claim to have found "the lost city of the Incas" in the eastern jungles and the truly breathtaking character of the remains sparked an interest that remains unabated today. Following on Bingham's work was a series of studies in the 1930s and 1940s at the capital of Cuzco and its environs. Most of the work was conducted by Peruvian scholars, notably Luis Valcárcel, Jorge Muelle, and Luis Pardo. Valcárcel's work at Cuzco and Saqsawaman were especially important in setting out the early chronology of the Inca heartland. Those investigators were primarily concerned with monumental sites, describing material culture, and working out cultural sequences that had not yet been defined. Their studies were supplemented by Paul Fejos's work at sites in the Urubamba (1944) and by John Rowe's (1944) seminal paper on the archaeology of Cuzco.

A complementary set of data was collected through the Shippee–Johnson air expedition of 1931, which shot some 3,000 images of the Peruvian archaeological landscape. Among their subjects were important archaeological sites, such as Machu Picchu, Pisaq, and Cuzco itself. Although only a subset of their images has yet been published, that photographic record provides an invaluable source of information on the archaeological and natural landscape of the time – much of which has been heavily modified through modern developments.

1960–2010

Starting about 1960, a transformation began to occur in the study of Inca provinces. Throughout the preceding century, archaeologists working in local contexts had been recording Inca sites, but those were consistently interpreted in the context of the written sources and a Cuzco-centric view of the Andes. In a pivotal article written in 1959, Dorothy Menzel recognized that the Incas had formed a variety of relationships with the societies of the south coast of Peru. She inferred that Inca rule had been adapted to existing local conditions, which was a major step forward in interpreting an empire that had previously been assumed to be essentially homogeneous. The year 1963 saw the initiation of the Huánuco Project in Peru's central highlands. That was the first major investigation to systematically integrate historical and archaeological research in a regional study called "A Study of Provincial Inca Life." The circumstances for the investigation were exceptional, for the Huánuco region could lay claim to both the most spectacular provincial center in the empire and two Spanish inspections, from 1549 and 1562. The research team, led by John Murra, Donald Thompson, and Craig Morris, took great advantage of the conditions, producing a series of publications that remain the standard against which all provincial research is compared.[10] I will refer to the Huánuco project on numerous occasions throughout this book.

Not until the UNESCO project at Cuzco, published in 1980, did professionals make a concerted effort to identify, map, and conserve the existing Inca architecture in and around the capital (Agurto Calvo 1980). Until recently, those interests – site mapping, architectural description, ceramic analysis, and culture history – have dominated the archaeology of the Inca heartland. The Peruvian National Institute of Culture (INC) has been engaged in a long-term, full-coverage cadastral registry of archaeological remains in the greater Cuzco region. Research conducted under its auspices by Peruvian scholars has investigated an impressive array of archaeological sites, for example Machu Picchu (e.g., Valencia Zegarra and Gibaja Oviedo 1992), Maras (Gibaja Oviedo 2000), Moray (Quirita 2002), and Tipón (INC 1999). A number of other projects have made important contributions in this milieu, for example, at the estate at Chinchero (e.g., Alcina Franch 1978) and manors in the Cusichaca region (e.g., Kendall *et al.* 1992, Kendall 1996). Those studies are matched by research on many other individual sites, such as the royal estates of Ollantaytambo (e.g., Protzen 1993), Yucay (Niles 1999), and Machu Picchu (Burger and Salazar 2004).

A major shift of the archaeology of the Inca heartland occurred with the application of systematic regional survey over the last twenty-five years, complementing the work of prior scholars. Five major surveys of the greater Cuzco region have been completed: Bauer's (1992) seminal study of the Paruro region, Heffernan's (1989) work in the Limatambo area, Bauer and Covey's (2002) Cuzco Valley survey, Covey's (2006b) study of the Sacred Valley, and Kosiba's (2010) survey of the Ollantaytambo region. Even so, no complete survey of the archaeology of the Cuzco region has yet been published (although see Bauer 2004).

Those studies give us a much better understanding of the full range of the archaeological record. That point is crucial, because the archaeological landscape consists not just of major sites, but of carved natural features, roads, terracing and canal networks. Even places with no obvious modification may have been significant – sight-lines, mountain peaks, springs, and the like. From the written sources, we know that the Incas lived in a socialized landscape that was inscribed with history and populated by various beings or forms of consciousness. Andean peoples envisioned humans as inhabiting an animated space that included the earth, its surface, the waters, and the heavens. Our interpretation of that landscape needs to take the full range of its elements into account, not just the obvious sites, but viewscapes, paths of travel, and apparently empty spaces. A number of studies have taken on such topics, working from the premise that explaining the relationships between the Incas and their history requires study of the sacred elements of the landscape (e.g., Bauer 1998; Van de Guchte 1990). Collectively, those investigations have greatly advanced our understanding of the nature and genesis of the Inca polity. Just as important as their empirical contributions has been the expansion of the range of questions that researchers are trying to address and the technical tools that they can bring to bear on the subject. Satellite imagery and geographic information systems, for example, have helped considerably in mapping out large-scale patterns.

The gains from research around Cuzco have been matched by a proliferation of studies on the Inca provinces by scholars throughout the Andes (e.g., Burger *et al.* 2007; Malpass and Alconini 2010). Such works are too numerous to mention individually, but their interests take us into topics that were seldom considered before. Most importantly, they are fleshing out how Cuzco interacted with the hundreds of local societies under its dominion and are investigating elements of life that were often outside direct state control. We can now recognize stability and change in community life that were beyond our reach until a couple of decades ago. Work on household archaeology permits scholars to examine how symbols of status, diet, architectural styles, life expectancy, and household labor were impacted (if at all) by the advent of imperial rule (e.g., D'Altroy *et al.* 2001). Biological techniques (e.g., DNA analysis, trace element chemistry) also now facilitate the study of population movements, health, and social identity in ways that had previously been inaccessible (e.g., Verano 2003; Shinoda in press).

A final array of studies is taking us into new territory. As noted earlier in this chapter, some scholars are making forays into the ways that the Incas perceived and thought about their world. For example, they are exploring the relationships between Andean linguistic and visual communication and ways of codifying information (e.g., Cummins 2007; González and Bray 2008). The work on *khipus* has been particularly fruitful in this regard (e.g., Urton 2003; Salomon 2004; see chapter 5 here), but ideas of performance, knowledge, memory and power have also been making inroads (e.g., Abercrombie 1998; Coben 2006). Throughout this book, I will try to keep the theoretical discussion to a modest level, but posing new and sometimes provocative questions leads us to understand more about old topics. All in all, such advances by hundreds of scholars in the land once called Tawantinsuyu continue to make this an exciting time to study the Incas.

Notes

1   Those figures are based on the royal fifth of 2,600 lb of gold and 5,200 of silver (McQuarrie 2007: 124), using a July 2012 price of $1570/oz for gold and $26/oz for silver.

2   Titu Kusi Yupanki (Titu Cusi 2005), who was born in 1529 and thus was probably not old enough to remember an independent Tawantinsuyu, has left us a chronicle. Regrettably, he described only the era after the Spanish invasion.

3   *amauta*: "perhaps from *ama uta*, house of memories" (Szemiński 2008: 429).

4   This sections ventures a little more into theoretical questions than did the first edition, in part as a response to requests from internal reviewers. To readers for whom this is heavy slogging, my apologies.

5   I obviously do not share this notion, or I would not be writing this book. Even so, I think it necessary to consider both points of view – the comparative and the internally generated (i.e., the hermeneutic) – to provide a balanced explanation of the past.

6   Or "subaltern."

7   See Morris 2007 for an excellent review.

8 I especially recommend the new three-volume study edited by Pillsbury (2008); see also Means 1928; Levillier 1940: 207–486; Rowe 1985b: 207–16; Porras Barrenechea 1986; Pärssinen 1992; Pease 1995; Hamilton 1996.

9 Segovia 1968; Cabello Valboa 1951; Molina 2011; Albornoz 1989; Murúa 1986.

10 Even so, an enormous amount of information from the Huánuco project is still in the process of being published (Morris *et al.* 2011). Much material, including 5,000 photos and reams of field notes, are currently being analyzed by scholars for publication (Barnes 2010).

Chapter Two

The Land and Its People

At first glance, the rugged lands of western South America seem like an improbable place to give birth to grand civilizations. Compressed within a narrow band along the Pacific Ocean lie the highest peaks in the western hemisphere, a coastal desert that may go for years without rain, and dense tropical jungles. As forbidding as the setting seems, a closer look shows that the land contains a mosaic of productive micro-environments and natural resources. The Andes mountains form the continent's most commanding geographic feature. Running 8,000 km along the length of the land mass, they ascend so rapidly that the continental divide lies only 100 km east of the shoreline at Lima, Peru. For a seasoned hiker, the climb up to the high passes takes about a week, but a passenger in a long-distance taxi can reach the divide in just three memorable hours. The descent from the eastern snow-caps to the upper reaches of the Amazon jungle is even more precipitous in some places. To appreciate how geography has condensed the ecology, we may visualize a path across central Peru from the ocean to the forest. In a trip that would cover about 200 km by air, we would pass over twenty of the world's thirty-four major life zones (Burger 1992: 12). In this compact vertical arrangement, which is not duplicated anywhere on the planet, distinct ecological belts may lie less than an hour's walk apart.

The early inhabitants managed to flourish in the demanding conditions, for the Andes contain the richest biota of any zone of its size in the world (Luteyn and Churchill 2000). People first entered the continent at least 15,000 years ago, when hunting and gathering were the way of life everywhere. Over the millennia, they devised a wide variety of foraging, farming, and herding strategies. The marine fisheries of the bone-chilling inshore waters could be exploited with simple technologies, while llama and alpaca herding became both a successful adaptation and a source of wealth for mountain peoples. Although people still foraged for some

The Incas, Second Edition. Terence N. D'Altroy.
© 2015 John Wiley & Sons, Ltd. Published 2015 by John Wiley & Sons, Ltd.

Plate 2.1   Prehistoric terraces in the Colca Valley, Peru. Source: reproduced by permission of the American Museum of Natural History. Neg. No. 334671, Shippee–Johnson Collection.

resources after states appeared about two thousand years ago, all of their staple foods and industrial crops had been domesticated by 3000 BC. They modified features of the landscape through irrigation, terracing (plate 2.1), and draining wetlands, at the same time that they adjusted the rhythms of their lives to the demands of the climatic cycles. Despite these successes, however, life in the Andes was never easy. Even in some of the most densely occupied highland zones, crops could fail two years out of three (Polo 1965b: 71), while earthquakes, floods, erratic rainfall, disease, and a host of other natural forces periodically brought disaster to subsistence systems.

The Inca empire – a latecomer to Andean civilizations – thus built upon millennia of adaptation, tradition, and innovation in carving out its domain. For the most part it was a rural society, as most people lived in small towns and villages and spent their time farming and herding. To set the stage for the rise of Tawantinsuyu, this chapter sketches out the Andean natural environment and the ways that people exploit its resources. That outline is followed by a synopsis of Andean prehistory before the Incas.

The Natural Setting

The Andes

The Andean environment has been molded by a conjunction of geography, geology, and climate. Over the last five million years, the oceanic Nazca plate has been sliding eastward under the South American plate, raising the mountains and creating a deep trench off the coast (Wicander and Monroe 1989: 157; Windley 1995: 105–12). Two parallel mountain ranges dominate the central Andes – the Cordillera Oriental (or Blanca) on the east and the Cordillera Occidental (or Negra) on the west. The peaks of the eastern range are about 1,000 m higher than those of the west; they are also wider and more continuous, but both are effective barriers to the moisture-bearing trade winds. In the north, transverse ranges called *nudos* (knots) break up the landscape into a few large drainages and many small valleys. The highest snowcap in the Americas – Mount Aconcagua (6,960 m) – lies along the Chile–Argentina border. It was just one of more than fifty peaks that the Incas revered by building a shrine near the summit.

Periodically, the movement of the earth's plates touches off catastrophic earthquakes. In 1970, a temblor centered near Lima claimed about 70,000 lives. In the quake's most dramatic event, a mountain face sheared off in the Callejón de Huaylas, triggering an avalanche that wiped out the town of Yungay and most of its 4,000 residents in a few minutes. Plate tectonics have also created three active volcanic zones along the spine of the mountains from central Colombia to central Chile. Even though vulcanism is less of a threat than other natural forces, eruptions can still have a major impact on life. On February 19, 1600, for instance, the volcano called Huaynaputina, near Arequipa (Peru), produced an explosion that took more than a thousand lives and devastated the socioeconomic infrastructure of a large area of southern Peru (de Silva and Alzueta 2000). Fifteen kilometers west of the volcano, the fall was 2 m thick, and Peru's coastal wine industry never fully recovered. The effects of the eruption were felt worldwide, as it may have been the major factor in producing the coldest summer (1601) of the last 500 years. The eruption may also be implicated in the two-year famine that followed the severe winter of 1601–2 in Russia, which killed 500,000 people and possibly contributed to the overthrow of the tsar (see Verosub and Lippman 2008). Layers of ash in archaeological deposits attest to analogous, though perhaps less catastrophic, events in prehistory.

The Andes abound with mineral deposits, including the volcanic glass called obsidian that was widely used to make cutting tools. Copperbearing deposits are found along the entire mountain chain, while tin is concentrated in Bolivia and northern Chile. One of the most famous mines of the Colonial era was the silver operation at Potosí, Bolivia, which enriched a few Spaniards at a notable cost in Andean energy and lives. Gold also was found in plenty, much of it along the eastern side of the mountains where it was recovered from veins and placer mining (Berthelot 1986; Windley 1995: 111–12).

Climate

The climate has contributed in important ways to Andean life by conditioning the annual round of life for farmers and herders and helping to determine the locations that could support settlements. Broadly speaking, two climatic trends are found in western South America: from the temperate south in Chile to the tropics in Colombia, and from the arid west to the humid east. Those patterns result from the interaction of the ocean currents, mountains, and trade winds. The Chile–Peru trench, which lies just off the shoreline, provides a conduit for the Humboldt Current's frigid waters flowing north from the Antarctic. As the waters well upwards, they bring up nutrients that sustain rich beds of plankton. These tiny plants form the first link in a biotic chain whose fisheries were among the world's most productive until they were over-exploited in the twentieth century. The coastal waters are especially rich in anchovies and sardines, and in larger fish, such as tuna, salmon, and sea bass. Sea lions, seals, and fishing birds such as pelicans and cormorants are sustained in large numbers by the fish. Both the rocky and the sandy littoral zones provide many kinds of shellfish; their remains are piled up to 5 meters deep in scores of pre-ceramic sites. Even with traditional techniques like the simple nets and reed boats called *caballitos* ("little horses"), the inshore waters have been a bounteous source of food for the last five thousand years.

The climatic cycles produce two wet and dry seasons each year north of Peru, but only one each in the central Andes, the heartland of the Inca empire. From June to November, the prevailing oceanic winds blow in from the southwest. As the air warms up over the land, the relative humidity drops so quickly that rain almost never falls near the coast. Instead, a heavy fog (*garúa*) straddles the shoreline, trapped in place by an upper layer of warmer air. During the rest of the year, when no temperature inversion occurs, the air flows up the sharp Andean escarpment and the moisture falls out as rain. Since most precipitation falls above 1,600 m, it can be used for farming only after the water runs back down and is tapped off for irrigation. On the other side of the central Andes, the equatorial easterlies bank up against the mountains, cool, and drop their abundant moisture on the forested mountain faces. All the rain that falls east of the continental divide helps to swell the Amazon, which discharges more water than any other river on the planet – about fifteen times the volume of the Mississippi (Burger 1992: 15, 21).

The regular cycles are intermittently disrupted by a phenomenon called El Niño ("the Child"; also known as ENSO for El Niño Southern Oscillation), so named because it normally peaks around Christmas (Diaz and Markgraf 1992). When an event occurs, the trade winds slacken as part of a global weather pattern. Warm equatorial waters flow south along the Peruvian coastline, suppressing the upwelling of cold southern waters. In strong events, like that of 1997–8, the effects are catastrophic. Torrential rains destroy coastal crops and wash away canal systems, roads, and exposed settlements. Fish and birds die in massive numbers or migrate out of the range accessible to traditional methods of capture. Because the environment can take several years to recover fully, some archaeologists suggest that El Niño and other natural forces may have helped trigger social upheavals by disrupting food production (Moseley 1983). At the same time that the coast suffers downpours, the highlands receive less than average rainfall. Since El Niño occurs at intervals of two to eleven years, prehistoric people could not predict its cycle, but could be sure that its damaging effects would recur.

Intriguingly, however, potato farmers of the high Andes from Bolivia to Peru can anticipate a mountain drought for a given year by gazing at the stars (Orlove *et al.* 2002). A study of twelve communities that use this method found that it provided more accurate forecasts than modern meteorologists can currently make for the region. When the star group called the *qollqa* ("granary," i.e., the Pleiades) appears over the horizon about June 24, farmers climb to the high peaks to assess their visibility. If the stars are obscured by the high clouds that precede an ENSO event, the farmers know that dry times are coming and irrigate their crops or delay their planting. Clear skies mean that the rains will come in November and they plan accordingly. The same knowledge was present among the people of Huarochirí about 1600, recorded in a native account called the *Huarochirí Manuscript* (Salomon and Urioste 1991: 133).

Environmental Zones

Over the years, geographers have developed many ways to classify the Andes' natural environments. A widely used scheme, devised by Javier Pulgar Vidal (1987), combines native terminology with modern biotic classifications to divide the central Andean environment into eight zones (figure 2.1). From north Peru to central Chile, the entire coast (*chala* or *costa*) is a sere desert, punctuated only by drainages that cut ribbons of green through a pastel landscape of drifting sands and jagged rock formations. Where irrigation is practicable, the valley bottoms are lush croplands, but seepage and evaporation can cost canals as much as 85 percent of their water (Shimada 1994: 42). Among the most important indigenous crops are maize, squash, gourd, and cotton; in the twentieth century, sugar cane became a major export crop. Other foods included algarrobo (pods of the carob tree) and fruits such as chirimoya and lúcuma, which is used today to make a popular ice cream flavor that tastes vaguely like caramelized milk. Protein in the coastal diet was enhanced primarily with shellfish and fish. Above the coastal plain lies the warmer *yungas* zone (300–2,300 m). The most important crops here are coca and *ají* (pepper), along with fruits, such as chirimoya, guayabo, avocado, and lúcuma. Together with maize, coca has long been a common element in gifts and sacrifices, and was given in vast quantities to Inca subjects in a kind of obligatory state largess. Another *yungas* band lies on the eastern side of the Andes above the Amazonian jungles; it may have been even more productive than its coastal counterpart.

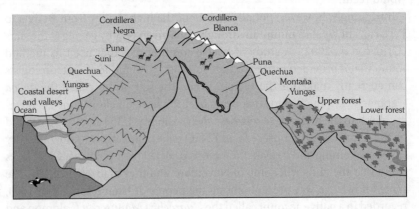

Figure 2.1   Cross-section of the major life zones in the central Andes. Source: adapted from Burger 1992: 21.

The temperate *quechua* band (3,100–3,500 m) is the most productive highland ecozone. In the valley bottoms, dry-farming produces maize, beans, garden vegetables, the native grains quinoa and cañihua, a variety of tubers such as potato, ulluco, oca, and mashwa, and the legume called talwi. Today the Asian grains of wheat and barley are often sown in place of the native crops. Even apparently modest elevation changes can have a significant effect on the viability of crops, as each 10 m of elevation gain effectively reduces the growing season by a day and a 300 m gain in altitude reduces it by a month (Earls and Cervantes in press). For that reason, irrigation at higher elevations is often intended to accelerate the beginning of the agricultural cycle as much as it is meant to get water to plants.

Above these lands lies the *suni* zone (up to 4,000 m), which features cold hills, ridges, and deep valleys. This zone is especially productive for the Andean tubers, quinoa, and talwi. Today, more than 4,000 varieties of potatoes have been identified, many of which are far tastier than the outsized spuds found in supermarket bins. In prehistory, this was also a prime zone for hunting, especially deer, and was home to the Andean condor, the world's largest bird (plate 2.2). Above this land lies the *puna* (up to 5,000 m), an alpine tundra that is the natural habitat for the Andean camelids. The weather is usually cold and damp, with heavy fogs and

Plate 2.2 Andean condor.

Plate 2.3   A llama caravan, the principal beast of burden and source of meat for Andean peoples.

violent storms that roll over the ground during the wet season. This zone was used for herding llamas and alpacas (plate 2.3) and hunting guanacos, vicuñas, and Virginia and white-tailed deer. Although the puna is marginal for most agriculture, some frost-resistant tubers can be grown, such as bitter potatoes and maca. Even higher is the bone-chilling cold of the *janca* zone, which features permanent snowcaps and glacial lakes, along with abundant mineral wealth. At about 4,700 m, the modern communities near the pass called Ticlio (Peru) are the highest permanently inhabited towns in the world; they are serviced by the world's highest railroad (4,900 m). It is a testament to human resilience that every town has its own football field.

Down the eastern Peruvian slopes lie the upper Amazonian jungles, called the *montaña*, and the lower forest, called the *selva*. The upper edge of the Amazonian forest itself is known as the *ceja de selva* or "eyebrow of the jungle." The steep terraces and valley bottoms of the montaña produce maize, coca, fruit, pepper, and other warm-weather crops. Although this zone was sparsely populated in prehistory, it was still important economically. The verdant Amazonion forest below contains fertile plains where the root crop called manioc is a staple. During Inca times, jungle societies were scattered and simply organized, but the Incas attempted to draw them into the empire, for they coveted the gold, wood, and brilliant feathers that the lowlands yielded.

To the north, Ecuador's coastal mangrove swamps and western woodlands proved inhospitable to the Incas and they never managed to draw them effectively into the empire. The intermontane valleys, in contrast, enjoy such a delightful climate that they were chosen for the northern Inca capital, called Tumipampa. Intermixed in the highlands are the rolling grasslands called the *páramo*, which were suitable for camelid pasturage though generally not part of their natural range. South of Peru, the high cordilleras are bridged by the *altiplano*, a windswept plain that runs through upland Bolivia into northwest Argentina. Potatoes and chenopods are the main cultivars in this cold land, but the great flocks of camelids were more important culturally, for they provided wool, meat, cargo transport, and wealth for their owners. At its north end, the plain encloses Lake Titicaca (3,800 m), the world's highest navigable lake. South of the altiplano on the eastern side of the peaks lie the dry intermontane valleys (*valliserrana*) of Argentina; to the west are the Atacama desert and central Chile's temperate uplands. The southern Andes were less fertile than lands to the north, but they still supported towns in areas where snow-fed rivers could be tapped for irrigation.

Such modern land classifications only partially mesh with folk understandings of the land and people's relationships with it, of course, for they live in a world teeming with all manner of powers. Traditional Andean peoples (*runakuna*) use both their own cultural visions and understandings compatible with a scientific viewpoint. As Catherine Allen (2002) beautifully describes in her ethnography, *The Hold Life Has*, the landscape is alive to the *runakuna*. Every distinct element of the topography has a name, a personality, a will, and a history. The herding and potato-farming people of Sonqo, less than a day's trip from Cuzco, know the land's most important features as the *Tirakuna* (Sacred Places). Collectively, they form a society parallel to the human one. Each one of them constantly watches and depends on the other for its well-being. The most powerful beings are the snowcapped mountain peaks, such as Ausangate, but even the most humble hill, plain, promontory, or spring has meaning and a social relationship with its human and non-human neighbors. The dealings between people and places are constantly negotiated and reinforced through prayer and ritual, so that the weather will be propitious, the crops and herds bountiful, and the Tirakuna satisfied and beneficent (Allen 2002).

The *runakuna* today also distinguish between areas where the residents maintain good relations with the ancient land or have lost their character through incorporation into modern society. The people of Sonqo both envy and mistrust the more hispanically assimilated residents of nearby Colquepata and even more those living in Cuzco (Allen 2002). To dress correctly in home-made clothes and to chew, exchange, and make offerings of coca are key markers of the *runakuna*, the people of the high lands. As someone becomes *mestizo*, he or she dons factory-made clothes and discontinues using coca. In Peru's Ayacucho region, the *quechua* zone is the land of agriculture and civilized people (Flannery *et al.* 1989: 21–4). The puna is where the camelids live, farming is insignificant, and the people are primitive. The snow-capped peaks are home to the *apu* or *wamani* – powerful spirits who control the weather and own the flocks. For many societies of the late prehistoric Andes, the summits were the origin places for the ancestors, whose spirits still roam the earth (Reinhard 1985; Salomon 1991; Allen 2002). In Andean eyes, successful relations with the environment call for an intimate knowledge of the landscape, a keen eye for weather, and a congenial relationship with the land's many inhabitants.

Traditional Land Use Today

Farming

Traditional communities in the central Andes are organized around a kin group called the *ayllu*,[1] just as they were in Inca times. Members of an *ayllu* believe that they share a common ancestor and place of origin. They hold their productive resources collectively and allocate them to families according to their size and status. Whenever possible, an *ayllu* will include a variety of farmlands and pastures in its holdings. Each household will ideally have access to a full complement of production zones, so that its members can produce all the basics of life themselves in concert with their neighbors/relatives. *Ayllu* usually contain two or three opposing parts, often called upper (*hanan*) and lower (*hurin*), or left-right-center (*ichuq-allawqa-chaupi*). *Ayllu* members typically take their spouses from another division and thus keep resources within the larger group.

The ethics and practice of traditional communities are built on mutuality and interdependence. Labor is reciprocally shared, so that many tasks are performed by teams, often organized by sex. The married couple are inseparable parts of a unit, since neither a man nor a woman is whole without the other. What we refer to in English as husband and wife is treated as a joint entity in Quechua called *warmi-qhari* (wife-husband; Allen 2002: 54). As Allen (p. 54) explains for the community of Sonqo, male and female roles are conceptually distinct but interdependent. Tasks, materials, and spaces are identified with one or the other sex. The largely domestic and agro-pastoral roles of women tend to keep them around the house and children, or at outpost houses, while men's work is conducted farther afield. Women and men also tend to socialize among people of the same sex, in both cases mostly keeping the company of family members or relatives by marriage (Allen 2002: 54). Even with the strongly sexualized division of roles, performance of some tasks may cross over gendered lines. For example, men and boys may spin thread and weave or the occasional widow may choose to pick up the tasks performed by her late husband rather than remarry. This overall approach to life means that a couple may spend a lot of time apart, sometimes weeks or months at a time, especially when one or another is off tending herds at high elevations (women) or seeking day-labor (men).

To take advantage of the varied natural environment and achieve self-sufficiency, communities distribute their members across the landscape (Brush 1977). In steep lands like those of the eastern Andes, the main settlement lies at a mid-elevation between maize and tuber lands. Smaller hamlets are placed in the puna for herding or in the lowlands to grow coca, pepper, and fruits. In some cases, the main and offshoot communities lie a week's travel or more apart across the lands of other ethnic groups. This *archipelago* settlement pattern can be employed to exploit resources such as coca, salt, and guano; sometimes members of several different communities share access to the same resources (Murra 1968, 1972; Masuda *et al.* 1985). Where the gradients are gentler – for example, in the Urubamba Valley where the Inca royalty built estates – the population is spread more evenly across the terrain to take advantage of broader areas of arable land.

William Mitchell's (1980) studies in Quinua, near Cuzco, show how altitude and the local ecology affect agricultural practices. During the most important growing season, crops are planted in November and December. Sowing moves downhill from the highest plots so that the last planting coincides with the first rains. The members of several households may share labor in long-standing relationships of reciprocal assistance. By irrigating crops before the rains arrive, the farmers can move the harvests forward and beat the killing frosts. This approach to land use both increases harvests and reduces risk, because the conditions that cause crops to fail in one zone may produce a bountiful crop elsewhere. The staggered agrarian cycle also uses household labor efficiently, since planting and harvesting are spread out over time.

Several million of Tawantinsuyu's subjects also lived along the Peruvian coast, where the ecological setting, as well as some social and economic features, differed in important ways from the Incas' mountainous heartland. In prehistoric times, the steep terrain and hydrology limited the amount of the major drainage basins that could be farmed to no more than 17 percent (Kroeber 1930; Shimada 1994: 42). Even so, the rich bottom lands of entire valleys were irrigated by the beginning of the first millennium AD. The most extensive irrigation systems in the Americas lay along Peru's north coast, where sets of adjacent valleys were linked by canal networks. Once in place, the irrigation networks – and the social systems that depended upon them – could be disrupted by coastal uplift, earthquakes, El Niño events, river channel downcutting, salinization of the aquifers, and wind-blown sands (Moseley *et al.* 1992). Under the circumstances, building and maintaining canal systems was a continuous challenge.

Herding

Pastoralism has been the indispensable complement to farming in the Andes for millennia. Of the four native camelids, only the llama and alpaca were domesticated, while the guanaco and vicuña remain wild. Recent mtDNA analyses suggest, still controversially, that the llama was likely domesticated from the guanaco and the alpaca from the vicuña about 6,000–7,000 years ago (Kadwell *et al.* 2011). Moreover, there may have been more species diversity in late prehistory than is seen today. Llamas are best suited to elevations above 3,000 m, while the alpaca's core range lies above 4,200 m (Gade 1977: 116). Archaeological studies indicate that the presence of camelids on the coast or in most of the *páramo* grasslands of northern Peru and Ecuador was a direct result of human intervention (Miller and Gill 1990). Drovers have been taking caravans to the coast for thousands of years and some scholars suggest that herds were tended there in prehistory.

Researchers have taken an intense interest in traditional pastoralists in recent years, because they are one of the few groups who practice lifeways much like those of their pre-Columbian forebears (Flores Ochoa 1977). The alpine tundra contains a patchwork of useful microenvironments, including turf, tallgrass, and moor puna, even if frost falls on the bleak land nine to twelve months per year (Flannery *et al.* 1989: 16). Modern herders often live in small, widely scattered units called *kancha*, the Quechua word for "enclosure." In this case, things have changed since prehistory, for Peruvian herding settlements in Inca times housed hundreds of residents (Parsons *et al.* 1998). Like farmers, the herders maintain a network of group assistance and ritual for herding, shearing, and butchering. They move their small herds of eighteen to thirty-five animals from pasture to pasture following a seasonal round (Flannery *et al.* 1989: 50–1). The puna's residents also tend fields in lower reaches to make freeze-dried potatoes, called *chuño*, a delicacy of dubious flavor to a foreign palate. *Chuño* is made by alternating freezing the potatoes and then stamping out their moisture (Flannery *et al.* 1989: 78–81). A similar process of freeze-drying meat produces *ch'arki*, a word that has been adopted into English parlance as "jerky." *Chuño* and *ch'arki* are long-lasting and lightweight foods that are used on trips when travelers carry much of their food. They were staples of the Inca armies on the move.

Both llamas and alpacas produce useful wool, but the light weight and fineness of alpaca wool make it preferable for clothes and other textiles. The wool of vicuñas, prized for its silky warmth, was a royal prerogative under Inca rule; today, vicuñas are a protected species. The llama is used more for meat (100 edible kg for a buck llama) than its smaller relatives and is the only camelid used for cargo. Even though it can tolerate extreme cold and heights and forages for its food, a llama still has its limitations as a beast of burden. A male buck will carry a load of about 30 kg for 20 km per day and it is usually rested one traveling day out of three by carrying no burden (West 1981). Animals break down even with good care and, when tired, will refuse to budge. Their unhurried pace means that a round trip from the altiplano to the coast can take almost two months. Consequently, even though military caravans could contain thousands of llamas, Murra (1980b) judges that human porters carried the bulk of the cargo in late prehistory (chapter 10).

Human Physiology in the Andean Environment

The human occupation of the high Andes is impressive not just because of the challenges of getting adequate food, but because of the physiological stresses the body endures. Today, over ten million people live at elevations between 2,500 m and 5,000 m, while about two-thirds of the Andean population lived above 3,000 m in 1532. At 3,000 m, the partial pressure of oxygen is only about 60–70 percent of the pressure at sea level, which can put severe strains on the human cardio-pulmonary system. Individuals adapted to coastal conditions suffer from shortness of breath, headaches, and nausea at altitudes where highlanders play football or run marathons. In some cases, altitude sickness (called *soroche* or *puna*) can be fatal. Studies of the bioenergetics of modern sierra peoples show that they have a caloric intake much lower than that of most people living in Western society. Brooke Thomas's (1973) research in Nuñoa, Peru, shows that an adult male of about 55 kg expends on average 2,094 kcal per day, while an adult female of 50 kg expends 1,610 kcal per day. Those figures are much lower than the 2,500 kcal/day typically recommended for Western adults or the 3,500 recommended for US soldiers or estimated for other ancient societies (Van Creveld 1977: 21, 24; Engels 1978: 123; Hassig 1985: 20–1).

Although individuals can adjust to elevation changes and many factors affect stature, some physiological characteristics among native peoples vary genetically. Andean highlanders tend to be shorter and have larger chest capacities than their coastal neighbors. Large lungs especially have been selected for among the highlanders in the 800 or so generations that they have lived in the upper reaches. Intriguingly, some differences also exist between highland groups of Quechua and Aymara ancestry who occupied similar locales in the Titicaca basin. This indicates that choice of mates among ethnic groups also had a hand in creating the biological character of modern Andean peoples.

Predecessors

Archaeologists have made great strides in identifying and explaining the major changes that occurred in Andean prehistory, but readily admit that we still have a long way to go in accounting for the emergence of complex societies. Theories tend to focus on a few key issues in seeking explanations for the appearance of social classes, economic specialization, formal institutions of religion, and the political institutions that crystallized into early states. Among the most frequently cited factors are population growth and the concentration of people in more urbanized settlements. As societies expanded and nucleated, their interactions made it harder to maintain social order and obtain adequate food. Successful societies were those that met the organizational challenges of sustaining a larger population in the face of increased internal strife and external conflict. On the other hand, the close interaction of larger numbers of people provided a setting that fostered intellectual life and creativity. Increases in food production, specialization of labor, and coordination of labor for tasks ranging from erecting monuments to warfare were also crucial. When found together, they indicate that society had centralized leadership and that its members were interdependent for their livelihoods in ways that fed back on one another to produce even more complexity.

Socially, the most important change was the appearance of inherited status differences. This shift signaled differences in access to power and prestige that were ascribed at birth and laid the foundations for class society. Formalized ideologies explained humanity's place in the cosmos and provided rationales for life, but the beliefs also often legitimized social inequality by proposing separate origins for the elite and common members of society. The religions thus simultaneously bonded societies and justified disparities in rank and power. The beliefs were elaborated through monumental architecture, such as pyramids, palaces, and open spaces, in art, and in ceremonies that could venerate the dead as if they were still among the living. In terms of political life, the creation of offices with specific duties allowed a privileged few individuals or kin groups to control the accumulation of information and thus to wield disproportionate power within society. Those elites gathered and guarded information, set policy, and made day-to-day decisions; all of those actions were facilitated by the invention of standardized recording systems.

Each of those features was well established in the Andes more than a thousand years before the rise of Inca power (figures 2.2, 2.3). Until the Incas, however, we only get glimmers of what the people of the time thought about themselves and the forces that surrounded them, and how those views affected the ways that they ordered their lives. Colonial-era documents provide great insights into Andean thought in the sixteenth century, but it is a chancy business to push those ideas too far back into the past. Most of the information came from a few elites with their own viewpoints and positions to protect. Translators, scribes, and administrators whose own convictions were woven into the documents introduced their own biases and filters. Because Andean world views are such a rich field, I will just sketch out pre-Inca history here and save an exploration of Andean beliefs for a later point (esp. chapters 5 and 8).

The earliest reliably dated occupations of South America go back as far as 13,000 years ago. The earliest peoples were small bands of foragers who relied on a diverse array of resources to sustain life, often shifting

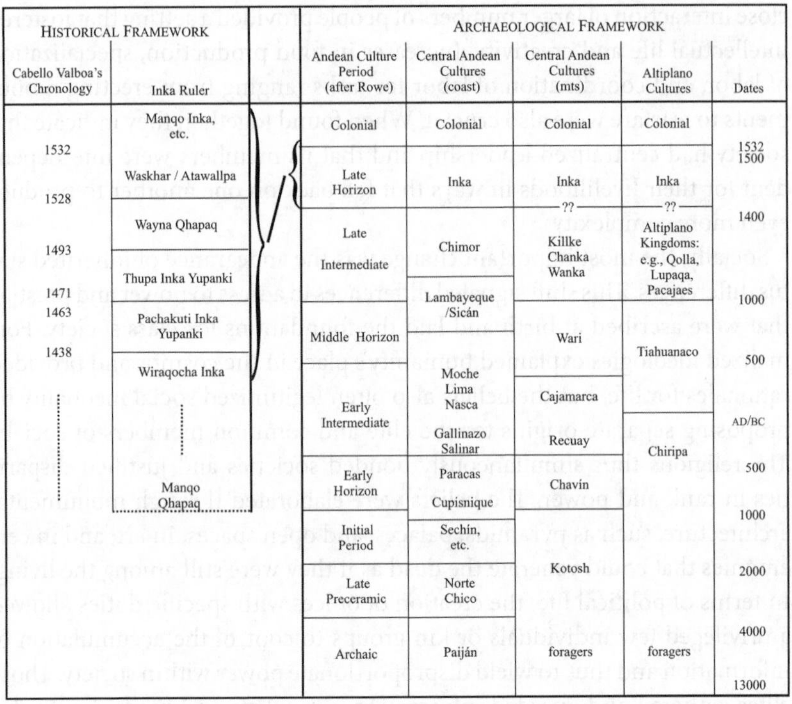

HISTORICAL FRAMEWORK		ARCHAEOLOGICAL FRAMEWORK				
Cabello Valboa's Chronology	Inka Ruler	Andean Culture Period (after Rowe)	Central Andean Cultures (coast)	Central Andean Cultures (mts)	Altiplano Cultures	Dates
	Manqo Inka, etc.	Colonial	Colonial	Colonial	Colonial	
1532						1532 1500
1528	Waskhar / Atawallpa	Late Horizon	Inka	Inka	Inka	
				–??–	–??–	1400
1493	Wayna Qhapaq	Late Intermediate	Chimor	Killke Chanka Wanka	Altiplano Kingdoms: e.g., Qolla, Lupaqa, Pacajaes	
1471	Thupa Inka Yupanki		Lambayeque /Sicán			1000
1463	Pachakuti Inka Yupanki	Middle Horizon		Wari	Tiahuanaco	
1438	Wiraqocha Inka		Moche			500
⋮	⋮	Early Intermediate	Lima Nasca	Cajamarca		AD/BC
			Gallinazo Salinar	Recuay	Chiripa	500
	Manqo Qhapaq	Early Horizon	Paracas	Chavín		1000
			Cupisnique			
		Initial Period	Sechín, etc.			2000
		Late Preceramic	Norte Chico	Kotosh		
						4000
		Archaic	Paiján	foragers	foragers	13000

Figure 2.2 Chronological chart of Andean prehistory.

their residence in a seasonal round. Following a long period of slow, local developments, important changes began to occur rapidly between 3000 and 1200 BC along Peru's coast. The most significant changes have been most clearly identified in the Supe Valley and its neighbors (Huaura, Pativilca, and Fortaleza). The peoples of that area built an impressive array of architecture in thirty large communities that are arguably the New World's first urban settlements (Shady Solís, Haas, and Creamer 2001; Haas and Creamer 2006; Shady Solís 2006, 2008).[2] Major towns such as Caral, Vinto Alto, Porvenir, and Caballete, cover as much as 100 ha or more and may have housed thousands of residents.[3] They contained impressive arrays of monumental architecture along with adjoining residential neighborhoods. Shady Solís's intensive studies at Caral (65 ha) illustrate the complexity of the era's settlements. That site, like a number of others, boasted half a dozen large terraced platform mounds adjacent to plazas and circular ceremonial structures. Individual truncated pyramids at such sites could contain over 100,000 m³ of earth. Differences in scale and quality of the residential

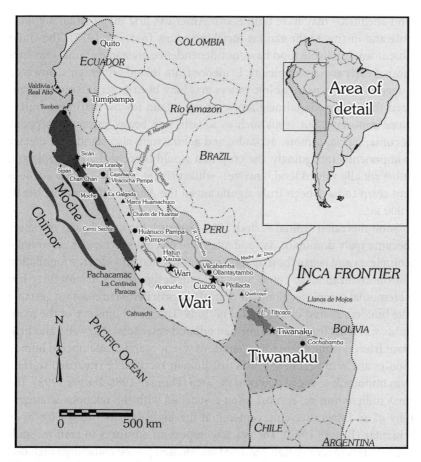

Figure 2.3 Locations of major pre-Inca sites and culture regions described in the text.

compounds suggest that social distinctions may have been taking root. At Aspero, dedicatory caches in mounds include human burials, spondylus shell from coastal Ecuador, bird feathers, beads made of shell, bone, plant, and stone, and unfired clay figurines.

The era's activities are notable not just for the scale of labor investment or the organization required. Remarkably, they occurred before people used pottery vessels or relied heavily on domesticated foods, two features that we often consider essential elements of early complex societies. The dense marine remains at many coastal sites have been taken as evidence that communities relying heavily on rich inshore resources – e.g., anchovies, sardines and shellfish – may have built South America's first major ritual architecture and instituted the earliest social inequality (Moseley 1975). They infer that it was a reliable food base, not dependence on staple grains, that supported early social complexity. Evidence from inland settlements, however, suggests that towns in the low valleys may have been larger and more urbanized than their coastal neighbors. At the inland towns, marine resources were important, but crops such as squash, jack beans, capsicum peppers, lúcuma, guava, camote, avocado, and achira were also significant dietary components. Intriguingly, the crop that would become the key staple and most ritually valued food – maize – while present as early as 5000 BC, does not seem to have been truly significant in the Andean diet until as late as 1000 BC.

Soon thereafter (Initial Period: 1800–800 BC), the inland parts of valleys became truly dominant, as residents there erected spectacular ceremonial complexes and began the irrigation agriculture that provided the foundation for the civilizations to come. Similarities in design among at least forty-five ceremonial complexes along the central to north Peruvian coast suggest that the builders shared cosmological notions. The visual imagery of the pyramids was truly imposing. Some had pillared entrances, stairwells, and brilliant friezes, while a gruesome parade of warriors and dismembered human bodies at Cerro Sechín suggests that human sacrifice or ritualized warfare was important to social power in the area (Donnan 1986; Burger 1992). The first millennium BC is most often associated with the religious iconography of an integrative cult, centered at the highland site called Chavín de Huantar (Burger 1992). The era saw important advances in craft technology. Potters made ornately modeled and incised pieces; metallurgy included soldering, sweat welding, repoussé, and silver–gold alloying; and weaving innovated use of the heddle loom. The most dazzling textiles from the prehistoric Americas date to the end of this period, from cemeteries on the arid Paracas peninsula.

Between about 300 BC and AD 800, the first state and urban societies in the Andes arose on Peru's north coast. The first major societies of this era are now called the Salinar and Gallinazo, who occupied the coast during the last three centuries years BC. Many people lived in nascent cities, and began to erect monumental complexes in several adjoining valleys. The largest Gallinazo settlement was probably the dispersed Gallinazo Group in the Virú valley, which contained as many as 30,000 rooms distributed across about 8 km². By this time, most valleys contained large-scale irrigation networks and the smallest were essentially fully irrigated.

Those developments were rapidly eclipsed by those of the Moche peoples (AD 100–800), who occupied about 500 km of coastline from the Nepeña to Lambayque valleys (see Shimada 1994; Pillsbury 2001). In recent years, the Moche have been second only to the Inca in the intensity of interest that their society and artistry have provoked. The Moche transformed Andean life, building both extensive cities and enormous ceremonial complexes. At least two Moche states and, at times, perhaps several reigned simultaneously within the culture region. Evidence from burials and iconography suggests that the leaders of Moche society blended sacred, military, political, and social roles without developing the distinct administrative institutions seen in other pristine states, such as Uruk Mesopotamia. The most graphic Moche imagery was not just metaphorical. Sites such as Sipán, Huaca el Brujo, and San José de Moro have yielded spectacular burials containing individuals dressed as major figures in a frequently illustrated scene called the (human) Sacrifice Ceremony. The Sipán tombs have yielded the most spectacular burials ever excavated professionally in the New World (Alva and Donnan 1994; Castillo and Donnan 1994).

At the site of Moche, two grand ceremonial constructions flank a flood-scoured plain that contained a large residential community, which could have housed well over 10,000 inhabitants. On one side of the settlement lies the so-called Pyramid of the Moon, a complex of ascending platforms and cloistered rooms. Its many façades boast brilliantly colored clay murals, which depict warriors and prisoners, a decapitator god and other deities, and maritime motifs. The Pyramid of the Sun, situated across the town, is the largest adobe structure in the prehispanic Americas. The date of its construction remains unclear, but it was probably begun after the Pyramid of the Moon and much of it may have been built as late as AD 600. The platform (340 × 160 × 40 m) contained about 143 million adobe bricks. In 1603 treasure-seekers diverted the Moche River to erode away two-thirds of the Sun pyramid from its back side; they recovered 2,788 kg of precious metals in the process.

The intensive Moche agricultural economy supported artisans who crafted exquisite objects for elite patrons, and others who mass-produced items for a more general public. The north coast was the heart of metallurgical craftsmanship in the Americas (Lechtman 1984), so much so that the Incas resettled peoples from the coast to Cuzco to create objects for them. Intriguingly, creativity in metal served symbolic, status-related, and decorative ends for the most part, although copper tools such as needles and tweezers were also made. Moche ceramics also stand out as some of the most exquisite objects made in the prehispanic Americas. They illustrated a bewildering array of images, from portraits of prominent individuals at various life stages, to textile workshops, burial ceremonies, mountain deities, plants, animals, and sexual acts (Donnan 2004).

This was also the era of the Nasca culture of Peru's south coast (200 BC – AD 600; Silverman and Proulx 2002). The urban center of Tambo Viejo rivals its northern counterparts, but the society was probably less hierarchically structured in a political sense. The Nasca culture is best known today for its geoglyphs, which were created by removing stones from the ground surface (Aveni 2002). The most spectacular set is the Nasca Lines, first recognized from the air in 1926 by Alfred Kroeber, but there are many others, from the north coast of Chile to central Peru. Since their discovery, the immense natural figures and arrays of lines have been the subject of professional study and popular myth. While interpretations are vigorously disputed, it seems most plausible that the figures represented constellations, while the straight lines could have been ceremonial pathways or occasionally sight-lines charting astronomical passages. Since convergent line centers seem to be associated with watercourses, it has also been suggested that they marked the flow of water under the desert surface.

About the same time that Moche flourished, two great cities arose in the highlands. Tiahuanaco, which lies just south of Lake Titicaca, became fully urban by about AD 375 and extended ties or founded colonies on the coast, the Bolivian lowlands, and northwest Argentina (Kolata 1993). Both Tiahuanaco and Lake Titicaca were revered in the Inca view of the world, since their origin myths narrated that the Creator God, the sun, the moon, and the stars had all emerged from the lake. The capital included temples and a pyramid oriented along the cardinal directions, and an expansive residential community. The Gateway of the Sun (plate 2.4) and outsized human statues were incorporated into Inca mythology, while the town was recognized as one of two symbolic capitals in a level just below Cuzco. Below the city was a complex array of smaller settlements. The basin was justifiably renowned for its vast flocks of llamas and alpacas, but the populace was also supported by an extraordinary array of raised field systems built along the lake's shoreline.

In southern Peru, Wari rose to power in the Ayacucho basin about AD 500 – 1000 (Schreiber 1992). At its peak, the city housed scores of thousands of residents, but it lacked the formal planning or ceremonial core found at so many other Andean cities. Its leaders expanded their dominion by erecting far-flung, planned settlements in locations where they could

Plate 2.4 Gateway of the Sun at Tiahuanaco. Source: reproduced by permission of Alexei Vranich.

control transport and communications. By this time, simple knot-records were already in use as a device for precise data recording. Hundreds of years later, the Incas adopted some of the same principles of statecraft and even appropriated some of Wari's roads.

Wari and Tiahuanaco shared iconographies that were remarkably similar, so much so that even scholars sometimes mistake one for the other. Even so, we have essentially no evidence for direct political, economic, or other kinds of active relationships between the members of the two polities. The two cities seem to have had radically differing approaches to governance, as Tiahuanaco apparently tried to attract visitors and extend its influence as a ceremonial center, whereas Wari tried to export its power (Isbell and Vranich 2004). At some point, each city seems to have exceeded its abilities to maintain itself, either through environmental stresses or organizational challenges. In any event, both cities were essentially finished as regional powers by about AD 1000.

As Wari and Tiahuanaco collapsed, the Peruvian coast resurged as home to the dominant Andean polities. By AD 1400, a group called the Chimu had emerged in the old Moche valley heartland and united the entire north coast (Moseley and Cordy-Collins 1990; Moore and Mackey 2008). The aristocrats who lived in the main city, called Chan Chan, formed the wealthy apex of a highly stratified society. An enormous social and economic gulf lay between the aristocracy, their retainers, and the rest of the population who lived in more rural settlements. The elites apparently made considerable efforts to set themselves apart from the common folk. The capital covered about $20 \, km^2$ and housed as many as 30,000 inhabitants. The core of the city was taken up by compounds assumed to be royal residences, intermediate elite housing, and housing for retainers and artisans. To govern their 1000-km long coastal domain, the Chimu lords oversaw the construction of a series of provincial installations and major agricultural projects, such as canals and drained field systems. Sometime in the fifteenth century, the empire of Chimor and its million-plus inhabitants fell to the Inca armies. Minchançaman, the last emperor, was taken to Cuzco, and the empire was dismantled. With him went many of his smiths, renowned as the most skilled in the Andes.

The Incas themselves emerged from a highland political environment that was fragmented into hundreds of independent societies by AD 1000. Figures 2.4 and 2.5 illustrate the distribution of many of the major ethnic groups (*etnías*) that were drawn into the Inca empire. The cultural landscape would look different, however, if we changed the scale of our focus. In the

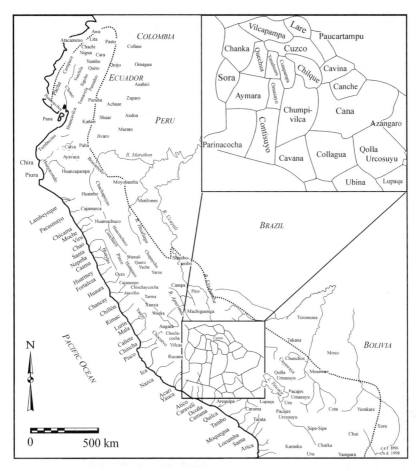

Figure 2.4 Distribution of the major named ethnic groups in the central and north Andes. Source: adapted from Rowe 1946: inset map; Saignes 1985; Fresco, personal communication 1998.

pre-Inca era, many ethnic groups had internal social divisions or included several autonomous polities, called *señoríos* by the Spaniards. Although the Inca provinces were usually built on existing *etnías*, groups were often recombined for administrative convenience. These maps therefore provide only an approximation. They follow Rowe's (1946: 185–92, inset map) convention of identifying regions along the Peruvian coast by valley name, rather than by the many named groups living there.

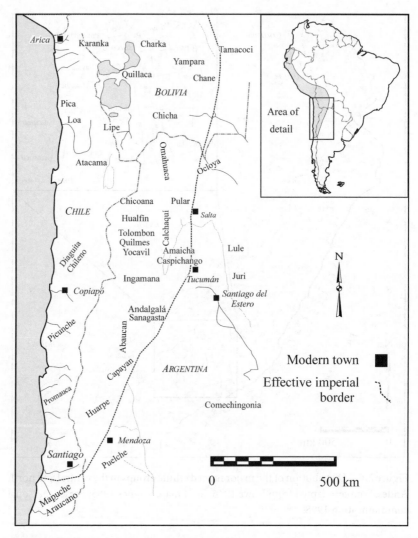

Figure 2.5 Distribution of the major named ethnic groups in the southern Andes. Source: adapted from Berberián and Raffino 1991; Lorandi, personal communication 1998.

Both oral traditions and archaeology suggest that warfare was rife in the sierra from Ecuador to Argentina after AD 1200 or a bit later. Many communities settled on the peaks in protected villages well above the best farmlands. Some of the most powerful societies of the time, including the

Lupaqa and Qolla, lived around Lake Titicaca. In the early Colonial era, they called their pre-Inca rulers kings, but they do not seem to have attained a state level of organization. Instead, the region's societies seem to have lived in considerable instability, in which local conflict played a major role in both begetting chiefly alliances and fracturing polities (Arkush 2011). Radiocarbon dates suggest that the settlement pattern shifted radically about AD 1300, which may have been a result of a significant growth in conflict among neighboring communities (Arkush 2011). Groups living in the populous Peruvian sierra, such as the Wankas, lived in towns that contained as many as 4,500 densely packed circular houses and may have housed 10,000 or more people. Significantly, the shift to defensively situated communities occurred about the same time in that region as had occurred in the Titicaca area, suggesting that similar processes were in play in both areas (D'Altroy *et al.* 2001). In the south Andes, the largest towns contained a few thousand people, but regional polities still held no more than 20,000.

One of the factors that may have contributed to the contentiousness of the Late Intermediate Period was a change in climate that reduced precipitation in the central Andes for the period AD 1250–1310 (Thompson *et al.* 1985). The drought was coupled with colder conditions, with a glaciation occurring *c.* AD 1290 (Seltzer and Hastorf 1990: 402). As a result, climatic conditions were depressed as much as 150 m from modern levels in central Peru (Seltzer and Hastorf 1990: 405). Put another way, Seltzer and Hastorf estimate that about 29 percent of the land suitable for potato agriculture today in the Mantaro valley – the most productive area for farming in the Peruvian highlands – would have been lost during the cold, dry era that characterized the second half of the Late Intermediate Period. The effect on maize would have been even more dramatic, as about 54 percent of the land currently used for maize agriculture would have been unavailable for that crop. Those more challenging conditions likely would have helped set into motion an array of competitive and cooperative strategies over access to both natural and human resources.

By AD 1200, the Cuzco area itself may have been an oasis of relative tranquility, already integrated under pre-state Inca rule (chapter 3). That development set the stage for the meteoric rise of Tawantinsuyu (chapter 4). Even this sketch illustrates that complex society had been developing for millennia before Cuzco's ascendancy. The Incas saw things another way, of course, insisting to the Spaniards that they had brought order and civilization to a chaotic world. Conversely, some of their subjects complained that their own cultures had been irrevocably disrupted by barbaric conquerors, Inca and Spaniard alike, but their voices were not so clearly heard.

Languages

The question of the Incas' language used to have a straightforward answer. Pretty much from the moment the Spaniards first set foot in Tawantinsuyu, everyone understood that the Incas spoke Quechua. During the imperial era, they spread it for use as a *lingua franca*, that is, a language used to communicate among peoples who spoke different tongues. The earliest Spanish writers generally understood Quechua to be one of the three principal languages of the land, along with Aymara and the now-defunct Puquina of the Titicaca basin. Scores of other languages also fell into disuse in the Colonial and historical periods.[4] Like so much of our understanding of Andean prehistory, however, scholars have turned conventional knowledge on its head. Linguists have recently arrived at the view that the Incas may have adopted Quechua for imperial rule precisely because it was already widespread. Before then, the Incas spoke one or two other languages, most likely Aymara and possibly Puquina. To understand how perspectives have shifted, we need to explore the linguistic terrain of the Andes a little bit.

The language that the Incas used to administer their domain is commonly known today as Southern Peruvian Quechua, but its speakers knew it as *runasimi*, or human speech. Quechua is more properly a language family than a language, as several variants existed that were not fully mutually intelligible. Today scholars classify Quechua in several ways; one system recognizes two major variants while another has yielded seven separate lexicons and grammars. In modern Peru, Quechua and Spanish are the two official state languages and the native tongue remains an important or even exclusive language of about ten million people (King Kendall and Hornberger 2006: 178). When I worked in the Mantaro valley of Peru's central highlands from 1977 to 1986, field assistants born by 1945 were fluent in Quechua, but few of those born later spoke it in everyday conversation. Sadly, the trend toward disappearance of the language is increasingly rapid – only about 5 percent of the children of Quechua-speaking parents speak Quechua today (Heggarty, pers. comm., November 2011).

The term *Quechua* itself was probably imposed early in the Colonial period by Spaniards who mistook the word *qheswa* (valley) in the phrase *qheswa simi* (valley speech) for the name of the language (Mannheim 1991). Native peoples then adopted the term back into their own tongue in various forms, including the word for the mountainous ecological zone described earlier. I use the term throughout this book as it is commonly applied, to describe the Incas' administrative language and its close relatives. Quechua was entrenched by 1532 as the language in which all official business was supposed to be conducted. Because of that situation, both the public and most scholars thought that the Incas themselves were responsible for the spread of Quechua throughout Tawantinsuyu (e.g., Rowe 1946). In keeping with their penchant for order and standardization, according to this view, the Incas found it convenient administratively to impose a single language on their realm. The language that they chose, of course, was that of their own heartland.

Many historical linguists no longer accept that argument as valid (e.g., Adelaar and Muysken 2004; Cerrón-Palomino 2008; Heggarty 2008). Instead, they generally agree that the home region of Quechua lay along the central Peruvian coast (figure 2.6a). The language had split into two major branches and was already widely distributed in the highlands at least five centuries before the Inca rise to power.[5] The variant that the Incas adopted appears to have been Chincha Quechua. Its roots lay on the south-central coast, but it was used in parts of the Andes from Ecuador to south Peru (Adelaar and Muysken 2004). The Incas' major contribution to the geographic spread of this form of Quechua was in the south Andes, and even some of that distribution can be attributed to Spanish Colonial practices (DeMarrais 2012).

As just noted, the Incas' dominant pre-imperial language may thus well have been Aymara (figure 2.6b). Drawing from historical linguistic and toponymic (place-name) evidence, some linguists suggest that the Incas probably spoke Aymara well into the early imperial era, since that was the language of the southern Peruvian highlands in late prehistory and Aymara place-names are even found as far north as the central Peruvian highlands (Adelaar and Muysken 2004; Cerrón-Palomino 2004, 2008; Heggarty and Beresford-Jones 2012; figure 2.6b). Quechua and Aymara speakers apparently interacted a great deal, to the extent that the two languages now overlap about 30 percent (e.g., in lexicons).[6] Such a scenario raises the questions as to when the Incas adopted Quechua as their administrative language, and why. The leading Andean linguist today, Rodolfo Cerrón-Palomino (2012), suggests that the shift may have occurred as late as the rule of Wayna Qhapaq, that is, no more than three or four decades before the Spaniards' arrival, because its widespread use in the lands to the north made it an effective sociopolitical tool.

Intriguingly, a few chroniclers (e.g., Garcilaso, Murúa) reported that the Incas maintained a secret language that only they were allowed to learn. Many scholars have dismissed that idea as fancy, but those who accept its existence have settled on Aymara or Puquina as the most likely candidates. Cerrón-Palomino (2004, 2012) tentatively favors the latter, drawing on etymologies and toponyms for support. That language dominated in the

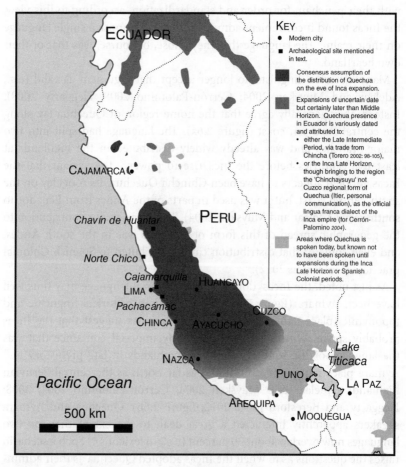

Figure 2.6 Distribution of (a) Quechua language at the eve of Inca expansion; and (b) current and assumed distributions of Aymara, by nature and strength of evidence. Source: Heggarty and Beresford Jones 2012.

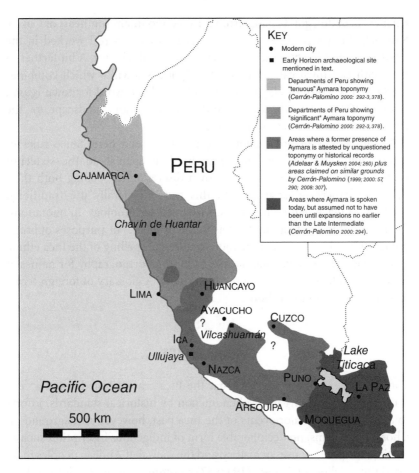

KEY

● Modern city

■ Early Horizon archaeological site mentioned in text.

Departments of Peru showing "tenuous" Aymara toponymy (*Cerrón-Palomino 2000: 292-3, 378*).

Departments of Peru showing "significant" Aymara toponymy (*Cerrón-Palomino 2000: 292-3, 378*).

Areas where a former presence of Aymara is attested by unquestioned toponymy or historical records (*Adelaar & Muysken 2004: 260*) *plus areas claimed on similar grounds by Cerrón-Palomino* (*1999; 2000: 57, 290; 2008: 307*).

Areas where Aymara is spoken today, but assumed not to have been until expansions no earlier than the Late Intermediate (*Cerrón-Palomino 2000: 294*).

Figure 2.6 (*continued*)

Lake Titicaca region at the time and only disappeared from the linguistic landscape in the nineteenth century. As we will see later, key Inca terms for sacred places (the capital *qusqu*, lake *Titicaca*) or beings (e.g., the Sun deity Inti) arguably have Puquina origins or were filtered through mixed Aymara–Puquina structures (Cerrón-Palomino 2004, 2012).

Even if the Incas did adopt Quechua late in the game, the impact of using that language for state business is written today in place-names from Ecuador to Argentina. As part of the imperial stamp, the Incas renamed mountains and other natural features after revered locations around Cuzco. For example, the peak named Huanacauri that overlooks modern

Cuenca, Ecuador, got its name from a sacred mountain southeast of Cuzco. Similarly, the town in Salta province (Argentina) where I worked in the 1990s is named Cachi – the Quechua word for salt (*kachi*). A bit farther to the south is a town called Sanogasta – "potter's town" – which combines the Quechua word for clay (*sañu*) with the Kakano word for town (*gasta*; Lorandi 1984). In truth, today's Andes are a memory landscape for the language that the Incas took as their own.

A comment is in order about the spellings used here. Since rules of orthography had not yet been formalized in Spanish in the sixteenth century, the chroniclers used their own discretion in spelling both their own and American languages. In this text, I generally use traditional spellings of place-names, but modernize other terminology. In quotations, the names of individuals are kept as in the original. For purposes of broad recognition, I have retained the more traditional spelling of the Inca ethnic group, but otherwise use standardized Quechua orthography for names of important individuals, such as the Inca rulers. A glossary of foreign terms is found at the end of the book.

Time Frames

The available evidence suggests that the Inca empire lasted about a century, making it a short-lived phenomenon by historical standards. Efforts to assign dates to major events of the Inca past, however, run aground on a host of problems: no decipherable form of indigenous inscription such as writing, the political uses of history, and the ways that Andean peoples reckoned time. Following Rowe's (1944: 57) recommendation, modern authors often cite the last part of the chronology proposed by the cleric Miguel de Cabello Valboa (1951) in 1586. Cabello estimated that the imperial era began about AD 1438 when the Incas repelled an attack by the Chankas, a people who lived to the west of Cuzco. He reckoned that the successions of imperial rulers occurred about 1471, 1493, and 1526. Lacking any way to determine absolute dates in 1944, Rowe judged that Cabello's chronology was the most plausible to be found in the chronicles. Rowe made his recommendation cautiously, based on a close analysis of many sources, and considered Cabello's pre-imperial succession dates to be unlikely.

Even though we do not know the cleric's sources, it helped matters that his dates were supported indirectly. Most chroniclers reported that the imperial era lasted through the reigns of Pachakuti Inka Yupanki, Thupa Inka

Yupanki, and Wayna Qhapaq, followed by a civil war between two of Wayna Qhapaq's sons. The conquest sequences recounted in Cuzco also often coincided with those recorded in the provinces, albeit with some discrepancies (Pärssinen 1992). In addition, members of several ethnic groups living around Cuzco in the 1570s recalled that their ancestors a generation or two back had been brought in by the three emperors named above. Together, those lines of evidence suggest that Cabello may have been pretty close to the mark.[7]

For other scholars, use of Cabello's or any other historical chronology has been as much a matter of convention as conviction. The Spanish accounts that drew on Inca narratives produced at least four date sequences other than Cabello's (Covey 2006a). Sarmiento's official history, for example, was based on interviews with more than a hundred record-keepers in Cuzco and read publicly before the nobility, who assured its veracity. Even so, the process yielded dates that are patently unbelievable, as numerous rulers lived to be well over 100. Rowe himself considered Cabello's pre-imperial chronology to be unreliable, for much the same reason.

From the Inca perspective, a specific number of years may well have been incidental. Since eminence and great age went hand in hand, it was only fitting that the rulers had lived well beyond the natural life span of normal human beings.[8] Part of the imprecision can also be traced to the fact that the Incas seemingly did not keep close track of the accumulating years, even though they traced annual cycles carefully (Rowe 1946: 274).[9] Cobo (1979: 252–3) explained that,

> When they are asked about things of the past, if something happened more than four to six years back, what they usually answer is that the incident occurred *ñaupapacha*, which means "a long time ago"; and they give the same answer for events of twenty years back as for events of a hundred or a thousand years back, except that when the thing is very ancient, they express this by a certain accent and ponderation of their words.[10]

When the Incas described events that were written down in Spanish court records, they seem to have used other well-known events as temporal anchors for their accounts. For instance, conquests were described as having occurred during the rule of a particular ruler, or under the leadership of named generals, not at a specific chronological moment. Similarly, Wanka testimony about provisions given to the Spaniards in the first couple of decades recorded that a certain set of materials had been provided when thus and such a Spaniard had been present, or when a particular military action was underway (Espinoza Soriano 1972). To complicate matters further, the Spaniards heard differing accounts of the Inca past (see chapter 1), while the organization of the *khipu* knot-records limited their ability to construct history as they knew it. Since the *khipu* histories were organized partially by hierarchies of power and space as well as by sequence, some scholars judge that translating the oral sagas into European histories with a firm time frame is a futile endeavor.

Archaeologists have therefore turned to radiocarbon and thermoluminescence dating methods in efforts to pin down the emergence of the empire. Even under the best conditions, however, those techniques contain an intrinsic error term. Dates are reported as brackets of years before the present (BP, i.e., before AD 1950 for radiocarbon), based on probabilities, and are then calibrated to calendrical dates through a variety of means.[11] The lack of certainty in the dates leaves some scholars skeptical that current radiometric evidence can improve on the historical estimates, while others judge that enough information exists to permit some tentative statements about the timing of the Inca era.

At this point, scholars have collected and analyzed hundreds of dates from Inca contexts in an effort to resolve the problem. While the controversy remains, my own view is that there is enough evidence to suggest that the first major surge of Inca expansionism occurred early in the fifteenth century, a few decades years earlier than Cabello's historical chronology reckoned (Bauer 1992; Adamska and Michecsynski 1996; Bauer and Covey 2004; Covey 2006a). A particularly intriguing set of dates was taken recently from deposits at the site of Chokepuquio (McEwan and Gibaja O. n.d.). At this site, which was home to a major Inca foe in the Lucre basin late in the era of Inca state formation, a major burning event separated the pre-Inca from the imperial era. The reported suite of dates puts that event between 1400 and 1430 (with a 95 percent degree of confidence). If we accept the proposition that the conflagration occurred after the town fell to Inca forces, then we can infer that the Incas took control sometime early in the fifteenth century, not close to mid-century as the historical readings put it. A few decades is not a major shift in calendrical time, but it does imply that we need to be careful in taking the historical chronologies too literally.

Despite the discrepancies, the chronometric evidence and the historical accounts both suggest that the empire was a late prehistoric phenomenon that lasted somewhere close to a century. Archaeology also indicates that there was a roughly contemporaneous extension of Inca material culture across the Andes in the fifteenth century, with the exception of potentially early materials the Lake Titicaca region (see chapter 3), as we might expect from a polity that was rapidly expanding. Beyond those broad conclusions, however, we cannot refine the chronology any more than to say the empire arose quickly, probably early in the fifteenth century, and lasted for only a few generations.

Notes

1 The word *ayllu* actually has a far more complicated connotation than this brief description, a point that will be taken up in chapter 9, on family and class. As Salomon (1991: 22) explains, the term is best thought of as constituting a kind of relatedness among people or even things, not a particular set of related people. So the term can be applied to any of a range of groupings, depending on the context. He writes (1991: 22): "It has no inherit limits of scale; in principle, it applies to all levels from sibling groups to huge kindreds, clanlike groups, or even whole ethnic groups defined by reference to common origin and territory." Allen (2002: 82–7) adds that today's peasant *ayllu* are constituted in conjunction with a particular locale. People can move in and out of an *ayllu*, and an *ayllu* can be defunct and then reconstituted when people move back into a vacated locale.

2 Archaeologists working in this era disagree on whether the north coast was alone in early urban and monumental constructions, or if similar sorts of sites were also built along the central coast, but were later buried under the even more monumental sites of the Initial Period. Even more contention exists over exactly what happened or how to account for it, issues better left for another venue.

3 As a point of reference, that is a little less than Washington's National Mall (80 percent), or roughly 200 American football fields, 270 soccer fields, 250 acres, or one-third of New York's Central Park. A hectare (ha) = 1.59 acres.

4 The most important, especially the Muchik of Peru's north coast, may have been spoken by a million or more people.

5 Heggarty and Beresford-Jones (2012) have argued that the spread of Quechua can be most reasonably linked to the expansion of the Wari empire in the mid-first millennium AD. Their position is being debated as this text is being written.

6 People borrowed a fair amount from one another across languages in the greater Andean region. For example, the lowland Arawakan languages lent some words (e.g., of tropical forest animals), word-suffixes (e.g., month names), and linguistic structures to the highland languages of Quechua,

Aymara, and Puquina (Adelaar and Muysken 2004; Adelaar pers. comm. 2011).

7   Recently, historians have re-examined the documentary sources to see if the historical time frame can be refined (Julien 2008; Rowe 2008). Rowe did not address the issue of the inception of the regional or imperial Inca polities, but does suggest that Betanzos' account provides a reasonable set of reconstructable dates for events in the latter decades of the empire. Those dates coincide with others from complementary documents, so Rowe judged that the historical chronology that he proposed using in 1944 was still a fairly reasonable framework for the imperial era. Using the same documents, as well as the Probanza, Julien suggested that the conquest of the south coast occurred somewhat earlier in the imperial era than Rowe had first inferred. Since the Late Horizon as a chronological period had been based on the inception of Inca presence in the Ica valley, she deduces that the Late Horizon began earlier calendrically than had previously been accepted, but sees no reason to extend the imperial era per se any earlier.

8   Witnesses made implausible and erratic claims about their own ages as well. For example, two noble witnesses claimed ages first of 120 and 132, and then of 86 and 86, in depositions presented a week apart in 1569 (Urton 1990: 64).

9   In his analysis of Betanzos' (1996) chronicle, Rowe (2008) argues that the Incas did indeed keep close track of event sequences and their duration, even if they did not calculate ages precisely. He suggests that the Spaniards were less accurate in their calendrical determinations than the Incas. This contention is not fully accepted by Inca scholars, since it requires admitting some documents or parts of them as chronologically accurate and discarding others. Another adherent of the historical chronologies, Julien (2008: 172, 174), accepts the sequence of events for the conquest of the south coast recorded in the 1558 Chincha document. She observes that the document puts the inception of that conquest about 150 years earlier, that is, *c.* 1408, but does not accept that date as accurate. Similar examples may be cited to underscore the complexities of reconstruction, but this is too arcane an argument to take up further here.

10 There is a little evidence that the Incas made some effort to keep track of the life spans or reigns of the most recent rulers. Two royal descendants of Pachakuti and Thupa Inka Yupanki, interviewed in Cuzco in 1570–2, consulted an illustrated wooden board and *khipu* (knot-records) to report that Pachakuti died at 100, Thupa Inka Yupanki at 58 or 60, and Wayna Qhapaq at 70. Pachakuti's age is pretty clearly a nicely rounded figure intended to mean that the empire's founder had lived to a grand old age. Other witnesses said that Thupa Inka Yupanki died young, between youth and old age, and old. Regarding Wayna Qhapaq, they said he died at about 60 or 70, very old, or with some grey hair, anywhere from two to ten years before the Spanish invasion (Toledo 1940: 92, 118, 140, 148, 157–8, 166, 173, 200, 202, 203). As we will see in chapter 5, how

the Incas thought about time played into their lack of precision in accounting for the passage of the years.

11   The techniques are also subject to a range of other problems that may arise, for example, from re-use of materials or misidentified contexts. It is particularly vexing that there is a wiggle in the correction curves for radiocarbon dates just at the crucial era of the early Inca expansion.

Chapter Three

The Incas before the Empire

Setting the Stage

Considering the impact that the Incas had on the Andes, it is astonishing how little we knew about their pre-imperial society until recently. We still do not know when the Incas began to identify themselves by that name, for instance, or how they came by it. By the late imperial era, the word *Inca* meant *lord*, but we cannot be sure of any earlier meanings.[1] We can lay some of our plight at the doorstep of the royal narratives, which were grand epics designed to exalt the heroic and supernatural creation of Inca society. Constantly reshaped in the telling, they flowed smoothly from the mythical origins of mighty ancestors to the lives of people the Spanish conquistadores met in the flesh. As for archaeology, the imperial building programs wiped out many of the pre-imperial Inca (Killke[2]) settlements of the Cuzco basin. Until archaeologists began a vigorous study of the early Incas in the last couple of decades, it was hard to envision what kind of society gave birth to the Americas' greatest indigenous empire. Even with the recent advances, explaining the grand trajectory still calls for some informed conjecture, but happily our explanations today are much better grounded than they were a short time ago.

The legendary character of the earliest part of the Inca narratives makes it difficult to build a credible history for that era. At best, we can examine the stories for themes and internal coherence as they progressed through the generations. The politics they describe for the first few rulers after the Incas' genesis and sojourn to Cuzco are consistent with a kind of society called chiefdoms, which we are familiar with through ethnographic studies. Chiefdoms have internal social and political hierarchies, so that some families or lineages have more status and power than others. Over the generations, the power of the more privileged members of society – over resources, the ability to make group decisions, or to provide sacred, military

The Incas, Second Edition. Terence N. D'Altroy.
© 2015 John Wiley & Sons, Ltd. Published 2015 by John Wiley & Sons, Ltd.

and political leadership – tends to become increasingly concentrated in a restricted set of hands. The most complex chiefdoms have incipient social classes, so that a person's status is largely determined by whose family he/she is born into. They are unstable formations, often exhibiting predatory warfare, inter-group marriages, fragile alliances, and population realignments to new leaders and their resources. By about the sixth to eighth rulers in the conventional list of thirteen, the Incas seem to have developed many of those features, while they were flexing their muscles in regional expansionist ventures.

Many Incas told the Spaniards that they rose to power from an uneasy regional balance only about four generations before Francisco Pizarro's unwelcome arrival in AD 1532. The Jesuit chronicler Miguel Cabello Valboa judged that a pivotal transformation had occurred about AD 1438, a date that is often still used as a benchmark (see chapter two, section entitled "Time Frames"). At that time, he wrote, the Chanka people attacked Cuzco from their home in Andahuaylas, about 150 km to the west. In the face of the assault, the Inca ruler Wiraqocha and most of the town's other residents fled to a nearby redoubt.[3] Prince Inka Yupanki refused to cede his home to the assailants, however, and crushed them in a series of divinely aided battles. The prince then deposed his father and took the title *Pachakuti* ("Turning over of space–time"), an act that symbolically claimed a regenesis of history. Soon after seizing power, Pachakuti began to annex neighboring societies, some of them no more than a few kilometers away from Cuzco. His pursuit of wealth, glory, and power snowballed with each success, as he rapidly began to establish the imperial realm.

That celebrated tale may hold a lot of truth, but there are also sound reasons to doubt some aspects of it. For one, archaeology suggests that the Incas had been building power over several centuries before Pachakuti's generation (Bauer and Covey 2002, 2004; Covey 2006b). Their ascendancy began sometime after AD 1000, when they were just one of many highland societies jockeying for position following the decline of Wari and Tiwanaku. By about 1300, the Incas had dominated the greater Cuzco area and were well on the way to establishing a state, with an urbanized elite class at its core. That is, their experiences over 300–400 years provided an organizational foundation for the rapid imperial expansion of the fifteenth century. In comparison, no fifteenth-century Chanka settlement could rival Cuzco, nor did their home country in Andahuaylas contain an urban hierarchy like that of the Incas (Bauer *et al.* 2010; see chapter 2 this volume).

We can also raise an eyebrow about the Chanka narrative for historio-graphic reasons. It helps to keep in mind that the Inca history that is so widely cited today – and that foregrounds Pachakuti – was not settled on until the 1550s or even later, decades after the empire's collapse (Covey 2006a; Pease 2008a). Inca informants told the Spaniards several other versions of their past that were shunted aside as a conventional history took shape. A few alternate rulers appear in some histories but not others,[4] for example, and the narratives vary as to who annexed which subjects (see below and chapter 4). Some authorities wrote that the Inca victory over the Chankas took place one or two generations before Pachakuti (e.g., Cobo 1979: 121–5), and there is even reason to think that Inka Yupanki and Pachakuti may have been different people (Dean 1999).[5] In the face of such inconsistencies, many scholars look askance at the idea that a Chanka attack *c.* AD 1438 set off the Inca imperial expansion.[6] While the Incas and Chankas may well have fought at some point, the narrative particulars may also have been tailored after the fact to favor one iconic figure and his descendants.

If we look at the question from an anthropological viewpoint, an expla-nation that relies on a single trigger or figure is surely unsatisfactory. It is far more likely that an interplay occurred between historical and other circumstances. Political and economic conditions, ideology, military capac-ities, wrangling among kin groups, and maybe even the climate were all implicated. It is impossible to do justice to all of those issues here, and that isn't the goal of this book. But we do need to be aware that there is no straightforward version of the Incas' past that they, the Spaniards, and mod-ern scholars would ever agree on. So this chapter will take a brief look at the available evidence and then sketch out a composite view that tries to reconcile the different kinds of information.

Narrative Origins

The earliest Inca history consists of genealogies and narrative tales, rooted in primordial time (Urton 1990; Bauer 1991). Those annals customarily begin with the deified Manqo Qhapaq and continue through twelve or thirteen rulers (figure 3.1; table 3.1). Like many Andean peoples, the Incas understood that their ancestors had emerged from a natural feature of the landscape. Such a place – a cave, a lake, a mountain peak – was known as a *paqarisqa*. In ancient times, went the main Inca legend, there was a cave called the House of Windows (*Tampu T'oqo*) at the Inn of

Figure 3.1 The Inca royal lineage, as illustrated by the native chronicler Guaman Poma (1936).

Table 3.1 The Inca ancestors, according to Sarmiento; glosses after Urton (1990: 21).

Brothers	Sisters
Ayar Manqo ("first ancestor") also known asManqo Qhapaq ("first rich [ancestor]")	Mama Ocllo ("shapely [plump] mother")
Ayar Awka ("ancestor enemy")	Mama Waku ("cheek [jaw] mother"; "grandmother")
Ayar Kachi ("ancestor salt")	Mama Ipakura / Kura ("maternal aunt/daughter-in-lawcastration mother")
Ayar Uchu ("ancestor chili pepper")	Mama Rawa ("[?] mother")

Dawn (*Pacariqtambo*).[7] The Creator God Wiraqocha summoned the four brothers and four sisters who became the Inca ancestors from the central cave, called the Rich Window (*Qhapaq T'oqo*). He then called forth the Maras and Tambos peoples from two adjoining caves, called *Maras T'oqo* and *Sutiq T'oqo* (Sarmiento 2007: 60).

The eight Incas were paired off as couples either at their first appearance or soon thereafter. In Diez de Betanzos' (1996: 13–14) version, the richly dressed primordial ancestors emerged as couples, each husband preceding his wife. A little later, they decided to seek the fertile lands that they coveted to make them rich. The principal couple, Manqo Qhapaq and Mama Oqllu, found a ready ally in the Tambos, who they organized into two sets of five kin groups called *ayllu* (table 3.2). The company then set off, stopping every now and then along the way, but they never found land quite productive enough to persuade them to settle down. At one resting spot called Tamboquiro, Mama Oqllu gave birth to Zinchi Roq'a, destined to become the second Inca ruler. The travelers' lives were complicated along the road by the actions of an unruly Inca brother named Ayar Kachi, who fought with the people they met and smashed mountains into ravines with the stones he flung from his mighty sling. So the other siblings tricked him into re-entering the origin cave by claiming that they had forgotten some golden vessels, seeds, and other things inside. When Ayar Kachi fell for the ruse, his kin sealed him in forever with a large stone (Sarmiento 2007: 65).

The company's meandering journey eventually led them to the top of a mountain beyond which they could see a fruitful valley graced by a rainbow – a manifest sign of their long-sought home. Before they could descend the slopes, however, brother Ayar Uchu was transformed into a stone. (Both the stone and the mountain became known as Huanacauri and were revered as shrines of surpassing sanctity; the stone was even granted a house of its own in Cuzco during the early Colonial era.) At Matagua,

Table 3.2 The ten *ayllu* formed at Pacariqtampu, according to Sarmiento; spellings after Urton (1990: 25).

Hanan Cuzko ("Upper Cuzco")	Hurin Cuzko ("Lower Cuzco")
Chawin Cuzco Ayllu	Sutiq-T'oqo Ayllu
Arayraka Ayllu Cuzco-Kallan	Maras Ayllu
Tarpuntay Ayllu	Kuykusa Ayllu
Wakaytqaui Ayllu	Maska Ayllu
Sañuq Ayllu	Oro Ayllu

Mama Waku – some said Manqo Qhapaq – cast two golden rods into the valley. When the first did not stick firmly in the soil, they knew the land was not fertile. But when the second rod plunged deep into the earth at Wanaypata, the Incas knew they had found their land. As the company entered Cuzco, Manqo Qhapaq called Ayar Awka to him and said,

> "Brother! Do you remember that we agreed that you should go to take posses-
> sion of the land we are to settle? So now look at that rock!" Showing him the
> boundary marker, he said, "Fly over there" (because they said that he had grown
> wings), "and sit there and take possession of the very place where that boundary
> marker is so that we can then go to settle and live there!" (Sarmiento 2007: 69)

Ayar Awka flew to the designated place just as he had been commanded, and transformed himself into a stone pillar that marked the Incas' claim. Inconveniently enough, people were already living in the valley, so the Incas took up a campaign to dislodge them. Mama Waqo personally inflicted terrible cruelties on the Guayllas people, tearing one man apart with her bare hands and inflating his lungs by blowing into them. Despite occasional setbacks, the Incas finally expelled the local people and set themselves up as lords of the valley. They then divided Cuzco into four parts and built the first house of the Sun at Inticancha. (The story continues with the life and times of the early Incas in Cuzco, described later.)

This narrative exemplifies how many elements of Inca social relations and cosmography were woven into their view of history. Like so many other imperial lords, the Incas claimed a creation separate from the rest of humanity, even the non-Inca lineages of Cuzco. Bauer (1996) notes that the story recalls the image of the wandering stranger-king endowed with mystic powers, a tale found in many other societies (Sahlins 1981). That union of exotic and separate creation allowed the Incas to distinguish their supernaturally blessed line from all other peoples. Cuzco's social hierarchy also gathered legitimacy from the tale, since the grouping of the non-royal kin into two divisions of five each foreshadowed the social structure that the Spaniards encountered in 1533. The sanctification of space – marking the pilgrimage route and the division of Cuzco into four parts – also let the Incas claim specific landmarks as part of their past and started to fashion the sacred geography that defined their relationship with the natural world (chapter 8). Finally, the tale grounded imperial sun worship in primordial times by crediting the first solar temple to the ancestor Manqo Qhapaq. All in all, the Inca myth of their own creation provided a neatly refined tradition that legitimized the sixteenth-century present.

By the time the Spaniards arrived, the Incas had turned their origin place into a shrine. In response to Crown inquiries, they said that the site was located about 30 km south of Cuzco. Bauer (1991, 1992) describes two sites in the Paruro region with imperial Inca components that fit elements of the legend. One is a stone outcrop known as *Puma Orqo* ("Puma Mountain") and the other is a settlement called *Maukallaqta* ("Old City"). At Puma Orqo, several boulders form a cave just as the story of *Tampu T'oqo* recalled. The outcrop's summit was modified by Inca-era carvings of horizontal planes and two puma figures, while Bauer's excavations recovered Wari-era material remains beneath an adjacent Inca building. Maukallaqta, which fronts Puma Orqo, contains more than 200 finely built structures in the imperial style, including some elegant cut-stone walls. Excavations there recovered both Wari-era and imperial Inca materials. Among the latter were a human skeleton, marine shell, a gold llama, a silver *tumi* knife, and two silver *tupu* pins, reminiscent of the kinds of offerings interred in the important *qhapaq ucha* ritual (chapters 7 and 8). Bauer infers that the constructions and carvings at this location enshrined the earliest Inca *wak'a* and bonded royal history to the landscape.

The Early Reigns

According to their narratives, the Incas often fought their neighbors during their early years in Cuzco. Some protagonists, such as the Ayarmaca ethnic group, were named after natural resources, such as salt (*kachi*), quinoa (*ayar*), and a tuber crop (*maca*) (Rostworowski 1999: 8 – 11; see Sarmiento 2007: 68 – 74; cf. Cobo 1979: 108 – 12). The Incas thus claimed to have subdued both the peoples of Cuzco and through them the products of the earth. Once conquered, the Ayarmaca largely disappeared from the narratives, although rulers even as late as Pachakuti were said to have vanquished them. The exploits of Manqo Qhapaq, the Inca ancestor, mainly concerned his divinely inspired origin, the sojourn to Cuzco, and the founding of the first settlements (chapter 8). Most stories about his son and successor, Zinchi Roq'a, said that he was renowned more for his wisdom and generosity than physical valor. His reign featured peaceable relations with the neighbors, which were cemented when he received his wife Mama Kuka from the town of Saño, which lay a few kilometers to the east of Cuzco.

Lloq'e Yupanki ("Left-handed"), the third Inca, became ruler even though he had an elder brother. Like his father, Lloq'e Yupanki was usually credited with expanding Inca influence through acumen rather than war. Late in life he married the local beauty Mama Kawa, who gave birth to the redoubtable Mayta Qhapaq, the fourth Inca. The legends told that Mayta Qhapaq was an aggressive leader who was repeatedly embroiled in fights – first with other Inca boys and then with nearby peoples. Through marriage with a daughter of the lord of Collaguas, he sired a number of sons, one of whom, Qhapaq Yupanki, eventually succeeded to leadership (Sarmiento 2007: 81–4; Cieza 1967: 109; Callapiña *et al.* 1974: 30–1; Cobo 1979: 115–20; Diez de Betanzos 1996: 18; Murúa 1986: 60–4). Like most Inca successions, Qhapaq Yupanki's accession may have been indirect. Some narratives said that he was the eldest son, but Sarmiento's (2007: 84) witnesses agreed that he had an older brother named Conde Mayta, who was so ugly that he was thought unfit for rule.[8] For his wife, Qhapaq Yupanki took Mama Qori Willpay ("Golden Jewel"), who hailed either from Cuzco itself or from the neighboring Ayarmaca.

Their son Inka Roq'a was credited with transforming Inca life in several substantial ways (see Sarmiento 2007: 87–9). In the social context, he reportedly closed off the addition of new lineages to Lower Cuzco, the older and less prestigious of the two royal Inca kin groupings.[9] He then founded Upper Cuzco (*Hanan Cuzco*), the grand royal moiety to which all of the imperial-era rulers belonged. He also saved the city from drought, by plunging his hand into the soil where he heard running water. The canal networks that were subsequently built to water the Cuzco valley and nourish the city itself were assigned to kin groups following his lead. In this context, it may be significant that Inka Roq'a is the earliest ruler whose descendants claimed a royal estate in the early Colonial era.

Some Spanish-authored accounts wrote that, following his marriage, he dispatched expeditions into the Vilcanota valley, where they seized towns as far afield as Quiquijana, about four leagues (~20 km) away (Cieza 1967: 115–22; Murúa 1986: 69). Sarmiento's witnesses said that he also vanquished the two principal Inca foes in the Lucre region, the Pinahua and Mohina, thus solidifying Inca control over much of the linked Cuzco–Vilcanota valley drainages. Cobo's (1979: 121–5) chronicle added that Inka Roq'a also conquered the valley of Andahuaylas, some 34 leagues (~170 km) west of Cuzco. There, they vanquished the Chankas, with mercenary help from the Canas and the Canche, who came from lands to the southeast of Cuzco. Intriguingly, some narratives that drew closely from indigenous viewpoints credited the Incas with even greater accomplishments at this point. Guaman Poma (2006: 38), for example, wrote that

Inka Roq'a conquered the lands to the southwest of Cuzco and southeast all the way to Lake Titicaca. Garcilaso was even more effusive, writing that by the time Inka Roq'a was through, the Incas had annexed essentially the entire southern highlands of Peru and the adjacent south coast.[10]

The royal couple gave birth to four or five sons, the eldest of whom (Titu Kusi Wallpa) became ruler. In his youth the prince was kidnapped by some neighbors in revenge for Inka Roq'a's marriage to a maid their lord had coveted. The boy was reprieved from a death sentence when he miraculously cried tears of blood. This event later gave rise to the name that he assumed as ruler, Yawar Waqaq or "He Who Cries Bloody Tears" (Cieza 1967: 123–7; Sarmiento 2007: 89; Murúa 1986: 71; Cobo 1979: 126).[11] Upon his father's death, Yawar Waqaq took vengeance on the enemies of his youth, who had also murdered one of his sons. He followed this triumph by seizing land from many groups (Sarmiento 2007: 96–8). Some said that he waged successful battle into the Valley of Pisaq and beyond, some 30 km northeast of Cuzco, although others attributed those conquests either to his father or to Wiraqocha Inka, the next ruler.

Cieza's (1967: 125–7) less flattering version of Yawar Waqaq's reign said that he was caught unawares by warriors from Condesuyu at a festival he was hosting in Cuzco, in preparation for an expedition against the powerful Qolla of the Lake Titicaca basin. The guests first clubbed the ruler over the head and then killed him in a general slaughter as he tried to flee to the sanctuary of the temple. While the Incas prepared to abandon the city, the skies opened and a mighty storm drove the assailants away. The Inca survivors took advantage of the celestial reprieve to regroup; they recovered their dead and buried Yawar Waqaq without any of the honors conferred on previous royalty. With the leadership in disarray, Cieza wrote, the third of Yawar Waqaq's sons assumed rule under the name Wiraqocha Inka. He added that a pivotal regional conflict to the west of Inca territory was also being resolved about that time. The Quechuas had been bent on expanding their domain, but saw their designs crushed when they lost a decisive battle to the Chankas. At this point, the tales take on an increasingly imperialist tenor with the exploits attributed to Wiraqocha Inka. This historical summary will accordingly pause here, leaving the descriptions of the great conquests to the next chapter.

The Origins of "Cuzco"

A question that we have yet to take up concerns how the Inca capital came to have its name. As with so many things Inca, different sources tell different stories. Some of the earliest Spanish authors took the term *el Cuzco* ("the Cuzco") to refer to a person, not a place (Ramírez 2005: 14–23). As early as 1535, however, the Spaniards were shifting to using the word for the capital, occasionally noting that they were correcting an error (e.g., Oviedo 1959 [1535–45]: 91). Even so, Ramírez argues that the ruler may actually have been called "the Cuzco" in lieu of his proper name or other titles, and that speaking the emperor's name may have been proscribed except in ritual circumstances.[12] In support of this position, she notes that the phrase was typically applied to the sitting ruler in the first accounts: Wayna Qhapaq was called "the old Cuzco," and his successor, Waskhar, was referred to as "the Cuzco."

Ramírez's argument fits with two ideas concerning how the Incas referred to their rulers. One is that the king and his principal wife had an assortment of descriptive titles designed to show their power and benevolence. The second is that the names we have for the imperial rulers today were not their given childhood names, but were actually titles they assumed when taking the throne (see chapter 1, table 1.1). If we pursue this line of reasoning a little further and accept that the ruler was the state (or the city) personified, then wherever and whoever the ruler happened to be was Cuzco at that moment. While this argument has a defensible logic, the view that the word Cuzco was actually a title, and not an early misinterpretation by ill-trained translators and uninformed Spanish writers, remains a minority position among scholars.

Concerning Cuzco as the name of the city, explanations abound. Diez de Betanzos (1996: 70) wrote that the early village lay in a swampy area at the foot of Saqsawaman, the majestic site on the elevation overlooking the urban center. In modern Cuzco Quechua, the word *qosqo* has been glossed as "dried-up lake bed" (Hornberger and Hornberger 1983: 191). In contrast, many of Sarmiento's (2007: 69) witnesses agreed that the town's name referred to a stone territorial marker, called a *cozco*. They also recalled that the founding ancestors had set out four divisions between the Saphy (Tied River) and Tullumayo (River of the Bone), which formed the capital's core when the Spaniards arrived. The divisions were called *Q'enti Kancha*, or Hummingbird Enclosure; *Chumbi Kancha*, or Weaver Enclosure; *Sairi Kancha*, or Tobacco Enclosure; and *Yarambuy Kancha*, a district of mixed Puquina–Quechua linguistic origins, meaning Enclosure of the Yellow Flowers (Rostworowski 1999: 7; Cerrón-Palomino, pers. comm. 2011). The mestizo chronicler Guaman Poma (2006: 34) later added that the town had been called Acamama before being recast as Cuzco. Yet another mestizo writer, Pachacuti Yamqui (1993 [1613]: 8), saw the name's origin in a term for "rocky outcrop." Recently, the linguist Rodolfo Cerrón-Palomino has suggested an alternative etymology. He proposes that the name originally arose from a combined Puquina–Quechua term that referred to Ayar Awka's miraculous sprouting of wings referred to earlier in this chapter. The phrase *qusqu guanca* (falcon + rocky outcrop) was shortened to *qusqu* and later was hispanicized as *Cusco*.[13]

Whatever the source of the capital's name, scholars often view the claims of extensive early Inca triumphs sketched out above as grandiose legends. They were told in ways that usually cast the Incas in a favorable light, but that were also peppered with defeats and shameful incidents. It is striking that the different accounts vary so widely with respect to the scope and timing of pre-imperial Inca ventures. Some histories held that they stuck fairly close to the Cuzco basin, while others claimed that the Incas ranged over one or two hundred kilometers beyond Cuzco in the pre-imperial era. As Rowe (1946: 206–9) and others have inferred, some of those claims may have arisen from confusion over duplicate names or embellishments of history. It also seems that a few societies saw every generational change of Inca leadership as an opportunity to cast off Cuzco's yoke. As a result, several different rulers could claim to have defeated the same peoples. Alternatively, some of the differences could stem from the self-serving histories that each Inca royal kin group apparently kept. We may now look at the archaeological record to see how its evidence matches the stories the Incas told themselves.

The Archaeological Picture

For many years – starting in the mid-nineteenth century when Inca sites first drew serious attention – the archaeology of the heartland was the study of the grand and the imperial. That should be no surprise, on many counts. Only a handful of sites anywhere in the Americas are the peer of Cuzco, Saqsawaman, Machu Picchu, Ollantaytambo, or Pisaq. Exquisitely sculpted architecture, flowing arrays of terraces, an infrastructure of roads, bridges, and waterworks, and intricate landscaped stonework all crave attention. Adventurers and explorers such as Ephraim Squier, Adolph Bandelier, Charles Wiener, and Hiram Bingham, and the pioneering archaeologists Max Uhle, Julio C. Tello, Luis Valcárcel, Jorge Muelle, and John Rowe, all focused their study on the major sites and basic chronological issues. We are greatly indebted to their work, because it provides the foundation of Inca archaeology today. In keeping with the climate of the time, those investigators thought that archaeology could never provide fine-grained information on time or meaning that could supplant the written evidence. For them, documents allow us to interpret archaeology, rather than the two sources complementing one another.

They had ample reason to see things that way, and many historians today remain dubious about any archaeological interpretation that contravenes the written record, even for the pre-imperial period. Part of the archaeological challenge in understanding Killke (early Inca) society stems from the actions of the Incas themselves. They told the Spaniards that Pachakuti stripped the capital of its population so that the sacred center of the world could be built from scratch (Sarmiento 2007: 119–21). That program all but wiped out visible evidence of the Killke era. Moreover, when the Incas besieged the city in 1536, they torched it in a vain effort to drive out the Spaniards. The Colonial remodeling already underway accelerated soon afterward, but a devastating earthquake in 1650 took additional toll on the material remains.

Archaeologists hardly gave up the effort to unearth the Inca past, however. Since the 1950s, they have conducted over seventy excavation programs in Cuzco, incrementally bringing new evidence to light (Farrington 2010: 87). Others have been systematically surveying the greater Cuzco region since the 1980s, recording over 2,000 sites in the process (see esp. Bauer 1992, 1998, 2004; Heffernan 1989; Bauer and Covey 2002; Covey 2006b; Kosiba 2010). Their research has worked in tandem with a host of site-specific studies at Saqsawaman and the royal estates of Chinchero (Alcina Franch *et al.* 1976), Ollantaytambo (Protzen 1993; Bengtsson 1998b), Yucay (Niles 1999), Machu Picchu (e.g., Burger and Salazar 2004), and Tipón (Wright *et al.* 2006), for example. Collectively, they have rethought the nature of the pre-imperial Incas and the forces that led to their emergence as an imperial power.

We can begin here by considering the place of Cuzco in a regional context from AD 1000 to 1400. Intensive surveys have shown that the valley's population grew markedly after about AD 1000, as Cuzco began to dominate a developing urban hierarchy (Bauer and Covey 2004). Below the center were maybe ten towns, twice as many smaller villages, and well over a hundred hamlets and other small sites. While the existing communities grew, people also started to use other areas that had been mostly vacant. That trend was especially visible on the north side of the valley, where several large new villages were established (Covey 2006b: 124–5). Those settlements were generally unfortified and lay in open positions, a pattern at variance with the defensive planning of most highland settlements of the time, even places nearby. At Larapa, new canal and terrace systems enhanced production in thousands of hectares of land, an effort that Bauer and Covey rank among the largest agricultural projects ever carried out in the valley. They suggest that new Inca elites directed the construction and benefited disproportionately from the increased output. The labor needed for the work may have been raised as a tax (*mit'a*). In essence, a mixed agrarian–urban aristocracy was taking shape.

The traces of pre-imperial Cuzco itself are unfortunately still mostly buried, a common problem in urban landscapes, but archaeological studies are incrementally fleshing out the character of the early settlement. Valcárcel (1934–5) made a major advance in understanding the early settlement through his extensive excavations in the early 1930s at that site. There, he recovered abundant ceramics, about one-quarter to one-third of which were later determined to be pre-imperial Inca (Killke style). Rowe found similar pottery a decade later in his excavations within the Qorikancha, the Incas' most sacred temple. In a benchmark publication, he first formally defined the Killke style and also refined the classification of the later imperial ceramics (Rowe 1944). Continuing studies by Peruvian archaeologists have recovered Killke pottery from at least seven more locations, distributed across an area that approximates imperial-era Cuzco.[14] Their work in and around the Qorikancha has yielded exceptionally high-quality pottery (Bauer and Covey 2004: 77–8). The planning of parts of the early town apparently foreshadowed the imperial capital's layout. Building foundations under the present-day Hotel Libertador were found to have orientations like those of nearby imperial masonry. From that evidence, we may infer that at least part of the most prestigious imperial layout overlaid an existing design. In turn, that suggests that there was some sort of conceptual continuity from the pre-imperial to imperial eras (González Corrales 1984; Hyslop 1990: 30–4).

During the Killke era, the Incas were slowly extending their dominance over neighboring peoples, with varying degrees of success (Bauer and Covey 2004; Covey 2006b). Several hundred Killke sites have now been recorded within about 60 km of Cuzco, many in the Apurimac and Vilcanota drainages (figure 3.2). Societies living to the south and west of Cuzco came under the Inca wing relatively early, while the people living to the north and east had a more fractious relationship and maintained their independence longer. About 30 km south of Cuzco, the Paruro area was occupied by at least three named ethnic groups: the Chillque, Maras,

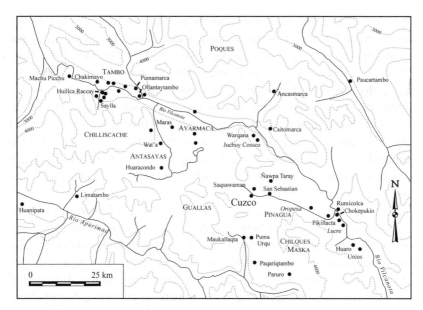

Figure 3.2 Distribution of early Inca (Killke) sites in the Cuzco region. Source: adapted from Kendall 1994; 1996.

and Tambo.[15] The largest Paruro sites were no more than hamlets (Bauer 1992: 94–108), many of them situated on small exposed knolls or lower valley slopes, near rich bottom lands suitable for maize farming. The area just west of the Cuzco Valley was inhabited by the Anta and Ayarmaca, among others (Bauer and Covey 2004: 78–9). The Killke sites there were also quite small, and were usually situated near productive lands, typically on mid-elevation ridges or peaks (Heffernan 1989). The long-term stability of the settlement pattern into the imperial eras suggests to Heffernan that the region may not have suffered overly from the endemic warfare seen elsewhere.

To the east and north of Cuzco, the situation was more problematic for the Incas. The societies living in the Lucre basin, about 30 km east, were rivals to the Incas right up to the inception of the imperial era as well (Dwyer 1971; Parsons and Hastings 1988: 224; Bauer and Covey 2004: 84–7). Two main ethnic groups lived in the basin: the Pinahua and Mohina. Choquepukio was the most important settlement in the valley (McEwan 2006). Occupied by the Pinahua, it was quite an impressive town and may have even approached Killke-era Cuzco in scale and grandeur. Its ruins cover 60 ha on a low ridge and boast architecture bordering on the monumental – large stone enclosures and multi-storey buildings. There were many other settlements in the Lucre area; some of them, such as Minaspata and Coto-coto, were almost as large as Choquepukio (Dwyer 1971: 41; Glowacki 2002: 271). Since those towns likely housed several thousand people each, the populace collectively posed an ongoing challenge to Inca hegemony. Sarmiento's (2007: 87, 96, 99) informants said that four successive Inca rulers – from Inka Roca to Pachakuti – all took up arms against them, but only the last was able to finally subjugate and then disperse them. Because of the extended animosities, it is no surprise that the Oropesa area that lay between them was an unoccupied buffer zone for much of the early era (Bauer and Covey 2004: 84–7).

North of Cuzco, things were also complicated. The Vilcanota river seems to have formed a boundary between people closely linked to the Incas early on (south side) and those who resisted for a longer period (north side). The Incas recalled that their rulers fostered amicable relations with the residents of the south through intermarriage. The people living on the other side of the river however, maintained a distinct material culture in both pottery and architecture. Bauer and Covey (2004: 82–4) found that the whole area's population grew markedly in the Killke era. A number of large villages were inhabited, most of those on the north side set on ridge tops at high elevations. Between about AD 1250 and 1350, the largest town in the area, Pukara Pantillijlla (10 ha), grew notably. Heavily protected by encircling terraces, the town began to exhibit Inca-style architectural forms, such as the rectangular buildings already found in Cuzco that would later typify the imperial Inca style.

The village of Wat'a (Huata), high above the Cusichaca valley, was also protected by surrounding walls. It was extensively burned at one point, implying that worries about defense may have been well founded (Kendall 1976, 1985). Kosiba's (2010) research at this site has shown in detail how the Incas incorporated newly subjected communities. At the most important spatial position in the community, the Incas appear to have razed existing structures and ordered the construction of a new terraced and enclosed plaza. The fill used to create that plaza's foundations included Inca vessels, suggesting that the new rulers had deliberately conducted ceremonies that made the town's occupants its subjects. Toward the end of the Killke era, people living in the area's high settlements shifted to lower elevations. They also began to undertake massive land improvement projects, such as canalization of the Vilcanota river and construction of irrigated terraces along the lower valley slopes (Bauer and Covey 2004).

Over time, many other communities beyond the Cuzco basin started to raise buildings that presaged the imperial style of architecture. Several important sites overlooking the Vilcanota river are especially interesting, because their ceramics, plans and architecture mark the Killke/proto-imperial transition. Among them are Pumamarca, Markasunay, Qhapaqkancha, Juchuy Cossco, and Pisaq; the last three sites became royal estates during the imperial period (Covey 2006b: 127–34). Included in the important shifts were selective adoption of a rectangular floor plan and the construction of palatial or institutional buildings (Kendall 1976; Niles 1980). Covey infers from this evidence that the Incas were beginning to dominate the public or institutional life of the communities over a wide area.

The dating of the Killke era from AD 1000 until about 1400 is still based on relatively few radiocarbon dates, but they are consistent with one another (Dwyer 1971; Kendall 1985; Bauer 1992; Adamska and Michecsynski 1996). Carbon dates taken from Pumamarca architecture end in the fourteenth century (Hollowell 1987), while the Inca-style rectangular and ceremonial constructions at Pukara Pantillijlla are also earlier than we would expect from the historical chronology (Covey 2006b: 163). In light of the early dates, Bauer (1992: 47) has ventured that some structures usually thought to belong to the imperial era were actually raised during the Killke period. As noted in chapter 2 (section entitled "Time frames"), carbon dates suggest that the transition from the pre-Inca to Inca eras at Chokepuquio seems to have occurred 1400–30, which is in keeping with the idea of a late incorporation of the Lucre region.

Some archaeologists have also been rethinking the relationship between the Killke and imperial polychrome ceramic styles. Using stratigraphic associations, Kendall (1996) suggests that the polychrome style may have appeared well before 1400 as an elite ware that was subsequently transformed into the imperial style, but that inference has yet to be widely accepted. Killke artifact styles themselves barely hint at the form of imperial manufactures. The rise of state society often features innovative styles of crafts and architecture, especially in elite, ritual, and administrative contexts. Their creation reveals the elite's interest in controlling the objects that represent the status, perquisites, and tools of power. Imperial Cuzco's tapestry tunics, polychrome pottery, and architectural style are classic examples of that attention to material culture (chapters 6, 13). The varied Killke material assemblage, in contrast, shows no evidence of central management of artisanry. Some of the Killke ceramics do presage imperial

Inca motifs (e.g., nested triangles, pendant rows of solid triangles) and vessel shapes, but the varied and sloppy execution contrasts starkly with the standardized and often elegant imperial pottery (Dwyer 1971; Heffernan 1989; Bauer and Stanish 1990). None of the other Killke artifacts, which are only briefly described, indicates that they were produced either at large scales or under central management either.

Stylistic similarities between imperial Inka and Lake Titicaca basin pottery has been recognized for decades (e.g., Julien 1993: 190–8). Scholars generally infer that the Incas admired the ceramic (and stone) products of the lake region and incorporated elements into their own goods, probably in the latter half of the fifteenth century. Even so, archaeologists working at both ends of the Cuzco–Titicaca spectrum have sometimes proposed that the imperial Inca style has much earlier roots. Kendall and colleagues (1992), for example, reports imperial-style pottery in the archaeological record much earlier in the Inca sequence than is usually accepted. Moreover, new arguments are being made that the style appeared in the Lake Titicaca basin well before the rapid expansion of the empire (e.g., Pärssinen and Siiriäinen 1997; Pärssinen in press).

A Sketch of Pre-Imperial Inca Society

It seems pretty reasonable to modern eyes to assume that the Incas neither appeared out of thin air nor emerged fully grown from caves to found the royal lineages, both of which would have been perfectly sound explanations for Andean people. As a result, the issue of how the Incas appeared as a self-identified people still remains an open question. In some senses, taking up that subject will always be a fruitless endeavor, since we can attempt to trace any society back indefinitely and it's not always clear what that kind of inquiry gains us. So a better question may be whether we can identify any antecedents that the Incas thought were essential to their roots or that provided a foundation to their imperial society.

Over the years, scholars have pointed to the Lake Titicaca basin as indispensable to the Incas' identity. Their mytho-history, style of stone-carving, and political organization all cite the altiplano in significant ways. For example (see chapter 8), an Inca origin myth alternative to the one cited above claims that Manqo Qhapaq was originally called forth from the Island of the Sun in Lake Titicaca and subsequently traveled underground to Cuzco. The origins of the celestial bodies and the starting points for the travels of the Creator God Wiracocha and his assistants were also situated in the lake. Similarly, the human monoliths at Tiwanaku have been linked to the Inca myth of petrified giants, while the central figure on the Gate of the Sun has been interpreted to be the model for the Inca sun god statue. Many scholars have also pointed to the similarities in the styles of stereotomy (stone-carving) found at Tiwanaku and Cuzco, while others have raised doubts about their lineal relationship (e.g., Protzen and Nair 2013; see chapter 13 here).

Those problematic lines of argument have recently been supplemented by historical linguistics and biology. As described earlier (chapter 2), Cerrón-Palomino (2004, 2012) infers that the Incas spoke Aymara and Puquina before adopting Quechua. Their linguistic affiliation thus lies with the peoples of the Lake Titicaca basin. While the jury is still out on some linguistic questions, new biological evidence mirrors that picture. Shinoda and his colleagues (Shinoda *et al.* 2006; Shinoda in press) compared the DNA from over 100 Inca-era skeletal remains from the area around Machu Picchu and Cuzco with the DNA from ancient skeletal remains from coastal and other highland locales.[16] They found that the Inca matrilineal gene pool is more similar to that of modern and past altiplano peoples than to those of the north coast or the highland area around Wari. They infer that the Incas (or colonists they brought in) had altiplano ties. Intriguingly, the Inca-era populace of the Cuzco area differs from earlier residents of the same zone; the latter group is biologically more closely affiliated with the Wari region. That evidence supports the idea that the Incas were latecomers to the Cuzco area, after AD 1000. Even so, they also found that some human remains recovered from Saqsawaman (just above Cuzco) had closer links to more northerly and coastal populations. They deduce from this evidence that there may have been some genetic mixing as a consequence of imperial programs (Shinoda in press).[17] The complexity of this patterning emphasizes the difficulties of sorting out Inca history, whether political or biological. Overall, however, the suggestion that the Incas had a strong pre-imperial link to the Lake Titicaca area is far better supported now than it was a short time ago, even if we cannot quite argue that the issue is settled.

If we turn to the Cuzco region itself, the written and archaeological sources paint a fairly coherent picture of long-term development for the pre-imperial Incas, despite some important divergences. Both sources are compatible with the idea that, sometime after AD 1000, the Incas experienced 300–400 years of slow development from an incipiently hierarchical society into a nascent state. As an urban hierarchy arose, the lands near Cuzco were progressively developed for more intensive exploitation. The archaeology also indicates that, by the fourteenth century, the Incas had extended a kind of collaborative or imposed rule over the Cuzco basin and were turning their intentions outside the valley.

From an anthropological perspective, setting aside some of their more fabulous elements, the narratives of the pre-imperial era contain many features compatible with a chiefdom society. At the heart of the polity was a set of elite kin groups that oversaw both the emerging city and its surrounding agrarian landscape. It appears possible that the Incas were even forming distinct social classes, fostered by strategic marriage alliances. The theme's repetition suggests that a union between one local lord and the daughter of another may have helped to build political relations among the region's elites and separate them from the remaining populace. If so, their actions would have contrasted with those of the general populace, who conventionally married across divisions within their own extended kin group, or *ayllu*.

The marriages were honored with gifts or exchanges of fine textiles and valuables that both confirmed the lords' generosity and created social debts. Inca myths touted their ancestors' largess, because it helped to legitimize their elevated status. Speaking more generally, a chief's position often partly depends on his ability to control labor and its products, without owning the natural resources themselves. Since gift-giving advertises a leader's productive capacity, it can attract new adherents and create public obligations. Among the Incas, ritualized generosity may have helped to mediate political alliances and residential shifts among the Incas and their neighbors. Some authors also suggest that the Inca largess underwrote their local rise to power because it put the gifts' recipients in an inferior social position (Rostworowski 1999: 38–47).

Many accounts also highlighted early military ventures. When the ruler himself did not take the lead, his close kin did, a practice that continued through the entire imperial period. Stories of the era often said that warlords incited their followers by promising them glory and plunder (Sarmiento 2007: 73; Cobo 1979: 130; Diez de Betanzos 1996: 20). There are few allusions to lands as benefits of war, although Sarmiento surmised that land conflicts underpinned feuds between the newly arrived Incas and the people already living around. Considering the small scope of most highland societies *c.* AD 1000–1400, few lands may have actually been seized and held until late in the pre-imperial era. Instead, the tales' emphasis on capture of booty and labor may have been closer to the mark. Some years ago, Richard

Schaedel (1978) drew attention to a slow shift in the motivation and practice of warfare that occurred through the early Inca accounts. The early plundering was augmented by demands for tribute and then replaced by seizure of productive resources. Capture of labor was also important, although it too shifted, from abduction to extorting production. In Sarmiento's (2007: 99) account, Wiraqocha Inka innovated the practice of occupying the lands of defeated neighbors, rather than just pillaging them. If those trends in the tales approximate the changing goals of war, then the shift to annexing vast territories in the imperial era grew from long developing practices.

An evolving elite ideology may have also underpinned Inca leadership, but it was transformed so much that we cannot be sure when any particular story or claim became part of the canon. The image of the stranger king – seen first in the founding ancestor Manqo Qhapaq – was so potent that some Inca elites told Cieza that Wiraqocha Inka was also an outlander. Other aristocrats, who had their own interests to protect, dismissed the story as puffery. Claims to leadership, though based on genealogy and ability, also gained legitimacy from religious sanction in the royal narratives. Most early kings were imbued with magical qualities granted by the Sun or Creator God. Their deeds exhibited precocious military valor or supernatural assistance, combined with visions of the future. Mayta Qhapaq's life, for instance, was so filled with wondrous feats that the Spaniards used Hercules and Merlin as reference points for their European audiences. He was reputedly born with his teeth intact after only a three-month pregnancy, could walk at birth, and had reached the stature of an 8-year-old at just one year (Sarmiento 2007: 81–4). When an Inca ruler took the throne, he also assumed a new, sometimes supernaturally inspired, name. As noted above, Titu Kusi Wallpa received the name "He Who Cries Bloody Tears" (Yawar Waqaq) for weeping blood, an act that was famously repeated by the "Tired Stone" above Cuzco (chapter 7). We cannot fix when particular narratives became royal doctrine, but the invention of elite dogma was an ongoing process that most likely had some roots in the Killke era.

The question remains as to what triggered the Incas' local successes, rather than a collapse into a simpler polity, as so often happens with chiefdoms. A likely contributing factor was simply the successful pursuit of gain by leaders of particular kindreds in the warfare that pervaded the highlands at the time. By the time the state began to form, the peoples of southern Peru and the northern altiplano had been enmeshed in conflicts and alliances for centuries. The narratives suggest that the political climate put a premium on military leaders who could deliver security and spoils and that the warlords and their adherents benefited especially from predatory warfare. With each success, war may have increasingly concentrated power in the hands of a few families. The Incas and their neighbors may also have seen that it was to their benefit to join forces against the marauding actions ascribed to other neighbors. Finally, it is possible that early Inca ideology contained exhortations for conquest or evangelism. Those features were present in late imperial doctrine, but often enough they sound like justifications after the fact rather than catalysts for expansion.

Even if this sketch of pre-imperial society contains some conjecture, the information now available is consistent with a society moving toward statehood earlier than was long thought. A great deal of crucial evidence remains to be developed, to be sure, but some of the kinds of material culture seen in the imperial styles were apparently taking form by the middle of the fourteenth century or maybe even earlier. More importantly, the strategies that the Incas formulated to draw the region's peoples into a unified polity over several centuries provided the organizational foundation for the great expansion that was to come (Bauer and Covey 2004).

Notes

1 The earliest appearance of the word Inca appeared in a 1526 publication by Gonzalo Fernández de Oviedo y Valdés, entitled *De la natural historia de la Indias* (*On the Natural History of the Indies*). He wrote "Solo al superior señor le llaman Inga" ("Only the supreme lord is called Inca"). Oviedo y Valdés never visited the Andes, and the source of his information is unclear, since the Spaniards had only made the most tentative of inroads into the land that forms modern Colombia and Ecuador by that point. Sarmiento (2007: 61) provided the same rendering of Inca as lord in 1572, presumably drawing that information from his aristocratic witnesses in Cuzco.

2 The Killke period was named after the ceramic style, first called Canchón, identified by Rowe (1944: 60–2).

3 Caquia Xaquixaguana, also known as Juchuy Cuzco ("Little Cuzco").

4 The interpretation of the accuracy of the royal narratives is a matter of ongoing contention among Inca scholars. My own sense is that both Spanish and Inca politics played a role in determining which narrative became the dominant story. The development of a standardized history had as much to do with (1) Spanish concerns about the legitimacy of its sovereignty over its American holdings and suppression of non-Christian subjects at home and abroad, as it did with (2) indigenous political infighting and claims over aristocratic holdings in Peru (see Covey 2006a). It was in the interests of the Spanish Crown to

show the illegitimacy of Inca rule, so that it could be rightfully supplanted. It was similarly in the interests of the surviving Inca royalty to establish a fixed history that recognized their rights to resources, if not to rule. Paradoxically, the creation of a standard, canonical history met both those conflicting goals, at least for the parties who emerged successful in the process.

5 Conversely, Cabello himself thought that Pachakuti and Thupa Inka Yupanki were the same person.

6 Such skepticism is hardly universal, however. Many people working in the field still accept the Chanka narrative as the key event in the ascension of Pachakuti to the throne and thus to the emergence of Inca imperial power (e.g., Davies 1995; Niles 1999; Julien 2000; McEwan 2006; see also Burger *et al.* 2007).

7 The traditional *ayllu* of Pacariqtambo today tell a cycle of stories about the ancient past, divided into the pre-Inca, Inca, and Spanish eras. In their telling, the Incas emerged from a cave before migrating to Cuzco, and after the Spanish conquest, returned to live inside the cave as small people who grow golden corn. Among the marks they left were the creation of extension irrigation networks and the town of Maukallaqta, where they lived (Urton 1993).

8 Another story recalled that Qhapaq Yupanki's brothers hatched a plot to supplant him with another brother named Tarqo Waman, but the ruler was able to forestall the coup attempt with a memorable speech. Intriguingly, the well-informed magistrate of Cuzco, Juan Polo Ondegardo, reported that Tarqo Waman actually ruled the Incas for some time, but was displaced by Qhapaq Yupanki. Many sources also said that an Inca named Qhapaq Yupanki had greatly expanded the Inca domain. The issue is complicated by the fact that the ninth ruler (Pachakuti) had brothers named Qhapaq Yupanki and Inka Roq'a, namesakes of the fifth and sixth monarchs. As a result, the chronicles differed as to whether some conquests should have been attributed to those rulers or to Pachakuti's generals.

9 There were two royal Inca moieties – each of which contained five royal lineages – at the time of the Spanish entry.

10 In a contrasting story, the Pacariqtambo Quipucamayos stated that Inka Roq'a did not expand the domain at all, but devoted himself to pious activities, religious constructions, and improving lands (Callapiña *et al.* 1974: 32). Such differences may be the result of the competing versions of the past presented by different kin groups.

11 In Betanzos's (1996: 18) story, Yawar Waqaq received his name because he was born crying blood.

12 There is even a case where local lords on the north coast were apparently disconcerted when the ruler was referred to by his name, and not title (Ramírez 2005: 22).

13 Cerrón-Palomino (pers. comm. Nov. 27, 2011) recently modified his published interpretation (2004: 12) of *qusqu* from owl to falcon, based on an alternative

reading of the Puquina term. As he observes, the falcon was a bird of power for the Incas.

14 Among the scholars who have conducted research at the Qorikancha, confirming the pre-imperial importance of the location, are Luis Barreda Murillo, Arminda Gibaja Oviedo, Alfredo Valencia Zegarra, and Raymundo Béjar Navarro (Bauer and Stanish 2001: 10).

15 The Maras and Tambo were named in the origin myth sketched out earlier.

16 The study focused on mitochondrial DNA, which traces the matrilineal gene pool.

17 The Sacsayhuaman populations may have included people buried before and after the Spanish conquest.

Chapter Four

The History of the Empire
Narrative Visions

When war is declared, Truth is the first casualty.[1]

Ponsonby 1928

The meteoric rise of Inca power was filled with charismatic leadership, arduous campaigns, spirited opposition, divine aid, heroism, treachery, and wise rule – in short, all the elements of history's grand sweep as told by the victors. About fifty accounts of the Inca past were written down in the early Colonial era, but distilling out an accurate record of the empire's formation may still be impossible today. Even the accounts that transparently drew from *khipu* records could present conspicuously different visions, so that the chroniclers had to choose which stories to preserve for posterity. Modern scholars are split between those who assume that the chronicles captured a core of truth that can be discovered through close comparisons (e.g., Rowe 1946; Pärssinen 1992) and those who judge the chronicles to be too colored by Andean concepts of time and social hierarchy for use as linear narratives (e.g., Zuidema 1982; Urton 1990).

A further split can be seen in the sources themselves. Several authors with at least one foot firmly planted in the indigenous camp, in the sense of having Andean ancestry, placed some Inca expansions earlier in the royal genealogy than the prevailing modern view of a late imperial development that started with Pachakuti. Among the indigenous or mestizo writers championing earlier expansions are the Quipucamayos de Vaca de Castro, Blas Valera, Garcilaso de la Vega,[2] and Guaman Poma. Their viewpoint was countered by the accounts drawn from Andean sources of information, but written by Spaniards, whose chronology has been more widely accepted in the last several decades.

My own view is that the accounts are fraught with so many problems that we will probably never come to an authoritative resolution for the earliest stages of the imperial era using the historical sagas alone. On the other hand, it defies credibility that Inca history was invented wholesale after the Spaniards arrived. It appears more likely that different interest groups – royal families, ethnic groups – tailored a generally understood past to suit their own political ends, even when describing events that had occurred at the edge of the Colonial era. If we accept this view and keep in mind the limitations of the sources, we can sketch out the empire's trajectory, at least as the Incas chose to remember it. The internal conflicts were so deep and the Inca notions of recording the past so different from European conventions, however, that many of the details of the prehispanic era will always be beyond us.

What I present in this chapter, then, is a composite account of the impe-rial expansion as described by the principals' descendants. Rather than dun readers with repeated comments about the legendary tenor of the stories, I simply ask them to keep in mind that this is a synthesis largely composed of Inca sagas filtered through many Andean and Spanish voices. We also need to keep in mind that the information preserved in the existing documents heavily favors both the actions of the later Inca kings and their military valor, rather than diplomatic successes.

Expansionist Designs and the Crisis in Cuzco

The reign of Wiraqocha Inka, the eighth ruler on the standard list, usually marks a narrative transition from raiding and alliance to attempted terri-torial expansion. He is often described as a man bent on amplifying his power through conquest and intrigue during a tumultuous era in the cen-tral Andes (Cieza 1967: 125 – 8; Diez de Betanzos 1996: 19; Sarmiento 2007: 98 – 104; Cobo 1979: 130 – 1). Soon after ascending the throne, Wiraqocha Inka took his wife from the Anta, who lived a bit to the west of Cuzco, per-haps to cement a local alliance. The Incas were flexing their muscles locally in this era, during which the political stakes were being raised through-out the region. Sarmiento's witnesses recalled that several of Wiraqocha Inka's sons accompanied or led expeditions against their neighbors. Among them were the brothers Inka Urqon and Inka Yupanki (later Pachakuti), who would soon feud over the throne. Wiraqocha Inka's ambitions led him to the altiplano, where the powerful societies of the Lake Titicaca basin were locked in a struggle for regional ascendancy (Diez de Betanzos 1996: 20; Cieza 1967: 142–3).[3] As the basin's hostilities escalated, both the Lupaqa and Qolla leaders solicited the Incas' aid. After consulting his oracles and counselors, the Inca ruler chose to favor the Lupaqas but hedged his bets by promising aid to both sides. He then set out for the altiplano with an army, leaving his son Inka Urqon in charge of Cuzco. Before the Incas arrived in the lake region, however, the Lupaqas won a decisive victory. Their lord Qari thus met the Incas from a position of strength and they sealed an alliance by drinking from a golden cup.[4]

The Chanka Wars

Many chroniclers wrote that the repulsion of Chanka assaults on Cuzco propelled the Incas into their imperial phase, but they disagree on when that happened.[5] In Diez de Betanzos's (1996: 19–30) history, which is largely a heroic biography of Pachakuti, the Chankas attacked when Wiraqocha Inka arrogantly presumed to take the name of the Creator God as his title. The Chankas assembled a grand army for a three-pronged attack on lands south of Cuzco, into the altiplano, and against Cuzco itself.[6] Wiraqocha Inka fled to a fortified refuge in the face of the attack, along with his heir designate Inka Urqon and most of the aristocracy. The intrepid prince Inka Yupanki spurned retreat, however, and rallied three lords to hold their home. With the battle impending, either the Creator or the Sun appeared in a vision to the prince and promised to send warriors to aid him in defeating the Chankas. At a critical moment in the battle, the vision came to fruition as warriors appeared as if from nowhere and the Incas proved victorious. Several chroniclers reported that the stones from the fields had metamorphosed into warriors, which were later venerated as shrines called *pururaucas* ("hidden thieves"; Polo 1917: 46; Pachacuti Yamqui 1993: 219; Cobo 1979: 128–9; see MacCormack 1991: 286–301).

Diez de Betanzos continued that Inka Yupanki took the prisoners and spoils of victory to his father, so that Wiraqocha Inka could tread on them in the customary gesture of triumph. The ruler was so perturbed at the prince's newly achieved stature, however, that he orchestrated protocol so that his other son Inka Urqon was treated as if he were already enthroned (see chapter 5). He declared that Inka Urqon must have the first honor with the plunder, but Inka Yupanki refused to let his hardwon victory be defiled and departed for Cuzco. When the irate ruler organized an ambush to kill the defiant prince, it was discovered and thwarted by the young man's loyal captains. Soon thereafter, the two other Chanka contingents attacked Cuzco, but Inka Yupanki emerged victorious once again. The Inca celebrated his victory by hanging and beheading the defeated enemy, flaying them and stuffing the skins with ashes. The conquistadores who entered Cusco later told Cieza that they had seen the skins on display.

Despite the tensions, prince Inka Yupanki implored his father to return to Cuzco. His efforts were in vain, but the elder man was willing to accept an offer of assistance in building a fine estate at his refuge (*Caquia Xaquixaguana*). For his part, Inka Yupanki kept busy by expanding and organizing the Inca realm; twenty years alone were spent renovating Cuzco (Diez de Betanzos 1996: 44 – 55, 69 – 73). Once the capital was completed, the court persuaded Wiraqocha Inka to travel to Cuzco and place the fringe of rulership on Inka Yupanki's head. The prince himself had refused to visit his father's manor, declaring that he would take the fringe from Inka Urqon only if the head came along with it. So Wiraqocha traveled to Cuzco, where he gave his son the title "Pachacuti Ynga Yupangui Capac Yndichuri, which means 'change of time, King Yupanque, son of the Sun'." The new monarch was not content with this gesture, however, and forced his father to drink *chicha* from a filthy jar while deriding him as a woman. In the end, Pachakuti accepted his father's apologies for past transgressions and invited the aged ex-monarch to participate in Cuzco's festivities, which he did until his death some ten years later (Diez de Betanzos 1996: 74 – 9).

Despite the many accounts of the Chanka wars, scholars disagree about their authenticity. Part of the skepticism arises from the discrepancies concerning the succession to the throne and the timing of Inca conflicts with their western neighbors. Cieza (1967: 114 – 15, 125 – 7, 146 – 9), for example, understood that Inka Urqon had been truly installed as ruler while Wiraqocha Inka was still alive – an assertion later repeated by the native chronicler Pachacuti Yamqui. Moreover, different sources say the Chankas came under Inca rule during the reigns of the fifth, sixth, eighth, and ninth rulers, or do not mention them at all.[7] Duviols (1980) takes an especially skeptical view, suggesting that the Chankas may have been built up as the consummate but largely mythical foil, used to glorify Pachakuti and to provide a divinely inspired foundation for the empire.

A recent, integrated archaeological and historical study of the Chanka homeland in Andahuaylas helps to clarify the situation (Bauer *et al.* 2010; see also Kellett 2010; chapter 3 here). Systematic survey of the Chanka region recorded a wide range of Late Intermediate (pre-Inca) communities, some of which were clearly fortified. None of the Late Intermediate Period or Late Horizon Chanka towns, however, remotely approached contemporary Cuzco in scale or elaboration. The largest Chanka community of the Late Intermediate Period was no more than about 15 ha, while Cuzco and several other towns of its region were up to four times that size. Acknowledged Inca rivals closer to Cuzco, such as the peoples of the Lucre region occupying major settlements like Choquepukio, also outstripped the Andahuaylas area occupations. Scale alone is not a perfect measure of a rival's potential threat, of course, but the archaeological data do cast doubt on the Chanka peoples' ability to mobilize a serious threat to an Inca polity that was already a state. It remains plausible that the Chankas were a crucial early enemy, perhaps repeatedly, but the sagas of the Chanka wars may still be mostly a glorious epic invoked to burnish the image of the empire's father.

The Major Expansions: Pachakuti and Thupa Inka Yupanki

The sagas tell that Pachakuti began to expand his domain once he had firmly established his power, although they differ on the details. It is striking that they often begin with a litany of battles around Cuzco itself, even some that attributed conquests much farther afield to earlier rulers.[8] From our vantage point, it is hard to say if the Incas really had to reassert local control with every succession or if the chronicling of local triumphs was a narrative device used to ascribe the empire's creation to Pachakuti. If the latter were true, the conquests may have been fictitious or merely symbolic. To help readers follow the subsequent expansions from a historical perspective, figure 4.1 presents Pärssinen's (1992) reconstruction, based on review of a wide array of provincial documents.

Expeditions Southward

We often think of the Inca empire in association with the Peruvian mountains, but the earliest rich targets for Cuzco's expeditions lay in the altiplano. Most chroniclers agreed that the Incas had established a presence in the Titicaca basin during Wiraqocha Inka's reign, either through their alliance with the Lupaqa or through conquest (e.g., Diez de Betanzos 1996: 92–6). The Qolla remained a potent force in the basin, despite their reported defeat at the hands of the Lupaqa. One version of Pachakuti's exploits told

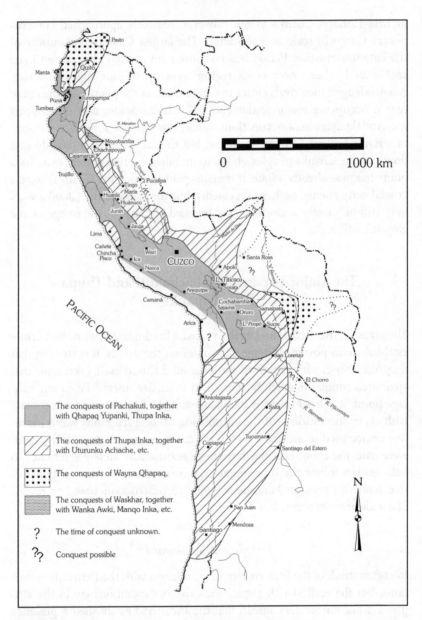

The conquests of Pachakuti, together with Qhapaq Yupanki, Thupa Inka,

The conquests of Thupa Inka, together with Uturunku Achache, etc.

The conquests of Wayna Qhapaq,

The conquests of Waskhar, together with Wanka Awki, Manqo Inka, etc.

? 　The time of conquest unknown.

?? 　Conquest possible

Figure 4.1　Pärssinen's (1992) reconstruction of the Inca expansion, redrawn from the original.

how the ruler himself defeated the Qolla and their allies by taking a fort in which he then installed an Inca garrison. The Qolla ruler was taken to Cuzco where he was beheaded in a public triumph. In contrast, Cieza (1967: 55–6, 160–1, 177–84) wrote that Pachakuti dispatched two Chanka lords at the head of their own soldiers to subdue the Qolla. Although a series of victories advanced Inca interests in the basin, the region had not been fully secured before Chanka forces deserted a parallel Inca campaign in the central Peruvian sierra. As a precaution, Pachakuti recalled the Chanka forces from the altiplano and discharged them. Only after the end of the sierra campaign and expeditions into the montaña did Pachakuti himself venture into the basin to subdue the Qollas and Ayaviris. A number of other sources reported that Pachakuti eventually conquered through south Bolivia before turning his eyes northward (e.g., Callapiña 1974: 39; Diez de Betanzos 1996: 112–14).

The Peruvian Sierra and Coast

Many chroniclers reported that an early campaign into central Peru started to bring the agricultural heartland of the realm into Inca hands, but engaged Cuzco with unintended and dangerous foes. The expedition's mixed success also prompted a crisis in Cuzco typical of the political animosities that erupted periodically. There are three versions of the story, but the gist is as follows (see Rowe 1946: 206). At some point, Pachakuti dispatched forces northward, supported by Chanka soldiers pressed into service. They advanced through several hundred kilometers of difficult territory, subduing many redoubtable *etnías* through intimidation, pitched battle, and siege. The Incas and Chankas fell out along the way, apparently because the Incas were embarrassed by the Chankas' superior valor in taking a fort. Before the Inca commander could recoup his honor by punishing the Chankas, they escaped northward. The Incas advanced to Cajamarca in their pursuit, where they defeated the local lord and his coastal allies, the Chimu. After leaving a garrison in Cajamarca, the army turned back to Cuzco laden with booty.

On the return trip, the army took a route through the lower slopes of the western Andes. That venture was the first or second of four or five separate descents described for Inca armies until the entire coast was finally taken (see below). Whether the privileged Chincha valley and its neighbor, Pisco, were taken at that time is unclear. Cieza wrote that Pachakuti sent an army under his brother Qhapaq Yupanki to secure Chincha, but the foray was rebuffed. Chincha's own residents told the Spaniards that the fifth ruler, also named Qhapaq Yupanki, peacefully secured vows of allegiance with gifts of fine cloth and golden beads (Castro and Ortega Morejón 1974: 94–103). Their relationship was later solidified by Thupa Inka Yupanki and Wayna Qhapaq (Rostworowski 1999: 71).

When the returning army approached Cuzco, Pachakuti had its generals executed at Limatambo (Cabello Valboa 1951: 317–18; Murúa 1986: 80; Polo 1917: 115). He used the Chanka desertion as a rationale, but his motivation is sometimes conceived as fear that the soldiers could use their triumph as leverage to unseat him. Cabello Valboa (1951: 318) wrote that the remaining commanders organized another expedition north as a way to flee Pachakuti's awful presence. The prince Thupa Inka Yupanki, too callow to take command, accompanied his more experienced relatives as a symbolic general and military apprentice. Diez de Betanzos typically did not mention any such murders by the hero of his saga. Instead, he wrote that another general named Yamque Yupanki led a pair of expeditions north to relieve Cajamarca. On the first trip, he served as military mentor to his underage brother Qhapaq Yupanki and then to the youthful Thupa Inka Yupanki on the second.

One of these northern expeditions turned toward the north coast, descending through Huamachuco toward Pacasmayo. It is uncertain if the first invasion brought down the Chimu empire or if that formidable foe fell to a later campaign heading south from Ecuador. Rowe (1948: 44) has suggested that a first engagement broke Chimor's power and that a later invasion solidified Inca control of the coast. Cabello Valboa (1951: 320–1; see Rostworowski 1999: 78) wrote that Thupa Inka Yupanki used the stratagem of threatening to cut off the coastal water supply to render the coastal populace helpless. At the end of the expedition, the Chimu paramount Minchançaman was taken to Cuzco as a hostage.

Advances into Ecuador

Fairly early in the imperial era, an Inca expedition reportedly pressed into Ecuador in a grand sweep of the north Andes. The achievement of Inca dominion there required numerous campaigns spread over a half century or more. More than a few operations ended in crashing defeats – at least from the Incas' point of view – and even in 1532, many areas bordering the central valleys lay beyond Inca control. In most accounts, while Pachakuti was still ruler, expeditions under Thupa Inka Yupanki's titular leadership worked their way into central Ecuador. The northern limit of the initial push was apparently reached in the southern Quito basin. The advance was a halting, arduous affair, as the forces returned to Cajamarca to reform and supply themselves between expeditions (Diez de Betanzos 1996: 116–21; Cieza 1967: 187–9; Sarmiento 2007: 146–8; Cabello Valboa 1951: 320–1; Murúa 1986: 81; *RGI* II: 265, 275, 279; Cobo 1979: 143).

The sequence of ventures to the Ecuadorian coast is confusing, since campaigns are described for Pachakuti's, Thupa Inka Yupanki's, and Wayna Qhapaq's reigns (Cabello Valboa 1951: 320–30, 392–3; Sarmiento 2007: 1512; Cieza 1967: 156, 217–22; 1984: 157; Cobo 1979: 150; Murúa 1986: 82, 92; Rowe 1985b: 224; 1946: 207; Pärssinen 1992: 91–4). At one point, however, Inca forces reportedly descended into the coastal tropics in the Manta region and crossed to the Isla Puná. During that endeavor, one of the more fabled events of Inca history is said to have taken place – a voyage by Thupa Inka Yupanki to the Pacific islands of Anachumbi and Niñachumbi. Sarmiento wrote that some 20,000 soldiers sailed with him on balsa rafts. When the voyage stretched out for close to a year, the commander of the land troops mistakenly presumed that the leader had been lost. His premature celebration cost him his life when Thupa Inka Yupanki returned. Despite the Incas' efforts, coastal Ecuador was never well integrated into the empire, perhaps because it was viewed as unhealthy by the highlanders (McEwan and Silva 1989).

More Ventures onto the Peruvian Coast

The timing of conquests along the coast from Nazca to Mala is hard to pin down even as reconstructed narrative occurrences (Callapiña *et al.* 1974: 32; Rowe 1985b: 224; Cobo 1979: 139; Cieza 1984: 217; 1967: 199–202; Polo 1917; Sarmiento 2007: 160–2; Cabello Valboa 1951: 331, 338–9; see also Rowe 1946: 207; see Rostworowski 1999: 73–6; Pärssinen 1992: 87–9; Rowe 1946: 207 for further discussion). One version suggests that a third coastal campaign occurred before Thupa Inka Yupanki's montaña ventures, described below. Another put the conquest of the south and central coasts after the conquest of the south Andes. Whatever the sequence, the campaigns reportedly took years and constituted one of the most noteworthy Inca achievements. In a familiar pattern, the sources differed over the balance between peaceful submission and stiff resistance by the residents of individual valleys.

There was general agreement, however, that the Incas met a resolute foe in the Lunahuaná and Mara peoples of the Cañete valley. After an abortive first campaign, the Incas withdrew to the highlands to escape the summer heat and attendant illness among the soldiers. Cobo (1979: 138–9) wrote that the armies alternated contingents of 30,000 soldiers between the coast and highlands, because the coastal lands were so unhealthy for the people of the sierra. Some coastal forces who had been pressed into service took the failure as a sign of Inca weakness and defected. An angered Thupa Inka Yupanki then mounted campaigns for three years from the settlement of Inkawasi, which was built expressly for that purpose (Hyslop 1985). The town was called the "New Cuzco," with streets and districts named after those of the capital. The facility sustained the army on its annual campaign and housed a garrison to maintain pressure on the locals. According to one story, after all assaults failed to take the local fortress of Ungará, the Incas duped the residents into leaving their redoubt by feigning withdrawal and leaving sacrifices by the sea. The besieged forces foolishly left their strongholds to celebrate, only to be butchered on the beach and in the water. The local people were thereafter called the Guarco – a name derived from the Quechua word for "hang," since many unfortunates were hanged from the fort's walls (Cabello Valboa 1951: 339). At the end of the campaign, Thupa Inka Yupanki ordered another settlement built, probably the site now known as Cerro Azul (Hyslop 1985: 12), and installed a governor and colonists. The valley's inhabitants were deported and more compliant peoples from the neighboring Chincha and Coayllo valleys were brought in to occupy their lands (Rostworowski 1990: 455–6).

Further Ventures into the Eastern Lowlands

The narratives describe several ventures into the Peruvian and Bolivian jungles and plains late in Pachakuti's reign and again at the beginning of Thupa Inka Yupanki's (Cieza 1967: 173–5, 205; Rowe 1985b: 225; Sarmiento 2007: 158–9; Cabello Valboa 1951: 334–5; Murúa 1986: 87–8; Cobo 1979: 135–7, 143; see Saignes 1985; Pärssinen 1992: 107–19). The *selva* proved a recurrent nightmare, as the highland armies were ill-suited to jungle warfare. Thupa Inka Yupanki reportedly led at least two expeditions, one as Pachakuti's general on a mission of conquest and one as emperor to subdue an uprising following his father's death. In Diez de Betanzos's narrative, the first expedition was only modestly productive, yielding gold, feathers, honey, and exotic animals. Shortly thereafter, Pachakuti died and Thupa Inka Yupanki spent a year in mourning, followed by a major campaign back to the jungles. Leaving Yamque Yupanki in Cuzco as governor, the new ruler took two brothers along as military leaders.

In countering the expedition, the Incas' opponents made a fatal tactical error by massing their forces, instead of harassing the highland troops and fading into the forest, a method that caused the Incas all kinds of distress on other campaigns. Despite his reported military successes, Thupa Inka Yupanki found little of value and opted to turn back to Cuzco. In an alternative version, Sarmiento's witnesses explained that the emperor Thupa Inka Yupanki had initially called the warlords of the montaña to Cuzco to pay homage. Once there, the guests took offense when they were required to deliver soil from their lands for the service of the Sun Temple and turned homeward. Thupa Inka Yupanki then assembled a large army divided into three parts, but the Incas found the eastern lands a den of horrors. Many of the men in Thupa Inka Yupanki's contingent perished from hunger and disease as they wandered about lost, until Uturunku Achachi's ("Tiger Ancestor") men found and led them out. How far into the lowlands the Incas penetrated is uncertain. The Chunchos and Mojos peoples east of Lake Titicaca are often mentioned, but the *llanos de Mojos* cover an immense territory. Some sources even mention places down the Madre de Dios river as far east as the border between Bolivia and Brazil (chapter 10; see Pärssinen 1992: 107–19).

Rebellion in the Altiplano

Most early accounts agreed that the Qolla and Lupaqa lords of Hatunqolla, Chucuito, and Azángaro led a major uprising in the altiplano during one of the Incas' eastern campaigns (Diez de Betanzos 1996: 143–7; Cieza 1967: 53, 174–84, 204; Rowe 1985b: 225–6; Sarmiento 2007: 160–2; Cabello Valboa 1951: 335–6; Cobo 1979: 143; Murúa 1986: 88–9). Although the chroniclers differed as to whether the rebellion occurred under Pachakuti's or Thupa Inka Yupanki's rule, they agreed that the latter led the punitive force. The altiplano uprising was a serious matter, but was only one of several that periodically threatened Inca hegemony. The Aymara-speaking societies were split in the war, with the Cana and Canche siding with the Inca forces (Rowe 1946: 207; Cieza 1967: 175–9). In a commonly reported version, a Qolla soldier named Coaquiri deserted the forces in the montaña and fled to the altiplano, where his report that the paramount was lost touched off a rebellion. Such periods of succession or uncertain leadership were often unsettled, as many subjects saw a chance to reassert their independence, which they initiated by killing the resident Inca authorities. Once Thupa Inka Yupanki had been extricated from the jungles, he left

Uturunku Achachi as governor and headed directly toward the altiplano to deal with the situation. Because the Incas did not have standing armies, a major mobilization was required. Diez de Betanzos (1996: 143–53), who wrote the most detailed account of the events, noted that the situation was complicated by the untimely death of Yamque Yupanki. Determined to take no chances with security elsewhere, the Incas reportedly detached 20,000 men from Antisuyu, along with 20,000 Canas and Canches from Kollasuyu, to help maintain order in Chinchaysuyu. Ten thousand men from Antisuyu, Canas, Quivios, and Canches, were allocated to Cuntisuyu. Diez de Betanzos wrote that for his campaign Thupa Inka Yupanki took 100,000 soldiers from Chinchaysuyu, and a personal guard of 5,000 from the Cuzco area. Even if those figures were largely symbolic fiction, the reassertion of Cuzco's dominion over the altiplano societies was a major undertaking that required years of campaigns, at least as recounted in the royal sagas. Over time, the Incas invested and overran a series of fortified settlements sequentially occupied by the retreating Qolla and their allies. The Inca forces ultimately prevailed at the Desaguadero river, which flows out of the south side of Lake Titicaca. They took memorable retribution by flaying the defeated altiplano lords, impaling their heads on poles, and fashioning their skins into drums.

Advances into Argentina and Chile

Most sources ascribed the annexation of the southern Andes to Thupa Inka Yupanki, although those expeditions formed the most schematic slices of the Inca histories (Callapiña *et al.* 1974: 40; Diez de Betanzos 1996: 148–52; Cieza 1967: 204; Polo 1917: 116; Rowe 1985b: 226; Sarmiento 2007: 160–2; Cabello Valboa 1951: 336–7; Murúa 1986: 90–1; Guaman Poma 1980: 89; Cobo 1979: 146–7; see Lorandi and Boixadós 1987–8; Pärssinen 1992: 120–36). Because the Spaniards met fierce resistance in that sparsely occupied part of the Andes, they were slow to assimilate it and take down accounts of local history that could be compared to the chronicles. Some areas resisted Spanish rule for 130 years, by which time local peoples had been free of Inca rule for much longer than they had been subjects. In most accounts, once the Inca armies had secured the Lake Titicaca basin, they pressed south through the altiplano into northwest Argentina and Chile. According to Diez de Betanzos, the sequence of southern conquests began with the occupation of Guasco and Coquimbo territory and the establishment of a fort and garrison at Coquimbo. The Inca expedition then engaged the Chiriguanos (Guaraníes) and Zuries, east of the Andes, along what would become the troublesome southeastern frontier. Diez de Betanzos explained that the army found the rough eastern terrain impassable, especially the Río de la Plata out on the plain. So they shifted back to the high country and crossed over to Chile in pursuit of gold and mineral wealth at Porco, Tarapacá, and Carabaya.

The force then reportedly headed still further south, with a vanguard pressing forward beyond the Río Maule, near Santiago. Diez de Betanzos (1996: 148–9) wrote that rapacious Thupa Inka Yupanki asked the populace ten days' journey north of the river where they had procured their gold. The natives described a watercourse and the dense human and small camelid populations, six days beyond. The army pressed southward for 15–20 leagues (70–90 km) and a contingent was sent forward to scout the river. At that point, Thupa Inka Yupanki decided that he had been away from Cuzco for quite a while and had seen enough. In contrast, Cobo (1979: 146–7) explained that the allied forces of the bellicose Mapuche and Araucanian societies who lived beyond the river repelled the invasion, killing the Inca commander and most of his soldiers. That setback provided the Incas sufficient motive to turn back north.

In Diez de Betanzos's (1996: 150–2) account, after settling garrisons in Chile, Thupa Inka Yupanki's forces set course back to Cuzco, divided into four parts. One took the coastal plain to Arequipa; one marched into the central highlands through the lands of the Carangas and Aullagas; and the last went to the east through the lands of the Chichas. Thupa Inka Yupanki himself headed the fourth contingent, following an eastern route. The troops reportedly suffered enormously crossing the desert and endured grave losses in battle en route north. Before arriving in Chucuito, Thupa Inka Yupanki's soldiers established dominion in the province of Ilipa and in Chuquisaca, home to the Charkas, a province that his father had already reportedly conquered. In that march, his forces founded the *tampu* of Paria, above Cochabamba, and compelled tribute of great quantities of gold from the residents of Chuquiabo (La Paz). The easternmost army meanwhile lost about one-third of its personnel in its campaign to secure Chicha territory, in the south Bolivian altiplano. In that endeavor, the Inca army also passed through the modern province of Santa Cruz, establishing fortified settlements at Pocona, Samaipata, and Cuzcotuiro, along a hardened eastern perimeter (Rowe 1985b: 226). The ultimate extension of Inca authority or activity in that region probably fell 100 km or more beyond the string of forts (see chapters 10 and 11).

According to a number of sources, Pachakuti died during Thupa Inka Yupanki's campaigns in the south Andes, although Sarmiento's account can be read as though the father died before his son's first venture into the montaña. The campaign south may have been Thupa Inka Yupanki's last military venture. However, both the *khipu kamayuq* of Pacariqtambo and Sarmiento report that much of the empire had rebelled during the southern conquests, so the Inca had to return north to resecure those rebellious lands (Callapiña *et al.* 1974: 40; Sarmiento 2007: 160). Sarmiento specifically mentioned the defiant Chachapoyas in that regard. The consensus, however, is that Wayna Qhapaq was the protagonist in the Incas' efforts to finally pacify that troublesome people.

Consolidation of the Empire: Wayna Qhapaq

The transition from Thupa Inka Yupanki to Wayna Qhapaq was reportedly just as turbulent as earlier successions, involving both intrigue and murder among royal kin groups (see chapter 6). Once his kin were in control, Wayna Qhapaq was said to have balanced his reign between military and administrative affairs (Callapiña *et al.* 1974: 42; Diez de Betanzos 1996: 165–85; Cieza 1984: 157, 229, 1967: 211–29; Polo 1917: 114; Rowe 1985b: 224–6; Sarmiento 2007: 173–86; Murúa 1986: 107–31; Cobo 1979: 152–6; Cabello Valboa 1951: 361–405). The major expansions were already completed, so his campaigns involved securing perimeter territories and dominating the far north. With his brother Awki Thupa Inka installed as co-ruler, Wayna Qhapaq spent two years in Cuzco before setting out on his first military venture against the Chachapoyas. Using Cajamarca as a base of operations, Wayna Qhapaq's forces ultimately spent years subduing the peoples of that land. Sometime early in his reign, Wayna Qhapaq inspected his domain, for new rulers had to re-establish their supremacy physically and symbolically. He set off to the south, having entrusted his uncle Waman Achachi ("Hawk Ancestor") with the northern half of the empire. During the tour, the emperor passed through Cochabamba, in eastern Bolivia, where a vast set of state farms was created at his behest (chapter 12). He also ordered the eastern frontier at Pocona hardened against a threat of invasion from the east, by renovating a fort built during Pachakuti's reign. The Incas also mounted an expedition onto the plains of northwest Argentina through Tucumán, but like many marches into the eastern lowlands, the venture ended with the army retreating ingloriously to the mountains. The Incas nonetheless formed an alliance with the natives of Tucumán, who served as internal colonists and as a frontier buffer against depredations from the east in return for Inca protection (Lorandi and Boixadós 1987–8; Lorandi 1988).

After an organizational respite in Cuzco, Wayna Qhapaq set off for new conquests in the north. Cieza (1967: 214) placed the total number of soldiers at an improbable 200,000, not counting servants. The forces were sent out in contingents to ease the logistical problems involved in moving so many men and their camp followings. The sovereign's journey was a suitably prolonged affair, as he often paused along the way to tend to affairs of state. In the Mantaro valley, Cieza (1967: 215) heard that the ruler had settled a long-simmering quarrel among the Wanka and Xauxa over the borders of their lands, while Cobo (1979: 154) referred to Wayna Qhapaq's settling of a dispute over grazing lands in Kollasuyu. Wayna Qhapaq took quite a few Xauxa along with him to the Ecuadorian campaigns, an episode that their relatives were still complaining about half a century later, since many had never returned. The sojourn also solidified control over fractious *etnías*, including the perennially unruly Chachapoyas, who reportedly succumbed only after three new operations (see Cobo 1979: 153).

Wayna Qhapaq's forces reportedly conducted as many as six to eight arduous campaigns over two decades in Ecuador, but his efforts enjoyed only mixed success (see Niles 1999: 95–105 for a discussion of his military exploits). They established a base of operations at Tumipampa and, in especially trying regions, such as the Pasto territory at the north end of the empire, they built or took over existing forts as forward bases. There as elsewhere, where the Incas could establish a clear field of battle against a massed opponent or could invest a stronghold, they stood an excellent chance of success over time. Where the enemy proved elusive or held difficult terrain, especially in forested country, Inca military efforts often miscarried. The Brazamoros proved insuperable, sending the Incas packing back to their base camps. Cieza (1967: 188, 217–18) wrote that another force was routed even before arriving at the targeted forts, and two others also retreated in the face of native resistance. One of the latter expeditions was led by Atawallpa, whose precipitous flight greatly shamed his father. Only after even more failed efforts led by other officers did Wayna Qhapaq himself take personal command in the field, according to Cabello (Cabello Valboa 1951: 368; see also Diez de Betanzos 1996: 182–3).

The campaigns against the Otavalo and Caranqui included some of the most celebrated battles of late Inca history (Sarmiento 2007: 177–83; Cabello Valboa 1951: 369–70; see also Murúa 1986: 119–20). In one conflict, the Incas met concerted resistance in efforts to take a citadel and Wayna Qhapaq was unseated in an unexpected counterattack. He was saved only by the heroic action of his personal guard composed of *orejones* (literally "big-ears," so named for their pendulous ear lobes in which they inserted large earspools), Cuzqueñans who formed the army's elite. In the aftermath of the battle, the ruler and *orejones* quarreled when he chastened them for letting him fall into mortal danger. The humiliated warriors organized to return home, and were only dissuaded from doing so by personal entreaties from the image of the emperor's mother, sweetened with gifts. Ultimately, the Incas prevailed only by feigning withdrawal and catching the hapless defenders as they poured out of the fort. Most of the defenders were pinned against a lake, where they mistook Inca efforts to capture them as a continued attack. When they resisted, they were slaughtered in the water, thus giving the lake its name – *Yaguarcocha*, or Lake of Blood. Wayna Qhapaq then retired to Tumipampa, but the Incas were continually plagued by a warlord named Pinta, who had escaped with a "thousand" Kañari and raided for some time from a fort at Chillo. When the defiant Pinta refused pardon after he was finally captured, his skin was made into a drum that was played as a gesture of respect in festivals in Cuzco honoring the Sun (Cabello Valboa 1951: 382).

Wayna Qhapaq received news about that time that the southeastern frontier at Cuzcotuiro, Bolivia, had been invaded. He dispatched the commander Yasca to assemble a force to counter the incursion of Guaraníes (Chiriguanos), accompanied by the Portuguese adventurer Alejo García. The general headed south, beginning to gather his army in Cajamarca and picking up soldiers along the way. Although Yasca's forces met noteworthy resistance, they ultimately re-established the frontier, rebuilt the forts, and installed garrisons (Cabello Valboa 1951: 383–4; Sarmiento 2007: 183; Murúa 1986: 130–1). In the meantime, Wayna Qhapaq's forces pressed northward into the lands of the Pasto and Quillacinga. They placed the empire's northernmost territorial markers at the Río Angasmayo or a little farther north, near the border of modern Ecuador and Colombia. A vanguard was sent further, but returned with tales of an impoverished land populated by naked cannibals, a description sometimes applied to areas where the Incas could not establish control (Cabello Valboa 1951: 384; see *RGI*: 210, 279; see Salomon 1986). At that point, Wayna Qhapaq descended to the coast himself. The Incas advanced only under great hardships, fighting debilitating battles along the way. How far his army traveled is a matter of some dispute, but most sources report an advance no farther than southern Ecuador (Cieza 1967: 221–2; Sarmiento 2007: 184; Cabello Valboa 1951: 392–3). While in the lowlands, Wayna Qhapaq heard of an epidemic that was killing many of his relatives – probably hemorrhagic smallpox (Cook 1981: 62) – and quickly headed back to the mountains. Early in 1528, while in Quito or Tumipampa, he was fatally stricken himself. The death of his heir designate Ninan Cuyuchi of the same pestilence soon precipitated a conflict over succession.

Dynastic War: Waskhar and Atawallpa

The succession to Wayna Qhapaq's throne suffered the conflicting claims, fratricide, and pitched battle that often attended the transfer of imperial power, in part because of Ninan Cuyuchi's untimely death (e.g., Callapiña *et al.* 1974: 47; Diez de Betanzos 1996: 182–5; Cabello Valboa 1951: 394; Murúa 1986: 140; Cobo 1979: 160–1; Sarmiento 2007: 185). Waskhar and Atawallpa, two royal sons by different mothers, fought a savage war that ended just as the Spaniards arrived in 1532. In fact, Pizarro's men captured Atawallpa in Cajamarca just as the disgraced Waskhar was being ferried north. Three Spaniards actually had an audience with the fallen emperor shortly before he was murdered along the road, in which he vainly pleaded to be released. The dynastic war split the Andean peoples, providing a wedge that the conquistadores quickly recognized and exploited.

Most accounts agree that Waskhar was enthroned in Cuzco with the assent of the royalty. This view was unsurprisingly countered by Diez de Betanzos (1996: 183–4), who was married to Atawallpa's sister/wife. In Diez de Betanzos's version, Wayna Qhapaq successively named Ninan Cuyuchi, Atawallpa, and Waskhar as the next paramount, while in his deathbed fever. Only because Atawallpa rejected the throne was the fringe to be passed on to Waskhar. Shortly thereafter, his half-brother Atawallpa challenged his authority from a base of power in Ecuador, where the Incas' most seasoned army was stationed. It is uncertain if Atawallpa intended to claim the northern part of the empire at first, or if he did so only after Waskhar's murderous behavior (described in chapter 6) led him to fear for his life. In the context of the narratives, Waskhar's lethal actions toward his immediate male kin would have given any survivors cause for fear. It bears remembering, however, that most of Waskhar's adherents were eliminated at the end of the war, so that he left few supporters to tell his side of the story.

Cabello (1951: 394–474; see also Sarmiento 2007: 186; Diez de Betanzos 1996: 184) wrote that word of the deaths of Wayna Qhapaq and the prince was sent ahead to Cuzco, while the funeral cortège was mounted. The emperor's organs were removed and the body cured in the sun and air. His attendants then dressed him in precious robes and placed him on a fine litter adorned with feathers and gold to be transported back to Cuzco. Guaman Poma (1980: 93; see Rostworowski 1999: 90) wrote that the embalmed body was treated as if Wayna Qhapaq were still alive in an effort to allow insiders a chance to install a successor before opposition could be raised. Cabello reported that some members of the funeral party hatched a plot to kill the newly selected Waskhar and enthrone his brother Kusi Atachi, but the plot was foiled when the chief conspirator approached an uncle who remained loyal to Waskhar (Cabello Valboa 1951: 396–7; see also Murúa 1986: 143; Guaman Poma 1980: 93). Waskhar ordered the funeral train to stop outside Cuzco, according to Cabello (1951: 398) and Murúa (1986: 144–5), since it had already come within 20 leagues of the city. Perhaps mindful of the recent conspiracy to supplant him, Waskhar commanded the four executors of Wayna Qhapaq's legacy to enter Cuzco one at a time. He demanded to know why Atawallpa had remained in Ecuador, but even under torture, they simply said that Atawallpa did not want to affront the aristocracy with his wretched appearance. To everyone's horror, Waskhar ordered the executors killed, even though they were esteemed relatives from Upper Cuzco (i.e., *Hanan Cuzco*, the more prestigious half of Cuzco's aristocracy: see chapter 6). Many members of the funeral cortège fled immediately. Some carried the fearsome news to Atawallpa, while Waskhar symbolically divorced himself from Upper Cuzco in a fury (Sarmiento 2007: 187). Despite the tumult, Wayna Qhapaq's funeral was a prolonged, elaborate affair, with great pomp and copious drinking. Sometime thereafter, Waskhar took his sister Mama Chukuy Juypa as wife, but reportedly only after embarrassing entreaties and with the grudging acquiescence of her mother.

The chroniclers differed over Atawallpa's intentions in the early stages of Waskhar's rule, although most observed that he initially declared obeisance to his brother. His pledges were ill-received in Cuzco, however, for various messengers were maimed, tortured, or slain (Diez de Betanzos 1996: 193; Cabello Valboa 1951: 413–14; Sarmiento 2007: 187). As word of Waskhar's suspicions of treason got back to him, Atawallpa reportedly set about erecting palaces in Tumipampa and dressed in his father's vestments to visit Quito. The Inca governor of the Kañari reported those actions to an irate Waskhar, who perhaps rightly believed that Atawallpa was staking a claim

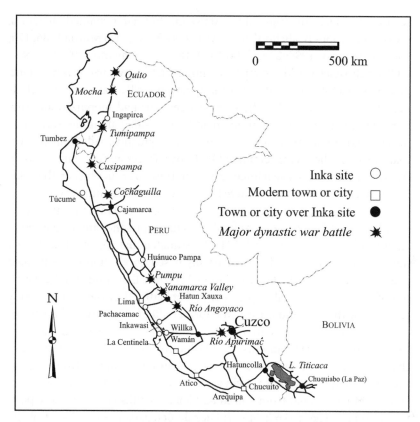

Figure 4.2   The major battles of the dynastic war between Waskhar and Atawallpa.

of legitimacy to the throne (Cabello Valboa 1951: 423). Rejecting counsel for restoring amicable relations, Waskhar decided on military action.

The first battles of the dynastic war were remembered in many ways (figure 4.2). Cieza (1967: 239–44) commented that he heard so many different versions that he would just go with the majority. He wrote that Waskhar sent Atoq ("Fox") north to assemble a local force of Kañari. Some reports said that Atawallpa was captured either by Atoq in battle or during an appeal to the Kañari for assistance. He was held prisoner in Tumipampa, from where he escaped with the aid of a silver lever or by transmogrifying into a serpent. In Cabello's account, Atoq's local army engaged Atawallpa's forces near Tumipampa. The Cuzco side prevailed, so Atawallpa's men retreated to the Río Ambato, south of Quito, which they had previously secured for such an eventuality. Atawallpa himself remained in Quito, rallying his troops (Cabello Valboa 1951: 429–31; see also Murúa 1986: 170; Diez de Betanzos 1996: 200; Cobo 1979: 164–5; Sarmiento 2007: 187–9).

Other chroniclers did not report an initial victory by Cuzco's forces. Diez de Betanzos (1996: 195–6) – ever the apologist for Pachakuti's kin, including Atawallpa – wrote that the southern generals had mobilized an army of 6,000 in Cuzco and picked up an additional 4,000 along the way. They provisioned the army at state centers along highland roads built for just that purpose. They were reinforced by Kañari forces at Tumipampa, while Atawallpa gathered his own forces in Quito. The two armies met on the fields of Mochacaxa or Riopampa, where the Ecuadorian forces under Atawallpa's personal direction won a resounding victory. One of Waskhar's two commanders was killed, but Kusi Yupanki was taken prisoner and converted to Atawallpa's cause. Cieza (1967: 241–3) estimated that 15,000–16,000 men died in the conflict, a judgment partially based on viewing the battlefield over a decade later. Cabello (1951: 428–32) wrote that Atoq and the governor of the Kañari were taken prisoner in that battle. They were subsequently executed with darts and arrows, the former after being tortured for information about Cuzco's intentions. Atoq's skin was then turned into a drum (Sarmiento 2007: 189) and his skull fashioned into a gilded drinking cup that the Spanish soldier Ruiz de Arce saw Atawallpa drinking from in Cajamarca. At that point Wanka Awki assumed command of Waskhar's forces, supported by *orejones* from Cuzco and soldiers enlisted from many parts of the empire (Cieza 1967: 245–7; Diez de Betanzos 1996: 206–8; Cabello Valboa 1951: 433–4; Murúa 1986: 172–5).

There were numerous diplomatic overtures along the way among Waskhar, Wanka Awki, and Atawallpa, but they ultimately miscarried, not least because Waskhar feared that Wanka Awki would defect. Cabello wrote that the great armies soon engaged each other in a second battle at a bridge controlling access to Tumipampa, where Cuzco's forces prevailed in a Pyrrhic victory. Atawallpa's men took refuge on a hill slope for the night, but sallied forth the next morning and forced Wanka Awki's men to retreat to Tumipampa. Finding that Atawallpa's soldiers were advancing toward him, Wanka Awki dispatched an army to engage them, but it was routed at a substantial loss of manpower (Cabello Valboa 1951: 433–5; see also Sarmiento 2007: 189–90). He then retreated to Cusipampa, where he set about constructing a fort.

Even during the war's early stages, the Quiteñan and Cuzqueñan sides were not always engaged with each other, as some ancillary campaigns reportedly followed the first conflicts (Diez de Betanzos 1996: 203–4; Cabello Valboa 1951: 433–8; Cieza 1967: 246–7). Part of the rationale may have arisen from their desire to secure their base territories before engaging one another. Cabello explained the forays of both sides as training exercises and as a means of keeping the massed forces occupied. Atawallpa reportedly worked hard to firm up military control and to expand his domain to the east. He exacted ghastly revenge from the Kañari for their allegiance to Waskhar, killing many, resettling some in Guambo, and transporting about 15,000 south for intended resettlement near Cuzco. Sarmiento (2007: 189–90) and Cabello (1951: 437–41; see also Murúa 1986: 176–9) also reported that armies under Wanka Awki undertook similar ventures with mixed results. According to Cabello, Wanka Awki's defeat on the eastern slopes was rewarded with a derisive present of women's clothes from Waskhar, which goaded him into taking on Atawallpa's men in an effort to regain lost prestige. However, he was defeated again at Cusipampa because his army was so drained after its ill-fated campaigns to the east.

Those defeats inaugurated a calamitous series of battles commanded by Wanka Awki as he retreated along the Andes. Modern analysts concur with Cobo's (1979: 165–6) assessment that the hastily mobilized southern forces, though immense, were no match for Atawallpa's seasoned troops, who had been honing their skills during twenty years of warfare. The continued losses by Wanka Awki both weakened his forces and reduced morale. Following the loss of southern Ecuador, his remaining army retreated to Cajamarca, in north-central Peru. There he was reinforced by an army of 30,000 fresh troops, whose core consisted of 10,000 of the redoubtable Chachapoyas (Diez de Betanzos 1996: 206–7; Sarmiento 2007: 190; Cabello Valboa 1951: 436–46; Murúa 1986: 183). Those men set out against the advancing forces of Quizquiz, one of Atawallpa's two principal generals, to do battle at Cochaguilla, in northern Peru, between Guancabamba and Guambos. According to Cabello, Quizquiz astutely recognized that the Chachapoyas were key to the battle and concentrated his forces on breaking them. Once the Chachapoyas were put to flight, the remaining southern army quit the field and many men crossed over to the opposition. Reinforced with those soldiers and others forcibly pressed along route, Quizquiz continued south with an army vastly larger than the one he had commanded when departing Quito.

At Pumpu, an important provincial center in the central Peruvian puna, Quizquiz prevailed once more; the southern forces fled to Hatun Xauxa, about 150 km to the south. The ill-fated Wanka Awki was then stripped of command by Mayca Yupanki, who led a considerable array of reinforcements (Sarmiento 2007: 190; Murúa 1986: 184; Cabello Valboa 1951: 448–9). The two contingents soon joined battle in the Yanamarca valley, just north of Hatun Xauxa. According to Cabello (1951: 449–50), Mayca Yupanki's inexperienced soldiers initially held the field, but at such great cost that they retreated to the pass over the Angoyaco (Mantaro river), about 70 km south of Hatun Xauxa. In the aftermath, thousands of corpses were said to have been strewn across the battlefield, their remains still visible to the Spaniards in March 1533 (Herrera 1952: 323). Following the victory in the Yanamarca valley, Quizquiz's forces took a recuperative break at Hatun Xauxa, after which they pushed on to the Angoyaco bridgehead. The constricted topography favored the defenders, but the northern forces ultimately took the pass either through a flanking maneuver or a massed attack.

Waskhar then determined to set out at the head of his own force. After the customary consultation of oracles, fasting, and sacrifices, his armies mobilized to entrap Quizquiz's men. The consensus among the chroniclers is that Waskhar divided his forces into three parts (Diez de Betanzos 1996: 223; Sarmiento 2007: 193–7; Cabello Valboa 1951: 453–9; Murúa 1986: 188). Cabello and Sarmiento wrote that the two forces on the eastern flank met before the major battle. In the conflict between the forces of the center, Waskhar's troops held the field but failed to press their advantage. They drove the northern forces onto grassy slopes to which they set fire, after which they retired to a state installation to rest. The northern commanders, in contrast, rallied their men during the night. Determined to finish things the next day, Waskhar divided his forces to trap his opponents. However, Sarmiento wrote, Challcochima, Atawallpa's other principal general, successfully employed a similar pincers tactic and routed one of the Cuzqueñan forces.

In a now familiar pattern, the histories differed on how Waskhar fell to Quizquiz's and Challcochima's men. In Cabello's account (1951: 457–9; see also Murúa 1986: 192), the emperor's litter was overthrown in a great battle. Seeing their ruler captured, his demoralized men took flight. Diez de Betanzos (1996: 225–7) and Sarmiento (2007: 195) wrote that Waskhar was drawn into an ambush with only a guard of 5,000. Tellingly, that guard was apparently composed of warriors from *Hurin Cuzco*, since Waskhar did not trust the upper half of Cuzco's royalty, whom he saw as being allied with Atawallpa. A small contingent of northerners placed themselves in his path, feigning sleep and then a disorderly retreat. As Waskhar pursued his apparent advantage, lateral forces closed the trap and took him prisoner. Challcochima then dressed a number of his men in Waskhar's clothes and ordered them to take up the fallen emperor's litter in a march toward the main Cuzqueñan army. When they approached Waskhar's forces, Challcochima's men revealed themselves as the victorious northern army, which so dismayed the Cuzqueñans that they surrendered.

However it occurred, that battle effectively ended the dynastic war. Challcochima and Quizquiz entered Cuzco, where they held Waskhar, his mother, and his wife prisoner. There is confusion over the sequence of events afterward, but the generals may have initially granted a general pardon. Some time later, Kusi Yupanki, Atawallpa's highest-ranking military officer and High Priest of the Sun, arrived in Cuzco. Under his supervision, Waskhar's wives and children were executed one after another in the most ghastly fashion as the lamenting ruler was forced to watch. The carnage was so thorough that only a handful of close relatives were spared or escaped. Kusi Yupanki also supervised the burning of Thupa Inka Yupanki's mummy and the virtual eradication of his descendant kin (see chapter 6 for a political explanation of this episode). Among the lucky few who escaped the carnage were Wayna Qhapaq's sons Manqo Inka, who would lay siege to Cuzco in 1536, and Paullu Inka, who collaborated with Spanish rule (Diez de Betanzos 1996: 243–4; Sarmiento 2007: 198–200; Cobo 1979: 168–9).

While the definitive battles were waged outside Cuzco, Atawallpa was slowly wending his way south from Tumipampa. He was in Cajamarca when word arrived that a contingent of strange, bearded men had arrived on the coast at Tumbes, where they were making a general nuisance of themselves by pillaging and killing. Atawallpa dispatched Rumiñawi ("Stone Eye") at the head of a force said to include 6,000 men to meet the Spaniards, who had begun to ascend the Andes by that point. The emperor himself elected to wait in Cajamarca for both his uninvited visitors and the defeated Waskhar. Confident in his victory, Atawallpa could not have foreseen that the arrival of the Spaniards spelled death for him and the end of his hard-won empire.

Explaining the Inca Expansion

Some important factors – especially political history and ideology – remain to be explored, but this is probably a good point to reflect on the causes of the great expansion. Although a prince's ambitions may have fanned the Incas' ardor, the rise of the empire cannot be assigned to that factor alone. Keeping in mind the poetic license of the narratives, we need to think in terms of the dynamics of chiefdoms, not states, for the early stages. Both settlement patterns and the legendary accounts suggest that the conflict endemic to Late Intermediate highland societies set the conditions for Inca expansion. Intriguingly, there are hints of pressure on productive lands in the last century or two before the first Inca expansion. The layers of ice in the Quelccaya glacier testify to a prolonged drought in the south Peruvian Andes *c.* AD 1245–1310 (Ortloff and Kolata 1989; see also Seltzer and Hastorf 1990). That situation may have threatened highland subsistence and put a premium on leaders who could defend or expand resources. The prospect of aggression by powerful neighbors to the south and west may have also genuinely threatened Cuzco's security, as the narratives recounted. Certainly the immense, walled settlements in the Titicaca basin suggest that the powers developing there were enmeshed in warfare. It thus seems plausible that the Incas' initial expansionist moves combined predation and self-defense.

Rowe (1946: 206) has plausibly suggested that the early Inca successes may have also committed them to hostile relations with powerful societies that they had not considered engaging, notably Chimor. Militarism may have played another, more indirect role, as military competence was conspicuously mentioned in the selection of Inca leadership (chapters 6 and 10). In the Late Intermediate period, the endemic conflict selected for warlords who could provide security and opportunities for plunder. This ethic carried over into the imperial era. Though the conquistadores' own careers as soldiers colored their views of Inca history, the image of rulers as great warriors pervaded the Incas' own descriptions. The succession process was intended to produce vigorous leaders, and the dynastic histories gave short shrift to rulers who failed to enlarge their domain.

There is no reason to doubt the Incas' own explanation that a quest for wealth also drove their expansion. A change from plunder to annexation of productive resources may have been crucial in the emergence of the expansionist state (Schaedel 1978; see also Rostworowski 1999). The gains realized from seizing resources likely benefited most Incas, but the methods may have concentrated power in a few elite lineages who needed to keep the flow of spoils in motion to maintain power. Booty was a prime motivator for the officers and rank and file soldiers throughout the Inca era, but some regions were most likely targeted for natural resources that could be intensified. The highlands of Peru were attractive for farming and pastoral production, whereas the altiplano was coveted for the wealth of its flocks.

Cochabamba, Bolivia, was developed for its productive farmlands (Wachtel 1982). The Incas also sought raw materials that could be used to sustain the elites' privileged position – minerals from the south Andes, gold and feathers from the jungles, and spondylus shell from tropical waters (chapter 13).

As for politics, the interplay between militarism and genealogy in Inca successions also contributed to the expansion (see also chapter 6). There is fragile balance in a practice of succession that selects for dynamic leadership while providing for continuity of rule. Perhaps recognizing the problems inherent in political instability, the later emperors adopted co-regency as a policy to smooth the transition across generations of leadership. As a consequence, royal successions set aristocratic kin groups against one another, in the names of potential heirs too young to assert their own claims. The transitions to Thupa Inka Yupanki, Wayna Qhapaq, and Waskhar/Atawallpa emphasize that the bloody politics of succession were played out by kin groups. While the paramount was reaching maturity, however, it remained for him to demonstrate competence through effective military leadership. Some late Inca campaigns, especially Wayna Qhapaq's grand tour and his campaigns in Ecuador, are therefore at least partly understandable as a play to royal politics.

Ideological motives often appeared in accounts of the expansion, but their role is complicated because the Incas continually reinvented their grand tradition. Charismatic leadership was almost certainly vital in both strategic and tactical command and the narratives certainly show that the Incas were aware of the utility of promoting a cult of the great leader. The narratives emphasized the importance of the Sapa Inca in decisive battles, even though many key expeditions were directed by other kin. The Incas also generated heroic and supernatural tales about the emperors even after the Spanish invasion. Nonetheless, the infighting among Cuzco's aristocracy should make us chary of crediting the emperor with too much power in describing how Inca rule actually worked. There is also some suggestion that the Incas drew inspiration from an evangelistic creed. Imperial ideology, as told to the Spaniards, contained an edict to civilize the world and we have every reason to believe that the Incas had faith in their gods and ancestors (chapter 8). Because we do not know how much of the imperial ideology was formulated late in the game, however, the degree to which evangelism actually drove the major expansions remains uncertain.

Some scholars have also inferred that the Andean practice called split inheritance drove the expansion (Conrad and Demarest 1984). In that custom, the individual who succeeded to the throne inherited the office and control over state resources. The deceased Inca's personal resources were kept by his kin group to venerate him in perpetuity. This proposition suggests that each new emperor had to expand the empire to feed the capital and build his own wealth, because the resources near Cuzco were soon exhausted. I find the argument unpersuasive, in part because Pachakuti and Thupa Inka Yupanki annexed virtually the entire empire, according to the sources used. Moreover, despite the ostensible shortages, even Wayna Qhapaq and Waskhar claimed areas in and near Cuzco for their own palaces and estates. The limitations of Andean transport technology also precluded long-distance shipment of food for daily subsistence. What is described as a concern about a shortage of resources is more plausibly explained as jealousy over royal estates (chapter 7). The situation may well have been cause for political infighting, but it does not work well in explaining imperial origins.

Notes

1   Samuel Johnson is credited with writing that "among the calamities of war may be jointly numbered the diminution of the love of truth, by the falsehoods which interest dictates and credulity encourages" in *The Idler* 30 of November 11, 1758   (www.theguardian.com/notesandqueries/query/0,5753,-21510,00.html [accessed December 11, 2013]). Ponsonby was more pithy, but apparently not original.
2   Garcilaso drew heavily from Blas Valera and thus cannot be considered to be a truly independent source.
3   The Quipucamayos of Pacariqtambo averred that he subdued the entire alti-plano through a mix of diplomacy and conquest, and then ventured northward to the Huánuco region of Peru's central highlands. They mentioned such regions as Paria, Pacajes, Carangas, Charkas, and Umasuyo (Callapiña *et al.* 1974: 32 – 3). According to that account, Yawar Qhapaq had already vanquished Chucuito, home to the Lupaqa. Guaman Poma (1980: 87) also wrote that Wiraqocha Inka conquered through the central highlands of Peru and some lowlands, including the Chincha and Ica Valleys of the south Peruvian coast.
4   Despite such detailed versions of Wiraqocha Inka's exploits in the altiplano, Pärssinen (1992: 82 – 4) points out that there appears to be no corroborative evidence for the king's adventures in the local documents from the region. Instead, the sources from the altiplano ascribe the conquests to armies operating during Pachakuti's and Thupa Inka Yupanki's reigns, which tends to support the notion of a very rapid imperial expansion, as Rowe originally suggested.

5 Not all accounts agreed with even these versions of the timing or importance of the Inca–Chanka conflicts described here, although the sources that had the most direct input from native traditions tended to place the conflict earlier than the now-standard version. The purportedly earliest account by royal historians, the Pacariqtambo *khipu kamayuq*, did not even mention the Chankas by name nor describe an attack on Cuzco. They did state that Qhapaq Yupanki, the fifth ruler, conquered the Vilcas, Soras, and Aymaraes regions to the west of Cuzco (Callapiña *et al.* 1974: 31). Guaman Poma (1980: 85) took the same position in his historical review. However, most modern scholars suggest that the Qhapaq Yupanki who conquered that region was actually a brother of Pachakuti, who commanded a major campaign through the central Peruvian sierra. The *RGI* documents from the region credit Pachakuti and Thupa Inka Yupanki with the conquests. Alternatively, the mestizo Jesuit Blas Valera also wrote that Wiraqocha conquered the Chankas. In the mid-seventeenth century, drawing from a variety of sources, Cobo first wrote that Inka Roq'a, the sixth ruler, had conquered the Chankas. He then amended his account to say that the Chankas had actually not really been conquered, but "had surrendered to the necessity of adapting to the times." It was actually Wiraqocha Inka who vanquished the Chankas after Yawar Waqaq fled Cuzco. Pachakuti nonetheless also had to subdue them during his reign, after pre-empting a rumored coup attempt by his brother Inka Urqon by having him secretly murdered (Cobo 1979: 124–5, 127–8, 137).

6 The leader of the Chankas, named Uscovilca, was described as an idol or as the mummified corpse of the deceased Chanka lord in Sarmiento's (2007: 105) account. Polo found the idol with Pachakuti's mummy (Rostworowski 1999: 107).

7 See, for example, Callapiña *et al.* 1974: 31; Guaman Poma 1980: 85; Cobo 1979: 124–5, 127–8, 137.

8 Sarmiento and Cobo describe an early sortie led by Pachakuti and Inka Roq'a down the Urubamba valley to Ollantaytambo and perhaps as far as Vilcabamba, about 200 km away (Ollantaytambo: Sarmiento 2007: 125–8; Vilcabamba: Cobo 1979: 135–7; see Rowe 1946: 206; Saignes 1985: 14–15; Pärssinen 1992: 107–19). According to Diez de Betanzos (1996: 85–91), that first venture took the Incas only as far as Xaquixaguana, in the Anta region west of Cuzco. They penetrated deeper on a later occasion when Pachakuti sent in a contingent after returning from wars to the west with the Soras, Lucanas, and Chankas. He continued that, after Pachakuti's first expedition, the Incas moved to annex lands south and west of Cuzco. Diez de Betanzos explained that Pachakuti first obtained obeisance from the Quechua, Omasayo, Aymaráes, Yanahuara, Chumbivilca, and Chanka. Following a sortie into Abancay, the army swung north to defeat the allied forces of the Soras, Rucanas, and unpacified Chankas.

Other chroniclers and local documents reported variations on the same ventures. Witnesses from the Alca division of Chumbivilcas named Pachakuti as their conqueror, whereas the residents of Colquemarca in Chumbivilcas and (Rucanas) Antamarcas witnesses named Thupa Inka Yupanki. In another area, Toledan witnesses in Huamanga stated that Pachakuti had personally conquered as far as the Soras lands. In contrast, another Toledan witness, testifying in Xaquixaguana and professing himself to be Thupa Inka Yupanki's grandson, recounted that the campaign to Soras had actually been commanded by Pachakuti's brother Qhapaq Yupanki, not by the paramount himself (Alca: *RGI* I: 214; Colquemarca: *RGI* I: 220; Rucanas: *RGI* I: 230; Rucanas Antamarcas: *RGI* I: 241; Soras: Toledo 1940: 40, 44, 61–2). Sarmiento's chronicle appears to agree with the last version. The campaign to Soras complete, Pachakuti returned to Cuzco triumphant, while two other armies set out south to Cuntisuyu and east to Antisuyu, where they captured some highland and coca-producing lands and brought jungle cats and snakes back to Cuzco. The first contingent conquered as far as Arequipa, defeating the Collaguas, Canas, and Urocache (Canches). The other troops headed 40 leagues (i.e., about 200 km) into the montaña, where they took the coca-growing province of Caxarona (cf. Diez de Betanzos 1996: 81–91; Cieza 1967: 174, 176).

Chapter Five

Thinking Inca

Everything should be made as simple as possible, but no simpler.
Attributed to Albert Einstein, apparently by Roger Sessions.[1]

Now that we have described the rise of the Incas as an imperial power, it seems like a good time to consider what they were trying to accomplish and how they thought they could achieve their goals. Let me start by suggesting that the Incas' imperial ventures had two integrated components. The more obvious aspect was the domination and exploitation of millions of people and the Andes' resources. Those ends required military, political, economic, and social actions, such as securing control, building an infrastructure, and establishing a sustainable form of governance. Part of the Incas' success in that arena occurred because the leadership's strategies changed over time, in accord with the shifting terrain of challenges and interests. In a second, simultaneous endeavor, the Incas devised a rationale for their place in the cosmos and its history, attempting to impose their own notions of social order on the world at large. The heart of the argument consisted of the ideas that they legitimately ruled the known world and were indispensable to relations between humanity and pretty much everything else. We can't be entirely sure of the ideas that governed the Incas' perspectives when they started, but by the sixteenth century, they almost certainly professed a more intricate set of beliefs, conducted far more extravagant ceremonies, and experienced a richer array of intellectual activities than they had a century earlier.

This chapter is an effort to explain that intellectual project, to examine how the Incas thought the world worked and how they believed they could be successful within it. In essence, I am trying to get at the *why* of the nature

The Incas, Second Edition. Terence N. D'Altroy.
© 2015 John Wiley & Sons, Ltd. Published 2015 by John Wiley & Sons, Ltd.

and history of the empire from an inside perspective, to lay the groundwork for the rest of the book. Because the Incas' ways of thinking about things were often so alien to European perspectives, we will have to explore a few challenging topics in some detail – thus the aphorism from Einstein cited above.[2] The task is complicated, of course, by the lack of prehispanic documents and the modest range of graphical representation of any other kind. So we are more reliant here on early Spanish documents composed from their own observations and native testimony, on ethnography, and on linguistics than we are on archaeology. A few of the problems that arise as a result may be ultimately be intractable, but let's give it a try.

The chapter contains three parts, any of which can be read separately. The first part provides an overview of the most important ideas that underpinned Inca thought. The second looks at the nature of existence, space–time, and things in more detail. The third part looks at the ways that the Incas worked with numerical thought. It considers not just mathematics and accounting, but the pervasive social dimensions of numerical ordering in the Inca world. If you are worn out by the end of Part I, don't worry. You can always check back for more detail when reading other chapters.

Part I: Framing the Questions

What Was the Inca Canon?[3]

Dozens of questions can be raised about the subject of Inca thought. One deceptively simple issue concerns what they understood knowledge to be. How did they distinguish what they thought they knew from what they took to be belief, assertion, proposition, or falsehood? When the Incas thought they knew something, why did they think that it was true? Did they entertain notions of ideal truth or unchallengeable, divine revelation, or did they have other ways of generating ideas and evaluating arguments? Who had the right to propose new ideas, who judged them, and how were they judged? What were life and death all about? How did they categorize or classify things? How did cause and effect work in human or other affairs, and what principles guided order in the world? In short, what kinds of understanding and logic did the Incas employ as they created and ruled their empire?

If we briefly consider other major early civilizations, the importance of those questions may become clearer. For millennia, numerous societies have assessed cultural or philosophical issues in light of a formal canon – a set of established, written works that describe the principles of life, morality, sanctity, divinity, knowledge, power, and legitimacy, among many other issues. The canon can be used to appraise the validity of any novel idea, by providing a set of axiomatic precepts and the kinds of logic that can be applied to new questions or situations. The writings of the Greek and Roman philosophers, the Old and New Testaments, the Torah and Talmud, the Quran, the Hindu Vedas, and the Analects of Confucius all provide canonical texts. Less well publicized are the ideas of prehispanic American civilizations, such as the Maya, Mixteca, Zapoteca, and Azteca. Their learned works, today called *codices*, set down calendars, royal histories, ritual cycles, astronomical and astrological information, medicinal practice, and the like. Their core ideas could provide the impetus and rationale for imperial action, and molded the character of rule once dominion was established.

As far as we know, the Incas had no canon encoded in the form of a readable text. The genealogies, histories, poetry, and ceremonial programs kept on *khipu* might be the closest approximation, but there is no indication that principles of moral behavior, sanctity, or philosophy were directly readable as such. So what did they have? If there was an Inca canon of knowledge, what form did it take, what did it contain, how was it maintained, and how was it accessed? Did people take their moral codes directly from teachers or elders, did they learn from performed narratives, or was something more complex involved? While the Incas were the most complex polity that never used a linguistically based writing system (although see below on *khipu*), many of the world's other pre-modern societies did not have a writing system either. That limitation did not inhibit them from developing sophisticated ideas and passing them on from one generation to the next. The question here, then, is what did the Incas think and how did they transmit those ideas? Most of the key ideas in the remainder of this chapter are introduced in the next section, and then are elaborated with examples afterwards.

The Nature and Basis of Knowledge

A basic issue concerns what the Incas' theory of knowledge may have been, or even if they had formally devised one. Broadly speaking, problems of knowledge and its assessment fall within the branch of philosophy called epistemology. That field deals with the questions of how you know something, and then how you know that you know it. To frame Inca thought on those issues, let me sketch out two ways of explaining the world – Western science and religion – that are often portrayed as though they were in direct conflict. That kind of opposition was lacking in Andean thinking, but starting here will help to explain how things worked in Tawantinsuyu.[4]

In general terms, science deals with a particular domain of knowledge – the empirical constitution of the universe – and the methods used to obtain information and test explanations about it. The approach assumes that reality exists and that its existence and nature are independent of human experience. Successful science also depends on the idea that its methods and conclusions can control for the effects of individual perception and culture. To put this point another way, reality exists whether we humans are here or not, and whether we perceive and interpret it or not. Within this framework, uncertainty and doubt are perfectly reasonable viewpoints. We are comfortable following logical arguments that lead to conclusions that upset our current understanding, since the unexpected can lead us to new insights (Maffie 2005). In fact, testing and potentially overturning presumed knowledge is a key scientific goal. We are willing to accept results provisionally that run against current thinking, if the premises, methods, and logic are defensible. There is no final truth, but a scientific explanation is robust if it systematically withstands repeated and varied efforts to show it to be wrong. In practical terms, of course, science tends to be messier than the idealized description provided here, but testing and independent verification remain at the heart of the method.

At the same level of generality, religion deals with origins, morality, ethics, and meaning. It has a special interest in humanity's relationships with the non-human aspects of the cosmos. It deals with the spiritual, the numinous, the sacred, and the divine. It encompasses everything holy or transcendent. In contrast to science, religion's methods rely on faith and on principles that provide coherent explanations within a cultural framework. Roy Rappaport (1971, 1999) has suggested that religions that endure are typically founded on what he calls ultimate sacred propositions (USPs) – unchallengeable, untestable premises that are accepted as truth. "The lord our God the lord is one" is an example. Such statements provide meaning, explanation, and emotional reassurance. By extension, any secondary concept (e.g., the Holy Trinity), order, or action logically drawn from a USP is legitimized by that association. Such derivatives might include liturgies, conventional prayers, gestures, ritual cycles, or religious orders. They may take in the sanctification of people, things, or places. In this framework, the adequacy of any explanation about things in the cosmos depends on its adherence to accepted truths. Any proposition, conclusion, or practice that runs against the core principles is likely to be challenged and found wanting. People may well be persecuted if their ideas' substance is overly disturbing or heretical. As the history of religious discourse, schisms, and war amply illustrates, however, religion is hardly free from constant internal questioning, close reasoning, dispute, or revision. Even so, both the domain of inquiry and the mode of knowing are often far removed from those of modern Western science. On occasion, they are dramatically in direct conflict with it, as evidenced by the trial of Galileo.

In Andean societies past and present, people have approached many issues addressed by science and religion from a unified conceptual framework, which we can call a worldview (Note *et al.* 2009). That is a broad cultural philosophy encompassing the principles that underlie almost every important idea in a single model. Among them are cosmological order, life, death, morality, virtue, vitality, time, space, being, causality, knowledge, and epistemology. It provides the means of both comprehending reality and orienting people within it. That is, a philosophy/worldview both explains life and guides people on ethics and matters about the world in a unified package (Note *et al.* 2009: 2).

Some writers suggest that contemporary Andean philosophy, drawn from both indigenous and Christian thought, is equivalent in intellectual stature to the great Eastern and Western philosophical traditions (especially Estermann 2006). While that proposal remains controversial, we may highlight two distinguishing aspects of Andean thought. The first concerns the ideas that form its basic content, which are discussed throughout this chapter. Equally important is that most people in the region understand life's principles much more through daily practice and periodic ceremony than through reflective contemplation, written documents, or formal instruction (de Munter and Note 2009). People do not generally mull over the core principles that guide their lives, but learn them through daily, moral experience. The idea that understanding is ingrained and transmitted across generations through practice (*cosmopraxis*) was commonplace among the non-literate peoples of the world, of course, who formed most of humanity until recently.

Today, it may be beyond our reach to know if any prehispanic Andean peoples thought that they held a formal philosophy with enumerated principles (akin to the Ten Commandments, for example). But there is no doubt that the Incas ended up with a systematic, coherent worldview. It also seems clear that their view was not the only one in play during their heyday. Members of different societies apparently disagreed vehemently about religious and moral issues. Among the points of contention were theological matters, such as the potential divinity of human beings, or the widely shared idea of the primacy of the Moon, which contrasted with the Incas' favoring of the Sun. Similarly, peoples differed as to what was properly comestible, such as dog meat or human flesh. The former was eaten on the north coast and the latter by some Amazonian peoples, such as the Quillacingas, but both foods were shunned by the Incas. Sexual matters also entered into the picture, for instance the desirability of zoophilia and human non-procreative sexual acts, or perhaps even their necessity for human vitality. Some north coastal populations followed those practices, much to the Incas' and Spaniards' mutual disgust.

Despite the rich diversity of Andean beliefs and practices, the commonalities and systematic ways of knowing things are of greater interest here. The Incas were certainly familiar with systematic, specialized knowledge, as the chronicles refer frequently to knowledge experts who were masters of particular subsets of information. The most prominent among them were probably the philosopher-wise men of the court, known as *amauta*, who were especially well versed in ritual, history, poetry, and calendrics, among other things. The masters of the knot-records, which will be discussed later in the chapter, were probably the most common knowledge experts. Called *khipu kamayuq*, they were found from small villages all the way up to the royal courts, passing their skills and information along to offspring or, more rarely, students (figure 1.2). Their principal domains of knowledge included accounting and history. The chronicles also mention famed architects and military experts, and we may assume from the ingenuity and regularity of the built environment that select individuals or groups were accomplished in landscape, hydraulic, and road engineering as well. The range of people with specialized knowledge of healing, divining, and communicating with non-human beings was also broad (Molina 2011: 18–20). The organizational principles running through so many different kinds of Inca practices and material constructions – performance, hierarchy, duality, mutuality, numerical order, and symmetry most prominent among them – suggest that a core set of ideas about natural and social order existed, which crossed over from one knowledge set to the next.

Some Fundamentals[5]

At the time of Spanish contact, the Incas believed that the cosmos operated in experiential, active, and relational terms. By that I mean that they thought that all things were related to everything else in specific ways that allowed them to interact with and affect each other. So far as we can tell, they did not imagine any transcendent, otherworldly, spiritual realities such as a Christian heaven and hell to which the souls of the dead disappeared. According to the Inca Garcilaso, they did recognize an upper world, a lower world, and the world in which people live (*kay pacha,* "this world"), but those were real, concrete places, not ethereal otherworlds. Neither did they contemplate separate realms of perfect ideas and imperfect physical existence like those envisioned by Plato and some Eastern philosophies. Garcilaso (1966: 84) made the key point explicitly: "They did not consider the other life to be spiritual, but corporeal, like this."[6] That is not to say that Andean peoples didn't work with abstractions or that ideal states or progenitors did not exist. But it does mean that things that were material and spiritual belonged to the same sphere of existence and experience.[7]

Vitality

The Incas, like many other Andean societies, thought that everything of material substance could at least potentially be charged with a kind of vitality (Taylor 1974). Among those things were living and dead humans, places on the landscape, celestial beings, and even objects that people had found or made. Called *camaquen,* the vitality was continually conferred to things on earth by paradigmatic beings called *camac.* For people, the *camac* would have been their human ancestors and, for camelids, the llama dark cloud constellation (Salomon 1991: 19). Animacy could be manipulated, transferred, or counteracted, but humans could not create something vital from nothing, for that was the preserve of the Creator God. Non-human beings (*waqa*) that had vitality could also be rendered powerless; an Inca official was charged with determining which ones still had power and which had lost it (Van de Guchte 1999).

In keeping with the idea of origin in a prototype, Andean peoples also thought that things composed of the same substance shared an inherent essence (Lechtman 1984). An object made of metal or stone, for instance, contained that essence as part of its being, even if it were covered, broken up, mutilated, or perhaps even incinerated. In the early Colonial era, fragments of sacred objects or the ashes of rulers' mummies continued to be treated as if they were equivalent to the whole, much like Christian relics.

An extension of the principles of animation was that things and people could share a mimetic relationship (plate 5.1). By that I mean that all things touched by a similar vitality were related to and affected each other. Since they lived in a pervasively social world, the Incas took those relationships to be much closer to literal than metaphorical. The kinds of practices that affected humans on earth, like eating, drinking, speaking, and sexual congress, similarly affected non-human agents. Things, beings, or places that did not fall within the civilized part of the cosmos were chaotic and dangerous. Among them were the people, animals, and land of the rainforest and the plains east of the mountains.[8]

Kinship and Sexuality

Some of the most important dimensions of human and non-human relationships were structured by extended concepts of the human body, gender, and kinship, as well as by location, direction, and movement. Constance Classen (1993: 3) suggests that the Incas used the human body as both a "symbol and mediator of cosmic structures." So places on the land were named according to parts of the human body, while a parallel was drawn between human blood circulation and the movement of water. An explicit analogical relationship existed between human semen and the mountain runoff water that fertilized the crops that arose from Mother Earth. Frank Salomon (1991: 15) memorably called that process "hydraulic sex." Other parallels are embedded in dual meanings for particular Quechua words. For example, *nawi* can be glossed as *eye* and *spring of water*, *uma* as *head* and *mountain peak*, and *wasa* as *back* and *the other side of the mountain* (Stark 1969: 8; Bergh 1993: 81). Similar bodily terminology is used today near Cuzco to describe stellar constellations, so that the same term is used for a particular cross and women's hips (Urton 1981: 130–2).

The ethnographer Catherine Allen (2002) writes that today's traditional communities still live in a pervasively sexualized world. That is, everything from daily practice to the physical features of the land is envisioned as having male and female aspects. The paired elements both oppose and complement one another, and both are essential to the whole. Given the range of subject areas for which parallel evidence can be found for the Incas (Silverblatt 1987), we have every reason to believe that a fully sexualized vision also characterized their world. Space, for example, was partitioned into female (household, earth) and male (external/public, water) domains. Depth and stability are associated with the female, while altitude and motion connote the male (Salomon 1991: 15). In Aymara, the right side is associated with the masculine and the left with the feminine

Plate 5.1 Two sets of stones at Machu Picchu shaped to mimic Mount Yanantin. Source: reproduced by permission of Stuart Schueler, Sandy Schueler.

(Bouysse-Cassagne 1986). The Creator God, Wiraqocha, had both male and female aspects, as may also have been the case for Inka rulers, at least in a state of death (Dean 2010b; see next section).

Kinship was another crucial axis of relationships between people and their world order. The political structure of Cuzco's royalty, for example, was classified by the kin groups' positions with respect to the sitting ruler. Every group's standing changed from one generation to the next, because the members' relationship to the new king had shifted from the status that they had enjoyed with his father (chapter 6). Some non-human features of the land were also thought to form a kin-based society parallel to humanity's. Other places were ritually linked to particular kin groups, so their status could also change across the generations. Generally speaking, places in the landscape were explicitly related to one another through events long past (e.g., origins, descent) and recent history (e.g., miraculous or pivotal events, or shifts in the political structure).

Since human and nonhuman societies depended upon each other for their well-being, a lot of knowledge revolved around how to make things work in a shared space. All of the actors needed the others' goodwill and actions for a successful existence, and harmony required mutual obligations and balance. A relationship could be among peers or unequals, but it still needed to be reciprocal. As a result, both everyday and august practices were dedicated to ensuring that all the suitable parties in the matter – human and otherwise – were accorded their due. The expectation was that they would do their part in return. For example, humans took care of the living places on the landscape with coca, food, and drink, so that the places would also care for them. The roles of many agents – people, peaks (plate 5.2), springs, stones, celestial beings, ancestors – were laid out in hierarchies, and acting out of turn was a serious breach. Individuals or even non-human actors, such as oracles, could be ostracized or neutralized if they failed to meet expectations.

As Andean peoples understood it, the dead were prominent actors in such reciprocal activities. The goodwill of the original ancestors was essential for human well-being for each society, but so was that of all past members. It would be almost impossible to overemphasize the importance of the local kin group and its ancestry in social identity. The living people and their predecessors formed an unbroken chain from their genesis to the present, embedded in the landscape.[9] Among the Incas themselves, the deceased rulers and their principal wives played an especially important role in human affairs (figure 5.1). In fact, the dead were such weighty

Plate 5.2   The glacier Nev. Sahuasiray, a powerful mountain being, overlooking the Sacred Valley at Urubamba.

players in the game of politics and power that the continued existence of royal mummies could threaten the living leadership.

Motion

Movement was another important element that was integrated into Andean thought in complex ways. Broadly speaking, the Incas were more attuned to *practice* (socially learned ways of doing things) and *performance* (public presentation) than to abstract reflection in organizing their thoughts. Information was encoded, ideas were realized, and social relations were put into action through various kinds of personal and group movement, along with linguistic activity such as speech and song. People passed on information in social performances, not through self-contained objects, like books or tablets, that could be consulted by anyone with the appropriate skills or status, at any moment. Speech was also closely tied to social interaction, whether in narratives or political discourse. That is, one principle of the Inca canon was doing things in an orderly fashion in social space and time.[10]

Figure 5.1 Mummy being carried on a litter, illustrated in Guaman Poma's (1936) chronicle.

We will come back to this topic when looking at quantitative thinking, but some examples of *doing* will help show how things worked. A widespread Andean idea is that social relations flowed around constant exchanges of labor, coca, and beer. Second, a great deal of religious practice was built around processions and pilgrimages, as one collective ritual after another was performed in specific space-times in an annual cycle. Legitimization of changes in the social order, transfers of power, and certain kinds of knowledge entailed the same kind of movement from place to place, where group rituals ratified the new state of being by seeking the approval of the powers that held sway there. The cosmos also worked through circulation and flows. For instance, the Milky Way (which they called *mayu* or river) and the Vilcanota river, which ran through the Inca heartland, both flowed southeast-northwest. The Incas understood that parallel to be part of a unified cosmic structure. The rains that nourished the earthly watercourse were drawn from the heavenly river by the Weather God and then the water returned after flowing underground back to the east (see Urton 1981; Bauer and Dearborn 1995).

Shifting contexts, but staying with motion, the practices of accounting and arithmetic also appear to have been intimately linked to gesture. For example, recording information usually required the manipulation of knots in an array (*khipu*), while adding and subtracting were accomplished through movement of pebbles or other small objects. Today, Quechua speakers studied ethnographically do their arithmetic mentally by envisioning the geometry and motions of weaving (Urton 1997). Whether the Incas used the same kind of mental abacus in prehistory is an intriguing possibility, but I am unaware of any information to that effect. In a more abstract notion, Urton also shows how number systems in Quechua are inherently social and generative (see below). A related idea is that particular kinds of actions that we might consider to be essentially mental in a Western context are phrased in Quechua with verbs of active motion. For instance, "telling" a story is parsed in both Inca and modern Quechua as "to take from the memory" or "to take from the head" (Urton 1997: 154). In Aymara, such ideas are melded in the profuse use of textile metaphors in the recounting of narratives (Platt 2002), an idea we use in the English phrases, "weaving a story" and "narrative thread."

Space-Time

Another core idea is that space-time was an integrated whole, called *pacha* in both Quechua and Aymara.[11] The early Quechua lexicographer Gonzalez Holguín (1952: 268) illustrated the unity by glossing *pacha* as *time, ground, place*. Space and time each retained some of its own distinguishing features, which I will touch on throughout the book, but I would like to highlight a couple of key implications of *pacha* here. One is that the Incas envisioned things as happening in a particular location and moment. In fact, expression in the Quechua language itself is strongly couched in the idiom of space and social relationships (Allen 2002; Howard 2002).[12] People typically remember and talk about the past through reference to places on their local landscape. In Quechua narratives, speakers make a crucial distinction between what happened in their visible, known landscape and what happened outside their view and thus is less certain. The flip side of that way of talking about the past is that people understand their landscape by its past and present residents, and by what happened on it. Thus, landscape and history work mutually to constitute one another.

Individual places were described by their vitality, their social being, and their relationships to other places. They could also be situated in relation to movements by humans, such as the paths of the original ancestors, or to the form and motion of celestial entities such as the Milky Way. What the Incas apparently did not do, even when making models of the landscape, was organize space by cardinal positions or any other fixed spatial framework, like a map projection. For example, the entire empire, Tawantinsuyu, consisted of four parts whose existence was defined by their spatial relationship to Cuzco. Similarly, sacred places around myriad towns, including Cuzco, were envisioned in radial, hierarchical arrays stretching outward from the community's central place. Space was therefore not positioned absolutely, but was composed of places where interrelated social things existed or events had occurred. Moreover, each society had its own understanding of the social history through which places came to be known. So their world was a constant series of space–times that people both lived in and influenced. Even so, the Incas replicated the fundamentals of spatial order when they created a number of New Cuzcos, as conceptual replicas of the capital (chapter 11).

Language and Knowledge

Finally, returning briefly to questions of epistemology, it will be useful if we consider just one aspect of how people phrase statements that transmit information in the Incas' languages. In Quechua, speakers regularly make fine distinctions in what they are saying as to whether or not they saw what they are describing, and how sure they are about the content (Faller 2006). Without going into too much detail, there are two basic kinds of introductory authentications of Quechua statements that let the listener assess the validity of what is to follow (Salomon 1991). One of them is first-hand testimony and the other is more like hearsay: that is, "I saw it" versus "it is said that" (Howard 2002). Similarly, Aymara grammar shows the source of information in a statement: the speaker, someone who told the speaker, or an indirect inference (Hardman 1986). Levin (2006) adds that, "(w)hereas most Indo-European languages are more concerned with locating an event in time, Aymara prioritizes how much responsibility a speaker assumes for the information in a speech act." While it's possible to be ambiguous, Selder (2007: 106–8) suggests that identifying the correct source of information is just as serious a matter as is correct citation in a professional publication in the West.

What we need to take from this way of passing on information is that being there and participating provided a greater degree of certainty than having been told. The very structure of linguistic expression invites witnessing as a way to provide the greatest confidence in any statement. To put the point another way, a canon that people can see, hear, and perform will be more persuasive than one ascribed to a distant, unseen figure (like a pope). Similarly, concepts housed in an object that can be read by anyone literate (like a tablet or book) carry less weight than do ideas invested in objects that are socially and visibly performed (like a *khipu*). We can now turn to a few ideas in more detail to see how the Inca view of the world might have affected their notions of what an effective imperial project ought to do.

Part II: Existence

Vitality

We noted earlier that the Incas thought that a single kind of life force – *camaquen* – could potentially animate any material. The Creator God, Wiraqocha, was the only being capable of calling things forth to life, but humans could manipulate vitality once it existed. The meaning of his name provides some insight into how his powers were interwoven with things on earth. Although (predictably) there is some difference of opinion on the subject, Andean specialists often gloss *Wiraqocha* as "Sea Fat" or "Foam of the Sea."[13] Another one of the Creator's names, *Wiraqocha Pachayachachi*, would be rendered as "The Sea Foam Who Makes"; yet a third name, *Ticci Wiraqocha*, would be "The Original Cause (or Foundation) Sea Foam."[14] Those translations find support in the range of Andean societies that drew a parallel between the generative powers of human semen and foam

(Bergh 1993: 82). In the preceding section, we saw how the water from the mountains was thought to be analogous to sperm, as it fertilized the female earth to bring forth the crops. Foamy beer (*chicha* or *aqha*) carried a parallel relationship with semen, so that pouring a libation to the dead was effectively plying them with a life-giving substance. Just as significantly, Wiraqocha was also called *Yachachiq*, or "Who Causes the World to Have Practical Knowledge or Language" (Diez de Betanzos 1987: 44; translation by Mannheim 1988: 239). In this name, we see the emphasis on knowledge and speech as the distinguishing features of human vitality.[15]

We can also understand how vitality worked by examining the Incas' views of rulers and their personal objects, some of which were living icons. Rulers could possess or appear in the form of several different vital items that were either made or found. Although the Spaniards described them as idols, the Incas considered them to be the ruler – that is, to share the same *camaquen* – not simply to represent or substitute for him in the absence of his person/mummy.[16] The most important item was probably a brother figure (*wawqi*) made of stone or gold, who accompanied him throughout life and after (chapter 6).[17] Various *wawqi* reportedly acted as the ruler in public events or on the battlefield. Cobo (1979: 141) described Pachakuti's "brother" and mummy this way:

> This king had a large golden idol called Inti Illapa, which, during all his lifetime and afterward up to the arrival of the Spaniards, was greatly venerated. He had it placed on a very valuable golden platform, and according to reports, the idol and platform were broken into pieces and taken to Cajamarca for the ransom of the Inca Atauhualpa [*sic*]; in addition, much more of the treasure left by Pacha-cutic [*sic*] was used for the same purpose. This king's body was entombed by those of his tribal group in Patallacta, from where it was moved later to Toto-cache, and there it was found by Licentiate Polo; the body was kept with great care, and it was so well preserved with a certain bitumen and concoction that it appeared to be alive. Its eyes were made of a thin golden cloth; its hair was grey, and it was entirely preserved, as if he had died that same day. The body was very well dressed with five or six magnificent mantles, the royal fringe, and some well-made *llautos*.

The icons of the rulers who preceded Pachakuti were made of stone, but both his and Wayna Qhapaq's "brothers" were fashioned out of gold (Cobo 1979; Sarmiento 2007: 186). Given that the Sun's own icon was crafted as a golden boy (Punchao), making the *wawqi* of the imperial era rulers from the same metal was almost surely intended to invoke the mimetic powers of the Sun. By extension, therefore, the royal *wawqi* could be seen as the Sun incarnate on earth.

The exact appearance of the images is a bit hazy, as no identifiable *wawqi* or other images of the rulers are known today. The cleric José de Acosta (1986: 323–4) wrote that the Incas made portraits of the rulers and also shaped the *wawqi* to represent them, but he seems never to have actually seen one (Dean 2010b: 32). Sarmiento (2007: 77, 78, 104) added that the *wawqi* were given names like Falcon, Fish, and Serpent, and that they were shaped to those forms. Certain humans and their *wawqi* were intimately related to one another in some ways. Cabello (1951: 365), for instance, reported that he had a golden image of his mother crafted for the palace of Mullukancha in Tumipampa, Ecuador, after her death. The ruler then placed his own afterbirth in the belly of the idol. From other accounts, it appears that the objects were actually often unworked stones, or were at least visually unremarkable to the Spaniards who saw them. It therefore seems likely that Acosta was projecting European notions of representational sculpture on Inca objects. For the Incas, the key issue concerned the essence of the stone material and less so its shape, since only in the case of Inka Roq'a does any document mention the sculpture's face. One Inca sculpture of a male head has been preserved, apparently adorned with royal headgear, but its identity as a companion piece to a ruler has not been established (Van de Guchte 1996). Numerous *wawqi* were discovered and destroyed in the late 1550s under Cuzco's administrator Licenciado Polo, who distrusted their potential as vessels for the devil's work.

Other objects that the Spaniards identified as idols also accompanied some of the rulers. During his lifetime, the Sapa Inca's hair and nail clippings were collected, so that they could be joined together as another living icon (Diez de Betanzos 1996: 138). Both the *wawqi* and second icon were called *bulto* by the Spaniards. When the ruler Wayna Qhapaq died in Ecuador in 1528, Atawallpa's adherents fashioned a *bulto* from part of his body (probably the heart) that they retained while the mummified remainder was sent on to Cuzco.[18] They used it as the foundational icon of an ancestor worship cult that directly challenged Cuzco's authority (Salomon 1995: 343). Pedro Sancho, one of the original conquistadores, described Wayna Qhapaq's mummy and the other images that accompanied it when he saw them in Qasana, the deceased ruler's palace facing Cuzco's main plaza.

[Wayna Qhapaq] was well obeyed and almost adored, and his body is in the city of Cuzco, intact, wrapped in rich textiles and only the point of his nose is missing. There are other images made of plaster or of clay, which have only hairs and nails which they cut and the clothes in which he was dressed in this lifetime; these images are so venerated among those people as if they were their gods. They bring them frequently to the main square with music and dances, and they attend them, day and night, chasing away the flies. When some important lords come to see the cacique, they first go to salute these figures and only afterwards the cacique. (translation from Van de Guchte 1996: 260–1)

After the king died, his internal organs were incinerated. The ashes were placed in the belly of the golden statue of a small boy (Punchao), which was kept in the Qorikancha, the realm's most sacred temple in the core of Cuzco. Salomon (1995: 331) argues that the mummy and brother played different roles. The former was the ruler's civic presence, while the latter was a more personal being that was enshrined as the ancestor of the ruler's kin group (*panaqa*). Dean (2010b) takes a different tack, suggesting that the mummy represented the female side of the ruler, while the stone represents the masculine side.

After his death, the mummy was kept in state either in an urban residence or a country estate. The multiple meanings of the Quechua word for mummy – *mallki* – illustrate the ways that the Incas linked life forms. *Mallki* could be used to mean a planted thing, a sprout ready for planting, any fruit-bearing tree, or a sapling (Santo Tomás 1951: 314; González Holguín 1952: 224). Those varied meanings fit the idea that the mummy would regenerate as a living being after death.[19] The notion of the ancestors as generative plants was also represented graphically by the mestizo chronicler, Pachacuti Yamqui, who drew the original male and female ancestors as trees with roots. One ruler's mummy continued to carry a particular generative power long after death. The sixth king, Inqa Roqa, reportedly saved Cuzco from a drought by finding underground water and channeling it to the city. In later droughts, his richly garbed mummy was carried in a procession through the fields and puna to induce rain (Cobo 1979: 125).

The link between mummies and plants takes us into the issue of birth and rebirth. Chapter 2 described how the Incas, like many other Andean peoples, thought that their ancestors had been called to life at a specific place in the landscape. The Quechua term for that location – *paqarisqa* – is generally glossed as "the place of dawn," but the same word root is used to mean "birth."[20] When a person died, his/her spirit sought to return to the origin place, to spend eternity in a purified state. The living relatives helped the spirit to return over the course of a year, during which the soft, liquid-saturated flesh of the living being gradually turned into a harder state that endured forever. According to the native Huarochiri text, when the spirit of the body emerged, often in the form of an insect, it flew back to the people's origin point (Salomon 1995: 325).[21] As a matter of common practice, the ancestors' bodies were mummified or, once naturally dried or defleshed, were placed in special above-ground tombs (*chullpa*). There, they were thought to form a vital society parallel to that of living humanity.

When the Spaniards investigated in the Huamanga region, they found as many as 2,000 mummified ancestors in individual cemeteries, an observation that met its archaeological counterpart in the ~1,300 mummies found at Inca-era Puruchuco-Huaqerones, near coastal Lima (Cock and Goycochea Diaz 2004). Because the dessicated dead were perpetually thirsty, they were plied with copious amounts of beer to keep them hale and well disposed (Gose 1993: 494). In some cases, their descendants built conduits into the tombs to allow liquid to be poured in. In many communities, the most important tombs adjoined central plazas, while other ancestors were placed near residential units or in caves, so that the community could readily interact with them from that point onward. Past members of a community thus became part of the landscape, forming a society of their own whose goodwill was essential to the well-being of their descendants.

The Andean idea of an intimate relationship between soft, impermanent, living humans and hard, eternal ancestors was also related to the view that human and lithic beings could morph into one another (see Dean 2010b). In chapter 2, I summarized a commonly told Inca origin story, in which two of the four founding brothers were transformed into stone objects at Cuzco. The founding ancestor Manqo Qhapaq himself was thought to be embodied in a stone, which also had a stone "brother" icon. Conversely, other narratives told that stones in the field turned to soldiers to help the Incas repel the Chanka assault on Cuzco and trigger the Incas' imperial era (chapters 3 and 4). Those collected stones (*puruaucas*) were revered among the holiest of items. Even more stones (*wanka*) situated in the fields were identified as petrified ancestors. We might use the term transubstantiation today to describe that kind of a change, but the Incas likely thought that the substance of both person and stone was the same.

A final point about manipulating vitality is that the capacity was extended to include various objects. Cummins (2000) notes that the Incas felt that some things used to make other objects had the power of *camay*, that is, the ability to infuse something else with animacy. Tools such as the ceramic molds that were used to make figurines possessed that capacity. More provocatively, Verónica Cereceda (cited in Platt 2002: 253) has suggested that the *khipu* knot-records were thought of as living beings. That is, they were sentient repositories of information, whose knowledge could be called on as needed (see below). The sum of all those ideas about vitality is that the borders overlapped among animate things that were born, that were used to make other things, that could bring life to something else, that were capable of knowing, and that were part of the natural order of creation. In short, not all dimensions of vitality were found in all things alive, but anything animate could be related to anything else.

(Space–)Time

Let's look at the second half of the unified space–time concept (*pacha*) in a little more detail now. Since it is basically a measure of sequence, duration, and periodicity,[22] time may seem like a straightforward concept to define. But it isn't, of course, as there are profound differences in the ways that the exact sciences, humanities, and social sciences approach the topic. Anthropologists have their own take, focused on how societies understand temporality and then act on those ideas (e.g., Munn 1992; Gell 1998; Gosden 1993; Lucas 2005).[23] This section looks at how the Incas viewed time, and puts their ideas into a comparative context along the way (cf. Ziółkowski and Sadowski 1989).

Overall, a sense of constant progress or change as a natural state of affairs was less congenial to the Inca way of thinking than was a kind of punctuated equilibrium. Stability and continuity provided a framework for life, but moments of radical transformation also occurred. The change that did happen was rupture – witness the destruction of the four worlds of a thousand years that had preceded the Inka era. But it was not the essence of life, which accentuated continuity. Within a framework of stability within epochs, the Incas saw time as both cyclical and linear. The cycles occurred on a relatively short-term basis, for example on a daily, monthly, or annual basis. Those cycles were repeated over and over from the genesis of today's people up to the present and, presumably, into the future. More provocatively, at least to a Western mind, the Incas treated the past as if it were cumulative, since the beings and places of the constantly expanding past were always accessible for interaction. So rather than operate within a calendar in which the present moved forward inexorably from a known, fixed point, like the Julian and then Gregorian calendars of the west, the Incas seem to have worked with more flexible, interactive notions of time.

Language and time. Anthropologists have long thought that we can gain insight into the ways that people think about things by examining both their vocabulary and their grammar. In the Inca case, it turns out that Aymara and Quechua share some basic principles. Both treat the past and present as a unified entity, separate from the future. That unity works both in the way they think about things and in their verb tenses. To take the Aymara case, today's speakers think of time as existing along a continuum, but they use only two time-related grammatical tenses. One is used for the future and another covers past and present.

Second, both Aymara and Quechua use the language of space to talk about time, like many other societies.[24] In an unusual twist, however, the present and past lie in front of the individual, since that is what is visible; the future lies unrevealed behind him/her (Miracle and Yapita Moya 1981: 33; Nuñez and Sweetser 2006: 401).[25] In both language and gesture, the same spatial–temporal orientation is employed. For example, the Aymara term for "tomorrow" (*q'ipüru*) is a composite word that means "some day behind one's back."[26] Moments in time are positioned the same way in Quechua: past (*ñawpa*) in front and future (*qhepa*) in back (Bengtsson 1998a). A closely linked idea is that "(t)he Aymara view the speaker to be stationary and looking into the visible past while an unseen future passes by and recedes into the past. That is, time is moving rather than the speaker" (Levin 2006: 5). The difference between that notion and the modern Western view could not be starker. While space and time provide a framework where Western people live out their lives, people in the Andes often constitute the pivot around which space–time is oriented. To draw the Spanish–Inca distinction most clearly, the people who the Christians invaded were not preparing for a savior's coming/return; they were living in a constant today grounded in an ever-present and mutable past.

Temporal cycles. If we look at cycles on a short-term basis, the day figured prominently, as might be expected. The Aymara day today is divided into two basic parts, the sun time and the night time. In addition, there are many markers along the way, much like the English dawn, midday, sunset, dusk, and so on. The passage of the night is measured in part by stellar observations, with the planet Venus also playing a significant role from November to March, when it is visible (Miracle and Yapita Moya 1981: 235–9). Another set of time markers revolves around the daily cycle of tending the flocks. Markers for the passage of longer periods of time include lunar cycles for the months, and two annual seasons, rainy and dry. For the Incas, solstices and equinoxes were crucial in the annual ceremonial cycle. So was the 328-day appearance and 37-day absence of the Pleiades for the agricultural cycle, as we will see in chapter 12.

The longest term periods for the Incas were the cyclical creations and destructions of the world, each of which lasted 1,000 years. In chapter 3, I noted that the Incas thought that they lived in the fifth sun of creation, the one that saw the genesis of the living peoples of today and in which the Incas brought civilization to a disordered world. Various residues of prior creations were still to be found in the Andean landscape. Among them were the monolithic statues at Tiahuanaco and elsewhere, which formed the petrified remains of giants who the creator god had destroyed because they were either too large or had disobeyed him.

Calendar and duration. What about the Incas' concern for directional progress in time, or calendrical sequences, which have been highlighted for other great American cultures, like the Maya? While they may not have been overly concerned about multi-year calendars, the Incas certainly did pay close attention to annual cycles. They had a complex ritual calendar, tied to solar, lunar, and sidereal cycles, and to how those predictable changes meshed with seasonal cycles. We will explore those ideas further in chapter 8.

From my reading, the Incas thought about progress in broad episodic strokes, not as a gradual narrative. The five suns of creation certainly included a sense of development from barbaric and ignorant to civilized and knowledgeable. But there was little, if any, sense of a calendrical progression – things existed in one stable state until they were transformed to another. That is why precise sequences of events were less crucial than what happened in any given space–time episode, while duration was even less important. Those notions find expression in both the chronicles and today's traditional society. As described earlier, when a group of Inca litigants presented *khipu*-based testimony to narrate the history of their imperial ancestor to the Spaniards, they prioritized space over temporal order (Rowe 1985b). They listed everything that happened in each of the realm's four parts, in descending order of status. Their account, however, provides little concrete sense of how long it took for the conquests, nor how to integrate what happened in one part to what happened in any of the other three. Similarly, Allen's (2002) modern informants living near Cuzco were taken aback at the thought of stringing together series of events to make a narrative. To the contrary, they seemed to think of the circumstances of the moment as little capsules of life. I therefore suspect that the Incas would have been willing to argue that each space–time moment was often best understood in and of itself.

All that said, Andean peoples did recognize and represent a sense of temporal distance. Aymara, for example, makes grammatical distinctions that mark near and remote time, but Selder (2007) explains that the way that people talk about how long ago something happened depends on how they feel about it, and not on how it fits into a calendar. We may also recall Cobo's comment (1979: 252–3) that Quechua speakers generally did not distinguish times more than about four to six years back, except through different emphases on the sound of the words. So we can accept that people talking in Aymara and Quechua regularly expressed ideas about the near and distant past, while we also acknowledge that the lack of a precise, multi-year Inca calendar meant that no one knew just how old she/he was.

The one place where some degree of precision has been claimed lies in rulers' biographies. Some of the early sources, based on native testimony, recorded life spans, regnal years, and particular episodes in rounded numbers (Rowe 2008). For instance, events that took a few years to accomplish, such as a military or building campaign, were described as having taken thus and such a length of time, usually expressed in years. Being specific doesn't necessarily imply being accurate, however.[27] The life spans and years of rule of particular rulers cited by Inka informants were so different from one another that the multiple chronological schemes pieced together by the Spanish chroniclers vary wildly on the number of years involved (Covey 2006a).

A creative engagement with the past. The Inca stories that have come down to us today don't contain much of a sense of change within any given epoch, except for the last one, for which they had developed a history. The history was at least partially sequential, especially in the sense of tracing their own genealogies. Neither modern nor Inca-era Quechua narratives are conventionally linear, however, as several frustrated chroniclers pointed out when they wrote their own accounts (Cieza 1967; Diez de Betanzos 1996: 3; Harrison 2002). For example, the hospice priest Molina (2011: 20) wrote that his charges had no idea of the order in which things had happened before the Flood. While revealing his Christian and European convictions, his assessment is in keeping with the Andean habit of focusing more on the importance and content of space–time events, and less on any sort of strict sequencing or duration. Diez de Betanzos' chronicle, as close to a royal Inca view of their history as we have today, illustrates the problems the Spaniards ran into. Despite his self-professed best efforts to provide a fluid narrative, the text contains "overlapping events narrated several times from distinct perspectives" (Mannheim and Van Fleet 1998: 340).

More generally, the ways that indigenous Andean people treat history are less concerned with what actually happened than with "what should have been" (Harrison 2002: 28). "The future that 'could come to be' is created in narrative form out of the symbolic material provided by a past that never was" (Harrison 2002: 28). Another intriguing feature of southern Peruvian Quechua narratives is that they often seem fragmentary to our ears (Mannheim and Van Fleet 1998). They may start at any point in an event, without paying attention to chronological development. The chroniclers' comments indicate that those ideas probably also worked for the Inca view of the past/present. If so, sequences of space–times certainly existed for the Incas, but they did not have to be strung together in a Western chronological sequence to make cultural sense.

Harrison's point about a creative engagement with the past in narratives was also extended to Inca interaction with the past itself. Earlier in this section, I mentioned one of the odder aspects of Inca thinking about time: they dealt with the past as a cumulative phenomenon. Any past vitality that existed in the current "sun" (see p. 2) was always present and available to interact with and possibly be changed. What interests me here is that the Incas were inventive with the ways by which they periodically reorganized themselves and accounted for their dealings with the social, historical landscape. So long as fundamental principles of order remained intact, the sociopolitical organization could be modified. The history that generated the actual content of the present could then be dealt with flexibly. "Where/what are we?" was more of a concern than "How did we get here?" The latter could always be reassessed to make sure that the former made sense.

Time and larger frameworks. How do Inca notions of time fit into a larger comparative framework? Let's take a brief look at the question through two sets of eyes: (a) one that sees time as a universal dimension, appreciated and described differently from one field of inquiry or society to the next, and (b) another that sees time as constructed and lived in culture by culture.

A first thought is that our standard set of time's components – sequence, duration, and periodicity – were not equally important to the Incas. We just noted that space and hierarchy often took precedence over sequence in recording and recounting past events. As for duration, they apparently have paid little attention to what we would consider to be a realistic assessment of the length of most events. Periodicity, on the other hand, underpinned activities ranging from household chores and agricultural sequences to grand ceremonial cycles and cosmic regenerations.

How might the Incas have thought about two widely recognized time series: *past/present/future* and *before/after* (McTaggart 1908; Gell 1998)?[28] As I read it, the Incas' views drew from both series, while being strictly neither (see Mellor 1998: 7–18). The idea that the past was ever-present certainly implies a sense of continuity and, to some degree, duration. In addition, the division between the past/present and the future were clearly marked in both Quechua and Aymara. That view implies a separation between *the known that has come before and still is* and *the unknown which has yet to come*. More dramatically, the cataclysmic changes of the world-changing *pachakuti* also required a concrete sense of *before* and *after*.

Crucially, the Incas thought that it was both possible, and sometimes desirable, for humans to change the past and reset time. How did they do that? For one thing, political history could be changed by decree, a method known to both revolutionaries and despots.[29] Key actors were added, removed, or repositioned. Among them were aspirants to the throne, past and present rulers, royal kin groups, and at least one emperor's mummy. The political formation was re-sorted and ratified on at least one occasion – the ascension of Pachakuti – and probably more. At the same time, narratives were created or modified to make the new order the inevitable outcome of a reformulated past (chapter 6). To expedite things at the end of dynastic war between Waskhar and Atawallpa, the victors killed royal historians and destroyed their records (Callapiña *et al.* 1974). New moments in history were also inscribed on the landscape and then legitimized by including them in group ceremonies.

The Incas' view of rewriting the past included the radical notion that (space–) time itself was subject to human action. They expressed that idea early in the Colonial era, in the abortive *taki onqoy* ("dancing sickness") millenarian movement of 1564–72. The hospice priest Molina (2011: 85) wrote that people envisioned its anticipated fruition as another *pachakuti*.

[They said] that when the Marquis entered this land, God had defeated the *hua-cas* and the Spaniards [had defeated] the Indians. But now, the world had turned around, [so] God and the Spaniards would be defeated this time, and all the Spaniards [would] die, their cities would be flooded, and the sea would rise and drown them so that no memory would be left of them.

The movement's adherents thus thought that human actions would put a halt to this world order-existence and begin another era, if they did things right. They had done it before and could do it again.

So the Incas' notions of time can be assessed in comparative terms, but their ideas also work in culturally specific terms (see Durkheim 1915).[30] Here, we can draw on two other kinds of time that people invent for their own culture and then live in simultaneously (Evans-Pritchard 1939). The first one, known as *ecological time*, arises from human relations with the cycles of nature mostly at the household level. Among agro-pastoral peoples, it concerns how people order their rhythms of labor across the days, seasons, and years. The second, *structural time*, is moral in character. It concerns social relations written on the grander, multi-year scale, and treats issues like origins, genealogy, and membership in sequential age grades. So people are perfectly comfortable experiencing short-term cycles at the same time they pass through the phases of life and across generations.

Those ideas resonate with Inca life. Households, communities, and the state were all closely attuned to cycles in the sky and in the seasons for farming and herding. They arranged much of their ceremonial practice to annual, repetitive rituals that interacted with non-human beings (*ecological time*). Daily life was punctuated with small social exchanges, offerings, and gestures to the ancestors. They also thought that people passed through stages of life – the range of available age statuses was a given and people moved through them (*structural time*). The Inca enshrined the latter idea in the state census, which periodically classified everyone in the realm into one of ten male or ten female categories (chapter 9). A similar view of the political order can be seen in the ways that they reclassified royal kin groups across the generations, following a set of rules that had deep cultural roots, but were elaborated during the imperial era (chapter 6).

Objects, Things, and Stuff

For this section's last general topic, I would like to highlight a couple of points about material stuff that were touched on earlier; such things would include both made and found objects, and their constituent materials. Our own views of the issue aside, we can ask if the Incas thought that objects and images were animate entities with real power, or if they were inanimate things to which humans just attribute agency. There seems little doubt that the Incas came down on the side of the real. Their ideas of transferable vitality (*camaquen*), living places on the landscape, and sentient brother images of the ruler, all show that they had a broader view of consciousness, will, and agency than we do today (see Bray 2009; Sillar 2009).

How did that work in practice? One of the ways that the Incas felt they could affect things was through use of a model.[31] They seem to have thought that a model, icon, or graphical representation of a being or object carried the same essence.[32] Christie (2012), for example, explains why the apparent step sequences so prevalent in carved rocks were likely models of terraces. Their carving – often in association with springs or flowing water – was intended in part to reinforce interactions among the vital life forces of stone, crop, and water. The act of carving was intended to bring the power of *camay* into fruition. The Incas also created small objects, called *enqa*, that concentrated the power of whatever they represented (Allen 2002: 41–3).[33] Among the few *enqa* recovered archaeologically are the human and llama figurines primarily found in ritual caches on mountain peaks. Their materials invoke the powers of the Sun (gold), Moon (silver), and Sea (spondylus shell). Their forms – generic features, emphasizing sexual organs and hairstyles of humans, for example – highlight the essential features of the male–female pair and camelids. I am aware of only one context in which graphical representations of identifiable Inca rulers was reported. The origins and history of the Incas were painted on a series of wooden boards that were housed in the Qorikancha, the empire's main temple in Cuzco, along with histories of each subject people (chapter 7; Sarmiento 2007: 58; Molina 2011: 4). The existence of so few illustrations, and their protection in the most highly restricted building in the realm, suggests that they carried a special potency. In no other context were representations of the rulers present, either as statues, friezes, paintings, or objects in any other medium.

These ideas suggest that we need to pay attention to what constituted an object that made cultural sense in the application of power. Partial objects, or their essences, could have power, while other objects only fully existed as part of a group of things. In contrast, some beings (the ruler) or objects could be present simultaneously in various forms in multiple locations. That kind of thinking, of course, presents all sorts of challenges to the archaeologist, which I will try to address in part in later chapters. But one point is worth emphasizing here. Just as most parishioners of medieval churches almost never understood the Latin in which church services were conducted, or could even read for that matter, most Inca subjects likely never really grasped the detailed thinking that the Incas invested in their stuff. That means that for most people, the communication through objects may have been limited to the medium and the performance. Broadly speaking, the visibility of imperial power outside the heartland may have been more crucial than much of the internal content.

Part III: Numerical Thinking (Not Just Accounting or Arithmetic)

There are three kinds of people in the world: people who can count and people who can't.

Anonymous

The Incas clearly belonged to the first of those groups, as numerical thinking played an unusually active and integrated role in their lives. Any of a number of early societies developed sophisticated abilities in mathematics, geometry, and data recording, of course, along with architectural and civil engineering, and astronomical prediction. Proficiency in those arenas would therefore not be especially rare, as admirable as it may be. Nor is the issue here one of numerology or astrology to forecast the future. Instead, Inca culture actively integrated social order, geometry, and numbers, to a greater extent than any other pre-modern society that I know of.[34]

The best-known aspect of numerical thinking in Andean social life is the pervasive ordering of kin and political groups into matching parts (see chapters 6 and 10 for fuller descriptions). By far the most common is the division of the flexibly defined kin group called the *ayllu* into moieties, or matching halves. Those divisions were often termed upper (*hanan*) and lower (*hurin*), but some societies partitioned themselves into left and right parts. Among the Incas, the upper–lower division appeared more prominently in the grouping of Inca royalty into *Hanan Cuzko* and *Hurin Cuzko*. The same divisions were also often applied to the divisions of space matched to each social part, so that the city of Cuzco was similarly divided into *Hanan Cuzko* and *Hurin Cuzko*.

Triadic divisions into left, right, and center were also found, especially in central Peru. The Inca kinship system also contained a tripartite ranking of royal lineages' distance from the ruler. Such two- or three-part divisions were extended to larger political entities, such as ethnic groups or Inca provinces. The Incas also famously used a decimal system in two overlapping contexts. In one, every person was classed into one of ten male or ten female statuses for purposes associated with the census, such as labor mobilization. The other was the reorganization of many taxpaying households into a decimal administrative hierarchy that facilitated the assignment of adult males, and often their wives, to particular labor taxes (chapter 9).

Matching social divisions, labor taxes, or orderly administrations were hardly unique to the Inca empire, however. We need to look a little farther to see where they took their ideas to unusual ends before turning our attention to the *khipu* knot-registers. It turns out that, just as they ordered social life along numerical lines, Andean peoples invested social meaning in numbers and numeric operations. Gary Urton has phrased the issue nicely in the title of his book, *The Social Life of Numbers* (1997). In that work, he describes how Quechua speakers today treat human and cosmic order through a logic in which social and numerical orders are integrated.[35]

Let me try to clarify the point by drawing a contrast with Western society. We occasionally use numbers as descriptors in social positions, such as in first and second cousins or first- and second-generation immigrants. In those phrases, the numbers qualify relationships that were defined on other grounds. That is, the kin or social status exists first and then we can specify a distance. Among the Incas, social and numerical orders are more intimately related – both arise from deeper principles that structure everything in the world. Urton (1997: 145–6) explains that, for Quechua speakers, any kind of relationship or practice should be in a state of balance. If something is out of equilibrium, then people have to act to bring it back into balance. He suggests that this principle of maintaining order – which he calls "rectification" – applies to everything, whether it is personal attitude or emotion, material things, cosmology, or numbers. In arithmetic itself, integers share some social conditions with humanity. For example, integers come in pairs, not as a sequence of individual numbers. They are organized in terms of alternation between odd and even, with the even completing a set.[36] So just as completed humans exist as female–male sets, numbers come in odd–even pairs. From this perspective, arithmetic practice works in the same moral universe as social relations. Although Urton's study refers to the Quechua-speaking societies of today, the same principles arguably organized the Incas as well.[37]

In this kind of order in the world, the term *mama* ("reproductive female") works in many contexts. Among them are "numbers, colors, and the relations of hierarchy and succession in organizing numeral and non-numeral ordinal sequences" (Urton 1997: 116). For instance, the ordinal numbers 1–5 are envisioned as arising from the sexual reproduction of a genetrix (number 1), yielding her four successive offspring (2, 3, 4, 5). Two mothers and their eight offspring yield the base unit of 10. A parallel idea explains the ears of maize that appear successively on a stalk. Similarly, the sequence of pens used to hold a growing herd is conceived as having been reproduced by the mother corral. Intriguingly, however, herd animals are normally named, and not counted, as a way of keeping track of them. Counting separates the generative herd into its individual members, which can bring bad luck. In a pinch, when counting is necessary, only women are allowed to do it, presumably because of their generative role in society (Urton 1997: 103). Other sorts of things are also outside the realm of counting, like the colors of the rainbow or leaves of grass, which only exist as part of the whole.[38]

One of the most interesting parts of Urton's discussion concerns the relationship between counting and weaving, studied among the weavers of Tarabuco, Bolivia. In this context, *mama* (master weaver, always a woman) is thought of as the origin of numbers and colors. When the most complex textiles – women's skirts – are made, the warp threads are always counted in pairs; the central design panels always work in decimal units of warps (Urton 1997: 123). Girls in the community learn to count and carry out complex arithmetic operations in the mental framework of weaving. Since generation and hierarchy are built into weaving, arithmetic is similarly social and generative. In working with numbers, weaving is not simply a mnemonic metaphor substituting for a mental abacus.

Information Recording and Communication: A Problem and Its Knotty Solution

When the Spaniards arrived in Peru, both they and the Incas were amazed at the methods that the others used to record and recall information. The Spaniards' writing, which in their view manifested their superior intellect, surprised the Incas because it could turn graphics into speech in a way that they had never envisioned. Given the range of things that Andeans considered to have *camaquen* (vitality), it is tempting to wonder what kind

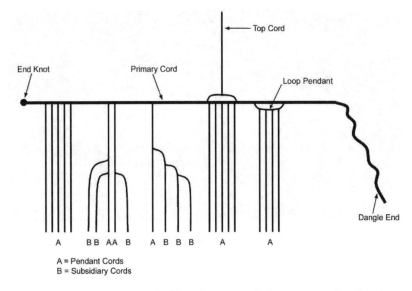

Figure 5.2   Basic structure of a *khipu* knot-record. Source: reproduced with permission of Gary Urton.

of animate power they thought resided in the invaders' documents. Conversely, the Spaniards were astonished at the accuracy, precision, and scope of information that could be called up from the Andeans' prodigious memories or through reference to indigenous recording tools.

The best-known tool is a fabric register called the *khipu*, or "knot" in Quechua, and *chinu* or "knot-record" in Aymara (figure 5.2; plate 5.3). For ease of recognition, I have been using the better-known term *khipu* in this text, except when referring specifically to Aymara-related contexts. Other visual media included painted sticks, designs woven into textiles or painted on ceramics, and illustrations painted on wooden panels.[39] Today, more than 850 *khipu* are known from archaeological deposits (Urton 2010: 55; pers comm. 2013). Largely because their materials do not last for long in the highland climate, most surviving registers are from coastal sites, where the dry conditions aided their preservation (Ascher and Ascher 1981: 68).

An individual *khipu* consisted of a longitudinal primary cord or, more rarely, a carved wooden bar to which a multi-colored series of knotted cords were tied. The cords, usually made of cotton and occasionally of wool, were twisted in different directions and a variety of knot forms were employed. They were dyed in hundreds of colors, or left in their natural hues, and each

Plate 5.3 A *khipu* from the Chachapoyas region, interpreted by Gary Urton to be a two-year register of labor obligations. Source: reproduced by permission of Gary Urton.

shade could have a specific meaning in a particular context. Of a set of 350 samples studied by Urton (2010: 55), individual *khipu* had from just a few pendant cords all the way up to 1,500; the average was 84. When all the combinations of position, number, order, color, and shape are considered, the possibilities for recording specific information become enormous.

The *khipu* is most often associated with Inca accounting, but it was borrowed from Andean traditions that were developed at least a thousand years before the Incas. Some scholars think that the earliest systematic use of the *khipu* as a recording tool occurred in Wari or other expansionist states. It may owe its genesis to institutional demands, such as keeping track of supplies (Quilter and Urton 2002; Brokaw 2010). If they are right, then the Incas elaborated a package of administrative techniques developed by their imperial predecessors.[40] It is certainly the case that the tool was well established across the Andes before the Inca empire came along, as different societies reportedly used a variety of knot-tying conventions. The chronicler Murua wrote that, "each province, as it had its own language, also had a different form and logic [*razón*] of quipo" (translation from Platt 2002: 229). In short, the Incas' challenge most likely lay in systematizing recording for state institutions and in bringing many thousands of knot-masters up to speed in the preferred format, not in developing a specific inscription technique for state interests from scratch. To that end, the chronicler Murúa (1986: 366–8) wrote that the last two years of a four-year curriculum for aristocratic youths in Cuzco were dedicated to training in the *khipu*.

How Did the Khipu Work? Figuring It Out

We don't know the answer to that one yet, but scholars have taken several different approaches to figuring things out.[41] For many years, the chroniclers' descriptions were the most important sources of information. Garcilaso, long considered an authority on Inca life, grew up in Cuzco and claimed to know how the *khipu* worked in detail. Augmenting his knowledge with Blas Valera's work, he described the organization of the knot-records at some length. He explained the way that information was organized hierarchically or as sums, what information was recorded, and what some of the color coding meant (Garcilaso 1966: 329–33). He also pointed out that the message transmitted by the *chaski* (messengers) often consisted of a short verbal message accompanied by a *khipu*. Given that the messengers were youths, probably untutored in the *khipu* codes, at least some knot-records must have been legible to a range of masters. Although many of his observations bear up under comparative scrutiny, he offered too few details to allow us to read the code(s). Moreover, some comments suggest that he may have exaggerated his description for better effect with his intended audience of Spanish elites. For instance, he wrote that the masters "treat(ed) their knots as letters," drawing a closer equivalency to European writing than anyone is willing to accept today. Similarly, he wrote (1966: 124) that "(t)hey added, subtracted, and multiplied with these knots," when we now understand that the *khipu* was a data register, and not a calculating device.

Writing in the early seventeenth century (1638), Antonio de la Calancha (1974) penned that he had conducted an extensive inquiry into the *khipu*, which he called their "writings, archives, and histories." His description of the coding technology focused on the existence of the knots themselves and the various thread colors. He echoed Garcilaso's (1966: 330) comment that specific colors were signs for known categories, such as yellow for gold, white for silver, and red for warriors, adding his own signs of black for time, green for the dead, and crimson for royalty; he wrote that lesser categories had no color marking. Again in agreement with Garcilaso, he said that items registered on the accounting *khipu* were recorded in descending order of status. Some of what those two chroniclers had to say stands up to cross-checking from independent sources. Among them are the decimal code, the placement of sums at the beginning of an account, and the descending rank order of items registered on accounting *khipu* (Locke 1923; Murra 1975). Even so, Urton (2003) judges their one-to-one correlations of specific colors with data categories to be too neat, direct, and European in flavor to capture the Andean complexities – an assessment I tend to agree with. And they still didn't give us specific enough information to read any particular *khipu*.

Understanding sat pretty much in that same state of affairs – with one claimed exception discussed below – until the twentieth century, especially the last couple of decades.[42] Locke (1923) made the first modern break-through when he showed that the structure of the majority of surviving *khipu* was based on a decimal positional system (see Ascher and Ascher 1981). On a pendant string, the position of the knot group farthest from the primary cord marked units, the next in marked tens, the next hundreds, and so on, just as Garcilaso (1966: 330) had said. A figure-8 knot in a group position marked a unit value; a long knot with the appropriate number of turns marked values from 2 through 9. A value of 10 was represented with a single "granny" knot and a value of 0 was represented by the lack of a knot in a particular position (Urton 1997: 180). The largest decimal position known to have been recorded on a *khipu* is 100,000, again echoing Garcilaso (1966: 330), although much larger numbers could have easily been regis-tered. Locke also showed that a string superior to the primary cord could represent the sum of several pendant cords. About one-third of known *khipu* do not appear to be based on the decimal structure, however, leading schol-ars to believe that they were likely dedicated to more narrative or historical, rather than accounting, information.

Using concepts drawn from mathematics and symmetry analysis, other scholars have deciphered a number of other elements of *khipu* structure. Ascher and Ascher (1981) have shown that the *khipu* could be organized hierarchically like a branching tree diagram. Within the first level of infor-mation, the order of the pendant strings attached to the primary cord signi-fied a ranking of information. Typically, the initial entry on an accounting *khipu* seems to have recorded the sum or summary of the more detailed data to follow. By extension, each subsidiary string farther away from the primary cord would record more specific information dependent on the level above. Similarly, various *khipu* could be tied together in a sequence or one could sum up others. This format is eminently well suited to data such as census records. For instance, a *khipu* could record the census data for a province; levels of information on pendant and subsidiary cords could include data on decimal subdivisions, males and females, age-grades, marital status, and so on. Scholars have also shown that cords were arrayed in ways that made cross-reference to one another.

Another effort at decipherment focuses on working with people who still use *khipu*, especially to keep track of family herds (esp. Mackey 2002). The system that they use is so simple, however, that it does not provide direct insight into reading Inca records. More promisingly, study of the *khipu* from Tupicocha, in the highlands of central Peru, has been able to relate the knot-records to written information sources, like work records from the nineteenth century (Salomon 2004; Salomon and Niño-Murcia 2011). Conklin (2002) has gone at the problem through reverse engineering, looking at the physical structure of the *khipu* to see how they were fabricated and then added to or otherwise altered. He shows that there was a logical sequence to construction which must have closely replicated the hierarchy of decisions behind the registry of information. Among the essentials were choice of "materials, colors, cord construction, and cord placement, followed by knotting and attachment of supplemental cords" (Conklin 2002: 83). Presumably, each choice in the sequence would represent an increasingly detailed registry decision: e.g., general category of information, location, context of event, summary data, subsidiary categories, and detailed registry of items.

One of the most productive efforts to understand the *khipu*'s code(s) focuses on the patterning, organization, and content of legal papers and court testimony to the Spaniards. Some of that information coincides with the chronicles, but what we know about any specific *khipu*'s content today comes largely from disputes over resources or taxes. Fortunately, until they began to distrust the association of the records with diabolical or heretical knowledge, and by extension the Andeans' intellectual independence, the Spaniards found the accounts to be so reliable that they allowed witnesses to read their data in court as part of their testimony. As we will see in the next section, many documents contain information that is organized in a repetitive fashion, suggesting the logical structure of various categories of knowledge.[43]

Only recently, however, has anyone been able to plausibly suggest that a particular knot-record and a particular document contained the same information. In work unpublished as of this writing, Gary Urton (pers. comm. 2013) has made a potentially revolutionary advance by showing specific correspondences between six *khipu* from the coastal Santa Valley and a mid-seventeenth-century document. The document recorded a new tribute for 132 Recuay Indians organized into six groups, while the *khipu* contain 132 six-cord color groups. He notes that there is also "a coincidence between the amount of tribute demanded of the Indians (367+ pesos) and the sum of knot values on the first cord of the 132 six-cord groups." The potential rewards for working out the code are obviously enormous.

An earlier analysis by Urton (2001) provided the first persuasive interpretation of a specific non-modern *khipu* (plate 5.3), but it unfortunately lacks a corresponding document. While acknowledging that his explanation requires making certain assumptions such as duality in the knot-record's structure, he deduces that the *khipu* was a calendrical device that recorded a two-year solar calendar, lunar cycles, and various correlations between solar and lunar periods over several years. Part of the logic is that the total knot count (3,005) on the paired strings on the *khipu* corresponds closely to the number of local taxpayers (~3,000) reported to have served under Inca rule. Linking the two elements, Urton infers that the *khipu* may have registered a two-year cycle of tribute obligations to the state, kept by a Chachapoya lord named Guaman who provided census information to the Spaniards in 1535.

Information Recorded on the Khipu

Inca *khipu* were used to record a wide range of numerical data, from census records, to warehouse contents, counts of the royal flocks, tax obligations, land measurements, military organization, and calendrical information. They aided in keeping royal genealogies, conquest sequences, and myths, and were even used as aids for literary works, such as poetry. The everyday populace used them to keep track of such things as community herds, a practice that continues today. Each *khipu* was accompanied by an oral account memorized by a knot-record master, or *khipu kamayuq*. The position passed down from father to son, along with the oral information that was needed to read each record fully. The Incas made this position into a professional office and ranked the specialists according to the level or kind of information that they were responsible for. Since *khipu*-accounting was common, the Incas probably found it fairly easy to recruit individuals to fill the state offices in many places, but we do not know to what extent the Incas allowed local techniques to continue or standardized them across the realm.

Some Colonial documents help us to understand the cultural logic embedded in some *khipus*' structures in specific ways. Those containing rulers' biographies, for example, exhibit formulaic structures in the sequence of information called up. Brokaw shows that two documents that recount the Inca royal genealogy used the same format when telling the lives of Inca rulers. They (1) name the ruler as successor to the previous emperor: (2) list his conquests and achievements: (3) name his woman (*coya*, queen): (4) name his oldest male child: (5) name his younger children and the *ayllu* of their descendants: (6) describe the length of his rule (Brokaw 2003: 130).[44]

If we look at one presentation of a ruler's accomplishments, the details provide insight into how different kinds of historical information were sorted out. In 1569, the survivors of Thupa Inka Yupanki's descendant kin group filed a claim for the lands that they had lost in the aftermath of the dynastic war and Spanish conquest (Rowe 1985b). In their testimony, apparently dictated from *khipu*, they itemized the peoples and forts that Thupa Inka had conquered. The list was organized first by region and then by time. It told the complete story of the northwest, most prestigious part (Chinchaysuyu), then moved clockwise to the next, and again until it arrived at the southwest, least prestigious part (Cuntisuyu). Events within each of the four parts seem to have been described as if they were chronologically ordered. Such an approach to history meant that anyone attempting to create a unified history would need more information to intercalate events that occurred across the four parts. Inca history thus gave priority to space over time in a way that the Spanish chronicles do not, which caused the Europeans a certain amount of frustration as they gathered information.[45]

Other documents help us to understand the cultural values of labor and goods (see chapter 13). For example, writing in general terms, the Licenciado Falcón (1946: 137–40) listed thirty-two state duties for the people living along the coast and thirty-seven for the highlanders. Among the many nuggets found in those lists, we see that personal service to the rulers and mining gold and silver were more important than everyday craft activities. Similarly, herding took precedence over farming and making cloth was the most prestigious craft. Intriguingly, both Falcón and Murúa (1986: 402–4) distinguished between artisans who made fine objects and those who made more ordinary goods. Similar lists can be found in lists of specific provinces, both in the services provided to the Incas and the provisions given to (or stolen by) the Spaniards in the early decades of the occupation.

Overall, we can take away from these documents the ideas that status, space, category, event, sequence, and numbers were registered in systematic, but complicated, ways on the *khipu*. As we look at the way their information was organized, we can see why their manufacture and use have more conceptual depth than we might expect from a simple tabulating device. Most

importantly, Urton argues that the *khipu* carries the social concepts of hierarchy and rectification as an integral part of its being. He also thinks that the
decimal basis of Inca tabulations linked the social "model of fives" (*mama*
and four offspring) to the pervasive opposing/matching concept of duality.
We might also consider the meaning that is embedded in the term *khipu
kamayuq*. That term usually glossed as "knot-record master," but just what
does "master" mean here? If we return to the root word *camay*, it indicates
the ability to infuse with animacy, or to transfer vitality from one thing to
another (Salomon 1991: 19). So it seems probable that the mastery described
here involved something more than the simple registry of information. That
is to say, recording and rendering were ongoing social transfers, linking the
information, the instrument and the master.[46]

Was the Khipu an Instrument of Writing?

Good question. And – at the risk of offending pretty much everyone not in
academics – I'm going to have to say that it all depends what our definition of writing is. Before addressing that issue directly, however, let's put the
khipu into the broader context of the techniques that people have devised
to express information in a visual or material form. With just a moment's
reflection, it is easy to call up any of a number of ways that people encode
data visually so that they can be retrieved later, and yet do not directly register spoken language (Boone and Mignolo 1994; Cummins and Rappaport 1998; Boone and Urton 2011). Musical and choreographic notation, for
example, allows us to represent conventional sound and movement. In the
sciences, we use multiple kinds of notation in mathematical operations: e.g.,
arithmetic, statistics, linear and matrix algebra, calculus, graphical notation,
and binary coding. In other fields, three-dimensional drawings or models of DNA, cladistic models of genetic histories, engineering and architectural diagrams, Bohr's model of the atomic structure, and chemical notation
and models provide examples of widely used formats. Similarly, bewildering arrays of maps record spatial information in systematic, but distinct
ways; road and pedestrian signs use their own symbol systems, sometimes
to useful effect.

Certain kinds of information can be recorded with equal precision in
more than one notational system, and most of those mentioned can be read
out in verbal form across different languages. Even so, the formats do not
record language per se in the way that we think writing does today, or as the
Spaniards understood it. And none of those kinds of notation touches on

the powerful messages embedded in artistic symbols and images (not that they are so unambiguously interpreted). The extraordinary variety of ways that people have encoded ideas, and the ways in which they interact, has led to the suggestion that we should really be thinking about visual literacy, and not just reading literacy as it pertains to encoding information, even language (Cummins and Rappaport 1998).

Where does the *khipu* fit into such a flowering of human creativity in recording information? Is it writing? Some chroniclers, such as the Jesuit Blas Valera and Garcilaso de la Vega, suggest that linguistic representation was actually directly encoded in the *khipu*. We need to reserve judgment on their views, however, because they had a position to defend in favor of the intellectual accomplishments of native American civilizations, or they may have just been using a generous terminology. So the question takes us back to the contentious issue of what actually constitutes writing. Major studies of the world's writing systems often exclude *khipu* from discussion altogether (e.g., Daniels and Bright 1996). True writing for those scholars, who generally work in the Old World, is a form of symbolic notation that represents spoken language precisely and systematically (Urton 2003: 26–7).[47] They recognize that all sorts of steps exist between non-verbal symbol systems and writing that represents verbal expression directly, among them rebus symbols, logograms, ideograms, syllabograms, and alphabets, but they reserve the term writing strictly for the graphical representation of language.

In contrast, scholars who work with the forms of graphical representation found in the Americas often take a more expansive view of writing (e.g., Boone and Mignolo 1994; Boone and Urton 2011; Houston 2004). Boone (1994) and Urton (2003) both suggest that our most effective approach would be to maintain a distinction between language-based and meaning-based systems of information recording. Boone and Mignolo have proposed the phrase "writing without words" to cover the vast range of graphical representations that people have developed to express ideas visually, but not linguistically.

Quite a few prominent scholars have accepted the idea that *khipu* was an instrument of writing, broadly construed, and not simply a mnemonic device. To them, the *khipu's* structure indicates that it likely had widely shared logical and syntactical properties and semantic values, which would have allowed many people to understand the contents of a given register (see Urton 2003). Among them are the mathematicians Marcia and Robert Ascher, whose joint studies set the standard for modern research on the subject (Ascher and Ascher 1981, 1997). R. Ascher divides writing into thought or concept writing (the *khipu* format) and sound writing, while observing that they may cross over in some recording formats (Ascher 2002: 105; see also Boone 1994). Today's leading scholar of the *khipu*, Gary Urton, takes the position that the knot-registers can possibly be understood as a writing system, or perhaps better as some kind of a hybrid form. His key criterion is that they encode complex levels of meaning in a conventional, standardized format. He offers a series of suggestions as to how physical features of the records had the potential to mark signs, but there is a lot of room between possibility and actuality. So he withholds judgment on the degree to which particular knot configurations may have stood for particular labels or lexical references. An equally eminent scholar who has treated the *khipu*, Frank Salomon (2004, Salomon and Niño-Murcia 2011), is in general agreement that the knot-records lay somewhere between an idiosyncratic, personal code and a systematic representation of linguistic phonology.

How Did the Khipu Work? Today's Theories

We may now ask where we stand today on the nature of the *khipu*'s code(s). Salomon and Niño-Murcia (2011) group contemporary ideas into three basic models. One proposes that the codes were built around the syllables found in the Quechua language. A second works on the premise that language, per se, was not recorded; instead, a meaning-based (semasiographic) sign system was used. The last model suggests that the *khipu* may have been based on a content-neutral coding format akin to 8-bit ASCII sequences.[48] Each model has something to recommend it, and it is conceivable that more than one code was used by different knot-masters or ethnic groups. Regardless of the model that is proposed, there is a consensus that the order of the information recorded on the *khipu* probably matched the order in which oral accounts were presented.

　　Let's look at the syllabary model first, since it was proposed centuries ago and leads us into a contentious historical mystery. The essential point of this kind of a code is that an individual sign makes a direct reference to a syllable in the relevant language. So a specific knot in a particular place on a particular colored cord might correspond to a specific syllabic sound. Several early writing systems developed elsewhere in the world used signs for syllables, including Mesopotamian cuneiform, Egyptian hieroglyphics, and the Maya script. So the idea has clearly occurred to people on more than one occasion. Until recently, the earliest known suggestion of this means of coding for the *khipu* was proposed by Sansevero di Sangro in 1750, but the idea languished without much support for centuries (Salomon and Niño-Murcia 2011).

Then in 1996 a private Italian archive began to yield up a series of controversial papers, which are now known as the Naples documents (e.g., Laurencich Minelli 1998, 2007). One of them contained a code for "reading" the narrative *khipu*. It was based on a series of memorized lines, whose content suggested a way that words and Quechua's meaningful syllables could be marked.[49] Among the documents' many novel claims are that Blas Valera faked his own death and, along with his colleagues, wrote the chronicles of Garcilaso, Murúa, and Guaman Poma. The documents have not been released to the academic community for physical scrutiny at the time of this writing, and scholars are split over their authenticity. Some think they are authentic and revelatory (e.g., Laurencich Minelli), while others suspect seventeenth- or twentieth-century forgeries (see Hyland 2003; Urton 2003). Even more want to see the documents before passing judgment.[50]

If the Inca *khipu* was based on a Quechua-based syllabary, it is hard to see how people who spoke other languages might have used it. Recall that linguists now think that the Incas adopted Quechua to rule their empire; previously, they had spoken Aymara and maybe Puquina. The *khipu* could not have worked as a language-specific code, unless the Incas adopted a particular format when they began to use Quechua. One of the most persuasive lines of evidence against a linguistic model is that no Spaniard ever learned how to use or decipher the knot-records (Salomon and Niño-Murcia 2011). On the other hand, many Spaniards quickly became proficient in Quechua, Aymara and other native languages. Priests had to preach to their flocks, administrators had to communicate with the Crown's subjects, and Spanish estate-holders had to manage their affairs (Salomon and Niño-Murcia 2011). Spanish authorities also saw value in the use of *khipu* during the early Colonial decades, to facilitate administration and religious instruction. Yet no one claiming to be a Spaniard has left of record of knowing how the *khipu* worked, Calancha's claims notwithstanding. A number of writers well versed in Andean cultures specifically noted that they had never figured it out (e.g., Blas Valera in Garcilaso, Acosta). This situation strongly implies that there was no direct linkage between *khipu* and spoken language. Or, as Salomon and Niño-Murcia put it, a crucial distinction existed between speech and graphic communication.

Many scholars think that *khipu* probably used a meaning-based code (Salomon 2004; Brokaw 2010). Salomon suggests that entries on *khipu* that did not register numbers would signify "categories, acts, objects or any culturally recognized entity," but not words themselves. He suggests that the closest parallel in the modern *khipu* he studied[51] may have been Sumerian "proto-writing." Their registers included nouns plus number sequences. That kind of code works well across multiple languages, which would have been effective for a *khipu* code in the multi-lingual Andes. For example, an English speaker can still figure out most Japanese road signs. In writing systems, cuneiform was used in various forms for both ancient Sumerian and Akkadian, just as the Chinese written code works for Mandarin and Cantonese, and the alphabet used in English can be used for Romance or Slavic languages.

Finally, Urton (2003) has suggested that the core logic of the *khipu* may have drawn on a kind of binary coding. He began by observing empirically that essential features of *khipu* have two mutually exclusive states. Setting aside the color coding and the actual values recorded on the *khipu*, he points out that much of the logic could have worked in a way roughly analogous to the 1 and 0 of binary computer codes. Among those features are the twist and ply of threads and cords (z-twist and s-twist), the direction in which the cords were knotted, and the direction by which pendant cords were attached to the main cord. If we add the twenty-four named colors that he has identified in Quechua terminology, they would have had 1,536 distinct sign options – fully sufficient for recording a language. Whether they did so or (k)not is another question, an issue Urton is investigating.

Making Calculations

It is important to emphasize that the *khipu* was not a calculating instrument. To do their arithmetic with material things – as opposed to the mental weaving operations described earlier – the Incas manipulated piles of colored pebbles or grain, or moved counters about on a tray with rows of compartments (Rowe 1946: 326). Modern studies of those trays, called *yupana*, have focused on archaeological examples and Guaman Poma's illustrations (esp. Mackey *et al.* 1990). In one drawing (figure 1.2), Guaman Poma showed a *khipu kamayuq* with his cords, and illustrated what is most likely a counting tray of twenty boxes organized into four columns of five rows. The association of those two items in a single drawing emphasizes the linkage between mathematical operations and data recording. In the tray's right-hand column, each box has one dot, in the adjacent there are two, in the next three, and in the left-hand column five. Similar objects antedated the Incas by a considerable degree, and the same design can be found in a Moche illustration from over a thousand years earlier. The utility of the tool can be seen in that counting trays were still in use in the recent past (Radicati 1990). Acosta wrote in admiration of the calculating skills of the Andeans:

(They have) another kind of *khipu* that use maize kernels, a thing that is captivating. In order to carry out a very difficult calculation, for which an able accountant would require pen and ink, to see how much they have among so many, how much of a contribution, taking so much from there, and adding so much from here, with another hundred *retartalillas*, these Indians will take their kernels, placing one here, three there and eight I don't know where. They move one kernel from here, take three from there, and as a result come out with their calculation done precisely, without the slightest error. And they know how to apply their method and reasoning to how much one has to pay or give much better than we can with pen and ink. If this is not ingenious and if these men are beasts, let anyone judge as he will, (but) what I judge as certain is that to what they apply themselves they are much better than us. (Acosta 1986: 403)

Unfortunately, once again neither chronicler provided enough explanation for us to understand how the counting trays might have worked.

De Pasquale and Aimi recently proposed that Guaman Poma's illustration shows a base-40 counting system (De Pasquale n.d.; Aimi and De Pasquale n.d; De Pasquale and Aimi 2003a, 2003b). That idea has the benefit of combining decimal and quadripartite numerical elements. Their examination of fifteen preserved *yupana* indicates that they are all either base-10 or base-40. They infer that the calculating device was based on a Fibonacci sequence, in which each number is the sum of the prior two, and provides examples of how the calculations could have worked that coincide with Acosta's observations.[52] This suggestion is novel and as yet unproven, to my knowledge. Nonetheless, such an interpretation of the *yupana* conforms to another element of Andean mathematical thinking – that is, the idea that prior numbers give rise to subsequent numbers. So inquiry into this field continues.

Measuring Things

Inca measurements of distance, area, and volume were attuned to specific applications rather than being standardized in ways that might have facilitated relating length to area or volume, for example. Measurements of relatively short length were based on parts of the human body, while those pertaining to travel over any significant distance were related as much to time spent on the road as to a linear measure. Similarly, measurements of land area depended on productivity. The Inca official assigned to measure land was called an "*allpa tupuk apu, o cequek apu* ('measurer, or the one who partitions land')" Urton 2010: 56).

The shortest measure may have been the length of a finger (*rok'ana*), which is mentioned in Bertonio's Aymara dictionary (1956) but not in the early Quechua lexicons (Rowe 1946: 323–4). The next largest measurement was the distance between the tips of the outstretched index finger and thumb, which amounted to about 12–14 cm. Then followed the *ccapi*, about 20 cm and roughly equivalent to the Spanish *palmo*. The next largest measure was the *khococ*, which was about 45 cm. Finally came the *rikra*, which measured about 1.62 m; it was divided into two units. *Rikra* was also used to describe the load that could be carried in one arm (Urton 2010: 56). Rods a *rikra* long were reportedly used as a standard measurement for land and for constructions requiring precise lengths. In a test of this premise, Farrington (1984) found that architecture and terraces in Cuzco and on the Urubamba estates were regularly based on multiples of 1.6 m. Some of the central platform mounds at provincial centers along the main highway between Cuzco and Quito were similarly designed. The platform at Huánuco Pampa, for example, is 32×48 m at its base, while the best preserved side of the platform at Hatun Xauxa also measures 32 m. Even the platform at the Argentine center of Shinkal, over 2000 km to the south, measures precisely 16 m on a side (Giovanetti 2009).

The shortest unit used to measure travel distance was the pace (*thatki*). Rowe (1946: 325) suggests that it was counted as one step with each foot and may have equaled about 1.3 m. Another term, *tupu*, was used both for longer distances and for units of area. The length of a *tupu* is uncertain, since it was often described in the early sources as

1.5 times the Spanish league, which itself was a measure of uncertain distance. The chronicler Murúa wrote that 6,000 *thatki* were equal to a *tupu*, and Hyslop's (1984: 296–7) review of the literature suggested that a league usually fell between 4.1 and 6.3 km. If we work with those numbers, then a pace would have fallen between about 1.0 and 1.6 m and a *tupu* would correspond to about 6.2–9.4 km. Hyslop (1984: 294–303) points out, however, that Andean concepts of travel distance were influenced by the amount of time needed to traverse a stretch. Rough terrain would have shortened the linear distance assigned to a *tupu*, while flat surfaces would have extended it. The Incas may have also used the concept of a day's walk, since that distance was supposed to lie between adjacent *tampu* along the road. Although there was a substantial amount of variation, Hyslop found that the majority of *tampu* lay 15–25 km apart. Since that is less than Andean people can easily traverse in a day, he suggests that the spacing was tightened up to accommodate the distance that a llama caravan would normally cover.

The *tupu* as a measure of area was probably a flexible unit that was adjusted to the agricultural productivity of the lands that it was measuring (Rostworowski 1960a). Some of the chroniclers used European terms to describe the *tupu*, but they varied in the expanses that they cited. Cobo said that it was 50 fathoms by 25 fathoms, while Garcilaso suggested that it was equivalent to 1.5 Spanish *fanegas*. Garcilaso's estimate (0.94 ha) unfortunately works out to about three times that of Cobo's (0.33 ha). Although Rowe suggests that Cobo was more likely to be right, Murra (1980a) points out that Andean farmers often resisted fixing their land area according to European measures. Instead, they considered a *tupu* to be the amount of land a couple needed to support themselves for a year, as Garcilaso noted. Since the land's agricultural output varied markedly from one ecozone to the next, the area encompassed by a *tupu* would have varied accordingly. Terms were also used to denote half a *tupu* (*checta*), a quarter (*sillcu*), and an eighth (*cutmu*), illustrating that dual partitioning was extended into space in various contexts (Urton 2010: 56). Cobo also wrote that the Incas had no unit of liquid measure, but did have one for grain. That measure was usually a large gourd that contained about half a Spanish *fanega*, that is about 28 liters. The Incas also seem to have used the Roman balance, which they may have borrowed from coastal peoples, but do not seem to have developed a set of standard weights (Rowe 1946: 325; Rostworowski 1960a).

They also seem not to have taken up the idea of currencies that combined the four standard functions of money: medium of exchange, repository of value, standard of accounting, and standard of value. Even so, coca was widely used as an exchange good in the Andes and the Incas dispensed it as part of their obligation to the taxpayers who put in their labor duties to the state. Along the coast and in Ecuador, there was also a long pre-Inca tradition of fabricating bronze axe-monies (*hacha*) in units of 2, 5, and 10 (Hosler *et al.* 1990). It is not certain if the axe-monies were still in use by the Inca era, but shell and gold beads (*chaquira*) used as media of exchange were certainly in circulation in Ecuador and along the north coast. In neither case, however, did the Incas adopt the currencies into their economies.

Conclusions

Much of the Incas' intellectual project concerned working out the principles used to organize their realm, and then figuring out how to make things work. I do not mean to imply that the Incas had sorted out their full array of ideas at the outset of their imperial era. They had only gone a certain distance along that road by the time their supremacy was rudely interrupted, but their efforts were written along the length of the Andes. What does their way of thinking about vitality, space–time, the past, and trajectory mean for the nature of the empire? Much of the rest of this book deals with this question, but let me venture a few ideas at this point.

One principle is that, in the Inca way of thinking, reality is what exists now. That idea meant that order had to be constantly replenished, whether by the beings that granted vitality to things on earth or by humans through their ceremony and social intercourse. Conversely, on a grand scale, the Incas thought they could stop and restart history. They could manipulate existing space–time and the things within it to their own ends, placing themselves at the heart of all power. A result of that way of thinking was that history served the interests of the present. As the Spaniards found out, the Incas themselves kept several divergent views of the past, each serving a particular interest group and its allies. And as we will see in the next chapter, the available evidence suggests that they reshuffled Cuzco's sociopolitical order several times, and were on the verge of another radical change in 1532. In order to ratify the new present, the Incas needed to alter the past, which required new ceremonies and new sacred places on the landscape.

A second general conclusion is that the world the Incas lived in was a complicated place, with many kinds of beings interacting with one another. My sense is that agency (the ability to make things happen) and vitality (having life force) existed as continua and admixtures, and not as absolute states. A distinction between human and non-human beings and things existed, but it was not a difference among sentient creatures with souls, animals without souls, and objects or materials. Something like water could be vital without being conscious of having volition. Tools used to make other things could have agency, but not vitality. Selected rocks and mountain peaks could have the whole package, as could the human ancestors. Nonetheless, Andean peoples do not seem to have argued that rocks per se had human agency, unless they were changed from or into humans. Rather, they had their own kind of agency. To put the point another way, non-human agents did not act in precisely the same way as humans do – holding ceremonies, making offerings, manipulating time, and the like. The non-humans had other capacities, such as affecting the weather and replenishing vitality in other living beings.

A related idea shaping the empire was that they could and should turn social and non-human disorder into order. That crucial principle is nicely captured in a ritual poem invoking the creator god Wiraqocha. Juan de Santa Cruz Pachacuti Yamqui, a provincial native lord, recorded the words in 1613 (translation from the Quechua by Mannheim 1988: 238).

> Sun
> Moon
> Day
> Night
> the season of ripeness
> the season of freshness
> do not simply exist
> [but] are ordered.

As part of their imperial credo, the Incas asserted that they had the capacity and mandate to replicate, on the earth, the Creator God's actions for the cosmos. Among the many things they did to that end was to intervene in subjects' history and space, by inserting themselves as the intermediary, or at least superior power, between those people and their own ancestry.

That point brings us to a final thought for the chapter: the ideas described here permeated most contexts of Inca life. Borrowing from Gertrude Stein, Ascher and Ascher (1981) call this principle *cultural insistence* – the incessant application of the same concepts and practices across all sorts of contexts.[53] By the time the Spaniards showed up, key aspects of the organization of people, space–time, non-human beings, history, architecture, objects, linguistic construction, numerical operations, and biota were all envisioned through a unifying, repetitive set of motifs. It would be an exaggeration to suggest that the motifs applied to all subjects, but there was considerable interplay across categories of things that the Western world would consider to be radically discrete. Most everything that mattered was social, spatial, concrete, ordered, and connected. Things or situations that lacked order – the pre-Incaic Andes, extra-Incaic space – were chaotic or dangerous, which was basically the same thing. That said, the Incas were hardly averse to innovation or trying something new, so a lot of the organizational principles were surely invented along the way, or elaborated from existing ideas. And it is also true that a great deal of space lay between the ordered vision and the tolerated reality. But we can understand much of what the Incas were about if we see their treatment of people, rocks, mountains, food and cloth through the same lens.

Notes

1   According to http://quoteinvestigator.com/2011/05/13/einstein-simple (accessed December 11, 2013), Einstein's original comment was given in the Herbert Spencer lecture "On the Method of Theoretical Physics" at Oxford in 1933: "It can scarcely be denied that the supreme goal of all theory is to make the irreducible basic elements as simple and as few as possible without having to surrender the adequate representation of a single datum of experience." Sessions abbreviated it for clarity, ironically enough, to the more quotable "everything should be as simple as possible, but not simpler."

2   Other scholars have addressed this issue, sometimes at much greater length than I do here. Classen (1993), Pacheco Farfán (1994), Abercrombie (1998), Allen (2002), and Estermann (esp. 2006) stand out in this regard. While those authors and I have some divergent interests, our readings of the material coincide on important points, which are cited when appropriate.

3   I have raised and examined these same questions elsewhere (D'Altroy in press b), and draw from that discussion here.

4   I am keenly aware that the terms science and religion can raise hackles, red flags, and blood pressures among philosophers, scientists, theologians, anthropologists, and lay readers alike. I am also aware that distinct kinds of approaches to explanation (contentiously) lay a claim to being science. It is not my intention here to explore the full range of ideas on or even definitions of science and religion, because such a diversity of opinion is involved in the subjects. Just a brief discussion can quickly lead into a quagmire of terminology or invite caricature. Among the serious treatments, an animated discussion has occurred in recent decades as to whether science as a discipline is or can be exempted from the constraints of culture, history, sociopolitical systems, or personal relationships (e.g., Popper, Habermas). A number of scholars contend that the entire notion of science as a separate way of knowing things is a recent, Western intellectual product, situated in its own cultural time and place and dependent on its own myths of objectivity (see, e.g., Foucault 1972; Latour 1993). On another question, some thinkers consider the domains of science and religion to be inextricably interlocked, over the issue of first causes, for example (Gould 1997). Other researchers argue that all human experience and knowledge are predicated on the reception of information through the human senses (Merleau-Ponty), or that the processing of information is subject simultaneously to biological networks and symbolic frameworks, and that such filters inevitably configure any explanation or knowledge system. Yet others argue that the past is truly unknowable, as many pasts are constructed either by individuals or by groups with their own interests to advance in the present (e.g., Shanks and Tilley 1987). On a slightly different note, the ways in which we may know things predictively (future) or retrodictively (past) may use different kinds of logic. All that said, and acknowledging the mind-boggling array of issues at play, science and religion work as terms of convenience for introducing core aspects of Inca thought. As there is no way to engage with the philosophy of science in a serious way in this book, I am punting on any further discussion of the topic.

5   Some of the metaphysical ideas are explored more fully in D'Altroy (in press b), especially those concerned with the complexities of space, time, vitality, and death.

6   That quotation (Garcilaso 1966: 84) is from a passage that attempts to make Inca belief as compatible with Christianity as possible, which led him to make a variety of misrepresentations, such as the existence of heaven, hell, and the devil. What is of most interest here is Garcilaso's point that the spiritual and corporeal were not segregated in indigenous religion. Drawing from her ethnographic work, Allen (2002: 178) puts the same point this way: "there are no disembodied essences in the Andean universe."

7   The ethnographer Billie Jean Isbell (1978: 353) refers to this type of viewpoint as a "'science of the concrete,' whereby perceived order in the environment is the basis for systems of classifications, epistemological structures, and cosmologies."

8   Michael Taussig (1993) has examined the relationship between these two states of being at length, in his book *Mimesis and Alterity*. Among the central points that he makes is that, in many societies, things and people that cannot be controlled or subsumed within the existing cultural framework are viewed as dangerous. They are feared, shunned, and caricatured, but their power and freedom may also be envied. A similar idea is express by the concept of the "other" – that is, not us. Edward Said (1978) stimulated much of the post-colonial intellectual and political movement with his book *Orientalism*, which charged the West with cultural arrogance in its attitudes toward Middle Eastern societies in particular.

9   The anthropologist Marisol de la Cadena (2010) even suggests that the kin group and the landscape formed a cohesive, unified kin group.

10 Urton (pers. comm. 2013) observes that "violation of that principle was known as *hucha*, which had to be confessed (to an *ichuri*) and expiated." He further notes that the Spaniards came to equate their notion of "sin" (*pecado*) with *hucha*, which is a misunderstanding of what the Incas considered to be sinful.

11 The list of societies that consider space and time to be inextricably linked is actually pretty long, ranging from the Hopi and Apache of the American Southwest (Malotki 1983; Basso 1988) to the traditional Chinese (Maffie 2005; see Munn 1992; Gell 1998) to many Andean peoples. The particulars vary, of course, but the notion that an integrated space–time is part of reality was invented in many times and places.

12 The linguist-ethnographer Rosaleen Howard (2002: 30) has written that "a cognitive relationship [exists] between land and language that I believe holds the key to the way the oral tradition is continually regenerated in human memory, and a study of which can reinforce our appreciation of the significance of the landscape in all aspects of Andean thought."

13 E.g., Urton (1981: 202) uses that translation, while Rowe (1960) adamantly disagreed with it. Hornberger and Hornberger (1983) gloss *wira* (adj.) as fat and *qocha* as lake, pond, lagoon. González Holguín (1952: 353) provides the following meaning: "Era epicteto, del sol honrroso nombre del Dios que adorauan los indios y de ay ygualandolos con su Dios llamauan a los españoles viracocha." That phrase may be rendered as "He was Epictetus (AD 55–135, a Greek Stoic philosopher) from the sun, honored name of God who the Indians adored and confusing them with their God they called the Spaniards Wiraqocha."

14 In Sarmiento's (2007: 60–1) history, the Creator God was named Viracocha Pachayachachi and Ticci Viracocha. González Holguín (1952: 361, 340) glosses *Yacha chik* as "He Who Makes," or "the maker" (*El que la haze, o hazedor*),

and *Ticci* as origin, beginning, base, foundation, cause (*Origen principio fundamento cimiento caussa*).

15 What may have existed before the creation of the first sun is unclear. A number of scholars think that the notion that Wiraqocha created something from nothing represents a Christian imposition, and that the Incas simply left the question unasked or unanswered.

16 A couple of ways of reading the Inca logic here can be suggested, either one of which can find some support in the early accounts. One idea is that the ruler was divisible into multiple parts, each of which acted as him, simultaneously in several places if need be. In the anthropological literature, the divisible individual is known as a partible person and each element of that person is a dividual (Strathern 1988). Mosko (1992) examines the implications of the divided or expanded person. Conversely, as a divine being, he could be transubstantiated into many different things or substances, each of which embodied his person.

17 The creation of the *wawqi* was not limited to the Inca rulers, but was also applied to certain deities and other people (Van de Guchte 1996).

18 Alternatively, Garcilaso reported that Wayna Qhapaq's heart was retained in Quito, where it was buried (Garcilaso 1966: 578).

19 That idea is found explicitly in the native Huarochirí account of traditional highland beliefs (Gose 1993: 494; Dean 2010b). The generative powers of the dead had a long history in Andean thought. For example, among the Moche people of the north coast, whose culture prevailed from *c.* AD 100–800, modeled ceramics show human females of reproductive age in a variety of sexual acts with skeletal males. The idea seems to have been that the ancestors brought vitality to their descendants.

20 González Holguín (1952) provides the following lexicon: (p. 266): Paccarin. Amanecer [dawn]. Pachayuracyan, 0, paquitman, 0 lliukñin, Pacca pacca rinrac, o tuta tuta mantarac. Temprano de mañana antes de entrar el dia [Early in the morning before day breaks]. Paccarini, paccarimuni. Nacer [To be born]. (p. 404): Amanescer [dawn]. Paccarinpacha yurakyan paquit man cakñin.

21 Among Aymara people today, death is a continuous process with various stages along the way (Miracle and Yapita Moya 1981: 44). The stages of death exhibit a mixture of traditional and Christian beliefs. A recently deceased individual is a "new cadaver." While the soul is freed from its earthly ties after three years of All Saints' Day remembrances, it takes a full ten years for the ultimate passage to a status akin to returning to the soil.

22 Some scholars suggest a more teleological definition, which is that time is what clocks measure.

23 Anthropology generally does not consider the complications introduced by relativity, quantum physics, mathematics, astronomy, philosophy, and the other disciplines that lie well outside the scope of this text. Even so, the range of anthropological questions proliferates so quickly that Nancy Munn (1992: 93)

compared reviewing the disciplinary literature on the subject to Borges's *Book of Sand*, whose titular volume expands itself infinitely when it is opened.

24 An inverse relationship between space and time existed in another context, however. As described in the section on measurement (this chapter), when referring to distances that required travel, the Incas estimated the distance by the amount of time it took to walk from one point to another. That approach made eminently good sense to someone like me, who went to graduate school in Los Angeles, where distances between points are described with phrases like "about an hour from here," referring, of course, to a point about ten miles up the freeway.

25 The representation of time through spatialized language – "the future lies before us" – is found in many societies. The Andean spatial conception of time of the future lying behind us (e.g., Nuñez and Sweetser 2006; Nuñez 2011) is also present among some traditional societies of North America (Deloria 2003: 61–76) but it appears to be a rarer perspective. Psychologists have recently conducted experiments to determine if using the language of space to describe time is simply a common metaphorical device or if there is a deeper grounding in the nature of human thought. Casasanto and Boroditsky (2008: 579), for example, argue that a series of experiments provides "evidence that the metaphorical relationship between space and time observed in language also exists in our more basic representations of distance and duration. Results suggest that our mental representations of things we can never see or touch may be built, in part, out of representations of physical experiences in perception and motor action."

26 Similarly, (quoting an Aymara speaker) "The phrase, 'from here behind,' means from here into the future" (Miracle and Yapita Moya 1981: 35).

27 The Quipocamayos document stated that Waskhar had ruled two years and four months, a kind of precision rare in accounts said to be based on khipu.

28 The first framework (A-series) emphasizes continuity and duration, while the second (B-series) focuses on succession or moments, and is necessary for arguments of causation (Lucas 2005: 21).

29 Wiping out knowledge of the past history to create a more congenial lead-up to the present was hardly the sole province of the Incas. The first ruler of a unified China, Qin Shi Huangdi, ordered to be burned all books that could be found that espoused a philosophy that contravened his views.

30 Durkheim (1915) proposed that each culture actually lives in a time of its own making. According to his view, people experience the world through categories that they themselves create through cultural conventions and practices, one of which is time (Gell 1998: 11).

31 There are many different ways to create a model: linguistic description, graphic representation, physical miniature, use of the same materials, or use of physical parts of the original, for example.

32 That idea can be found in numerous places in the world, for example, among the Middle Kingdom Egyptians, for whom inclusion of a model of food, people, animals, or anything else came to substitute for the actual things that had previously been placed in graves. A similar notion underlies the concept of sympathetic magic, where actions taken upon an item that stands in for an original (like a voodoo doll) will act in a similar manner on the original.

33 Allen (2002: 43) observed the impact of such talismans today. One her informants, upon seeing a large carved penis in a Cuzco museum, exclaimed "The living one itself!" Urton (pers. comm. 2013) also wonders to what degree a census *khipu* actually represented the people themselves for the Incas. That is, was there a mimetic relationship between the substance of the people and the substance of the information about them embedded in the register? I don't have a ready answer for that question here, but the fact that it can be reasonably asked for the Incas highlights the intimate relationships that they saw between categories of things that we consider to be utterly discrete.

34 Perhaps the Maya and the early Chinese civilizations come closest to the Incas in terms of their concern for numerically structured spatial ordering.

35 Much of the discussion in this section is based on Urton's exceptional publications, in which he explores issues of arithmetic, language, and social relations in far greater depth than I can hope to outline here.

36 As Urton (2003: 89) puts it, Quechua speakers think of integers as "organized at their most basic level in terms of the alternation between what are considered to be two related social states of being: *ch'ulla* (odd; alone) and *ch'ullantin* (even; pair; the odd one together with its natural partner)."

37 Urton takes pains to identify the distinct contexts in which bilingual Quechua–Spanish speakers conduct their numerical operations in one or the other language. Greatly simplifying his explanation, we can say that numerical activities that have a social and moral component are conducted in Quechua and those having to do with money and markets are carried out in Spanish. Such a separation reinforces the idea that much of Quechua arithmetical procedure and cultural context today can be used judiciously to think about Inca-era numerical activities.

38 Those ideas raise all sorts of questions about what constituted a thing for an Inca – an individual item, a pair, an assemblage of (reproductive) things, a part of something we would consider to be a distinct object today, or the essence or vitality of a thing. We will take a closer look at those issues later in the book in chapter 13 on things and their masters.

39 None of those techniques, however, was ever cited in early Colonial documents as an analog to European writing (see Cummins 2011).

40 Other scholars suggest that knotted string records, perhaps antecedents to *khipu* are identifiable in urban contexts from sites dating as early as the third

millennium BC (Shady Solis 2008), but that remains a controversial and minority position.

41 The fact that we cannot yet decipher the code(s) of the *khipu* should not be taken, by itself, to preclude its inclusion as a potential writing system. The determining issue ought to be more one of the nature and content of the coding, rather than our current ability to understand it. After all, the Indus script and Minoan Linear A are still beyond us, the Maya glyph system has only recently been largely broken, and cuneiform and Egyptian hieroglyphs were not effectively translated until the early nineteenth century.

42 The most significant modern volumes that analyze the *khipu* are Locke (1923), Radicati di Primeglio (1976?), Ascher and Ascher (1981), Mackey *et al.* (1990), Boone and Mignolo (1994), Quilter and Urton (2002), Urton (2003), Salomon (2004), Brokaw (2010), Boone and Urton (2011), and Salomon and Niño-Murcia (2011).

43 Pärssinen and Kiviharju (2004) have recently published a two-volume set of early documents that give the appearance of having been dictated directly from *khipu* records.

44 Hyland (2007: 100) also finds a similar format in the biographies of some rulers in the anonymous Andean history that recorded ninety-three pre-Inca and eleven Inca kings, preserved by Fernando de Montesinos. Intriguingly, even though that document was likely recorded by a native of the northern Andes whose first language was probably neither Quechua nor Spanish, it used the same format that structured histories recorded both in or closer to the heartland.

45 Not all of the Spanish chronicles generally worked along a strict timeline. For example, Cabello Valboa's 1581 account was salted with numerous "meanwhile back at the ranch" episodes, as he wove a love story into his history.

46 Urton (esp. 1997, 2003) explores the idea of the social dimensions of classifying, recording, and calculating at length in his work.

47 True writing: "systems based on phonograms [i.e., a symbols representing a spoken sound], which are the various types and levels of graphemes [letters or other symbols] that denote the sounds of a language" (Urton 2003: 26).

48 Among modern scholars, Urton (2003) favors the 8-bit code, which he proposed, while Salomon (2004), Salomon and Niño-Murcia 2011), and Brokaw (2010) favor a semasiographic argument. Urton (1998: 409) has also argued that "*khipu* signifiers contained a high level of syntactic and semantic information."

49 A very broad letter-based analogy can be found in the English sentence, "The quick brown fox jumped over the lazy dog," which contains all the letters of the alphabet. If we put each word in a separate line and then assign each letter a sequential number, anyone knowing the code could quickly and easily read 1/2–1/3–8/1–5/4, with the right punctuation mark, as "Help!"

50 One valuable suggestion that has come out of the discussion is Hyland's (2003) argument that a real Quechua-syllabary based *khipu* system may have existed, but that it was invented in the Colonial era, likely by the Jesuits. Andrien (2008) provides a useful, and notably skeptical, description of the documents.

51 Which were similar to Inka *khipu*.

52 A functioning calculating machine has apparently been built based on this logic, suggesting that the method could well have worked. Again, whether it did work that way or not remains another open question, and I will have to leave that assessment in part to mathematicians.

53 The Aschers (1981) note that the concept parallels the idea of structure in Marxist terminology. Urton (2003) elaborates on the idea with respect to the *khipu* and other aspects of Andean life.

Chapter Six

The Politics of Blood in Cuzco

Since the days of the Spanish conquest, the Inca government has often been pictured as a finely tuned machine. Whether they admired or deplored Inca rule, authors usually agreed that Cuzco's crowning success was its orderly administration (Rowe 1946; Moore 1958). In the popular view, an omnipotent emperor presided over a vast bureaucracy that was mostly composed of local elites who had been recruited into state service. By applying the same policies everywhere, the Incas soon molded a cultural patchwork into a homogeneous society. Virtually everything the peasants did from birth to death was supervised by state officials, who called on taxpayer labor to meet state economic and military needs. The officials spoke Cuzco Quechua in public affairs and the people adopted some Inca customs into their daily lives. As for religion, the people's beliefs were eclipsed by a state ideology that elevated the ruler to the status of a god on earth. Since the Incas' society had been simply organized before the great expansion, they had invented a state to rule an empire.

Portraits of the realm that emphasize general themes are still common in overviews (e.g., Davies 1995; McEwan 2006), but an image of uniform and ubiquitous control is an illusion based largely on Cuzco's view of the world. We should not be surprised at that, since both the Incas and their conquerors were preoccupied with the life and times of royalty. While the Spaniards did ask hundreds of petty lords about life before and under the Incas, they gave far more weight to the views expressed by Inca aristocrats, which included a fair measure of propaganda. From the early seventeenth to the mid-twentieth century, Garcilaso's (1966) idealized treatise on the uniform and benevolent society of his ancestors was especially influential. His credibility was based largely on his lineage, however, and not necessarily on the accuracy of his account.

The Incas, Second Edition. Terence N. D'Altroy.
© 2015 John Wiley & Sons, Ltd. Published 2015 by John Wiley & Sons, Ltd.

Research over the last few decades has shown that some societies were transformed by Inca rule while others continued much as before (e.g., Malpass and Alconini 2010; Morris and von Hagen 2011). Their duties to the state notwithstanding, most subjects spent their lives in everyday activities focused around family and community, and many of them seldom saw a real Inca. And while the Incas did apply standard policies, the land outside Cuzco was actually a mosaic of societies to which they had to adjust their methods (chapters 2, 11). Cuzco's political history also affected the nature of Inca rule. The oral traditions that were dominant in Cuzco from about 1550 onward said that the government was largely the product of Pachakuti's divine genius. In accounts that unabashedly burnished his image, Pachakuti's descendants described a visionary who personally invented the social, political, and ceremonial order of the Inca world. While elements of this vision were surely hyperbole, it is true that the Incas did rule their empire for only a few generations. It is reasonable to believe that a few individuals were instrumental in the design, although the details of Pachakuti's inspired role are still open to question. One reason to raise an eyebrow is that the Incas periodically modified both the ruling hierarchy and the history that accounted for its legitimacy. They were, in fact, just at the point of changing things again when the Spaniards arrived. Because the Incas lacked a writing system and used their past as a political tool (see chapter 5), it is hard to disentangle myth from reality – especially for times more than a generation or so removed from the Spanish invasion. The narratives also warn us that Inca rule cannot be explained simply by describing the system that existed in 1532. Tawantinsuyu was in a dynamic phase at the time of its collapse, but it was not the first time that a political cataclysm had occurred.

Tawantinsuyu: The Four Parts Together

Like many Andean peoples, the Incas envisioned their society, history, and land as a unified whole. Their world and its people consisted of four parts (*suyu*) whose political and cosmic center lay at Cuzco (figure 1.1). In fact, the name of the realm – *Tawantinsuyu* – means "The Four Parts Together." Each of the parts was headed by a great lord (*apu*) who advised the emperor in Cuzco and directed affairs for his division (Cobo 1979: 199). The most populous of the four parts, called *Chinchaysuyu*, took its name from the respected Chincha *etnía* of Peru's south-central coast; it encompassed the lands and peoples of the Peruvian coast, the adjacent highlands, and the north Andes. *Antisuyu* lay to the north and northeast of Cuzco; it was named after the warm forests of the montaña, known in Hispanic form as the Andes. *Kollasuyu* formed the largest part of the empire; it ran from Peru's southern highlands through the altiplano all the way to central Chile and adjacent Argentina. This division took its name from the Qolla (Kolla, Colla) peoples who lived on the north side of Lake Titicaca. *Cuntisuyu*, the smallest part, took in the stretch of land that ran southwest from Cuzco to the Pacific; its name corresponded to a province in the same region. Following the logic that arranged the whole empire into four parts, Upper (*Hanan*) and Lower (*Hurin*) Cuzco also contained ranked parts. The Upper part included Chinchaysuyu and Antisuyu, while the Lower included Kollasuyu and Cuntisuyu.

Until recently, we did not know where the borders among the four divisions lay around Cuzco. Then, in 1977, Waldemar Espinoza published a document prepared for Viceroy Toledo exactly 400 years earlier, which listed the affiliations of many villages near the capital. A plot of their locations and the positions of known shrines shows that the four parts were laid out neither symmetrically nor along the cardinal directions, even though the Incas had the knowledge to do so. Observers have known since the sixteenth century that the *suyu* took in markedly different fractions of the empire as a whole and this evidence shows that the *suyu* probably differed in size even near the capital (Espinoza 1977; Zuidema and Poole 1982).

Cuzco's Political Organization

Stripped to the bones, the Inca government was a monarchy in which rule passed from father to son. A layer beyond the skeleton, however, takes us into an elaborate hierarchy that fused Inca kinship and ancestor worship with ethnicity and a rigid class structure. In the Inca regime, the mummies of long-dead kings and queens, as well as oracular idols, participated in affairs of state through cults staffed by their descendants. To many Spaniards, this was proof positive of the devil's handiwork, but to the Andeans, their roles were natural, since the world was shared by the living, the dead, the gods, and other sentient beings of the land.

The emperor and his family stood at the apex of power, below whom were two classes of aristocratic Inca kin and one class of honorary Inca nobility. In 1532, the most exalted aristocrats were ten royal kin groups called *panaqa*. In theory, a new *panaqa* was created with each royal succession as part of a convention called split inheritance. In this custom, the "most able" son of the deceased ruler became the new sovereign, while his other descendants became the custodians of his properties, usually under the leadership of one of his brothers. A *panaqa*'s duties included perpetual veneration of its ancestor and care for his assets through a cult founded around his mummy (see below). Below the *panaqa* were ten noble Inca kin groups who were considered to be distant relatives of the royalty. Cuzco's final elite class were called the Incas by Privilege. They were made up of ethnic groups who had lived in the region when the founding Inca ancestors arrived, according to their accounts of the past (see Bauer 1992; 2004). Figure 6.1 illustrates the relationships among these social levels.

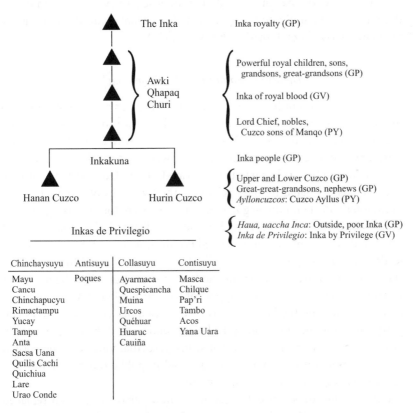

Figure 6.1   A schematic model of the social hierarchy of the Cuzco region in 1532. Source: adapted from Bauer 1992c: 32. GP: Guaman Poma; GV: Garcilaso de la Vega; PY: Pachacuti Yamqui.

The elite kin formed matching divisions that were called Upper and Lower Cuzco. When the Spaniards arrived, each half included five royal and five non-royal kin groups. This design probably resulted from one of the periodic reformations that occurred as Cuzco's society grew and changed over time, but it is difficult from our present vantage point to be sure when specific changes occurred. In late prehistory, the *panaqa* of Upper Cuzco were the more powerful and enjoyed the greater fruits of the imperial expansion. Their members lived in the higher part of town and took precedence in politics and ceremony. They dominated the civil, military, and religious hierarchies and their estates were far grander than those of Lower Cuzco. Pachakuti's descendants (*Hatun ayllu*; aka *iñaqa panaqa*) and Thupa Inka Yupanki's scion (*Qhapaq ayllu*) were especially powerful in the last prehispanic years. The narratives told of an intense rivalry that carried on for decades, which culminated in *Qhapaq ayllu*'s virtual eradication just as the Spaniards arrived (Ziółkowski 1996; see below).

The Ruler: Sapa Inca ("Unique Inca")

In the final version of Inca government, the king was an absolute ruler – a divine being with a celestial mandate to rule the world. In practice, however, the very human monarch had to work closely with Cuzco's contentious aristocracy to take the throne and rule afterward. The royal epics recounted time and again how rulers had been elevated, counseled, assisted, deposed, and even assassinated by their relatives. The two faces of monarchy – the omnipotent ideal and the negotiated practice – were found throughout the oral histories. Because the Incas drew no neat distinctions among different aspects of power, the emperor melded political, social, military, and sacred leadership in a single person. Ideally, his existence passed through three stages (Gose 1996a). Early in life, he had to show himself to be a warrior worthy of his lineage and the support of Cuzco's noble kin. Once anointed by the Sun to rule the land, he was revered as a deity whose powers and perquisites were unique among the beings who walked the earth. In death, however, his descendants accentuated his perpetual vitality, as he feasted and conversed with the quick and the dead in public during the day and retired to his quarters for repose at night.

When a ruler took office, he assumed a new personal title that replaced his given name. Diez de Betanzos (1996: 72) wrote that the sovereign was to marry his principal wife at that same time, so that the coronation actually installed a new royal couple. According to narrative tradition, the custom began with Thupa Inka Yupanki, who also instituted the practice of marrying his full sister. The ruler's many titles were intended to advertise his lineage, power, and generosity. The most prominent epithets were *Sapa Inca*, which means Unique Inca, *Intip Churin* or Son of the Sun, *Qhapaq Apu* or Powerful Lord, and *Huaccha Khoyaq*, or Lover and Benefactor of the Poor (Garcilaso 1966: 59–60, 62–4; Rowe 1946: 258). In the Andean view of things, the king's generosity was just as important as his sanctity and valor, for he embodied the state as a magnanimous patron. All of royal Cuzco lived from his largess both symbolically and literally, since they regularly received provisions from the central storehouses that he controlled. The ruler's relations with provincial lords and subjects also drew on his image as a gift-giver on a grand scale. His principal wife held parallel titles, including *Qoya* or Queen, and *Mamancik*, meaning Our Mother (figure 6.2). Garcilaso explained that *Sapa Inca* and *Qoya* were matching honorifics, as were *Huaccha Khoyaq* and *Mamancik*. Secondary consorts and other royal women were called *palla*, while princesses or other daughters of royal blood were called *ñusta*.

When the emperor traveled, he was carried on an elegant litter borne by the Rucanas, who were selected for this prestigious duty because they were thought to have an especially even pace. His fine clothing was often woven for him by the *mamakuna*, members of the land's highest women's institution. As befit his station, the emperor's activities were filled with ritual, pomp, and feasting. Among his most important duties of protocol were presiding over the regular feasts in the main plaza in Cuzco, where he hosted the assembled guests from the Upper and Lower parts. According to Inca law, anyone approaching the emperor had to remove his footwear and carry a burden. He often sat behind a screen and spoke through an intermediary when receiving visitors or conducting affairs of state. This official was called "*Apo Ynga randi rimaric*, which means 'the lord who speaks in place of and in the name of the king'" (Diez de Betanzos 1996: 106). His attending court was meticulously organized. When the Spaniards had their first audience with Atawallpa at the baths near Cajamarca, he received them while seated on a low wooden throne (*duho*), surrounded by wives and lords who were all positioned according to their rank. The invaders reported that no one dared raise his eyes in the sovereign's presence (H. Pizarro 1959: 85).

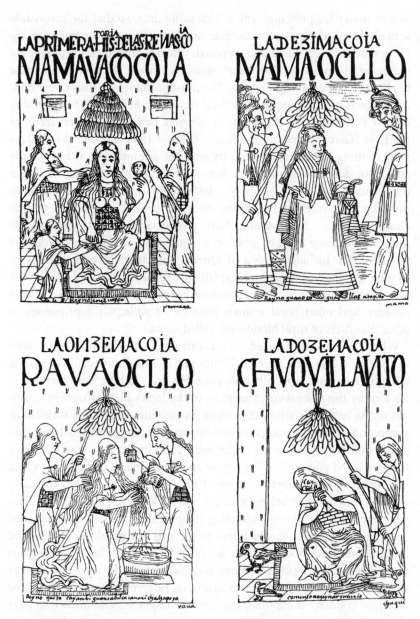

Figure 6.2   Guaman Poma's (1936) stylized illustrations of four Inca queens.

We do not know what the individual rulers looked like – even in a stylized format – except for Atawallpa and Waskhar, who were described by the conquistadores. The Incas did have a tradition of illustrating their history and kings on wooden panels, and Viceroy Toledo sent a number of portraits or tapestries to Spain, but they have since been lost (Acosta 1986: 323; Julien 1999; Molina 2011: 4). Chroniclers also recorded oral descriptions of other rulers, but what remain today in graphical form are the illustrations by Guaman Poma and Murúa, who were clearly influenced by European cultural traditions. Guaman Poma's drawings retain many indigenous Andean elements, for he often took considerable care to represent the clothing and adornments of the individuals. His work is consequently an irreplaceable visual source regardless of the mixture of Andean and Spanish elements and the generalized visages of the persons illustrated.

An emperor had an array of insignia and personal adornments, along with elaborate customs, that marked his office (see Rowe 1946: 258). His most important personal effect was a headband of braided cloth (*llauto*), which was sometimes adorned with feathers. It was positioned so that a thick tassel (*mazcaypaycha*) covered his forehead. He wore uniquely large earspools, a symbol of prestige that also marked Cuzco's aristocrats, who were called *orejones* or "big-ears" in the Colonial era. Another important royal symbol was a staff (*sunturpaucar*) that was completely covered with tiny feathers and adorned with three larger feathers that projected from the tip; it was sometimes used at the head of ritual processions to represent the ruler's power. The king had military insignia as well, most importantly a golden mace (*champi*) and a royal standard made of cloth that was painted until it stood stiff (Cobo 1979: 244–7). When Atawallpa arrived at Cajamarca's square just before his capture, a soldier placed the standard in front of one of its buildings to declare the royal entry, unaware that the tense Spanish troops were inside, awaiting the order to attack.

The conquistadores' observations while Atawallpa was imprisoned help us to understand the emperor's deportment. The Spaniards saw him in daily life and personal political relations, although for obvious reasons they never saw him conduct grand assemblies as head of state. They were duly impressed with his aura of gravity and august manner. Even while captive, Atawallpa received lords who came to pay obeisance and to receive instructions on managing the empire's affairs. Miguel de Estete wrote, "When they arrived before him, they did him great reverence, kissing his feet and hands. He received them without looking at them. It is remarkable to record the dignity of Atawallpa and the great obedience they all accorded him" (translation from Hemming 1970: 51). He was described by an eyewitness as being

> a man of thirty years of age, of good appearance and manner, although somewhat thick-set. He had a large face, handsome and fierce, his eyes reddened with blood. He spoke with much gravity, as a great ruler. He made very lively argument: when the Spaniards understood them they realized that he was a wise man. He was a cheerful man, although unsubtle. When he spoke to his own people he was incisive and showed no pleasure. (Hemming 2012: loc. 592–593/14166 [Kindle edn.])

At the time he met the Spaniards, Atawallpa wore a cloak over his head, covering his ears, apparently to hide an ear that had been damaged when he was captured early in the dynastic war. Pedro Pizarro (1986: 67–8) recalled how carefully Atawallpa was attended while he ate:

> (H)e was seated on a wooden duho [stool] little more than a span [9 inches] high. This duho was of very lovely reddish wood and was always kept covered with a delicate rug, even when he was seated on it. The ladies brought his meal and placed it before him on tender thin green rushes … They placed all the vessels of gold, silver and pottery on these rushes. He pointed to whatever he fancied and it was brought … He was eating in this manner one day when I was present. A slice of food was being lifted to his mouth when a drop fell on the clothing that he was wearing. Giving his hand to the Indian lady, he rose and went into his chamber to change his dress and returned wearing a dark brown tunic and cloak. I approached him and felt the cloak, which was softer than silk … He explained that it was made from the skins of bats that fly by night in Puerto Viejo and Tumbes and that bite the natives. (Translation after Hemming 1970: 50)

Atawallpa added a regal coda: "Those dogs from Puerto Viejo and Tumbes, what else did they have to do except catch the bats and make clothes for my father?" (Hemming 1970: 50). The conquistador Juan Ruiz de Arce attested to a further royal touch [of *noblesse oblige*?] – that Atawallpa spat into the hand of an attending woman rather than onto the ground, "out of grandeur" (Hemming 2012: loc. 624/14166 [Kindle edn.]).

Anything that touched or came from the ruler was treated with special concern for the potential mischief that could be put into play. Ruiz de Arce, for instance, said that the hairs that fell onto his clothing were eaten by his female attendants to prevent sorcery against him. Pizarro explained that all the clothing that Atawallpa had worn, the bones of the animals and the ears of corn he had eaten, in short all things that he had touched, were gathered and stored in chests. They were to be burned later in an annual ceremony similarly intended to thwart witchcraft against his royal person. The issue came to Pizarro's attention, predictably enough, when the ruler complained that a Spanish soldier had been rifling through the chests.

The installation of a new emperor was attended by all the pageantry that might be expected for the deified ruler of the world. Cobo (1990: 154–7) wrote that all the eminent lords of the land who could make the trip attended the ceremonies, which were held once the lamentations for the deceased ruler had been properly observed. As a cleric, the chronicler focused his description on the ritual rather than political dimensions of the ceremonies. He wrote that the participants gathered in the central plaza called Awkaypata, along with the statues of the Sun and other major gods and representatives of all of the important *wak'a*. The sacrifices took the lives of 200 children aged 4 to 10 and great numbers of camelids, along with elegant clothing, seashells, and many golden and silver serving vessels and statues. The priests made sacrifices to each of the shrines in the city and designated materials for sacrifice in each shrine in the four quarters of the land. Their most important offerings were dedicated to the Creator God Wiraqocha, whose aid was solicited in granting the emperor health and a long life, victory over his enemies, many children to succeed him, and peace in his time. Once they had completed those prayers, the priests of Wiraqocha strangled the children, and then buried them with the gold and silver objects on a hill called Chuquicancha, above San Sebastián. The camelids, cloth, and other materials were burned.

The death of a ruler was supposed to be celebrated in an equally majestic manner. Following the format of Inca epic history, Diez de Betanzos (1996: 134) explained that Pachakuti put a great deal of thought into planning his funerary rites and the disposition of his remains after death. He first ordered that all of Cuzco should spend a year dressed in mourning once he had expired. As described in chapter 5, a year was the period of time thought necessary for a newly deceased human to pass into the more permanent state of animated death. At the end of that time, royal Cuzco was to perform a month-long sequence of ceremonies that cemented his passage into the everlasting. They began by visiting all the lands where the Inca had planted or harvested crops, carrying his clothing, weapons, and adornments. At each place, they were to cry out to him, "Look here at the garment that you used to wear" or "'See here your weapon with which you won and subjected such a province and so many caciques who were lords there' … The most important lord of those who were going there would answer, saying he is in heaven with his father, the Sun" (Betanzos 1996: 134). A great ceremony was then held in the main plaza of Cuzco, toward the end of which squadrons of warriors from Upper and Lower Cuzco staged a mock battle in the main compound. The side from Upper Cuzco won the battle, symbolically recapitulating the ruler's actions in life.

The penultimate act to the ceremonies was to be a grand series of sacrifices (Diez de Betanzos 1996: 138–9). All the clothing that had been used in the mourning rituals was to be consumed in a bonfire in the main plaza, along with a thousand camelids decked out in fine clothes, and a thousand newborn camelids. The throats of two thousand other llamas were to be slit and their meat fed to his supporters, while another thousand were sacrificed and burned in all the places where he had gone in his lifetime. Pachakuti further instructed that "a thousand boys and girls will be brought and will be buried for me in the places where I slept and where I usually enjoyed myself." Finally, all of his table service of gold and silver was to be buried with him and his livestock and stores burned. Once all of the funerary rituals had been completed, Pachakuti's survivors dressed his mummified remains in finery and kept it in state at Patallacta, probably the site now known as Q'enqo. Diez de Betanzos wrote that his personal golden idol, known as his brother (*wawqi*), was placed upon his tomb, so that people could worship it. His fingernails and hair had been carefully saved during his lifetime and were now formed into a statue, called a *bulto* by the Spaniards. This statue was held in as much reverence as his mummy (*mallki*) itself and could serve as a surrogate for the deceased lord in public affairs.

The overt goal of all of those ceremonies and sacrifices, repeated in reduced form until Polo discovered his mummy in 1559,[1] was to ensure that the ruler had food, drink, and servants aplenty in a secure afterlife. In addition to ensuring that transition, however, the array of ceremonies had a crucial political role to play. The waiting period of a year was a window in which the competition over succession to the throne was resolved. As we will see shortly, no imperial-era succession occurred smoothly, repeating a pattern seen on several occasions earlier. Instead, each change was punctuated by palace intrigue, murder or even outright war. Whether by design or not, the year provided a time during which the succession could be worked out and the new political order installed. Everyone of consequence still standing in the aftermath then participated in the grand rituals, legitimizing the new reality.

From his newly sanctified plane, a dead Inca emperor continued to participate actively in Cuzco's ceremonial and political life. The mummies of past rulers were customarily kept in houses in town or in sanctuaries on royal estates. Cobo (1990: 39–43) wrote that the mummies and other images of the early rulers had once been kept in dedicated chapels within the main temple. Over time, however, their descendants decided that it would be more proper for each deceased ruler to reside in his own house where he could be better served. When the main Spanish force first entered Cuzco, the scribe Pedro Sancho de la Hoz saw Wayna Qhapaq's mummy comfortably seated in his palace, fronting the main plaza. The dead kings and queens were regularly feted and consulted on matters of importance. Pedro Pizarro (1986: 89–90) recalled:

> (m)ost of the people [of Cuzco] served the dead, I have heard it said, who they daily brought out to the main square, setting them down in a ring, each one according to his age, and there the male and female attendants ate and drank. The attendants made fires for each of the dead in front of them with firewood that was worked and cut until it was quite even, very dry, and lighting [them], burned everything they had put before them, so that the dead should eat of everything that the living ate, which is what was burned in these fires. The attendants also placed before these dead certain large pitchers … of gold or silver or clay, each as he wished, and here they poured out the *chicha* that they gave to the mummies to drink, showing it to him, [and] the mummies toasted each other and the living, and the living toasted the dead. When the vessels were full, they emptied them over a circular stone they had for an idol in the middle of the plaza, around which there was a small channel, and the beer drained off through underground pipes.

The mummies or their surrogates were accompanied by a variety of other icons and armaments. And, so that they might communicate their wisdom or make their wishes known, each ruler or *qoya* was served by a male and female medium. The mummies attended only the most solemn festivals, sending their brother icons out for less important occasions. As Pizarro explained, the mummies or icons were arranged according to their rank in a row in the main plaza, where they were offered sacrifices and *chicha*. When the urge took them, the mummies and their retinues also visited one another or their living relatives for festivities – a hospitable gesture that was, of course, later returned.

The Spaniards marveled at their preservation when they found several in 1559 (table 6.1). The young Garcilaso apparently saw the mummies when

Table 6.1 Inca emperors: their mummies and icons, according to Sarmiento (2007), Cobo (1990), and Betanzos (1996).[1]

Ruler	Name of brother icon (wawqi)	Icon	Place where mummy or icon maintained or found	Mummies' and icons' fate
Manqo Qhapaq	Indi	falcon	Indicancha or Wimpillay (image)	–
Zinchi Roq'a	Guanachiri Amaro	fish	Wimpillay; house named Acoyguaci	found by Polo in 1559
Lloq'e Yupanki	Apo Mayta	–	Wimpillay	–
Mayta Yupanki	–	–	Wimpillay	found by Polo in 1559
Qhapaq Yupanki	Apu amayta[2]	–	Wimpillay	found by Polo in 1559
Inka Roq'a	Vicaquirao[a]	–	Larapa (mummy)	found by Polo in 1559
Yawar Waqaq	–	–	Paullu	not found
Wiraqocha Inka	Inga Amaro	serpent	Caquia Xaquixaguana (i.e., Huchuy Cossqo: mummy and icon)	mummy burned by Gonzalo Pizarro; ashes collected in jar, captured by Polo along with icon in 1559
Pachakuti Inka Yupanki	Chuqui illa, Indi illapa	lightning, viper	Patallacta (Totocache; mummy)	mummy found and sent to Lima by Polo in 1559; icon broken apart and sent to Cajamarca as part of Atawallpa's ransom
Thupa Inka Yupanki	Cuxi churi	happy son	Calispuquio (icon)	mummy burned in dynastic war in 1532; ashes collected in jar, captured by Polo along with icon in 1559
Wayna Qhapaq	Guaraqui Inga	–	house near Saqsaywaman (mummy)	mummy found and sent to Lima by Polo in 1559
Waskhar	–	–	–	none created
Atawallpa	Inga Guauqui; Ticci Capac	–	–	–

Notes

[1] The icons may not have been represented in shapes that the Spaniards could have necessarily identified, since the essence of the object, not its appearance, was most important to the Incas.

he went to say goodbye to Polo in 1560 before leaving for Spain (Hemming 1970: 298). Almost fifty years later, he (Garcilaso de la Vega 1966: pt. 1, bk. 5, ch. 29; pt. 1, bk. 3, ch. 20; from Hemming 1970: 298) recalled that:

> (T)heir bodies were so perfect that they lacked neither hair, eyebrows nor eye-lashes. They were in clothes such as they had worn when alive, with *llautas* on their heads but no other sign of royalty. They were seated in the way Indian men and women usually sit, with their arms crossed over their chests, the right over the left, and their eyes cast down … I remember touching a finger of the hand of Huayna-Capac. It was hard and rigid, like that of a wooden statue. The bodies weighed so little that any Indian could carry them from house to house in his arms or on his shoulders. They carried them wrapped in white sheets through the streets and squares, the Indians falling to their knees and making reverences with groans and tears, and many Spaniards taking off their cap.

The High Priest (Willaq Umu)

In 1532, the High Priest of the Sun (*willaq umu*; "priest who recounts") was probably the second most powerful individual in the empire. According to several chroniclers (e.g. Diez de Betanzos 1987: 45), the office was created or elevated during Pachakuti's reign. Intriguingly, no matter what kin group he was born into, when he took the office, he reaffiliated himself with Lower Cuzco (Gose 1996b: 401). That shift provides just one, albeit prominent, example of how the Incas reorganized people at moments of transition, to make sure that certain structural arrangement continued across the generations.

Part of the High Priest's power stemmed from his role in confirming the selection of the new emperor in office, but he was also in charge of the most revered icon of the Sun, Punchao, in the temple of Qorikancha (Sarmiento 2007: 114). His pious duties hardly restricted him to ceremony, however, for both Atawallpa's and Manqo Inka's chief priests were also their field marshals in the last dynastic war and the neo-Inca era, respectively. At one point, the emperor Wayna Qhapaq deposed the priest and took the office for himself, perhaps to ensure that he could appoint his own successor.

The Royal and Aristocratic Kindred

The emperor was theoretically an absolute monarch, but Cuzco's royal kin groups (*panaqa*) were still a political force to be reckoned with. They formed an advisory court and provided many of the officials who devised and applied state policy. Because the *panaqa* could influence the selection of royal successors, candidates and kin groups likely negotiated with one another constantly in the quest for power. The murderous intrigues that punctuated royal successions gave the kin a great deal of leverage in deciding the future direction of the empire (see "Succession Crises," below). The highest ranking *panaqa* were the kin closest to the current emperor, not to the most ancient. Earlier, we noted that ten royal *panaqa* and ten non-royal *ayllu* formed Cuzco's elite when the Spaniards arrived. The most widely accepted view today is that a new *panaqa* was added to Cuzqueñan society every royal generation as a result of split inheritance. This custom should have modified the political arrangement, but we cannot be sure how things worked in practice, since one tradition suggested that all ten groups had actually been present from the pre-imperial era (e.g., Diez de Betanzos 1996: 69–73). In an alternative vision, the royal kin of Lower Cuzco were descended from the first five Inca rulers, while the kin of the later kings formed Upper Cuzco. If that was true, then history was written continuously into the social structure and political hierarchy. In yet a third version of Inca history, Pachakuti organized Cuzco's existing kin groups into a new dual design when he invented the imperial order. Following this view, Rowe (1985a) suggests that one of Upper Cuzco's royal kin groups may have been shifted to Lower Cuzco every two generations, to preserve the balance between the moieties (tables 6.2a, b).

Table 6.2a　The ten royal kin groups (*panaqa*) of Cuzco at the time of the Spanish conquest (modified from Rowe 1985a: 64); note that Qhapaq Yupanki's *panaqa* has been shifted from Upper (*Hanan*) Cuzco to Lower (*Hurin*) Cuzco with the addition of the ninth and tenth *panaqa*.

Hanan Cuzco		Hurin Cuzco	
Ruler	Descendant kin group	Ruler	Descendant kin group
10 Thupa Inka Yupanki	*Qhapaq ayllu*	5 Qhapaq Yupanki	*Apu Mayta panaqa ayllu*
9 Pachakuti Inka Yupanki	*Hatun ayllu (Iñaqa panaqa)*	4 Mayta Yupanki	*Uska Mayta panaqa ayllu*
8 Wiraqocha Inka	*Zukzu panaqa ayllu*	3 Lloq'e Yupanki	*Awayni panaqa ayllu*
7 Yawar Waqaq	*Awqaylli panaqa ayllu*	2 Zinchi Roq'a	*Rawra panaqa ayllu*
6 Inka Roq'a	*Wika K'iraw panaqa ayllu*	1 Manqo Qhapaq	*Chima panaqa ayllu*

Table 6.2b   A hypothetical structure of the eight royal kin groups (*panaqa*) of Cuzco in the epoch of Pachakuti (modified from Rowe 1985a: 71).

Ruler	Descendant kin group	Ruler	Descendant kin group
8 Wiraqocha Inka	*Zukzu panaqa ayllu*	4 Mayta Yupanki	*Uska Mayta panaqa ayllu*
7 Yawar Waqaq	*Awqaylli panaqa ayllu*	3 Lloq'e Yupanki	*Awayni panaqa ayllu*
6 Inka Roq'a	*Wika K'iraw panaqa ayllu*	2 Zinchi Roq'a	*Rawra panaqa ayllu*
5 Qhapaq Yupanki	*Apu Mayta panaqa ayllu*	1 Manqo Qhapaq	*Chima panaqa ayllu*

As with so much Inca history, however, any view is beset by all sorts of niggling problems (see below, "Two Inca Kings?"). For example, Rostworowski (1983: 141–5) points out that some royal kin groups seem to have fallen by the wayside over time. In addition to the core set of ten royal kin groups, the chronicles named several other kin groups that were either called *panaqa* or claimed status as a royal kindred. She suggests that political maneuvering may have removed some *panaqa*, or that some that had existed before the formation of the empire were not included in its original political design. Each option suggests a different way that structure and history could have interacted to produce the system that existed in 1532. Although the data are conflictive, I am most comfortable with the idea that kin groups were added or dislodged over the generations, and that stories of the Inca past were revised to rationalize the organization as it existed at any point. Whichever view best explains the situation, the political arrangement described to the Spaniards was a snapshot – the design as it was frozen in time by the European invasion.

Two Inca Kings?

A number of scholars support Zuidema's proposition that Inca government may have been a diarchy (Zuidema 1964: 127; Duviols 1979b; Rostworowski 1983: 130–79, 1999: 177–81). That is, there were always two Inca kings, one from Upper Cuzco and one from Lower Cuzco. His proposal starts from the observation that Andean social organization, including Cuzco's, featured opposing halves, each of which had its own leader. In addition, the generally reliable chronicler Cieza (1967: 111) said that Inca aristocrats claimed that there had always been two kings of Cuzco. Several chroniclers also wrote that Manqo Qhapaq was considered to be the founder of both social divisions. Without taking the latter premise at face value, Zuidema infers that the names of *panaqa* may have been titles for groups holding a particular status, not the names of kindreds in a historical genealogy. From his viewpoint, the narratives described relations of power, not linear accounts of history. His model of Inca government more closely approximates the diarchy illustrated in figure 6.3, than the standard design. If Zuidema is correct, then we cannot assume that each *panaqa* corresponded neatly to a generation (Zuidema 1983; Rowe 1985a; Rostworowski 1983: 141–5). Gose's illustration of three perspectives shows how the same basic information can be used to support different views of the central Inca political design (figure 6.3). Although the structural and diarchy models have points in their favor, they remain a minority viewpoint because they require elevating individuals to the Inca king lists who are virtually, if not altogether, absent from most lists of Inca royalty cited

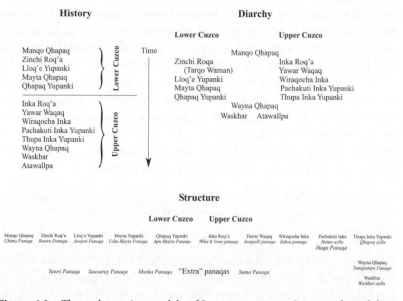

Figure 6.3   Three alternative models of Inca government. Source: adapted from Gose 1996a: 386, incorporating Zuidema's (1983) diarchy model.

in the chronicles. In addition, while Lower Cuzco almost certainly had a paramount figure, studies of kin-based political systems throughout the Andes show that the leader of one social division invariably stood higher in rank than the other and spoke for the group as a whole in external relations and global decision-making.

Royal Alliances: Political Marriages and the Power of the Queen

Women, especially the sovereign's principal wife (*qoya*), were powerful figures in royal life (see especially Rostworowski 1983, 1999; and Ziółkowski 1996: 177–214). According to Diez de Betanzos, the *qoya* had to be of pure Inca blood. She had to be "one of his sisters or first cousins" (Diez de Betanzos 1996: 72). The *qoya* brought a great deal into the marriage, including counsel, status, legitimacy for offspring, and wealth. Once in the alliance, she wielded some independent power and was also a persuasive political adviser for her husband and son who succeeded him. Even though she may well have been voicing the interests of her kin group, a *qoya* mother could also impede the marriage of her daughter to the king. Similarly, a prospective *qoya* could reject the proposal. Both Wayna Qhapaq and Waskhar suffered from this rebuff, at least temporarily. The outstanding feature of Inca royal marriages before the imperial era was probably the bond that they formed with other ethnic groups. In the imperial era, the ruler continued to take many women of other ethnic groups as wives, often with political intent, but only in a secondary status. The later emperors were credited with having hundreds or even thousands of wives or concubines of various statuses. When Wayna Qhapaq traveled north for his Ecuadorian campaigns, for example, he was said to have taken along a mere 2,000 consorts, leaving the other 4,000 behind.

In the political arena, women were instrumental in promoting the case of a selected son as royal successor. The lineage of the candidates' mother was crucial, because sitting rulers did not belong to their father's kin group. Instead, they founded their own *panaqa* and identified closely with their mother's. Those affiliations had enormous significance for alliance formation and for the actions of Atawallpa's generals at the end of the war, described below. The rulers' wives seem to have been the main liaisons between their husbands and their own kin, and the king's mother was also influential, alive or dead. During an Ecuadorian campaign, for example, Wayna Qhapaq berated the military nobility for having let him fall in harm's way and refused them the gifts to which they felt entitled. When they packed up in a huff to go home, the king recruited his mother's image to entreat them to stay; a Kañar woman spoke as the image's medium (Ziółkowski 1996: 177–207).

Two changes in marriage practices illustrate how the Inca rulers worked to concentrate power in the face of Cuzco's growing aristocracy (Rostworowski 1960b). One was to designate a principal wife whose male offspring would constitute a small pool of legitimate heirs. While it is hard to know exactly when that shift became formalized, it was sometimes described as one of Pachakuti's reforms. A second innovation was marriage between the ruler and his full sister – a practice that drew mythic legitimacy from the coupling of founding sibling ancestors. Thupa Inka Yupanki may have been the first emperor to wed his full sister (see figure 6.4a).

Waskhar's ascent to the throne leads into a report of one of the most peculiarly Andean of weddings. According to the native chronicler Pachacuti Yamqui, Waskhar had his mother officially marry his father's mummy, to provide the young ruler with full genealogical legitimacy. Since Wayna Qhapaq's mummy was regarded as animate and could voice his thoughts through his living mediums, the wedding would have been seen as an expression of his wishes. Whether this story was faithful to the facts is beside the point. What is important is that, in the Inca view of power, the act was plausible and maybe even necessary. The story also highlights the role assumed by the deceased kings and queens in choosing spouses for members of their kin groups. The ancestors and living *panaqa* could advance their mutual interests by forging marriages between the current ruler and the *panaqa*'s women (Rostworowski 1999: 106–7; Gose 1996a: 4). The ancestral lord and his principal wife, through their mediums, regulated the choice of marriage partners among the *panaqa*'s members and, if fortunate, created marital bonds with the king.

The stature of women in royal politics may also be appreciated by considering the unhappy fates of female relatives of royal combatants. When Wayna Qhapaq's kin elevated him to power in a coup, the displaced heir may have been only banished, while both his mother and another female relative who had forwarded his case were executed (Murúa 1986: 107; Ziółkowski 1996: 189, 351). In the next generation, Waskhar's power was threatened by a coup, which was to be touched off by his mother's assassination. According to some chroniclers, once Waskhar was finally defeated in the dynastic

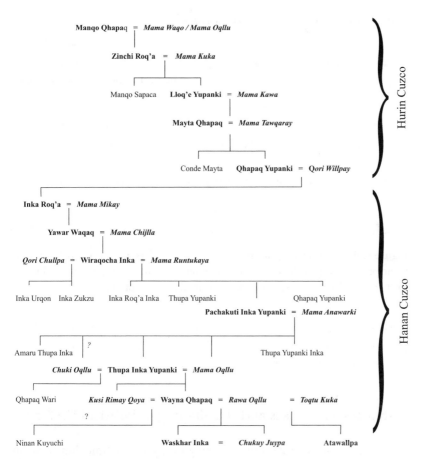

Figure 6.4a   A genealogy of the traditional Inca rulers (bold), their principal wives (italics), and principal offspring.

war with Atawallpa, the only three individuals taken into custody were the ruler, his mother, and his wife. A general pardon was issued to everyone else on Waskhar's side and only later were the bloody mass reprisals carried out. These stories emphasize that adversarial parties viewed women as crucial figures and took steps to remove them at an early opportunity.

The roles of royal women thus suggest that the ruler's principal marriage was not a simple joining of a couple to produce legitimate offspring or the forging of a political alliance. The royal couple formed a ruling pair with complementary roles. Within the marriage, the *qoya* enjoyed wide latitude of choice in some matters and owned significant personal resources, which

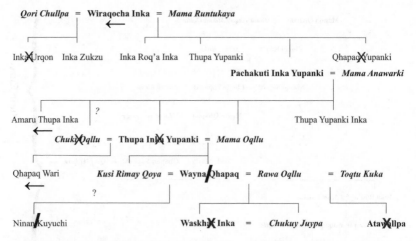

Figure 6.4b   A genealogy of the traditional Inca rulers, their principal wives, and principal offspring, with political acts highlighted (arrow = displaced; X = killed in Inca era; / = death by pestilence; X = executed by Incas or Spaniards).

she could bequeath as she wished (chapter 7). And once the monarch had passed on and his son was installed, the stature and influence of a surviving wife – and later her mummy – may have actually increased.

Succession Crises and the Shaping of Political History

The Incas' political system undoubtedly evolved over time, but their history's flexibility makes it hard to pin down the timing and nature of the changes. Still, the chronicles are our best source for insight into how the practices of power helped to shape the government's structure. They suggest that the royal successions and marriages were the pivotal moments for conflict and maneuver, although certain rulers also tried ideological reformations that would have enhanced their positions. Rostworowski (1960b) drew attention to the bloody infighting inherent in royal successions, and observed that the situation arose because Andean rules of succession typically favored vigorous actors. Often, a lord passed his station to the son who showed himself most able regardless of birth position, but it was not uncommon for a number of able brothers in a generation to hold office successively. Among the Incas, factional competition meant that successful aspirants won the throne through political intrigue, coup, murder, and even war. mboxSpanish writers often had trouble grasping the idea that there was no rightful candidate genealogically, because they saw primogeniture as the only legitimate path of succession. Native lords quickly learned to exploit their confusion by claiming rights based on Andean and European customs as the situation warranted. Members of the royal kin groups, for example, soon began referring to eldest-born sons as "legitimate" heirs and discrediting others as "bastards" when the circumstances favored that position. At other times, they asserted that a younger son had been tapped by the sitting ruler and installed as co-regent during the elder's lifetime. Their disputes contributed to the varied Inca histories that are preserved today. Rostworowski (1983, 1999) and Ziólkowski (1996), among others, have paid careful attention to sorting out the political struggles, which are too detailed to cover in more than a sketch here.

If we look at the outline of the imperial successions (figure 6.4a, b), we can gain a sense of the infighting that characterized royal politics. All the sources concur that the transition from Wiraqocha to Pachakuti was contested, but we do not know if Wiraqocha's displaced son Inka Urqon was simply designated as heir (Sarmiento 2007: 113; Cabello Valboa 1951: 298–9), treated as if he were all but emperor (Diez de Betanzos 1996: 27–9), or actually enthroned (Cieza 1967). In any event, Inka Urqon did not figure in the standard king list in the Colonial era nor did he leave a *panaqa* that was incorporated into Upper Cuzco.

Thupa Inka Yupanki's ascension was also convoluted, beginning with his replacement of an elder brother named Amaru Thupa Inka who had fallen short of expectations (Sarmiento 2007: 141; Pachacuti Yamqui 1993: 228; Cabello Valboa 1951: 334–5; Rowe 1985b: 221–3; Murúa 1986: 224, 317–26). Even though the younger prince had served a military apprenticeship on the northern campaigns, his ascendancy may not have been fully endorsed by Cuzco's families. In Sarmiento's account, Thupa Inka Yupanki required all of Cuzco to pay homage to him upon pain of death. Despite his precautions, the ruler was challenged (unsuccessfully) by another brother and he may eventually have been murdered. According to some accounts, Thupa Inka Yupanki may have designated his son Qhapaq Wari for the throne, but the heir was thrust aside in a bloody palace coup staged by Wayna Qhapaq's kin (Cieza 1967: 206; Sarmiento 2007: 171–2; Murúa 1986: 101–3). Since Wayna Qhapaq was still thought to be too callow to govern, his early political career was managed by two paternal uncles. The first of them tried to usurp power for his own son, but he was foiled by the other uncle, who then co-ruled with Wayna Qhapaq until the youth was mature enough to assume the throne alone. Guaman Poma (1980: 93) added that this ruler also followed the time-honored expedient of murdering a couple of his brothers to consolidate his position.

The final prehispanic succession was the passage of power to Wayna Qhapaq's sons, which culminated in the great dynastic war between Waskhar and Atawallpa. This conflict brought to a head a long-simmering rivalry between Pachakuti's *panaqa*, named *Hatun ayllu*, and that of Thupa Inka Yupanki, named *Qhapaq ayllu*. Through their mothers, Atawallpa was closely identified with *Hatun ayllu* and Waskhar with *Qhapaq ayllu* (Rostworowski 1999: 106–7). By all accounts, Waskhar's behavior as ruler was deplorable. In addition to repeatedly breaching royal courtesies and abusing the aristocracy (sometimes fatally), Waskhar jeopardized the entire system of privileged wealth when he threatened to bury the mummies of the past kings and alienate all the royal and religious properties. The most politically shocking of Waskhar's moves may have occurred when he divorced himself from Upper Cuzco (including his own kin) and declared his reaffiliation with Lower Cuzco. Using personnel from Lower Cuzco, Waskhar then set about building a new town at Calca, where he planned to live (Diez de Betanzos 1996: 195). When Atawallpa's men took Cuzco, his field commander Kusi Yupanki personally supervised the massacre of Waskhar's kin and carried out reprisals against Lower Cuzco. He also directed a house-by-house search in which *Qhapaq ayllu* and many of its priestesses and service personnel were killed. The most telling act occurred when *Hatun ayllu's* forces dragged Thupa Inka Yupanki's mummy out of its house and reduced it to ashes (e.g., Cabello Valboa 1951: 464). Nothing could have been more potent, for Atawallpa's agents had effaced both the living icon of his grandfather's reign and the people who maintained his legacy. The survivors' attempt to maintain some semblance of power and dignity by scraping the mummy's ashes into a jar seems a forlorn gesture indeed.

The different ways that the succession crises were memorialized illuminate Inca politics. Whatever the accuracy of any account, successions involved plotting, successful and failed coups, murder, and a host of other political delicacies. That situation is typical of imperial history everywhere, but the competition that was woven into the fabric of Inca politics virtually guaranteed periodic upheavals in Cuzco. In a polity intent on expansion, selection for leaders in this way may have yielded effective rulers, but in an established empire the practice could be ruinous, as it was in the final dynastic war. Over time, the Incas tried to limit the damage by consolidating power in a small circle of family members. Seen in this light, the marriage of the ruler to his full sister makes perfect sense, since royal incest reduced the pool of claimants in the next generation. Moreover, who but the daughter of a god was best suited to marry the son of the Sun? The devastation visited by the last dynastic war suggests that these designs had only a modest effect. It is hard to say with present information if the scope of the final blood-bath was unique in Inca history. Even so, the narratives suggest that the descendant kin of three (or four, if we count Inka Urqon) enthroned rulers were either wiped out (Thupa Inka Yupanki, Waskhar) or were delayed in their entry into Cuzco's formal hierarchy (Wayna Qhapaq) by successional conflicts. When we consider that those rulers were said to have reigned for as much as two-thirds of the imperial era, that is quite an impact.

Note

1   The ruler's mummy was sent to Lima on the orders of the Viceroy Cañete, along with those of Inka Roq'a, Wayna Qhapaq and four *qoya* (Hemming 1970: 298; Bauer and Coello Rodríguez 2007).

Chapter Seven

The Heartland of the Empire

The heart of the Inca empire beat in Cuzco, a small city of thatched-roof palaces, plazas, and terraces in high mountain valley (plate 7.1). Designed to be the hub of the known world, the capital was both the empire's seat of authority and its architectural masterpiece. The town's center was dedicated to temples, ceremonial spaces, and housing for the empire's royalty, nobility, and their retainers. Provincial lords and colonists were settled nearby in a dozen neighborhoods that echoed their position in the empire. Tawantinsuyu's most hallowed shrines lay in and about the city on a landscape whose every feature integrated a living past with the present (figure 7.1). In a more extended region that took in the lands within the next 60 km lay country homes for living and dead rulers, their descendants, other Inca aristocrats, and privileged social groups. The heartland also housed all the service personnel that the elites needed to keep their lives running smoothly – domestic staff, temple attendants, accountants, and farmers, along with the weavers, metal smiths, potters, and other artisans who crafted objects in a distinctive style that symbolized imperial power.

Cuzco was Tawantinsuyu's center of power when the Spaniards arrived, even though a strong late rival to its pre-eminence was rising at Tumipampa (Ecuador), where Wayna Qhapaq erected a second planned capital. Today, the local tourism industry, with only a bit of hyperbole, proclaims the city the "archaeological capital of the Americas." The urban core was a planned settlement, covering about 40 hectares (figure 7.2). Pachakuti is often credited with devising the plan after turning over command of the armies to his brothers and son Thupa Inka Yupanki (chapter 4). As his descendants explained it to Diez de Betanzos, Pachakuti ordered the entire basin vacated and had much of the existing architecture razed. The ruler then modeled his concept of the central city in clay and assigned architects to execute it. Whether we accept all the details of this vision or not, the

The Incas, Second Edition. Terence N. D'Altroy.
© 2015 John Wiley & Sons, Ltd. Published 2015 by John Wiley & Sons, Ltd.

Plate 7.1 View looking eastward over Cuzco and the valley toward Ausangate in 1931. Source: reproduced by permission of the American Museum of Natural History. Neg. No. 334756, photo Shippee–Johnson collection.

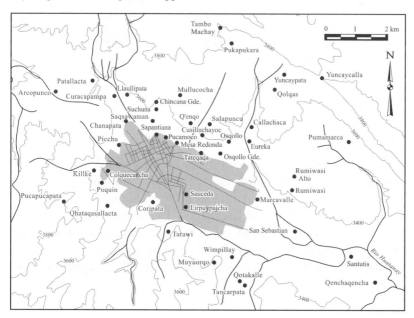

Figure 7.1 Distribution of important Inca sites near Cuzco. Source: adapted from Agurto Calvo (1987).

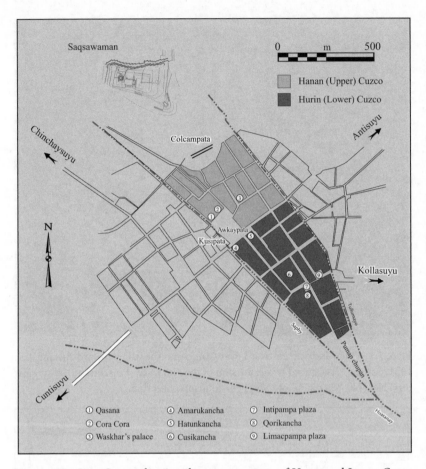

Figure 7.2   Inca Cuzco, showing the two core areas of Upper and Lower Cuzco, the twelve surrounding residential districts, and the roads leading toward the four parts of the empire.

city's core was certainly rebuilt during the imperial era following a carefully considered design. The town and its suburbs still incorporate many structures, terraced fields, and intricate networks of canals and baths. Hundreds of cultural and natural landmarks – including hilltops, carved rock formations, temples, and fountains raised over springs – formed elements of a socialized geography that radiated outward from Cuzco's center. Small wonder that Garcilaso said that the Incas called their capital the "navel of the universe."

Our knowledge of Cuzco is more patchy than that of the nearby royal estates, because it has been continuously occupied as the region's most important urban center for the last 800 years. We understand the basic plan because it was described in the chronicles and was preserved during the Colonial era with some modifications, but many important elements have been lost. The Spaniards began to alter the face of the city soon after taking control in 1533, as they officially assigned palaces to the officers, granted house lots to the soldiers, and designated other spaces for public use in 1534. A conflagration that was deliberately touched off in 1536 during Manqo Inka's effort to evict the invaders and an earthquake in 1650 also ravaged the capital. As they began to recognize the sanctity of some architectural elements, and suppressed rebellions by their own compatriots, the Spaniards took deliberate steps to dismantle particular structures associated with discomfiting circumstances. Other features stand as discordant reminders of the cultural clashes that occurred over the years. The main temple, for example, was converted to the monastery of Santo Domingo and a remnant wall of Wayna Qhapaq's palace now holds planters in a tourist restaurant.

In view of the hundreds of years of modifications, it is difficult – from standing archaeological remains alone – to gain a sense of what the city looked like during the height of Inca power. Historians and archaeologists have been working at the problem for decades, plumbing the archives and conducting more than 70 excavation programs since the 1950s (Farrington 2010: 87). Even so, they are only now producing a comprehensive architectural and settlement analyses and a fine-grained chronology for the valley's imperial occupation.[1]

The Setting and Urban Plan

Within the constraints imposed by a rugged natural setting, the Incas shaped Cuzco and its surrounding landscape to be the pivot of the cosmos and to symbolize their elevated place within it. The city itself lies at an elevation of 3,450 m (about 11,300 ft). From our contemporary perspective, we can see that the surrounding valley lands were well suited to growing a standard array of highland crops, while pastures can be found nearby in both rolling uplands and the steeply dissected terrain bordering the valley. The valley's streams are fed by numerous springs whose waters flow through the city in channelized courses and then merge in the eastward-flowing

Huatanay river. After passing through the Oropesa and Lucre basins, the Huatanay discharges into the Vilcanota's narrow gorge about 20 km east of the capital; in its lower course as it flows into the forest, the river is known as the Urubamba. To the west of Cuzco lies the marshy Pampa de Anta, while the Apurimac river gorge provides a formidable barrier on the south. During the imperial era, the Incas modified the region's topography through landscape engineering, especially for the royal manors along the constricted valley lands and hillslopes of the middle Vilcanota/Urubamba. Much of the surrounding land was cultivated and storage facilities were built to hold raw materials, produce, and crafts.

Once again, if we take the Incas' view of their world into account, the terrain looks much more complicated than that. They memorialized pivotal events of myth and history by modifying the landscape, erecting estates and building shrines that honored a social landscape populated by a parallel society. The most prominent features were the grand snow-capped peaks sweeping from east to west in the range to the north of the Sacred Valley. The most elevated was Ausangate, due east of Cuzco, but Sinakara, Colquepunku, Sahuasiray, Verónica, and Salkantay also populated the horizon. Closer to the valley, on the south side, lay Huanacauri, the final resting place of the petrified original ancestral brother. Springs, rock out-crops, watercourses and their confluences, passes, terraces, and fields – any of a vast array of distinctive features of the terrain – were alive or conscious in some sense. They had names, histories, and power and as such, they were active agents in the Incas' relationship to their land's past and present. The capital was thus situated not just in a splendid physical landscape, but in the midst of a dynamic social space, which was constantly politically contested (see Kosiba and Bauer 2012).

Cuzco was unquestionably the grandest center of its time in South America.[2] While the capital formed a spatial metaphor for Inca society and their world, it was also the hub of imperial political, social, and ritual activity. To the visitors who were granted access, the city's elaborate ceremonial life must have provided stunning witness to the power of the Incas and their gods. Its architectural elegance deeply impressed the Spaniards who saw the capital before events changed its face permanently. Pedro Sancho de la Hoz, Pizarro's secretary, compared it favorably with cities of his homeland in Spain. His companion, Juan Ruiz de Arce (1933: 368; translation from Hyslop 1990: 34), wrote that "(t)he city ... would have four thousand residential houses between the two rivers surrounding it and they are on a slope of a mountain, and at the head of the city in the same mountain there is a fort [Saqsawaman] with many rooms." Cuzco is better thought of as extending well into the valley, however, rather than consisting just of the dense core. Sancho de la Hoz (1917: 194; translation by Hyslop 1990: 35), who appreciated the layout better than his fellow, explained that "(f)rom the fortress one sees around the city many houses out to a fourth of a league, half a league, and a league, and in the valley in the middle surrounded by mountains there are more than one hundred thousand homes." Sancho's estimate should be taken as an impressionistic figure, since the conquistadores often used that number to describe a multitude of people or things.

In 1980, UNESCO published the results of field studies that identified many buildings but also confirmed that destruction and erosion have been too severe to permit more precise demographic estimates than the eyewitness accounts (see Hyslop 1990: 29–68). As Ruiz de Arce's description suggests, the city core covered a small area, about 1 by 0.6 km between the Ríos Saphy and Tullumayo (Hyslop 1990: 36). It was divided into two sectors. *Hanan Cuzco*, or Upper Cuzco, referred to both the last five royal *panaqa* and the sector of Cuzco northwest of the main plazas, where they lived. It was socially and topographically elevated above *Hurin Cuzco* (Lower Cuzco), which lay to the southeast (figure 7.2). Twelve districts surrounded the central sectors, three for each of the four *suyu*, or divisions of the empire (Agurto Calvo 1980: 122–8; Hyslop 1990: 64–5). The UNESCO report's author, Santiago Agurto Calvo, surmised that the population of the central sector was about 15,000–20,000 people, with an additional 50,000 in a ring of immediately surrounding districts. He estimated, very roughly, that 50,000–110,000 more people may have occupied the suburban area that extended about 5 km beyond the urban neighborhoods. While the evidence to support any population estimate is thin at best, we may judge that greater Cuzco housed somewhere between 100,000 and 150,000 people. The city was thus smallish by the standard of ancient imperial capitals.

The Incas said that they had built their city in the form of a puma, but even sixteenth-century writers were uncertain if that was meant literally or metaphorically. In the official history that he prepared for the Viceroy Toledo, Sarmiento (2007: 167) accepted a literal view. According to his informants, Pachakuti designed the city so that the puma's body took in the area between the Saphy and Tullumayo rivers. The confluence of the two rivers is still called *pumap chupan* or the "puma's tail," after the Inca toponym. Pachakuti, in this account, did not construct the animal's head himself, but left the task to his son Thupa Inka Yupanki. The young man took up the challenge with a vengeance, transforming a rocky prominence above the city into the feline's head. On it he built Saqsawaman, the most elaborate single architectural complex in the entire empire (see below). The metaphorical conception is supported by other passages in the chronicles that suggest that the image applied to the people of the greater Cuzco region, not to the layout of the city core. Diez de Betanzos's (1996: 74) account is probably the closest to a royal vision of any we have. He wrote: "to the whole city together [Pachakuti] gave the name 'the lion's body,' saying that those neighbors and inhabitants of it were the members of said lion, and that his person was the head of it." Some scholars take such comments to mean that the puma was intended as an allegory that has been misunderstood by most chroniclers and modern authors alike (see Hyslop 1990: 50–1).

The street plan consisted of straight roads that were irregularly arranged to fit the topography of the sloping land and perhaps the puma figure. The central district contained two main avenues that ran the length of the city and were crosscut by six other streets. None of the central blocks formed by their intersection was square and they varied greatly in size, with a general range of about 30–40 m wide by 45–70 m long (Agurto Calvo 1987; Hyslop 1990: 37–42). The streets themselves were narrow, as befit a city in which wheeled or mounted traffic were not concerns. Many were paved with stones and contained stone-lined water channels running down the middle. A persistent Spanish complaint about the city was that there was space for only a single mounted horseman on either side of the canals.

The Central Plazas

Two adjoining plazas, separated by the Saphy river, lay at the center of ancient Cuzco. *Awkaypata* ("Terrace of repose")[3] was a main locale for open-air ceremonies. *Kusipata* ("Fortunate terrace") lay just to the west across the watercourse; less well known because it was largely built over during the Colonial era, it included the space now covered by the Plaza de Regocijo. Measuring about 190 by 165 m (~3 ha), Awkaypata occupied the space that is today covered by the Plaza de Armas. It was diminished by about 30 percent by the Licenciado Polo, as he began the construction of the main cathedral (Bauer 2004: 113). It is fronted today by two cathedrals that have replaced important Inca buildings. In a gesture that brought the mother sea to their capital, the Incas covered the space with a layer of Pacific coast sand at least two and a half palms thick, into which they interred gold and silver figurines and vessels (Polo 1916: 109–10). When he was magistrate of Cuzco, Licenciado Polo realized the significance of the sand and ordered it to be removed, to desanctify the space in Inca eyes. He gave the some of the sand to the church, and used some in the construction of four bridges, as well as some other works (Polo 1965b: 118–19; see Bauer 2004: 113–14). A gilded stone was also situated in the plaza next to which the Incas installed a much-celebrated basin.[4] *Chicha* and other liquids poured into the aperture during rituals drained out through an underground canal system.

Awkaypata was the most important open space in the entire realm.[5] It often hosted the mummies or icons of dead rulers and their wives for a wide variety of ceremonies of state. They were seated according to their rank and fêted as though they were in living attendance. Major festivals in the annual ritual cycle took place there, such as the June solstice ceremony of 1535 witnessed by the Spaniards, and the investiture of new rulers, as well as military assemblies and ritual battles. Kusipata was more heavily impacted by the Spanish occupation of Cuzco. Only a fraction remains visible, as most is now occupied by Colonial-era architecture. Morris and his colleagues (2011: 33) suggest that the provincial counterparts to the plazas at Cuzco were the most important architectural elements of the *tampu*, because it was there that Inca rule was actively implemented in the context of ritual hospitality.

Until recently, it was thought that the Spanish efforts had eradicated any traces of Inca constructions within the great plazas. However, excavations in Awkaypata in 1995, associated with the municipal refurbishment of the Colonial fountain, uncovered wall footings as well as a quantity of Inca ceramics and four camelid figurines – one made of gold, two of silver, and one of spondylus shell. Underground canals were also found in the plaza and in nearby locations, including the terraces between the Sun Temple and the Saphy river (Farrington and Raffino 1996: 73). And recently, a ceremonial *qhapaq ucha* burial was found within the Casa de Concha, in central Cuzco. Collectively, those finds suggest that there is still much to be learned about Inca Cuzco beneath the modern city.

The Major Architecture

Royal palaces and religious compounds dominated the central architecture. Most were surrounded by a wall that limited access and vision into the interior. The Awkaypata plaza in particular was bordered by impressive compounds or buildings on three sides, but there is no comparable

Plate 7.2   Central Cuzco in 1931, with the Colonial Plaza de Armas overlying the Inca Awkaypata ("Terrace of repose") in right-center of photo. Source: reproduced by permission of the American Museum of Natural History. Neg. No. 334796, photo Shippee–Johnson collection.

evidence for monumental Inca constructions adjoining Kusipata (plate 7.2; Rowe 1991: 84). The two compounds on the southeast of Awkaypata were probably the most impressive. *Hatunkancha* ("Great enclosure") was a magnificent construction with a single entrance that gave onto the plaza.

Adjacent to the Hatunkancha lay the *aqllawasi*, which was the house of the *mamakuna* or *aqllakuna*, the most privileged women's orders (Bauer 2004: 128–30). One of the structure's walls along modern Loreto Street, known as the Street of the Sun, still contains beautifully cut stonework (plate 7.3). Garcilaso (1966: 195) described it effusively, observing that it gave out onto the Awkaypata and was bordered by three streets, so that "it occupied an island site between the square and these three streets." The combination of central location and spatial isolation was characteristic of the compounds dedicated to the women's orders.

The other grand compound on the southeast, called *Amarukancha* ("Serpent enclosure"), was attributed to a number of rulers by the early sources. Sarmiento (2007: 187) among others assigned it to Waskhar,

Plate 7.3 Finely cut regular ashlar masonry on the exterior of the Hatunkancha compound, facing the more uneven masonry of the Amarukancha compound.

along with another city palace at Colcampata, whereas Garcilaso favored Wayna Qhapaq. Bauer (2004: 124–6) judges Waskhar the more likely builder, which would have made this palace the last erected in the city. Amarukancha apparently contained a great hall that gave onto the plaza, but we know little else of its internal features. It was subdivided early in the Spanish occupation and its buildings were destroyed (Bauer 2004: 124–6).

Wayna Qhapaq's palace (*Qasana*) lay on the plaza's northwest side. It consisted of a series of important structures, enclosed by a large wall (Niles 1999: 232; Bauer 2004: 117–21). The complex housed the ruler's mummy when the Spaniards first entered the city. Its entrance held such significance that a shrine in Cobo's (i.e., Polo's; Cobo 1990: 58) list of 328 *waqa*, in Cuzco's *zeqʾe* system, was situated there. Garcilaso claimed that a courtyard within the complex was large enough to accommodate exercises for sixty mounted Spanish horsemen, and that a great hall could hold as many as 3,000 people (Garcilaso 1966: 261, 321). In front of the palace were two round structures, with tall thatched roofs, that extended into the plaza. It was bordered on the north by another royal palace, called the *Cora Cora*. According to some sources, it was a city property where Pachakuti used to sleep (Rowe 1991: 87–8), but Garcilaso (1966: 425) associated it with Inqa Roka (Bauer 2004: 122).

An elevated terrace lay at the northern corner of Awkaypata, behind and above which lay Waskhar's spacious palace; this compound has been largely destroyed (Farrington 1983). Scholars are not entirely sure of the precise location of Waskhar's palace, but it seems to have been near the Cora Cora, perhaps directly adjacent to it (Bauer 2004; Farringon 2010). The nature of the architecture on the northeastern side of the plaza is uncertain. The Triunfo church was built on the site of a large Inca hall, which was converted into the city's first Spanish church. The Inca building has often been associated with the name Wiraqocha, either as the king's palace or as the Creator God's temple (*Kiswarkancha*), but modern scholars generally do not accept either proposition (see Hyslop 1990: 40–1; Rowe 1991: 86–7). Two other palaces of note, whose location is uncertain, were Pachakuti's residence called Kunturkancha and Thupa Inka Yupanki's urban palace, which may have been found at Pukamarka (Rowe 1967: 61; Cobo 1990: 55).

There were also residences for the royal kin groups. The ten *panaqa* maintained residences in Cuzco, while the non-royal *ayllu* lived in settlements beyond the center. Within the suburban neighborhoods lived members of a variety of ethnic groups, arranged according to their position in the empire, creating an ethnic microcosm of the realm. For example, the non-royal *ayllu* who had (legendarily) migrated northward with the Incas from Pacariqtambo lived in Cayoache, a neighborhood on the south side of the city. The Chachapoyas and Kañaris, whose homelands lay in the empire's northwest part, were settled in an analogous position in the city. (Conversely, some groups such as the Chilque and Qolla had limited or no access to the city, apparently because of their historical resistance to Inca rule.) Each great lord of the empire was supposed to keep up a house in Cuzco, where he was expected to spend four months a year. One of his sons was also required to live in the capital continuously, so that he could learn Quechua and become enculturated in the ways of the Incas. While in the city, the provincial nobles were expected to maintain themselves with their own servants, who lived nearby (see Rowe 1967).

Temples

Allusion to religious architecture or space in Cuzco is almost a redundancy, for so much of the city was intrinsically sacred or the place of important rituals. Even so, a few buildings occupied a special position in the performance of the official religion. The most important complex by far was the Qorikancha, or Golden Enclosure, more commonly known today as the Temple of the Sun. The last term is a partial misnomer, since all of the major celestial beings were worshiped there and important royal mummies were also venerated in the inner sanctums (Rowe 1967: 62, 70; Hyslop 1990: 44–7). Located a couple of blocks to the southeast of Awkaypata, the temple was the focal point in the Incas' vision of sacred geography. At the same time that the temple was the empire's most important shrine, the compound enclosed several other sacred objects and locations that were venerated individually in the ceremonial cycle (chapter 8).

The western exterior of the compound was graced with the most famous wall in the realm – an elegant curve of ashlar masonry (plate 7.4). The interior of the complex contained four to eight rectangular rooms of similarly cut stone. Some of the walls were adorned with gold plate, which the first three Spaniards to enter the precinct prised off the walls to take back to Cajamarca. There were probably also several other buildings within the compound, since priestesses and other temple personnel lived there. The temple's rooms housed a variety of effigies, most importantly Punchao or the image of the Sun itself. This statue was brought out into a patio during the day and then returned to its quarters at night. Nearby lay a maize garden with birds interspersed among the plants; the garden was accompanied by a herd of camelids attended by their keepers. All were executed in precious

Plate 7.4 The exterior of the Qorikancha ("Golden Enclosure"), known popularly as the Temple of the Sun, over which the Spaniards erected the monastery of Santo Domingo.

metals (chapter 13). Despite considerable architectural study and several excavations, we still do not have a secure understanding of the chronology of the Qorikancha. In legend, the original Temple of the Sun was built when the founding ancestor Manqo Qhapaq settled in Cuzco. The epics also recounted that Pachakuti rebuilt the temple when he undertook his ambitious remodeling of the capital and its environs. The excavations that have been conducted do indicate that there was a pre-imperial Killke component in the location, but have not found clear evidence of a Sun Temple before the imperial era (Rowe 1944; Hyslop 1990: 32). The problem has been compounded by the early transformation of the Inca sanctuary into the monastery of Santo Domingo and its subsequent remodeling.

Two other important temples within the city were *Kiswarkancha* ("Enclosure of the kishwar tree") and *Pukamarka* ("Red Town"). The first, as noted above, was a temple dedicated to Wiraqocha the Creator God. Some early writers said that it was situated on the northeast side of Awkaypata, but Molina's more trustworthy account suggests that it was a little bit removed from that core area. The second temple contained shrines to the Creator and to the weather/thunder deity, Illapa.

Saqsawaman

On a rocky promontory above Cuzco lay Saqsawaman, the grandest architectural complex in the empire (plate 7.5). Depending on the oral tradition, either Pachakuti or Thupa Inka Yupanki was responsible for inaugurating

Plate 7.5 Artistic reconstruction of the main architecture at the Saqsawaman complex. Source: reproduced by permission of Ricardo Mar.

its construction as the head of Cuzco's puma design. L. Valcárcel's (1934–5) work in the 1930s recovered a great deal of preimperial Killke pottery, indicating that the site was occupied by the Incas even before the imperial era. According to Cieza (1967: 169–71), Pachakuti began the work and it was carried on by all his successors. He wrote that the ruler ordered 20,000 workers to be sent in from the provinces on a rotating basis. Four thousand of them quarried stones and another six thousand hauled them into place, while other workers dug trenches or laid the foundations.

Cieza wrote that Saqsawaman was originally founded as a Sun temple, but the facility was actually a combination of religious architecture, fortress, magazine, and ceremonial complex (Mar and Beltrán-Caballero in press). Unfortunately, much of the architecture was dismantled for use in the Spanish remodeling of Cuzco even before Cieza saw it, but some early witnesses provided vivid descriptions. Pedro Sancho wrote, in part:

> (T)here is a very beautiful fortress of earth and stone with big windows that look over the city and make it appear more beautiful. In it are many chambers and a main round tower in the center made with four or five stories one on the other ... There are so many habitations, and the tower, that one person cannot see it all in one day. And many Spaniards who have seen it who have been in Lombardy and other foreign kingdoms say that they have not seen another construction like this fortress, nor a more powerful castle. Five thousand Spaniards might be able to fit inside. On the side facing the city there is only one wall on a rugged mountain slope. On the other side, which is less steep, there are three, one higher than the other. These walls are the most beautiful thing that can be seen of all the constructions in that land. This is because they are of such big stones that no one who sees them would say that they have been placed there by the hand of man. They are as big as pieces of mountains or crags ... These stones are not flat, but very well worked and fit together ... These walls have curves so that if one attacks them one cannot go frontally but rather obliquely with the exterior. (Translation from Hyslop 1990: 53–4)

Sancho went on to describe the remarkable array of materials that were stored in the complex, including arms, quilted armor, clothing, pigments, cloth, tin, lead, silver, and gold. Recent excavations at Saqsawaman confirm this description, as archaeologists have unearthed a variety of sumptuary craft goods, including *tupu* pins, knives, other metal objects, and polychrome pottery (Valcárcel 1934–5; Rowe 1944; Van de Guchte 1990: 127–9).

The zig-zag walls of Saqsawaman are still one of the archaeological wonders of the Americas (figure 7.3). The terraces between the walls were wide

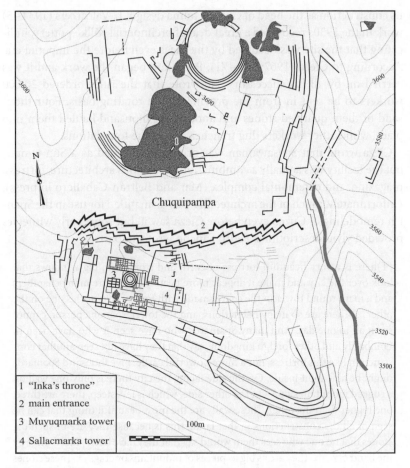

Chuquipampa

1 "Inka's throne"
2 main entrance
3 Muyuqmarka tower
4 Sallacmarka tower

0   100m

Figure 7.3 The ceremonial-fortress complex of Saqsawaman, above Cuzco. Source: adapted from Gasparini and Margolies (1980).

enough for three carts to pass side by side and today provide a vantage point for re-enactments of Inca sun ceremonies (chapter 14). As grand as they were, the walls formed only part of the facility. Across a grand plaza to the north lay another complex on a rocky hilltop, called Suchuna ("slide"), which contained aqueducts, cisterns, terraces, patios, stairs, and other buildings. One of the most elegantly carved stones in the empire is found on this hill. Popularly called the "Throne of the Inca," it consists of a series of step-planes cut into the bedrock. Beyond that complex is an immense, stone circular enclosure ("lake") and an array of small architectural features.

Many of those features consist of carved stones, terraces, or waterworks; frequently, those elements are combined, emphasizing the Incas' interest in manipulating those parts of the land that they viewed as being sentient. One of the most famous of the carved lithic beings was the "Tired Stone," a boulder that grew tired on its journey to Cuzco and began to cry bloody tears (chapter 8).

Other Features

Cuzco was not limited to residential and religious compounds, as a series of sacred agricultural fields also lay scattered throughout the city (Bauer 1996). One field was dedicated to the ritual planting of the first maize, while the harvest of other plots was reserved for various shrines of the city. Cuzco's outskirts also boasted a great quantity of storehouses (*qollqa*). The goods kept there were used to provision the city's residents, ostensibly every four days, and to supply the incessant ceremonial feasts. The *qollqa* also kept supplies for the capital's artisans as well as their finished products (chapters 12 and 13). Unfortunately, little evidence of the storehouses remains today.

Greater Cuzco

The imperial capital is best understood as an area extending outward from the urban core for a distance of several kilometers. Within this zone were aristocratic and service residences, hundreds of shrines, agricultural fields, and canal systems. A few estates lay in the Cuzco basin, although the *panaqa* of emperors after Thupa Inka Yupanki held no lands there. Sancho's estimate that more than 100,000 buildings were found in the entire valley is surely an exaggeration, but much of the valley was part of the grand imperial plan. Unfortunately, this surrounding area has not yet been well studied and we do not yet even have a full inventory of the sites. Susan Niles' study of Callachaca, one of several estates owned by Amaru Thupa Inka (brother of emperor Thupa Inka Yupanki), provides an exception to the general lack of detailed information about estates near Cuzco. The manor, which stretched along about 1.5 km of hillslope north of the city center, contained about fifty buildings loosely grouped in four clusters on terraces (Rostworowski 1962; Niles 1987).

Cuzco's organization was also closely tied to both the landscape and the cosmos through an array of at least 332, and probably more than 400 shrines (*wak'a*). Many of the shrines were springs, stones, and mountain peaks, each with its own name and link to Inca history. Jeanette Sherbondy (1994: 73–5) has identified over a third of the *wak'a* as water sources or other features associated with hydraulic works. During a year-long ritual cycle, the *panaqa* and affiliated *ayllu* took their appointed turns venerating the powers of the shrines with which they were associated. *Hanan Cuzco* controlled the water sources and canal systems of the upper half of the valley and *Hurin Cuzco* the lower. Each water source for the major irrigation canals was a shrine on a line assigned to the *panaqa*, whereas the less important networks received their water at shrines assigned to the lesser kin groups. Particular canal segments were cared for by specific kin groups. For the most part, the waters that ran through each canal system were used to irrigate the lands belonging to the associated group. The landscape, its production, and the social order of the valley's inhabitants were thus integrated through a ritual and agricultural cycle.

Royal and Aristocratic Estates

The imperial expansion put vast resources in the hands of the Inca elites, some of which were converted into private reserves for living and dead emperors and other aristocrats (table 7.1). Every province set aside lands for each ruler, but the most elegant estates lay in a 100-kilometer stretch of the Vilcanota/Urubamba drainage between Pisac and Machu Picchu (figure 7.4). This picturesque valley, which lies beneath snowcapped peaks, is often called the Sacred Valley of the Incas (plate 5.2). It contains many of the most spectacular archaeological sites ever erected in the Americas – not just Machu Picchu and Pisac, but Ollantaytambo, Wiñay Wayna, Patallacta, and others. The royal estates were used to support the monarchs in a manner suited to their deified stature. Not incidentally, they also provided sustenance and wealth for their descendants and underwrote their political and ceremonial activities. Those needs were weighty, since living and dead rulers and their kin spent a great deal of time visiting each other and performing rituals. Cobo (1990: 40–3) commented at length how those visits were needed to rationalize the *panaqa*'s ownership of such expansive resources and their fondness for lazy debauchery.

Every ruler from Wiraqocha Inka onward owned countryside properties, and even earlier monarchs may have also had private manors. Inca Roq'a and Yawar Waqaq's descendants, for example, lived in villas near Cuzco where they venerated the mummies of their royal ancestors (Sarmiento

Table 7.1 Principal royal holdings near Cuzco, primarily in the Vilcanota/Urubamba drainage (expanded and modified from Niles 1987: 14–45; Niles 1999: 76–7).

Ruler	Estate	Location	Comments	Sources
Inka Roqʼa	Rarapa	near San Jerónimo	mummy found there, estate not confirmed	Sarmiento 2007: 89; Cobo 1979: 125
Yawar Waqaq	Paullu	near Calca	mummy found there, estate not confirmed	Cobo 1979: 129
Wiraqocha Inka	Tipón	Oropesa		Bauer and Covey 2004: 86–7
	Paucartica	near Calca		Rostworowski 1970: 253
	Caquia Xaquixaguana	site of Huchʼuy Qozqo	mummy found there	Cobo 1979: 132; Rostworowski 1970: 253
	Pumamarca	eastern Cuzco valley		Rowe 1997: 279–80
Pachakuti Inka	Pisac	Pisac		Rostworowski 1966: 32; 1970: 253
	Guamán Marca (Huamanmarka), Chuñobamba, Pisiguay	Amaybamba		Rostworowski 1963; Kendall 1985: 458; Rowe 1997: 280
	Ollantaytambo (Tambo)	Ollantaytambo		Sarmiento 2007: 121; Rostworowski 1966: 32; 1970: 253
	Patallacta	Cusichaca	mummy kept there for a time	Betanzos 1996: 138; Sarmiento 2007: 140; Cobo 1979: 141
	Wiñay Wayna			Protzen 1993: 53
	<26 named parcels	valley below Machu Picchu		Glave and Remy (1983); see Rowe 1990b
	Machu Picchu	lower Urubamba	inferred, not specifically named	Glave and Remy (1983); see Rowe 1990b
	Urubamba valley	from Torontoy to Cochabamba (km 91.5 and km 149 respectively)	includes some parcels named above	Rowe 1997: 278

(continued overleaf)

Table 7.1 *(continued)*

Ruler	Estate	Location	Comments	Sources
Thupa Inka Yupanki	Chinchero	Chinchero		Sarmiento 2007: 169; Rostworowski 1970: 253, 258
	Huayllabamba	Urquillos canyon		Villanueva 1971: 38–9; Rostworowski 1970: 253
	Urcos	Urquillos canyon		Villanueva 1971: 38–9; Rostworowski 1970: 253
	Calispuquio		ashes of mummy hidden there	Sarmiento 2007: 171; Rostworowski 1966: 32
	Cozca	Yucay valley	arbor	Rowe 1997: 282
	Tiobamba	near Maras		Rowe 1997: 282
	Condebamba	near Amantuy		Rowe 1997: 282
	quebrada of Sorama		held with wife Mama Ocllo	Rowe 1997: 282
	Piscobamba	Urubamba valley	held with wife Mama Ocllo	Rowe 1997: 282
Wayna Qhapaq	Quispiguanca	Yucay valley	mummy kept there for a time	Villanueva 1971: 38–9; Rostworowski 1970: 253
	Urubamba			Villanueva 1971: 38–9; Rostworowski 1970: 253
	Zurite, Jaquijaguana	Limatambo area		Rostworowski 1983: 141
Waskhar	Calca	Calca		Murúa 1986: 163; Rostworowski 1970: 253
	Muina	site of Kañaraqay		Murúa 1986: 142; Rostworowski 1970: 253
	Pomabamba			Rostworowski 1962 [1555]: 134

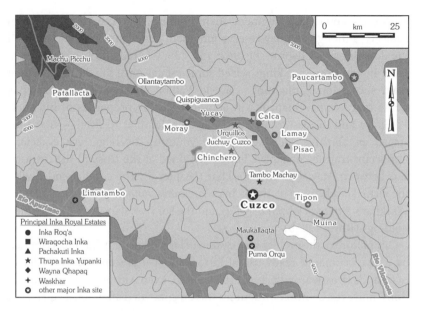

Figure 7.4 The distribution of the major royal estates and other land holdings in the Vilcanota/Urubamba drainage.

2007: 88; Cobo 1979: 125, 129; Rowe 1967: 68 n. 21). Rulers claimed their properties in many ways, including carving out new estates and commandeering expanses that had already been developed. Rowe (1990b: 143) suggests that Pachakuti founded estates at locations such as Pisac and Ollantaytambo to commemorate his military victories. According to the Inca narratives, this ruler even spruced up an estate at Juchuy Cuzco for his father Wiraqocha Inka, where the deposed monarch could live out his years in relative comfort (Kendall *et al.* 1992).

Thupa Inka Yupanki followed his father's example by claiming five strongholds that he had captured in the altiplano as personal estates. Rulers could expand their personal holdings at the expense of state institutions and royal competitors. Waskhar, for example, converted state lands and personnel into his own estate, when he claimed a region east of Huánuco in the last few imperial years (Julien 1993: 209–11). In an especially interesting twist, Thupa Inka Yupanki won some estates through a game of chance played with the Sun himself (Albornoz 1989: 175, 182; Cobo 1979: 149). He deliberately lost some lands to a son in a later game to give the youth a head start on building his own wealth. Monarchs and aristocrats could also augment their holdings by accepting gifts from subjects, although we may reserve judgment about the optional nature of the donations (Rostworowski 1962: 134, 136; Conrad and Demarest 1984: 139). In addition, Inca kings seized some estates once the dust had settled from successional infighting. Cabello Valboa (1951: 360), for example, wrote that Wayna Qhapaq's kin appropriated the properties of his uncle Wallpaya and his associates – and put their families to death – after they staged an abortive coup against the youthful sovereign. An especially important transfer may have been envisioned at the close of the dynastic war between Atawallpa and Waskhar (chapter 6). The conflict ended with the virtual eradication of Thupa Inka Yupanki's *panaqa* (*Qhapaq Ayllu*) and Waskhar's *panaqa* (*Waskhar Ayllu*) and the survivors' loss of their families' holdings (Rowe 1985b).

Our picture of the prehispanic system of land ownership has been clouded by native claimants' ready use of European legal precepts to gain control over lands (Rostworowski 1962, 1963, 1966). Even without those complications, however, control of resources was an entangled affair. Inca rulers, kin groups, institutions, and other elite men and women held estates and there may have been some discretion involved in passing them on. Most importantly, a deceased ruler's estates were normally left to his *panaqa*. Following the custom of split inheritance (chapter 6), the throne passed on to a successor who had to develop his own kin group's resources. The lands of the queen (*qoya*) were held separately; when she died, they were left to her own relatives. The natural complexity of the ecology and the slow development of the estates meant that parcels belonging to rulers, aristocrats, and local communities were intermingled among one another (Rostworowski 1962, 1963, 1966; Rowe 1990b, 1997). Since the Inca elite were linked through blood and marriage in many ways, ownership of some lands was especially complicated. Personal choice may have also played a role in inheritance, as claimants in early Colonial litigation testified that some bequests skipped generations at the wish of the benefactor. Over the generations, the number and types of claims that could be placed on particular plots must have created fertile ground for intrigue.

From a physical viewpoint, some estates were created through formidable engineering works. Wayna Qhapaq's holdings in Yucay were largely reclaimed from swamp and Waskhar's estate at Pomabamba was developed by diverting a river to create new land (Rostworowski 1962: 134–5; Villanueva 1971; Niles 1987: 13). Even though parts of the estates attributed to early monarchs boasted major land improvements, the riverine reclamation projects may have become increasingly important because the best field lands had already been spoken for. At one point, Waskhar groused that land tenure customs meant that the dead "had all that was the best of his kingdom" and that no decent expanses were left for him to claim (P. Pizarro 1986: 54). His gripe may have arisen from political rancor linked to his conflict with Atawallpa, but he may have also had legitimate grounds for complaint about limited access to prime lands for rural manors. His proposed solution was to abolish or confiscate both familial and institutional (Sun) estates, with an eye to appropriating them himself. As can be imagined, his threat to destroy all the mummies and seize their lands was not well received by Cuzco's powerful interests.

The archaeological remains along the Vilcanota/Urubamba valley provide magnificent witness to the resources and artisanry devoted to royal estates. The Incas' penchant for melding land forms and structures is one of the most distinctive features of their approach to designing the manors. All exhibit elegant terracing, waterworks, and masonry that is seldom approached in the rest of the empire. The estates were designed to provide access to a wide range of resources. Wayna Qhapaq's holdings in Yucay, described below, contained crop lands, pastures, settlements, forests, parks, a pond and marsh, a hunting range, and salt fields (Villanueva 1971; Farrington 1995). The number of workers committed to the manors was remarkable. At Yucay, 2,400 men and their families were dedicated to Wayna Qhapaq's holdings (Villanueva 1971: 94, 98, 136, 139; Rowe 1982: 100; Niles 1987: 13–15). Even more impressively, Thupa Inka Yupanki had 4,000–4,500 workers at each of three locations in the empire (Rostworowski 1966: 32). The assets found on individual estates may be best exemplified by the case of two of Wayna Qhapaq's secondary wives. According to one story, the ruler was unable to pacify the restive populace of the Huayllas region of highland Peru. Finally, he obtained peace by marrying daughters of each of the two regional lords. As part of the pre-nuptial agreement, each wife – upon giving birth to a son – was reportedly granted an estate with 6,000 tributaries free of state obligations (Ziółkowski 1996: 206).

A description of some of the estates attributed to the last four emperors before Waskhar will provide a more concrete sense of their nature. One of Wiraqocha Inka's estates was developed at Caquia Xaquixaguana, which archaeologists today identify as the site called Juchuy Cuzco ("Little Cuzco"). This site is spectacularly positioned at 3,650 m on a rock prominence some 600 m above the Urubamba river, with a grand view northward to the white-capped *cordillera oriental* and eastward toward Pisac. As at many estates, an enclosing wall restricted access to the site's core, which lies amidst elaborate sandstone terracing extending to sets of storehouses and smaller sites. The main architecture contains three groups of buildings that include elite dwellings and probable retainer housing. The site plan was modified at least once during the imperial era, when a standardized monumental style was imposed and sandstone walls were replaced by finely worked dacite incorporated into adobe walls. Ann Kendall and her colleagues suggest that the changes generally fit the historical account describing a major renovation during the imperial era (Kendall *et al.* 1992: 231). Soon after the Spanish invasion, Gonzalo Pizarro found Wiraqocha Inka's mummified remains and a golden treasure there. He looted the tomb and burned the mummy, but Wiraqocha Inka's caretakers gathered the ashes into an urn. They guarded them along with his personal idol until 1559, when Polo seized them in his campaign to root out vestiges of idolatry and to destroy enduring symbols of imperial power (Sarmiento 2007: 104; Kendall *et al.* 1992: 191).

Another impressive early estate was constructed at Tipón. In the Killke era, prior to the rise of the imperial Incas, the site was a fortified settlement high above the abandoned valley floor between the Cuzco and Lucre basins (Bauer and Covey 2004: 86–7). One of the very few defensively constructed late prehistoric sites in the area, it was reportedly captured by Wiraqocha Inka, who subsequently converted it into a personal holding. Colonists were installed in the valley lands below to care for cult of the dead Inca and the Sun (La Lone 1985). Tipón boasts some of the most beautiful canals and terraces of any of the royal manors. Water was channeled to the site from three intakes in the Río Pukara, about 1.4 km away, and distributed throughout the 200 ha garden-like manor (Wright *et al.* 2006). Among the main constructions at the estate were residential structures, storage buildings, and a temple sector.

Several of the most spectacular Inca sites have been identified as royal estates of Pachakuti. Most prominent among them are Pisac, Ollantaytambo, and Machu Picchu (see box). Pisac lies about 30 km north of Cuzco, on a rocky promontory extending into the Urubamba valley (Angles Vargas 1970). The site's principal architecture consists of a set of residential structures and a temple complex built around a large carved rock. The slopes below the settlement are graced with splendid terraces that cascade hundreds of meters downslope (plate 7.6). Across a ravine to the west, the face of an escarpment is pocked with scores of looted tombs, mute witness to the pillaging of the empire. Ollantaytambo, 40 km downriver, exhibits a

Plate 7.6   Terraces at Pachakuti's royal estate called Pisac, about 30 km east of Cuzco.

striking combination of regular layout and architecture tailored to rugged land forms (Gasparini and Margolies 1980: 68–75; Gibaja 1984; Hollowell 1987; Protzen 1993). The site was a planned residential settlement with palaces, religious and defensive structures, storehouses, roads and bridges, terraces, and waterworks (Protzen 1993: 14). Much of the site lies on an alluvial fan straddling the Río Patakancha just above its confluence with the Río Urubamba. The settlement was protected by forts and high terraces, while entry was channeled across bridges and through narrow gates. Its center is dominated by a trapezoidal street grid on the alluvial fan, which still forms the plan for the modern town. The town blocks are formed by enclosed *kancha* compounds, consisting of up to six one-room buildings facing onto an open patio (figure 7.5). Canals running through the streets provided fresh water and may have carried away effluent.

To the west, a grand set of terraces cascades down a steep hill, where the complexes now called the Fortaleza and its Temple of the Sun were erected (plate 7.7). The architecture on this spur is the subject of controversy among Inca scholars. The six exquisitely worked vertical ashlars of pink rhyolite that form the centerpiece of the temple are unique in Inca construction

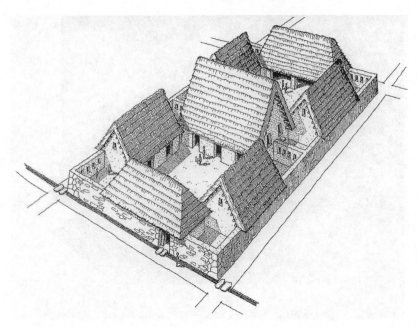

Figure 7.5   A *kancha*: residential compound of houses facing onto a courtyard.
Source: reproduced by permission of V. Lee.

Plate 7.7   The Fortaleza and Temple of the Sun at Ollantaytambo.

Plate 7.8 Pink rhyolite monoliths in the unfinished temple complex at Ollantaytambo.

(plate 7.8). They contain design details that recall masonry at Tiahuanaco, the great city on Lake Titicaca's southern margin. Some scholars contend that the reported use of Qolla masons, from the Titicaca basin, to build the site (Sarmiento 2007: 138) and the similarities in construction and design details (e.g., the step-fret; T-shaped sockets for binding stones together) show that the Inca cut-stone style was a direct outgrowth of Tiahuanaco's architecture (Gasparini and Margolies 1980; Hollowell 1987; Pärssinen in press). Others doubt that the link was so clear, citing stylistic differences and an apparent break of several centuries between the demise of Tiahuanaco and the rise of Cuzco (Protzen 1993). Whatever the cultural derivation, the finest stereotomy at the site is found at the temple and in nearby walls.

The treatment of the nearby landscape epitomizes the Incas' efforts toward socially and physically ordering the entire space within which they lived. Among the occupations outside the core urban complex, Kosiba and Bauer (2013: 82) found a fine-grained hierarchy of residential siting. The people in the fancier housing lived closer to more highly valued places and lines of sight, like "productive maize land, glaciated peaks, and spaces for collective memory." Within the surrounding settlements, lines of sight, entry to plazas, and other movements were controlled by construction of walls and constricted routes of transit. The intent was to filter access to high status activities. They note that such efforts to emphasize exclusion typified the architecture of royal estates, both in their cores and nearby areas, throughout the heartland.

In the physical domain, Ollantaytambo also exemplifes their bent for modifying the terrain and adapting their designs to existing land forms. Taking advantage of a meander in the Urubamba, engineers diverted the water flow from the left bank to the right and back again and also channelized the Río Patakancha where it flowed through the site (Protzen 1993: 22). The eleven expansive terraces that face the settlement gracefully blended in with the natural slope of the piedmont. In 1536, their steep stone walls helped to repel the Spanish expedition sent against Manqo Inka. The Incas even used the waterworks in their defense, as they flooded the valley where the Spaniards were attacking, handing them their only real defeat of the campaign (P. Pizarro 1986: 146–8).

Ollantaytambo's architecture also exemplifies the paradoxes of archaeology in the heartland. Although *panaqa* ostensibly had an inviolate right to control their estates, both Pachakuti and Thupa Inka Yupanki were said to have ordered the construction of important buildings. Hollowell's and Protzen's work indicates that the settlement's design was changed over time. There were at least three major construction phases in the imperial era, and structures were still being erected when the Spanish conquest put an abrupt cessation to the labors. The architecture contains at least seven kinds of stone, each seemingly worked in a distinct style with differing degrees of craftsmanship; rarely was more than one kind of stone used in a single cut-stone building. Over time, early structures were dismantled, and many stones were reworked, repositioned, or both (Hollowell 1987). The implications of the evidence are the subject of lively debate, but it is clear that the design of an estate was not inviolate, even when the property pertained to the founding emperor and his *panaqa*.

Machu Picchu

The magnificent site of Machu Picchu is justly celebrated as one of the archaeological splendors of the world (Bingham 1930; K. Wright and Valencia Zegarra 2000; Burger and Salazar 2004).[6] Although much of its stonework was beautifully crafted, it is the spectacular setting high on cliffs in the jungle and the graceful melding of land forms and architecture that impart such grandeur to the complex for today's visitors (plate 7.9). The Incas almost surely also appreciated the setting's aesthetics, even if we do not have any direct testimony to that effect. To understand the place of the settlement in their era, however, we need to place it in the context of their politics and their understanding of how human and non-human cultures interacted.

Plate 7.9   Setting of Machu Picchu, view from the Sun Gate. Source: reproduced by permission of Darryl Wilkinson.

Public perceptions to the contrary, Machu Picchu was not a last-line citadel on the jungle frontier. The Incas built numerous sites and paved roads well beyond the site, the last ones as far as 100 km down river into the forested slopes. Scholars now accept that the settlement formed part of a warm-lands estate held by the descendants of the founding imperial ruler, Pachakuti. That view is largely based on a sixteenth-century legal document brought to light by John Rowe in 1990 (Rowe 1990b). While the settlement itself is not specifically called *Machu Picchu* ("old hill"), its description and the use of the name *Picchu* for a place in that area in several documents leave little doubt as to the identity of the ruins. *Picchu* itself was identified in Rowe's document as a valley bottom property of Pachakuti and his descendent kin group, *Iñaqa panaqa*. Scholars infer that the site on the hill above was part of the same extended holding (Salazar 2004: 26). Sarmiento's chronicle, among others, suggests that Pachakuti had the settlement built to commemorate his conquest of the region, just as he had done with other estates, such as Ollantaytambo (Salazar 2004: 26; Niles in press). If we can take that assessment at face value, then Machu Picchu was established as both a royal retreat and a material statement of domination.

Rediscovery

In 1536, the nominal Inca ruler, Manco Inka, fled Cuzco and set up a new royal capital in the forested slopes to the north in an area called Vilcabamba. While it is known today as the neo-Inca state, the Incas saw their new home as the legitimate continuation of their empire. In fact, the third ruler, Titu Kusi (2005), vainly petitioned the Spanish king for recognition as co-equals. The independent Inca polity was a persistent thorn in the side of Spanish rule for thirty-six years, despite alternating attempts to conquer the holdouts and to lure them into peaceful fealty. Finally, the last independent Inca ruler, Tupac Amaru, fell to the Spaniards and was executed in Cuzco in 1572, by the order of Viceroy Toledo.

The royal settlements of Vilcabamba were largely abandoned and soon began to recede under the forest canopy. For centuries, few people paid attention to finding the "Lost City of the Incas," as the last capital came to be known. Then in 1865, the adventurer Antonio Raimondi identified Choquequirau (plate 7.10), another estate in the region, as the last Inca court (Lee 1999: 71). Little about the site actually fit the descriptions left by the Spaniards who had seen the capital, however, and so the search continued. Machu Picchu came to the world's attention when Hiram Bingham III,[7] a young historian from Yale, made the electric announcement in 1912 that he had finally found the lost Inca capital.

The discovery was years in the making. While in South America in 1908 for a scientific conference, Bingham had visited Choquequirau. Although impressed by what he had seen, he was not persuaded that it

Plate 7.10 Choquequirau: royal estate northwest of Cuzco. Source: reproduced by permission of Darryl Wilkinson.

was Vilcabamba. Taken by the spirit of adventure, he arranged an expedition to search for the elusive city. After some days of travel through difficult terrain, he and his Peruvian military custodian were guided up to Machu Picchu by Melchor Arteaga, a young local farmer on July 24, 1911. Bingham was not expecting to find much, and did not even bother to pack a lunch, thinking that he would be back down the hill after a brief visit. In short order, however, he was astonished by the architectural splendor that was revealed to him (plate 7.11).

> Without the slightest expectation of finding anything more interesting than the stone face terraces … I entered the untouched forest beyond, and suddenly found myself in a maze of beautiful granite houses! … Under a carved rock the little boy showed me a cave beautifully lined with the finest cut stone…. To my astonishment I saw that this wall and its adjoining semicircular temple over the cave were as the finest stone work in the far-famed Temple of the Sun in Cuzco. (Bingham quoted in Salazar 2004: 24)

Plate 7.11   Machu Picchu, probable royal estate of the emperor Pachakuti, in the lower Urubamba river drainage. Source: reproduced by permission of Darryl Wilkinson.

Despite his remarkable discovery, Bingham's expedition did not stop at Machu Picchu. They continued even deeper into the forests, visiting Vitcos (Rosaspata) and Espíritu Pampa, two neo-Inca royal settlements much farther along. Bingham's initial view was that Machu Picchu was the origin place of the Incas, in part because he took the Temple of the Three Windows to be the mythical origin caves at Pacariqtambo (Salazar 2004: 24; plate 7.12; see chapter 2). Based on some more faulty reasoning – and maybe wishful thinking because of the beauty of the setting – he later concluded that Machu Picchu was the last Inca capital. Scholars today, in contrast, accept Espíritu Pampa as that site (Lee 1999; see chapter 14 here).

Although he is widely credited for discovering Machu Picchu, Bingham's actual contribution lay more in initially publicizing its existence and then in assembling an interdisciplinary research team. Over the next few years (1912–16), they cleared and excavated large areas, in addition to studying the local environment. The reports from

Plate 7.12   Temple of the Three Windows at Machu Picchu. Source: reproduced by permission of Darryl Wilkinson.

those expeditions – lectures, articles, and books – quickly catapulted
the site into a prominence that it has never lost. As is so often the case
when a discovery is made public, however, several other people (or
their descendants speaking on their behalf) seem to have gotten there
earlier, in the late nineteenth or early twentieth centuries (see Mould de
Pease 2001).[8] Among them were a British missionary, Thomas Payne,
a German engineer, J. M. von Hassel, and a German treasure-seeker,
Augusto Bern. Moreover, Agustín Lizárraga, Gabino Sánchez, and
Enrique Palma, three Peruvians from the region, had visited the site
on July 14, 1901. In 1913, Bingham (in Burger and Salazar 2004: 13)
himself noted that a "local muleteer" named Lizarraga had left a graffito
on a wall marking his visit in 1902. Because an 1874 map shows the
name Machu Picchu in the area and Bingham's own papers contained
a copy of Berns' governmental authorization for exploration, as well
as an ascription of discovery to Lizárraga, scholars conclude that he
was well aware of other people who had walked the same path earlier

(Mould de Pease 2001). All of this, of course, sidesteps the fact that the site had never really been lost. People living in the area were well aware of its existence, but they were not in the adventure, mining, or academics businesses, so no one in any professional domain credited their knowledge with more than a nod.

Machu Picchu in the Landscape

Just as Cuzco made best sense to the Incas in its relationship to the cosmos and the landscape, so did Machu Picchu. Several architectural features, described below, were oriented to places on the horizon, such as mountain peaks, and to astronomical observations. Similarly, the Incas invested a great deal of effort in venerating – or perhaps bounding the powers of – certain features of the landscape, especially stone outcrops, caves and water. The three most significant features of Machu Picchu's setting were the mountainous landscape, the sky above, and the river below (Reinhard 2007: 21–41). One of the most prominent and revered peaks on the southern horizon is Salcantay, sometimes considered to be the brother of Ausangate, the only higher peak in the Cuzco region. The two summits lie almost exactly at 180° from one another with respect to Cuzco. Mount Verónica (*Waqaywillka*), which lies due east of Machu Picchu, was understood to be the female partner to Salcantay in the Colonial period (Reinhard 2007: 27). When viewed from Machu Picchu, the Southern Cross, one of the most important constellations in the Inca cosmos, traversed Salcantay, rising on one side and setting on the other (Reinhard 2007: 28). Moreover, the entire Milky Way forms an arc over Salcantay, intersecting the horizon line at the points of the December solstice sunrise and sunset (Reinhard 2007: 30). From the vantage point of the Intiwatana stone (see below) in the center of Machu Picchu's temple complex, the point of the solstice sunset is directly behind Pumasillo, another high peak on the horizon (Reinhard 2007: 34).

The third prominent landscape feature is the river below, called the Vilcanota in its upper course and the Urubamba in its lower.[9] The river was thought to be a terrestrial mirror of the course of the Milky Way. Reinhard (2007: 51) favors a translation of the Aymara word *Vilcanota* as the phrase "house of the sun" or "house where the sun was born," in deference to its rising in the east as seen from Cuzco. *Urubamba*

(Quechua) may be glossed as "worm plain," perhaps because of its sinuous path. The path of the river envelops Machu Picchu and Huayna Picchu, providing witness to the watercourse's importance in the manor's positioning.

With respect to the site's position in the built landscape, numerous features come into play: the road and nearby settlements, observation points, and apparent sanctuaries. The main access into the settlement from Cuzco is an elegant, paved road (plate 7.9). It would have taken about three days to traverse the distance between the two royal locales. Entry to the estate was guarded by a single gate, today called the Gate of the Sun, through which any travelers would have had to travel. In 1999, another road into and out of the site was found on the steep, terraced, eastern slope (K. Wright and Valencia Zegarra 2000). That road, containing well-built staircases, would likely have provided a link between Machu Picchu and the Vilcabamba region, perhaps through the coca estates below. There were actually three separate routes from Machu Picchu into Vilcabamba (Lee 2010), so the notion that the estate lay at the end of the line is given lie to simply on that basis.

Many other Inca sites were erected nearby. Among them are the valley-margin installation upstream at Patallacta, which scholars often consider to be part of the same extensive estate as Machu Picchu (Kendall 1984). A series of small high-slope or peak sites dots the nearby landscape, some of which may have been shrines. Among them are Wiñay Wayna, Llactapata, Cerro San Miguel, and Palcay (Reinhard 2007). Lee (2010) has also shown that a string of sites running around a loop from Choquequirao to Machu Picchu are sequentially intervisible. He suggests, following Garcilaso (1966: 328), that they may have served as part of an extensive rapid signaling network that used smoke and fire to transmit messages.

The Settlement's Layout

Machu Picchu's design illustrates the range of activities pursued at royal retreats. The core of the estate contains three main sectors: two central residential sectors bordering the main plaza; extensive stone-faced terraces; and a temple complex. Above the main architecture on a sugarloaf is the terracing and likely ceremonial architecture of Huayna Picchu.

On the back side of Huayna Picchu is an elegantly carved cave. The stone quarry, from which most of the granite blocks to erect the buildings were mined, lies adjacent to the main architecture on the west.

Much of the dense architectural sector on the northeast side of the site and the sector bordering the plaza on the southwest were probably temporary residences. Four compounds of the finest architecture were likely dedicated to elite housing, when they came to visit during the cold weather in Cuzco. The royal compound, which Bingham called the King's Group, lay in the southwest sector of the residential architecture, set apart physically from the other domestic architecture (Salazar 2004: 30). It is not especially large, in keeping with the Inca practice of not investing heavily in large-scale palatial structures on their country estates. Even so, it was provided with first access to the springwater that the canal system fed into the settlement, and lay adjacent to the curved Torreón (see below). Three other elite compounds lay across the plaza, adjacent to one another. Bingham named two of them the Ingenuity Group and the Three-Doors Group, while the third is now known as the Upper Group. They are enclosed by high walls with double-jamb entrances, and contain a variety of interior constructions, including gabled-roof structures and shrines. Bingham thought that they could be associated with distinct royal kin groups, but it is more likely that different families belonging to the same royal kin group occupied the compounds. At a maximum, they could probably have housed a few score people at a time. In contrast, the sets of one-room buildings facing onto enclosed patios on terraces were more likely the residences of retainer personnel.

A great deal of the effort put into Machu Picchu went into what we think of today as religious constructions. The principal complex lay north of the royal palace. It contained the Temple of the Three Windows and the Main Temple, and at the apex of a small hill, the carved *intiwatana* stone ("place where the Sun is tied"). Much debate has circulated around the possible uses of the *intiwatana* for astronomical observations, but astronomers and archaeologists have not reached a resolution satisfactory to all. Other constructed or modified features, however, clearly were intended to be used in conjunction with the landscape for astronomical and adoratory purposes. The curved wall of the beautifully constructed Torreón has two windows that may have been placed for that purpose (plate 7.13). The east-facing window provided a view to a notch in the horizon that lined up with the June solstice. A plumb dropped from the middle of the window would have cast a shadow precisely along a cut stone in the building interior. The south-facing window would have provide an alignment with the sighting of the Pleiades star group over the horizon, after its annual thirty-seven-day absence. That group's reappearance in August was the signal for the official inception of the agricultural year. Beneath the upper structure lies a small cave, whose interior surfaces were both dressed and inset with finely carved ashlar masonry. The precision and grace with which the newly introduced stone was set into the prepared bedrock suggests that the Incas thought of the act as one of grafting vital materials together (Dean 2010a; plate 7.14).

Plate 7.13 Torreón within the royal sector at Machu Picchu. Source: reproduced by permission of Darryl Wilkinson.

A number of other elements of the site graphically illustrate the Incas' engagement with stone. As MacLean (1986: 72) has pointed out, the architects designed many structures expressly to incorporate natural outcrops. The most striking are the carved rocks whose profiles

Plate 7.14   Melding of worked bedrock and inset blocks below the Torreón.

mimic that of Mount Yanantín, a powerful presence on the eastern horizon (plates 5.1a, b). Numerous other outcrops were modified, enclosed, or both. The so-called Temple of the Condor complex, which integrates shaped bedrock and laid ashlar masonry (so that a condor may be envisioned from one vantage point), is another beautiful example of the melding of natural and built stonework. It lies just above the smoothly worked "slide" outcrop, both of them in the northeastern residential sector (see R. Wright and Valencia Zegarra 2001: 84–7). Bingham (1913: 471) immediately recognized the reverence with which the Incas treated the stones. Enclosing and dressing the stone probably reflects both the Incas' esteem for the parallel society that inhabited the landscape and their interest in civilizing that world.

Construction Engineering: Water and Terracing

The spectacular nature of the visible architecture aside, some of the most remarkable aspects of Machu Picchu can be found in the site's construction engineering. While the central part of the site today gives the appearance of having been built on a relatively flat surface, that perception is the product of an enormous investment in modification of the land surface. The central part of the estate appears to have been largely designed and executed as part of a single plan, although the plaza contains some subsurface architecture that indicates either an early modification or an effort to stabilize the ground. The late director of the site, Dr. Alfredo Valencia Zegarra, has classified the stonework into eighteen distinct types. They range in degrees of preparation, dressing, and installation, from simple fieldstone (*pirka*) constructions to the finally cut ashlar masonry for which the royal architecture is so justly renowned. One of the most remarkable aspects of the construction is the fluid melding of outcrops, boulders, and bedrock with superimposed walls. The effect – and probably the intent – was to unify the human building with the living features of the land.

K. Wright and Valencia Zegarra (2000: 68) suggest that the designers took water management into account as their initial consideration, to ensure that the royal residence was the first to receive fresh water from the main supply. They deduce that the placement of the royal sector may have followed a study of the way in which water would be brought to the site. As noted just above, the royal bath is the first location where water arrives at the settlement, after being conveyed 749 m from a seep-age spring. The water that could be carried was about twice that which was needed for the daily demands of 300 people. Giving the royal sector precedence in access to pure water would likely have been a signifi-cant element in the site's design, but that bath is just the first of sixteen sequential fountains at the settlement running down a staircase adja-cent to the residential sector (plate 13.4). Each fountain was enclosed and could be blocked at the exit.

One of the most arresting features of Machu Picchu is the array of stone-faced terraces that both stabilized the central part of the site and provided land surfaces for agriculture. The terraces are not extensive, covering only 4.9 ha; they could have produced enough food to sustain just a fraction of the population, perhaps 15–20 percent of the permanent residents (K. Wright and Valencia Zegarra 2000). It is likely that the valley bottom lands and nearby settlements actually con-tributed most of the food to both the permanent and visiting populace.

The terrace construction, based on multiple layers of differently sized gravels, provided effective filtration and resistance to damage from earthquakes. Even so, some 129 drain outlets were needed to moderate the effects of the ~1,950 mm of rain that falls on the site every year. Despite their construction skills, the Incas still ran into problems with landslides and wall slumping. Their troubles are most notable at the main temple, which apparently was not completed because of settling and other problems with the foundations (K. Wright and Valencia Zegarra 2000: 74).

Who Lived at Machu Picchu?

Machu Picchu is often described as a city in the jungle, but in reality the main settlement could only support about 750 people on a permanent basis (Burger 2004). Some estimates of the resident populace put it at no more than 300 (K. Wright and Valencia Zegarra 2000: 21). Who were they? We should start by acknowledging that we cannot treat the populace who were buried there as a reliable cross-section of the settlement's occupants. Most of the people entombed at Machu Picchu were probably support staff and families, not society's top echelon. Cuzco lay only about three days' walk away, so any elites who died while at the site would likely have been taken elsewhere for final treatment.

The osteological expert on Bingham's expedition, George Eaton, judged that the majority of the skeletons recovered from cave burials during the early excavations were from young women or effeminate men. By his estimate, there were about four times as many females as males among the skeletons they unearthed. Unfortunately, Eaton was a mammalian expert, not a human osteologist, and he did not have access to the kind of comparative collections on which scientists rely today, so his evaluations seem to have been flawed (Burger 2004). Even so, Bingham enthusiastically promoted the idea that the settlement's principal residents were from a female religious order, the *aqllakuna*. They were girls coming of age, who lived in sequestered quarters and performed duties for the state. They spent much of their time making cloth and brewing and serving beer, before becoming partners in high-status marriages. The notion that Machu Picchu was largely occupied by "Chosen Women" (or even "Vestal Virgins") remains popular today, largely because of Bingham's salesmanship and the idea's romantic appeal.

John Verano (2003), a leading human osteologist who recently re-analyzed the human remains, tells a different story (see also Burger 2004). He determined that the collection contained a minimum of 174 individuals, distributed across a wide range of ages. Among the mortuary population whose age could be determined were a fetus, twenty people under 15, sixty-seven people of maturity (15–49 years), and fourteen adults of the ripe old age (for the time) of 50+. The ratio of females to males was not 4 : 1, but 1.46 : 1, and a number of the women had given birth. Put together, that information makes the notion of a settlement populated by young virgins hard to sustain.

Both biological and cultural sources of information provide clues as to the people's origins. One approach is based on the idea that people are what they eat and drink, so the composition of a person's teeth and bones should provide clues as to where he or she lived at various stages of life.[10] It turns out that the dead of Machu Picchu had consumed food and beverages from widely separated locations. In a study of the tooth enamel composition of seventy-four adults, Bethany Turner and her colleagues found that people from both arid coastal and wetter highland environments had been interred at the site (Turner *et al.* 2009). More specifically, the dental and skeletal chemistry "*tentatively* suggest that the Machu Picchu population was comprised primarily of individuals from the southern Peruvian/northern Chilean coast and the Lake Titicaca region, with some possibly from the northern Peruvian highlands, the coast of northern Peru and/or southern Ecuador, and highland Bolivia beyond the Titicaca region" (Turner *et al.* 2009: 330).

Similar results arose from study of the cranial deformations of the Machu Picchu dead (Verano 2003) and from analysis of the DNA of bones from nearby sites that are assumed to be part of the same extended estate (Shinoda *et al.* 2006; Shinoda in press). Both archaeologists and the early Spanish writers have observed that people in different parts of the Andes altered the shapes of their infants' heads in distinct ways, most likely as a kind of beautification. When Verano looked at the head deformations of the dead at Machu Picchu, he found that people from diverse coastal and highland locations had been represented. For its part, the DNA of the seventy-seven skeletons analyzed from Inca sites in the Machu Picchu Archaeological Park (largely from nearby Patall-acta) suggested that they were most similar genetically to people from the southern Peruvian highlands and Lake Titicaca region. The DNA evidence may be interpreted as providing insight into deep genetic history, as well as recent population resettlement. In either case, it seems safe to infer that the people of the estate complex were largely from areas to the south of Cuzco.

The burial artifacts add a complementary kind of insight. Lucy Salazar's (2007) analysis of the site's grave lots shows that several cultural groups were represented. The tombs themselves, located in 104 caves and rock shelters, were modest in their construction and contents. The corpses were interred in a typical Inca style, instead of their home societies' styles. The bodies were left above ground, so that they could easily breathe and be cared for with food and drink, as they were still thought to be living beings (Salazar 2007: 174). The kinds of artifacts recovered and the nature of stresses on the skeletons suggest that the workers were not involved in heavy agricultural labor, but were more likely artisans with a special focus on metallurgy. Salazar's (2007: 171) study of the artifact styles shows that over half of the dead had come from areas surrounding Lake Titicaca (Colla, Lupaqa, Pacajes). The Chimú of the Peruvian north coast and the Kañari of highland Ecuador were also well represented, and people from Chachas (central north Peru) and elsewhere were also interred. Significantly, the number of people from the Cuzco area proper was quite small. Salazar interprets the evidence to mean that the royal family that developed and owned the estate most likely populated it with service personnel brought in from various places in the empire, on either a temporary or permanent basis. Overall, then, her cultural research and the biological studies support the same conclusions.

The people who lived and died at the site by and large enjoyed good health (Verano 2003; see also Burger 2004: 88–94). They show little evidence of the arthritis common to people who work at hard labor, while the growth disruptions produced by severe childhood illnesses or food stresses were also missing. No skeleton has any indication of a skull fracture, a common occurrence in the Andes among people involved in combat. However, the frequency of dental caries points to a carbohydrate-rich diet, probably including maize for 60–70 percent or more for their food (Burger 2004: 88–94). In contrast to patterns in central Peru, where males had more access to maize (e.g., Hastorf 1990), both sexes at Machu Picchu had equal access to the prestigious food. George Miller's analysis of the sparse animal bone suggests that over 95 percent of the meat consumed at the site came from the llama and alpaca (Miller 2003, cited in Burger 2004: 92).

Machu Picchu Today and in the Future

Today, Machu Picchu is recognized as one of the world's patrimonial treasures, by both cultural heritage professionals and the public. Protected since 1981 as a Peruvian Historical Sanctuary, it was named to the UNESCO World Heritage list in 1983. And, in 2007, it was chosen as one of the New Seven Wonders of the World in an internet poll.[11] Even while Bingham was conducting his work, Machu Picchu became a focal point for debate over national and international interests in human patrimony, particularly in the context of countries that had once been European colonies (e.g., Salvatore 2003). One point of contention came to a head recently when the Peruvian government lodged a claim against Yale University, with the objective of repatriating the collections that Bingham had taken to New Haven. After some give-and-take over the ethics and legalities of custody, thousands of objects were returned to Peru by the Peabody Museum (Swanson 2008–9).

The site's splendor and popularity are a double-edged sword. More than half a million visitors travel to see the site annually, providing the core of a supremely important tourist industry for Peru and especially the Cuzco region. Even with increasing custodial care to limit access, to provide improved services, and to mitigate the impact of accumulated trash and other waste, the site will suffer the depredations of heavy use. In part to ameliorate the effects, the National Institute of Culture has been promoting tourism to other Inca sites in the general vicinity. Even so, if sufficient measures for protection cannot be fully implemented, the magnificent patrimony of the greater Inca heartland is threatened with permanent damage. Setting the question of tourist use aside, Machu Picchu lies in a region that is active tectonically. The dangers posed by earthquakes and rainfall-induced landslides are real, despite the ingenuity of the site's construction engineers. Many scholars from the world's scientific community have focused their attentions on the attendant problems, and the results for general stability seem reassuring (e.g., K. Wright and Valencia Zegarra 2000; Vilímek *et al.* 2007). Nonetheless, not even the best intentions and efforts will be able to completely stabilize architecture at a micro-level in such a volatile landscape.

Thupa Inka Yupanki's best-known estate was a rural villa at Chinchero about 30 km northwest of Cuzco, studied by a Spanish team in the 1960s and 1970s (Alcina Franch *et al.* 1976) and more recently by Stella Nair (2007). The relatively high elevation of the settlement, about 3,400 m, afforded a less hospitable climate than the estates in the Urubamba valley. Even so, it benefited from a microclimate in a small ravine, which was more favorable for agriculture than other nearby locations at the same elevation. Like other sites described as manors, Chinchero was a planned settlement, containing a large central plaza and a platform mound and enhanced with both agricultural and residential terraces. Besides the royal residence, the estate included compounds that Diez de Betanzos (1996: 159) said were built to house Cuzco's nobility when they came to visit. Chinchero was apparently entirely remodeled in the imperial era, as the fill deposits from landscape architecture contain quantities of Inca polychrome ceramics (Rivera 1976: 28). In 1540, the site was burned by Manqo II, but was later reoccupied and rebuilt during the Colonial era.

Wayna Qhapaq's main estate in Yucay was centered at the residence called Quispiguanca. The valley enjoys a reputation as a pleasant location, as its floor lies at 2,850–2,910 m, some 500–600 m below Cuzco. The estate is celebrated for its arrays of terraces, but most of the hillsides were actually farmed as sloping fields and lynchets (Donkin 1979: 111–14; Farrington 1995: 57). Chosen by Francisco Pizarro as one of his *encomiendas*, the estate became the subject of contentious land claims in the early Colonial era, records of which provide many details about its nature (Villanueva 1971: 37–9, 51–3; Rowe 1990b: 144). The manor was a place of recreation that existed only because of major feats of Inca ecological engineering. Much of the estate consisted of tracts claimed from swamp through channelization of the main river and several tributaries (Farrington 1983). The holdings included forty named parcels where maize, sweet potatoes, and the warm-weather crops of coca, chili pepper, cotton, and peanuts were cultivated. It included woods that were home to deer, while fish and reeds were grown in an artificial pond. Several of those plants are from environments that are lower, warmer, and more humid than those naturally found in Yucay. Their presence suggests that the Incas were aware of how to manipulate terracing systems to create micro-environments, and used their heat- and moisture-retaining capacities to devise a mini-montaña near Cuzco for the emperor's pleasure. The estate also boasted a facility, called Maras, that produced salt from a saline spring and which is still in extensive production today.

The architecture of Quispiguanca is modest in comparison to the estates of other emperors, perhaps because Wayna Qhapaq's most elaborate lodgings were in Tumipampa, Ecuador, far removed from Cuzco. The manor (10.4 ha) contains three sectors on a series of terraces and an alluvial fan: an agricultural area, a structural or residential zone, and a lakeside house complex (Farrington 1995). Like other rural retreats, the settlement was obviously executed according to a plan. It exhibits a large central plaza, a platform mound, and residential structures, with a large enclosing wall, along with several sets of nearby storehouses (Niles 1999). One building contains fine polygonal, fitted stonework, as do some of the terrace and enclosing walls. Although it was not nearly as ornate as some of the sites described earlier, Quispiguanca displays some distinctive architectural details of the kind typically reserved for royal constructions, such as human-sized wall niches and elegant staircases in the terraces.

On a plain opposite Quispiguanca, just above the Sacred Valley, lie the terraces of Moray (plate 7.15). Enthusiastic travel writers who salt their archaeological descriptions with adjectives like *mysterious, enigmatic* and *unique* can almost be forgiven if they apply them to this locale. Nothing else in the Inca world is quite like it. The site consists mostly of three sets of stone-faced, concentric terraces built into natural sinkholes (*muyu*). Like a number of other important archaeological sites, such as the Nasca Lines, Moray is best appreciated from the air. Of all of the images from the Shippee–Johnson photographic expedition of 1931, their Moray shots were the most striking for the immediacy of international discovery and the appreciation of an entirely new view.

Recently, Wright *et al.* (2011) detailed Moray's engineering and agricultural capacities. The largest terrace group (A) is monumental: almost 120 m in diameter, with a southern oval extension that reaches an additional 100 m, and a maximum depth of 36 m. At least twelve terraces ascend the slopes, most of which have recently been restored by the National Institute

Plate 7.15 Sinkhole terraces at Moray, in the hills on the south side of the Sacred Valley.

of Culture. The smallest, bottom terrace is about 32 m across. Two other terrace arrays (B, C) are smaller and less elegantly constructed, with six terraces each, and a much smaller, fourth sinkhole (D) contained only two terraces. While some impressive water features were present, such as an aqueduct, the terraces themselves were not irrigated, perhaps because the site was still under construction when it was abandoned. Overall, only about 5.5 ha could have been used for agriculture, with a best annual production of about 8.7 tons of maize. That output could have supported only about forty-five people for a year, so clearly food production for a significant population was not Moray's main purpose (Earls and Cervantes in press).

Then what was the point? For both local residents and professional archaeologists, ritual use is a perennial favorite.[12] While that phrase is a handy fallback when no other explanation springs to mind, we should not dismiss it out of hand. The Incas often integrated the human and non-human aspects of the world by melding modified land surfaces, watercourses, and stone. A second suggestion has been agricultural experimentation, since the temperature and humidity regime potentially varied from the bottom to the top of the terrace sets. Because of problems of water management (e.g., drainage), soil salinity, and adverse slopes on some terraces, Wright *et al.* (2011) conclude that intensive agriculture was not feasible. They favor ritual use, in part because of the unusual design and the array of carved stones found in and around the settlement. A third idea is that it was part of a royal estate, most likely that of Wayna Qhapaq at nearby Quispiguanca. The faces of the terraces contain step-tenons, for example, which were reserved for royal estates.

Earls and Cervantes (in press) more adventurously suggest that it was a weather/climate station. By tracking the passages of shadows associated with the June solstice sunrise, they deduce that the terrace layout could have been a solar calendric device. They also infer that the site's microclimatic variations could have been read as indicators of macroclimatic trends in the heartland. While the argument is intriguing, my own take is a little less adventurous. I judge that the site was probably part of a royal holding, which often contained sectors dedicated to ceremonially focused agriculture and interactions with the landscape. The produce itself may have had special meaning, like that from the Sun's field at Sausero or from the Copacabana maize plots, but we cannot make that inference securely with present knowledge.

Royal Coca Estates

Of all the Andean crops, only coca could compete with maize for equal cultural stature. The leaf lay at the center of a host of activities that resonated throughout life from the smallest family relationship to the grandest acts of the Inca royalty. In her study of the traditional community of Sonqo, near Cuzco, Catherine Allen (2002) details how exchange of the leaf permeates daily activity. Acceptance of an offering of a packet of coca, for example, signals approval of a marriage proposal. Exchange marks social acceptance among friends, and reinforces relationships of inequality between social statuses. Coca is invariably a central part of any offering to the ancestors, the mountains, and the earth. No other substance bonds the social fabric with greater constancy or necessity than coca.

Since a comparable value was placed on the leaf in prehistory, it is small wonder that the Incas coveted access to productive fields. No land suitable to growing the crop lay within the pre-state Inca homeland, however, so gaining a foothold in the appropriate ecozone must have been

Plate 7.16   Coca estate in the Amaybamba drainage, north of Cuzco, now used for tea cultivation. Source: reproduced by permission of Darryl Wilkinson.

an important goal for the nascent expansionist polity. The best climate lies at 1,200–1,900 m above sea level, in strips along both sides of the Andes. Fortunately for the Incas, good lands on the eastern slopes lay only about 100 km away from Cuzco. During the imperial era, the royal families installed hundreds of colonist families in small estates in places like Paucartambo and Amaybamba (plate 7.16). In the latter area, which lies over the mountains beyond (north of) Machu Picchu, workers built small farming settlements every couple of kilometers, clearing out the jungle underbrush to make room for the coca bushes (Wilkinson 2013). Those lands were the focus of familial competition, as Wayna Qhapaq's kin vied with other royalty for the limited surfaces that were congenial to growing the crop. The mark of royal estate construction can be seen most clearly at the site of Wamanmarka, which boasts double-jamb doorways, an *usnu* platform, and stone-faced terraces with step tenons. All of those construction details highlight the presence of royal design and ownership, as seen at higher elevation estates such as Ollantaytambo and Pisaq.

Summary

Overall, the royal estates exemplify elite life in the heartland during the imperial era. Their designs, which modified and adapted to natural features, symbolize an intensive interaction between humanity and the powers of the cosmos. They epitomize how prime resources were converted into private domains held first by the ruler and, after his death, nominally held in a trust for his reverence. On an empire-wide scale, the resources committed to the estates were not especially great, but the manors exemplify how an endogamous and exclusionary upper class concentrated power and wealth at the empire's heart.

Notes

1   A new book by Ian Farrington (2013), which was in production at the time of writing the present volume, promises to assemble the disparate array of evidence on prehispanic Cuzco.

2   An excellent description of the character of Inca Cuzco may be found in Bauer (2004: 107–137). The present summary covers many of the same points, in distilled form.

3   Rostworowski (1999: 50) conversely suggests that the name arose from the Quechua word *auca*, meaning soldier or enemy.

4   It was called an *usnu*, even though most structures of that name were platforms either in or adjoining the main plazas of Inca settlements.

5   Morris *et al.* (2011: 33–58) provide a fine description of the role of plazas in Inca centers, especially Cuzco and Huánuco Pampa.

6   As with so many things Inca, a number of the best professional and most accurate lay publications on Machu Picchu have appeared recently: e.g., K. Wright and Valencia Zegarra 2000; R. Wright and Valencia Zegarra 2001; Burger and Salazar 2004; Reinhard 2007.

7   Although Bingham is remembered today almost exclusively in the context of his archaeological discoveries, he had a distinguished career in other fields later in life. He was elected Governor of Connecticut, but served only one day, as he won a separate election to serve as a US Senator in 1924 to replace the sitting Senator Frank B. Brandegee, who had died by his own hand. He was re-elected to a full term in 1926, but suffered the same fate as many Republicans in 1932, when he failed to win another term: http://bioguide.congress.gov.

8   Simon Romero wrote a useful review in the *New York Times* in 2008: www.nytimes.com/2008/12/08/world/americas/08peru.html?pagewanted=all (accessed November 15, 2013).

9   I have been assured by various experts on the region that the place where the
     name changes from Vilcanota to Urubamba is either well below Machu Picchu
     or above it. In general, it has seemed to me that people who live and work in
     the Vilcabamba region use a lower-course name change, while those who live
     and work upstream favor a higher change.

10   Broadly speaking, and with many caveats, the chemical composition of the soil
     substrate where food is grown is taken into the plants that both people and their
     food animals eat. Human bone and tooth enamel chemistry can therefore be at
     least partially traced to general locales of origin. Significantly, since the enamel
     from different sets of teeth and from human bone are largely set permanently
     at different ages, it is possible to determine where people came from and if they
     might have moved in their childhood, youth, and adulthood.

11   Sources: UNESCO: http://whc.unesco.org/en/list/274; Seven Wonders: http://
     world.new7wonders.com/new7wonders-of-the-world-page/new7wonders-of
     -the-world/ (accessed November 15, 2013).

12   John Rowe (1944), the earliest professional archaeologist to visit and write
     about the site, took a characteristically cautious view of the site's function,
     reserving judgment pending further research.

Chapter Eight

Inca Ideology

Powers of the Sky and Earth, Past and Present

The Incas, like the rulers of many ancient societies, promoted an official ideology that inspired their actions and gave meaning to their lives. Although the tenets of the state doctrine were intended to justify their supremacy, the beliefs that the Incas professed were filled with the paradoxes that so often arise when dogma and politics collide. For example, while they fervently worshiped the sun, a line of divine kings, and sacred landmarks from their past, they also consciously manipulated the history that legitimized their rule. Royal families reimagined the past for political gain and, at least to the Spaniards, ridiculed claims of divinity by kings belonging to other kin groups, even while they actively interacted with their own animate ancestors. Dead rulers who mediated with the supernatural were a common enough phenomenon in ancient societies, but the Inca royalty enjoyed unusually energetic careers after death. With the help of a coterie of assistants, kings and queens carried on as though life had never left them. Royal mummies ate, drank, urinated, visited one another, sat at councils, and judged weighty questions. The mummies were such potent figures that, at the end of the last dynastic war, Atawallpa's men destroyed the mummy of Thupa Inka Yupanki as part of an effort to efface the existence of the ruler and, by extension, eradicate history. In the official religion, the Sun cult was the dominant institution, but many other beings were also worshiped and there was even competition among the different deities and their adherents. At times, the Incas sacrificed humans to their gods and ancestors, but the scale of offering never approached the tens of thousands who met a similar end in Aztec Mesoamerica. More commonly, Inca practices demanded immense quantities of goods and llamas for sacrifice.

Those practices illustrate that, in order to explain Inca ideology, we have to think about how tradition, history, and politics were interwoven with belief.

The Incas, Second Edition. Terence N. D'Altroy.
© 2015 John Wiley & Sons, Ltd. Published 2015 by John Wiley & Sons, Ltd.

As with so many elements of their culture, Inca religion drew extensively from local and great traditions. Many Andean peoples believed that they shared the cosmos with the animate dead, the gods, and the beings of the landscape. They paid careful heed to those powers through ritual, offering, and prayer – and that was wise, because they saw countless signs that human well-being depended on the other powers' goodwill. The skies were filled with gods, omens, and archetypal animals that controlled the weather, augured the future, and constantly reanimated the living beings on earth. People created mythic cycles, measured time, planned their crops, and celebrated festivals based on their knowledge and thinking about the heavens. On the earth, stones could come alive and people could be petrified, so that a mountain peak, a rocky outcrop, or a spring could be an ancestor or a guardian. In Andean eyes, the different beings co-existed as kin or rivals in a world where history was imprinted on the countryside. Their relationships were negotiable, for humans could worship, consult, supplicate, battle, abduct, or even incapacitate gods, oracles, and shrines. The Incas captured all of these things within a single concept – *waka* – that is, any thing, being, or place with transcendent power.

A great deal of Inca religious practice was dedicated to promoting their own legitimacy as the supreme interface between humanity and all other powers. That contention was captured in two prayers recorded by Molina (2011: 46–7), which began as follows:

> O Merciful Creator! [You] who are at the end of the world, who ordered and deemed it proper for there to be a Lord Inca ...

> O Sun! My Father who said, "Let there be Cuzcos and Tambos." [Let] these sons of yours be victorious and despoilers of all peoples. [I] pray to you so these Incas, your sons, are blessed [and will] not be vanquished or despoiled, but rather will always be victorious, since you made them for this.

Innumerable offerings, rituals, processions, invocations, fasts, and other aspects of religious practice were dedicated to promoting that core idea in Cuzco and the provinces. In support of that end, the organized ideology could call on institutional resources that were second only to those of the state, in the person of the ruler, and may have challenged or even surpassed those of the aristocratic families.

Despite Cuzco's might, religious practice among the general populace still revolved around local beings, shrines, and narratives in the sixteenth century. Most people thought that their founding ancestor had emerged from the landscape at a particular spot, called a *paqarisqa* (hispanicized as *paca-rina*; see Bauer 1991). They worshiped their progenitors through pilgrimages, offerings, and periodic commemoration of funeral rites when they reopened graves to make new offerings. Some graves were even built with conduits so that libations could be offered to the dead. The original ancestor for a local society was often embodied in an idol whose capture or destruction could spell disaster. The Incas took this belief quite literally, for they held ancestral idols hostage in Cuzco so that subjects had to travel there to worship their founders and renew their people's vitality. When challenged, the Incas would publicly whip the idols of rebellious provinces until they bowed to Cuzco's will. Local oracles also abounded. Some, such as Chavín and Pachacamac, may have been consulted by pilgrims for one or two thousand years before the Incas incorporated them into their domain.

The Spanish conquistadores soon recognized that the Incas worshiped the sun and that the rulers were thought divine. They also saw people revere idols and converse with oracles – all of this clear evidence to the Christians that the devil had been at work. But the invaders were slower to absorb the complexities of indigenous beliefs. The rifts between imperial and local religion were lost on most Spaniards, as were the intricate relations among ritual, an animate nature, and social power. In their efforts to come to grips with Andean beliefs, the early Spaniards relied on the cultural referents they had at hand. They referred to Inca temples as mosques and drew on Christian and classical analogs to explain what they saw. Clerics tried gamely to reconcile Andean creation myths with Christian theology, or assigned Andean deities individualized natures like those of the Greek gods, when the native gods were actually multi-faceted and overlapping (see MacCormack 1991).

It took about fifteen years for the Spaniards to begin inquiring closely about Inca religion, but that was unfortunately more than a decade after Cuzco's last major Sun ceremony. Among the first to make the effort were the soldier Cieza and the interpreter Diez de Betanzos, but they were soon followed by the lawyer Polo, Viceroy Toledo and his assistant Sarmiento, and the priests Molina, Albornoz, Arriaga, and Acosta, among others. Some Spaniards made earnest efforts to record myths, describe religious practices, and explain Andean views of life, death, and the supernatural. They also worked hard to discover the locations of shrines and mummies so that they could stamp out idolatry. Sadly, they rarely saw an important ceremony – such as Manqo Inka's investiture in 1534 or Cuzco's June solstice festival (*Inti Raymi*) in 1535 – and so they relied on the memories of informed survivors. By the time the Spaniards sought detailed information, however, the Incas had realized the perils of public celebrations and practiced much of their religion in secrecy. It was not until the beginning of the seventeenth century that the native authors Garcilaso de la Vega, Guaman Poma, and Santa Cruz Pachacuti Yamqui wrote about indigenous beliefs, and they all wrote as Christians trying to explain a coherent, though theologically flawed, system to a Spanish audience. The existing descriptions are thus heavily filtered, but they still manage to convey images of an elaborate ceremonial life. As with so much of Inca lore, we again need to remember that our information most often comes from Cuzco's fallen aristocrats. When the Spaniards wrote down the knowledge that they had gained, they often conveyed the idea that Inca imperial religion was Andean religion, which was far from the case.

Origins of the Cosmos and Humanity

Stories of the origins of the world and humanity were as abundant as the Andean peoples themselves. In the mid-seventeenth century, an exasperated Cobo (1990: 11) said that he had come across a "thousand absurd stories" that people told about their origins; "each nation," he wrote, "claims for itself the honor of having been the first people and says that everyone else came from them." Today, some forty cycles of Andean origin tales are found in the early sources (Urton 1990: 18). The Incas themselves told a variety of stories about the creation of the cosmos, whose contradictory elements even well-informed authors like Diez de Betanzos could not sort out.

Most Inca creation myths begin at Lake Titicaca, and run something like this (mostly following Sarmiento 2007: 45–9; see also Diez de Betanzos 1996: 7–11; Urton 1999: 34–7; Molina 2011: 4–11). In ancient times before there was light, the Creator *Wiraqocha Pachayachachic* ("Creator of all things") fashioned a race of giants to see if it would be good to make humans at that scale. Because he found them too large, however, he decided to make humans in his own size. But they were filled with hubris and greed, so the Creator turned some to stone and others to diverse forms, while even more were swallowed up by the earth or sea. And he caused a great flood to cover the land, destroying all that was upon it, save for three men, whom he saved to help him create humans anew. Later, on an island in Lake Titicaca he caused the sun, moon, and stars to come forth. The sun was jealous that the Creator had made the moon brighter than he, so he cast ashes in her face and thus she remains with her brilliance dimmed.

Wiraqocha then crossed over to dry land at Tiahuanaco, where he carved and drew images of all the nations that he thought to create on some large stones. He ordered his two servants to memorize the names of the people and the places where they were to appear on the earth. Then he sent one to the coast and the other to the eastern slopes. Wiraqocha himself took the central path, calling out the people from the lakes, springs, valleys, caves, trees, caverns, rocky outcrops, and mountains. He appeared to be a man of normal size, dressed in a white robe, carrying a staff and a book in his hands. At Cuzco, he called forth the Alcabizas and Inca nobles, gave Cuzco its name and continued north. Finally, he reached the Ecuadorian coast, where he told his servants that his messengers would return one day. Together they walked out over the water until they disappeared in the west.

The variations on this narrative suggest that the Incas found it necessary to change their theology to bring it into agreement with their expanding world. Rowe (1960) points out that different versions placed the Creator's point of departure on the south coast, at Pachacamac on the central coast, and in Ecuador. He suggests that the different locations probably reflect the retooling of the myth as the empire grew and the Incas had to account for more peoples and places. In a way, the situation paralleled the Spanish experience in the New World, when they suddenly discovered that their theological map covered only a fraction of the world. However we interpret the accounts, there is little doubt that the Incas were content to tell conflicting versions of their origins without suffering the angst felt by some chroniclers.

The Inca Pantheon

Wiraqocha, the Creator

The loftiest Inca deity was the Creator god just mentioned, who had no formal name, but a series of titles (see chapter 5).[1] The Spanish chronicles usually referred to him as *Wiraqocha* or *Viracocha* (table 8.1). Although Wiraqocha was generally removed from daily affairs, he appeared to Inca rulers on a few auspicious occasions. He revealed himself, for example, to the Inca prince Hatun Thupa Inka, who subsequently took the god's name in his imperial title Wiraqocha Inka (Sarmiento 2007: 98). Later in that king's life, the Creator (or Sun) appeared to prince Inka Yupanki (i.e., Pachakuti)

Table 8.1 Major Inca deities and regional oracles (sources: Rowe 1946: 293–396; Demarest 1981; Bauer and Dearborn 1995; Bauer 1998).

Deity	Meaning	Image or associated icons	Themes and roles	Region or culture
Major Inca deities				
Ilya-Tiqsi Wiraqocha Pacayaciq; Wiraqocha	ancient foundation, lord, instructor of the world	male and female aspects; golden statue, puma	creator of heavens, earth, living beings	Inca
Inti	Sun	male; Punchao: golden statue of young boy; golden disk (questionable)	father of royal Inca lineage; patron of empire	Inca
Inti-Illapa	Thunder	male wielding a sling; cat, puma	meteorological phenomena: lightning, thunder, rainbow	Inca
Mama-Quilla	Mother Noon	female	wife of sun; calendrics	Inca
Qollqa	storehouse (Pleiades)		preserve seed	Inca
Urcuchillay		parti-colored male llama	watch over flocks	Inca
Chaska Cuyllor	shaggy star (Venus)			Inca
Pachamama	Earth Mother	female	protect and make fields fertile	Inca
Mamacocha	Mother of the Lakes (and Sea)	female	supports earth, source of water	Inca
Important regional deities or oracles				
Apurimac	Lord Oracle		oracle	Inca: south west of Cuzco
Vilcanota			place where the sun is born	Inca: 40 km east of Cuzco
Thunupa	Thunder	male	creator; meteorological phenomena, puma	Titicaca region
Pachacamac	Earth Maker	statue	creation, oracle	Lurin valley, central coast of Peru
Catequilla		stone statue	regional patron, oracle	Huamachuco (north Peru)
Wariwillka	sacred ancestor[??]	stone statue	regional oracle	Upper Mantaro (central Peru)

who used the revelation to legitimize his claim to the throne. The chroniclers often portrayed the Creator Wiraqocha as one of a triad of Inca gods, along with the Sun (Inti) and Thunder (Inti-Illapa; see Duviols 1977; Demarest 1981; MacCormack 1991). The idea that the three formed a trinity was a Christian imposition on Andean religion, but the gods were clearly intertwined. All three were worshiped in Cuzco's main temple (Qorikancha) and were multi-faceted celestial beings with overlapping powers. In Molina's account, some prayers began with the joint invocation, "O Creator and Sun and Thunder." Despite Wiraqocha's importance, the Incas devoted relatively little energy or resources to his worship. No major ceremony seems to have been devoted to him, he had no endowment or elaborate priesthood, and only a few of the shrines in and around Cuzco were dedicated to his sacrifices (Demarest 1981). His most important temple lay between Cuzco and Lake Titicaca.

Inti, the Sun

Worship of the Sun was a centerpiece of official Inca religion. By 1532, Inti outshone all other Inca deities combined in worship, institutional scale, and properties. Although solar deities had long existed in Andean religions, the Incas' innovative emphasis on solar observations tied in neatly with their claims to cosmological supremacy. It placed crucial sacred knowledge in their hands and backed up their pretensions to be vital to the world's well-being (Pease 1973; Duviols 1977; Ziółkowski 1996). The Inca ruler could claim a direct genealogical link to the Creator through the Sun, since the Creator fathered Inti, who in turn sired the king. In Diez de Betanzos's account, Pachakuti was touted as the main force behind the Sun cult, but Sarmiento's sources named Wiraqocha Inka as the ruler who set the Sun's elaborate worship in motion. Pachakuti's contributions, according to most sources, included rebuilding the main temple and fabricating the principal solar idol (Demarest 1981: 49).

Inti was a male being reportedly represented as a golden disk or statue. The solar disk, often cited as an authentic Inca creation, was illustrated by the two mestizo authors Guaman Poma and Pachacuti Yamqui. A Spanish soldier named Mancio Serra even claimed that he carried it off from the temple and later lost it at gambling. Even so, Duviols (1976) makes a plausible case that the disk was actually a Colonial-era image adopted by native Andeans and that an elaborate mythology was built up around spurious claims and misapprehensions. The statue was a seated figure of a boy, called Punchao

("Day"). Diez de Betanzos (1996: 47) described its creation by Pachakuti as follows:

> he ordered them to fashion a boy of solid gold cast in a mold. This statue was to be the size, height, and proportions of a one-year-old boy in the nude ... [Its caretaker] dressed it in a tunic of very finely woven gold and wool in a variety of styles. He put a certain band on its head, according to their style and custom. Then he put on it a fringe like the one used by lords, and on top of it a gold disk and on its feet *ojotas*, as they call shoes, also of gold.

Sarmiento's witnesses said that solar rays projected from his head or shoulders; he was adorned with earspools, a pectoral (chest ornament), and a royal headband; serpents and lions projected from the body, much like Pachakuti's vision. Demarest (1981) has pointed out that those features recapitulate the distinguishing adornments of the central figure on Tiahuanaco's Gateway of the Sun, thought to be Thunupa, the Aymara Weather God. Conversely, Rowe (1946: 295, n. 30) suggests that the parallel lies between Thunupa and Inti-Illapa, his Quechua counterpart (see below). Whichever link is correct, it is another reminder of the altiplano's crucial role in the foundations of Inca culture.

Punchao tangibly bridged the gulf between humanity and the Sun since the vital organs of deceased rulers were incinerated and cached in his hollow stomach. The figure was housed in the main temple where it was brought out to a patio during the day and returned indoors at night. Molina wrote that it was kept together with the golden images of his wives Inca Ocllo and Palpa Ocllo. The Spaniards never saw Punchao during the conquest, though they searched for it vigorously, because its custodians had spirited it away. In 1536, Manqo Inka took the idol to Vilcabamba to help stage his resistance to Spanish rule. When Viceroy Toledo captured Thupa Amaru, the last ruler of the neo-Inca state, in 1572, the Spaniard boasted that he had finally seized the idol as well. He initially suggested sending it to the pope, but then reconsidered; unfortunately, we do not know what ultimately happened to Punchao (Duviols 1976: 167).

Inti was the patron of the empire and of conquest. It was the Sun to whom the Incas dedicated innumerable ceremonies intended to ensure the ruler's welfare and to foster bountiful harvests. On a twice-daily basis, offerings of grain, small birds, and *chicha* were consumed in a golden brazier before Punchao, wrote Diez de Betanzos (1996: 47). He added that, because access to the temple in which the idol resided was so restricted, a gilded sugar-loaf stone was placed in the main plaza, so that the lesser people could worship the Sun themselves. The foremost priest in the land was the High Priest of the Sun, who was usually one of the ruler's close relatives. The Incas set aside vast human and natural resources for Inti throughout the empire. The temple in Cuzco highlighted Sun worship, although numerous other images were also revered there (chapter 7). Every major installation in the provinces had a Sun Temple served by its coterie of male and female priests. One house of the *mamakuna* (or perhaps the *aqllakuna*, i.e., "chosen women") stands at coastal Pachacamac, where the building has been reconstructed rather more enthusiastically than accurately (Hyslop 1990: 255–61). Every province was supposed to dedicate lands and herds to the Sun, and the church had its own set of storehouses that were used to keep supplies for its personnel and sacrifices. The most expansive set of resources dedicated to the church's holdings may have been found on the north side of Lake Titicaca, where an entire province may have been given over to the institution (Julien 1993; chapter 11 below).

Mama-Quilla, "Mother Moon"

The second great deity of the heavens was the Moon, the wife of the Sun. Just as gold was the sweat of the Sun, so was silver the tears of the Moon. The Moon had its own temple in Cuzco and in the ceremonial complexes dedicated to cosmic origins, including one on the Isle of the Moon on Lake Titicaca. Each was served by its own cohort of dedicated priestesses. The Incas devoted a great deal of energy to sustaining a constant, mutually supporting dialogue between the Sun and Moon, in Cuzco's main temples and between the two isles on Lake Titicaca. Mama-Quilla was important in calculating time and in regulating the ceremonial calendar (Cobo 1990: 29–30), since many rituals were based on lunar cycles adjusted to the solar year. The Incas envisioned the moon in female human form and created an image of her that was tended by priestesses dedicated to her worship (Cobo 1990: 29). One myth accounted for the dark spots on her surface by explaining that a fox fell in love with the moon because of her beauty. When he rose up to the sky to steal her, she squeezed him against her and produced the patches that we see today (Garcilaso 1966: 118–19). In a great number of societies, such as the coastal Chimu, the moon was more important than the sun (Rowe 1948).

Inti-Illapa, the Thunder God

Another important being in the Inca pantheon was the god of thunder, lightning, the rainbow, and virtually all other meteorological phenomena.

He was visualized as a man in the sky who wielded a war club in one hand and a sling in the other. The thunder was the crack of his sling and the lightning flash the glitter of his shining garments as he moved. Lightning bolts were the sling stones that he cast and the Milky Way the heavenly river from which he drew the rainfall (Cobo 1990: 32). His image, Chucuylla, was kept in a temple called Pukamarka, in the Chinchaysuyu part of Cuzco, which also held an image of the Creator God (Bauer 1998: 58, 63). Inti-Illapa was the deity to whom prayers for rain were addressed (Rowe 1946: 294–5).

Other Important Deities

The Incas revered many other beings, including Pachamama, the "Earth Mother," to whom the Incas made offerings and prayed for successful crops. Cobo wrote that farmers commonly worshiped her at a stone altar that they placed in the middle of a field. Mamacocha, or "Mother of the Lakes (and Sea)," was also revered by the Incas, although she was less important than for coastal peoples, for whom she ranked as high as any deity (Cobo 1990: 32–4). An especially important regional being recognized by the Incas was Pachacamac, or "Earth Maker," a coastal oracle with two millennia of history before the Incas appeared. In Inca lore, the subjugation of the coast was fully accomplished when Pachacamac realized that he was a lesser power than Inti, and bowed to his domination.

The Incas also wove elaborate narratives around stars, constellations, and planets (Bauer and Dearborn 1995: 101–40; see also Ziółkowski and Sadowski 1989). They visualized figures in both stars and black spaces in and about the Milky Way, which passes high in the sky in the central Andes. The Incas' reverence for the stars and planets was nothing unusual in the Andes, for they were tracked and worshiped before, during, and after Inca rule. The Pleiades and the stars known as Orion's Belt or the Three Marys in western lore were especially important on Peru's north coast (Bauer and Dearborn 1995; Rowe 1948; Salomon and Urioste 1991: sections 372–8). About 1559, Polo composed an extended treatise on native beliefs of which only the abstract remains. He wrote that, "in general they believed that for each [kind of] animal and bird on earth there was a similar one in the sky who was in charge of its procreation and increase" (Polo 1965a: 2–5). Herders revered a star that they recognized as a parti-colored male llama (Urcuchillay) that constantly revitalized the animals, along with two others they saw as a ewe and a lamb. Forest peoples venerated particular stars for protection against jaguars, bears, pumas, and snakes.

Cobo, who used Polo's full treatise, wrote that all peoples sacrificed to Qollqa [*qollqa*, granary], or the Pleiades. The constellation was honored because it gave rise to all other stellar patrons of earthly things, and thus they called it "mother." He continued that "all the power that conserved the animals and birds flowed from this group of stars" (Cobo 1990: 30). Its reappearance over the horizon after a thirty-seven-day absence signaled the beginning of the agricultural year. They also revered a cross, although we cannot be sure that it was the four stars now known as the Southern Cross, since several constellations of that form are known in Quechua star-gazing (Bauer and Dearborn 1995: 107–10; Urton 1981: 129–50). The Incas also recognized the visible planets. They grouped them in with the brighter stars (*chaska*, shaggy hair) and distinguished all of those from lesser stars (*cuyllor*, star). They took special note of Venus (Chaska Cuyllor), whose passage along with that of the Pleiades was related to the agricultural/calendrical cycle.

Calendrics and Astronomical Observations

Solar and Lunar Calendrics

The Incas knew a great deal about celestial cycles.[2] They had a good fix on the solar equinoxes and solstices, for example, and seem to have kept track of zenith passage of the sun (i.e., the point where the sun is directly overhead). They also knew that the midsummer sun casts no shadow from a vertically aligned pole on the equator. As for the moon, they understood the lunar cycles and timed many of their celebrations according to the appearance of the new moon. Moreover, they had solved the cycles of Venus and some star groups.

The Incas' annual calendar was based on solar cycles, while festivals were largely built around twelve lunar cycles (table 8.2). The two do not mesh well, since there is an eleven-day disparity between twelve lunar months (29.5 days each) and a 365-day solar year. Several chroniclers noted that the Incas knew that twelve lunar months fell short of a solar year and made a correction every winter solstice month. Ziółkowski and Sadowski (1989: 167–96) have designed a plausible Inca-era calendar in which each lunar month began on a new moon and a short intercalation month was used to bring the solar and lunar years into agreement. Bauer and Dearborn (1995: 61–2) express doubts about such a scenario, because it would have

Table 8.2 The twelve lunar months of the Inca calendar, according to the chroniclers Betanzos, Polo, and Guaman Poma, modified from Bauer and Dearborn 1995: table 2; and according to Rowe's (1946) synthetic rendition.

Month (approx. beginning date)	Betanzos [1557]	Polo de Ondegardo [1585]	Guaman Poma [1615]	Rowe (1946)	Comments[1]
January (December 23)	Hatumpo Coiquis	Camay	Capac Raymi, Camay Quilla	Qhapaq Raymi	"Magnificent Festival"; summer solstice
February (January 22)	Allapo Coiquis	Hatun Pucyu	Paucar Uaray Hatun Pocoy Quilla	Kamay	disposal of year's sacrificial remains
March (February 21)	Pacha Pocoiquis	Pacha Pucuy	Pacha Pocuy Quilla	Hatoñ Poqoy	"great ripening"
April (March 23)	Ayriguaquis	Antihuaquiz	Ynca Raymi Mamay Quilla	Pawqar Waray	"earth ripening"
May (April 22)	Haucai Quos Quiquilla	Hatun Cuzqu Raymoray	Atun Cusqui Aymoray Quilla	Ayriwa	harvest of sacred maize field
June (May 23)	Hatun Quosquiquilla	Aucay Cuzqui	Haucay Cusqui Quilla	Aymoray	"great cultivation"
July (June 23)	Caguaquis	Chahua Huarquis	Chacra Conacuy Quilla	Inti Raymi; also Awqay-Koski	"Sun festival"; "Warrior's Cultivation"; winter solstice

August (July 23)	Carpaiquis	Yapaquis	Chacra Yapuy Quilla Quilla	Cawawarkis	sacrifices to water sources
September (August 23)	Satuaiquis	Coya Raymi	Coya Raymi Quilla	Yapakis	sowing of sacred maize field at Sausero
October (September 22)	Omarime Quis	Homa Raimi Puchayquis	Uma Raymi Quilla	Sitowa	Qoya Raymi: "Queen's Festival"; Citua: "Purification Festival"
November (October 22)	Cantaraiquis	Ayamarca	Aya Marcay Quilla	K'antaray	rain ceremonies
December (November 22)	Pucoy Quillaraimequis	Capacraymi	Capac Ynti Raymi	Ayamarka	preparations for Qhapaq Raymi

Note:

[1] There are apparent discrepancies in the sequences of months here because the chroniclers were not always precise or disagreed about the correspondence between Inca and Christian calendars. For example, Polo said that *Qhapaq Raymi* was the first month and corresponded to December, whereas he may have meant that it began in that Christian month. The comments here generally follow Cobo and Rowe.

put one of the solstices and its associated ceremonies out of synchrony every year. Instead, they infer that the Incas likely used thirty-day months (as Diez de Betanzos said) and made adjustments on a month-by-month basis, to ensure that the ceremonial and celestial cycles stayed in agreement.

Some time ago, Tom Zuidema (1982) proposed a controversial third calendar, based on the movement of the moon with respect to fixed stars.[3] The sidereal period of the moon is twenty-seven and one-third days, and twelve sidereal months total 328 days. Zuidema took note of the fact that the number 328 figures into two other important aspects of Inca religion. First is that the number of shrines around Cuzco on Cobo's main list was also 328, just as 328 is the number of days of the year when the Pleiades are readily visible in the region. (The last number occurs because there is a thirdy-seven-day annual span when the Pleiades are too close to the sun to be seen easily.) As observed above, the rise of the Pleiades over the horizon after their absence signaled the start of the agricultural season, marked by grand earth-breaking ceremonies. Given the Inca penchant for numerical order, Zuidema reasoned that such correlations were not likely to be simple coincidence, and that it was possible to bring the lunar and solar calendars into annual congruence. Although his calendar has met with some support, most scholars are skeptical about its prehispanic reality (Sadowski 1989; Ziółkowski and Sadowski 1989; Bauer and Dearborn 1995: 64–5). Two major objections to the calendar are that (1) the chroniclers consistently refer to lunar calendars based on phases of the moon (synodic calendar), and (2) the 328-shrine list does not constitute Cobo's complete catalog, since other sources indicate that there were many additional shrines in the area.

The Incas measured the solstices by making observations from points in or near Cuzco to stone pillars erected on the horizon. Several chroniclers described the four pillars on the hill called Picchu, which forms the northwest horizon from central Cuzco. Unfortunately, their reports of the columns' dimensions and purposes do not coincide, but Bauer and Dearborn (1995: 69–76) judge that two accounts make good sense. The pillars could have been used to define either (1) the June solstice sunset or (2) a specific sunset in August, as viewed from the Awkaypata plaza, for the inception of the planting season. A few other stone structures in the empire were also likely used for astronomical observations or calendrical purposes (Hyslop 1990: 226–9). The most famous is the Torreón at Machu Picchu, next to the royal living quarters in the upper sector. This D-shaped building contains a window that is oriented toward the Pleiades rise azimuth (65°) of the fifteenth century. Intriguingly, the edge of a cut stone in the floor may have been used as a solar device. The edge would have lined up nicely with the shadow cast by a plumb line dropped from the window, as the sun rose over a low point in the horizon on the June solstice (Dearborn and White 1983; Dearborn *et al.* 1987).

Eclipses and Comets

Unlike some Mesoamerican societies, Andean peoples had not worked out the cycles of earth, sun, and moon that would allow them to predict eclipses, so these were frightening events that called for a vigorous response. Between 1440 and 1570, twenty-seven total or annular solar eclipses and about twice that many partial eclipses passed over lands within the Inca empire. A lunar eclipse would have been visible from one location almost every year (Bauer and Dearborn 1995: 142), so the events were likely to have caused frequent distress. Cobo (1990: 27, 29; see also Garcilaso 1966: 118–19) wrote that when a solar eclipse occurred, the Incas would consult their diviners, who usually determined that a great prince was about to die and the Sun had thus gone into mourning. He continued that the Inca reaction was to sacrifice boys, girls, and livestock; the priestesses dedicated to the Sun went into mourning themselves, fasted, and made frequent sacrifices. Lunar eclipses were thought to occur because a puma or a snake was eating the moon. The corrective was to frighten the beast away by shouting, blowing trumpets, beating drums, hurling spears and other weapons toward the heavens, and whipping dogs until they howled.

The Incas also thought that comets were augurs of momentous events. One was seen in Cajamarca during Atawallpa's imprisonment there by the Spaniards. Francisco de Xérez (1985: 156), Pizarro's secretary, wrote that Atawallpa foretold the passing of a great lord of the land – and was dead himself within two weeks. About fifteen years later, Cieza de León (1984: 201) confirmed the report through interviews with men who had been at Cajamarca. He commented that Atawallpa had also said that a comet portended Wayna Qhapaq's demise. Dearborn and Ziółkowski have independently concluded that a comet probably passed overhead in January of 1528. That timing corresponds well with the report that Pizarro had landed on the South American coast before Wayna Qhapaq died, during an exploratory trip that lasted from 1527 to early 1528 (Ziółkowski and Sadowski 1989; Dearborn and Schreiber 1986; Bauer and Dearborn 1995: 147–51).

The Ceremonial Cycle

The Incas celebrated ceremonies tied to both the solar and lunar cycles, as well as irregularly scheduled rituals that were associated with particular events.[4] The lunar months were given a variety of names by the early chroniclers, examples of which are listed in table 8.2. The most important ceremony of the regular cycle fell in the first month of the year, which included the December solstice. The *Qhapaq Raymi*, or "Magnificent Festival," was both the year's first festival and its greatest. During this celebration, the noble Inca boys went through the puberty rites that marked the passage from child to adult (chapter 9). A number of public ceremonies included dancing, drinking, and eating cakes of maize and llama blood said to symbolize the food of the Sun. As this was the year's most solemn event, provincial subjects were required to leave the city for the duration of the rites.

Inti Raymi, or "Warriors' Cultivation," took place in the month that coincided with the June solstice. Like the *Qhapaq Raymi*, this celebration was intended primarily to honor the Sun. In recent years, this festival has been revived as a grand show in Cuzco that merges rekindled tradition with events staged for tourists. In 1535, a few months after Manqo Inka's coronation, the Spanish cleric Bartolomé de Segovia was among those who witnessed the last great Inca festival to the Sun, which lasted eight or nine days (Segovia 1968: 82). His account conjures a vivid image of a grand state ceremony in which all the major figures were involved – the Sun, the Inka, the effigies of past rulers, the nobility, priestesses, and people of Cuzco. Segovia wrote that,

> they brought out all of the effigies from Cuzco's temples onto a plain at the edge of Cuzco, toward the area where the Sun dawned. The effigies with the greatest prestige were placed beneath rich, finely-worked feather canopies, which had an elegant appearance … The space [between the canopies] formed an avenue over thirty paces wide, and all the lords and other principal figures of Cuzco stood in it.

The lords, dressed in all their finery, were arrayed in two rows of about 300 each. As the sun rose, the Inca ruler led off a chant that ascended in volume till noon, and then slowly diminished as the sun descended. Throughout the day, offerings of meat were consumed in a great fire and great amounts of *chicha*, coca, and other materials brought out by maidens were given in sacrifice. At one point, a number of llamas were set loose and the common Indians leaped to catch them in a scramble that everyone enjoyed as great sport. As the sun completed its descent, the Incas expressed great sadness and humility. After sundown, the effigies were returned to their quarters and the canopies that had sheltered the nobility were packed up for the night. At the end of eight or nine days of similar celebrations, the Incas brought out foot plows and Manqo Inka took the lead in breaking the earth. Through this act, wrote Segovia, the Incas inaugurated the plowing season (chapter 12).

According to several chroniclers, during the month known as the *Qoya Raymi* ("Queen's Festival") or *Citua*, the Incas performed a rite of purification. Cobo explained that the ceremony was performed in the rainy season, because that was when people were prone to fall ill. Cuzco's residents began the rituals by striking each other with torches and shaking clothing outside their doorways, as if to rid themselves of malignity. Molina's account explains how social hierarchy and ceremony were played out over space. At one point, four groups of 100 people ran out of the city carrying sacrificial ashes in the four directions. The procession began with priests in the Temple of the Sun and fanned outward. Members of three royal *panaqa* and three non-royal *ayllu* carried their burdens out on the Kollasuyu and Chinchaysuyu roads, while two of each kindred did the same in the other two parts, Antisuyu and Cuntisuyu (Molina 2011: 30–4). When they reached a certain spot, they passed their burdens to people of lower status and so on outward from the city. The last carriers bathed in four major rivers many kilometers away to divest the city and its people of disease and other impurities.

Cuzco's Network of Shrines: the Zeq'e System

Few aspects of the Inca empire have excited as much interest or mystification as Cuzco's network of shrines. Andean people often envisioned geography and features of the landscape in terms of sacred space. Among the Incas, this idea took form initially as a world composed of four parts that converged at Cuzco. The land around them teemed with spirits, while their history was inscribed on the terrain in mountains, springs, caves, stones, and buildings. Hundreds of holy places (*wak'a*) were joined together to form the most elaborate ritual complex in the native Americas – the *zeq'e* (line) system of Cuzco.

The Spanish authorities had known about some major shrines for decades, but their scope and significance really began to dawn on them about 1558–60, when Polo began inquiries into Inca religion. As magistrate of Cuzco, Polo found that the Incas worshiped at more than 400 shrines in and around the city (see Bauer 1998: 16–19). As they delved into Andean religion, the Spaniards found that Cuzco's network was only one of untold numbers that native people used to structure their interaction with a sanctified terrain. Polo ventured at one point that every town in the Andes had one. Other Spaniards were also alerted to the complexity of native shrine systems. During an inspection of Chinchaysuyu, the crusading cleric Cristóbal de Albornoz found more than two thousand *wak'a* in the lands of the Chanka and Aymara and recorded them in local ecclesiastical records. The most complete account of Cuzco's shrines is in Cobo's (1990: 51–84) magnum opus, into which he copied a list of 332 *wak'a*, probably from Polo's lost manuscript.[5] The catalog includes descriptions of the position and social affiliations of the shrines, their mythical history, and the sacrifices practiced at them (table 8.3).

In outline, the design was straightforward. Shrines distributed across the landscape were linked by *zeq'e* lines radiating out from central Cuzco; most lines originated in or near the Sun Temple. Each line was assigned to a particular social group in Cuzco, which conducted rituals at the appropriate shrines following a ceremonial calendar. Bauer's field research shows that most ran for about 5–11 km and contained between three and fifteen shrines. Some lines were essentially straight, while others jogged to adjust to the positions of the *wak'a*. That sounds simple enough, but the system's complexity quickly becomes so baffling that many otherwise diligent scholars have been reduced to scratching their heads and trusting someone else's judgment (see below). In fact, Cobo wrote that over one thousand record-keeping specialists were needed in Cuzco to memorize the lore of the holy places, their prayers, rituals, and sacrifices (Cobo 1990: 9; see MacCormack 1991: 190). To help readers visualize the system, figure 8.1 provides a map of the system's geography, figure 8.2 represents its organization schematically, and table 8.3 lists some of the most important shrines and their roles.

Table 8.3 A selection of important shrines in and around Cuzco, in Cobo's (1979: 51–14) list; spellings of shrines according to original, information following Cobo and Bauer (1998).

Name of shrine	Designation	Gloss	Modern identification	Social affiliation (royal founder)	Form	Ceremonies or significance
Chinchaysuyu						
Inti illapa	Ch. 2: 3	Sun – Lightning	exact location unknown	Vicaquirao	golden idol	idol of sun taken as brother idol by Pachakuti
Nina	Ch. 3: 1	Flame	near Qorikancha	*mamakuna:* priestesses	stone brazier	sacrifices to Sun every morning
Collaconcho	Ch. 4: 6	Large Cut-Stone Work	Tired Stone, above amphitheater in Saqsaywaman	–	carved stone	got tired on trip to Saqsaywaman
Cusicancha	Ch. 5: 1	Happy Enclosure	opposite Qorikancha	*Iñaqa panaqa*	house?	where Pachakuti was born
Pucamarca	Ch. 5: 2	Red Town	on Maruri Street, Cuzco	*Iñaqa panaqa*	temple	idol of Thunder worshiped there
Haucaypata	Ch. 5: 4	Terrace of Tranquility	Cuzco's Plaza de Armas	*Iñaqa panaqa*	plaza	main plaza of Inca Cuzco
Sabacurinca	Ch. 5: 6	Unique Golden Inka	"Throne of the Inka" above Saqsaywaman	*Iñaqa panaqa*	carved stone	gives view of six sacred mountains of Cuzco
Pucamarca (proba-blyQuishuarcancha)	Ch. 6: 2	Red Town (Kishwar Tree Enclosure)	on Maruri Street, Cuzco	Arayraca	temple complex	sacrifices to Pachayachachi (Creator)
Cajana	Ch. 6: 5	Place of Ice	northwest corner of Plaza de Armas	Arayraca	palace	palace of Wayna Qhapaq; sacrifices to wind made in doorway *Guayra* ("wind", Ch. 6: 4)
Quiangalla	Ch. 6: 9	Near the Rust-Colored (Sunset)	near Cinca, on western horizon of Cuzco Valley	Arayraca	stone pillars	marked sunset at beginning of summer

(continued overleaf)

Table 8.3 (continued)

Name of shrine	Designation	Gloss	Modern identification	Social affiliation (royal founder)	Form	Ceremonies or significance
Antisuyu						
Turuca	An. 1: 2	Deer (Stone)	in Qorikancha	zukzu panaqa (Wiraqocha)	round stone	idol of Ticci Viracocha (Creator God)
Amaromarcaguaci	An. 1: 7	Serpent Town House	Amaro	zukzu panaqa (Wiraqocha)	house, carved rock outcrop?	house of Amaru Thupa Inka, eldest son of Pachakuti
Tambo Machay	An. 1: 9	Lodge Cave	Puca Pucará site	zukzu panaqa (Wiraqocha)	house and enclosures	hunting lodge of Pachakuti
Quinoapuquiu	An. 1: 10	Quinoa Spring	Tambomachay site	zukzu panaqa (Wiraqocha)	two springs and architecture	universal sacrifice, save children
Chuquimarca	An. 3: 4	Gold Town	Salonpunca or Cusilluchayo site	–	carved stone	various sacrifices to Sun
Mantocallas	An. 3: 6	Near Red Paint (Tree)	Salonpuncu site	–	carved stone	important rituals for Sun, esp. for Inti Raymi ceremonies
Susumarca	An. 5: 8	Reed Town	above Callachaca	Sanoc?	spring	may be Susurpuquio, where Pachakuti had vision of Creator or Sun
Chuquicancha	An. 6: 3	Gold Enclosure	Rumi Huasi Alto	–	stone outcrop with buildings	sacrifices to the Sun for Inti Raymi and qhapaq ucha ceremonies
Pilcourco	An. 8: 11	Many-Colored Hill	near Larapa	Ayarmaca	stone	girls sacrificed for enthronement of new Inka

Kollasuyu

Limapampa	Co. 2:1	Plain – Speaker	plaza east of Qorikancha	Aguini	open area	maize sowing and harvest festivals
Sausero	Co. 2:3	?	terrace in Cuzco	Hahuanina	maize field	primordial field in Cuzco; initiation of agricultural season
Taucaray	Co. 4:2	(Funerary Bundle) Continually Piling Up	Taucaray hill	Apu Mayta (Qhapaq Yupanki)	tomb	place where dead assembled periodically
Huanacauri	Co. 6:7	Royal Scepter of Expiation	Huanacauri hill	–	stone on hill	petrified brother of Manqo Qhapaq; various pilgrimages, esp. for boys' initiation rites
Matoro	Co. 7:5	?		Usca Mayta Panaqa (Mayta Qhapaq)	mountain slope	birthplace of Zinchi Roq'a; boys' initiation rites

Cuntisuyu

Sabaraura	Cu. 1:1	Unique Flame	in Qorikancha	Anaguarque	stone	*pururauca* (petrified stone warrior)
Anaguarque	Cu. 1:7	Exquisite Wavy (Feathered Hawk)	Anaguarque hill	Anaguarque	large hill	boys' initiation rites
Tanancuricota	Cu. 8:1	Valiant, Gold Coca (Warrior Woman)		*qollana*	stone	petrified female warrior: Chañan Cori Coca
Chinchincalla	Cu. 13:3	Near – ?	Chinchincalla hill	–	hill with some Inka remains	stone pillars marked December solstice sunset

Other

Coricancha	–	Gold Enclosure	Santo Domingo/Qorikancha	–	temple	main shrine to the sun and other important deities
Tocoripuquiu	–	Provincial-Governor Spring	near headwaters of Saphy River	–	spring	source of Cuzco's water, found underground by Roq'a Inka

Note:

Ch. = Chinchasuyu; An. = Antisuyu; Co. = Collasuyu; Cu. = Cuntisuy.

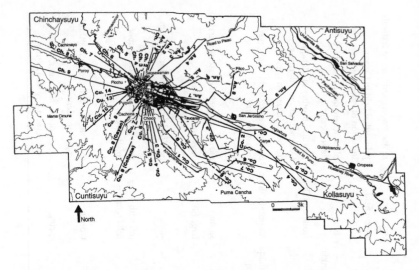

Figure 8.1 The layout of the Cuzco *zeqʼe* system of lines radiating outward from the city's center. Source: reproduced by permission of Brian Bauer.

Deciphering the *Zeqʼe* System of Cuzco

Modern study of Cuzco's shrines began with Paul Kirchhoff's (1949) work in the 1940s, followed up by Manuel Chavez Ballón's mostly unpublished work. Beginning in the 1960s, Tom Zuidema (1964, 1983) proposed that the system simultaneously reflected Cuzco's kinship and marital customs, cosmic space, and ceremonial calendrics. He saw a year-long clockwork in the layout that included sighting lines for the solar calendar and other astronomical phenomena. Zuidema has worked with the astronomer Anthony Aveni to test certain of his ideas; some have met acceptance, while others remain controversial. His student, Jeanette Sherbondy (1992, 1994), has shown how kin groups high in Cuzco's social hierarchy claimed rights to water and land through the spring-shrines and canals under their authority. Another student, Maarten Van de Guchte (1990), explored how the Incas carved stone shrines to mediate their relationship with the animate landscape. Rowe (1979a, 1985a), conversely, has tried to trace out the system's historical development in accordance with royal genealogies. His view challenges Zuidema's approach, which treats the system as

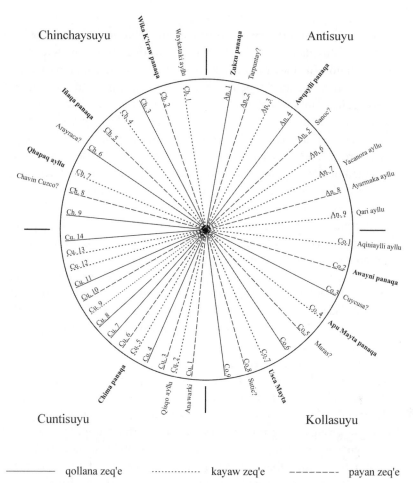

Figure 8.2 The schematic organization of the Cuzco *zeq'e* system.

if it were largely static. In the 1990s, Brian Bauer (1998) conducted the first comprehensive study of the system that integrated history and archaeological fieldwork. He identified many shrines in the field, correlated them with historical discussions of Inca religion, and tested proposals about how the system worked.

To illustrate the complexities, let me expand a little on the main text here, condensing primarily from Bauer's (1998) work. Chinchaysuyu, Antisuyu, and Kollasuyu contained nine lines of shrines each (figure 8.2). The fourth part, Cuntisuyu, contained either fourteen or fifteen lines. In total, then, there were forty-one or forty-two lines. Cobo's enumeration of lines runs clockwise for three of the four parts and counterclockwise for Chinchaysuyu. Within each part, the *zeqe* lines were grouped into sets of three lines (figure 8.3, top left). Each triad was assigned a status according to a rank order (*qollana–payan–kayaw*, in descending order) based on the Inca kinship system (e.g., *qollana* in figure 8.3, lower right). Individual lines in each triad were also assigned one of the three ranks. In Cobo's list, twenty-three lines were assigned to social groups in or around Cuzco, but we do not know if the assignments were extended to every line. Each social group carried out the sacrifices and other ceremonies associated with the shrines along its *zeqe*. In many cases, one line within a triad was assigned to a royal kin group (*panaqa*) and another to a non-royal *ayllu*.

One of the most striking things about the array of shrines is the status differentials among the four parts, which essentially projected Cuzco's socio-spatial hierarchy out toward the horizon. For example, all of the specific lines that are associated with Upper Cuzco's royalty were found in the two most prestigious parts, Chinchaysuyu and Antisuyu. Lower Cuzco's *panaqa* were associated with lines in the lesser two parts. Significantly, the two most powerful kin groups in Cuzco's aristocracy were linked to lines in the top-ranked part, Chinchaysuyu. They were Pachakuti's (*iñaqa panaqa*) and Thupa Inka Yupanki's (*Qhapaq ayllu*) descent groups, longtime adversaries and principal parties to the last dynastic war. Conversely, the least prestigious part, Cuntisuyu, is dominated by lines that were assigned to neither a royal nor non-royal Inca status. The one royal kin group linked to a line in Cuntisuyu is that of the Inca founder, Manqo Qhapaq (*Chima panaqa*). We might think that putting the original ancestor's group in the lowest-status spatial division is a bit odd. However, it mirrored the order of processions in Cuzco in the early Colonial era, as the kin groups most recently in power preceded those of the older, less prestigious groups.

Considering that entire books have been written on the subject, it should be clear that these features only sketch out the system. Scholars are still uncertain if the asymmetries in the layout arose from historical changes, oddities of the Inca social structure, or recording error. Another issue concerns whether the *zeqe* were straight lines or moved

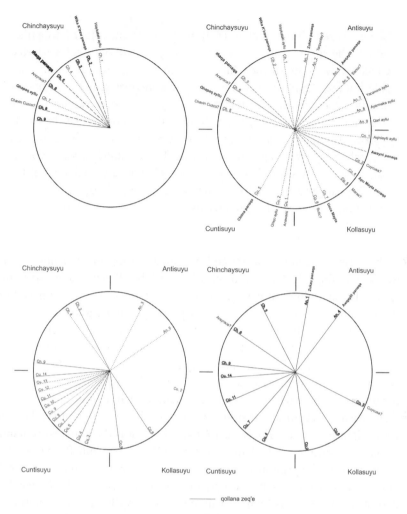

Figure 8.3 The *zeq'e* system partitioned: (top left) three triads in Chinchaysuyu (NW part of empire); (top right) paired royal and non-royal lines; (bottom left) "other" non-Inca lines; and (bottom right) highest-status kin group (*qollana*) lines.

erratically across the landscape. Many of the calendrical and astronomical proposals that have been put forward assume that a significant number of lines were straight. Some sight-lines almost certainly were, but

Bauer's work indicates that others took crooked paths. Since only a fraction of the shrines have been located, not all proposals can be tested conclusively. Some shrines, like the main Sun Temple, are unmistakable, but the identity and position of others are open to debate. Another question concerns how flexible the structure was. We can appreciate the adaptability that may have been required if we consider that the whole system of social ranking reported to the Spaniards may have worked only when Wayna Qhapaq was emperor. The unfulfilled addition of his *panaqa* to Cuzco's social system would probably have shifted all of the ranking categories, added new shrines, and maybe displaced or promoted one of the existing kin groups.

The shrines included natural and modified features of the landscape as well as buildings. Not all can be clearly typed, but Bauer groups many on Cobo's list as follows: ninety-six springs or sources of water, ninety-five stones, thirty-two hills and mountain passes, twenty-eight royal palaces and temples, twenty-eight fields and flat places, ten tombs, seven ravines, three caves, three quarries, three stone seats, three sunset markers, two trees, and two roads. The two most important shrines were the Qorikancha and Huanacauri. As the Qorikancha has already been described (chapter 7), the discussion here will look briefly at Huanacauri and other shrines.

Huanacauri, an uncarved stone, was one of the most potent symbols of Inca origin narratives. The Incas thought that it was the petrified remains of one of the four original Inca brothers ("Ancestor Chili Pepper") who emerged from the primordial cave at Pacariqtambo; it was thus the second oldest *wak'a* in Inca mytho-history, after the origin cave. Cobo (1990: 74) described the stone as being "of moderate size, without representational shape, and somewhat tapering." For solstitial festivals, it was adorned with fine clothes and taken to the hill southeast of Cuzco that was its namesake. Intriguingly, there was little architecture on the hill to indicate its status within the Inca pantheon. The peak has maintained its status as an important terminus for local ritual pilgrimages into modern times (Sallnow 1987). The stone was also often taken to war as the patron of the noble warriors (chapter 10). It accompanied the Incas to Ecuador, but was returned to Cuzco with Wayna Qhapaq's mummified body. The Spaniards later turned it over to the custody of their royal ally, Paullu Inca, who built a special house for it in Cuzco. It resided there comfortably quite a number of years, until the Spaniards figured out the profoundly disturbing (to them) vitality that was attributed to the stone and confiscated it. The name Huanacauri was applied repeatedly to locations around Cuzco and to important peaks in the empire, as the Incas imprinted their past on an expanded domain (Van de Guchte 1990: 53–4).

Many other stones were also important in the array of shrines. At least fifteen of them were the *pururaucas*, the stones venerated as the warriors who helped the Incas repel the Chankas (chapter 4). Among the carved stones are the beautiful planes of the "Throne of the Inca" above Saqsawaman and the Moonstone (*Quilla Rumi*) of the plain of Anta, west of Cuzco. The designs on some carved outcrops are astonishingly intricate. The Stone of Sayhuite, found just to the west of Cuzco's network, is a single boulder that exhibits an elaborate symbolic scene of humanity and the natural and built landscape (plate 8.1). It contains pumas, serpents, lizards, birds, monkeys, maybe lobsters, humans holding beakers, maize stalks, a miniature building illustrating traditional canons of Inca architecture such as trapezoidal

Plate 8.1   The Stone of Sayhuite, whose figurative landscape may represent a map of the Inca cosmos. Source: I, AgainErick GFDL (www.gnu.org/copyleft/fdl.html), CC-BY-SA-3.0 (http://creativecommons.org/licenses/by-sa/3.0/) via Wikimedia Commons.

niches or doorways and a stone staircase, and canals, among other things. Van de Guchte (1990) suggests that its nine-part figurative landscape may have been a graphical metaphor for the Inca world. Another carved stone of note is the "Tired Stone" (*Collaconcho*) above Saqsawaman; according to myth, the stone became fatigued on its way to be incorporated into the Inca fortress, shed bloody tears, and stopped in its tracks.

The site of Q'enqo is one of the most spectacular small archaeological complexes near Cuzco. According to Inca lore, it was likely the death house of Pachakuti called Patallacta (*terrace town*; Diez de Betanzos 1996: 138). Its core (Q'enqo Grande) contains a large boulder whose surface has been carved in steps, zig-zag channels, and gnomons (plate 8.2). On the interior of the boulder is a superbly cut passageway with a stone altar, which may have been a tomb. Other nearby outcrops and boulders are also carved in geometric planes. Adjacent to the stone, just to the north, lies a small amphitheater of finely cut stonework and an enclosed monolith, set on a small platform (*usnu*). A nearby spring and associated waterworks (Q'enqo Chico) are also part of the complex. Recent work by the Peruvian Ministry of Culture shows that the site was even more expansive, including terracing and architecture (Qochapata) to the north across the modern road (Christie 2012). Key rituals celebrating Pachakuti's death were probably carried out at the location (Christie 2012) which was likely shielded by more elaborate architecture than remains today. Those kinds of performances inscribed history onto the landscape in acts that gave material substance to and memorialized history, thus legitimizing the Incas' familial political structure (Niles 1999: 35–7, 45–8; Christie 2012; see chapter 5 here).

Several carved outcrops elsewhere may have been markers that divided the Incas' civilized world from the barbarity beyond. Samaipata, which lies along the eastern Bolivian frontier, contains a remarkable worked rock, carved in planes, steps, niches, channels, and other figures. Coyuctor, in southern Ecuador, is like a small-scale Samaipata; it reportedly contained a stone carved in the form of a park of animals that has been destroyed (Figuencia Pinos 1995; Hyslop 1990: 102–28; Van de Guchte 1990: 220). Ingapirca, a nearby Inca center, contains both finely carved Inca architecture and sculpted figures and designs in nearby rock outcrops. Many of Cuzco's shrines were enclosed or canalized springs (Bauer 1998: 86–7). Among the most important was Tocoripuquiu, which was the source of the stream that flowed through Cuzco. Another was Susurpuquio, where it was said that Pachakuti had experienced his vision of the Creator God or

(a)

(b)

Plate 8.2   The site of Q'enqo, above Cuzco, which may have been the death house of Pachakuti called Patallacta: (a) exterior, (b) interior of cave.

the Sun on the eve of the battle with the Chankas. A third, now a popular tourist attraction known as Tambo Machay ("Lodge Cave"), was probably called Quinoapuquio ("Quinoa Spring") by the Incas. This lovely little spot contains a spring that has been adorned with dual channels, niches, and terraces of fine stonework. Among the other landscape features in the *zeq'e* system were caves, fields, open places, hills, and viewpoints where Cuzco disappeared from sight as the traveler left the valley.

The built environment had its fair share of shrines as well, within and beyond the main temple of the Qorikancha. One important location was a brazier called Nina, just outside the Qorikancha, where female attendants of the Sun made burnt offerings each morning. Another was Cusicancha, an enclosure that Pachakuti's descendant kin worshiped as his birthplace. A number of the shrines were portable. Next to Huanacauri, the most important was probably a golden idol named Inti-Illapa, which was set on a gold litter in a house or temple in the Toto Cachi district (Bauer 1998: 54). Pachakuti reportedly took the idol to be his *wawqi*, or symbolic brother (see Ziółkowski 1996). It traveled with him when he went to war and in death accompanied his mummy in the house of eternal repose at Patallacta.

On Cobo's list, the common offering made to the *wak'a* was the sea shell called *mullu*, which was especially important in ceremonies designed to induce rain (Bauer 1998: 27). Other sacrificed materials included llamas, guinea pigs, precious metals, textiles, and coca. The most celebrated of Inca offerings – human children – were apparently rarely consecrated and were mostly associated with Sun worship and important events in the life of the Inca (see "Human Sacrifice," below). Overall, the system of lines and shrines provided a conceptual map for Cuzco's society, the empire, and the cosmos, while the worship of shrines and ancestors grounded Inca history in the landscape. The system organized the annual round of ceremonies that the Incas thought vital to their well-being, and gave the social groups in the capital a place in maintaining relations between humanity, the ancestors, and other sacred powers. Rowe and Bauer point out that as concrete as the system sounds, however, it was actually dynamic. Since it encapsulated history and power, both of which were forever changing, the system had to adapt. The Incas themselves historically associated at least nineteen shrines with Pachakuti; various others were associated with his wife Anawarki and later figures such as his eldest son Amaru Thupa Inka and younger son Thupa Inka Yupanki. Even Wayna Qhapaq's and Waskhar's palaces were *wak'a* on *zeq'e* lines, illustrating that shrines were added even in the empire's last years.

In fact, we would be hard put to find a better Andean example of a continuously invented ritual order (Rowe 1979a; Bauer 1998: 155–61).

Human Sacrifice: The Qhapaq Ucha and Itu Rituals

The Incas offered human sacrifices for ceremonies of great solemnity dedicated to the Sun, to the ascendancy, well-being, and death of an emperor, and to military victory (see Besom 2009 for an extended discussion). Specific *waka* around Cuzco, such as the petrified ancestor Huanacauri, Pachakuti's birthplace, and shrines dedicated to his wife, could also receive human sacrifices. In all, Cobo reported that 31 of the 332 shrines he described in and around the capital were owed human sacrifice (Dearborn and Schreiber 1989: 51). Calamitous events such as earthquakes, eclipses, and epidemics called for the ultimate offering as well, as did critical divinations. The victims were usually boys and girls chosen for their beauty and recruited from the entire land. Prisoners taken in war were also sometimes executed in a gesture that paid homage to the Sun and symbolized Inca power. On infrequent but dramatic occasions – such as the death or investiture of a ruler – the victims could number in the thousands. Even so, the scale of sacrifice never approached that of their imperial contemporaries, the Aztecs of Mesoamerica, among whom a single unusual event may have consigned as many as 80,000 victims to their deaths. The Andean chroniclers referred to maximal sacrifices of 1,000–4,000, and even those figures may have been more symbol than reality.

The rationale underlying human sacrifice in Inca ideology has not been as clearly laid out for us as it was in Aztec religion. Myths from Mesoamerica recount that humans owed a debt of creation to the gods that could only be paid with frequent offerings of human blood. There are no comparable myths in Inca lore, but the chroniclers did explain that the intent was to ensure that humanity's best was sent to join the Creator, the Sun, and other deities, as well as to accompany rulers into death. Cobo (1990: 8) reasoned that they could not have sacrificed their own children without expecting some reward, which is a different logic from one in which humanity was repaying an endless debt.

Two Inca rituals stand out in particular for their gravity and attendant human sacrifice – the *qhapaq ucha* and the *itu*. According to Polo and Cobo, the *itu* was conducted in times of great need, against such natural disasters as drought, epidemic, and earthquake. It could also be a positive celebration. For example, a provincial lord whose daughter was being received as wife by the ruler could be granted the right to celebrate the festival. The *qhapaq ucha* epitomized imperial ideology. Nominally, it paid homage to the Creator and Sun, but it also reinforced the legitimacy of the Inca lineage, Cuzco's social structure, and pan-Andean shrine networks. *Qhapaq ucha* ceremonies could be focused in and around Cuzco, but the grandest events encompassed the entire realm. They were reportedly invoked to seek the support of the Sun and other powers at pivotal political and military moments (Cieza 1984: 100–1; Diez de Betanzos 1996: 42, 132; Cobo 1979: 235–7; 1990: 54, 58–60, 67, 70–3, 78, 80–2, 154–7, 170; Sarmiento 2007: 69, 119, 138, 140, 144, 227, 233).

The fullest description of a *qhapaq ucha* comes from Molina (2011: 77–83), who placed it in the context of a monarch's ascension. He wrote that all of the towns of the empire were called upon to send one or two boys and girls about 10 years old to the capital, along with fine cloth, camelids, and figurines of gold, silver, and shell. The boys and girls were dressed in finery and matched up as if they were married couples. The ceremony began with sacrifices in the main temple and an assembly in the main plaza, where the victims paraded solemnly around Cuzco's notables – living, dead, and graven. Molina wrote that the ceremonies in Cuzco included sacrifices to the Creator God Wiraqocha, asking for health, long life, peace, and perennial victory for the new ruler. Some children were strangled while others had their hearts torn out and their blood painted across the faces of the images. Similar sacrifices were made to the Thunder, Mother Earth, Mother Cloud, and the petrified ancestor Huanacauri. Sacrifices of other kinds were then made to all of the other *wak'a* of Cuzco.

Priests were then dispatched to the four quarters with sacrificial items and orders to make offerings to all *wak'a* according to their rank. The parties left the city in straight-line paths, deviating for neither mountain nor ravine. At some point, the burdens were transferred to other porters, who continued along the route. The children who could walk would do so, while those who could not were carried by their mothers. The Inca himself traveled the royal road, as did the flocks. At each shrine in the provinces, the devotees interred gold, silver, and shell objects, while children were sacrificed only at the most exalted locations. And thus the parties continued with their travels and sacrifices, until they reached the markers that defined the edge of the civilized world, at a distance of 500 leagues (~2,000 km) or a little less. To keep account of everything, wrote Molina, the Incas maintained mnemonic specialists (*khipu kamayuq*) and keepers of sacred things (*villcakamayuq*). They also required knowledgeable provincials to be present in Cuzco or in the provincial centers so that the ceremonies could be conducted appropriately, since they were changed from time to time.

Archaeologically, the evidence to support sacrifices at that scale is still lacking. In his fieldwork among the *wak'a* of Cuzco, Bauer (1998: 31) found surface evidence of human burial at three shrines, but nothing approaching the thousands of victims described in the chronicles has yet been reported. Since systematic excavations at the shrines around Cuzco have yet to be undertaken, he notes that the issue is still open. Even so, Molina's comment that the rituals paid special attention to high peaks has been supported by the archaeological finds about to be described here. The principal offerings recovered from those sites – gold, silver, spondylus shell, and children – also nicely match the priest's account.

Shrines in the Provinces

Cuzco's *zeq'e* system formed only a tiny portion of the shrines and ritual pathways found in Tawantinsuyu. For instance, a case has been made that many of the radial patterns among the famous Nasca Lines, which antedated the Incas by about a millennium, were ritual pathways organized like those around Cuzco. All told, thousands upon thousands of water sources, peaks, or unusual land forms that had some ritual significance for local peoples were linked together in spatial arrays throughout the Andes. There were also several especially renowned non-Inca oracles or shrines. One lay at coastal Pachacamac, which had been an urban center since the early first millennium AD. According to most accounts, the Incas took control of the area under Thupa Inka Yupanki. While they respected the oracle's power, they also built a Sun Temple, a house of the holy women, the so-called pilgrim's plaza, the "Painted Building," and the Tauri Chumbi sector at the site (Hyslop 1990: 255–61). Intriguingly, coastal myths recorded that the presence of the Inca Sun god had been accepted by Pachacamac himself in deference to his inevitable supremacy and the two gods co-existed in an uneasy relationship. Even so, he demanded human sacrifice in return for the intrusive presence. Atawallpa apparently consented to the idol's destruction by Hernando Pizarro with satisfaction, since Pachacamac had mistakenly predicted Waskhar's victory in the dynastic war (MacCormack 1991: 55–61).

The most important imperial shrine outside the heartland was surely the complex at the Isles of the Sun and Moon, near Copacabana, on the south side of Lake Titicaca. The stone outcrop called *Titikala* on the Isle of the Sun was one of the most sacred rocks anywhere in the entire realm. According to Inca narrative, it was the place where the Creator God Wiraqocha had called forth the Sun to light the current world. Because of its long-recognized status as a major ritual center site, luminaries such as Squier, Wiener, Bandelier, Ibarra Grosso, and Ponce Sángines all studied the area's archaeological remains over the last century and a half. Building upon that work, Bauer and Stanish's (2001) survey and excavations have been able to chronicle the development of the islands and adjoining mainland over the long term. Their work suggests that the *Titikala* stone was a focus of ceremonial activity before AD 500, long before the Incas rose to power. The standing of the location for religion took off under Tiahuanaco's dominion, however, when an architectural complex was erected on the Isle of the Sun and the island's settlement organization was reconfigured (Bauer and Stanish 2001). The complex fell into disuse as a state facility after the demise of Tiahuanaco, *c.* AD 1000, but regained stature under Inca rule.

The Incas put notable effort into constructing new ceremonial complexes leading to and on the Island of the Sun, and founded an entirely new facility on the nearby Island of the Moon. The seventeenth-century author Ramos Gavilán wrote that members of forty-two different ethnic groups were brought in to staff the complex. When their origin points are mapped out (figure 8.4), we can see that essentially the entire empire was represented. Bauer and Stanish's (2001) study shows that access to the sanctuary areas on both islands was controlled through passage along roads through terraced landscapes, settlements, and checkpoints. Much of the Inca-era occupation of the Island of the Sun itself consisted of small residential sites scattered on domestic terraces near good agricultural land. The more significant architecture includes a wall setting off the sacred rock and the Chincana (labyrinth) complex. A number of features, such as a pair of natural stone pillars bridged by another stone at the Horca del Inca, were apparently designed as observatories to mark the June solstice. The maize that the residents carefully tended on the island, at altitudes well above normal limits, was especially revered throughout the empire (Garcilaso 1966: 191) On the Island of the Moon, the Incas built a temple complex focused around a large plaza (Bauer and Stanish 2001). The site called Iñak Uyu was almost surely the main religious and residential facility for the women's order. Overall, as much as any place in the empire, the ceremonial and pilgrimage facilities at Copacabana and the islands stamped the Incas' vision of the origin of the cosmos on the land.

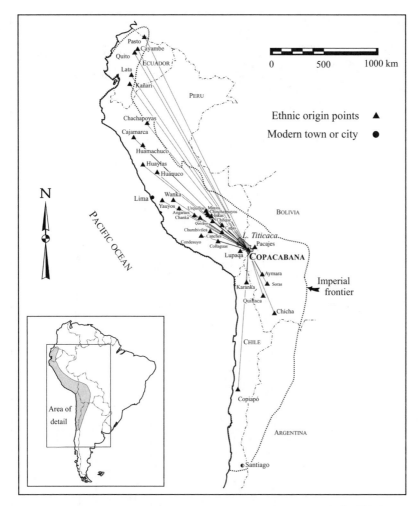

Figure 8.4 The identifiable locations from which people were sent to staff the sanctuary at Copacabana, according to Ramos Gavilán.

Mountaintop Shrines

The attention that the Incas devoted to animate places in the land is visible in a number of small ceremonial sites at unusually high elevations (figure 8.5). Both archaeologists and alpinists have investigated the mountaintop shrines, many of which have been damaged by looters and natural

Figure 8.5　The distribution of high-elevation shrines in the southern Andes. Source: adapted from Reinhard 1985.

processes such as lightning strikes (Beorchia 1987; Schobinger *et al.* 1966; Schobinger 1995; Reinhard 1985; 1993; Ceruti 1997; Reinhard and Ceruti 2005; 2010). Reinhard notes that all 50+ sites that have been recorded over

5,200 m lie south of 15°S latitude. This distribution has led some scholars to consider the truly high sites a south Andean phenomenon that the Incas borrowed from local peoples. Reinhard points out, however, that all of the culturally identifiable remains found above that elevation so far are Inca. Heffernan (1996) also notes that there are some mountain peak sites in Peru, but the highest peaks in the north are permanent snowcaps or glaciers, while many high summits in the south are exposed seasonally.

Erecting the sanctuaries was a daunting task that challenged even the Andean physiology. The Incas lessened the difficulties by building staging stations a few hundred meters below the peaks on the sheltered sides of the mountains, and made paths to the summits (Reinhard 1985). Thus the final pilgrimage and sacrifice could be accomplished expeditiously, once the propitious moment had arrived. Even among people hardened to life at altitude, however, the toll that working under such extreme conditions took may have been heavy. Beorchia (1987: 40–1) reported finding sixteen young males buried at 4,900 m on the ascent up Mount Lllullaillaco. As they were buried in common clothing, without apparent ceremony or special offerings, it has been inferred that they died in the process of constructing the complex of sites leading to the peak (Reinhard and Ceruti 2005: 16).

The existing remains at the high-elevation sites consist of small platforms, fieldstone structures, and enclosures. Their deposits contain human hair, camelid bones and dung, pottery, wood, grass, coca leaf, rope, carbon, and feathers. The most elaborate artifacts are usually paired human statuettes and llama figurines, modeled in gold, silver, and spondylus shell (plate 13.5). Johan Reinhard, the leading investigator of the shrines, infers that there was a consistent rationale behind the creation of the deposits, because no other kind of figurine is found at the high sites. It seems most likely that the combination of the two sexes and precious metals was intended to pay homage to the male Sun and female Moon, while the spondylus invoked Mother Sea. A similar cache of richly dressed figurines has also been found in a structure atop a pyramid at Túcume, on Peru's north coast (Heyerdahl *et al.* 1995).

Strikingly, but rarely, the sites contain frozen bodies of children, adolescents, and adults of both sexes, who were probably sacrificed in the *qhapaq ucha* ceremony described above. They are known from Cerro el Plomo and Copiapó (Chile), Cerro del Toro, Aconcagua, and Llullaillaco (Argentina), and Nevado Ampato, Sara Sara, and Mount Ausangate (Peru). A similar cache with a human sacrifice has been found on Isla la Plata, off the Ecuadorian coast (McEwan and Van de Guchte 1992). Similar *qhapaq ucha* interments have been found around Cuzco, as well. One was recently unearthed beneath the *Casa de Concha* (House of the Shell) in the center of Cuzco, and another in Choquepukio, a major early competitor to the Incas in the Lucre basin, about 30 km east of the capital (Andrushko *et al.* 2011). The last included the remains of seven children aged 3 to 12, who were buried in a single event underneath stone slabs in an Inca building erected at the heart of the site. They were accompanied by an array of high status goods of particular symbolic import, including silver and spondylus figurines of humans and llamas, fine ceramics, metal pins, and cloth.

One of the best-described sites is Nevado Ampato, Peru, excavated and reported by Reinhard and his colleagues, at an elevation of 6,300 m (Reinhard 2005). Nicknamed Juanita, the teenage girl was adorned with rich textiles, including a dress tied up by a belt and a bright red and white shawl that was fastened with silver pins. Her pigtail had been tied to her waistband by thread of black alpaca, from which carved wooden miniatures of a box, two drinking vessels, and a dog or a fox dangled by threads. Among the other offerings that accompanied her into death were female statuettes adorned with textiles much like those that the girl herself wore, coca leaves in a feather-covered bag, and maize. The girl most likely walked voluntarily to her next life, which came to pass when she was struck on the head while she was in a drunken stupor. The bodies of two other children – probably a boy and a girl – were found a bit below at a staging point along the path to the top. Four statues were found with the burials, each of which was clothed in Inca-style textiles, along with a spondylus necklace and silver llama figurine. Many of the artifacts in the two burials appeared in pairs. The excavators suggest that the two may have been buried as a symbolically married couple, just as the chroniclers described for the *qhapaq ucha* ceremony.

Among the shrines with human offerings is the world's highest archaeological site: Llullaillaco, in Salta Province, Argentina, at 6,739 m. The Inca presence on the volcano actually consists of a series of sites, including a waystation at 5,200 m, a series of staging stations trending upward from there, and a ceremonial complex on the summit. Reinhard's collaborative studies began with surveys in 1983 and continued periodically through 1999. Excavations conducted by Reinhard and Ceruti in 1999 (2005, 2010) focused on the summit, where they recovered the remains of three children, two female and one male, and a variety of accompanying offerings. One female mummy was extraordinarily well preserved (plate 8.3), while the other two had been damaged by lightning. The boy was dressed in a red tunic and had a headdress of white feathers; he wore leather moccasins

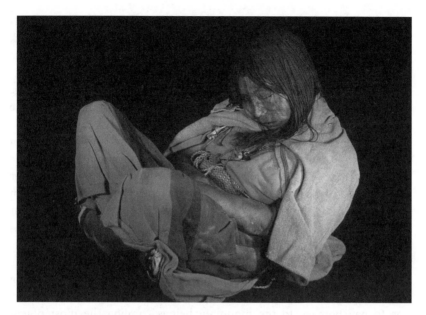

Plate 8.3 Mummy of young female from Llullaillaco, Argentina. Source: reproduced by permission of Johan Reinhard.

and had a silver bracelet. The girls wore dresses, fastened with belts around the waist and pins at the shoulders; the older girl was also adorned with a feather headdress. Radiocarbon dates taken from the last mummy indicate that she died during the period AD 1430–1520, precisely within the time frame of the Inca empire (Wilson *et al.* 2007: 16457).

Chemical analyses of the mummies help us to understand the lives of the people given up to the gods. The Llullaillaco mummies, for example, show that the children had a diet especially rich in highly valued foods over a period of time leading up to their deaths, most likely meat and maize (Wilson *et al.* 2007). The different stable isotope compositions of body parts that change fairly quickly over time (e.g., hair) also show that the children had originally come from diverse locations, but had spent the last few months living in the same, or similar, conditions. The older girl seems to have spent upwards of a year in preparation, judging from the enrichment of her diet during that period, over what it had been earlier in her life. Changes in the composition of her hair further suggest that she spent about 4.5 months in her final sojourn, which probably began in Cuzco. Unlike the two girls interred on Ampato and Sara Sara, who were killed with blows to the head, the cause of death for the three Llullaillaco children remains uncertain (Wilson *et al.* 2007). DNA analyses preliminarily suggest that the Ampato girl, Juanita, had no affiliation with contemporary people living nearby in the Colca canyon (Reinhard and Ceruti 2005). Conversely, the oldest Llullaillaco girl did show a maternal side affinity with one of the Colca individuals, while the closest affiliation for the Llullaillaco boy was from people of the Mapuche region, toward the far south.

Studies of the composition of the pottery recovered from a range of high-elevation shrines also show that there were clear status differentials in the offerings (Bray *et al.* 2005). At both Ampato and Llullaillaco, for example, the highest status vessels were interred with the main human sacrifice, at the summit. Those ceramics were made in either the Cuzco or Lake Titicaca region, both of which were renowned for their high-status pottery. Conversely, imperial-style vessels buried with the individuals found nearby at slightly lower elevations were made from local clays.

Overall, the high-elevation sites provided a wonderful means of meshing religious and political goals. A primary reason for building them, of course, was to pay homage to the mountain beings – among the most potent non-humans to share the cosmos with people. They were the source of weather, origin points or ancestors for many societies, providers of water, owners of the flocks, and oracles, among many other things (see Besom 2009: 117–45). The peaks were also the perfect context to stake an imperial claim. By building the shrines, the Incas interposed themselves as the mediators between human society and the other beings of the world. Since humanity's well-being depended on their relations with the living land and other great deities, the shrines let the Incas lay claim to the cultural foundations of the area's residents. The sanctuaries in this way formed a deft analog to the abduction of ancestor statues. At a broader scale, the shrines also focused attention on the mountain peaks in a way that could have draw devotions from a much larger audience than the local one that had paid its attention to specific peaks (Wilson *et al.* 2007: 16460).

A Native View from the Provinces

Only one known document, from the highlands east of Lima, describes indigenous religious traditions in a native Andean language. Written in Quechua, the Huarochirí Manuscript was prepared for the cleric Francisco de Ávila, who used it to help in his campaigns against the very traditions it described. As Frank Salomon (1991: 1) explains in an introduction to the English version, the manuscript tells of the ancient times of the mountain deity Paria Caca and his sister Chaupi Ñamca, when humans were immortal and when cannibal gods preyed upon them. It describes a landscape alive with spirits, recalls the Inca conquest, and tells of the coming of the Spaniards with their gods who displaced the children of the ancient deities. Although the manuscript is very much a Colonial-era document, it is also a lively testament to the memories of ancient traditions. The author begins his account of human origins in this way:

> In very ancient times, there were *huacas* named Yana Ñamca and Tuta Ñamca.
> Later on another *huaca* named Huallallo Caruincho defeated them.
> After he defeated them, he ordered the people to bear two children and no more.
> He would eat one of them himself.
> The parents would raise the other, whichever one was loved best.
> Although people did die in those times, they came back to life on the fifth day exactly.
> And as for their foodstuffs, they ripened exactly five days after being planted.
> These villages and all the others like them were full of Yunca [i.e., warm valley lands, their biota, and their people].
> When a great number of people had filled the land, they lived really miserably, scratching and digging the rock faces and ledges to make terraced fields.
> These fields, some small, others large, are still visible today on all the rocky heights.
> And all the birds of that age were perfectly beautiful, parrots and toucans all yellow and red.
> Later at the time when another *huaca* named Paria Caca appeared, these beings and all their works were cast out to the hot Anti lands by Paria Caca's actions …
> Also, as we know, there was another *huaca* named Cuni Raya.
> Regarding him, we're not sure whether he existed before Paria Caca or maybe after him.

However, Cuni Raya's essential nature almost matches Vira Cocha's. For when people worshiped this *huaca*, they would invoke him, saying,

> "Cuni Raya Vira Cocha,
> You who animate mankind,
> Who charge the world with being,
> All things are yours!
> Yours the fields and yours the people."

And so, long ago, when beginning anything difficult, the ancients, even though
they couldn't see Vira Cocha, used to throw coca leaves to the ground, talk to
him, and worship him before all others, saying,
"Help me remember how,
Help me work it out,
Cuni Raya Vira Cocha!"
And the master weaver would worship and call on him whenever it was
hard for him to weave.

The manuscript continued, in chapter 4:

In ancient times, the sun died.
Because of his death it was night for five days.
Rocks banged against each other.
Mortars and grinding stones began to eat people.
Buck llamas started to drive men.
Here's what we Christians think about it: We think these stories tell of the dark-
ness following the death of our Lord Jesus Christ.
Maybe that's what it was.

Concluding Comments

Some years ago, Roy Rappaport (1971) suggested that belief systems are
compelling because they draw meaning and legitimacy from untestable
premises that are accepted as truth. As they created their official ideology,
the Incas put this idea into action. Within the context of Andean beliefs,
state dogma plausibly accounted for both cosmic and human history. The
Incas embellished traditional ideas of ancestor worship and veneration of
the powers of the earth and sky by elevating an existing divine being – the
Sun – to a position of pre-eminence and by making worship of their
ancestors reverence for humanity's past. This does not imply that Inca state
ideology was the religion of the people, however. In many regions, it was
an alien and unwelcome presence. As soon as the empire disintegrated,
Sun worship and use of the solar calendar quickly abated outside Cuzco.
The Sun temples and the religious orders fell apart, and the lands tended
for the Inca gods were abandoned. Only among the Incas proper did the
royal mummies and idols retain the potency that the polity had lost – and
they were defended with a desperate vengeance for decades. During the
tumultuous early Colonial years, Inca and local beliefs were reformulated

as part of resistance movements, but the Sun cult and worship of Manqo Qhapaq's descendants were exposed as a recent veneer laid over hundreds of more resilient local religions. This fact, more than anything else, underscores that the official Inca ideology was as much a political instrument as it was a belief system.

Notes

1 One title was Ilya-Tiqsi Wiraqocha Pacayaciq, which Rowe (1946: 293) translates as "Ancient Foundation, Lord, Instructor of the World," eschewing the more common rendering of of Wiraqocha as "Sea Foam."

2 This section summarizes material from Bauer and Dearborn 1995, unless otherwise noted.

3 Zuidema (2010) has recently published a mammoth new work on this subject, which I have not yet had the opportunity to examine in detail.

4 Unless otherwise noted, this description of monthly ceremonies comes from Polo 1965a, b, c, d; Molina 2011; Cobo 1990; and Rowe's synthesis (1946: 308–12).

5 Molina and Polo are generally considered to be the most likely authors of Cobo's source list. Whereas Rowe (1979a) and Hamilton (1990) conclude that there is insufficient evidence to assign authorship, Bauer (1998: 21) judges that the evidence weighs heavily in favor of Polo, a position that I concur with.

Chapter Nine

Family, Community, and Class

By 1532, Inca dominion had imposed a host of new noble statuses and a stratified social order on people who still relied heavily on traditional family and gender relations in their home communities (see table 9.1). For the vast majority of people, daily life revolved around the kin with whom they shared social ties and economic risks and obligations. Nonetheless, overlays of class and ethnic ranking reorganized life on the grand scale, so that many societies that had been without an aristocracy now enjoyed all the mixed blessings of their presence. Most of the highland societies were headed by hereditary local lords, called *kuraka*, who were part of the region's social fabric. Only along parts of the Peruvian coast, especially in Chimor, had people been living in an imperial state where aristocrat and commoner stood on opposite sides of an unbridgeable gulf.

For centuries, Garcilaso's and Cobo's chronicles provided most of the information that was used to describe Inca social relations. Since they knew the heartland best, much of what they had to say was most relevant to the Incas proper. Things changed in the late twentieth century, as historians delving into the archives found evidence for many different kinds of social relationships across the Andes. Among the most valuable texts are Spanish inspections and court cases about rights to office, resources, or inheritance, which often show how family and kin relations worked in one region or another. Archaeology has also broadened our understanding of social relations, for example through the study of architecture and settlement planning, which provide avenues for analyzing social interaction. Similarly, mortuary analysis lends insight into how people envisioned social status, gender roles, identity, and relations with the afterlife. Recently, household archaeology, which studies the residues of daily life, has also begun to shed more light on the domestic life of the general populace and relations between local nobility and their peoples.

The Incas, Second Edition. Terence N. D'Altroy.
© 2015 John Wiley & Sons, Ltd. Published 2015 by John Wiley & Sons, Ltd.

Table 9.1 Quechua and Aymara terms referring to the nobility (after Rostworowski 1999: 140–3).

Quechua: Santo Tomás' (ST) and González Holguín's (GH) dictionaries			Aymara: Bertonio's dictionary	
Capac or *Capac Capa*	ST	king or emperor	*Hakhsarañani apu*	lord of great majesty
Capac Apo	ST	sovereign ruler	*Ccapaca Suti*	royal name or great ruler
Çapay Apu	GH	supreme lord	*Ccapaca cancaña*	king or lord, an ancient term no longer used with this meaning
Çapay Auqui	GH	the principal of or noble gentleman	*Ccapaca*	wealthy
Hatun Curaca	GH	the highest-ranking lord, best known, oldest, richest man	*Apu*	lord, *corregidor*, prince
Hatun o Akapac Curaca	GH	great lord	*Apu Cancaña*	*señorío*, domain
Appo	ST	great lord	*Auqui*	father or lord
Appocac	ST	great lord	*Taani*	fieldmaster, provider of something, such as a banquet
Yayanc	ST	lord, generic	*Pachpa marcani mayco*	rightful and natural lord of the people
Curaca	ST	lord, principal of subjects	*Cchamani, Sinti, Ataaani*	captain
Atipac	ST	powerful	*Hilacata*	the principal or head of the *ayllu*
Appocta, Sayani, gui	ST	to be standing before a great lord	*Hisquiquiri*	rich or noble gentleman
Auquicuna	GH	the lower nobles, lords	*Huallpani*	captain, or the one in charge of banquet preparations and other aforementioned
Rinriyoc Auqui	GH	*orejón* nobles	*Laa Mayco*	intrusive chief, or one without the right to the position

(continued overleaf)

Table 9.1 *(continued)*

Quechua: Santo Tomás' (ST) and González Holguín's (GH) dictionaries			Aymara: Bertonio's dictionary	
Curaca	GH	the lord of the people	*Mallco vel. mayco*	*cacique*, lord of subjects
Curaca Cuna	GH	the principals or those who execute what he orders	*Maycoña vel. mayco*	domain, royal authority
Llactayoc Apu	GH	the lord of the people	*Tataña*	one who plays the role of lord
Llactacamayoc	GH	deputy *curaca* or one who executes his orders		
Appo Ayllon	ST	lineage of lower nobility		
Llactayok	GH	lords of owner of camelid herds		
Michini Runacta	GH	govern or rule men or be of higher rank		
Ccoripaco Ccorinrincri	GH	the *orejón* captains		
Appoycachani, gui	ST	to outrank		
Mussoc Capac or Mosso Cappo	ST	newly crowned emperor (young)		
Pacuyok	GH	commoners who were made *orejones* in war		

The different kinds of evidence underscore that an ideal of mutuality and balance permeated social life, whether between males and females, among extended kin, or between people of different social rank. A fundamental symmetry between male and female roles lay at the heart of Andean society. Attuned as they were to Spanish mores, the chroniclers tended to focus on men and their activities, but indigenous cultures generally saw the two genders as complementary parts of a whole, not as a hierarchy. A household was not only conceptually incomplete without a married couple at its center, but the division of labor put any unmarried adult at a great disadvantage in performing the tasks of daily life. At a broader level, kin owed each other assistance, while the nobility owed leadership and generosity to their people, who in turn owed labor and allegiance to their lords. The degrees of ranking varied from one society to the next, but the traditional links between people of different statuses were stronger than the divisions that separated them. As the Incas imposed a class-based structure, the obligations remained, but the social gulf often widened.

The Elites

The most elevated classes in the realm consisted of the Incas themselves and their closest subjects. As described in chapter 6, the topmost ranks included the royal family, the descendant kin (*panaqa*) of past rulers, the non-royal ethnic Incas, and the Incas by Privilege. Both Quechua and Aymara have rich vocabularies for other elites, as did the Muchik language of the Chimu (Rostworowski 1999: 138–44).[1] In addition to the decimal officials, the diverse nobility included those whose statuses were distinguished by their lineage, military stature, civic role, or source of wealth (table 9.1). All of those terms were distinguished from the occupational specialists found among the commoners, called *kamayuq* ("master," chapters 5, 13). The terms for the nobility suggest how some social transformations may have occurred, but we need to remember that the lists were compiled decades after Spanish rule began and that there is some borrowing across languages. Rostworowski points out that some terms incorporate the word for "father" (*yaya*), and suggests that traditional kin terms were modified as society became stratified; the terms may have also carried the implication of lord as father/patron. Terms also existed for commoners elevated to noble status for their performance in war, and for individuals who usurped power or who simply played the role.

Peasant Communities

Despite the elites' prominence, peasant families living in towns and villages – farmers, herders, fishers, and artisans – made up about 95 to 98 percent of Tawantinsuyu's population. There were several layers of ranking or social divisions within peasant communities, but by and large, sharing and mutual responsibility typified their social relations. A highland community (*llaqta*) in the central Andes usually contained one or more *ayllu*, the most important kin grouping in traditional society. The sizes of *ayllu* varied from one to the next, but the largest could contain several lineages and hundreds of households. The *ayllu* were often divided into two parts and their lineages could also hold statuses of different social ranks. The households themselves typically included a male head of the family, his wife, children, and unmarried or widowed adult kin. As described in chapter 2, the *ayllu* and its member households often distributed their members across the landscape to take advantage of several ecozones so that they could be self-reliant for their daily needs (see below, "Making a Living").

The guiding ethic for those communities combined self-reliance, kinship, gender balance, social hierarchy, and mutual obligations. Taking a modern traditional community as an example, we can postulate how many decisions might have been made in the Inca era without the intervention of elite leadership. When the people of the Isle of the Sun and environs are about to make an important decision about a community action, they make offerings of a coca leaves and other materials to the earth (Bauer and Stanish 2001: 78). A ritual leader is chosen to made the offering (*pago*). If the consensus of the community, reached through prior discussions, is in favor of the terms of the agreement, then the offering will be successful. If not, then the offering is read by the ritual leader as unsuccessful, and new terms are worked out. Thus, an outcome acceptable to the community as a whole can be achieved, without anyone in particular being held responsible. Such an approach maintains social cohesion to the degree possible.

The remains of prehispanic peasant settlements are scattered throughout the Andes, but have become subjects of archaeological research only since the 1980s. In the Upper Mantaro Valley, my colleagues and I have recorded more than 125 Inca-era settlements within about a day's walk of the provincial center of Hatun Xauxa. The largest of those towns, Marca and Hatunmarca, each contained about 4,500 residential structures. We estimate that their populations were probably in the order of 4,000–5,000, a reduction of maybe 60 percent from the largest communities in the pre-Inca era. Both study of the settlement patterns and household archaeology illustrate the impact of the Inca occupation on village society (D'Altroy *et al.* 2001; Parsons *et al.* 2013). One major change was a shift of the villages from defensible, high-elevation peaks, to more dispersed communities near the valley bottoms. That shift was reflected in the diet that people consumed, which favored more maize under Inca rule (chapter 12).

During the pre-Inca Late Intermediate Period, the architecture at those communities reflected more of a consensual than hierarchical approach to decision-making. Even the largest communities contained no monumental, public architecture – just centrally organized public spaces between two residential sectors. Remnants of feasting paraphernalia were found adjacent to the plazas. While the most important political activities were conducted at the nearby Inca center of Hatun Xauxa, high-status families adopted some of the canons of Inca status into both the architecture and insignia of prestige. The elites also had access to hundreds of thousands of Inca ceramic vessels, with which they probably sponsored ceremonial feasts partly as representatives of the state and partly as traditional ethnic lords among their own people (chapter 12).

The Stages of Life

The Incas kept track of people's ages by following them through stages of life, not by counting their years, which they did not pay much attention to. They were most concerned with a person's ability to work and marital status. Of all the chroniclers, Guaman Poma probably portrayed the customary age-grades the best. He described ten grades each for males and females, which ran parallel to or perhaps in tandem with one another.[2] Although he was actually trying to describe the Inca census categories for each sex (table 9.2), some of the age-grades he listed were likely based on pre-Inca customs. Rowe (1958: 516–17) suggests that he may have split the youngest categories to round the number up to ten, which was the base for Inca accounting. Guaman Poma's first three age-grades included the warriors and their wives, followed by old men and women who were still productive, and then the deaf and drowsy ancients. The chronicler drew the first man as a valiant warrior clutching an enemy's decapitated head (figure 9.1), while the woman is industriously weaving (figure 9.2). Later in life, men could still carry burdens and the women could still weave, but the community's eldest members just whiled away their time. The fourth category, or "road" of life, took in all of the people who were unproductive because they were ill or disabled. The last six roads ran from adolescents to infants, in descending order of their ability to contribute. Guaman Poma showed the marriageable girl in the fifth road spinning, while her male counterpart is drawn as a messenger. Then come female herders, flower gatherers, and girls who could carry burdens, paralleled by

Table 9.2 The "roads," or life stages, of males and females, according to the native chronicler Guaman Poma, as summarized by Rowe 1958: 514–16.

"Road" (lifestage)	Male			Female		
	Term	English gloss	Approximate age	Term	English gloss	Approximate age
1	awqa-kamayoq	warrior	25 (or 33) to 50	awque-kamayoqpa warminãwqayoq warmi	warrior's womanwoman who has a warrior	33 years
2	pureq-machu	old man who can walk	60 or 70	payakuna	old women	50 years
3	roqt'u-machu	deaf old man	80, 100, or 150	puñoq-paya	old woman who sleeps	80 years
4	'onqoq-runa'upañaw zamakim p'akisqahank'at'inri wayaqak'umuch'eqta zenqa	sick person, dumb man, blind man, person with a broken arm, lame person, dwarf, sack, hunchback, split nose	people with various infirmities	ñawzakunahank'a'u pawiñay'onqoqt'inri wayaqak'umuch'eqta zenqaq'aqya	blind people lame, dumb, always sick, dwarf sack hunchback, split nose, tuberculosis	people with various infirmities
5	sayapayaq	helper, companion	18, 20	'allin zumaq sipaskunapurum thazki	very beautiful girls of marriageable age virgin girl	13 years

6	*maqt'akuna*	adolescent youths	12, 18	*qhoru thazkikunarutusqa thazki*	girls with their hair cut short, girl with her hair cut	12, 18 years
7	*toqllakoq warmakuna*	children who set net snares	9, 12	*pauau pallac*	[unknown] gatherer	9, 12 years
8	*pukllakoq warmakuna*	children who play	5, 9	*pukllakoq warmi wamra*	female child who plays	5, 9 years
9	*llullu lloqhaq warmakuna*	tender children who go about on all fours	1, 2, 3 to 5 years	*lloqhaq warmi wawa*	female infant who goes on all fours	1, 2 years
10	*wawak'irawpi-kaq*	infant one who is in a cradle	1 month, new born	*llullu wawa warmi k'irkawpi-kaqwawakuna*	tender infant girl who is in a cradle infants	1 – 5 months

Figure 9.1   Guaman Poma's stages of life ("roads") for males in the Inca realm.

Figure 9.2   Guaman Poma's stages of life ("roads") for females in the Inca realm.

male herders and hunters. As he illustrated, even children younger than five were expected to contribute something to the family.

Guaman Poma's list suggests that life's progress was based on the tasks thought appropriate for particular ages and sexes, but the arrangement also ties into the ways that Quechua speakers do their arithmetic. In a study of modern Quechua mathematics, Gary Urton (1997: 85–9) has found that the Incas' modern heirs think about ordinal numbers in terms of kinship and descent. When they are putting things into a sequence, the eldest or highest in rank comes first, followed in descending order by the remaining elements. Typically, a set of ranked numbers will be envisioned as a mother and her (four) offspring; two sets of five then make ten, which matches the Inca decimal base. In this way of thinking, adults logically come before children and infants, not the other way around. To put the situation another way, instead of thinking of life stages in terms of the order that we pass through them (i.e., the European way), the Incas classified age-grades in terms of a hierarchy of importance (i.e., a line of stature).

Birth and Childhood

Large families were welcome in Inca society both for the emotional attachments that children bring and because of their productivity. Even so, pregnancy and childbirth themselves did not draw much public attention. Women worked right up to the time of childbirth, although it was thought to be bad luck for a pregnant or menstruating woman to walk through a sown field (Cobo 1990: 176). As the mother went into labor, she would confess and pray to the *wak'a* for an easy birth. The husband and sometimes the woman would fast until the child was born. Women usually gave birth without the help of a midwife. Immediately after the baby arrived, the mother would wash both the infant and herself in the nearest stream, providing a chilly welcome into their mountainous world (Garcilaso 1966: 212). Cobo (1990: 200), who was greatly dismayed at the injury done to God's creations, wrote that many people bound their infants' heads to shape them into forms that they found attractive. The Qolla of the altiplano, for instance, wrapped strips of cloth around the head for four to five years to mold them into a cone shape – the better to fit their brimless hats, he commented. Archaeologists sometimes find evidence of such cranial modification practices, which can provide a way to help track the movements of ethnic groups under Inca rule (Haun and Cock Carrasco 2010).

Cobo wrote that the babies were wrapped in swaddling clothes four days after birth and placed in a cradle. Relatives were then called in to visit and have a drink, but no more elaborate ceremonies were celebrated at that point. The tiny bed was made of a board with four feet; a folded blanket padded the surface and the child was lightly bound to the cradle. It was used to rock the baby to sleep and was also strapped onto the mother's back for travel. Garcilaso (1966: 212) recalled that children were treated sternly during their earliest years to make sure that they were up to the rigors of Andean life.

> Every morning when [the baby] was wrapped up it was washed in cold water, and often exposed to the night air and dew ... The mothers never took the babies into their arms or on their laps either when giving suck or at any other time. They said that it made them crybabies, and encouraged them to want to be nursed and not to stay in the cradle ... The mother reared the child herself, and never gave it out to nurse, even if she were a great lady, unless she were ill. During this time they abstained from sexual intercourse, considering that it spoiled the milk and caused the baby to pine and grow weak.

When a child was about 2 years old, it was weaned and given a name in an elaborate hair-cutting ceremony called the *rutuchicoy*. Since many infants died of respiratory and intestinal diseases and half the children would probably not reach adulthood, we can understand why people might postpone a naming ceremony for a couple of years. Friends and relatives gathered for drinking and dancing, after which the relatives, starting with the eldest and most respected uncle, took turns in cutting off locks of hair and fingernails with a flint knife. The cuttings were gathered and safeguarded, for they were thought to carry the person's essence and a sorcerer could seriously injure or even kill someone by performing witchcraft on the materials (Cobo 1990: 201). Most children learned their parents' skills, but did not receive any other special education. Boys were typically taught to hunt and to make the craft objects that their fathers were adept at manufacturing. Girls learned to make thread, to weave, and to perform all the duties of a wife, such as cooking and maintaining the household. Farming and herding, and some crafts such as potting or weaving, were sometimes performed by both sexes, often as complementary tasks.

Children of Inca and provincial nobility enjoyed a more elaborate education. The sons of high provincial lords were sent to Cuzco as hostages, where they were trained as future officials of the realm and were inculcated with Inca values and culture. Along with the sons of Inca aristocracy, they were taught the use of arms, Quechua, Inca religion and history, and *khipu* accounting. Garcilaso says that they were taught by wise men called *amautas*, who passed along their knowledge of the sciences, poetry, music, philosophy, and astrology. Following Blas Valera and Murúa, he described the training as a formal school with a four-year curriculum (Garcilaso 1966: 226–7; Rowe 1946: 282–3; Rowe 1982).

The only girls to receive formal instruction were the *aqllakuna* (Chosen Women), who were trained throughout the realm (figure 9.3). They were attractive girls taken from their families at about age 10 and placed in Inca settlements under the supervision of the provincial governor. In the sequestered House of the Chosen Women (*aqllawasi*), they were taught religion, weaving, cooking, and *chicha*-making by lifelong virgins dedicated to the religious institutions. Cobo said that as many as 200 women of various ages could be found in the largest *aqllawasi*. Although they were well protected, the girls and women were not entirely confined, since they participated in many ceremonies at locations outside their quarters. After about four years, the girls were ready to serve as *mamakuna* (priestesses) or to marry men who merited the honor for their service to the Inca (Cobo 1990: 172–4; Rowe 1946: 283). The cloth they wove and the *chicha* they brewed were consumed in great amounts in festivities and sacrifices to the Sun. They began the *chicha*-making process by chewing maize or other plants; the mash was then spat into a jar where it fermented for a few days. Once decanted, the heady, sweetish brew was ready to be quaffed. Archaeological evidence for a large *aqllawasi* has been found at the provincial center of Huánuco Pampa, on the high grasslands of north-central Peru (Morris *et al.* 2011). There, excavations recovered large quantities of the remains of the jars used to brew *chicha*, along with spindle whorls, which would have been used to make the thread for cloth. The compound's controlled entry and its placement directly facing onto the main plaza, from the north side, both speak to the Incas' interest in limiting access to the inside.

Growing Up

Both boys and girls went through rites of passage in their early teens that marked their transition from childhood to adolescence. A girl celebrated individually at her first menstruation, which occurred at the age of about 13 or 14. Although a girl's ceremonies (*quicuchicuy*) were less elaborate than the boys' collective affairs, they were equally valued. She was required to fast in seclusion for three days, on the last of which she received just a little raw maize. On the fourth day, her mother washed and dressed her in fine clothes made for the occasion. The relatives then came to visit for a couple of days during which the girl served them food and drink. Her most notable uncle gave her an adult name and counseled her to live right and serve her parents well. Favored names for girls emphasized beauty and purity, for example, Star (*Cuyllor*), Egg (*Rontu*), Pure (*Ocllo*), Mark (*Cimpo*), Gold

Figure 9.3 The *aqllakuna*, or "Chosen Women," by Guaman Poma (1936); they were girls taken from their families and trained as weavers and *chicha* makers in provincial centers.

(*Qori*), and Coca (*Koka*; Rowe 1946: 284). The ceremonies concluded as the uncle and the other relatives gave her gifts according to their means (Cobo 1990: 202–3).

Boys' maturation ceremonies were probably simple for common folk, but were very elaborate for the scion of Inca aristocrats (see Rowe 1946: 283–4; Cobo 1990: 202). The rite of adolescent passage (*waracikoy*) was celebrated once a year for a community; in Cuzco it coincided with the December solstice festival, called the *Qhapaq Raymi* (chapter 8). Boys who had reached the age of about 14 were given their breechclout at this time, woven by their mothers. They also received their adult names during these rites. Among the preferred names for Inca boys were Condor (*Kuntur*), Snake (*Amaru*), and Hawk (*Waman*). The royalty were given names that included Happy (*Kusi*), Powerful or Wealthy (*Qhapaq*), Honored (*Yupanki*), and Jaguar (*Uturunku*), among many others.

The ceremonies for the sons of Inca nobility and royalty featured pilgrimages, sacrifices, and physical feats of daring and prowess. A month before the main ceremonies, the boys made a pilgrimage to the sacred mountain named Huanacauri to seek approval to go forward with the rites. During the preparations, the boys made slings and helped to chew maize for the *chicha* that would be consumed during the festivities. A second pilgrimage to Huanacauri marked the beginning of the month-long ceremonies; the journey was highlighted by sacrifices of camelids and was followed by a dance in Cuzco's central plaza. Additional pilgrimages to other nearby mountains continued throughout the month, where the boys made sacrifices of llamas, their wool, and other materials. Periodically, their adult sponsors would whip them on the legs, admonishing them to be brave and to serve the Inca and the Sun with honor. One of the high points of the month was an hour-long race down a mountain face that often resulted in injury. The boys were spurred on by young maidens, who waited at the bottom with *chicha*. As the rituals came to a close, the boys received gifts from their adult male relatives – each one accompanied by a single whip stroke – and had their ears pierced for the large earspools that marked them as nobility. Thus they were known in adult life as *orejones*, or "big-ears."

Marriage and Adult Life

Marriage marked the passage to full adulthood. In pre-Inca times, most young people probably chose their mates with the consent of both sets of parents. It was important to find someone from the other side of the (flexibly defined) *ayllu*, so that resources could be kept within the large kin group. In traditional society, marriage bonded both the individuals and their extended kin groups; the relations between in-laws were important links that could be activated when assistance was needed. Men typically married at some point between their late teens and mid-twenties, while the girls married somewhat younger. After the Incas asserted their rule, marriages were supposed to be approved by the provincial governor. In some regions, he reportedly lined up the eligible young men and women in separate rows and let the boys choose mates one by one. If two boys wanted to marry the same girl, the official would investigate who had the superior claim and settle the matter. Elsewhere, the boys made arrangements with the parents of their prospective wives, but the governor's sanction was reportedly still required. In practice, official supervision may have been applied unevenly (Cobo 1990: 204–10; Rowe 1946: 285–6). The marriage ceremonies were typically simple and varied from one society to the next. In the altiplano, wrote Cobo (1990: 206), the groom presented a bag of coca leaves to his future mother-in-law. When she accepted it, the marital bond had been secured. The new couple took up residence in their own household and were counted among the taxpaying populace. Although trial marriages were common in many places, full marital status could only be achieved with the formal sanction of the Inca or his delegate.

Love Poetry and Other Oral Literature

Andean peoples enjoyed composing and reciting oral literature that included love poetry, ballads, narrative history, myth, and religion. The Incas held accomplished orators and storytellers in great esteem. There was a special group of orators in Cuzco called *amautas*, who wove together the deeds of past kings and queens into captivating sagas recited at the court's request. The Incas also seem to have performed dramas in their public ceremonies and dances, but no securely pre-hispanic piece is known (Rowe 1946: 321). In his manuscript to King Carlos V, Guaman Poma recorded some verses that were preserved from Inca times or composed in the prehispanic style early in the Colonial era. The following love poem is an example of Quechua verse from the Colonial period (Guaman Poma 1936: 317; translation by Rowe 1946: 322–3).

> What evil fortune separates us, queen?
> What barriers separate us, princess?
> My beautiful one, for you are a chinchiroma flower,
> In my head and in my heart I would carry you.
> You are like the sparkling water,
> You are like a mirror of water.
> Why don't I meet my loved one?
> Your hypocrite mother causes our unbearable separation;
> Your contrary father causes our neglected state.
> Perhaps, queen, if the great lord God desires,
> We will meet again and God will bring us together.
> The memory of your laughing eyes makes me sicken.
> A little, noble lord, just a little!
> If you condemn me to weeping, have you no compassion?
> Weeping rivers, over the cantut lily, in every valley,
> I am waiting for you my little beauty.

Among the ethnic Incas, the marriage ceremony took place after the harvest was in. Cobo wrote that the groom and his relatives visited the bride's home, where all of her relatives had assembled. He placed a sandal on her foot, of wool if she were a virgin or of ichu grass if she were not, and then he took her by the hand. The whole group then made their way to the groom's house, where the bride presented him with a fine wool tunic, a headband, and a metal ornament, which she had secreted under her sash. After the groom had donned his new apparel, the elders counseled each of them on the responsibilities of marriage. The pact was sealed with gifts from both sides of the family and celebrated with feasting and drinking.

Among Inca and provincial nobility, the men could have several wives, but only one could serve as his principal wife. The rest had the status of secondary wife, even if the principal wife had died. The most prestigious way a man could receive a secondary wife was through the order of the emperor. A man who had several wives was considered wealthy, because of the household labor that he could command. A commoner whose wife died was in serious trouble. Not only had he lost his life partner, but there was no one present to maintain the household. Even worse, a wife's death was often treated as suspicious and he was blamed. Not until he remarried was he back on his feet socially and economically. Divorce of the principal wife was not possible if it had been sanctioned by the Inca, at least in theory, but secondary wives could be divorced easily (Rowe 1946: 285). Not surprisingly, the sources that provide detailed information on the married rights of men are essentially silent on the lives of women who were divorced or widowed.

Death and the Afterlife

In the high Andes, a common person's status changed when he died, but he did not ascend into an incorporeal heaven or sink into eternal torment. As described more fully in chapter 5, the thirsty spirit of an ancestor still inhabited the land, requiring libations of beer and other attentions (Gose 1993). Despite the spirit's continuing presence, relatives dressed in black mourning clothes and grieved at the death of a family member; the nobility wore black for a full year. Cobo (1990: 250–2) wrote that the lamentations for the dead could last for a considerable number of days, depending on the status of the deceased. Accompanied by flutes and drums, mourners would sing laments, fortified by drink and foodstuffs provided by the surviving family members. Women would cut off their tresses or tear out their eyelashes in a gesture of grief. The funeral party would visit the places that the deceased had enjoyed the most or where he had achieved his greatest successes; there, they recounted the key events of his life for everyone to hear. Cobo said that lords were dressed in their finery for burial and were accompanied into death by their wealth and occasionally by wives and servants. A commoner's burial furniture was considerably less extravagant, and some of his belongings may have been burned at the time of his interment.

Archaeologists have long recognized that the mortuary context provides the perfect opportunity for making social statements about the living and the dead. Rather than being a mirror of one's position in life, a burial is an idealized synthesis of the images that the survivors wish to convey. While the Incas' mountaintop shrines are an exaggerated version of this practice, their combination of *chicha* jars, cups, and individualized serving plates, gender-appropriate clothing, and offerings to the Sun, Moon, and Sea, epitomized what was considered valuable in Inca culture (Reinhard and Ceruti 2010). Many other graves in Inca times also contained artifacts that were associated with one gender or the other, for example, weaving kits and fastening pins for women. Similarly, the continuity between the ancestors and their surviving descendants was emphasized time and again by the preservation of mummies in caves and the periodic reopening of tombs for offerings. The variety of burial customs recorded archaeologically throughout the Andes is so complex as to defy description. Regrettably, however, the conquistadores and their successors were so effective at sacking Inca tombs that we have almost no mortuary evidence from the Inca elite classes themselves. An entire cliff-face at the royal estate at Pisac, for example, is pockmarked with looted tombs. The relatively few burials recovered intact by Eaton (1916) at Machu Picchu, tend to contain the remains of service or institutional personnel, not the aristocracy (Salazar 2004). The evidence from those burials and the few cemeteries at provincial sites that have yielded much material indicate that individuals were buried with goods appropriate to their ethnic group and duties to the state.

Recent excavations at Saqsawaman and Chokepukio, coupled with analyses of thirteen tombs excavated in 1933–4 by Luis Valcárcel, have significantly enhanced our information on Inca burial in the Cuzco heartland, however. In the Suchuna sector of the first site, Solis (1999; cited in Paredes 2003) encountered about eighty graves of the commoner populace.[3] Subsequent excavations in 2001 found an additional fifteen funerary contexts containing the remains of members of the elite populace (Paredes 2003). The Saqsawaman mummy bundles tended heavily toward older, adult females, whereas the Chokepukio cemetery, 30 km to the east, contained a cross-section of the population. This contrast suggests that there was a selection process involved in allowing people to be interred in the higher-status burial ground near Cuzco (Julien 2004; Andrushko et al. 2006). The Saqsawaman burials contained objects considered to be typically Inca, such as paired ceramic plates, bottles, and jars, along with pedestal dishes and tripod toasters. Interestingly, objects often associated with gender identity, like women's clothing pins, were recovered from tombs of both sexes. However, no gold was recovered, suggesting that the interred individuals were not among the most elite members of society. Instead, the archaeologists argue, many of the females were more likely members of an elite Inca women's order, the *mamakuna*. The high status of the Saqsawaman individuals did not protect their health, as they appear to have suffered from the effects of infectious diseases, while the individuals interred at Chokepukio showed the effects of increased heavy labor under Inca rule (Andrushko et al. 2006: 78–9).

In contrast, Morris (1972) observed that one of the outstanding features of Inca provincial centers is their apparent lack of a cemetery. He attributed that situation (reasonably in my view) to the fact that even the ethnic Incas considered their presence there to be temporary. Andean peoples considered their proper burial place to be their ancestral kin's homeland, so many individuals may have been transported home for proper treatment after death. As a result, many of the burials with Inca material culture that have been recovered intact in the provinces come from ceremonial contexts, such as the high-elevation shrines described in chapter 8. At the oracular coastal site of Pachacamac, the Incas sacrificed and buried about a score of young women at the entrance to the Sun temple and in the temple itself; some of their burial goods suggest that they may have been from coastal societies (Cornejo 2000). Similarly, about a century ago, Juan de Ambrosetti excavated 202 burials at the site of Puerta de La Paya, Argentina, where he recovered the most spectacular array of Inca grave lots yet found in northwestern Argentina. The goods that were recovered include hundreds of Inca-style ceramics, bead strings, and thirty-five metal objects. Most of the metal was tin bronze in such forms as axes, awls, tweezers, and *tumis* (crescent knives); only one silver and two gold objects were included in the inventory. More interesting were the thousand-plus spindle whorls and other tools for carding wool, spinning, and weaving, found in the tombs of young women. These burials almost certainly contained the remains of *aqllakuna* set to work by the Inca (Ambrosetti 1902, 1907–8–8; Calderari 1991; González 1979; González and Díaz 1992).

In the provinces, Inca-era mortuary practices varied widely in the degree to which they modified traditional practices to incorporate Inca elements. Among the Lupaqa of Lake Titicaca, the lords adopted rectangular floor plans and the cut-stone ashlar masonry characteristic of the finest Inca architecture into their above-ground crypts. The goods interred with these favored lords included a significant proportion of fine Inca polychrome vessels (Hyslop 1990: 247–9). In Peru's Upper Mantaro valley, where the local lords were also highly esteemed, tombs of the elite included cooking, serving, and storage vessels in the Inca style, as well as a variety of metal goods, such as tumi knives, also in the imperial style (Owen and Norconk 1987). Nonetheless, the majority of the tombs contained objects primarily in the local style.

Gender and Kin Relations

Male and female roles were inseparable complements in Inca life (see Silverblatt 1987 for an extensive discussion; see also chapter 5 here). We saw earlier that age grades paralleled one another and that rites were celebrated for each sex at various stages in the life cycle. In some Andean kinship systems, descent was reckoned through both male and female lines (ambilineality), so that men were thought to be descended from their fathers and women from their mothers. Among the Inca royalty, the female line was especially important, because sitting emperors were most closely identified with their mother's kin group and drew their wives from the same kindred. In contrast, the non-royal *ayllu* of the Incas proper seem to have been patrilineal rather than ambilineal, and most other highland peoples also reckoned descent through the male line (Rowe 1946: 253–6; cf. Zuidema 1964; 1977; Rostworowski 1999: 19).

Various kinds of labor were envisioned as efforts shared mutually by men and women. In agriculture, men broke the soil and women planted the seeds, while mining teams recorded in Colonial documents sometimes contained equal numbers of men and women (chapter 12). Certain other tasks were apportioned to each sex. In the mountains, women made beer, collected firewood, and did most of the spinning and weaving, while men hunted and were responsible for military duty, often accompanied by their wives. In some tasks, such as pottery manufacture and metallurgy, both sexes seem to have been involved. Control over the products of labor was not necessarily equally divided, however. For example, women controlled the household larder, while the men controlled the distribution of most status and politically related goods.

The balance between male and female was enshrined symbolically in many ways. As we saw in chapter 3, the origin myths told of four pairs of ancestral sisters and brothers who emerged from the origin place at Pacariqtambo. The Creator God Wiraqocha was conceived as having both male and female aspects, while the two most powerful celestial beings, the Sun and the Moon, were married. Two of the most powerful terrestrial deities were females: Pachamama ("Earth Mother") and Mamacocha, or "Mother of the Lakes (and Sea)," while the earthquake deity (Pachacamac) and weather deity (Inti-Illapa) were male. The various deities' human servants included both male and female orders. Silverblatt (1987) suggests that females were generally associated with symbols of fertility, although the male spirits of the mountains (*apu* or *wamani*) were also intimately associated with fertility as the owners of the flocks and the source of the water that inseminated Mother Earth.

Despite the many parallels between men and women, their relations were not entirely equal. Public roles, such as access to political office and power and the disbursement of natural resources that arose from those positions, were generally reserved for men. Among the Incas proper, there is no evidence for a queen as ruler and the presence of a woman as the paramount leader in other societies was rare enough to warrant special mention (Rostworowski 1999: 73–6). Even so, the Queen Mother and the Queen were enormously powerful figures, immediately below the sitting ruler in authority (chapters 6, 7).

The terms that individuals used to refer to one another depended on the sex of the speaker and that of the person to whom he or she was referring, as well as on their generational relationship. Broadly speaking, Inca kin terminology was ego-centered, meaning that kin terms depended on the speaker. In some contexts, however, the terms were defined in relationship to an important personage. For example, the status of royal Inca kin groups was defined by their kin relationship to the sitting ruler. Within families, a father used different terms for children of different sexes (son: *churi*; daughter: *ususi*), but the mother used only one term (*wawa*) for all children. Both sexes called their father *yaya* and their mother *mama*. Brothers called each other by a reciprocal term (*wawqi*) and their sisters by another word (*pana*), just as sisters called each other by a reciprocal term (*ñaña*) and their brothers by another (*tura*). Those and other terms were extended out to other relatives in different ways. First cousins, for example, were called "brother" and "sister," while father's brother was called "brother" and father's sister was called "aunt." By the time that a young man and woman had reached three or four generations of separation (i.e., they shared a great- or great-great-grandfather), they were thought to be distantly enough related that they could marry (Rowe 1946: 249–51; Zuidema 1964; 1977; Lounsbury 1986).

For the Incas, their kin terms were not simply a way of describing social bonds, but provided a conceptual vocabulary for all kinds of relations. As we have seen in other contexts, for example, Inca rulers kept statues as their alter egos. Called *wawqi* ("brother"), the statues could stand in for the ruler in ceremonies and accompanied them into death. Similarly, celestial beings and features of the landscape were envisioned as ancestors, while the deities themselves were kin to one another. Today, Quechua speakers carry out their arithmetic and weaving designs in kin-based terminology, which is probably a legacy of prehispanic times (Urton 1997). Kinship, gender balance, and hierarchy thus permeated Inca relations with all of humanity and nature.

Making a Living in the Highlands

Farming

In Inca times, highland peoples followed land use practices much like those used by today's Andean peasants (chapter 2). A family had the right to farmlands and pastures because one of its adults was an *ayllu* member by birth. The amount and kinds of land they had depended on the family's status and size and on how productive the lands were. Garcilaso (1966: 245) wrote that each newly married couple received a *tupu* of maize land, which was the area they needed to feed themselves for a year. He equated that to 1.5 times the Spanish *fanega*, which was a little more than half a hectare.[4] As convenient as that conversion sounds, it was probably too simple, since the size of a *tupu* varied according to local ecology, especially the length of a fallowing cycle. Andean farmers often resisted describing their holdings in European measures, because the Spaniards tried to fix areas that should have remained flexible in the native view of things. According to one Cuzqueñan farmer, for example, warm potato lands could be sown only one year in five and the coldest only one in ten. As a result, a farmer needed twice the area in a cold-lands *tupu* than in the warm lands, to allow him to rotate among fallow and cultivated plots without degrading the soil (Murra 1980a: 280–1).

Garcilaso (1966: 245–6) went on to say that a married couple received another *tupu* when a son was born, but only half a *tupu* came with a new daughter. When the children married and formed new households, their natal family's allotment would be reduced and the land reverted to the *ayllu*'s communal holdings. When the last member of a family generation died, the rights to the resources also went back to the *ayllu*, so that the lord could distribute them as needed. Although the Incas themselves apparently passed most rights from father to son, inheritance varied widely among Andean peoples. Among some societies, for example, a husband brought use rights from his father's *ayllu* into the marriage, and the wife brought rights from her mother's kin group (bilateral inheritance; see Murra 1980a).

Early Colonial inspections suggest that higher-status households held more lands in a wider range of zones than did most common folk (Tomka 1987). The elites' right to more than one wife also meant that lords could have more children, which in turn reinforced their prestige, and household labor force. Before the time of the Inca, the highland lords were entitled to pastoral, agricultural, and household service. In return, they were supposed to provide authority in war and peace, ceremonial leadership, and wise judgment in settling community disputes. The lords confirmed or modified land use rights for each household annually and assigned rights to newly formed families. When we take the variations described for different regions into account, Garcilaso's formula is too neat, but he was still on the mark about the core principles of peasant life – use rights were based on kinship, status, and family size.

Farmers' tools were simple – principally a foot plow, a hoe, and a clod breaker. Men wielded the plow, called a *chakitaqlla*. It was made of a pole about 2 m long with a pointed end of wood or bronze, a handle or curvature at the top, and a foot rest lashed near the bottom (Rowe 1946: 211). The farmer drove the point into the ground using both arms and a foot, and then levered up to break the soil. Both the hoes and clod breakers were typically made of river cobbles. The hoes were hafted like adzes while the clod breakers were attached to the end of long poles. When a hoe became blunted, it could be resharpened simply by knocking off a few flakes with a hammerstone after which it could be reused until it was exhausted. In Peru's central highlands, some farmlands are still littered with thousands of fragments of the hoes and clod breakers (Russell 1988).

Farming was a social activity that was celebrated with rituals, sacrifices, and songs (Garcilaso 1966: 244; Cobo 1979: 213–14). Typically, a team of seven or eight men from a family or neighborhood group would work in a line to prepare the fields. Each man used a plow to break the soil and the women followed in another row, breaking the clods and planting the seeds. By teaming up, the work group could share the labor and lighten their burdens. While they worked, they sang and chanted, striking the earth in unison. Cobo recalled being able to hear their singing from a distance off, and Garcilaso professed that the Spanish priests found the songs so pleasant that they were incorporated into church services. During the growing season, the hoes were used to weed the plants as needed. Harvesting inspired the same kinds of labor-sharing as planting did. Once the harvest was in, it was a time of public celebration, called the *Aymoray* (Rowe 1946: 213–16). Such gender-based teamwork remains a common sight in the highlands where traditional farming implements are used. Among modern farmers, it is not unusual for them to go for days with little sleep when it is time to get the harvest in ahead of the frosts.

Managing Water: The Tragedy of the Commons?

Managing water is an essential part of living in the high Andes, in both its ecological and social dimensions (Mitchell and Guillet 1994). Although enough rain often falls to support agriculture without irrigation, precipitation is not sufficiently predictable to ensure a healthy annual crop. Neither does it always fall at the best time of year to make sure that frost-sensitive crops like maize ripen in time for a secure harvest. In addition, managing moisture in the highlands is not simply one of getting water to crops but may be one of storage, or reducing humidity so that crops do not rot in the fields.

In contrast to coastal valleys, in which large-scale irrigation systems were in place thousands of years before the Incas, highland water management practices are usually local in nature. Although the Incas were responsible for significant land and water improvements in many areas, the last few centuries before the Incas' rise to dominance saw major upgrades of various kinds of facilities. It should be noted that the water management was not solely dedicated to growing plants, but also contributed to maintaining pastures for the flocks, and to storing water for use during potential warfare. Immense complexes of drained field lined the edges of Lake Titicaca during the Middle Horizon, for example, in some areas covering as much as 100 km². Scholars debate how much of the planning and labor involved was a product of state or community involvement, but there is no doubt of the vast scale of effort involved (e.g., Kolata 1991; Erickson 2006). Large-scale arrays of terraces were built during the Late Intermediate Period in the Colca valley of the southern Peruvian highlands, many of them irrigated, while smaller but still impressive systems were erected in the *valliserrana* region of northwest Argentina. The central and northern Andean highlands saw the construction of lengthy irrigation canals that fed irrigation networks, as well as reservoirs and drained field systems, all of which complemented lands dedicated to dry farming (Hastorf 1993; Lane 2009). Even so, the small-scale, spring-fed canal systems that were most common in the highlands generally fed no more than about 1,000 ha (i.e., 3.86 mi.²; Hunt 1988, cited by Trawick 2001: 361).

The problem of managing access to water within a social group or among communities sharing a watershed can be enormously vexing to everyone involved (e.g., Trawick 2001). Many issues arise from the ubiquitous problem of how to deal with a commonly held essential resource, such as water, pastures, fuel, clay and stone quarries, salt sources, and the like. Who gets water in what order, how much they get, who is responsible for allocation, how different sectors of the common facilities are built and maintained, are how transgressors are dealt with are just a few of the issues that recur constantly. For example, will water be allocated head-to-tail (i.e., canal intake to end of the line) or tail-to-head? In coastal communities, water is often distributed to the tail first, to ensure that the lowest-lying fields are not left dry. In contrast, in the vertical highland landscape, water is generally distributed trending downward, because the higher elevation fields need to get an earlier start in the agricultural cycle in order to beat the frost.

The principles underlying the contributions and benefits of the various kinds of waterworks are those that governed so much of late prehistoric Andean life. One had both access to and responsibility for water by being a member of a social group, either through birth or marriage into a kin group (*ayllu*). In some cases, dual systems of resource access and maintenance exist side by side, in keeping with the pervasive Andean principle of duality (Mitchell 1976). Garcilaso (1966: 248) wrote that water was allocated in turns in times of scarcity, favoring neither elite nor commoner families, and those who failed to water their lands at the appropriate time were punished accordingly. While he may have been wearing at least rose-tinted glasses here, another mestizo chronicler, Guaman Poma, concurred with his description.

In modern communities that use traditional social and physical techniques, Trawick (2001) found that transparency and social pressure can be effective measures in ensuring equitable distributions of both benefit and obligation, just as Garcilaso implied. While a particular individual may have primary responsibility for organizing things (on a rotating basis), a community may do much of its own policing through constant observation and conversation. Such an approach not only keeps thieves and layabouts in line, it also acts as a check on potentially corrupt officials, who are members of the same community after all. The lack of state involvement in such community affairs is beneficial to both parties. The state would not have to invest any effort, except when major disputes arose, while the social group could organize its own moral economy of water (Trawick's phrase) according to local conditions.

Herding

Many chroniclers accepted the Incas' broad claim that they owned all of the flocks in the empire, but there is little doubt that the empire's subjects had herds of their own (Murra 1975: 117–44). The chroniclers refer to herds owned by both individuals and the community, and there were probably several kinds of ownership practices among Andean peoples. It seems especially likely that the lords retained their rights to personal herds under the Incas. Most clothing came from the herds' wool, but camelid meat was not part of normal daily fare, despite the abundance of the animals. It was reserved instead for local elites and for special occasions (Garcilaso 1966:

202). Tending the herds was primarily the task of the adolescents and children of the community. Guaman Poma wrote that boys up to about 20 years of age and girls up to about 18 saw to their care, a view affirmed by other chroniclers (Guaman Poma 1980: 180–1, 200–1; Cobo 1979: 246). Adults were certainly involved in their husbandry, especially during birthing and shearing, but the day-to-day rounds were in the hands of the young.

Exchange of Labor and Goods

Local autonomy was the ideal, but Andean households depended on each other for a host of activities. And, since not all communities could produce everything they needed, exchange networks linked people living in complementary ecozones. Native witnesses in the Huánuco region, for example, said that people who had lands in only a few zones would produce extra coca, *ch'arki* (jerked, or freeze-dried meat: chapter 2), or other local specialties, which could be exchanged with trade partners elsewhere (Ortiz de Zúñiga 1967: 31, 63, 73, 179, 219, 329). Altiplano peoples traded llamas, *ch'arki*, and wool for lowland products, including cotton, pepper, and coca (Burchard 1974). In one of the more intriguing practices, some special resources such as salt and coca were obtained from colonies who lived several days' walk from their home communities, in what is called an archipelago settlement pattern. In some cases, the colonies housed members of several ethnic groups, who kept up their affiliation with their homelands (Murra 1972; Masuda *et al.* 1985). Families also arranged labor exchanges with real or fictive kin or through links to people of different social statuses. Close relatives often pooled their labor efforts for farming, herding, rituals, or house construction, working on each household's tasks as needed. This kind of balanced exchange, known as *ayni*, is still a common practice. In the asymmetric relationship called *minka*, a family head would work for his in-laws or a low-status household would work for a higher-status family; their labors were repaid with a share of the produce (Alberti and Mayer 1974).

A particularly important kind of mutual reliance came into play when workers were away, for instance when they were called up for military duty for the Inca. At those times, their fields were tended by their neighbors and the products were stored, so that when the soldiers came home, they found their produce nicely stored away and awaiting them. Similar extensions of neighborly support were extended to community members who could not fend for themselves, such as the aged and infirm without family.

A household that could call on the labor of a full nuclear or extended family could work a wider range of lands than one formed of old, single, or orphaned individuals. The smaller households had to rely on social relations to get what they needed, or they would have to do without. Cobo commented approvingly that the Lake Titicaca villages that kept up the mutual support practices a century after the Inca collapse were especially well-off and organized.

Relations between local lords and their subjects also provided ways for households to get goods that would otherwise be hard to obtain. Beyond his political, military, and ritual leadership, a good lord was supposed to be a generous host. To the degree that he could, he would dispense cloth, *chicha*, or other valued materials through ritualized generosity. He might also distribute products such as coca and peppers which could be procured only from great distances, sometimes from the colonies mentioned above. Some of the most noteworthy colonies of the sixteenth century exploited the guano islands off the south coast of Peru. The products were usually gathered or produced by people who worked directly for the lords, who then distributed them along social or political lines. It needs to be stressed that this largess did not substitute for subsistence production or a market system. Instead, it bonded groups, reinforced unequal statuses, and provided commoners with special products.

Domestic Activities

Household life revolved around family care, cooking, and weaving. Within the household, the woman was the dominant figure. Each household produced most of its own food and daily goods, although more extended kin often worked together and shared in the products. A typical complete household included a male head of family (*hatun runa*), his wife, children, and unmarried or widowed adult kin. It was normally part of the larger kin group called the *ayllu*, which held its farmlands, pastures, and other resources in common. Like their modern descendants, prehistoric *ayllus* sought access to several ecozones, for example, maize, potato, and herding zones in the highlands, and coca lands lower down. This allowed most families to be self-reliant for their daily needs.

Women and girls spent a great deal of time collecting firewood or llama dung to be used for cooking. The foods that they made were predominantly vegetarian. Cobo wrote that maize was toasted or cooked in small cakes; popcorn was thought to be a delicacy. Potato dishes were reconstituted from freeze-dried *chuño* or were made with fresh dried potatoes (Cobo 1979: 27–8; 1990: 198–9; see Rowe 1946: 220–1). Grains such as quinoa and *cañihua* were also staples of the highland diet, along with other tubers, such as oca, mashua, and maca. Many of the dishes were flavored with herbs and chili peppers obtained from distant plots or through exchange. Stews made with fish were popular, but meat was reserved for special occasions and for the elites, although *ch'arki* (freeze-dried meat) was a staple on the road. The maize and other foods were ground with rocker mortars or mortar and pestles. Fermented beverages, broadly called *chicha*, were so much part of the cuisine that Cobo said that being forced to drink water was a form of punishment. Families typically ate twice a day, once at about 8 or 9 in the morning and again an hour or two before sunset (Cobo 1990: 198). When a commoner family ate, the dishes were placed on the floor, but a lord would eat off a cloth spread on the ground. The husband and wife sat back to back and she served the food and drink as he requested.

Archaeological evidence from twenty-nine late prehistoric households in the Upper Mantaro valley, Peru, paints a similar picture (D'Altroy *et al.* 2001; see below). All households, whether elite or commoner, shared a basic set of tools: cooking, storage, and serving pottery, grinding stones, weaving tools, and casual flaked stone tools for cutting and scraping. Just before the Inca conquest, most of the Xauxa populace lived in high-elevation settlements that were protected by defensive walls. Christine Hastorf (1990) has been able to show that plant remains recovered from their residences closely matched a set of crops that could be grown nearby, mostly tubers and quinoa. Where maize was found, it was concentrated in the elite houses. Similarly, Elsie Sandefur (2001) has shown that the people who ate in elite households – whether the residents or their guests – got finer cuts of camelid meat. Under Inca rule, many people moved downslope into areas better suited to maize farming, which was reflected in household botanical remains. Not everybody gained equally, however. Analysis of human bone collagen shows that adult males benefited more than anyone else because, Hastorf suggests, the Incas gave them maize beer as part of their institutionalized generosity (Hastorf and DeNiro 1985). The status differences in meat consumption disappeared under the Incas, but we do not know if the diets were really equalized or if the elites were eating meat elsewhere, such as at the nearby provincial center. In any event, the elites still managed to display their rank through food, for they roasted much of their meat, while the commoners ate theirs in less prestigious stews.

Household Crafts

Despite the scale of state production (chapter 13), most goods and tools produced under Inca rule were made, used, and discarded in village economies in which the Inca had no interest. The written record took little notice of those activities, because they were marginal to Inca or Spanish concerns. With respect to the bigger picture of Andean life, however, household remains are a reflection of most people's daily affairs. The discrepancy between a vision of the Inca state involved in all aspects of domestic life and household residues could hardly be more conspicuous. The typical Andean household had no access to the cultural equivalent of Fabergé eggs, Wedgwood china, Chinese silks, or sterling silver. Instead, householders made their own homespun clothes and made or traded for the whole range of tools and utilitarian goods that they needed for daily life. Cobo said that a person owned just one set of clothes, which he or she never changed or washed; the peasants' state of constant filth offended his sensibilities. Even where we know that the local population was organized to perform state duties, goods of state manufacture are rare. The difficulties of identifying Inca-era occupations at local settlements is a key reason that we still do not have as fine an understanding of subject life under the empire as we would like.

This situation does not mean that daily life among Andean peasants did not change under Inca rule, but that the shifts were more subtle and less pervasive than imperial propaganda might lead us to expect. For a case study, we return to the Upper Mantaro (D'Altroy *et al.* 2001). To get most of their craft goods, peasants in the Mantaro relied on a mix of their own manufactures and regional exchange. In the classic vision of an Andean woman, whether sitting at home, nursing a baby, or walking, she was invariably spinning wool to make cloth. Archaeologically, the ubiquity of spinning and weaving is confirmed by the ceramic spindle whorls found in all households and by other bone tools and bronze needles (Costin 1993).

It is less widely appreciated that families relied on chipped stone tools right through the Inca era, for cutting, chopping, drilling, and scraping. Bronze tools complemented lithics, but did not replace them entirely. All households seem to have made casual stone tools for cutting and scraping, and some villages also made certain tools for exchange with neighboring settlements. Glenn Russell (1988) has shown, for example, that both before and during Inca rule, the Mantaro town nearest the main chert quarry made special blade tools that were probably used for the grain harvest. The scale of production was prodigious, as more than a million tool blanks were roughed out before being taken home for finishing work during the centuries that the quarry was mined. However, almost none of those tools found their way to Hatun Xauxa, the Inca center. In fact, stone-cutting and scraping tools are uncommon at Inca installations throughout the empire. The reasons for this are unclear, but it may be that the crafts pursued at state centers did not require them or that lithics were considered low status and were replaced by objects made of bronze. Many Mantaro households also contain vitrified sherds (wasters), which are evidence of the manufacture of pottery. As with the chert blades, large-scale potting was focused in single towns before and under the Incas. In contrast, the valley's finest pottery style was a special product made to the south that was replaced by Inca polychromes under Cuzco's dominion (Costin 1986, 2001).

The Mantaro evidence shows that craft production before Inca rule, where specialized, was organized along community lines. With Inca rule, the state intervened only in crafts that were part of the political economy, that is, in metals, prestige ceramics, and textiles. They seem to have utterly ignored the production of stone tools, which were essential to agriculture. None of the lists of labor assignments includes lithic tool production, and the farm workers seem to have carried their own tools to state fields. Overall, the pattern suggests that some village specialization was treated as part of local self-sufficiency, which the Incas were more than content to leave alone.

On the Coast

The social and economic relations of coastal communities were intimately linked, just as they were in the highlands. The decapitation of the Chimu empire along the north coast did not completely dismantle the strict social hierarchy, however. Some coastal lords owned entire valleys and their subjects had access to lands only through their relationship with the lord, not through the communal land holdings that prevailed in the mountains (Rostworowski 1999: 152). There were differences in other rights, too. For example, coastal farmers measured both field size and standing crops by the number of feeder canals that watered them and not by the flexible highland measure called *tupu*. People of higher social status had preferred access to the finer lands, especially those toward the canal intakes, which could yield more than one crop per year (Netherly 1978: 288; 1984: 239).

In sharp contrast to the mountains, entire communities could specialize as potters, weavers, farmers, fishers, traders, and sandal-makers. Rather than being self-sufficient, they would exchange their products for those gathered, grown, or made by other communities. One of the other interesting distinctions lay in the production of maize beer. On the coast, men made *chicha* for trade or to present to their lords, while women made the beer in the highlands for communal or institutional uses. Rostworowski shows that kin groups often gained access to diverse resources by organizing their holdings lengthwise within valleys. Access to more distant resources could also be enhanced as lords up and down river exchanged the rights to cultivate maize and coca fields in one another's territories (Rostworowski 1977: 240–1; 1990).

Another important difference lay in the long-time presence of special-purpose money and more sophisticated weights and measures than those found in the central Andean highlands. It is not clear how widely the currencies were used in prehistory. There is no evidence, for example, that land or labor could be purchased until the Colonial era (Hosler *et al.* 1990; Salomon 1986; 1987; Netherly 1978). The Incas themselves did not adopt the currencies for the state economy, although they used large amounts of the shell and gold for political and ceremonial ends. Instead, they either left things alone or manipulated the situation politically to give favored groups an advantage. Coastal life thus differed in important ways from that of the adjacent highlands. Overall, however, the ideas of community focus and collective resource management, along with mutual commitments between lords and subjects, typified the coast as much as they did the highlands.

Notes

1   Quechua: Santo Tomás 1951; González Holguín 1952; Aymara: Bertonio 1956; see also Rowe 1948.

2   Rowe (1958) describes a number of distinct models of the age-grade categories, including one that entailed twelve stages of life, not ten as Guaman Poma depicted. Rowe's close analysis of the sources led him to accept the base-ten model as the one most likely used by the state census-takers, an assessment that seems most reasonable to me.

3   Only a sample of the burial population was investigated, totaling forty-one to forty-three individuals (Paredes 2003; Andrushko *et al.* 2006).

4   Haggard and McLean 1941: 77; Cobo said a *tupu* was 50 × 25 brazas, or about 90 × 45 m, which is about 0.4 ha; see also Polo 1916: 70.

Chapter Ten

Militarism

Diplomacy, reward, and enculturation were essential ingredients in the Incas' formula for creating Tawantinsuyu, but warfare still lay at the heart of the process both symbolically and practically. Triumphant campaigns put untold resources at Cuzco's disposal, showered glory on the elites, and gave common folk a rare chance to better their station in life. Although the Incas negotiated dominion over many societies while shedding little blood, their armies met considerable opposition and a few especially redoubtable societies fiercely resisted Inca rule for many years. Effective Inca military strategy thus required mobilizing thousands of military and auxiliary personnel for campaigns that could last months or even decades. To meet their military goals, the Incas created a network of internal garrisons, frontier forts, and a remarkable logistical system of roads, support facilities, and depots. Those military activities collectively placed enormous, though sporadic, demands on the human and natural resources of the Andes throughout Inca rule.

The earliest chroniclers wrote extensively on military affairs largely because they were fortune-seeking soldiers themselves. Despite the Spaniards' initial successes, the course of events rapidly compelled their respect for the Incas' military prowess. Besieged Spanish forces in Cuzco and Ciudad de Los Reyes (Lima) narrowly escaped annihilation in 1536, and several expeditions were wiped out in the mountainous terrain. Under the circumstances, it is small wonder that Inca militarism gained a conspicuous place in early accounts. Some modern authors nevertheless suggest that the conquistadores' martial bent and the Incas' efforts to glorify their history have biased our views toward militarism as the power that forged Tawantinsuyu. They point out that the Incas formed many ties through ceremonial exchanges and that the same stories of conquest and rebellion tended to be repeated from one chronicle to the next (e.g., Pease 1982; Rowe

The Incas, Second Edition. Terence N. D'Altroy.
© 2015 John Wiley & Sons, Ltd. Published 2015 by John Wiley & Sons, Ltd.

1982; Morris 1982; 1998; Rostworowski 1999: 65–86). Their persuasive skills notwithstanding, the Incas' power and their own self-image hinged on their military capacities. The recitals of accomplishments by past sovereigns highlighted their conquests, and the names of forts captured in military campaigns were memorialized in *khipu* accounts. After his death, an emperor's funerary rites celebrated his life through pilgrimages to the sites of his great victories, while rulers without military conquests to boast of were not honored as were the more vital leaders. Gose's (1996a: 4) characterization of Inca rulers is apt: "(A)n Andean king began his career as a living warrior and matured into a dead deity."

In this chapter, we will explore how Inca militarism worked. At the outset, we need to recognize that the Incas owed much of their success to strategy and logistics, not to tactics, training, or technology. It was in their preparatory organization that the Inca military excelled, for their battlefield command and conduct drew from traditional methods applied on a grander scale. Even in 1532, the army consisted mostly of modular units of conscripts, using their own weapons and led by their own lords, waging war as labor duty to the state. That method of recruitment, along with linguistic barriers and the challenges of transportation, limited the Incas' tactical options, which they partially addressed by creating a support system and professionalizing the army over time. Even so, the dynastic war between Waskhar and Atawallpa was fought largely by farmers and herders pressed into duty.

Military Strategy

We are on firmer ground in discussing the Inca military strategy of the early sixteenth century than for earlier eras, but clues about pre-imperial warfare can be found in the royal sagas and archaeology. As described earlier (chapters 2, 3), the settlements of the Late Intermediate Period were situated on high peaks throughout much of the Andean highlands, suggesting that localized conflict was endemic (e.g., D'Altroy *et al.* 2001; Covey 2006b; Arkush 2011). To judge from the narratives, early Inca war was indistinguishable from that of other highland contemporaries. The tales portray the local leaders as warlords, called *zinch'i*, who mobilized their kinsmen and communities for booty and glory. Pillaging the neighbors' crops, wealth, and women was said to have been the main goal of war, along with the social stature that martial glory brought. The offensive and defensive elements of early Inca militarism were mutually reinforcing, because successful raids could provoke retaliation or dissuade attacks.

When the Incas expanded out of the Cuzco region, they faced great obstacles, for they were neither the most populous, the most powerful, nor the richest people of the central Andes. The Qolla and Lupaqa of the Lake Titicaca basin probably surpassed them in most ways and the coastal Chimu polity was vastly larger, wealthier, and more complex. The military situation dictated that the Incas economize in their use of force, because they lacked the resources to enforce hands-on control over all the societies that they dominated. The early imperial-era successes probably owed much to alliances, conscription of defeated foes, and confrontation of target societies with overwhelming force (e.g., Bram 1941; Rawls 1979; Espinoza Soriano 1980; Rostworowski 1999). The shift from looting to annexation was probably a decisive change in policy. Most chroniclers ascribed the policy to Wiraqocha Inka and Pachakuti, although some said that Inca lords had begun to attach lands three or four generations earlier (see chapter 4). The practical methods of annexing new subjects coupled diplomacy and coercion. Customarily, an army that was mobilized in the agricultural off-season approached a targeted *señorío* with overwhelming force. Messengers sent by the Inca commander would offer favorable terms of surrender. Compliant subject elites received gifts and could expect to retain or enhance their status, while communities were allowed to keep many of their resources (e.g., Cieza 1967: 163–4; Toledo 1940: 19–20). Along the central coast, for example, the highland Huarochirí people were awarded coca lands that had previously belonged to lowland peoples (Makowski and Vega Centeno A. 2004). A key to early success lay in the inability of Andean *señoríos* to coordinate resistance to Inca advances. In most confrontations, the Incas could marshal armies capable of overpowering whatever force the opponents could muster. The newly subjected populace would have to pledge loyalty to the Sapa Inca, agree to supply labor service, and pay homage to the Sun.

Tawantinsuyu's rapid expansion may have thus owed as much to perceptions of Inca power as it did to the reality. The general principle was to be generous with those who capitulated, and to punish harshly those who resisted. Many stories describe ethnic groups succumbing in the face of Cuzco's forces, if not meekly, at least without pitched battle (Rostworowski 1999: 69–72). For example, several valleys along Peru's southern coast from Chincha to Moquegua were said to have been absorbed through diplomatic ventures, although the sources disagreed over the particulars. Similarly, an army of 30,000 soldiers reportedly took much of the agriculturally rich Upper Mantaro valley of central Peru and its 200,000 residents without opposition. Only at the Xauxa stronghold of Siquillapucara – probably the archaeological site called Tunanmarca – did the residents resist fiercely. There the Incas were said to have won a desperate battle, after which they deported their adversaries en masse (Cieza 1967: 163–4; Toledo 1940: 19–20; Espinoza Soriano 1972: 38; Rowe 1985b: 224). The archaeological data fit the notion of a forced abandonment of the area, as Inca remains are lacking in Tunanmarca and several nearby Late Intermediate Period towns, even though well over a hundred other sites with Inca ceramics lie within half a day's walk (Earle *et al.* 1987; D'Altroy *et al.* 2001). The success of the Incas' diplomacy elsewhere similarly hinged on their ability and willingness to crush resistance. In part to deter rebellions and perhaps to make examples, they massacred some especially obdurate foes, such as the Guarco of coastal Cañete and the Cayambe of Ecuador (chapter 4).

As the empire matured, the Incas moved from expansion to more stable dominion. Governance shifted from a low-intensity, low-control approach in most areas toward a high-intensity, high-control strategy, especially in the central and northern highlands (Rawls 1979; D'Altroy 1992: 71–83). Broadly speaking, the goals of military policy shifted from acquisition toward pacification and securing frontier areas. These goals were met in part through founding garrisons, resettling restive societies, and fortifying frontier hot spots. One effective tactic pursued along the southeast seems to have been to recruit favorably disposed peoples from the frontier region to serve the Incas' interests, in return for benefits and security (e.g., Lorandi and Boixadós 1987–8; Alconini 2010). The need to sustain large forces at great distances from home for extended campaigns also favored development of a network of storage depots along the roads, especially in the northern part of the realm (see "Logistics," below). Even so, incidents of resistance, alliance, submission, and rebellion combined with the nature of existing societies and geography to make distinct policies appropriate in different times and places. Shifts in Inca military policy are thus better understood as changes of emphasis in regional theaters than as a sequence whose phases occurred concurrently throughout the empire (Dillehay and Netherly 1988).

The policy that was in place at the time of the Spanish invasion generally conforms to a strategy of defense-in-depth (Rawls 1979: 146). That approach relies on self-contained strongholds toward the edges of imperial control, supported by mobile forces deployed among or behind them. Forts formed hard points in a defensive perimeter that was intended to impede passage into the territory, if not stop it altogether. Defense-in-depth offers more security for the provinces than a strategy that relies on threat and retribution, but it reduces flexibility in the disposition of resources and requires an investment in fortifications and supply facilities (Luttwak 1976). If we can accept the narratives, elements of that strategy may have been introduced fairly early in the imperial era. Even though frontier problems were a concern, the principal threats to the stability of the state after the major conquests were insurrections and dynastic wars of succession (Murra 1986). Some Lake Titicaca societies like the Qolla and the north Peruvian Chachapoyas were reportedly prone to reasserting their independence at every opportunity. The persistence of such rebellions led the Incas to install loyal colonists, who provided control over refractory subjects, and to disperse the troublesome peoples in provinces away from their homelands. The move toward a more professional force of militarily specialized ethnic groups also helped meet the need for a dependable army (see "Military Specialists," below).

The provincial centers between Cuzco and Quito aided military activity by facilitating movement of goods, people, and messages between regions. The centers often lay at the intersection of natural conduits of travel, adjacent to open valleys or plains where armies could be conveniently bivouacked. Because many provinces were never truly secure, Hyslop (pers. comm. 1990) has suggested that major centers were situated partially as a tactic to reduce the threat of uprisings and to support reprisals when they did occur. As the support system was developed, the state's ability to mobilize large armies was markedly improved. Even so, armies could not be moved simply at the will of the commanders, and the resources of the immediate vicinity of the conflicts were occasionally exhausted even in well-planned campaigns. The development of roads, storehouses, and waystations was therefore fundamental to Inca military strategy.

Fortifications and Garrisons

Fortified strongholds are not abundant in most of Tawantinsuyu. Forts were built near hostile frontiers, but the Inca realm did not have a fixed border in the sense that modern nation-states do. Instead, the Incas maintained flexible relationships with societies beyond their control, leaving the frontiers permeable or hardening them as the situation warranted. The limits of effective Inca rule often lay at retrenched positions, to which the troops had withdrawn after exploratory ventures. In fact, most areas lay at or near a frontier at some point and incorporation was an irregular process (Morris 1988). As a result, some front-line forts eventually lay 1,000 km or more behind the empire's limits. The restricted use of forts makes sense in terms of the largely offensive or pacifying character of Inca warfare. The Incas did not have to defend a home territory against invasions by major powers, as did many Old World empires. Instead, they usually carried the offensive battle to the enemy, or dealt with insurrections, so that military construction was often attuned to logistics. Forts were used as forward bases of operations for campaigns, field camps in hostile territory, front-line redoubts used to support frontier advances, hard-point defenses, perimeter guard posts, and occasional internal garrisons. That is a varied list, to be sure, but strongholds were more important in the military arsenal of the Incas' targets than they were for Cuzco's strategy.

Few truly fortified Inca sites are known for the heartland, though many sites north and east of Cuzco lie in strategically and topographically defensible positions. Two important sites that played military roles in the early Colonial wars – Saqsawaman and Ollantaytambo – may have been only partly designed as fortified redoubts, if at all, but they served that purpose well enough when the need arose. Scholarly opinion is split about the military functions of the estates and other settlements lining the Vilcanota/Urubamba valley for 200 km below Cuzco. Some writers note that they could have served to limit traffic into the heartland, even if they were not specifically designed as fortifications (Rawls 1979). It has sometimes been proposed that the walls that enclosed the spectacularly situated Machu Picchu were intended for defense, but MacLean (1986: 34–40, 82–6) argues that they are better understood as barriers protecting sacred or private spaces or as terrace support walls needed because of the precipitous terrain. Even without any explicitly military architecture, however, the settlements placed the stamp of Inca dominion on the eastern slopes.

Despite the rarity of strongholds away from the frontier in highland Peru, garrisons at major centers were important even near the heartland. Their lack of defensive architecture suggests more that the Incas did not expect the centers to come under military threat than that they had no military functions. The structures most appropriate to military uses are *kallanka*, large rectangular buildings that sometimes served as barracks. Vilcaswaman was said to house 30,000 soldiers, but archaeological studies have found no fortifications there (González Carré *et al.* 1981). No Inca fort is known in the

Upper Mantaro valley either, even though an army counted off at 35,000 was stationed at Hatun Xauxa in 1532–3. Similarly, there are no fortifications at Huánuco Pampa (Morris *et al.* 2011) or Pumpu (Matos Mendieta 1994), while the Spaniards found Atawallpa's army in Cajamarca quartered in an orderly array of tents, but mentioned no fortifications.

In their earliest campaigns, the Incas may have made use of existing facilities, such as Cuismancu's fort at Cajamarca, Peru, or the series of redoubts built by the altiplano societies alongside Lake Titicaca. Nonetheless, documents and archaeology both suggest that the permanent forts were mostly a late phenomenon. The perceptive Polo (1916: 98–9) provided a brief list of the regions where the Incas conducted warfare that corresponds neatly to both the locations of known forts and Wayna Qhapaq's campaigns. Excepting a few prominent sites in Peru, such as Saqsawaman above Cuzco and Inkawasi in the coastal Cañete valley, the forts cluster mostly in northern Ecuador and along the perimeter of Kollasuyu, in Bolivia, Argentina, and Chile (Hyslop 1990: 146–90) (figure 10.1).

An especially high concentration of forts lay near Quito, where the Incas engaged in a seventeen-year-long effort to subdue the Cayambe (Connell *et al.* 2003). In total, thirty-seven forts identified archaeologically have been attributed to the Incas' Ecuadorian occupation. Plaza Schuller (1976; 1980) suggests that many were originally built by the indigenous societies, but were then taken over by the Incas to sustain their advances farther north. The complex of fourteen fortified hilltops at Pambamarca, 32 km northeast of Quito, was by far the most extensive array of strongholds concentrated in one region (plate 10.1; Hyslop 1990: 165–73). The site was probably the historical settlement of El Quinche, where the Incas installed colonists from half a dozen Peruvian and Ecuadorian societies (Salomon 1986: 163; see Espinoza Soriano 1975). Recent research at the Pambamarca sites highlights the importance of their intervisibility across the rugged terrain, which would have facilitated communications and thus defense (Connell *et al.* 2003). While a number of the sites in that array of fortresses contained residential architecture, the most prominent features of the sites were generally open spaces enclosed with walls, platforms, and rectangular *kallanka* structures. The site of Quitoloma, mapped and excavated by Connell and Gifford, is one of the more elaborate fortresses (plate 10.1). In addition to the basic features just noted, its internal configuration contained an array of other buildings, probably dedicated to more permanent habitation.

The concentration of fortified sites in the southern Andes also reflects an intense Inca concern for military security. Among the most important

Figure 10.1   The distribution of known Inca fortified settlements.

fortified sites east of the altiplano were Incallajta, Pocona, Batanes, and Inc-ahuasi. Inkallajta was unusual in that it seems to have been both a regional administrative/ceremonial center and a fortified stronghold (Hyslop 1990: 176–82; Coben 2012). While it lay hundreds of kilometers above the most easterly Inca settlements at the modern Bolivia/Brazil frontier (Pärssinen in press), researchers working at the center have long taken note of its defensive positioning and features. The zig-zag wall enclosing the site on the north

Plate 10.1 View of Unit 12 at Pambamarca, Ecuador. Source: reproduced by permission of Chad Gifford.

side, along with its baffled entrance, speak to a concern for protection. At the same time, the double-road leading to and from the site, and the control gate that straddled it, are indicative of a symbolic or status-related threshold that people entering the installation would have had to cross (Coben 2010). The grand double-gabled *kallanka* adjoining an immense enclosed courtyard is the largest in the empire; its longest sides measure about 75 m (Coben 2012; plate 10.2). Clearly, the Incas' intent in building this facility was not simply to establish a hardened perimeter, but to imprint the Inca ideal on the social landscape. Coben (2006) aptly analyzes Inca practice in making and using the installation as performance in an imperial theater.

In northwest Argentina, the easternmost array of forts also lies along or just below the crest of the mountains, beyond which roads, waystations, and farms extended for well over 100 km (Raffino 1993: 213–34). Several major sites in Kollasuyu's intermontane valleys were also fortified, among them the stronghold at Cortaderas, which was transformed into an administrative complex as their hold on the valley became more secure (Hyslop 1984: 175–7; D'Altroy *et al.* 2000; 2007; Acuto 2010). Pucará de Andalgalá and

Plate 10.2   The *kallanka* adjoining the central plaza at Inkallajta, Bolivia. Source: reproduced by permission of Lawrence Coben.

Pucará de las Pavas are impressive Inca citadels in the Bolsón de Andalgalá, and numerous other forts were also built or coopted. The Chilean forts at Cerro del Inga, Chena, and Angostura stand out as local sites at the southern margins of the empire that were taken over by the state (Stehberg 1976; Planella *et al.* 1991). Many of the strongholds formed a line of defense well inside the eastern margin of the empire; beyond them the Incas maintained economic or cultural relations for distances of several hundred kilometers. Until we have finetuned the chronology better, it will be hard to assess if the positioning of those sites represented an early stage of the Inca occupation, beyond which economic activities were extended, or if the intent was to provide a cordon of hard points behind the active frontier.

Most frontier fortresses were neither large enough nor manned with personnel adequate to preclude all potential incursions by outside forces. Instead, they seem to have been designed to deter raids or cut them off from behind. Forts were typically positioned to control traffic through key natural points of transit, especially mountain passes. Pambamarca (Ecuador), Incallajta (Bolivia), Cortaderas and Pucará de Andalgalá

(Argentina), and Cerro del Inga (Chile) were all situated in such locations. In some cases, the forts may have been no more than temporary facilities, such as the encampments that Wayna Qhapaq's armies built in their descent into the woodlands of northern Peru and Ecuador (Cieza 1967: 187). The site of Inkawasi, in the coastal Cañete valley, was the most elaborate temporary facility erected expressly for military purposes (Hyslop 1985). According to Cieza, it was built when entreaties and assaults failed to take the local stronghold at Ungará. A planned settlement containing about 800 structures, Inkawasi was one of several installations christened a "New Cuzco." The site housed a small garrison during the summer, when the highland armies suffered from the heat and withdrew to the mountains. When campaigns were conducted in the cooler months of several successive winters, the site was the regional base of operations. Inkawasi was abandoned when the campaign drew to a successful close, suggesting that forts were not a central part of the Inca strategy for ruling within their relatively secure lands.

Permanent Inca forts were usually not elaborate affairs, though they were well tailored to the kinds of threats that Andean armies could mount. The Incas could expect attacks with projectiles of limited range and power, such as arrows, spears, and sling stones, but did not have to cope with explosives, mounted attacks, or siege machinery, such as battering rams or catapults. Frontal attack by shock troops was the preferred method of taking a stronghold in Andean war, so forts were designed to repel waves of soldiers in close combat. They usually consisted of walled enclosures with broad open areas and spare architecture, set on hilltops or at the crest of steep slopes. Many had several concentric walls, moats, and revetments. The encircling walls were often built with bends and salients to gain multiple shooting angles on assaulting troops (Hyslop 1990: 163–90). Behind the walls, the Incas typically erected elongated platforms and cached piles of sling stones. Entry was channeled through doorways that were sometimes offset or laid out in zig-zag patterns to foil massed attacks. The largest forts each encompassed no more than about 10 ha, which limited the number of people who could seek refuge, but kept the perimeters relatively short. They were not designed to bivouac large numbers of soldiers for any length of time, and armies on the move typically slept in tents.

Overall, then, forts played a crucial role along the imperial frontiers, but relations were complex and attuned to local conditions. Reliance on overt militarism through fortified bastions played a crucial role in securing peace along the empire's edge at particular locations, but it was hardly the only strategy employed. Economic and cultural outreach across borders and recruitment of willing allies were also crucial tools for the Inca along their thousands of kilometers of borderlands.

Military Organization

Even in 1532, the Inca command structure was not complex by the standards of ancient empires. Much of the command's simplicity arose from the lack of a standing army for most of Tawantinsuyu's history, the drafting of peasants as soldiers, and the difficulties of communication in the polyglot empire. The emperor was the commander in chief and occasional field general. Below him was a hierarchy of officers ranging down to ethnic leaders of the fighting units. The highest officers were usually royal kin, although non-Inca ethnic elites sometimes held high ranks. Choosing relatives may theoretically have ensured common interests between the ruler and his officers, but delegating command of a large army to competent soldiers with a potential royal claim was a chancy business. The more effective a commander was, the more potent a threat he posed, since the military often held the key to settling claims to the throne.

In light of this situation, it is intriguing that the military commanders executed by sitting rulers were those whose power or glory potentially threatened the throne, not those who had failed in their duties. A celebrated case occurred when Qhapaq Yupanki, Pachakuti's brother, returned to Cuzco after vainly pursuing the deserted Chankas through the central highlands of Peru (chapter 4). Sarmiento suggests that Qhapaq Yupanki was killed nominally because he had failed to keep the Chankas in line and because he exceeded the territorial limit that Pachakuti had set for the expedition. Rowe (1946: 206) points out, however, that Pachakuti may have seen his brother's victories as a threat and decided to take preventive action. According to Sarmiento, Pachakuti also ordered the execution of one or two of his own sons who had accompanied his heir designate, Thupa Inka Yupanki, at the close of the great northern campaigns. The rationale was that they had kept the young man away from Cuzco for so long, but Sarmiento (2007: 153) offered the opinion that the ruler was jealous of their glory and riches. In contrast, failed generals seem to have been relieved of command in disgrace, but not executed. Wanka Awki's string of resounding defeats from Tumipampa to Xauxa, for example, resulted only in his humiliating dismissal.

The king's military role changed in emphasis from battlefield command to strategic planning as Inca warfare shifted from chiefly predation to imperial expansion. Many chroniclers wrote that Pachakuti increasingly delegated military command to his brothers and finally ceded it entirely to Thupa Inka Yupanki, his son. Thupa Inka Yupanki in turn was acclaimed for leading the armies, but the northern campaigns typically ascribed to his leadership occurred before he assumed effective military command and his uncles seem to have kept the heir a safe distance from the battlefield. Such protective action is not to say that heirs apparent were always removed from peril, however. Candidates for the throne accompanied military actions to represent the crown and to learn the dangerous practice of war. Atawallpa's disastrous sortie into the Ecuadorian forests provides a case in point (see chapter 4).

The rulers did go on campaign selectively throughout Tawantinsuyu's reign and even put themselves in the midst of conflict on a number of storied occasions, such as Wayna Qhapaq's miscarried assault on the Caranqui, when he was unseated. Atawallpa's first battle at Tumipampa, when he was captured and his ear damaged, and Waskhar's final defense on the banks of the Apurimac also saw the principals on the battlefield. In those situations, the paramount's role as charismatic leader and perhaps tactician may have been crucial to the success of the ventures. Despite his frequent absence from the battlefield, the king's presence on campaign was important, as leaders accompanied their men into some of the most difficult lands that the Andes have to offer. Even so, Inca monarchs only intermittently got close enough to the action to be in much personal danger. They usually directed operations from a headquarters some distance removed from the battlefield. Campaigns in northern Peru under Thupa Inka Yupanki's titular leadership and in highland Ecuador under Wayna Qhapaq were directed from Cajamarca and Tumipampa, respectively. Expeditions sent into unfamiliar lands were often headed by subordinate officers, for example into Pasto territory in the north, the temperate forests of the Araucanians in the far south, and the eastern lowlands of Bolivia and Argentina. Similarly, except for the first few and the last engagements of the dynastic war, neither Waskhar nor Atawallpa was present at the battleground.

In keeping with the dual organization that pervaded Inca rule, two or four commanders were often appointed to lead a campaign or army. How authority was divided among the commanders is uncertain. If military practice followed social convention, one individual was dominant. The chroniclers used distinctly European terms to describe such individuals, but their expressions may conceivably reflect the broad scope of duties assigned each position. Cabello Valboa (1951: 430, 442), for example, described Atawallpa's two commanders in the war against Waskhar as Field General or Field Marshal (Challcochima) and Master of the Camp or General Administrator of the Army (Quizquiz). At least in late campaigns, military units were organized in a decimal structure, which also had civil applications. The units were usually made up of soldiers from particular ethnic groups led by their own lords. The smallest unit contained ten heads of household (*hatun runa*), under the command of a *chunka kamayuq*. The next order up was 100 soldiers, under a *pachaka kuraka*. One thousand men were commanded by a *waranqa kuraka*, and 10,000 by a *hunu kuraka*, but it is not clear how often that many men were ever fielded at one time from any ethnic group. Each division contained two halves, each with its own leader.

For practical reasons, ethnic elites led their own men on the battlefield. There were scores of distinct languages in the domain and even the main dialects of Quechua were not mutually intelligible. Using Cuzco Quechua as a *lingua franca* among the elites helped matters, but most of the common troops could not be expected to speak it. Linguistic and personal familiarity between commanders and their troops was therefore necessary for effective battlefield conduct. Moreover, group cohesion and competition with other fighting units fostered an esprit de corps. The downside of using compartmentalized fighting units and scores of ethnically distinct low-level officers was a limited flexibility in battlefield command. Almost certainly, there were severe limits on the kinds of tactical control over the troops that come with standardized, professional, training exercises, such as those practiced by the Roman legions. Although maneuvers were planned and the troops were arrayed according to their weapons, once a battle was engaged, only the simplest changes in plan were possible based on up-to-the-minute information.

Scale of the Armies

Both Inca oral histories and Spanish accounts state that the Incas could field armies in excess of 100,000 at a time, although we should view the high-end estimates skeptically. Regrettably, only a couple of the figures seem to have been taken directly from *khipu* tabulations. In one case, Atawallpa's force at the battle of the Yanamarca valley was tabulated as 140,000 men, plus servants and porters, whereas the opposing army was estimated to include 130,000 soldiers (Cieza 1967). The other tally involved Challcochima's contingent, which was bivouacked at Hatun Xauxa following Atawallpa's final victory. When the first Spaniards on the road to Cuzco paused there, the army's *khipu kamayuq* counted off 35,000 soldiers for the visitors' benefit (H. Pizarro 1959: 89). At the same time, Quizquiz headed a force of 10,000 at Cuzco, having dismissed the other 30,000 under his command (Xérez 1985: 121).

For armies seen first-hand by the Spaniards, estimates of many scores of thousands are common, although we need to be cautious about the accuracy of any figure, since the participants on both sides were prone to exaggerate for effect. Cristóbal de Mena (1937: 84) reported that there were more than 80,000 effectives at Cajamarca when the Spaniards arrived, while others put the figure at about half that or a little more (see Xérez 1985: 92, 108; P. Pizarro 1986: 32; Trujillo 1985: 202; see Hemming 1970: 36). Drawing from interviews fifteen years later, Cieza (1967: 128) wrote that Atawallpa's army had totalled 87,000 men: 12,000 in a vanguard, then 5,000 to capture the Spaniards' horses, and 70,000 in the main body. He added that 30,000 servants, plus women, were also present. Such a profusion of porters and camp followers, common in Inca warfare, added to the size and unwieldiness of the imperial forces (see below). Some of the largest Inca armies may have been those under Manqo Inka that set siege to Cuzco in 1536. De Mena gauged that 100,000 soldiers and 80,000 auxiliaries were present. Pedro Pizarro put the figure at 200,000, which is the same figure that Molina cited for the army that Manqo Inka was preparing to mobilize for a renewed summer siege.[1] At the same time, an immense force assembled on the outskirts of Ciudad de los Reyes (Lima). Even after the siege of Cuzco collapsed, remnant armies in the eastern Andes reportedly contained upwards of 20,000 soldiers.

Estimates for earlier eras should be taken even more guardedly. The figures for armies of conquest range from the 10,000 Thupa Inka Yupanki was said to have used to take the Mantaro valley (Toledo 1940: 19) to the less credible 250,000 reported for Thupa Inka Yupanki's first campaigns against the Kañari and Quitos (Sarmiento 2007: 150). Even if we take these grandiose estimates with a large dose of salt, the two *khipu* accounts and the scale of forces besieging Cuzco and Lima give us ample reason to believe that scores of thousands of soldiers could be mobilized for individual campaigns and that more than 100,000 effectives may have been engaged in single battles.

Recruitment of Personnel

General Mobilization

Military service under the Incas was a broad, but not universal, labor duty of adult males (Polo 1916: 98–9). In principle, all sound married males whose age-grade fell in the range of 25–30 to 50 years were subject to call-up on a rotating basis. Those men, called *awka kamayuq* ("warriors"), formed the bulwark of the army as foot soldiers. They were often accompanied on campaigns by their wives or other close kin, who cared for their personal needs. On long campaigns, it was not unusual for children to be born and travel with the soldiers. Unmarried men whose age-grade fell in the range of about 18–25 (*sayapayaq*) bore messages and cargo (Guaman Poma 1980: 171, 179; *RGI* I: 346; Murúa 1986: 362–5; Rowe 1958; Murra 1980b: 89; Spurling 1982: 3).

Some chroniclers explained that boys were trained in the martial arts in their home communities so that they would be capable warriors when called upon. Bartolomé de Las Casas (trans. from Bram 1941: 46), perhaps with some exaggeration, wrote that "(i)n every settlement there were instructors in the art of fighting and manipulating weapons. They had charge of all the boys from ten to eighteen, who at certain hours of the day, were ordered to fight among themselves in serious or sham battles." Cobo (1990: 215) reported a more likely scenario, that many captains and officers were found in the provinces to train the youths. Ritual battles in Cuzco were part of the young men's initiation ceremony (Guaman Poma 1980: 231; see Rowe 1946: 308–9). The battles helped distinguish the best warriors, who would later be tapped for duty. Such staged conflicts were widespread in the Andes well into the Colonial era and have even been recorded in the ethnographic present; the blood that was spilled and occasional fatal outcomes were thought to add potency to the rituals (Gorbak *et al.* 1962; Sallnow 1987: 136–9).

Typically, when a campaign was being planned, the military leaders sent out word to the lords of selected ethnic groups to mobilize the personnel required. Because some Inca campaigns were raised against rebellions, the call to duty could come at disconcertingly short notice. The disruption caused by rapid mobilization was likely greatest for campaigns whose timing was unpredictable, but any military service was surely a burden for a farming populace, especially if one or both parents were taken away from children who could not travel with them. The lands of those on duty were supposed to be farmed by the remaining members of the community. Fractions of ethnic groups were called to service by the state, not individual heads of household. The actual proportion called up at any point undoubtedly varied, but some idea may be gained from information gathered for Spanish inspections. In 1549, the Chupachu and Yacha of Huánuco, Peru, reported that about one-eighth to one-quarter of the heads of household were committed to military duty. Out of their 4,108 households, they provided 200 guards against the Chachapoyas, 200 more for Quito, and 68 for Huánuco Pampa. Five hundred also reportedly went with the king to Quito and elsewhere, but it is not clear if the last figure was a summary or a separate tabulation (Ortiz de Zúñiga 1967: 306–7). Similarly, the Lupaqa of the altiplano stated that they had sent 6,000 soldiers out of their population of 20,000 households to the northern campaigns. Of those, only 1,000 returned home, for a net loss of a quarter of the adult male populace (Diez de San Miguel 1964: 106). As Murra (1982: 53) observes, such burdens were truly onerous.

Warriors recruited from the Upper Mantaro valley for Spanish military operations in the early Colonial decades were taken in proportion to the population of the province's three political divisions (Murra 1975: 246). The working figure (266) is very close to 1 percent of the tabulated taxpaying populace, estimated in 1586 to have been 27,000, suggesting that it was a standard proportion for calling men to war. Gifts and supplies presented to the Spaniards were also tendered in proportion to the population of the three provincial subdivisions, but porters were not. Remarkably, the baseline for mobilizations remained intact during the demographic catastrophes of the first twenty-five years of Spanish rule. The resilience of the system after the Inca collapse is testimony to its utility, and it is a fine irony that it was used so effectively against Cuzco's dominion.

The Inca's Personal Guard

Drawn from Cuzco's aristocracy, a few thousand *orejones* ("big-ears") trained from youth as warriors, formed the army's elite corps and emperor's guard until late prehistory. Perhaps mindful of the not so latent threat posed by their close kin, later rulers also supplemented their guard with warriors from other *etnías*. Thupa Inka Yupanki reportedly enlisted Charkas, Karakaras, Chuis, and Chichas from the southern altiplano, while Wayna Qhapaq used Kañaris and Cayambes from Ecuador along with Chachapoyas from northern Peru, and Waskhar employed Kañaris,

Chachapoyas, and the central Peruvian Wankas (Espinoza Soriano 1980: 175; Spurling 1982: 9–11). In the neo-Inca era, Manqo Inka used the cannibalistic Quillacingas from Ecuador in that capacity (Hemming 1970). The Quillacingas had earlier proved their terrifying worth when they ate the bodies of three Kañari lords at Atawallpa's request before their defeated troops (Diez de Betanzos 1996: 201). The use of non-Inca subjects to protect the emperor may be a telling comment on the trustworthiness of Cuzco's nobility. When Wayna Qhapaq reviled the *orejones* for letting him fall into danger against the Caranqui, he may have inflamed tensions that had been building as Cuzco's military elites found themselves increasingly removed from unimpeded access to the ruler.

On campaign, the guard was a well-ordered force in the low thousands.[2] Cristóbal de Mena (1937: 83) recalled that Atawallpa's lodgings near Cajamarca in 1532 were "surrounded by squadrons of pikemen and halberdiers and archers; and another squadron had Indians with throwers and slings; and others with clubs and maces." The honor guard preceding Atawallpa for his entry into the center consisted of 1,000 soldiers in a dazzling livery of red and white tunics that vividly reminded the Spaniards of a massive, mobile chess set. Atawallpa himself said that 7,000 of his guard were killed in the square when he was captured (Ruiz de Arce 1933: 261).

Military Specialists

Inca armies included few military specialists other than officers and the *orejones*. The notion of a voluntary career soldier or mercenary in the rank and file was outside the scope of Andean military practice, but the Incas instituted two policies that moved them toward a more professional military. They created islands of loyal *mitmaqkuna* in areas otherwise hostile to the Inca; they were especially important in Ecuador and along the frontiers. Late in their rule, the Incas dedicated especially redoubtable ethnic groups to soldiery (Espinoza Soriano 1975; 1980). Murra (1986: 53) has suggested that general conscription lost its attractiveness over time as a recruiting principle, perhaps because of the increased distances that the armies had to travel to campaign or because recruitment was hard to enforce. Moreover, the great conquests had been completed, so that the common soldier's economic and prestige incentives for military service had become curtailed. Standing out in military roles were the Chachapoyas and Kañari, long-time Inca foes in the northern Andes who were subdued over the few last decades of the empire. Ultimately, up to half of the two ethnic groups was dispersed as permanent military personnel. Some were installed in the Yucay valley (Cieza 1967: 189; Murra 1986: 55–6), just north of Cuzco, while others formed garrisons elsewhere, such as in the Upper Mantaro valley (Toledo 1940: 22). A particularly privileged duty lay in acting as personal body-guards to Wayna Qhapaq (Murra 1980b: 159). In the civil war, both ethnic groups sided with Cuzco, for which Atawallpa exacted horrific revenge on the Kañari. When the Spaniards met Atawallpa in Cajamarca, he had 15,000 Kañari in his camp, apparently destined for resettlement.

Exemptions from Service

As useful as they are, individual cases cannot be extrapolated directly to determine how armies were mobilized. The notion of equally apportioned, universal service masks the actual recruiting practices. As we have just seen, some ethnic groups suffered oppressive levies while others were dedicated wholesale to military duty. In contrast, many adult males were exempted from service, because they were privileged, were assigned other duties, or were thought unreliable. Even among the groups that contributed many troops, the Incas separated out the better warriors and dedicated others to auxiliary duties such as portage. The most sweeping exclusion included most of Peru's coastal societies, which removed a third or more of the empire's populace from the rolls. When the Spaniards arrived, the peoples of the north coast were forbidden to carry arms, ostensibly because the Chimu lords had rebelled (Zárate 1862: 472). That edict was part of a policy, intended to reduce the Chimu threat, that included the dismantling of the coastal empire into its constituent valleys. Coastal troops are almost never listed among those who contributed to Inca conquests or the civil war, and they were conspicuously absent from the army that set siege to Lima in 1536.[3]

Apart from being untrustworthy, or holding favored statuses as did the Chincha, the lowland peoples may have fared poorly at high elevations. The converse is certainly true – the highland soldiers suffered from heat and dis-ease in campaigns on the coast (Marcus and Silva S. 1988: 27). Several high-land ethnic groups were also partly excused from military duty. Speaking generally, Cobo (1979: 234) wrote that groups rich in particular resources or skills could work off their entire obligation to the state through intensive exploitation and thus presumably were not obligated for military duty. Polo (1916: 98–9) mentioned that the Rucanas were exempted because they had a good pace for litter-bearing and the Chumbivilcas were exempt because of their dancing skills. The much-despised Urus of Lake Titicaca were little used because they were thought inept.

Ritual and Ideology

Ritual and ideology pervaded Inca militarism from strategy to tactics. The Incas themselves proclaimed that they were driven by a divine mandate to spread the religion of the Creator God Wiraqocha, the Sun god Inti, and the other deities, to the rest of humanity. Rowe (1946: 280) notes that such a directive sounds suspiciously like crusading Christianity, but that there is little doubt of its aboriginal character by the early sixteenth century (Polo 1940b: 132). What we cannot resolve from our present vantage point is how much such a charge truly galvanized the expansion or formed a rationale developed over time.

The preparation for campaigns incorporated divination, fasts, feasts, and sacrifices. In an effort to see the future, the Incas sacrificed black llamas that had been starved for some days. Polo (1916: 38) wrote that the weakening of the llamas' hearts was thought to correspond to the loss of the enemy's courage. If certain flesh near the heart did not diminish from the fasting, it was an ill omen for the coming campaign, and a number of dogs were then sacrificed to overcome the bad fortune. An especially solemn ceremony called the *itu* was performed when the emperor went to war. For two days, everyone in Cuzco fasted and refrained from sex. After all the provincials and women who had dogs and other animals were sent out of the city, the images of the gods were brought into the Awkaypata plaza. Two llamas and sometimes children were sacrificed, followed by processions by boys under 20, resplendently garbed in red tunics of *qompi* cloth, feather crowns, and shell ornaments. During the processions, coca was scattered on the ground and, once the ceremonies were complete, there was an enormous feast with copious drinking (Cobo 1990: 151–3; Acosta 1986: 377–8; Rowe 1946: 311–12). On occasion, children were also sacrificed in the *qhapaq ucha* ceremony as a precursor to war (see chapter 8). Other divinations were also undertaken to ascertain the result of military ventures. According to Montesinos, "(i)f the King desired to learn of the outcome of some war, or battle or some other event, they [the priests] placed the [maize] grains as usual [in a large flat ceramic vessel called a *kallana*], naming the captains and saying certain words. The grains themselves then had a great fight, some against others, until the conquered were driven out of the vessel, and then the wizard told the outcome as if he had seen it" (Montesinos 1920: 88–9, bracketed interpolations by this author).

Priests played key military roles, in keeping with Inca practice that did not neatly divide responsibilities into civil and military or religious and secular categories. Atawallpa's chief priest, Kusi Yupanki, for example, led an expedition against the province of Rata, Ecuador, and directed the execution of Waskhar's kin at the end of the dynastic war (Diez de Betanzos 1996: 200, 242–6). Later, Manqo Inka's chief priest of the Sun (Willaq Umu), likened by many chroniclers to the pope, accompanied Almagro and Paullu Inka to Chile but then organized the siege of Cuzco in 1536 (Anon. 1934: 6, 15; Hemming 1970: 177, 187).

Religious belief and ritual practice also had an effect on battle tactics. For example, the Incas reserved the night of the new moon for ceremonies, even during campaigns. The Spaniards were quick to recognize the practice and used it to their advantage in the siege of Cuzco, capturing Saqsawaman on the night of the new moon on May 18 or 19, 1536. Whenever the Incas marched into battle, they carried an array of icons with them. The most important were the images of the Sun and Thunder, and the stone icons of the founding ancestors Manqo Qhapaq and Huanacauri. Each emperor also had his own named battle idol (Ziółkowski 1996: 136–40). The *wak'a* were items of great potency, as they were not simply symbols of a society, but embodied beings. Seizing the enemy's idols signified capture of his power. The Incas kept the captured icons in Cuzco so that their subjects would recognize their domination and have to travel to the imperial capital to worship their own gods. A sense of the reverence the people held for the idols may be seen in the phrasing both Sarmiento and Murúa used to describe General Yasca's mobilization of an army to retake the troublesome Guaraní frontier about 1520. As the chroniclers put it, Yasca took the *wak'a* from various regions with him and the people came along with the icons (Sarmiento 2007: 183). Similarly, when Atoq left Cuzco to engage Atawallpa in Ecuador, he took the statue of the Sun with him and made the Kañari swear allegiance to Waskhar before it (Cabello Valboa 1951: 427).

The Army on Campaign

On the Road

When the Incas set off on campaigns, they dispatched multiple contingents, stretching out their departures. The staggered approach to the march moderated the impact on the supplies and support personnel along the way, as well as limiting the turmoil inevitably entailed in moving large forces. Wayna Qhapaq's major campaigns in Ecuador began with an inquiry into the state of affairs in the provinces, followed by notice sent to all the societies along the planned route to prepare supplies and lodgings (Cieza 1967: 213–14). That communiqué prepared the way for a vanguard from Cuzco, after which larger contingents were dispatched over an extended period. The principal forces accompanying the emperor followed in a grand procession. Wayna Qhapaq reportedly took along 2,000 concubines and a vast array of servants, leaving another 4,000 wives in Cuzco. The main force was said to contain 200,000 men, plus servants and camp followers. Even allowing for some license in the estimates, the scale and character of such an army on the move had little to do with a lean fighting force (see below, "Logistics").

Porters, wives, servants, and other personnel formed a substantial entourage that may have approached the number of combatants.[4] Such large auxiliary groups relieved the soldiers' burdens by cooking and carrying loads, but they placed additional demands on the logistical system. It is little wonder that the Inca armies sometimes left their supply train and camp followers behind when pressed for rapid movement. That occurred at least once in the final battles of the civil war, when Atawallpa's army left its train at Vilcas in a rapid flanking move to the battlefield at Chaquixampa. The army paid dearly for the decision, because a contingent of Waskhar's soldiers found and sacked the camp (Diez de Betanzos 1996: 217–18).

Zárate's (1862: 483) description of the disposition of Quizquiz's forces across the mountainous terrain east of Hatun Xauxa in the 1530s provides a concrete example of how an Inca army on the move was organized. A Kañari *kuraka* warned the Spaniards that Quizquiz's army exceeded 12,000 members, a figure that Almagro dismissed at the time; it is not clear if he was referring to soldiers or total personnel. Zárate wrote that a vanguard contained 2,000 with 3,000 on the left flank and 3,000–4,000 more in a rearguard. He did not estimate the size of the main body of the army, which included many women and service personnel. The lead force preceded the main body by about two or three days' march, while the rearguard followed it by two days. During the march, the flanking contingent foraged among the towns in the region. In all, the troops were said to be spread over 15 or more leagues (60 km), which suggests that they were covering about 12–15 km per day. In a running conflict with Almagro, Quizquiz abandoned more than 15,000 animals along with more than 4,000 male and female prisoners, and burned all the textiles his forces could not carry into their hastily built high forts.[5]

The road and *tampu* system was designed largely to assist military operations, but even the provincial centers were not equipped to shelter thousands of soldiers. Settlements such as Huánuco Pampa and Pumpu did have barracks-like structures, called *kallanka*, but they could have lodged only a fraction of the assembled forces. The large armies apparently camped in tents, such as those the Spaniards observed at Cajamarca. The soldier Ruiz de Arce (1933: 359; translation by Hemming 1970: 32) wrote of his impression of a first view of the encampment: "the royal center of the Indians appeared on one side of the river, a very beautiful city, for they all had their tents ." Atawallpa's lodgings themselves were surrounded by white tents for half a league around (Mena 1937: 83).

Discipline among the troops was a mixed thing. While on the road, the soldiers were said to be forbidden to stray from the road or to take any goods from the countryside, on pain of death (Rowe 1946: 279). The Spaniards at Cajamarca were witness to capital punishment for disciplinary infractions, as thirty to forty of Atawallpa's guard were executed when they broke ranks in the face of a display of horse-charging bravado by Hernando de Soto (Ruiz de Arce 1933: 361). Atawallpa himself remained regally impassive when de Soto approached so close that his horse's breath fluttered the emperor's fringe (Mena 1937: 83). Regardless of the order exhibited on the march and in the camp, discipline broke quickly on the battlefield and looting was the order of the day following victory.

Logistics

Few aspects of the Inca empire impressed the conquistadores more than its supply and transport system. Besides the road network, the most renowned aspect of the Inca supply system was the array of storehouses, which stockpiled an enormous variety of food, arms, clothing, and other items throughout the empire (Morris 1967; LeVine 1992). Each soldier was supposed to receive a set of clothing and sandals annually, and some weapons were also provided. They were also issued blankets, maize, peppers, and coca leaf (Murra 1980b: 76, 102). The difficulties of transport in the rugged Andean terrain required that the storage facilities be replicated regionally. The massive scale of the system is best exemplified by the hundreds or even thousands of storehouses at each major center from Cuzco to Tumipampa, and adjacent to state farms in Cochabamba, Bolivia, and the Lerma valley,

Argentina (chapter 12). Each small waystation located every 20 km or so along the roads also stored goods for state travelers.

The Incas relied on llama caravans and human porters for transport. The state owned hundreds of thousands of llamas and on occasion individual pack trains could include thousands of animals (Zárate 1862: 483; Murra 1980b: 46). Although the camelids are supremely well adapted to the rigors of the mountains, there are limitations to their uses. For example, llama caravans cover only about 20 km per day, which is the average distance between *tampu*. Typically, two loads of 30 kg each will be rotated among three adult males, but they still break down with disconcerting frequency and refuse to budge when tired. As a consequence, humans may have actually carried the majority of baggage on their backs. They were more reliable and could carry heavier loads (Murra 1980b: 48), but had to be fed from local supplies or carry their own. Both Colonial and modern figures suggest that porters could carry upwards of 30 kg for 20–25 km per day (see Hyslop 1984: 294–8; D'Altroy 1992: 85–6). Both male and female porters accompanied the army on long-distance treks, the women usually as soldiers' wives. In 1575, Atienza (1931: 49–50) reported acerbically that Ecuadorian women customarily carried enormous loads alongside their unburdened husbands. In another routine, porters carried supplies from one end of their territory to the next, where their neighbors assumed the burdens. The second form of transport did not wear down the porters, but both forms required drawing on food along the road to transport the loads.

The slow transport, together with the bulkiness of foodstuffs, meant that the porters' food would have had to be replenished every few days with food from the countryside. Under those circumstances, the best solution to the logistical challenge was to develop a regionally based supply system and to mix pack trains and human porters. Armies and other state personnel could then travel in the expectation that their supply needs would be met without having to forage or make resented demands from the countryside.

Battle Tactics and Weaponry

Our information on Inca battle tactics comes mostly from the late prehispanic Ecuadorian campaigns, the dynastic war, and early encounters with the Spaniards, where the Incas followed a number of sound principles. In order to inform themselves as best as possible of what lay ahead, they attempted to spy out the land and made clay models of the terrain. The armies then presented an overwhelming force at the point of attack. When Manqo Inka's forces invested Cuzco in 1536, for example, he waited several weeks for his full army of 100,000–200,000 to arrive, even though they were attacking only 190 Spaniards and a few thousand native allies (Hemming 1970: 190–2). Most battles for which we have accounts were described as either great melees on open terrain or assaults on fortified strongholds. Two favorite tactics were feigned withdrawals coupled with pincers counterattacks, and flanking maneuvers. Both approaches indicate that the Incas used surprise to their advantage and concentrated force on the vulnerable flanks and rear of forces.

The battles were noisy, colorful affairs. The soldiers from each *etnía* were clothed in their distinctive martial vestments. Cobo (1990: 216) wrote that the warriors adorned themselves with finery: "Over this defensive gear, they would usually wear their most attractive and rich adornments and jewels; this included wearing fine plumes of many colors on their heads and large gold and silver plates on their chests and backs; however, the plates worn by poorer soldiers were copper." Before the actual fighting, both sides typically postured belligerently, trading insults and martial songs, sometimes for days. Passages in the narratives also record impassioned, if apocryphal, oratory by emperors or generals before their men, firing their ardor for the fighting to come. Various instruments fashioned from bodies of defeated opponents were used to terrorize the enemy. Guaman Poma (1980: 287) wrote that the soldiers celebrated their valor in song: "We will drink from the skull of the traitor, we will adorn ourselves with a necklace of his teeth, we will play the melody of the *pinkullu* with flutes made from his bones, we will beat the drum made from his skin, and thus we will dance."

The Inca battle formation was organized by ethnic group, each one of which specialized in its own arms (Mena 1937: 83; Cabello Valboa 1951: 308; Cobo 1990: 218; Rowe 1946: 276–7). Flurries of arrows, sling stones, and javelins preceded hand-to-hand combat by troops who wielded maces, clubs, and spears. Some stones were large enough to fell a horse or break a sword in half at a distance of 30 m (Hemming 1970: 192–3). The emperors were carried into combat on litters, wielding slings or spears (figure 10.2). The Incas' preferred weapon was a stone or bronze star mace mounted on a wooden handle about 1 m long. Another favorite was a hard, double-edged, palmwood club shaped like a sword. The bow and arrow were a late addition to the Inca army's repertoire as warriors from the jungle were drafted into service. Troops defending fortified locations responded with a similar array of weaponry, to which they added large boulders rolled down onto

Figure 10.2 Guaman Poma's illustration of the emperor Wayna Qhapaq wielding a sling as he is carried into battle against the *etnías* of highland Ecuador.

advancing forces. Piles of hundreds of sling stones lining the interior of defensive walls can still be found at various Inca forts, such as Cerro del Inga, Chile (Planella *et al.* 1991: 407). Soldiers often wore quilted cloth armor that was so effective against Andean weapons that many Spaniards discarded their own metal plate in favor of the lighter protection. Warriors also frequently carried shields and protected their chests and backs with plates of metal and their heads with cane helmets.

A sketch of one engagement will illustrate the kinds of tactics employed on fortified strongholds. In an effort to take a Caranqui fort north of Quito, the Incas prepared the field by taking control of the surrounding country and then launched a frontal assault (see chapter 4). The first strike was repelled and an unexpected counterattack unseated Wayna Qhapaq from his litter, and he was saved only by the heroic action of a number of *orejones*. After another unsuccessful assault, the Incas withdrew to Tumipampa, desolating the area around the stronghold (Sarmiento 2007: 180). According to Cabello, Awki Toma's forces then set siege, but a prolonged, bloody assault failed when he fell mortally wounded. When some of the besieging forces withdrew for lack of food, the defenders broke out to resupply themselves and reinforce the fort (Cabello Valboa 1951: 377–8; Murúa 1986: 122–5). Wayna Qhapaq led the next force himself, finally gaining victory by drawing the enemy out of their fort with a feigned withdrawal and pincers counterattack by hidden forces. The difficult terrain and the distances involved meant that the forces had to take circuitous routes and appear on the morning of the fifth day. At the appointed time, the Incas under Wayna Qhapaq attacked the fort frontally and then withdrew as if they had been routed. When the Caranqui pursued the fleeing enemy, they were set upon from the flank and rear by the two other forces. The defenders were then slaughtered in a nearby lake (called Yaguarcocha, or Lake of Blood), in which they had sought refuge. Similar surprise attacks and flanking maneuvers characterized a number of the battles, most notably the final battle on the Apurimac when Waskhar was captured by Atawallpa's men.

The attack on Lima in 1536 provides an example of late Inca tactics in open terrain. The general Quizo Yupanki had amassed an immense army on the surrounding hills in an effort to overwhelm the Spaniards by force of numbers. Accompanied by a brilliant array of banners, the army advanced from the north, east, and south. The general himself rode a litter and wielded a lance at the head of his hand-picked troops in the eastern force. The Spaniards waited until the army had begun to enter the streets of the town and then attacked with two contingents of cavalry. They chose the Inca command as their target, which marched at the army's head. In short order, Quizo Yupanki and forty officers were killed and the attack was broken. With their leaders gone, the native army melted into the hills that night and the siege was lifted. In addition to the Spaniards' superiority in such terrain, several features typical of Inca warfare stand out from this battle: the concentration of massed force, the physical leadership of the army by its officers, the three-pronged attack, and the collapse of the army's discipline with the loss of its command (Hemming 1970: 212–13, 575; Murúa 1986: 206).

Archaeological study of the enormous cemetery at Puruchuco-Huaquerones, about 12 km southeast of central Lima, provides graphic material witness to the effects of such conflict on the native populace (Murphy *et al.* 2010). The available evidence leans toward the inference that some of the 2,000+ people buried there were among the earliest victims of Spanish armaments, perhaps even from the thwarted attack on Lima. As the excavators Guillermo Cock and Elena Goycochea Diaz (2004) describe, many of the burials bear Inca-era hallmarks, but some were interred early in the Colonial era. Examples of the former include individuals who were wrapped in textiles and interred in a seated, flexed position facing northeast; among other items, the burials contained textiles, pottery, musical instruments, food, spondylus shell, and weaving tools. Numerous burials from the 57AS03 cemetery sector show anomalous features, however. Located toward the cemetery's peripheries and at levels near the surface, they were apparently interred hastily, without the careful preparation typical of the prehispanic era. They contained few items, often only one two textile wrappings, and the bodies were placed in supine or prone positions, or semi-flexed. About a quarter of the quickly buried individuals exhibit trauma that likely resulted from battlefield injury, such as unhealed fractures of the skull and ribs. The nature of some people's injuries suggests that Spanish arms, such as guns and swords, caused their deaths (Murphy *et al.* 2010). Although the lethal wounds were concentrated among males of fighting age, they were not limited to adults or men, illustrating that a wide range of people fell victim to Spanish violence.

Triumphs and Rewards

Victories in war were celebrated in grand fashion, most prominently by triumphs in Cuzco led by the generals or the emperor himself. To show off the defeat of a foe, the Inca trod upon his head in the Golden Enclosure or in the main plaza in front of the massed throngs of Cuzco's residents. Particularly dangerous enemies were killed, some by imprisonment in a dungeon of snakes, while others were sacrificed to give thanks for the victory (Rowe 1946: 279–80). In a highly personalized expression of victory, Inca rulers had the heads of obdurate foes fashioned into drinking cups. Cristóbal de Mena saw Atawallpa drink *chicha* from the skull of Atoq, the commander sent to confront him at the inception of the dynastic war. A golden bowl had been set in the general's skull and a silver spout emerged from his mouth. Defeated lords were also flayed and the skins of their bellies made into drums that were taken into battle or played at ceremonial events in Cuzco. Individual valor was elaborately rewarded, though clear distinctions were made between the awards granted to nobility and to commoners, reinforcing the class structure of Inca society. Clothing, gold and silver breast- or back-plates, and captured women, weapons, and flocks were rewards for commoners; marriage to an *aqlla* was a sign of special favor. Nobles, on the other hand, could be awarded administrative sinecures, lands, multiple wives, and privileges such as riding in a litter or sitting on a stool (Guaman Poma 1980: 164; *RGI* I: 177; Diez de San Miguel 1964: 106; see Rowe 1946: 279–80).

Summary

As the Inca polity developed, the leaders faced a shifting array of challenges that were addressed through military action. Up to the proto-imperial era, warfare was focused on localized raiding. Once the Incas shifted their goals to annexing lands, warfare – combined with alliances, diplomacy, ceremony, and gift exchange – became the linchpin of Tawantinsuyu's expansion. The emperor himself drew much of his personal prestige from his perceived success as a military leader, while valor in battle was the principal means by which commoners could move up the social ladder. In the latter decades of the empire, after the main conquests had been completed, threats to Cuzco's power came largely from insurrections, not from external attack. The commitment of relatively small forces to the perimeter and large contingents to internal garrisons and armies of pacification suggests that the Incas saw the greatest threat in rebellion, not invasion. Thus, the logistical infrastructure took center stage in most of the empire. Fortified military architecture was useful, but only for limited circumstances, primarily along the frontiers.

Notes

1   See Hemming 1970: 572–3; 2012 for a variety of estimates.

2   Diez de Betanzos (1996: 144) wrote that Thupa Inka Yupanki took a personal guard of 5,000 soldiers on campaign to suppress a rebellion on the altiplano, consisting of 1,000 *orejones* from Cuzco and 4,000 others from the immediate vicinity. A similar figure of 5,000 is named for Waskhar's guard in his final sortie in the battle on the Apurimac (Diez de Betanzos 1996: 223–4; Sarmiento 2007: 194).

3   A rare exception was the support that Thupa Inka Yupanki was said to have received in his first efforts to take the Cañete stronghold of Guarco, but that aid evaporated in the face of the Incas' repeated failures (Cieza 1967: 200–1).

4   During their assistance of the Spaniards in 1533, the Hatunxauxa and Lurinwanka provided 589 men, 437 women, 311 porters, and 110 servants, for a ratio of warriors to non-combatants of about 1 : 1.5. Between 1533 and 1548, 3,465 men, 1,915 women, and 7,131 porters were mobilized, for a ratio of 1 : 2.6 (Espinoza Soriano 1972; Murra 1975: 252, insert; D'Altroy 1992: 85). It is difficult to know in what ways the Spaniards' military needs may have distorted the ratio.

5   Sancho (1917: 142–3) and Ruiz de Arce (1933: 365) also reported that the Inca force of 15,000 initially retreated south in good order, down the Mantaro valley from Hatun Xauxa, following Challcochima's first conflict with Pizarro's men in October 1533. A baggage train and assembly of women lagged some four leagues (~24 km) behind the main group, in which groups of women, porters, and other auxiliaries were protected by organized contingents of 100 effectives each. From the information available, it is not clear if the formation was standard for armies on the march or whether it was more strictly a defensive formation used in hostile territory or on ordered retreat. In any event, the pursuing cavalry easily broke up the formation and routed its personnel into the nearby hills, although they failed to cut them off from their retreat across the bridges farther south.

Chapter Eleven

Provincial Rule

The Administrative System

As their domain expanded, the Incas were faced with the challenge of governing societies that ranged from villages to states and a population that ultimately outnumbered them by about a hundred to one. In chapter 1, I outlined a range of policies that imperial rulers have chosen to address similar problems, ranging from the extractive, indirect approach of the Aztecs to a full-fledged civil bureaucracy, such as that developed by Han China. The Incas opted for a mixed strategy, ruling the central part of the empire directly, but applying less intensive rule along the populous north coast, the eastern slopes, and much of the far north and south Andes. At the heart of the provincial system was an administration that is often – misleadingly – called a bureaucracy. In practice, the government consisted of an umbrella of Inca officials who oversaw a hierarchy of hereditary ethnic lords drafted into state service. Many taxpayers were assigned to units of 10 to 10,000 households in an organizational pyramid that was used to recruit labor for duties ranging from farming to military service. By 1532, millions of people had also been resettled for political and economic ends and to defuse threats to Inca dominance. To keep track of the population, the Incas took censuses, kept detailed accounts, and imposed an official language. And to provide a physical framework for their rule, they built a network of roads, provincial centers, and waystations.

As novel and rigorous as some of those policies may seem, the approach really consisted more of shuffling about existing ethnic groups than inventing a new government wholesale (Morris 1982). Political relations between the Inca and the provincial lords relied heavily on personal bonds, while supervision of the general populace meshed compulsion with ritualized exchange, pageantry, and state-sponsored revelry. Moreover, because social and political conditions differed from one place to the next, so did Inca

The Incas, Second Edition. Terence N. D'Altroy.
© 2015 John Wiley & Sons, Ltd. Published 2015 by John Wiley & Sons, Ltd.

policies. A single model of Inca rule thus fails to capture the nature of the empire, and some cases will be sketched out in this chapter to illustrate the variety of provincial relations.

A great deal of recent research has been devoted to figuring out how Inca rule worked outside the core. Just as investigations around Cuzco have changed our understanding of the emergence of Inca power, studies elsewhere have fleshed out our knowledge of provincial life. Since the area outside the heartland encompassed about 99 percent of the empire's people and space, adding nuance to descriptions of provincial rule has been a welcome development. In a case-based volume on the subject, Malpass and Alconini (2010: 2) describe five major areas of interest. The first highlights the vastly greater base of archaeological information we have on specific regions. We have better data than ever on the balance between stability and change in subject societies through study of their communities, household activities, foods, and general health. That knowledge has helped us rethink how to integrate the information found in documents and material remains. Because written records often provide insight on topics that are hard to study through archaeology – such as the rationales for action or particular beliefs, or activities that particular people carried out – they give us a privileged window into many aspects of life. On the other hand, the documents sorely neglected many topics that interest us today. To take one issue, the lives of the weak, poor, or oppressed (i.e., most of the peasant populace) held little interest for the early authors. In addition, the largest of the four parts of the empire, Kollasuyu, was visited by only a very few chroniclers; the land south of Bolivia is almost totally bereft of the detailed inspections that enrich our knowledge of the north. A third topic focuses on imperial–subject interactions, which were often negotiated in a case-by-case, fluid approach. Another issue concerns what may have been considered marginal spaces or social positions in the Inca world. While we may think of northern Ecuador as lying on the far fringes of the empire, for example, it was far closer to the emperor's seat of power in Tumipampa than was almost any place in the south, for at least the last couple of decades of imperial rule. Finally, Malpass and Alconini suggest that archaeologists, who worry about lots of methodological questions, are constantly trying to sort out what scales of analysis work best in studying empires: the realm as a whole, individual provinces, ethnic groups, communities, households, or some combination. Not surprisingly, the consensus to date is that the analytical scale depends on the problem, so that we are always working at multiple levels of space and order in our studies. Overall, those lines of research have both advanced our understanding and opened up fascinating new lines of inquiry.[1]

Organization of the Provinces

There were at least eighty provinces in the Inca realm, distributed unevenly among the four parts.[2] Chinchaysuyu (northwest) was the most populous, contained the most provinces, and was the most prestigious, while Cuntisuyu (southwest) was lowest ranked on all three of those dimensions. Antisuyu (northeast) was second in status, while Kollasuyu (southeast) was territorially the largest, probably second in population, and third in rank. The Incas thought of a province as an enumerated population which was most often based on the societies that were native to a region. As an extension of that logic, the colonists who were transplanted to distant territories were still counted on the census rolls of their homelands. Each province was composed of two or three ranked parts called *saya*. The parts also frequently corresponded in some way to ethnic divisions, although they could include more than one group or fractions of several. The goal was to create units whose composition came as close as was convenient to multiples of decimal figures (Murra 1958; Julien 1982, 1988). Ideally, each *saya* consisted of 10,000 heads of households, so that a province nominally contained 20,000 or 30,000 households.

After claiming a new region, the Incas defined the limits of the province and groups within it. Two kin groups from Cuzco seem to have had a special responsibility for surveying and setting out markers (Van de Guchte 1990: 323). Provincial subdivisions also had bounded territories, but officials sometimes had to intervene in land disputes that were frozen when Inca rule was applied (Cieza 1967: 215). Diez de Betanzos (1996: 110) wrote that when a local population needed more resources than were available to them, Inca officials were supposed to send a painting of the lay of the land to Cuzco, accompanied by the local lords, so that an equitable adjustment could be made and the markers reset. Those who lost land would be compensated as the Inca saw fit.

A governor (*tokrikoq*) conducted the affairs of each province with help enlisted from local elites and functionaries, such as record-keepers. The governor was usually an ethnic Inca, although the rare non-Inca could find a place near the top; ability was a prime consideration in making his appointment (Rowe 1946: 262; Wachtel 1977: 75–9; Schaedel 1978: 300–6). He had broad responsibilities and authority, most importantly supervising the census and mobilizing labor for whatever tasks his superiors required. He was supposed to administer the colonists, along with the lands of the state and maybe the Sun, but probably not the private estates of the Sapa Inca, the *panaqa*, or other aristocrats. Additional duties included making sure that the roads, bridges, and support facilities were in good order, so that people who passed through on state business would find their needs anticipated. He also judged all the cases that were related to state interests and had the authority to pass sentences up to and including the death penalty (Cobo 1979: 194–202; Moore 1958: 115).

The Decimal Administration

In much of the realm, the Incas organized able-bodied, male heads of household into units of 10, 50, 100, 500, 1,000, 5,000 and 10,000 (table 11.1; figure 11.1). Both Cieza and Polo, who inquired closely on such matters, credited Thupa Inka Yupanki with the design (Rowe 1958: 500). The Incas used the hierarchy to tabulate labor for both civil and military duties, including farming, herding, and artisanry, as well as portage, guard duty, and war service (Rowe 1946: 264; Murra 1958: 33–4; Wedin 1965; Julien 1982; 1988; LeVine 1987). The officials were responsible for maintaining state facilities and for leading their men into battle. Each unit was headed by a hereditary local elite called a *kuraka*. According to some chroniclers, no official took his post without the direct approval of the Inca or his governor, but Cobo wrote that those who had charge of 100 or fewer households were appointed by their lords of 1,000 (Cobo 1979: 201). In practical terms, individuals in line for positions under local customs generally filled state offices. The guiding rule seems to have been to keep power within elite

Table 11.1 Officials in the Inca decimal hierarchy.

Title of official	Scope of jurisdiction (heads of household)
hunu kuraka	10,000
pichkawaranqa kuraka	5,000
waranqa kuraka	1,000
pichkapachaka kuraka	500
pachaka kuraka	100
pichkachunka kamayuq	50
chunka kamayuq	10

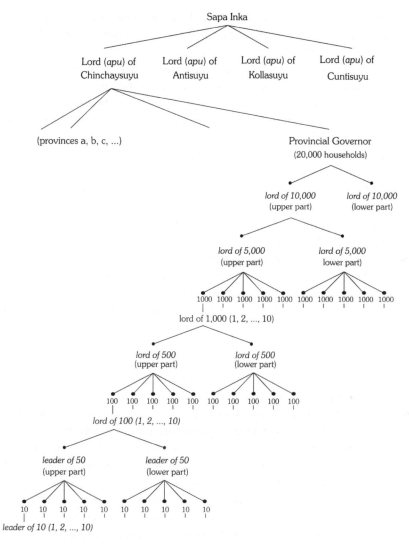

Figure 11.1   The Inca decimal administration hierarchy.

families by selecting the most appropriate adult male at times of transition. Most commonly, he was the most able son of the prior lord, but brothers of the past lord could hold the position until it passed on to the ablest son of the first. If an official was unwilling or unable to carry out his duties, the Incas replaced him with a more compliant individual who was usually also drawn from the local people. Drafting the *ayllu* leaders into the state hierarchy meant that the Incas could rule without interfering unduly in community life, but it also meant that the government reached deep into existing political order.

As might be imagined, the decimal hierarchy had to be adjusted to local conditions. It was installed throughout the central empire, but in the far north and south, it may have been regularly applied only among the colonist communities (Salomon 1986; Lorandi and Cremonte 1993). The program's uneven application probably arose from many factors. For one, it was simply not feasible to rearrange the empire's people into a neat structure by administrative fiat (Murra 1958). Local intransigence also played a role. The Chachapoyas, for instance, resisted Inca rule for decades but were finally subdued late in the empire's run. Their leaders were made into *yanakuna*, or personnel committed to serve the Inca personally for life, rather than decimal officials (Pease 1982). The populace was widely dispersed (figure 11.2), and many were converted wholesale into military specialists. Elsewhere, toward some margins of Tawantinsuyu, the population or resources may not have warranted the administrative effort. To date, scholars have found no evidence for officials with decimal titles in Chile and Argentina, for example (D'Altroy *et al.* 2007).

Lords of 100 households or more received benefits according to their standing. Although the sources vary on the details, in general their lands were worked and herds tended, and they were granted household service at a rate of one servant for every 100 households supervised. They could also receive wives and personal estates, whose maize, coca, and peppers fields were essential to the hospitality expected of a lord. Symbolic paraphernalia, such as wooden seats and elegant tunics, also marked the status of lords in the hierarchy. For especially meritorious service, an individual could be named an Inca by Privilege, although that designation was largely reserved for certain ethnic groups from the Cuzco area. The foremost provincial lords were supposed to make an annual journey to the capital, where they lived for four months supported by their own retainers. While there, they exchanged gifts with the Inca himself, especially cloth.

The Census

Because accurate census records were crucial to Inca administration, keeping track of births, deaths, marriages, and other changes of status was among the most important of official duties. People of each sex were assigned to one of ten categories that corresponded to their life stage

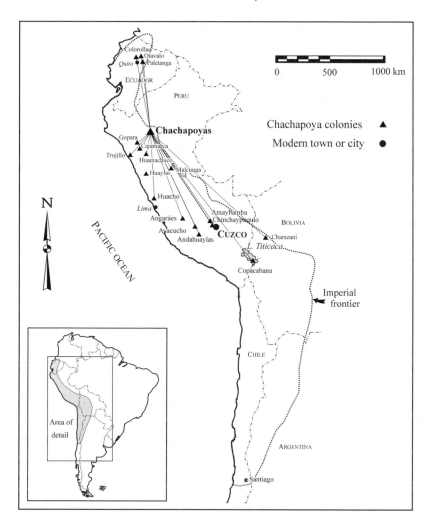

Figure 11.2 Representation of the places to which the recalcitrant Chachapoyas populace was dispersed.

or ability to do useful work, not to their chronological age (chapter 9). Registering males and females separately was vital because the members of each sex were recruited for different purposes. Some young girls were tapped for the women's orders, for example, while boys were destined for courier or hunting duties. Garcilaso (1966: 329–33) explained that the Incas kept separate *khipu* for each province, on which a pendant string recorded the number of people belonging to each category. He added that the *khipu kamayuq* would sometimes attach subsidiary strings to indicate, for example, how many men or women of a given age-grade had been widowed. The provincial officials were expected to report their tabulations in Cuzco annually at the December solstice festival, and an independent check on the census may have been made every three to five years (Polo 1965b: 55). Rowe (1958: 501) makes the reasonable assumption that the decimal hierarchy and the census were initiated together, since they were conceptually so closely linked.

Inspectors and Judges

Cuzco also appointed a centrally controlled set of inspectors (*tokoyrikoq*, "He Who Sees All") who checked on affairs in the provinces. Diez de Betanzos (1996: 110 – 11) wrote that the sons of the ruler were charged with the inquiries. The highest-ranking official may have been the "Inspector General" of the conquered territories, a position that was sometimes filled by the emperor's brother. The existence of these independent agents implies that the rulers evidently did not fully trust the provincial officials to conduct all affairs with the best interests of the Sapa Inca and the state in mind.

Establishing and Maintaining Social Order

For Andean peoples in general, social order was an integral part of cosmic order, while existing society arose from a constant regenesis of past society. The Incas built on those ideas, interjecting themselves as the linchpin of universal order, while leaving most of their subjects' community organization intact. That kind of logic let them claim that they were essential to sustaining civilized life at large. The scope of state interest was limited, however, even though the Incas aspired to regulate many aspects of life. For instance, they do not seem to have created a formal system of laws or a separate judiciary. Subject societies were also left to their own affairs to judge many disputes and misdeeds beneath the mantle of state oversight, since the Incas had neither the capacity nor the interest to govern the details of local life.

While we may recognize the limitations of Inca legal codes, the chronicles are still filled with social dictates and sanctions for unacceptable acts. Broadly speaking, the Incas applied many of their own notions of proper

relations to their subjects and invented new measures to protect the interests of the ruler, aristocracy, state, and religion.[3] Some specific rules were
intended to keep tabs on the populace. According to Cobo (1979: 206), a
resettled colonist was tortured if he returned home and a two-time offender
was executed. The existence of a second sanction indicates, of course, that
the resettlement policy met resistance. Additional rules governed conduct
that might be thought of as customary, such as the choice of clothing or
headgear, especially among colonists. The purpose again was to identify taxpayers and thereby control their movements. Other official strictures were
designed to guard specific symbols, property, and personnel of the elite. For
example, hunting on the Inca's lands, removing gold or silver from Cuzco
without permission, or having sexual relations with the women of the Inca
or the Sun were proscribed. Some status articles, such as *qompi* cloth, were
reserved for the Inca elite or members of the state institutions, unless the
right to use them was explicitly granted. The Incas assumed the right to
condemn individuals to death, and only the provincial governors and their
superiors had that authority.

Further aspects of law emphasized the cleavages of status found in
Inca society (Moore 1958: 74–5). In general, any individual in the state
hierarchy could be judged only by someone of higher rank. Moreover,
royalty and aristocrats were granted latitude to behave in ways that
were sanctioned for commoners. If an act was widely condemned, the
nobility were disciplined less severely. Various homicides committed by a
commoner were punishable by death, but an official who killed someone
under his jurisdiction was only disciplined physically for a first offense. If a
commoner male committed adultery with the wife of a commoner, he was
beaten, but if his partner was the wife of a noble, he was executed. Incest,
for which commoners were ostensibly supposed to be executed, resulted
only in reprimand for the nobility, and was required of the later rulers who
were supposed to marry their sisters. Despite his frequent regard for Inca
accomplishments, Cobo (1979: 207) commented acidly that the unequal
penalties were "due to an illusion … that a public reprimand was a far
greater punishment for an Inca of noble blood than the death penalty for
a plebeian."

Men and women were reportedly punished in different ways for the
same crimes. For example, incest committed by certain kinds of cousins
resulted in both being beaten and shaved, after which the man was sent
to the mines and the woman to temple service. Blas Valera's (1945: 58–9)
vivid description of the consequences of different kinds of rape or sexual

relations may be indicative of the Inca views on gender relations, but it is also notable for the Spanish clergy's absorption with scandalous behavior. Explicit sanctions also existed concerning property crimes and proscriptions against witchcraft and other misuses of supernatural powers. It was forbidden to move the markers that denoted boundaries, for instance, even among local peoples. Cobo (1979: 203) wrote that the entire household of a person who murdered through sorcery was executed along with the guilty party, on the assumption that they all knew the craft. The punishment was carried out as a public event to dissuade others from similar acts.

Even in a land of unequal rights, commoners were supposed to receive some protections. Soldiers on the march were prohibited from stealing food upon pain of death for themselves and their captains (Diez de Betanzos 1996: 108–9). Officials were ostensibly punished for abusing their subordinates, and the official who failed to ensure that the *tampu* under his jurisdiction were well stocked would be punished. He, in turn, would discipline those under his sway for their dereliction of duty. Among commoners, a man who killed his wife for adultery could be forgiven and an individual whose goods were stolen was entitled to restitution. Regrettably, it is hard to know if such rules were truly honored.

Moore (1958) has pointed out that most penalties involved physical punishment, such as stoning or torture, or public humiliation for nobles. Polo attributed the relative lack of economic sanctions to the rarity of private property, which was reserved only for the most elite. In one of the most fabled punishments, individuals accused of treason against the Sapa Inca, or other especially heinous acts, were thrown into a special dungeon stocked with snakes and other wild animals. Although we cannot track Inca law over time, one major change clearly lay in the state's removal of the right to resolve major disputes over property and life from the hands of the native elites. Murra (1958) recognized that enacting such policies did not end conflicts, but simply moved their resolution out of the hands of communities into those of the state. Blood feuds and local political violence were thus reduced at the cost of sovereignty. We do not know if specific rules were applied evenly throughout the realm, but a few chroniclers described some of the diversity in locally acceptable behavior. The peoples of the altiplano and the Chimu region, for example, reportedly engaged in sexual practices that the Incas found repugnant.[4] Not surprisingly, however, the codes of the pre-Inca Chimu state protected the persons, perquisites, and properties of the ruling class, just as Inca rules did (Rowe 1948).

The Infrastructure: Provincial Installations

Organization at the Grand Scale

The Incas managed provincial affairs of state through a network of regional centers and secondary facilities that were connected by a network of some 40,000 km of roads. Cieza de León, who saw much of the north, wrote:

> For it was their custom, when they traveled anywhere in this great realm, to go with great pomp and be served with great luxury, as was their custom. It is said that, except when it was necessary for their service, they did not travel more than four leagues [~20 km] a day. And so that there would be sufficient provisions for their people, at the end of each four leagues there were lodgings and storehouses with a great abundance of the things that could be had in this land; and even if it was uninhabited there had to be these lodgings and storehouses. (Cieza de León 1984: 237–8; trans. Morris 1982: 154)

All of the installations are usually called *tampu*, although the term refers most properly to lodgings. Hyslop (1984: 277; 1990), who studied the roads and settlements more extensively than anyone else, estimates that there may have been 2,000 or more *tampu*. Although no comprehensive list of the sites was recorded in the Colonial era, Vaca de Castro compiled a partial inventory in 1543 and Guaman Poma pictorially divided over 200 *tampu* into five ranks in the chronicle he sent to King Felipe III. At the apex of Guaman Poma's list lay cities with royal installations, followed by large towns with royal lodgings, smaller towns with royal lodgings, royal lodgings, and small lodgings. Unfortunately, his list contains enough significant errors that it is risky to trust his hierarchy too closely (Hyslop 1984: 278–9).

We do not yet have a reliable grasp of the system's development, but the available evidence suggests that upgrading the roads became policy during Thupa Inka Yupanki's reign and that many *tampu* and road sections were built at the same time. It also seems likely that the elaboration of the route between Cuzco and Quito owed much to Wayna Qhapaq's late campaigns in the northern Andes. By the early sixteenth century, both Cuzco and Tumipampa functioned as imperial capitals. Their roles diverged during Wayna Qhapaq's reign, for the political and military power lay in the north, while the royal kin groups and principal religious institutions were still concentrated in Cuzco.

The major provincial settlements were the seat of a provincial governor and administered large regional populations. The grandest centers lay along the main mountain highway. North of Cuzco were Vilcashuaman, Hatun Xauxa, Pumpu, Huánuco Pampa, Cajamarca, Tumipampa, and Quito. South of Cuzco lay Hatunqolla, Chucuito, Chuquiabo (La Paz), Paria, and Charkas. According to Sarmiento (2007: 166), Hatun Xauxa and Tiahuanaco occupied a symbolic second tier below Cuzco under Thupa Inka, as the residences of the two governor-generals of the land. None of their archaeological remains, however, suggests that they held such an elevated position. Along Peru's south-central coast, Inkawasi and Tambo Colorado stand out as planned installations. No important *tampu* were built on Peru's populous north coast and only a couple of military sites south of central Bolivia exceeded about 35 ha. Although archaeologists and architects have studied the network for decades[5] most centers have not been adequately investigated because they lie under later settlements. Of all the mountain centers, only Pumpu, Huánuco Pampa, and Paria are exposed and only Huánuco Pampa has been excavated intensively. Below those large sites were smaller provincial centers, such as Tarmatampu and Acostambo, and the main installations at provinces of lesser importance, such as Conchucos and Guaylas. At least a third and fourth level of smaller Inca settlements and waystations also lined the road system.

Hyslop (1990: 291–309) has suggested that, conceptually, several Inca networks of facilities may have lain on top of one another in the provinces. One consisted of the state administrative and ceremonial centers, another of sanctuaries and other religious facilities, a third of production and storage facilities, another of private estates, and a last of military facilities. In some places, several functions coincided, but often they did not. He infers that the Incas drew selectively from an array of principles – not a standard package – in making their decisions about the design of each site. Most important were the site's major activities, its topography, the amount and proximity of the local labor pool, and local cultural circumstances (Hyslop 1990: 306). He also suggests that the scale of each center was proportionate to the size of the regional taxpaying populace. LeVine (1985: 458) has noted a similar correlation between plaza size and regional population for some sites, but proposes that it arose from the intended scale of ceremonies. They may both be right.

While local conditions were surely taken into account in the positioning and design of the facilities, macro-regional issues were just as important, if not more so. Jenkins' (2001) network analysis of the *tampus'* relationships to one another along the road system provides insight into Inca global planning. His study showed that the Incas were adept planners for communication and control at the grand scale, from the center outward. Cuzco was the best-positioned center in the entire network for communication with any other Inca facility. It was also the second-best positioned, after nearby Vilcashuaman, in terms of its ability "to control the flow of information or goods between any two points." The major provincial administrative and supply center at Hatun Xauxa, at the second tier of imperial ranking, was also exceptionally well placed for both political and economic activities at the grand scale. The same cannot be said, however, for other major supply/storage centers at Cotapachi (Bolivia) and Campo de Pucará (Argentina), which were positioned toward the edges of imperial territory. Those two facilities, however, show little evidence of administrative responsibility and seem to have been dedicated to agricultural production for consumption elsewhere. Similarly, locales that were the source of lightweight, high-value goods such as spondylus shell, gold, and feathers, were often positioned toward the end-points of subsidiary lines on the network. If we extend Jenkins' logic into the military domain, we can see that the network of forts worked much like the ribs on a skeleton anchored to a spinal column. Inca installations at most of the empire's edges linked the periphery to the main interior imperial road system and not to one another. Only in a very few locations, such as among the forts guarding Ecuador's active Pambamarca frontier, do the Incas seem to have made an effort to create active lines of interaction paralleling the empire's edge.

Imposed Urbanism

In a classic study, Morris (1972) described how the provincial centers formed a kind of imposed urbanism that was quickly abandoned after the Inca collapse. As just noted, their positioning often reflects more concern for interregional contacts than for local affairs, for they lay at strategic points for long-distance movement. The major *tampu* were usually founded in locations without a significant local occupation, sometimes two or three days' walk from the people they administered. An underlying goal of that strategy may have been to moderate the impact of imperial rule on subjects' access to their traditional, nearby resources. Some regionally important facilities were also established at the borders between two neighboring groups. The secondary center of Tarmatampu, for example, lay at the existing frontier between the Wanka and Tarama peoples of central Peru

(Parsons *et al*. 2000: 138), while the textile and ceramic production center at Milliraya, just northeast of Lake Titicaca, lay at the border between the Qolla and Lupaqa populations (Spurling 1982). In both cases, the intent seems to have been to avoid apparent favoritism of one subject group over another.

The populace of the centers ebbed and flowed on an annual and fitful schedule. Morris suggests that during most of the year no more than about a quarter of the housing may have been used. The numbers swelled as workers came in for a few months during the agricultural off-season to discharge their labor obligations. At times, the centers also housed royal entourages or mobile military forces that numbered into the tens of thousands. The largest *tampu* additionally staged massive annual festivals for the region's inhabitants. After a few days of state-sponsored festivities, the people received their labor assignments for the following year.

The *tampus'* architecture often used local techniques and materials, but their layout, masonry, and material culture were largely foreign to the social landscape. The elegant cut-stone masonry seen in Cuzco is rare in the provinces. In most cases the architecture was built from locally available materials, especially the fieldstone used in *pirka* masonry. At coastal sites, the standard material was adobe. Such a result could be expected because most provincial installations were built and maintained by the labor of local residents. As a consequence, the architecture's materials and masonry could vary a great deal from one installation to the next. *Tampu* also lacked the kinds of independent craft, residential, or market activity that often appear in urban settlements that arise organically as a regional hub of activity. The great storage facilities and emphasis on temporary housing further underscore that they were designed to support traveling armies and part-time occupants. Finally, Morris notes, none of the centers on the main highway had a significant cemetery, emphasizing that even the Inca personnel felt that their presence was only temporary. In keeping with the idea that identity was grounded in a particular place, the homeland was the only place where a deceased person could enjoy a tranquil afterlife.

In practice, the centers worked to help project Inca notions of order onto both the human and non-human landscape of the Andes. Gasparini and Margolies (1980: 195–305) rightly called provincial constructions the *architecture of power* – buildings and spaces intended to reinforce the image of the empire's might – but it may be equally apt to refer to the *architecture of performance* (Coben 2006; 2012). At a macro-level, the *tampu* organized space and movement within the realm and the region, and integrated human society with the sentient landscape. They drew an ethnic mosaic into an imperial cultural space and rhythm through their labor duties, feasting, ritual battles, and political acts (Morris *et al.* 2011: 42). The point was not just to mobilize labor, but to convert the people into the Sapa Inca's subjects by compelling their participation in state-patronized functions. Conversely, the centers also paid reverence to or caged elements of the landscape within architecture, including the sentient stones that were often seen as vital beings (plate 11.1).

Unlike some other pre-industrial states, the Incas did not dedicate buildings to purely administrative functions, such as accounting or holding audiences. To the contrary, most centers reflect an intense preoccupation with ceremony and sacred space. At least six sites were called "New Cuzcos," built in the conceptual, if not actual, image of the capital: Huánuco Pampa, Quito, Tumipampa, Hatunqolla, Charkas, and Inkawasi. The idea apparently was to transpose the order of the heartland onto selected places throughout the entire domain. Models of spaciousness, the centers were laid out around immense rectangular or trapezoidal plazas that hosted

Plate 11.1   Enclosed monolith sometimes called the puma stone, as the focal point of the small amphiteater at Q'enqo Grande, illustrating how the Incas enclosed unusual rocks in platforms as a way of venerating them.

civic-ceremonial functions. At Huánuco Pampa the plaza measured 550 m by 350 m, that is, about 19 ha or almost thirty city blocks (Morris and Thompson 1985: 58; Morris *et al.* 2011). The pyramidal platform that was invariably erected in the center of the plaza or to one side of it was a stage from which officials could preside over state ceremonies. The imperial highway typically took a southeast-to-northwest passage through the plaza, just as it did in Cuzco.

Residential and work sectors surrounded the open areas, often enclosed by high walls. The most common Inca architectural element, called a *kancha*, is a rectangular compound that contained one or more one-room structures (Hyslop 1985: 282–4; 1990: 16–18). At residential sites, the *kancha* housed permanent residents, while at *tampu*, it provided housing and craft quarters. Special sectors of some centers were also designed to house the Sapa Inca and his retinue when they passed through. A second unit, called the *kallanka*, is an elongated rectangular building with an undivided interior space; one side opens onto a plaza (plate 10.2). Common in the north, the *kallanka* housed mobile groups, such as soldiers on the move, and provided space for feasts. In contrast, Inca sites in the south Andes often had a single *kallanka*. Hyslop has suggested that *kallanka* may have been built mostly along roads with large transient populations, especially the main highway that served Wayna Qhapaq's operations in Ecuador. A third form, most prevalent in the south, is a large structure (over 100 m long) divided into about twenty cells, whose function remains unclear (de Hoyos and Williams 1994). Other important architectural forms were religious structures, such as the temples to the Sun, and sequestered sectors devoted to the *aqllakuna*.

The Road System

The Inca royal highway (*qhapaq ñan*) was a wonder of Bronze Age engineering that unified the empire physically and conceptually. Built using wood, stone, woven, and bronze tools, and without benefit of precise surveying equipment or draft animals, the network linked together about 40,000 km of roadway (Hyslop 1984: 224). In a conceptual framework, the roads emanated from – and led to – the imperial capital of Cuzco. There were four main roads radiating from the city, but even in the heartland, the network was far more complex than that (plates 11.2, 11.3). At a grand scale, Hyslop's study, which built on the work of Raimondi and Balta (1874), Strube Erdmann (1963), and Regal Matienzo (1936; 1972), showed

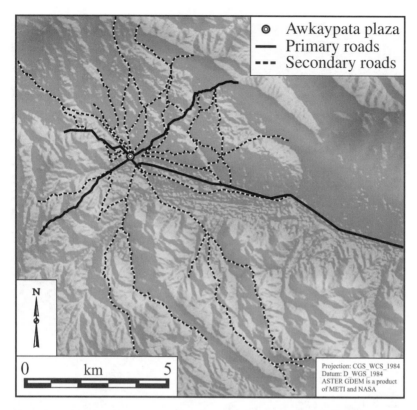

Plate 11.2 Inca road system in Cuzco heartland; base. Source: reproduced by permission of A. Vranich, A. Gonzales, and K. Floerke.

that the network was based on two north–south highways (see also Kosok 1965). The eastern route took a high path through the puna and mountain valleys from Quito (Ecuador) to Mendoza (Argentina). In most of the north, another artery ran along the coastal plain, but deserts made that route impassable in northern Peru and Chile. In those stretches, the road hugged the western foothills where water was more readily available. The major highways were bridged by more than twenty routes that traversed the western mountains, while other roads crossed the eastern cordillera and ran into the montaña and lowlands. Some of the lateral roads ran through passes that approach 5,000 m in altitude. Along the east, a few roads ran well beyond the last significant state sites into the jungles or plains, where they seem to have been used to aid military expeditions or as ties to people beyond Inca control. As work has progressed on the regional level, the

Plate 11.3 The main Inca road leading out of the Cuzco basin toward Antisuyu, the northeastern part (*suyu*) of the empire. Source: reproduced by permission of Kevin Floerke.

complexity of the road network is becoming increasingly apparent. Manzo *et al.* (2011), for example, have recorded at least ten transverse routes extending down the eastern slopes in just the southern Bolivian province of La Tarija, along which lay some 140 Inca installations.

To build their roads, the Incas claimed exclusive rights over numerous traditional routes, including some that had been built centuries earlier. Some sectors ran right through Wari centers such as Pikillacta and Azángaro, leaving no doubt as to their original cultural associations (Schreiber 1992). Even so, the Incas' unrivaled vision is exemplified by the highways built where none had previously existed and there was no local population to serve. A prominent new road ran through Chile's Atacama desert, for example, as well as alongside the Nudo de Azuay in the Ecuadorian *páramo*, on the Peruvian puna south of Huánuco Pampa, and along the western margin of Lake Titicaca (Hyslop 1984: 270–4; plate 11.4). Scholars have long commented that the central Andean roads were far more ostentatious than was needed for the practicalities of travel (e.g., Thompson and Murra 1966; Morris and Thompson 1985). The intent of the elaborate design may have been in part

Plate 11.4   Inca royal highway near Huánuco Pampa, Peru. Source: reproduced by permission of the American Museum of Natural History.

to impress travelers and workers called to the centers for labor service, and to provide a visible symbol of space from which people were excluded except by royal permission.

The roads provided conduits for rapid communication, personnel movement, and logistical support. Soldiers, porters, and llama caravans were prime users, as were the nobility and other individuals on official duty. Other subjects were allowed to walk along the roads only with permission and tolls were charged at some bridges. Relay messengers, called *chaski*, were stationed at intervals of about 6–9 km to carry everything from news from the battlefront to fresh marine fish for the ruler in the sierra (see chapter 5, "Measurement"). Rowe (1946: 231) estimates that they could cover about 240 km per day. Since a message carried from Quito to Cuzco would have required about 375 transfers (Hyslop 1984: 308), some means must have been found to reduce the garbling that would accompany an oral report transmitted by so many locally drafted couriers. Estete and Garcilaso said that the *chaski* carried *khipu* along with the spoken message, which implies that some knot-records could be read with minimal oral input (chapter 5). Despite the *chaskis'* renown, we cannot even be sure that the runners were used along all of the major highways, since Hyslop was unable to locate roadside relay stations (*chaskiwasi*) along several important and well-preserved stretches. He concluded (1984: 308) that we can only be certain that runners were stationed along the main highland route and a couple of routes to the coast, although additional surveys may turn up more sites.

Inca roads varied greatly in their scale, construction techniques, and appearance. For the most part, Hyslop found that road widths varied between about 1 and 4 meters. Thousands of drains and culverts channeled water alongside or under the roads and, where necessary, the Incas built buttressing walls or causeways over wetlands. The roads were flattened and clearly delineated by walls, stone markers, wooden or cane posts, or piles of rocks. In a number of locations, there were two or even three parallel roads. Although the highway has a reputation for ignoring obstacles in the interest of straightness, Hyslop found that straight stretches rarely ran for more than a few kilometers and that the roads are filled with minor adjustments to the terrain. The grandest highways were neatly paved with cobbles or flagstones, but much of the network employed dirt, sand, grass, and other natural surfaces. The finest paved roads were concentrated between the altiplano and Ecuador and along the routes that linked that stretch of highway and the coast. Some paved roads were also extended down into the eastern forests, for instance through the royal coca estates in the Amaybamba–Vilcabamba region. Early travelers, such as Cieza, marveled over the stone staircases that mounted the steep western passes. The technical skill seen in some roads was so great that they are still used for foot traffic or as the foundation of vehicular routes.

The dissected topography, rivers, and marshy areas of the Andes spurred considerable ingenuity as people sought ways to traverse watercourses. Polo commented that, "(o)f the four roads leaving Cuzco, there is none which is crossed by a river easy to ford unless by a miracle" (Polo 1965b: 52). In some important valleys, such as central Peru's Mantaro valley, crossing points over fast-running rivers lay 50 km or more apart, so that Incas and Spaniards ended up building their bridges at the same place (plate 11.5). To get over wide, meandering rivers along the coast and in the highlands, people commonly used rafts (Regal Matienzo 1972; Hyslop 1984: 317–34). In marshy highland areas, the Incas built bridges of stone or floating reeds. The suspension bridges were built of braided cables that supported floors of wood, fiber, and brush; some had full side walls. The most famous bridge spanned about 45 m across the Apurimac river, west of Cuzco (figure 11.3). Even when they were well kept up, the longer suspension bridges may not

Plate 11.5 Inca and Spanish Colonial bridges over Mantaro river, just upriver from Hatun Xauxa.

Figure 11.3 Woven suspension bridge spanning the Apurimac River west of Cuzco. Source: Squier 1877.

have been passable during much of the day, when winds set them swinging (see Squier 1877: 545). And when the breezes were still, most bridges could support only a few people at a time, although Cieza marveled that the most robust could sustain a soldier galloping on horseback. Those conditions meant that large numbers of soldiers or support personnel could not always travel easily across the landscape. Some chroniclers noted that many suspension bridges, like roads, were built in pairs; they suggested that the separate courses were designated either for the nobility and commoners or for each sex. The most unnerving means of crossing ravines was the hanging basket, or *oroya*. The basket could span greater distances than any bridge (over 50 m), but could move only a few passengers at a time; a single failure of materials spelled disaster (see Hyslop 1984).

Resettlement

No state policy affected the Andean social landscape more than resettlement. According to Cobo, Inca officials as a rule selected six or seven thousand families from each new province to be moved elsewhere. That figure is too general to be useful for any particular region, but his estimate that about a quarter to a third of the population was resettled may be about right on average. The most renowned program moved entire communities hundreds or even thousands of kilometers to create enclaves of settlers called *mitmaqkuna*. Occasionally, the Incas moved people to lands that were ecologically similar to their places of origin, presumably to ease the adjustment, or exchanged groups from two locations with one another. While the Incas' use of resettlement was ostensibly initiated by the founding ruler, Pachakuti, the practice built on long Andean tradition. Both the Wari and Tiahuanaco urban polities of the mid-first millennium AD established low-elevation colonies in Pacific coastal valleys, and Tiahuanaco also had a major presence in the warm eastern Cochabamba valley, where maize was easily grown. Some elites in the Late Intermediate polities of the highlands also may have had coca plantations on the eastern slopes (Murra 1972). Thus, both mountain and altiplano societies had centuries-long strategies of seeking direct access to resources outside their home environments.

The principal modern chronicler of the resettlement program, Waldemar Espinoza Soriano, has published many documents that detail the rationales and practices behind the Inca policy (see D'Altroy 2005 for a review). Broadly speaking, the goals concerned security, economics, and ideology, and both institutional and aristocratic interests were served. A principal reason for resettlement was to disperse societies that posed threats to Inca security. Many colonists were assigned to internal and frontier garrisons. Among them were the altiplano's Qolla, who revolted against Inca rule at the transition from Pachakuti to Thupa Inka Yupanki, and the Ayaviri, whose resistance was met by an essentially complete removal from their homeland in southern Peru. A similar fate met northern Peru's Chachapoyas, whose subjugation required at least three major campaigns; and Ecuador's Kañari, who put up stout resistance to the Inca invasion of their homeland. Many Chachapoyas were converted wholesale into a permanent military status, while others were dispersed throughout the northern half of the domain (figure 11.2). At the time of the Spanish invasion, Atawallpa had some 15,000 Kañari in tow, as they were being resettled out of the way toward the south.

A second goal was to congregate economic specialists dedicated to farm-ing, herding, artisanry and extraction, with the products destined for state, religious, or aristocratic use. Among them were artisans, such as the 1,000 weavers and 300 potters installed at Milliraya, Bolivia (figure 11.4). The placement of their community, at the border between two antagonistic peo-ples, suggests that political considerations played a role in the positioning of the colony (Spurling 1992). Farmers, such as those settled at the state farms at Abancay (Peru) and Cochabamba (Bolivia), were assigned to produce maize, coca, cotton, and peppers for the state. Elsewhere, herders, masons, and miners were installed. Wayna Qhapaq's rule seems to have seen the greatest development of the economic colonies, since he was named as the founder of the largest farms and artisan communities. Aristocratic estates also benefited from the production of economic *mitmaqkuna*. Among them were the 500 weavers installed at Wayna Qhapaq's estate at Lamay, in the Sacred valley, and the Chachapoyas resettled over the mountains to the north, in the warm Amaybamba valley, where they helped to populate the royal coca estates (Wilkinson 2013). Thupa Inka Yupanki's kin were reportedly served by 1,000 gold miners and 5,000 support families at a single colony established near the Bolivian frontier.

Another motive for resettlement lay in the Incas' interest in claiming a divine mandate over the Andes. That vision found its most conspicuous form in the ethnic microcosm created at Cuzco. Colonists from each of the four parts of the empire were resettled in twelve neighborhoods surround-ing the royal core, in a pattern that recapitulated their spatial positioning in the domain. The sanctuary at Copacabana also reprised imperial social space, as at least forty-two ethnic groups were assigned to serve the facilities (figure 8.4). Peoples from all over the empire were moved to communities and sanctuaries on the mainland, on the Island of the Sun, and the Island of the Moon (Bauer and Stanish 2001).

Colonists were generally supported from state resources only until they could sustain themselves on the lands they received – perhaps a year or two. The state's insistence on self-sufficiency even extended to people who had previously made their living largely by specializing in craft manufac-ture. Among them were the Ischma metal smiths from the central coast, who were resettled in the unfamiliar highland environment near Cuzco. The Incas went to some lengths to make sure that the *mitmaqkuna* owed their allegiance to the state. They were required to wear their traditional cloth-ing and to speak their own languages, and their interaction with the local societies was restricted. The colonists were often bitterly resented, since they

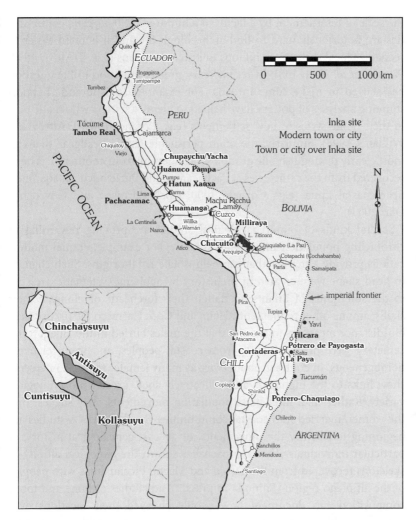

Figure 11.4 Colonies of artisan communities resettled by the Incas to produce textiles, ceramics, and other objects.

received prime lands at local expense. Even so, the *mitmaqkuna* sometimes forged relationships with their neighbors to obtain goods that they might otherwise have been unable to get.

Such a program might be expected to produce a patchwork quilt of ceramic types, house forms, and mortuary practices across the Andes as ethnic groups were intermixed. Surprisingly, however, if it were not for the many witnesses who testified to the program, we could easily underestimate the scale of resettlement by a factor of a hundred. *Mitmaqkuna* communities are notoriously hard to find archaeologically and it is often easier to recognize local shifts from hilltops to lower elevations (e.g., D'Altroy 1992; Parsons *et al.* 2011: 138). In recent years, greater attention to the question has started to make some inroads. For example, stylistic and chemical sourcing analyses of pottery have helped to identify settlers who made pots in their home styles in new settlements (e.g., Lorandi 1984; D'Altroy and Williams 1998). Similarly, the often perishable textile headgear that can most clearly distinguish one group's social identity from another's has been recovered from the cemeteries at Pachacamac and Puruchuco-Huaqarones, near coastal Lima (e.g., Cornejo 2000; Cock Carrasco and Goycochea Díaz 2004).

Several kinds of bio-archaeological studies are proving rewarding in chronicling population movements directly. For example, cranial modifications provide a marker that can help isolate natal origins. Such changes in head shape were created in prehistory by applying systematic pressure to the soft skulls of infants, to flatten their foreheads or elongate their skulls, among other refinements. Haun and Cock Carrasco (2010) use such bio-distance measures to suggest that the males buried in the Huaqarones cemetery were predominantly from coastal peoples, and were relatively homogeneous. In contrast, about twice as many females (43 vs. 25 percent) show links to the highlands and collectively show greater morphological variety. Rather than infer mass population movements, they suggest that the women married into coastal communities. Similarly, DNA studies are beginning to identify the movements, or at least genealogical history, of particular individuals. That approach has shown the biological affinity of skeletons recovered from the Cuzco and Machu Picchu areas with peoples of the altiplano region (Shinoda in press). And studies of bone and tooth composition can document how people changed their locations over time, since the foods they ate reflect the geology from which they came (Andrushko *et al.* 2006, 2009; Turner *et al.* 2009). This last method has even been able to partially track the journeys of children sacrificed on high mountain peaks in the southern Andes (Wilson *et al.* 2007).

Two recent studies of colonies have been especially fruitful. In the coastal Rimac valley, archaeologists have excavated a settlement apparently constructed by the Huarochirí populace, who traditionally occupied the adjacent highlands (Makowski and Vega Centeno A. 2004). Early documents reported that the Incas rewarded the highlanders by granting them some coca farmlands previously held by coastal societies that were unreceptive to

Inca rule (Marcus and Silva S. 1988). The architecture and ceramics of the town reflect an admixture of Huarochirí, Inca, and coastal styles, much as might be expected from a transplanted community. Similarly, on the eastern slopes of Bolivia, Alconini (2010) has identified frontier settlements built with Inca-style architecture but provisioned with local ceramic styles. She interprets that mixture to indicate a collaborative relationship between state and subject that benefited both parties. The Incas enlisted favored peoples from the area to carry out security functions, and backed them with the latent force of the state (see below, "Frontier Relations").

Local resettlement complemented the long-distance program. During the Late Intermediate Period, many densely packed villages had been situated at high elevations, often perched on hilltops. Once the Incas were in control, many a community moved downslope, which had the potential to serve everyone's interests (e.g., Parsons *et al.* 2013). The Incas gained by reducing their subjects' capacity to rise up and workers could be moved around more easily. From the local viewpoint, a loss of freedom was mitigated when lands became available that had been off limits earlier. A "neon lights" effect may have also been at play, as the lords and peasantry alike were attracted to the power, ceremony, or opportunities that a closer tie to the state provided.

The Varieties of Provincial Rule

To illustrate how the varieties of Inca rule worked in practice, we will take a capsule look at a cross-section of regions, beginning with the best-studied Inca province, Huánuco, Peru.

Huánuco, Peru

Huánuco's rich historical and archaeological records provide an exceptional opportunity to study life in the provinces under Inca rule (Helmer 1955–6–6; Ortíz de Zúñiga 1967; 1972; Morris and Thompson 1985; Morris *et al.* 2011). The elaborate regional center, Huánuco Pampa (3,800 m), is the grandest Inca site preserved anywhere outside the heartland. Guaman Poma called it one of the "New Cuzcos." Built on virgin terrain, the city covered about 2 km^2 and contained nearly 4,000 buildings. Pathways radiate out through architectural sectors from an immense rectangular plaza, so that the city can easily be divided into two, four, eight, or even twelve parts (figure 11.5). While an obvious analogy can be envisioned

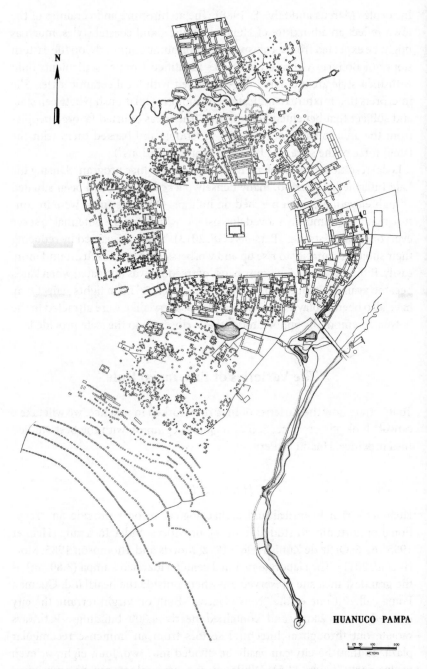

HUANUCO PAMPA

0 25 50   100   200
         METERS

Figure 11.5   Plan of the Inca provincial center of Huánuco Pampa. Source: reproduced by permission of the American Museum of Natural History.

between the layout and the four parts of the realm, Morris (1990) suggests that the design may actually have reflected the relationships among the ethnic groups administered by the settlement, in a scheme analogous to Cuzco's ethnic microcosm. The center could house up to 15,000 people, but the permanent population was probably only a fraction of that. Many people came in for a few weeks at a time to fulfill their labor duties or to participate in political and ceremonial functions.

The layout of the center gives the impression of rigorous planning, but only a fraction of the internal sectors were planned arrays (Morris *et al.* 2011). The most important were the compounds that served important political and religious functions and the buildings along the plaza that housed travelers or were dedicated to preparations for festivals. Two sectors were occupied more intensively than others: the palace and a residential zone. The palace occupied the eastern portion of the site, exhibiting finely cut ashlar masonry. In one of the more imaginative details in this sector, portals through eight unevenly angled walls line up neatly along the site's east–west axis. The alignment runs directly between a cut-stone bath in the royal sector and the central platform. Excavations within this part of the site recovered massive quantities of ceramics

Archaeological evidence suggests that many of the permanent residents were *aqllakuna*. A well-built compound in the north sector, with a single narrow doorway, contains fifty exceptionally regular buildings. Excavations there recovered weaving and spinning tools, along with large quantities of the kind of jars used to brew and store *chicha* – just the kind of remains one would expect from the Chosen Women's duties (Morris and Thompson 1985; Morris *et al.* 2011). The royal residence on the eastern side of the plaza also exhibits evidence for intensive occupation.

The elegant stepped platform (32×48 m at its base; plate 11.6) in the plaza's center was built with a façade of dressed stone, but the site's finest ashlar buildings lie in the royal residences of the eastern sector. This sector was probably rarely occupied, which surely reminded the other residents that there was a greater power elsewhere. Despite the site's elegance, the artistry was only skin deep, since even the finest stereotomy did not extend beyond the visible surfaces. Moreover, many structures toward the perimeter were circular buildings of rough fieldstone built in the local style. On the hill slopes south of the city, 700 storehouses ($\sim$30,000 m^3) were laid out in rows to house the supplies needed for state activities.

Huánuco Pampa had charge of several adjoining provinces, administering at least five, and perhaps many more, ethnic groups (Cieza 1984: 234). Inca

Plate 11.6   Pyramid platform (*usnu*) in the center of the great plaza at Huánuco Pampa. Source: reproduced by permission of the American Museum of Natural History.

rule among those societies reflects a full array of standard policies. That is, Inca officials oversaw local lords who held the offices for all units from 1,000 households on down (Julien 1982; 1993; Grosboll 1993). Julien (1993: 210) describes the effects on one ethnic group at the time of the last census, which probably occurred in the mid-1520s:

> First of all, 1,110 of the 4,108 Chupachos households were in Cuzco. Another 580 resided out of the province on a full-time basis. Another 918 were out of the province on at least a temporary basis, including the 500 assigned to army service. Those who remained, except perhaps the 500 assigned to do agricultural service, were permanently relocated to specialized communities within Chupachos territory.

In the empire's final years, Waskhar claimed the entire populace as a personal estate (Julien 1993: 206, 209–11; see Helmer 1955–6: 24, 26–8, 30–1, 35–6, 38). Altogether, Inca policies altered the social landscape in ways that would have been unimaginable to the indigenous peoples beforehand.

The province's roads and waystations were especially elaborate. The roads featured extended paved surfaces, paved staircases, stone drainage channels, retention walls, bridges, and causeways. In some areas, the paved highway was 15 m wide and one paved staircase was 16 m wide, while two roads ran parallel along some stretches. Hyslop (1984: 74, see 68–84) remarked of one 20-km section, that he "has never seen, nor is aware of publications reporting, such a monumental sector of Inca road anywhere else in the Andean highlands" (see also Morris and Thompson 1985: 109–18). Intriguingly, material evidence is slight for Inca rule away from the grand center and roads. Grosboll (1993: 74–5) observes that the Incas invested most effort in the northeast, which was favorable for maize and coca cultivation and for exchange across the frontier. That is where 200 ethnic Incas from Cuzco were settled and where the most elaborate irrigation and terracing systems are found. The only local village (Ichu) that contains much pottery or architecture in the Inca style was home to the highest ranking ethnic lord in the early Colonial period (Thompson 1967; Morris and Thompson 1985; Grosboll 1993).

Coastal Peru

Peru's north coast presented a different challenge, for this region had already seen 1,500 years of state society. Chimu resistance to the Inca advances was stout and the Incas distrusted most of the coastal populace. A key Inca goal was therefore to eliminate resistance orchestrated by native elites. To that end, they held the Chimu king hostage in Cuzco, while dividing control among local lords who each headed up a territory roughly corresponding to a valley (Rowe 1948; Netherly 1978; Hyslop 1990: 249–51; Ramírez 1990). Irrigation engineers were sent to the south coast to oversee canal systems, while other colonists went to work at *tampu* or to make pots in nearby mountain provinces (Espinoza Soriano 1975; Ramírez 1982; 1990; Rostworowski 1990). Two other policies deliberately weakened the coastal lords. First, coastal peoples were forbidden to carry weapons. Just as important symbolically, some upvalley coca fields were transferred to the jurisdictions of highland peoples, so that the lords lost some of their ability to dispense this vital product (Rostworowski 1983; 1990).

Inca rule on the dense north coastal populace often applied a lighter touch than that applied to adjacent highland populations, and may have been different in substantive ways. It may be surprising that there is little documentary information on the particulars of Inca rule in the region. However, recent work at a major Chimu center at Farfán, in the Jequetepeque valley, has identified an important Inca component (Mackey 2010). Rather than build a new *tampu*, the Incas used the existing center for their own ends, among them production of textiles and ceramics, along with storage. For those purposes, they built two new compounds and remodeled three others. In the process, they also constructed an *unsu* platform, which is the signature ceremonial element of Inca rule. They also dedicated areas to commensal hospitality, which is also at the heart of Inca governance. The result was a blend of construction styles, which Mackey calls "conciliatory or diplomatic architecture" (2010: 223). She interprets the evidence to suggest that the Incas ruled indirectly through local elites, actually increasing the number who were resident at the facility over those who had been present under Chimu rule. Nearby, up the valley, Kremkau (2010) has described new small residential communities and ritual activity focused on intermittently flowing water sources. In a complementary fashion, Hayashida (1999) has documented how the Incas mobilized artisans to make pottery for state interests, even while the potters made ceramics for their own ends.

In other valleys, the Incas appear to have governed from installations at least partway into the highlands. Generally speaking, sites built according to Inca canons are much sparser near the coast than inland. In the expansive Chillón valley, the main Inca site lay at Huancayo Alto, about 30 km up the valley. That small settlement lay in lands occupied by the Yauyos, a highland people who kept up good relations with the Incas and were granted the lowlanders' coca fields, much like the Huarochirí in the Rimac valley (Dillehay 1977; Rostworowski 1990). The Incas built no major centers along the north coast and, in fact, their most elaborate construction in some valleys was probably the *tapia*-walled desert road (Xérez 1985: 82 – 5; Hyslop 1984: 37 – 55). The lacuna is all the more striking when we consider that the coast is incredibly rich in archaeological remains, where the desert climate has preserved even delicate organic remains for millennia. Three important sites in the lower valleys with Inca elements are Túcume, Tambo Real, and Chiquitoy Viejo.[6] Each site had a prior occupation into which the Incas installed a state sector, like those at Farfán, but local architectural styles and artifacts still dominate (see Conrad 1977; Hyslop 1984: 49; 1990: 327, n. 6). The cache of brilliantly decorated Inca figurines found at the top of Túcume's main pyramid speaks more of an ideological claim to power in the productive Lambayeque valley than to direct administration.

The intensive rule on Peru's south coast contrasted starkly with these policies. The Chincha, for example, were so esteemed that their foremost lord fell at Atawallpa's side in Cajamarca's plaza. The Chincha were granted trading privileges along the Ecuadorian coast to obtain spondylus shell and other goods from extra-territorial peoples. A Spanish expedition ran into one such trading raft a few years before the invasion of Peru was mounted. On the balsa, they found shell, emeralds, and a host of other fine goods (Sámano-Xérez 1937: 65–6). The shell, called *mullu*, had many uses – as currency in the north, as decoration on cloth for the Incas, and as raw material for statues and rain ceremonies in the mountains. The Chincha grant was thus a major concession.

Physical evidence of Inca rule in Chincha is concentrated at La Centinela, where a small Inca sector was erected at the heart of the pre-Inca center. Like the compound at Túcume, it seems to have been intended for the ceremonial and political activities that legitimized both Inca rule and the privileges enjoyed by the valley's aristocrats (Morris 1998: 296–7; 2007). In the adjacent Pisco valley, the Incas built two new centers, called Lima La Vieja and Tambo Colorado (plate 11.7). The latter is the classic coastal Inca site. Its adobe architecture flanks a large trapezoidal plaza, with the platform situated at the downvalley edge. Traces of brilliant red and yellow clay still adhere to some walls, providing hints of the colorful vision the settlement presented when it was occupied. Two other sites were important

Plate 11.7   Coastal Inca center of Tambo Colorado, in the Pisco valley, Peru.

in Inca relations with coastal peoples. Inkawasi (Cañete), one of the "New Cuzcos," was built for the express purpose of conquering the resistant Guarco people. Once that goal was achieved, the site was vacated (Hyslop 1985). The other great site was Pachacamac (Lurin valley), which was an important city and oracle for 1,500 years before the Incas. There, the Incas intruded five architectural sectors, including a temple and enclave of priestesses, but allowed the local society an unusual degree of independence (Cornejo 2000).

The Lake Titicaca Basin

The Lake Titicaca region held abundant attractions for the Incas. While the lake lay at the center of the Incas' vision of their genesis, the altiplano's wealth made it an early target for Cuzco's expansionist aspirations. In 1532, the peoples living around the lake had been formed into about thirteen provinces. As a result of their early alliance with the Incas, the Lupaqa enjoyed a privileged position. The Lupaqa province was composed of two *hunu* of 10,000 households each, but the Incas adjusted to the local demography by organizing the hierarchy around seven population centers. Local Aymara-speaking lords held positions of power in all levels of the hierarchy. Resettlement and militarism devastated some of the other peoples of the basin. Since the Ayaviri had vigorously resisted Inca domination, they were savaged and the province was nearly vacated (Julien 1983: 88). Cieza wrote that the survivors "went through the sown fields calling upon their dead ancestors for a long time, and lamented their ruin with groans of profound emotion" (Cieza 1984: 271; see Julien 1983: 89–93). The rebellious Qolla were employed as masons and soldiers from Cuzco to Ecuador, while Thupa Inka Yupanki claimed five of their towns as personal estates. The most variegated pocket of colonists lay at Copacabana, where members of forty-two ethnic groups were resettled from all over the empire (Ramos Gavilán 1976: 43). In addition, seven altiplano groups south of the lake provided 14,000 workers for Wayna Qhapaq's farms at Cochabamba, Bolivia (Wachtel 1982).

The archaeological record also reflects the Inca impact on the basin. Cieza's report that the Incas forced the local societies to quit their fortified hilltops is supported by field studies that show that the populace on both the western and southern sides of the lake moved closer to the water's edge. Surveys along the western lakeshore found that most of the Inca-era populace lived there. Nevertheless, the uplands were still essential for the basin's economy, as vast herds were put to pasture there (Cieza 1967: 83; Hyslop 1984: 119; Albarracín-Jordan and Mathews 1992: 215–42; Stanish 1997: 210–11). The most prominent center in the northwest basin was Hatunqolla. This settlement, now buried by a modern town, covered about 50 ha, that is, about one-eighth of Huánuco Pampa's area (Julien 1983). Chucuito was even more spacious, covering about 80 ha. Both of those provincial capitals and likely all the Inca sites along the two roads that ran around the lake were founded in pristine locations. They were provisioned with both high quality Cuzco-style pottery and regional styles (Hyslop 1984: 116–25). The basin also contained many religious installations. The settlement at Arapa and maybe even the entire province of Chiquicache were dedicated to the Sun (Polo 1940b: 182; Julien 1993: 184). Likewise, the province of Copacabana, located on a promontory extending into the lake, was an Inca sanctuary (Ramos Gavilán 1976: 43; Bauer and Stanish 2001). The temples on the Islands of the Sun and the Moon provide witness to the importance of the lake in state ideology, and Cobo described Tiahuanaco as a universal shrine (Cobo 1990: 100). Another kind of state facility consisted of artisan colonies set to work making textiles and ceramics (e.g., Milliraya) and metals (e.g., Pila Patag; see chapter 13; Murra 1978; Espinoza Soriano 1987b; Spurling 1992; Hyslop 1984: 130–1). Altogether, the evidence from the basin illustrates that the Incas developed extensive independent facilities that were set apart from the local societies, no matter how privileged they were.

The South Andes

Southern Kollasuyu, the empire's southeastern and spatially largest part, is often considered marginal to Inca interests, because of its low population, relative lack of large installations, and distance from Cuzco (D'Altroy *et al.* 2007). That perception is in part well founded, but the region's thin documentary record (Bibar 1966; Valdivia 1960; Matienzo 1967) has led many scholars to overlook the richness of the Inca archaeological remains. Because some peoples resisted Spanish dominion for about 130 years, Inca rule was only a distant memory in oral traditions when the first written accounts were taken down. Even so, we may infer that the Argentine and Chilean lands were divided into only four or five provinces (Lorandi 1988; Lorandi and Boixadós 1987–8). There is no mention of the decimal hierarchy anywhere, but we do not know if that stems from gaps in our knowledge or if, as in Ecuador, the Incas never installed the hierarchy among native peoples. The prominent mention of *mitmaqkuna*, however, indicates that some important positions were filled by colonists.

The infrastructure was not as ambitiously developed as it was in the north, but it still reflects considerable effort carried out within a global conception. Regional surveys have now recorded well over 400 Inca sites or settlements with Inca sectors in south Bolivia, Chile, and Argentina. In recent years, field workers have found many previously unknown Inca sites by surveying high elevations, transverse road networks, and the eastern slopes (Raffino 1983; 1993; C. Vitry pers. comm. 1998; Manzo *et al.* 2011). A key Inca tactic was to found settlement clusters at agriculturally productive locations from which travel and communications could be controlled. At some settlements, such as Turi (Chile), Tastil, Quilmes, and Fuerte Quemado (Argentina), the Incas simply installed sectors within existing towns. Chile was mostly administered from sites high in the mountains, paralleling the indirect approach applied to Peru's north coast. In contrast to many important sites in the north, the Incas relied heavily on local material culture at their centers, so that ceramics or other artifacts made in the imperial style are far less common in the south.

The Incas intensified mining, farming, herding, and artisanry in and around the state centers. Raffino estimates that three-quarters of the Inca sites in the mineral-rich south Andes were involved in mining or metallurgy, but some large state farms also lay there. The Incas also improved security by erecting fortresses, such as Pucará de Andalgalá and Pucará de las Pavas, along the upper edge of the eastern slopes. On both the east and west, the line of forts lay well up in the mountains, above other Inca settlements and farms. It is hard to say at present if the lower settlements were founded only after the forts had assured security, or if the forts were a fall-back designed to foil any incursion into the mountains.

Resettlement also reshaped the demography of the south. In the Calchaquí valley, for example, the Pulares gained status and resources at the expense of the Calchaquíes, who resisted Inca rule. Settlers from Tucumán and Santiago del Estero of the eastern lowlands were moved into the intermontane valleys, while altiplano societies, such as the Churumatas and Chichas, were resettled along the eastern fringes. Canas and Canches *mitmaqkuna* from as far away as Peru (1,200 km) were also settled in Chicoana and Quiri-Quiri (Lorandi and Cremonte 1993). Finally, the Incas claimed the sacred landscape by constructing many shrines on the highest peaks (Schobinger *et al.* 1966; Beorchia 1987; Reinhard 1985; Ceruti 1997). In addition to their ritual purposes, the shrines served a political end by interjecting the state between the indigenous peoples and their founding ancestors, who were thought to have descended from the peaks.

Highland Ecuador

The Incas fused two extremes of imperial strategy in highland Ecuador: indirect rule through local chiefs, and construction of their second capital at Tumipampa, which took its name from Wayna Qhapaq's kin group (Salomon 1987: 172–86; 1987). The chiefdoms were often intransigent foes who occupied difficult terrain and posed administrative dilemmas. They were politically autonomous, but were linked to one another through regional marketing systems; many traded outside imperial territory for spondylus, gold, feathers, and other materials that the Incas wanted (Idrovo 1984). Salomon judges that, initially, the Incas found it effective to rule each area through a paramount chief who was sometimes elevated to represent a pooled set of smaller chiefdoms. Over time, Cuzco tried to shift toward a policy of social and political integration.

Some local elites resettled in Quito were granted estates and trading privileges, which gave them a vested interest in maintaining the state economy. Small versions of the state tribute and political systems were also set up within the chiefdoms. There is more evidence of those efforts around Tumipampa than in the north, which likely stems from the longer Inca occupation in the south (esp. Salomon 1986: 185; Idrovo 1988). Despite the Incas' efforts at civilizing the region, the decimal hierarchy was found largely among the colonists, not the natives (Espinoza Soriano 1975: 387; Salomon 1986: 172). The resettlement program altered the ethnic composition of the south Ecuadorian highlands as much as any part of the empire, as the entire landscape around Tumipampa was reformed (Truhan 1997).

There are notable Inca sites in Ecuador, but the recorded archaeological remains are inconsistent with the intensity of rule described in the sources. Tumipampa and Quito were the most important centers, but both unfortunately lie under modern cities. Tumipampa was also the locale of heated battles at the inception of the war between Atawallpa and Waskhar, when Inca armies deliberately destroyed much of the city (Hyslop 1990: 264–5). Documents indicate that Tumipampa (a "New Cuzco") shared several toponyms with the original imperial capital (Arriaga 1965: 24).[7] For instance, the core part of both sites was laid out between two rivers that flowed northwest to southeast, one of which was named Huatanay in each city (Idrovo 1984, cited in Hyslop 1990: 140–2). Only modest amounts of ashlar masonry are to be found in standing architecture, but Idrovo's excavations have uncovered deposits that suggest that cut-stone work was prominent. The fact that about 80 percent of the excavated pottery was in the Cuzco polychrome style underscores the site's high status (Idrovo 1984: 98). Ingapirca is more spectacular. Situated about 40 km north of Tumipampa, this site consists of an Inca ceremonial and residential complex built over an important Kañari settlement (Hatun Cañar) that had been occupied for several hundred years. Excavations indicate that the Incas demolished the existing surface architecture, perhaps in part as retribution against the recalcitrant Kañari. Fresco (1984) and Cobo (1990: 14–15) suggest that the rock prominence upon which the great oval structure was erected was considered to be the origin place of the Kañari. By building on the outcrop, the Incas may have been paying homage to the ancestral power while claiming precedence in mediating between this and other worlds (Alcina Franch 1978; Fresco 1984; see Hyslop 1990: 261–4). Other recorded sites are dedicated to military activities, transportation and communication, ceremony, and royal residence, but Inca settlements related to agricultural and craft production, herding, colonies, and residential sites with imperial ceramics are largely missing from Ecuador's archaeological register.

Frontier Relations

The Incas enjoyed a geographic advantage unique among pre-modern empires – at the apex of their power, no foreign competitor could threaten their dominance. There was no analog to the Tarascans for the Aztecs, the steppe nomads for the Chinese, or the Germans, Parthians, and Sasanians for the Romans. Even so, Tawantinsuyu's frontier traversed over 4,000 km of mountains, jungles, and plains, across which the Incas had to deal with scores of societies. The Incas maintained a flexible array of relations with those people and in many areas promoted economic and cultural ties beyond the limits of their military and political control (see papers in Dillehay and Netherly 1988). Regional hostilities called for a hardened border in some places, but for the most part the frontier was a permeable membrane across which the Incas regulated, but did not shut off, traffic.

The northern perimeter of the empire is conventionally set at the Río Angasmayo in Pasto territory, near the Ecuador–Colombia border, across which the Incas seem to have maintained open relations (see Salomon 1986). In the rough terrain of the eastern Ecuadorian slopes, Cuzco's armies ran into fierce resistance, and it appears that the relatively secure edge of the empire lay along an eastern cordon of forts bordering the Quito basin (Salomon 1986: 148–51; see Renard-Casevitz *et al.* 1986). In Chachapoyas territory, local documents state that Thupa Inka Yupanki once visited and claimed lands toward Moyobamba, about 100 km into the jungle (*RGI* I: 166–75). Recent survey in the region shows that the Incas built several small outposts well into the forest and there is historical mention of small forts along the borderlands in Huánuco (Schjellerup 1997: 112–67). Farther south, coca fields claimed by the Mantaro Valley societies lay about 50 km into the jungles, but no forts are known along the eastern slopes there (Vega 1965).[8] How far to the north and east of Cuzco the Incas applied their rule is also unclear, because survey of the eastern slopes has been rare. The *tampu* typical of highland provinces are unknown below about 1,800–2,000 m, but a section of Inca road has been found 200 km down the Río Urubamba from Cuzco. Several sources suggest that expeditions ventured well into the tropical lowlands now occupied by the Piro and Machiguenga, and societies within the empire traded there for forest products (Ortiz de Zúñiga 1967; 1972; Rowe 1985b; Renard-Casevitz *et al.* 1986: 68, 71; Pärssinen 1992: 107–18). Overall, it appears that the frontier in lands now part of Peru was not heavily defended and that the Incas tried to extend their relations into the jungles peaceably once conquest had failed.

In Bolivia, there is a great disparity between the locations of state settlements and the farthest Inca advances into a larger territory. As described in chapter 10, the Incas established a series of major installations in the mountains, such as Incallajta, which boast evidence of a significant concern for defense (Coben 2012). Even so, Thupa Inka Yupanki reportedly marched 800 km into the lowlands east of Cuzco, along the Madre de Dios river. The most distant named point, Paititi, lies about 400 km beyond the forts that line the eastern cordillera. Inca sites are also strung out along the upper Río Beni, suggesting that Cuzco may have tried to establish control into the *llanos de Mojo* (Saignes 1985: 18; Pärssinen in press). Samaipata is the easternmost major Inca site in the region. The Incas said that they had won over some groups even farther out through gifts and alliances, an effort that was stimulated by the discovery of gold. They sent 1,000 miners into the lowlands along with 5,000 *mitmaqkuna* to provide their sustenance, but the settlement was later overrun (see Saignes 1985: 20; Pärssinen 1992: 130–1).

The approach taken in the frontier zone southeast of Incallajta differed from that employed above or near Quito. Studies by Sonia Alconini (2004, 2008) at two Inca sites, Cuzcotuyo and Oroncota, indicate that the imperial presence in this zone was a "soft military frontier," not an overt military occupation. The complexity of the political, ethnic, and cultural map of the region (Alconini 2008: figure 2) shows a great variety of colonists and other ethnic groups living cheek by jowl. State installations included outposts and small centers built in the imperial style, which emphasized cultural interaction rather than domination and exploitation. Alconini's work shows that the Inca presence in this zone seems to have little to no effect on settlement patterns or the local economy. Instead, residents of the region were apparently recruited to work on the Incas' behalf in securing pacific relations. Intriguingly, that strategy was applied in an area that was at least periodically unsettled by the Chiriguano populace, who lived outside imperial control and who were the protagonists in an incursion in the 1520s into imperial territory.

A similar situation existed along the Argentine frontier – a string of forts in the eastern mountains, beyond which expeditions advanced onto the plains without annexing them (see Raffino 1983; 1993 for a review of Inca sites in the south Andes). In both Jujuy and Salta, the Incas gained enough control over the piedmont to establish extensive farms and associated facilities with hundreds of storehouses (Boman 1908; Fock 1961; González 1983; Mulvany de Peñaloza 1986; Mulvany de Peñaloza and Soria 1998). The people living in the Tucumán piedmont allied themselves with the Incas for protection against the plains dwellers, and were dispersed throughout the south Andes as military and economic settlers.

Writers from the sixteenth century to the present have puzzled over the empire's southern limit, placing it anywhere from the Río Maipu, just south of Santiago, to the Río Bío Bío, 300 km beyond. The most southerly major Inca site is the fort called Cerro del Inga, about 80 km south of Santiago in the Cachapoal drainage (Planella *et al.* 1991; Planella and Stehberg 1994). However, Inca-style copper axes and ceramics have been found as far south as Valdivia, 700 km beyond Santiago. Dillehay and Gordon (1988) point out that the problem of fixing a border in Chile evaporates if we drop the idea that political, military, and economic frontiers coincided neatly. For the far south, they suggest that economic and cultural ties with the Araucanians extended well beyond the military and political limits of the empire. Frontier relations at the fuzzy limits of dominion were thus complex and varied, because they met imperial needs that changed over time and space. It is especially interesting that the Inca advances to the north and south halted at the edge of rich agricultural expanses. The temperate lands of the Mapuche were richer and more populous than those farther north in Chile, and the societies of Colombia north of the Pasto were wealthy chiefdoms. It seems most likely that logistical obstacles, the great distances from Cuzco, and formidable local resistance combined to halt the progression of Inca rule.

Notes

1 The creation of new questions is a good thing on many levels, some of them whimsical. As the apocryphal Prof. Wotan Ulm (Oxford) points out in *The Long Earth*, "But then science is nothing but a series of questions that lead to more questions, or it wouldn't be much of a career path, would it?" (Pratchett and Baxter 2012: 8–9).

2 Cieza (1984: 223) mentioned thirty-nine provinces, while Pedro Pizarro (1986: 221) named thirty-three. Unfortunately, neither explained what he meant by the term and their lists are not remotely complete (see Hyslop 1990; Pärssinen 1992: 294–301).

3 For more extended discussions of this topic, see Moore (1958: 74–85, 165–74); see also Rowe (1946: 271–2). Some chroniclers provided explicit lists of the acts that the Incas considered illicit or punishable, but their accounts are often general or contradictory (e.g., Diez de Betanzos 1996: 108–9; Murúa 1986: 355–9; Guaman Poma 1980: 159–66; Cobo 1979: 203–7; Valera 1945). Of the modern studies of Inca law, Hermann Trimborn's (1925: 1937) and Sally Falk Moore's works provide treatments at the grand scale. Moore (1958) treats land tenure and taxes under the concept of law; the discussion here is reserved primarily for what she covers as criminal law. Trimborn sees a more systematic code than do Moore and I.

4 Among them were anal sex, fellatio, and miscegenation (e.g., Garcilaso 1966: 162). The long history of non-procreative sex among north coastal peoples is visible in the graphic pottery dating to the Moche society (AD 100–700) and its successors. It is not clear from the available information if the acts were undertaken for pleasure, for ritual purposes, or both, or if some of the representations were purely mythical.

5 E.g., Morris 1972; Gasparini and Margolies 1980; González Carré *et al.* 1981; Raffino 1983; Hyslop 1984; 1985; 1990; Morris and Thompson 1985; LeVine 1985; Raffino 1993; D'Altroy 1992; Matos Mendieta 1994; Burger *et al.* 2007; Malpass and Alconini 2010; Morris *et al.* 2011; Coben 2012),

6 For Chiquitoy Viejo, see Conrad 1977; Tambo Real: Hyslop 1984: 42; Túcume: Heyerdahl *et al.* 1995.

7 Colcampata (Cuzco) and Collca or Cullca (Tumipampa), Huatanay and Huatana, Monaycuna and Monay, Pumacurco and Pumachupan (both Cuzco) and Pumapungo, Cachipamba and Cachipamba, Calixpuquio and Calyxpogyo, Guanacaure and Guanacuri (Arriaga 1965: 24).

8 Among the places mentioned are Monobamba, Uchubamba, Paucartambo, Andamayo, and Comas, all well into the upper jungles.

Chapter Twelve

Farmers, Herders, and Storehouses

When the Inca settled a town, or reduced one to obedience, he set up markers on its boundaries and divided the fields and arable land within its territory into three parts, in the following way: One part he assigned to Religion and the cult of his false gods, another he took for himself, and a third he left for the common use of the people. It has not been possible to determine whether these parts were equal in any towns and provinces; however, it is known that in many places the division was not equal, but depended on the availability of land and the density of the population ... The Inca had the same division made of all the domesticated livestock, assigning one part to Religion, another to himself, and another to the community; ... he did the same with the grazing lands and pastures in which the livestock was pastured, so that the herds were in different pastures and could not be mixed.

Cobo 1979: 211, 215

Father Cobo's description of farming and herding, in which all resources were divided into three parts, is the classic sketch of an orderly Inca economy. In Garcilaso's more idealized account, no one ever went hungry, because the community and state provided for everyone's welfare from resources that were adequate for every need. The priest did not share Garcilaso's romantic vision, but did comment approvingly that communities that practiced the ancient ways of mutual assistance were far better off in the seventeenth century than those that did not. There was truth in both chroniclers' portrayals, but Cobo simplified things, while Garcilaso glossed over the effects of labor exploitation, loss of prime pastures and fields, and the forced removal of millions of people from their ancestral lands. For a more accurate view, we need to consider both the vast resources

The Incas, Second Edition. Terence N. D'Altroy.
© 2015 John Wiley & Sons, Ltd. Published 2015 by John Wiley & Sons, Ltd.

commanded by the state, church, and aristocracy, and those held by the common folk in the variegated Andean environment. Equally important, we need to disentangle utopian myths from the grind of daily life in a demanding land.

In some early empires, the heartland's economy was markedly more complex than that of the provinces and the capital was a vacuum for provincial production. The core cities of the Aztec Triple Alliance, for instance, housed great markets and quarters for artisans and merchants (Smith 2012). Their immediate hinterlands included garden-like farmlands and towns that specialized in particular crafts, such as pottery, textiles, or obsidian tools. Taxes in cacao and cloth from farther afield poured into the center, where elites consumed them or exchanged them for other goods. Similarly, Rome was the hub of a circum-Mediterranean marketing system (Garnsey and Saller 1987). Its populace, subsidized by a public dole, consumed much of the grain and wine output of entire regions, including Egypt, the Crimea, eastern Spain, and southern France. Many of its provinces shifted toward a more fully monetary economy, in part because some taxes were levied in widely used currencies. In these and other cases, the empire's economy was focused on consumption at the core.

Tawantinsuyu was unusual in these respects. The Incas did not have a large urban population to support in Cuzco, nor could they move bulk goods across great distances as part of a regular system of provisioning. Even so, the conquests gave them access to the labor of millions of workers, expanses of farmlands and pastures, and the Andes' mineral wealth. In organizational terms, how best to take advantage of the human and natural resources was the issue. When the Inca expansion began, economic activities in the highlands were organized community by community or at most by a regional polity. Highland societies did not typically have markets, taxation in goods, a temple economy, or any other institution that would allow the Incas to easily divert their products to Cuzco's ends. People living on the coast, on the other hand, had economies that were more specialized and interdependent, which the Incas were ill equipped to supervise directly.

Caught between societies with much simpler and more complex economic systems, the Incas chose to intensify the highland economies they knew best and left the more integrated systems largely alone. Beginning with his classic doctoral thesis, John Murra (1980b) has shown how the Incas used the language of kin-based production and exchange to represent their economy as if it were just an extension of familiar obligations. A few observers that he drew from, especially the astute Polo (1940b; see also

Falcón 1946; Garcilaso 1966; Cobo 1979), took pains to explain to their superiors how things differed from Europe. Some elements of Andean economics struck the Spaniards as novel, bizarre, or idolatrous, for example the ritualized exchange and hospitality that were intertwined with political relations, and the ceremony that accompanied everything from shearing wool to tilling the fields.

Polo and his compatriots described how the Incas claimed farmlands, pastures, and flocks, and all the wild and mineral resources of the land for themselves. The peasants paid their taxes in labor on a rotating basis, while the products of their own fields and flocks were untouched. In return, the state owed largess, security, and leadership in all its forms. To make the system work, the Incas periodically counted the empire's heads of household and organized many of them into a pyramid of taxpaying units that encompassed from 10 to 10,000 households (chapter 11). Over time, state officials also resettled entire communities of farmers and artisans who were set to work for particular needs. Although they annexed lands with markets, money, and specialized communities, the Incas did not adopt market features into their state economy. Instead, they created an independent set of state resources and institutions that provided for their needs.

In the process, the Incas altered both the social and biotic makeup of the Andean landscape (D'Altroy 2005; in press a). To make sure that sufficient labor was available at the right times and places, they assigned workers to agro-pastoral and artisanal production both in their home regions and in areas where the Incas' anticipated needs were greatest or where particular resources were available. As described in chapter 11, many thousands of workers were resettled in new locations, to exploit lands and raw materials like clay, salt, and gold, on behalf of the Inca. Modifications of the landscape through construction of terraces and irrigation systems have also left their mark, especially in aristocratic estates and state farms. Those practices changed the humidity and temperature regimes of micro-landscapes, effectively lowering the ecological altitude of highland crop lands. The impact of the Incas' focus on particular crops should not be overlooked either. Not only did they emphasize maize as a culturally important crop, but they introduced species into areas that previously had not seen them. Cuzco flint maize was widely distributed, for example, while quinoa was introduced into the far south as a novel cultigen (Rossen *et al.* 2010). They developed previously uncultivated lands on the eastern slopes for coca and other warm-weather crops, and practiced forestry management at upper elevations (Chepstow-Lusty and Winfield 2000). Overall, the practices put into place to sustain the Inca economy transformed the Andes as much as, if not more than, any other aspect of the Inca imperial endeavor.

Labor Service

Darrell La Lone (1994) has suggested an apt phrase for the Inca economy – *supply on command* – because it was designed primarily to meet institutional goals, rather than follow the supply and demand motivations of market economics. As they did with so many elements of their rule, the Incas drew from earlier Andean statecraft in designing their economy. The Moche, Wari, Tiahuanaco, and Chimu, for example, had all increased the intensity of farming, herding, and artisanry within their domains, often explicitly for state interests (e.g., Moseley and Cordy-Collins 1990; Schreiber 1992, 2001; McEwan 2006; Shimada 1994; Pillsbury 2001; Janusek 2008; Jennings and Bowser 2009; Jennings 2010; Quilter and Castillo B. 2010). Some of that intensification was dedicated to provisioning state activities or sustaining elite kin groups. Among the efforts leaving their archaeological marks were the Wari construction of agricultural terraces in subordinate valleys, the draining of coastal marshes or construction of vast irrigation systems in the Chimu region, the creation of vast drained field and irrigation systems by the Tiahuanaco in the Titicaca basin, and the establishment of low-elevation colonies by both Wari and Tiahuanaco. Some of those efforts were also undertaken to sustain the feasting (commensal hospitality) through which so much of Andean politics were conducted over the millennia. So there were a lot of models that the Incas could draw from.

Even with that deep history of intensification – and even though they relied on customary principles – Andean economics were radically modified under Cuzco's rule. By declaring that they owned everything, the Incas devised a rationale that gave people access to their traditional lands only in return for labor duty. The peasants' household output was untouched by Inca demands, but their resources and labor were not. Even so, Murra (1980b) observes that many people did not happily digest the idea that they could use their ancestral lands only by the grace of the Inca. Most of the services and products that the Inca state required were obtained through a corvée system that tapped the heads of households for rotating labor service, called *mit'a* ("to take a turn"). Cobo (1979: 234) explained the situation this way:

> One thing that should be pointed out with respect to the amount of tribute that they brought to the king, and it is that there was no other rate or limit, either of the people that the provinces gave for the *mita* labor service or in the other requirements, except the will of the Inca. The people were never asked to make a fixed contribution of anything, but all of the people needed were called for the aforementioned jobs, sometimes in larger numbers, other times in lesser numbers, according to the Inca's desire, and the result of those labors was the royal tribute and income; and in this way the people extracted all the gold and silver that the Incas and the *guacas* [*wak'as*, sacred objects and places] had.

To make things work, officials required current information about the size of the taxpaying population and the natural resources at their disposal. They also needed to be familiar with subjects' skills and to understand what goals could be met without undermining communities' self-sufficiency. Those needs were met through the census and a flow of information between the higher authorities and their subordinates (chapter 11). Where the data are preserved, the accounting of both labor and goods seems to have been proportionate to the numbers of households within the units (see below).

The labor tax was levied on male heads of household, called *hatun runa*. They were the married men who belonged to the age category that corresponded to about 25–50 years of age. Since they made up about 15–20 percent of the empire's population, the Incas could call on the labor of about two million workers. A householder's duties typically required two or three months of work each year, but Incas did not require that the *mit'ayuq* (laborer) work for a specified period or even discharge his obligations by himself. As a result, whole families could take on some jobs and the larger the family, the more quickly the task was done (Cobo 1979: 235). Thus, a man with a large family was thought to be well off. That advantage, among others, gave couples a strong incentive to have a lot of children.

Some early sources wrote that there were standard categories of duties, which were reported in an order that generally reflected cultural importance rather than the numbers of personnel involved. Falcón (1946: 137–40) itemized thirty-two duties for coastal societies and thirty-seven for the highlands, not counting general farming and military service, which claimed the greatest energies. Both his and Murúa's (1986: 402–4; see also Guaman

Poma 1980: 183) lists regularly distinguished between artisans who produced fine-quality objects and those producing more ordinary goods. From our present perspective, it is hard to be sure that the Spanish reports precisely reflected Andean categories of importance, since the lists do not conform exactly to the local labor assessments that are available.

All taxpayers were supposed to render some labor duty, but in practice many were exempt from the standard corvée service. Officials with responsibilities for 100 households or more were excused from labor service entirely and certain ethnic groups were favored for particular duties because they were thought to have special talents (chapter 10). Among the highland peoples, the Rucanas were employed as litter bearers, some of the Lake Titicaca Qolla as stonemasons, the Chumbivilcas as dancers, and the Chachapoyas, Kañari, Chuyes, and Charka as warriors (Rowe 1946: 267–9; Espinoza Soriano 1980). Rostworowski (1989: 273) suggests that all coastal artisans were exempted from rotating labor service and were put to work on their specific crafts for the state. Other groups were required to render natural products, such as the spears made of *chonta* palm and the gold dust produced by some jungle peoples. Still others were thought to be virtually useless for state purposes, but were put to work anyway. The Urus, who lived on the southern margins of Lake Titicaca and on the north side of Lake Poopó, were renowned for their ineptitude. The word *uru*, in fact, means "worm" in Quechua and was used as a pejorative by the Incas. The Urus were assigned to fish for the state, as well as to gather reeds and help make cloth, but did not participate in public works projects. In one of the more eccentric duties, one society with nothing else to render had to turn in a basket of live lice every four months, ostensibly so that they would learn the imperatives of service (Cieza 1967: 56).

Over time, the Incas modified the ways in which they extracted labor service from their subjects. Although they initially depended on the productive capacities of the general populace for their needs, over time they increasingly augmented and even replaced rotating corvée workers with permanent specialists (see Murra 1980b: 183–6). They also created several specialized labor statuses, the most important of which were the *mitmaqkuna* (colonists), *yanakuna* (lifelong servants), and the *aqllakuna* (chapters 10, 11). There was also some flexibility in the way policies were applied. According to Santillán (1968), local officials assigned duties to the taxpayers under their supervision. Polo (1916: 102) added that a new set of miners was called up at every royal succession to work alongside the miners still committed to the estates of the deceased rulers. Rather than select the workers, the new Inca left the choice up to the ethnic lords. Moore (1958) comments that this kind of discretion provided lords with a great deal of leverage in local relations, since notions of equal service could be construed in many ways in practice.

Our best evidence on how labor was assigned locally comes from Spanish inspections, called *visitas*, recorded in the first few decades of the Colonial era. The inspections of 1549 and 1562 in the Spanish province of León de Huánuco (Helmer 1955–6; Ortiz de Zúñiga 1967, 1972) and the 1567 inspection in Chucuito (Diez de San Miguel 1964) are especially rich in detail. Julien (1988) has shown that officials in both locales were supposed to apply duties according to the number of taxpayers on the census rolls and that labor duty rotated among households. In Chucuito, witnesses said that the Incas annually specified the area to be farmed, or the amount of seed to be sown, and the amount of wool to be woven by local communities. As was the case with the householders' rights within *ayllu*, we may suspect that those amounts were adjusted intermittently, but confirmed annually.

If we explore the numbers a little, we can see how the tax system worked locally. According to the first Huánuco inspection, the Chupachu and 300 Yacha together made up 4,108 households in the last Inca census, which probably dated to the mid-1520s. That figure included four units of 1,000 households (*waranqa*) made up of forty units of 100 households (*pachaka*). Julien (1988: 264–6) suggests that 1 percent of the taxpayers was the base for assessing levies, since many duties were assigned to forty households or a multiple. Table 12.1 shows the households dedicated to the wide range of services that were demanded of the Chupachu. Julien points out that we need to keep in mind that some duties, such as farming, lasted only a couple of months a year, while others, such as construction at Cuzco, required continuous duty. LeVine (1987) has also shown that when people made cloth, pots, and other goods, the levies were assessed evenly by units of 100 households. On the other hand, services such as guard duty and portage were assigned evenly among units of 1,000. The difference suggests that tasks that yielded products were tailored to local resources, but service duties did not have to take environmental detail into account.

For archaeologists, the figures are worrisome. Only one of every nine taxpayers performed work that produced architecture and pottery – the two kinds of remains that archaeologists rely on to study the Incas. More than 40 percent performed services that would leave few traces in the archaeological record, such as guard duty and portage. Moreover, every one of the 400 workers assigned to roads and buildings was sent to Cuzco, even

Table 12.1 Labor service provided to the Incas by the Chupachu of central Peru, as reported in 1549 and 1562.

Assignment	Total households	Extraction	Manufacture	Agriculture	Building/ maintenance	Service	1562
				1549			
gold miners: 120 men, 120 women	120	120					+
silver miners: 60 men, 60 women	60	60					+
construction (Cuzco area)	400				400		+
agriculture (Cuzco area)	400			400			
retainers of Wayna Qhapaq (Cuzco)	150					150	+
guards for body of Thupa Inka Yupanki (Cuzco)	150					150	
guards for weapons of Thupa Inka Yupanki (Cuzco)	10					10	
garrison in Chachapoyas	200					200	
garrison in Quito	200					200	
guards for body of the Inca (Cuzco)	20					20	
feather workers	120	120					+
honey gatherers	60	60					+
weavers of tapestry cloth	400		400				+
dye makers	40		40				
herders of Inca's flocks	240					240	+
guards for maize fields	40					40	+
pepper cultivators	40			40			
salt miners (varied: 40, 50, 60)	50	50					+

(continued overleaf)

Table 12.1 (continued)

Assignment	Total households	1549					1562
		Extraction	Manufacture	Agriculture	Building/ maintenance	Service	
coca cultivators	60			60			+
hunters for royal deer hunt	40	40					
sandal makers (Cuzco, Huánuco)	40		40				+
wood workers, products to Cuzco	40		40				+
potters, products to Huánuco	40		40				+
guards for Huánuco Pampa	68					68	
porters carrying loads to Huánuco	80					80	
guards for women of the Inca	40					40	
soldiers and litter bearers	500					500	
cultivators of Inca lands	500			500			
makers of weapons and litters (Cuzco)							+
processors of dried, salted fish							+
snare makers for the hunt							+
women in service to the Inca							
Subtotals	4,108	450	560	1,000	400	1,698	
Percentage		11.0	13.6	24.3	9.7	41.3	
Total	4,108						4,108

Sources: Helmer 1955–6, Ortiz de Zúñiga 1967; modified from LeVine 1987: 23, Julien 1988: 265; D'Altroy 1994b: 184–5. The figures for miners are ambiguous, since the inspection lists 120 and 60 individuals of each for gold and silver mining, respectively, whereas other figures appear to cite men only. Because this table represents households, I follow Julien in citing 120 and 60 households rather than 240 and 120 individuals.

though the people came from the province whose center, Huánuco Pampa, was the most elaborate in the empire. The disparities between the tabulated labor duties and archaeology remind us that the most visible remains of Tawantinsuyu are only indirectly related to what people were doing when the Spaniards arrived.

Farms of the State and the Sun

At some point after the Incas took over a territory, state officials set about ensuring a steady supply of food, *chicha*, textiles, and other supplies. Many of the state farms were located near provincial centers, but some were also created in especially favorable locales for particular crops (figure 12.1). State and Sun lands often lay next to one another, but the resources and their products were apparently separated both physically and administratively. For the most part, the farms were tended by corvée workers as part of their rotating labor duties, although thousands of colonists were also called upon for this purpose in the empire's later years (Murra 1980b). Both state and Sun lands were distinct from the royal and aristocratic estates created in many parts of the empire, even though they too were maintained by *mitmaqkuna* and *yanakuna* dedicated to lifelong service.

The state farms at Cochabamba, Bolivia, may have been the most extensive in the entire realm (Wachtel 1982; Gyarmati and Varga 1999). In a tour of the south soon after his coronation, Wayna Qhapaq ordered most of the native residents to be removed from the western part of the valley. Witnesses testified to Polo that 14,000 farm workers were brought in to work fields for the state, mostly from the adjacent altiplano. They said that both permanent colonists and corvée laborers from seven ethnic groups were employed, but did not explain how many people lived there year round or came in only for the peak seasons. The colonists were allocated tracts to support themselves and could also farm along the margins of the state's fields. The farms were divided into seventy-seven narrow strips that ran across the valley and particular groups were assigned to work specific strips. Polo was told that the farms were used to grow maize for the Inca's armies, although we may suspect that "maize" was a shorthand expression for a range of crops. In addition to more than a hundred known Inca-era sites in the valley, the Incas built 2,400 storehouses at Cotapachi, where the produce was stored before being shipped to Paria, Cuzco, and wherever else it was needed (Céspedes Paz 1982; La Lone and La Lone 1987).

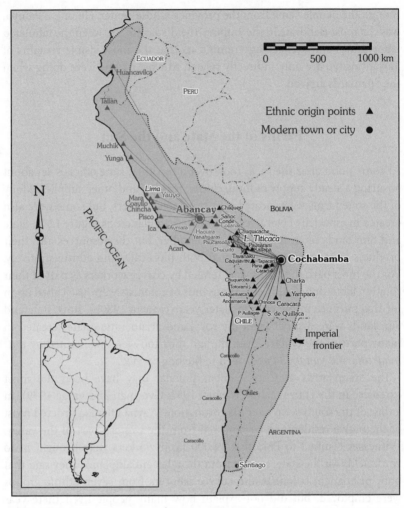

Figure 12.1   Locations of the major state farms at Abancay and Cochabamba, illustrating origin points of workers named in documents.

The permanent colonists had charge of the storehouses in addition to their agricultural labors.

Farms at Arica, Arequipa, and Abancay were also dedicated to military uses (Espinoza Soriano 1973; Spurling 1982: 14; La Lone and La Lone 1987). The farms in the warm Abancay valley were also said to have been founded by Wayna Qhapaq to help sustain his war efforts in the north.

Plate 12.1 Vast unfinished terrace system at Coctaca-Rodero, northwest Argentina, possibly an Inca state farm.

Rather than producing maize, the plots were principally dedicated to growing coca, cotton, peppers, and various fruits. The Incas claimed the best bottom lands for themselves and made hill slope fields available to the colonists brought in to work them. Extensive Inca farms have also been identified archaeologically in the Upper Mantaro valley, Peru, and in Argentina (plate 12.1). In the Upper Mantaro, productive lands within about 5 km of the provincial center (Hatun Xauxa) were virtually empty of subject villages (D'Altroy 1992: 154–78). The few that were present contained great numbers of farming tools, such as hoes and clod breakers, but no evidence of other kinds of production typical of villages, such as weaving, metallurgy, or potting. The same area contained thousands of state storehouses, suggesting that the zone surrounding the center was dedicated to Inca farms. At Coctaca-Rodero, Argentina, a massive terraced field system covers about 6 km² on the alluvial fans and piedmont (3,700 m) just below the altiplano. Because many terraces were abandoned before completion, it seems likely that the farm was developed late in the empire's run and may never have been put into use (Albeck and Scattolin 1991; Albeck 1992–3; Nielsen 1996). Large tracts may have also been farmed at the Campo de Pucará, in the Lerma Valley of Argentina's eastern piedmont (Boman 1908; Fock 1961; González 1983). Their location suggests that the area was peaceful enough that they could be worked with little danger from the mobile bands who lived on the eastern plains.

Fields were also supposed to be set aside for the religious institutions in every province. Some of those farms were well known and may have been quite large, while hundreds of small plots were also dedicated to the gods. Polo (1916: 58–9) mentions a farm for the Sun at Arapa, on the north side of Lake Titicaca, and the entire province of Chiquicache may have also been dedicated to Inti (chapters 10, 12). State and Sun farms were also established south of Cuzco near Raqchi, where a famous temple was built for the Creator God Wiraqocha (La Lone and La Lone 1987). Perhaps more typical were small plots dedicated to nearby temples. In Peru's Chillón valley, residents said that a small coca patch was planted for the Sun and its leaf was offered to the deity while it was still green (Murra 1982: 253). We cannot be sure how much land was committed to each kind of farm, but the Sun's resources were probably less than the state's. In one effort to resolve this question, Polo (1916: 58–9) compared the storehouses of the state and church in many locales and concluded that the Sun's holdings were much smaller.

Inca farms on the coast were apparently smaller than those in the highlands, and how the Incas got their coastal lands is mostly unclear. In their report on the Chincha valley, Castro and Ortega Morejón (1974) wrote that every 1,000 households ceded 10 *hanegadas* of irrigated lands to the Inca. Roughly speaking, that would have worked out to 190 ha,[1] which is not a small amount, but certainly nothing approaching the farms in the mountains. The Incas nonetheless did intensify some coastal production, as they transferred *mitmaqkuna* with experience in canal engineering from the north coast of Peru to the south (Rostworowski 1990).

If we took the chronicles at face value, we would imagine that maize and coca were essentially the only crops grown on farms of the state and the Sun, with the occasional exception of specialized farms like those at Abancay. The placement of major farms in warm valleys certainly fits that view, and there is little doubt that the maize consumed in *chicha* and the coca distributed to the armies and state workers were vital to state activities. The Incas even experimented with varieties of maize and appear to have distributed Cuzco flint maize throughout much of the realm. Because the reports to the Spaniards tended to emphasize what was culturally important, however, the emphasis on those two crops is probably misleading. Even on fertile soils, maize must be rotated with other crops to keep the nutrients from being depleted rapidly. Moreover, the botanical evidence from storage facilities suggests that the Incas grew a mix of crops that was locally suitable, even the low-status tubers (see below).

Ceremonial and Agricultural Cycles

The Incas approached farming with weapons in their hands and prayers on their lips. They envisioned agriculture as warfare – a victory claimed by disemboweling the earth (Bauer 1996). At the same time, successful crops could be assured only through supplication to the powers of the earth and the sky. Their agrarian cycle was arranged around a calendar tied to astronomical observations at Cuzco and to the turning of the seasons. It officially began with an August ritual, when the Sapa Inca turned over the soil in a sacred field called Sausero within the capital city. This plot, which belonged to the Sun, was revered because the primordial ancestors had first planted maize there. The Incas accompanied the tilling of the land with songs and rituals in which they sacrificed llamas and guinea pigs and poured libations of *chicha* onto the soil (Cobo 1990: 143–4). Garcilaso (1966: 151) wrote that the Incas sang verses

> which they performed in honor of the sun and their kings; all were composed regarding the meaning of this word "haylli," which ... indicates "triumph," in the sense that they triumphed over the earth breaking it and plowing it, so that it might produce. In those songs, they mixed refrains about discreet lovers and brave soldiers, all with the intent to triumph over the soil.

The emperor or highest Inca noble present took the lead in tilling the soil with a gold-tipped plow, and the queen and her ladies broke the clods. The king soon retired from his exertions and other lords took up the tasks according to their standing, after which everyone enjoyed a grand banquet. In the provinces, Cuzco's representatives performed similar rituals. The lowest officials and taxpayers worked all day, but farming for the state was festive even for the common folk, as the Incas displayed their generosity by plying them with food and drink at the end of their labors (Cobo 1979: 212). The close link among farming, reciprocal obligations, and ritual can be seen in two meanings of the Aymara word *haymatha*. This term is glossed both as "to go and work in the fields which are planted communally, like those of the lord ... or the poor" and as "to dance in

the ancient way particularly when they go to the fields of their leaders"
(Bertonio, translation by Murra 1968: 134).

To ensure that the life-giving waters continued to flow, the Incas prayed
and made sacrifices to the springs and rivers. Cobo (1990: 111) recorded a
typical entreaty:

> O source of water who have irrigated my field for so many years, and by means
> of this benefaction that you confer upon me I obtain my food, do the same this
> year, and even increase the amount of water so that the harvest will be more
> abundant.

When the crops were ready to be brought in at Sausero, the activities were
once again attended by elaborate rites. The harvest was begun by young men
who had recently made the ritual passage into manhood and was followed
up by all of the city's nobility. Cobo (1990: 140) wrote that the field was then
plowed and "they returned with great rejoicing to the main square, wearing
the tunics that they had won in war." Molina (1988: 118) commented that
the maize was used to make *chicha* for the cult of Mama Waku, one of the
founding Inca ancestors.

Several chroniclers explained that the Incas specified a strict order in
which the lands were to be worked. The sequence usually described for
the highlands said that the church's plots were tilled first, followed by the
state fields, and then those of the workers. For the coastal Chincha valley,
Castro and Ortega Morejón (1974) reported that the lands of the Inca came
first, then those of the state religion and the regional lords, and finally
the lands of the "poor," or general peasantry. Despite its repetition, there
are ecological reasons to doubt that highland farmers could have adhered
strictly to the sequence. Mitchell points out that the formulas run afoul
of conditions that require that crops be tended in a staggered sequence
according to elevation and maturation time (Mitchell 1980; see also Hastorf
1993). Higher fields normally must be planted before lower lands, because
of temperature and rainfall patterns. On a practical basis, farmers could
not have worked all state fields from the uplands to the valley bottoms
before turning to their own crops. It is possible that state lands were often
concentrated in a few ecozones near state centers, or that state lands in
any given niche were worked first, or even that the convention applied just
to maize fields, in which case the sequence could be a fair representation.
Nonetheless, as Mitchell observes, it is likely that the reported labor
sequences reflected the elite ideologies of hierarchy more than the details
of crop scheduling.

Landed Estates and Grants

Rural manors and other elite resources provide an important contrast to the institutionally and communally held resources. As described in chapter 7, the best-known estates were situated near Cuzco, many of them in the warmer Vilcabamba/Urubamba drainage. Some of the most celebrated Inca sites, such as Machu Picchu, Pisac, and Ollantaytambo, formed the nuclei of royal estates, but the facilities really extended over an expansive array of lands surrounding the residential and ceremonial cores. For example, the site of Patallacta, while treated as a distinct archaeological site, is now considered to be part of the Machu Picchu estate. Entirely new tracts of land were put into cultivation on the eastern slopes to ramp up the production of coca. Scores of new settlements dedicated to the leaf were founded in the Paucartambo and Amaybamba Valleys, among others, just over the mountains to the north of the Sacred Valley. The intensified production for the royal kindreds was part of a trend that converted prime resources into aristocratic holdings. Other royal manors were established throughout the empire; perhaps with some exaggeration, each ruler was said to have a personal estate in every one of the imperial provinces. The estates' productivity was needed to maintain the living and deceased emperors and their descendants, and to underwrite their political/ceremonial activities both at home and in provincial regions.

Grants of land or other resources were not limited just to the Incas proper. The Incas also used them as an instrument of policy to entice subjects to cooperate with Cuzco's rule. For instance, the Incas gave lands to people who had distinguished themselves in war or who had performed some service of special merit to the crown, such as building a bridge, canal, or road, or who had a valued skill. Children of lords could also receive grants. Polo (1916: 73–4) commented that such grants were concentrated in the Cuzco region and that they were passed on to the collective heirs, not to an individual (see also Cobo 1979: 213). In northern Ecuador, the Incas awarded lands near Quito to a number of local lords, thinking to draw them closer to imperial control. The lords balked at taking up residence, perhaps because the private gain would have exacted too heavy a political concession (Salomon 1986). Elsewhere, local elites did take advantage of the opportunities. The lords of the Upper Mantaro valley held lands in the montaña where their personal farmers grew coca and peppers (Vega 1965). Similarly, the paramount Lupaqa lords of the west side of Lake Titicaca sent colonists to live in the warm coastal valleys. There, they grew maize, collected guano, and cultivated or gathered other products that could be shipped up to the highlands for distribution at the lords' discretion. Even as late as 1567, colonists were working for them along the coast (Diez de San Miguel 1964; Murra 1968). Lords on the east side of the lake, in contrast, were awarded lands in the warm eastern valleys.

The Flocks of the Inca

In the Andes, camelids were wealth, transport, food, clothing, and prestige on the hoof (plate 2.2). Because the llama and alpaca lay at the heart of the Inca economy – both culturally and practically – it is small wonder that considerable energy was devoted to breeding large herds that could be used for the armies, sacrifices, and other ends. Unlike some of the lands turned into farms, however, the Incas could not cast about for under-used flocks, but had to requisition herds from conquered peoples (Polo 1916: 61–2). Murra (1980b: 52) suggests that, since the greatest flocks grazed in the altiplano, the Incas turned their eyes to that region in particular to enhance the herds already husbanded near Cuzco. In the early Colonial era, residents of the Charkas area and the Huamanga valley testily recalled how the Incas had taken herds from their ancestors. Herding for the state was at least partially a specialized duty conducted by adults. In some pastures near Cuzco, the herders were *yanakuna*, the lifetime servants (Murra 1980b: 56). Those situations contrasted with the typical community practice, in which children and adolescents tended the flocks.

Although the vast state and Sun herds were carefully tabulated, it is hard to come by reliable numbers. Román y Zamora (1897: 122) stated that the Sun had more than a million animals, a figure that may not have been meant literally. Nonetheless, a witness in Chucuito commented that even the altiplano's pastures were sometimes inadequate for the great flocks of the Inca era. In 1567, a middling lord there was reputed to have 50,000 animals (Diez de San Miguel 1964: 50; Murra 1968: 120), so an estimate of hundreds of thousands or even a million might not be out of line for the church's holdings altogether. The Incas certainly knew how many they had, for they did a census of state and temple animals every November that coincided with ceremonies intended to help the herds multiply (Cieza 1967: 101). They also made an effort to introduce flocks into areas where they were unknown as part of the indigenous economy, especially in northern Peru and parts of highland Ecuador (Cieza 1967: 52–3, 56).

The prime uses of the herds were military. Armies on the move regularly used trains of thousands of llamas to pack supplies and to supply food when they were no longer needed for portage. After Pizarro captured Atawallpa in Cajamarca (chapter 4), he ordered the town to be cleared of camelids, because it was filled with animals making a mess of the camp. Zárate also reported that Quizquiz abandoned some 15,000 animals in the eastern mountains after a battle in the first years of the Spanish conquest. The llamas and alpacas were also the principal source of wool and leather for state personnel, especially soldiers. Much of the wool sheared annually from the herds was turned over to women in subject households to spin and make into rough cloth that was turned back to state overseers. Many animals also found their end in myriad sacrifices and in feasts at state installations throughout the empire. To judge from the age profiles of camelid bones recovered from the Calchaquí valley, northwestern Argentina, Inca feasts featured cuts of meat from animals in the prime of life, rather than from the aged animals often eaten in local communities, once their working life was over (D'Altroy *et al.* 2000).

State Storage

A vast storage system provided the bridge between state-sponsored production and use throughout the empire. If we pause for a moment to consider the problems that transport posed to the Inca taxation system, we can see the kinds of challenges that they faced in financing their activities and why storage played such a crucial role. Economists often refer to the *range* of a good, that is, the distance that goods like food or valuables can be transported before their value is used up in the process (Hassig 1985). The higher the value and the lighter the weight, the farther something can be carried and still retain caloric or exchange value. So *chuño* and *ch'arki* were better than whole potatoes and fresh meat, at least for transport if not for taste. We can make an analogous argument for the range of a tax. High-weight, low-value goods, like bulky foods, can be rendered as taxes (e.g., a tithe on crops) or the product of labor (e.g., in the Inca case). They can be used up quickly in the process of transportation and so have low ranges, unless the transport technology is efficient. Because the Incas did not have inland boats or wheeled vehicles pulled by powerful draft animals, they could not regularly move bulky commodities over long distances as part of a subsistence economy. Nor did they have the purchasing power, flexibility, or transportability of money. Having committed themselves to a staple finance system, in which most supplies came directly from state resources, the Incas had to reproduce their supply system from one province to the next.

As with farms and herds, the state and church storehouses were separated from one another administratively and probably physically. Most of the storehouses, called *qollqa*, were built in just a few contexts: at Cuzco, at installations along the roads, and next to state farms. Cieza (1967: 143–4) provides us with a sense of the scale involved:

> in the more than 1,200 leagues of coast they governed, they had the delegates and governors, and many lodgings and great storehouses full of necessary things, which were for provisioning the soldiers. Because in one of them, there were lances, and in others darts, and in others sandals, and in others the remaining arms they had. Moreover, some storehouses were filled with rich clothing, and others with more goods and others with food and all manner of supplies. In this manner, once the lord was lodged in his housing, and his soldiers nearby, not a thing, from the most trivial to the greatest, was lacking, because it could be provided.

Cieza highlights the main uses of state stores: supply of the military, administrative, and religious personnel, specialists working for the state, and corvée laborers. Craig Morris (1982) has suggested that the Incas' approach to ceremonial politics provided another reason for stockpiling certain supplies. The relationships between the Incas and their subjects required hospitality and generosity on a vast scale, all lubricated by state food and drink. Another important, but irregular, use of state storage was as a fallback for the general populace in times of privation (Polo 1916: 127).

As ever, the Incas drew on centuries of Andean practice in devising their storage system. Several Wari sites, including Pikillaqta and Azángaro, contain hundreds of cell-like structures, many of which were probably used for storage (*c.* AD 600). Once the Incas adopted the idea, they elaborated it to an unprecedented scale. According to Diez de Betanzos (1996: 51), the Inca state storage system was initiated in the mid-fifteenth century, when Pachakuti ordered facilities built to expedite the construction of Cuzco. We may reserve judgment on that point, since the royal tradition that Diez de Betanzos relied on tended to attribute the origin of most everything in Tawantinsuyu to Pachakuti's energies and organizational genius.

In the 1960s, Morris initiated the archaeological study of Inca storage, working at facilities at Cuzco and provincial installations along the highway to Quito. The great provincial centers all contained hundreds of *qollqa* arrayed in rows on the hill slopes just above them, but the vast facilities in the Mantaro valley were unusual even for the Incas. The valley was a breadbasket for the highlands and home to a major provincial center. All told, 2,753 *qollqa* have been recorded in the basin, about half just above the center and the other half in forty-eight other sites lining the valley. Collectively, the buildings contained about 170,000 m^3 of storage space, making it one of the largest storage complexes recorded archaeologically in the prehispanic Americas (Browman 1970; Morris 1982; D'Altroy 1992; LeVine 1992).[2] Facilities adjacent to some of the state farms even surpassed those of most centers. Cotapachi, next to the farms of Cochabamba, contained 2,400 buildings in two sets, and the Campo de Pucará (Argentina) contained 1,717 (Snead 1992). Storage facilities of a few buildings up to several hundred have also been recorded at scores of other Inca installations throughout the Andes. In fact, a road station without storage would have been an anomaly. When we consider that there were more than 2,000 such *tampu* throughout the empire, the scale of state storage becomes astonishing.

The Spaniards were certainly impressed. One of our best eyewitness accounts of Cuzco comes from Pedro Sancho (1917: 194–5), a secretary who saw the empire while it still functioned.

> From this fortress [Saqsawaman], one can see many houses around the city, a quarter of a league, half a league, and a league away; and in the valley, which is surrounded by hills, there are more than 100,000 houses; and many of them are the houses of pleasure and recreation of the past lords and others are of the leaders of all the land who now live in the city; the others are houses or storehouses full of blankets, wool, arms, metals and clothing; and of everything that is raised and made in this land. There are houses that store everything that the vassals bring to the leaders; and there is a house in which more than 100,000 dried birds are kept, for from their many-colored feathers articles of clothing are made, and there are many houses for this purpose. There are shields, beams for supporting houses, knives and other tools; sandals and armor to provision the people of war in such quantity that it is not possible to understand how they had been able to supply so many and such diverse things.

The scale of the facilities at Cuzco is hard to estimate, because so many of the region's archaeological sites have been reduced to rubble over the centuries. Pedro Pizarro (1986: 99–100) remembered that they were so vast that it seemed impossible that the supplies could have ever been exhausted. Even granting some descriptive licence, the storage at the capital must have been enormous, if only because its residents were said to be supplied every four days from the *qollqa* (Polo 1940b: 147). A very few of the storage structures

Plate 12.2   Storehouses on the hill slopes overlooking the Urubamba. Source: reproduced by permission of Darryl Wilkinson.

are still visible in the Sacred Valley, on the slopes above Ollantaytambo and Urubamba (plate 12.2), for example, but they must represent just a tiny fraction of the facilities in operation in the time of the empire.

Accountants were responsible everywhere for keeping tabs of everything that went into and out of storage. Guaman Poma drew one of his relatives, Apo Poma Chaua, giving an account of the storehouse contents at Huánuco Pampa to Thupa Inka Yupanki (figure 12.2). In his hand, he holds a *khipu* from which he was presumably drawing his detailed information. The chronicler explained that the inspectors did not belong to the Inca nobility, but were among those residents of the Cuzco region elevated to the position he called "Inca by Privilege." The fact that storehouses were also attended by watchmen and surrounded by expanses of exposed ground suggests that theft was a concern.

In many ways, the storehouses epitomize state planning, since the design of the system aided accounting. *Qollqa* basically came in two modular one-room shapes, round and rectangular, which were laid out in discrete series paralleling the land's contours. Even though they varied

Figure 12.2 Guaman Poma's (1936) illustration of a storehouse accountant reporting to the emperor Thupa Inka Yupanki.

regionally, *qollqa* tended to be standardized within any region, as though a functionary had a measurement template and instructed local workers to replicate it. In the Mantaro, we have been able to use airphotos to measure the length of rows, divide that value by a standard length and distance between *qollqa*, and calculate exactly the number of structures in complexes containing up to 100 buildings. For structures built of fieldstone alongside maize and potato fields, that degree of replication is remarkable. Morris's (1967, 1982; see also D'Altroy and Hastorf 1984) excavations show that storehouse architecture was designed to preserve perishable contents as long as possible. Their placement on open hill slopes put the goods in cool, well-ventilated locations. Many structures were also built with gravel subfloors and drainage canals that kept the atmosphere dry and cool (Morris 1982). These practices allowed untreated foods to last a year or two without significant degradation, and freeze-dried foods about twice that long. Polo (1916: 59) said that some goods were kept in storage for up to ten years and were shuttled about from facility to facility as the need arose.

Exactly how much of which supplies were actually kept in the storehouses remains a bit of a mystery, although food probably headed the list in most places. Maize was the food most frequently mentioned by chroniclers, followed by *ch'arki*.[3] However, Morris's excavations at Huánuco Pampa found mostly potatoes, which were locally grown, and our own limited tests at Hatun Xauxa found quinoa most often. The disparities between documents and archaeology probably again stem from differences between cultural values and practice. Judging from tests in more than one hundred structures at Huánuco Pampa, Morris has suggested that maize was stored in circular structures and potatoes in rectangular buildings, although evidence from half a dozen buildings in the Mantaro did not match that pattern.

Remarkably, the Inca storage system continued to function for decades in some areas after the empire's collapse. When a Spanish force arrived in the Mantaro valley in late 1533, the Inca general Challcochima was bivouacked outside Hatun Xauxa with an army that the record-keepers tabulated at 35,000 soldiers for Hernando Pizarro's benefit. The valley's residents had unhappily been on the losing side of the war between Atawallpa and Waskhar and were ready to see the Spaniards as saviors. In one of the time's most curious acts, Challcochima agreed to accompany the Spaniards to Cajamarca where his sovereign was in bondage, thus consigning himself to his own death. Soon thereafter, his army was routed and the valley's lords began to supply the Spanish forces occupying Hatun Xauxa. The lords kept the production and storage system working until

1554, furnishing the Spaniards with food, prestige goods, and utilitarian supplies, even while rogue bands of soldiers periodically ransacked the facilities (Espinoza Soriano 1972). In 1547 – fifteen years after the fall of Inca power – President Gasca stayed in the valley for a hundred days with an entourage of 2,000 men. Collectively, they consumed 15,534 *hanegadas* (878 m^3) of supplies and commented with amazement that it was hard to tell that they had even made a dent in the stored goods. That is small wonder, however, when we consider that the northern valley's *qollqa* alone could have stored enough food to support Challcochima's entire army for many months.

After twenty years, the supplies in the storehouses finally ran out and the lords filed petitions in Lima's Royal Court to gain restitution. In their briefs, they listed all the goods and services that they had provided the Spaniards in specific episodes over the years. Murra (1975: 243–54) recognized that the lists, read directly into the record by *khipu kamayuq*, were apparently ordered by the goods' cultural significance. First came gold and silver, then adult and young camelids, fine cloth, blankets, maize, quinoa, potatoes, two kinds of sandals, bags, rope, large and small ceramics, game birds, rough and fine firewood, charcoal, grass, straw, *chicha*, "all fruit," salt, and fish. As early as 1537, the Mantaro natives had also started to supply goods of European origin, such as chickens. Significantly, the lords turned supplies over to the Spaniards in proportions that directly reflected the size of their taxpaying populations. That practice suggests that provisioning of goods, as well as labor service, was intended to be consistent with the number of households in each political unit. The Mantaro lords' ability to operate the supply system for two decades into the Colonial era also shows that they were thoroughly involved in its management during Cuzco's reign. Their status gave them the power and knowledge to make the arrangement work for their own interests long after the Inca state had been obliterated. Such was the Incas' repute, however, that Polo (1916: 76) suggested that many lords actually kept the system working because they feared that the Incas might return some day and call them to account.

Trickle-down Effects on Households

In closing this chapter, I would like to consider what happened to the household economy of the millions of people whose resources and labor were appropriated by the Incas. There is no doubt that the loss of lands disrupted many people's lives, especially in areas such as Cochabamba, Vilcashuaman, and Ayaviri, where the residents were moved out en masse. In some areas, however, production for the state may not have strained community resources as heavily as we might expect. The Incas often placed their fields in areas that were probably not used very heavily during the preceding period.[4] In some cases, farms next to the state installations were carved out of virgin terrain and new canals were built to water them. That approach must have moderated the impact on local villages, and the Inca peace even seems to have allowed farming and herding in areas that had been off limits during the bellicose Late Intermediate Period, especially in Peru's mountain valleys.

What about the impact of taxes? In states where peasants had to pay taxes in money or in kind, such as a tithe on grain, their food may have been stretched in lean years. The Incas' subjects did not normally give up their own produce, but they may have faced a different kind of shortage – disposable labor needed at crucial times in the agrarian schedule. The ecology of the mountains causes farmers to cultivate their plots in a sequence set largely by the choice of crop, the agricultural cycle, and location of the fields. Because the windows of opportunity for planting and harvesting can be counted in days, families may well have felt a labor squeeze at those times. Several responses were possible to such scheduling dilemmas, aside from ignoring calls to service. One option would have been to alternate working on state and personal tasks according to the job immediately at hand. Alternatively, subject households may have tried to increase their size to reduce their per capita obligations by having larger families or delaying marriage. Although data on this subject are scant, witnesses from the Mantaro area did say that their populace grew under the Incas (Toledo 1940: 14–37).

Recognizing the problems that ensued, the Incas may have seen that it was in their interest to create an independent economy. In that way, they could have met their production needs while minimally threatening the security of subject communities and improving obedience. Years ago, Murra (1980b) drew attention to the Incas' shift away from corvée-based production to state farms staffed by dedicated workers. That move would have reduced travel time between the villages and state lands at the same time that it ensure a ready labor source. In the final analysis, however, the Inca economy was still built upon the skills and hard work of their subjects and on resources taken from communities. The Incas tried to mask the exploitation by using the language of traditional obligations, but their subjects had memories long enough to complain to the Spaniards about how their flocks and fields had been taken away, decades after the Inca collapse.

Notes

1   30,000 households × 1.59 acre/*hanegada* (Haggard and McLean 1941: 77).

2   Among the other important storage facilities in the Peruvian highlands were those at Pumpu (Matos Mandieta 1994) and Vilcashuaman (Cieza 1984: 252).

3   In a review of 287 documentary references to the subject, Murra (1980b: 13, 25) found only eighty-six references to food. That figure is probably more a reflection of Spanish interest in exotica and armaments than anything else. Maize, with twenty-nine citations, and *ch'arki*, with twelve, were the most frequently listed foods.

4   E.g., at Huánuco Pampa, in the Upper Mantaro, the northern Calchaquí, La Quiaca, the Bolsón de Andalgalá, and the Lerma valley.

Chapter Thirteen

Things and Their Masters[1]

It's a fair bet that most people reading this book would agree that "a rock has no discernible opinion about gravity" – a thought ventured by the humorist Sir Terry Pratchett and his scientific colleagues (Pratchett *et al.* 1999: 10).[2] No doubt that assessment would have also been true in the Inca world, but only because Andean rocks didn't know about gravity at the time. Certain rocks would have voiced opinions on many other subjects, and some metal, cloth, and wood items could have also contributed to the discussions. Such ideas about sentient objects were entirely natural in the Incas' life space, because the cultural and natural worlds were inseparable elements in a unified cosmos. Andean people's view of consciousness and agency involved complex relations between humans and their material world that wouldn't occur to most Western observers (chapter 5). The scope of the non-human agents in the Inca world was staggering. In 1582, for example, the cleric Christobal de Albornoz complained that so many sentient outcrops, crags, and mountain peaks existed that he could not destroy them all, even if he set everyone in the land to the task (Dean 2010a: 27).

As an extension of the same logic, certain things that were either made or found could be much more than tools or status or display items. They could possess powers that could parallel or even exceed humanity's (Sillar 2009). The relations between humans and material things were so entangled that the Incas called people who worked with objects *master* (*kamayuq*) – implying a social dynamic – rather than something closer to *artisan* or *artist*. Only if we engage with that mode of thought can we really address how the Incas co-existed with material things.

But we also need to see things through Spanish eyes, because it was their writing that told us most of what we know about Inca practice and thought vis-à-vis objects and their materials. Pedro Pizarro's account of a mortuary

The Incas, Second Edition. Terence N. D'Altroy.
© 2015 John Wiley & Sons, Ltd. Published 2015 by John Wiley & Sons, Ltd.

trove highlighted the different registers with which the invaders and the Incas worked.

> In one cave they discovered twelve sentries of gold and silver, of the size and appearance of those of this country, extraordinarily realistic. There were pitchers half of pottery and half gold, with the gold so well set into the pottery that no drop of water escaped when they were filled, and beautifully made. A golden effigy was also discovered. This greatly distressed the Indians for they said that it was a figure of the first lord [Manqo Qhapaq] who conquered this land. They found shoes made of gold, of the type the women wore, like half-boots. They found golden crayfish such as live in the sea, and many vases, on which were sculpted in relief all the birds and snakes that they knew, even down to spiders, caterpillars and other insects. All of this was found in a large cave that was between some outcrops of rock outside Cuzco. They had not been buried because they were such delicate objects. (Translation modified from Hemming 1970: 132)

Where Pizarro saw precious metals, idols, pots, and rocks, the Incas would have seen living beings and the essences of deities. Like the Incas, the Spaniards saw animate forces in some objects and oracles, but they often thought of Inca manufactures as icons through which the devil let his voice be heard. Such divergent viewpoints between the two peoples characterized many other kinds of notions about material things. For example, both sides would have recognized that the provisioning of the conquistadores in the early Colonial era involved resources, labor, and logistics, but Andean peoples also saw layers of mutual social obligations that escaped the Spaniards entirely.

Our analysis can also benefit from a modern comparative perspective, which brings history, anthropology, archaeology, and other sciences to bear. In examining the ways things were made, distributed, and used, we might consider energetics, sourcing studies, labor organization, and manufacturing technologies. And since people traded with other people to get the things they didn't produce themselves, exchange practices should surely be involved. As with so many things Andean, however, money and markets entered the picture only tangentially. Even if some semi-monetary goods and some market exchange did appear within Tawantinsuyu, the Incas generally relied on other means to make and distribute material stuff. In this chapter, I would like to sketch out how the Incas dealt with material things, highlighting a few kinds of objects to show how things worked.

To begin, let's consider Pizarro's description, quoted just above. From the Spanish and modern viewpoint, those objects were the products of skilled artisans – smiths who crafted exquisite objects for the Inca and his relations. They made up just a tiny fraction of the craftsmen who worked for the Incas. The state retained artisans to create works of beauty, as a means of mass production, and as an instrument of policy. There were thousands of metal smiths, weavers, carpenters, sandal makers, lapidary workers, potters, pigment workers, and dyers. Others made weapons, drinking cups, earspools, and hunting nooses, all from raw materials that were reserved for the Incas' use. Yet others carved stones in place, or enclosed them in architecture, or dressed them for the close-fitting ashlar masonry for which the Incas are so justly renowned. In addition to their utilitarian value, many items expressed messages about social identity. In a land where status was often rigidly enforced, people used craft goods to make visual statements about their place in the cultural landscape – about their history, ethnicity, class, gender, occupation, and rituals. In Tawantinsuyu, standardizing some kinds of visual information became crucial because the people spoke so many different languages and had no common symbolic system. Textiles were the favored medium for such expression, but items executed in many other media also met the dual ends of practical use and symbol.

From an Inca viewpoint, however, some of those things were living beings or worked as an interface between humanity and their ancestors, and with the sun, moon, sea, and mountain peaks. Moreover, objects were not *made from* particular materials. They *consisted of* those materials, sharing an essence with other things made of the same stuff. Today, we may envision things that we make and use, such as machines, robots, and electronic devices, as if they had a life of their own. The sensibility may be unnerving at times, but it is still basically metaphorical. In the Incas' conceptual framework, such things *had* a vitality of their own, and shared space with people.

Production for the Incas

This chapter will focus on textiles, stone, metals, and ceramics. Those represent only a portion of the material arts, but they cross-cut mass produced and individually crafted items, goods that had symbolic and utilitarian value, things with life, portable objects and the built environment.

In thinking about Inca artisanry, it helps to keep in mind how intricately technologies were related (Melissa Hagstrum, pers. comm. 1997); just as ceramic innovations improved metallurgy, metal tools aided weaving and textiles were used for stone working. Feathers or beads of metal and shell were woven into some fabrics, while metals were inlaid with stone and shell, painted, adorned with feathers, or covered in cloth. To speak of individual media would often miss both the cultural point and the visual impact of many objects. In certain cases, one medium (e.g., cloth) could even transfer vitality from one object to another (rocks).

In addition, we need to be aware that Andean innovation often arose in the service of making ceremonial or status objects, not from efforts to make tools more efficient. Even metallurgy was only occasionally driven by improving the efficiency of weapons, farm tools, or transportation (Lechtman 1984). Mass production did not result from efforts to reduce costs in a market economy, although exchange was widespread. Instead, large-scale and individual production combined meaning, vitality, utilitarian value, social messages, and artistry in a wide variety of packages. The Incas do not seem to have created many works simply for display, but aesthetic expression is obvious in their material culture. With rare exception, items made for the Incas were more elegant than local wares and provided a conspicuous stamp of imperial presence. In contrast to other empires, where mass production often yielded simple and inelegant objects, crafts made for the Incas combined high quality with labor intensity and mass production. Inca artisans created a distinctive style for portable objects that drew initially from the pre-imperial Killke style of the Cuzco area and from the Titicaca basin and then was refined into a new style of its own. Despite regional variations, the consistency of the products suggests that state supervisors insisted that the artisans pay careful attention to the canons of the imperial style. The simplicity and repetition of the basic elements lent themselves to duplication by artisans throughout the empire. Designs on textiles and ceramics featured geometric forms in symmetric layouts, executed in bold, solid colors (see Morris 1991, 1995; Pasztory 2010). The realistic, personalized portraiture seen in earlier Andean styles, especially the Moche, is not preserved in known Inca art. The successions of kings were recorded on panels and tapestries, but we do not know how representational they were.

The system worked because the Incas put artisans skilled in all the arts to work in varied settings. It helped the Incas that many tributaries were already masters of a particular craft and that weaving was the essence of Andean women's skills. In the resettlement program, communities that could include hundreds of households that were moved en masse to new locations. Espinoza's studies of sixteenth-century court cases chronicle how the Incas restationed weavers, potters, smiths, and other craftsmen on lands alienated from the local peoples (chapter 11). Artisans who worked with different materials were sometimes placed nearby, but their workshops were separated physically and administratively. Specialized workshops seem to have been founded early in the imperial era, but many craft enclaves were part of a late change in economic organization orchestrated under Wayna Qhapaq (e.g., Espinoza Soriano 1970, 1973, 1975, 1976, 1983, 1987a, 1987b; Murra 1980b). Among the other specialists who went to work for the state and the Sun were members of the women's institutions. The products were then used to supply state activities or aristocrats or were distributed through ceremonial largess to favored elites or individuals who had distinguished themselves in service to the state.

The ruler and other lords also retained personal artisans who produced goods for household consumption or gifts. Even so, most artisans worked part time at their crafts, alternating farming and herding with seasonal or intermittent craft work. Full-time artisans working for themselves, the state, or elite patrons were rare, perhaps even in Cuzco or on royal estates. Because the early sources often did not distinguish neatly between the resources held by the Sapa Inca as the personification of the state and those he held in private, it is hard to estimate how many artisans were institutional or members of estates. The difference may not have mattered in many cases, since the ruler had rights over the possessions of the state.

The Incas obtained many goods by applying a household labor tax similar to that described for farming and herding (chapter 12). They put tributaries to work at their home communities or at provincial centers, using materials drawn from state and church holdings. Because the workers' skills were varied, officials sought out individuals, communities, and entire ethnic groups who had expertise in one craft or another. Some communities made certain goods because suitable resources were available nearby. In Huánuco, for example, certain villages made sandals, rope, or pottery, because the fibers or clay could be readily procured (see LeVine 1987; Julien 1993). Elsewhere, ethnic groups were assigned to gather items such as specially colored woods and bird feathers. Overall, while labor assignments were made on the basis of population, the state adapted its requirements for craft production to environmental variations.

The most common material made for the state in local communities was ordinary cloth. Every year, each family received wool from state stockpiles that the women used to spin yarn and then weave cloth. One shirt per year may have been the normal output. Cathy Costin's (1993) archaeological studies of Xauxa households in central Peru support this picture of a tax on women's labor. Densities of spindle whorls and related tools show that weaving doubled under Inca rule, even though most of the Xauxa had moved several kilometers away from good pastures. Common cloth ranked high among the materials that the valley furnished the Spaniards in the 1530s, but its production is missing from the forty or so labor duties on specific provincial lists. It is possible that household weaving was so much a part of the cultural landscape that it did not need mentioning, or that some women's work was not thought worthy of tabulation. Other evidence on the status of women's labor is mixed. Some activities viewed as women's work were often less highly valued than those performed by men. For example, there was no term for spinner, which was mostly a female activity, but there were several for weavers, who were drawn from both sexes. Women were listed for other standard duties, such as mining, and some women held high-status positions whose duties included fabricating material goods. The most outstanding of those were the *mamakuna*, who wove the most valued cloth in the realm (see below). Whatever the value of the work itself, as Costin (1993) points out, distributing the products seems to have been mostly under men's control.

Despite the scale of the imperial economy, we need to remember that peasants still produced and consumed most of the material culture of the Inca era in their own styles. They lost access to some resources, to be sure, but they were expected to be self-sufficient. Artisans sometimes copied elements of the Inca style into their own, emulating the power of the state, but the effects of imperial rule are virtually invisible elsewhere. In coastal Chimor and in many highland villages, artisans often rejected or were forbidden to use Inca stylistic elements in their own products. As a result, distinguishing pre-Inca and Inca occupations can be difficult, especially since real imperial goods moved in limited circles. One thing is sure, however – much of the archaeological record outside Cuzco does not bear the obvious imprint of state involvement, even at the empire's height.

Textiles

Weaving was almost surely the most valued art in Tawantinsuyu. Cloth was usually made from cotton on the coast and in the eastern lowlands and from wool in the highlands, but some coarse textiles were also made from rougher materials, such as maguey fibers. Unfortunately, textiles in the Inca style from the heartland are rare because organic materials disintegrate quickly in the highland climate. Most of the preserved Inca textiles come from the coast or from high-elevation shrines. The Incas also valued their cloth so highly that they burned it rather than let it fall into Spanish hands. As a result, relatively few Inca textiles are available for study, but Guaman Poma's drawings provide valuable information, because he took meticulous care to depict the tunics that were appropriate to individuals of particular social groups or statuses.

In 1962, John Murra wrote a classic paper that explored the roles of textiles in Inca culture and the imperial economy (see also A. Rowe 1978; J. Rowe 1979c; Morris 1991, 1995). He observed that woven materials had many functions, such as clothing, blankets, footwear, and carrying bags, but cloth took on its greatest significance in the social and ceremonial aspects of life. It was used in all rites of passage, for instance to celebrate the naming of a child or as gifts in puberty rituals. Weddings typically included the presentation of cloth by the groom and his kin to the family of the bride. Many societies buried their dead in specially woven new clothes, along with sandals, bags, headdresses, and, with women, needles, spindles and whorls, skeins of yarn, and the woven baskets that held them.

Making textiles in the Andes did not require complex tools. To make thread, the prepared (cleaned, teased, and organized) wool was wrapped around the wrist or placed on a distaff. The spindle was spun free in the air or rested on a pottery plate. For most Andean textiles, the thread was first spun clockwise (z-spun), then doubled, and twisted counterclockwise (s-plied). Special ceremonial cloth was sometimes spun and plied in the reverse directions (Cobo 1990: 223; Rowe 1946: 241). Needles were typically made of sharp cactus spines or bronze. Andean peoples used three different kinds of looms (Cobo 1990: 224–5; Rowe 1946: 241). The earliest and simplest was a backstrap or body-tension loom (see figure 9.2). In that technique, the weaver used two rods to support the longitudinal threads (warp). One was attached to a post or wall and the other was tied to a belt that passed around the weaver's back. A second type, used primarily among Aymara speakers, was a horizontal loom that consisted of two rods attached to posts set into the ground. The cloth was suspended above the ground. In both of these types, heddles were used to separate the warp threads that formed the ground weave structure, so that the weft threads could be passed through easily to form patterns. The third loom was a vertical frame of four poles that was used to weave the finest cloth.

The coarsest of the Inca textiles (*chusi*) was a thick cloth that was used for blankets and other materials that required a durable weave (Cobo 1990: 223–6; Rowe 1946: 242). A single length of *chusi* served as a bedroll and, when doubled back, as a blanket. Father Cobo was scandalized that the entire family was accustomed to sleeping under a single cloth. The next grade up was common cloth, called *awasqa*, which was simply dyed or decorated, if treated at all. Woven in large quantities by housewives, it was the most commonly made craft item produced for the empire.

A more elegant cloth, called *qompi*, was a tapestry weave made from both cotton and the finer wools. Some of the most luxurious *qompi* incorporated viscacha fur and bat hair. Feathered cloth and other paraphernalia, such as shields and lances, were especially associated with the military (Murúa 1986: 349–50). The most valued textiles were made with beads or bangles of gold, silver, and spondylus shell woven tightly into the fabric. Half a century after the conquest, Pedro Pizarro still remembered the storehouses of textiles and raw materials at Cuzco with wonder:

> There were deposits of iridescent feathers, some looking like fine gold and others of a shining golden-green color. These were the feathers of small birds hardly bigger than cicadas, which are called "pájaros comines" [hummingbirds] because they are so tiny. These small birds grow the iridescent feathers only on their breasts, and each feather is little larger than a fingernail. Quantities of them were threaded together on fine thread and were skillfully attached to agave fibers to form pieces over a span in length. These were all stored in leather chests. Clothes were made of the feathers, and contained a staggering quantity of these iridescents. There were many other feathers of various colors intended for making clothing to be worn by the lords and ladies at the festivals … There were also cloaks completely covered with gold and silver chaquira [beads], with no thread visible, like very dense chain mail, and there were storehouses of shoes with soles made of sisal and uppers of fine wool in many colors. (Translation modified from Hemming 1970: 135)

Inca tapestry tunics were standardized in decoration and structure (J. Rowe 1979c; A. Rowe 1997). Two common designs were black and white and "Inca key" checkerboards, while more elaborate patterns contained rows of square or rectangular geometric designs with internal repetition (plate 13.1). The designs, or rows of them, were known as *t'oqapu*. They were executed in bold colors of red, black, white, purple, orange, and yellow. Even the tunics'

Plate 13.1 Inca man's royal tapestry-weave tunic, decorated with character-istic *tokapu* design. Source: © Dumbarton Oaks, Pre-Columbian Collection, Washington, DC.

background hues apparently were significant, for Guaman Poma went to some effort to specify whose tunic had been executed in which colors. The designs' regularity has suggested to scholars that the encoded information was closely linked to the Inca social hierarchy. Some writers have even suggested that the codes approximated a writing system, but that interpretation is not widely accepted.

Uses of Cloth

The military were probably the major consumer of cloth and other woven goods, such as bags. Soldiers were regularly issued blankets, in addition to one or two annual sets of clothes and sandals. Murúa wrote that the *awasqa* cloth was typically given to soldiers. Warriors who distinguished themselves in battle were also awarded finer textiles, as well as camelids, drinking cups, and jewels (Murra 1962: 717). Some fabrics were reserved for the Sapa Inca alone, whose most important insignia was a red woolen fringe (*mascaypacha*) about an inch thick. It was placed on his head, concealing his forehead and shielding his eyes. According to Murúa (1986: 348–9), royal concubines wove the emperor's vestments, which were embroidered with gold, silver, and feathers; one room of the imperial palace was reserved for storage of his most ornate fabrics and jewelry. Each of the deceased lords of the empire was also dressed in the finest clothing, as were the statues of stone or nail clippings that represented them (Murra 1962: 719).

Many ceremonies and social interactions among Cuzco's nobility included exchanges or gifts of the finest textiles. When the Sapa Inca took a bride, he consecrated a woman's *qompi* garment and fastening pin, golden chains, and other objects in the Golden Enclosure. Accompanied by a musical procession, he made his way to the house of his bride's mother, where he presented the gifts to his betrothed. She reciprocated by giving him a tunic made by her own hand and they both donned the clothing. The rites of passage into manhood celebrated by Cuzco's aristocratic youths were also accompanied by gifts of clothing from relatives, which were changed at each step of the month-long ceremony. The colors, designs, and fabrics all made symbolic reference to royal genealogy and history (Murúa 1986: 382–3; Murra 1962: 719).

The Incas also consumed untold quantities of textiles in religious activities, especially ritual sacrifices. Santillán (1968: 111) wrote that camelids and cloth, both of which were burned, constituted the two principal offerings. Cobo added that fine clothing was part of nearly every major sacrifice and that both men's and women's garments were made expressly to be consumed in specific ceremonies. The maize harvest ceremonies on a hill outside Cuzco (Mantocalla) included the immolation of llamas on fires fed by "many bundles of carved firewood dressed as men and women and a great quantity of maize ears made of wood" (Cobo 1990: 117; see Murra 1962: 714). The children and youths or paired golden and silver statuettes buried in high-elevation offerings were also dressed in finery (Reinhard and Alvarez 1996).

Textiles were put to more explicitly political ends as well. The only way that a non-royal individual gained the right to wear *qompi* was through a gift from the Inca. Upon being incorporated into the empire, newly subjected lords would be given gifts of cloth, drinking cups, and jewelry. When provincial lords visited the capital, they were given gifts of cloth and other fine objects, just as they presented textiles and other crafts to the ruler. Cieza (1967: 74) wrote that transplanted colonists were awarded gold and silver bracelets, woolen and feathered clothing, women, and various other privileges, perhaps to help alleviate the pain of dislocation. As Rowe (1979c: 240) points out, the Incas typically made the quality of the gifts appropriate to the rank of the recipient. The reciprocal exchange of these items bonded the ruler and his subjects, while reinforcing the status differences that lay between them.

Clothing

Clothing signified group identity and social status among Andean peoples, while nudity was shameful among many coastal and mountain societies, though not among many peoples of the eastern lowlands. Cobo (1979: 196) wrote that:

> (t)he men and women of each nation and province had their insignias and emblems by which they could be identified, and they could not go around without this identification or exchange their insignias for those of another nation, or they would be severely punished. They had this insignia on their clothes with different stripes and colors, and the men wore their most distinguishing insignia on their heads; each nation was identified by the headdress.

To tolerate the cold and windy conditions in the highlands, both sexes dressed in layers of simple and untailored wool clothing. In the warmer lands, both men and women typically wore clothing woven from cotton. Women's clothing consisted primarily of a long rectangular cloth that was wrapped around the body and under the arms; its corners were pinned over the shoulders. A long sash, called a *chumpi*, was wrapped around the waist several times. Over this wrap, women wore a mantle which they fastened with thorns or a *tupu* pin made of copper (bronze), silver, or gold. Besides providing warmth, the mantle was an all-purpose carrying tool, used to haul everything from infants to potatoes.

The standard men's garment was a rectangular tunic (*unqo*) worn over a loincloth wrapped around the pelvis and groin. The loincloth became part of a male's wardrobe when he passed through a puberty ritual in his early teens. The tunic was a single piece of cloth that was sewn on both sides, with room left at the corners for the arms to pass through and a vertical slit left for the wearer's head. To fend off the cold, men would wrap themselves in a heavy cloak. Both men and women sometimes wore leather sandals, which were tied with cords of wool, cotton, or other plant fibers; its cords were often gaily decorated.

Weavers

The production of so many textiles required tens of thousands of people working at coordinated tasks. The raw materials came from state or church farms (e.g., cotton) or herds (llama and alpaca wool), or gathered resources (e.g., vicuña wool, hummingbird feathers, dyestuffs). In some instances, such as at Huamachuco and Chinchis, the weavers and herders lived nearby (Spurling 1992: 233). Elsewhere, the raw materials were accumulated, stored, and dispensed to the artisans as needed. Many of the tasks involved in making textiles were restricted by gender, but just about everybody in the family could get involved in some way. Young boys, for instance, collected bird feathers and girls the dyestuffs (Guaman Poma 1980: 182–3, 202–3).

Different kinds of cloth were woven by women and men (Murra 1962; Spurling 1992: 221–2). While male weavers (*qompi kamayuq*) wove many of the finer grades of cloth and the feathered textiles, the *mamakuna* made the finest, most valued *qompi* for sacrifices, idols, and the ruler himself (Rowe 1979c: 239). Other women holding special rank, especially *aqllakuna*, also made many textiles. At Puerta de La Paya, Argentina, Ambrosetti's (1902, 1907–8–8; Calderari 1991) excavations a century ago recovered over a thousand spindle whorls and other weaving tools from the tombs of young women. The wives of lords, even those of the Inca, also wove fine cloth. As Polo (1940: 146) reported, "(t)here was no one who was an administrative official who did not send the Inca every year a set of garments made for his person by the hands of the official's wives" (translation by Rowe 1979c: 239).

Specialized Communities

To meet an insatiable demand, the Incas set entire communities – up to a thousand households – to weaving. The best-known facility was Milliraya, situated just northeast of Lake Titicaca, described below. Other enclaves were installed on the altiplano, because of the region's weaving tradition and the proximity of the great herds (Spurling 1992: 234–6; Diez de San Miguel 1964: 106). Peru's central highlands also contributed many weavers to state institutions or royal estates. One Wanka lord claimed that his ancestor had presided over 500 weavers in the Yucay valley (Cuzco), where Wayna Qhapaq had an estate (Toledo 1940: 71). Chupachu witnesses from Huánuco also said that 400 of their members, i.e., 10 percent of the enumerated tax-payers, went to work as weavers for the Inca.

The Milliraya enclave lay on the border between two political divisions, but took lands from only one ethnic group (see Murra 1978; Espinoza Soriano 1987b; Spurling 1992). Spurling suggests that the point was to foster local tensions that would help prevent the reformation of an alliance that had put Inca rule in jeopardy a few decades earlier. One thousand tapestry and feathered cloth weavers and 100 (or maybe 300) potters were settled in different parts of Milliraya's lands under Wayna Qhapaq's direction. Rather than being brought in from afar, as often happened with colonists, the *mitmaqkuna* were transplanted from nearby altiplano communities. Each group received irrigated fields, pastures, lakeshore lands, and lowland maize fields, from which they were expected to support themselves (Spurling 1992: 182). The artisans worked under an Inca-appointed provincial governor, a Lupaqa lord named Cari. Spurling (1992: 197–203) points out, however, that none of the artisans was an ethnic Lupaqa – an early Inca ally – illustrating a way that the Incas rewarded cooperative subjects. Below the governor were an overseer (*jilaqata*) and an accountant-manager who kept the land and population records, apportioned clay to the potters, and told them what vessels to make. None of those officials actually lived in the town, but two pottery overseers did, as well as other lower officials who represented the settlers' *ayllu* of origin.

How did the Incas determine how much cloth to weave or how many potters to install? There are hints that some changes arose from the demand for specific projects. The weavers at Milliraya were reportedly installed to help outfit Wayna Qhapaq's campaigns in Ecuador, but the potters said that they distributed their products to other groups living around the north end of the lake. More generally, the Incas appear to have estimated their needs and put artisans to work until the required amounts were produced. If the amount produced did not match the quotas, they could add more workers. The output stockpiled from cadres of artisans such as these was remarkable. Xérez wrote that the storehouses that he saw at Cajamarca were filled with "so much cloth of wool and cotton that it seemed to me that many ships could have been filled with them," and people drew from the Mantaro valley stores for thirty years after the empire's collapse (translation by Murra 1962: 717).

Stone

The Incas had a complicated, often social, relationship with what we today call stone, or *rumi* in Quechua. Some stones appear to have been just inert rocks, while others were living beings. The Incas also recognized some differences based on their composition – such as ore-bearing or crystalline rocks – and on their form, function, and treatment (Dean 2010a: 25). Rocks left in place in their natural state, carved in place, enclosed in buildings, mined and shaped – whatever their physical condition – could be living, potent forces in the world. The shape was often irrelevant, because what mattered was the perceived substance. A few rocks had been humans in the past, notably the stones that were the original ancestors of living peoples. Even more rocks, which today we would consider to be metallic ores, contained the sweat of the Sun (gold) or the tears of the Moon (silver). And some rocks – the brother idols of the rulers and the oceanic beach sand that filled the Awkaypata plaza in Cuzco stand out – had special powers. The Incas' veneration of the sand so upset the Spaniards that they ultimately used it for mortar in a church (Dean 2010a: 4), inadvertently embedding Inca sanctity in the Catholic house of worship. From the perspective of archaeology, the most spectacular of Inca sites feature stone at their core, whether as architecture or terraces, or as the beautifully carved outcrops scattered across the landscape. Let's pick up our discussion with architecture and then turn to some of the more exotic aspects of the Inca relationships with stone.

Visitors to Cuzco and nearby sites are often astonished at the beauty and ingenuity of Inca stone working. Whether in architecture, sculpted boulders, or carved bedrock, Inca stereotomy was unsurpassed in the Americas and perhaps in the entire ancient world. The precision cutting and scale of Inca stone working are so confounding that writers have attributed the feats to everything from lasers to space aliens (see Lee 1990). Modern architects, however, have described a range of simple techniques that Inca masons could have used to shape their works (see especially Gasparini and Margolies 1980; Protzen 1982, 1993; Lee 1990; Agurto Calvo 1987; Hollowell 1987). Profuse clues to their methods are preserved in the quarries and the rocks themselves. The building blocks were shaped from existing rocks or hewn out of bedrock. The tools were usually simple – hammerstones, ropes, and logs. Distinctive scarring on the blocks' surfaces indicates that shaping was accomplished mostly through pounding, rather than abrasion or cutting. Unfinished rocks in the quarries and along the roads leading to Inca sites indicate that blocks were first shaped in the quarries and then finished on site. Abrasion marks suggest that the rocks were moved by dragging with ropes. That staging of work is illustrated by the constructions at Ollantaytambo, where cut stones prepared for later use still line the road from the quarry to the site or are laid out on the ground within the settlement. Similar techniques of pounding and, occasionally, polishing were used to carve rocks in place.

The work probably moved along more rapidly than one might suspect. Using hammer stones found at the Kachiqata quarry, which provided stone for Ollantaytambo, Protzen (1982: 189) dressed five sides of a small block in an hour and a half. Inca masons would likely have been quicker. Protzen's experiments have shown that the beveled edges that impart such beauty to Inca ashlar masonry may actually be a consequence of the dressing technique; their angles would have also helped prevent fracture of the edges during transportation and handling. Some questions still remain. How did the masons fit blocks so precisely that a knife blade often cannot be introduced between adjoining, unmortared stones? How were the gargantuan blocks installed (plate 13.2)? We do not have definitive answers, but Vincent Lee suggests a credible scenario, based on his study of construction sequences and shape details. Both he and Protzen infer that, in Saqsawaman and other sites, the rocks in an upper course were trimmed first and those in the course below were shaped to receive them. Each upper rock could have been raised with the help of dirt ramps and supported by a log scaffold. A scribe-and-cope (kept true with a plumb) could then be used to follow the contours of the upper rock and mark the fit on the rocks below. Once the bedding and rise joins were matched, the upper rock could have been lowered into place, attaining a neat fit without prolonged trial and error. This is an unromantic vision of Inca cyclopean masonry, to be sure, but it is a more persuasive scenario than shifting 15-ton rocks about in repeated experimental fittings, as is often proposed.

One of the unexpected implications of this approach to stereotomy is that regular courses of masonry – such as those on the famous curved wall of the Qorikancha (plate 7.4) – might have posed a greater challenge than the irregular shapes that seem such a marvel. A more beneficial result of the masons' painstaking work is the architecture's resilience to the earthquakes

Plate 13.2   Cyclopean ashlar masonry in the lowest tier of Saqsawaman.

that strike the central Andes with unnerving frequency. Despite many violent temblors, numerous Inca ashlar walls still exhibit no ill effects of the earth's movements, although they are not immune.

While we do not have much testimony on the subject, we can gain a sense of the Inca understanding of stone architecture from the planning and details of their sites. As described in chapter 7, Inca settlements in the heartland combined modular planning with accommodation to the natural terrain. Even Cuzco, with its layout ordered around the main plazas, was adapted to the channeled Saphy and Tullumayo rivers, and to the promontory above, on which they built Saqsawaman. In the heartland, royal estates such as Pisaq, Patallacta, Ollantaytambo and Machu Picchu, all meld Inca design with the flow of the landscape. And farther out in the provinces, stone architecture often provided a stage for the enactment of state ritual in an ordered space.

Earlier (chapter 5), I suggested that one of the driving forces in the Inca imperial effort was to civilize the world, both human and otherwise. That idea had many dimensions, but two of the key elements were the reduction of chaos/danger and the integration of the human world with its social counterparts in the landscape. Readers may recall that many Andean peoples told the Spaniards that their ancestors had been called forth from features of the landscape, including outcrops, caves, and peaks, to which people returned after death. Rock was the mediating substance between humanity and the land, so it should not be surprising that the Incas melded what they built with the living rock that shared their social space. The affinity between ashlar masonry and carved bedrock is often so intimate that Dean suggests that Inca stone construction was more grafting than building. As she puts it, "architecture very nearly becomes agriculture, as the grafted edifices grow from foundations of living rock" (Dean 2010a: 82).

The carefully adjusted relationship between stone and water was also a repeated motif in Inca construction, linking the two vital elements of the land (e.g., K. Wright and Valencia Zegarra 2000; Wright *et al.* 2006). For example, water channels were frequently divided into two and then reunified in a pool (plate 13.3). Royal estates abound with water that was

Plate 13.3   Tambo Machay, stone-faced fountain complex above Cuzco (probably the *waka* or sacred place known by the Incas as Quinoapukio [quinoa spring]; the tenth *waka* on *zeqe* 1 in the Antisuyu [NE] part of Inca space; Bauer 1998: 77). It pertained to *Zukzu panaqa*, the descendant kin group of emperor Wiraqocha Inka. Source: reproduced by permission of Darryl Wilkinson.

Plate 13.4 Fountain at Machu Picchu.

manipulated through sequences of cascades, such as the sixteen successive fountains built at Machu Picchu (plate 13.4). Stones were carved in ways that created channels for the controlled flow of fluids, and canals were engineered to ensure the movement of water through time and space in an appropriate manner. Overall, the use of stone to shape the flow of water seems as much like a negotiated, social practice as it does an effort to ensure access to a crop-growing, purifying, and life-giving liquid.

Readers may also remember that Inca sites also often incorporated unworked stones or outcrops into their architecture. Sometimes they were enclosed in buildings of their own, which was the treatment granted fourteen outcrops at Machu Picchu. In other places like Q'enqo and Inkallajta (plates 8.2, 10.2), the stones were enclosed by platforms, giving the appearance that they had been artificially elevated. Elsewhere, rocks or outcrops were elaborately sculpted in planes, channels, rounded forms, niches, or bestiaries. One of the most elaborate examples of such carving was the Sayhuite stone, just west of Cuzco, which may have contained a nine-panel representation of the Inca view of the world's ecology (plate 8.1). Similarly elaborate carving has been found at places as far afield as Coyuctor (Ecuador), Samaipata (Bolivia), and Ñusta Hispana, in the Vilcabamba region (Peru). While we still do not have a deep understanding of the ideas involved, the carved rocks seem to embody the idea that they represented a transition point between civilized space and that which lay beyond (Dean 2010a; Wilkinson 2013). In support of that idea is the frequent association between worked stone and water, another animating force of the land.

Finally, we should take note of the variety of stone objects that the Incas created. They ranged from the architectural models now on display outside the Qorikancha temple in Cuzco, to carved animals, counting trays, and vessels. The most potent of those objects may have been the *enqa*, the small objects thought to contain a mimetic relationship with those things that they represented.

Metallurgy

In Inca cosmology, gold was the sweat of the Sun and silver the tears of the Moon. To the Spaniards, the metals embodied earthly riches. Those differing values meant that a century's creativity in precious metals – modeled figures, idols, serving vessels, personal ornaments, and architectural adornments – disappeared into the Spanish forges in a matter of months. Today we know about Inca metallurgy from the few pieces that survived Spanish diligence, from eyewitness descriptions, and from inferences based on earlier objects, which are preserved in greater numbers.

To make their wares, the Inca smiths drew from millennia of Andean knowledge, which was the most sophisticated in the Americas. The smiths of Peru's north coast were especially proficient. By Moche times (*c.* AD 100–800), artisans were using sheet metals to create copper-gold and copper-silver alloys and had developed gilding and surface enrichment techniques (Lechtman 1984). The products that they made were primarily symbolic, decorative, and status-related, rather than utilitarian. Both archaeology and the art market show that many items reached a final resting place as grave goods with society's elite or with individuals who symbolized key ritual positions (Alva and Donnan 1994). Copper (actually copper-arsenic bronze) tools, such as needles and tweezers, were common but not very important culturally or economically. Later craftsmen created a remarkable array of pieces decorated with repoussé designs, filigrees, and inlays of shell, turquoise, lapis lazuli, and emeralds. Along the coast and in Ecuador, there was also a long pre-Inca tradition of fabricating bronze axe-monies (*hachas*) in units of 2, 5, and 10 (Hosler *et al.* 1990).

In Tawantinsuyu, precious metals were wrapped up in elaborate webs of meaning, which the Incas embellished to their own ends (Morris 1995). Because metals were considered to be the gift of the earth, the Incas prayed to the rich mountains as well as to large nuggets or ore-laced rocks, called *mama acha*. In one coastal Andean myth, the Sun came to Earth, where he placed a golden egg that gave birth to noblemen, a silver that bore noble-women, and a copper that bore commoners (see Rostworowski 1983: 147). Inca rulers, who called themselves "the son of the Sun," symbolically inaugurated the agricultural season by rending the soil in the primordial field in Cuzco with a gold-tipped plow. Appropriately, the most sacred temple in the land was "The Golden Enclosure," which housed a variety of icons made of precious metals. Nearby was the Temple of the Moon, where priestesses held the positions of honor. With such an array of beliefs built around the powers of the two celestial bodies, it is small wonder that the Incas placed great emphasis on mining and metallurgical artistry.

Metal Objects

Many of the treasures that the Spaniards saw before the sack of Cuzco would be the most remarkable products of Inca material culture in existence today, had they survived. The Qorikancha housed the golden sun image, named Punchao (Midday Sun), which was brought forth to greet the sun each day and then returned inside at night. This effigy held the ashes of the internal organs of past Inca emperors. The first Spaniards who arrived in Cuzco were astounded and delighted to see that the temple's interior had been covered with golden plates half a meter or more in length:

> These buildings were sheathed with gold, in large plates, on the side where the sun rises, but on the side that was more shaded from the sun the gold in them was more debased. The Christians went to the buildings and with no aid from the Incas – who refused to help, saying that it was a building of the sun and they would die – the Christians decided to remove the ornament ... with some copper crowbars. (Hemming 1970: 133)

The 700 plates that the Spaniards removed weighed about 2 kg each, which would be worth about \$38,684,800 today. When the main Spanish army arrived to sack Cuzco on Saturday, November 15, 1533, the temple was still filled with an array of metal statuary and vessels (Hemming 1970: 133). One golden altar that was still in place weighed over 19,000 pesos. The display that excited the greatest wonder was a full garden of maize, with birds flying among the plants, wrought in gold and silver. Nearby stood the flocks of the Inca, along with the herders, all executed to life-scale in precious metals. It is one of the great losses to the modern world that so few of those pieces escaped the furnaces to survive to the present day. Only because the conquistadores had the grace to send King Philip 18-carat golden figures of a woman and a llama along with other objects of precious metals (Hemming 1970: 131–2) did anything avoid the flames.

Many metal objects were serving vessels fashioned for the church and the royal families. The royalty were said to drink their *chicha* from silver and golden tumblers. It was primarily from the *panaqas'* assets that Atawallpa's ransom was gathered, since he specified that his father's assets were not to be touched. The amount of gold and silver that was fed into the forges at Cajamarca ultimately totaled 13,240 lbs of 22.5 carat gold and 26,000 lbs of good silver (Hemming 1970: 73). One elegant golden fountain, dismantled for transport to Cajamarca, weighed over 12,000 pesos by itself. At today's values, the gold would be worth about \$332,588,000 and the silver a little more than \$10,816,000. The take at Cuzco was even greater.

Because the Spaniards hunted down the Inca treasures so thoroughly, and perhaps because the Incas successfully hid what was left, only a few pieces are found in museum collections. Readers who have seen other publications on Inca artistry may have noticed a suspicious tendency for authors to use pictures of the same items. Scholars' habit of repeating each other

Plate 13.5 Silver and spondylus figurines from Cerro el Plomo, Chile. Source: reproduced by permission of Johan Reinhard.

aside, those objects appear because they are just about all that remains. Fortunately, recent discoveries of ceremonial offerings at high altitudes have begun to expand our knowledge. When metal objects are included, they usually consist of paired male and female figures made of gold or gold and silver, sometimes accompanied by llamas or alpacas executed in the same materials (plate 13.5). The idols are simply designed, with ovoid heads and stocky, unelaborated bodies. To judge from the well-preserved examples, they were usually clothed in gender-appropriate attire and decked out with feathered headdresses and other adornments (Reinhard and Ceruti 2010).

Mines and Mining

Chroniclers often reported that the Incas made a blanket claim to all mineral resources, but that was more an assertion of sovereignty than reality. Cobo's (1979: 249) comment is more to the point:

> Some of these mines were worked at the expense and under the auspices of the Inca himself, and others, constituting the majority, were worked at the expense of the caciques [lords] of the districts in which the mines were located. This was so that they would have things to give as presents to the Inca.

Berthelot's (1986) studies suggest that the Incas took the richest, most concentrated sources for themselves, while the community mines were more scattered. The Incas' mines were distributed throughout their domain; copper deposits are distributed in bands along the length of the Andes, but gold and silver occur in more restricted deposits. Tin, which was used widely in the empire to make bronze, was concentrated in southern Bolivia and northern Chile.

Just as they did with food, coca, and cloth, the Incas claimed raw resources for institutions and estates and set men and women tributaries to work on a rotating basis (Berthelot 1986). Santillán (1968: 39, 42, items 42 and 51) wrote that the standard practice in provinces where the Incas had mines was for the local lords to call up 1 percent of their taxpayers, although the numbers of miners actually varied in practice. Apparently distrustful of the lords' interest in rendering accurate accounts, the Incas installed their own supervisors to collect and weigh the ore daily as the miners left for home. One of the most elaborate operations lay about 100 km east of Samaipata, Bolivia, where the Incas reportedly installed 1,000 miners and 5,000 other colonists to support them (Pärssinen 1992: 130–1). When the Spaniards arrived in 1533, the gold operation at Chuquiabo (La Paz, Bolivia) totaled more than a hundred people of both sexes from four different tributary groups. The Huánuco inspection reported that the Chupachu committed 120 men and 120 women (3 percent of their tributaries) for the nearby gold mines and 60 more men and their wives for the silver mines in the adjacent Yaros territory (Berthelot 1986: 74–6). Betanzos, Sarmiento, and Pedro Pizarro all wrote that the main purpose of the Inca ventures into the south was to procure mineral wealth, although a little hindsight may have slipped into that explanation. Archaeological surveys support the view that the Incas took advantage of mineral wealth in the south. Raffino (1983: 243, 259–62) enumerates sixty-eight Inca-era sites in Argentina and fifty-eight in southern Bolivia and Chile that were involved in mining gold, silver, copper, galena, zinc, tin, and other minerals.

Some mines were apparently designated as the Sapa Inca's personal property. Polo (1916: 102) implied that an important fraction of all mining operations serviced the emperors, living and dead, along with their retinues. He wrote that when an emperor died, his successor sent out another battery of miners to start producing for his own estate, alongside those of the prior ruler. Thupa Inka Yupanki had one such mine on his estate at Asillo, north of Lake Titicaca. Local lords seem to have set their own tributaries to work their personal mines, as part of the regular labor service to which they were entitled (Berthelot 1986).

Mining techniques were simple. Where the ore was found in veins, the miners dug galleries that were so constricted that only one person could enter at a time. Fall-ins, poor lighting, and bad ventilation made tunnel mining a risky business, but gold, silver, and copper were all extracted that way. At some open-air mines, gold was recovered by sluicing river gravels (see Berthelot 1986: 77–80). As always, the Incas were prepared to invest enormous amounts of their tributaries' labor to achieve their goals. Confronted with a perpetual lack of water in ore-rich Tarapacá (northern Chile), they sent engineers to lay out a canal that would carry water from the altiplano to the coastal valley. The intent apparently was to improve the region's ability to support permanent residents, not to assist in mining operations per se. The canal was never finished, as its construction was cut short by the Spanish invasion (Berthelot 1986: 80; Núñez 1986: 31–2).

For the most part, mining was a seasonal affair, because of the extreme cold found at high elevations and because workers needed to tend their fields back home. Based on his experience in southern Peru and the altiplano, Polo (1940a: 165) stated that mining was solely a summer occupation. At Chuquiabo, they worked only from December to March and just from noon to sunset. Where the climate permitted, such as at Huánuco, mining could be a year-round enterprise (Berthelot 1986: 74–5).

Much of the ore was sent to Cuzco, where it was worked by the Incas' smiths and jewelers into service vessels, architectural adornments, and other objects. Some important state installations, including Hatun Xauxa (Peru), had resident smiths as well. Waste fragments of gold and bronze have also been recovered archaeologically from Inca centers in the south (D'Altroy *et al.* 2000).

Local Metallurgy under the Incas

Cuzco's rule left a heavy imprint on local metallurgy. Provincial lords lost control over many mines and much of the local product became part of the obligatory gift exchanges between the Inca and his subjects. Just as important was the loss of the artisans to state activities. The heaviest blow may have fallen on Peru's north coast, but the south Andes may have given over much of their artisans' labor as well. A major technological development was a broad shift from copper-arsenic bronzes to tin bronzes, even at local communities. Many copper deposits in the Andes have a high natural arsenic content, but a tin alloy is less toxic and makes the bronze more workable. Since tin was concentrated in a relatively small area in Bolivia and Chile and was under the Incas' control, this technological change was fundamentally a product of state intervention and supply (Lechtman 1984). The bronzes were often used to make tools, among them needles and chisels. Many of the decorative objects made and used by subject peoples were given Inca forms, in particular the *tupu* pins that were used to secure women's clothing (see Howe and Petersen 1994; Owen 2001).

A brief look at the Upper Mantaro valley will illustrate what happened in one province. Owen, Howe, and Petersen have shown that the Incas altered the local production and use of metals, but did not take over the craft entirely. Excavations in twenty-nine households recovered 267 objects of arsenic bronze, tin bronze, silver, and lead from the late pre-Inca and Inca periods. More than half of the items were used for adornment and display, such as *tupu* pins, pendants, and disks that were probably attached to cloth. Among the utilitarian objects were needles, bola weights used for hunting, chisels, ceremonial *tumi* knives, and a lead fragment that may have been used to repair a vessel. A substantial amount of metal production debris was also recovered, such as ore, sheet scrap, and casting debris. The debris was found in both elite and commoner households in both phases, suggesting that metalworking was a fairly common skill among the valley's inhabitants. Under Inca rule, bronzes shifted from native arsenic to tin alloy (Owen 2001). The amount of copper and lead in circulation increased, while the ratio of finished products to debris doubled, suggesting that some production was moved elsewhere or that the local populace received items made under state auspices.

In sum, metallurgy encapsulates the selective intervention of the Incas in Andean artisanry. While gold and silver provided a crucial symbolic link between the Incas and the cosmos, they were also alloyed with copper and their surfaces were often covered. The Incas claimed all mineral resources, but local societies maintained their own independent mining and metallurgical industries. And while those local industries flourished, the Incas both commanded many of the products and controlled the technology of bronze alloys.

Ceramics

Textiles and metals were more important in Inca culture, but Cuzco-style polychrome pottery is the archaeological hallmark of Inca presence throughout the Andes. Inca polychrome ceramics are abundant in the heartland and in provincial centers from Cuzco to Quito; they are also found in small amounts in thousands of local settlements. At some provincial sites, such as Huánuco Pampa (Morris and Thompson 1985: 71–80) and Hatun Xauxa (D'Altroy and Bishop 1990; D'Altroy 1992), provincial variants of Cuzco wares formed over 98 percent of the ceramic assemblage. On the coast and in the southern Andes, they often formed a small component, as the assemblages at state sites consist mostly of local types. Although it might seem odd that the distributions of Inca-style pottery and architecture only partially match, a lack of fit between them should not be that surprising, since they served different purposes (Hyslop 1993: 339; Morris 1995).

Inca pottery had a narrow range of uses outside the heartland. The vessels were to brew the beer, prepare the food, and to serve these items in state-sponsored feasts (Bray 2003). They were also used for long-term storage, to hold offerings of food, and as grave goods (Morris 1995: 523). The pottery's use at provincial centers emphasized the importance of the state as both the symbolic and the physical sponsor of political and ceremonial activities (Cummins 2002). Ceramics were also given to privileged lords, but Inca vessels were not used in the peasants' everyday affairs. The finer Inca ceramics were almost invariably the most elegant vessels in use, no matter the context. Such visual displays, like *qompi* cloth, were ways of expressing the state's presence, especially where many people could not speak the language of their rulers (DeMarrais *et al.* 1996).

The most distinctive Inca vessels are flared-rim jars with constricted necks (often called aryballoid jars or *aríbalos*: figure 13.1, plate 13.6a), open-mouth jars, open and closed bowls, plates with duck head and tail appendages (plate 13.6b), drinking cups or tumblers (*keros*; plate 13.6c), bottles, and pedestal-based cooking pots (see Valcárcel 1934–5–5; Rowe 1944: 47–9, figures 18 and 19; Rowe 1946: 243–4; Hyslop 1993: 340). The collection from Chinchero, one of Thupa Inka Yupanki's estates near Cuzco, has yielded twenty-eight distinct shapes of pots, illustrated here in figure 13.2 (Rivera 1976: 29). The full set of vessel forms found in the Cuzco area does not appear to have been reproduced anywhere else in the empire. That probably occurred, as Hyslop (1993: 339) suggests, because state personnel in the heartland were involved in a wider range of activities and held higher statuses than those in the provinces.

Inca pottery is usually distinguished by its high technical quality and regularity. It is generally well fired and burnished, contains low proportions of temper, and is decorated with lustrous, opaque slips. As with the textiles, motifs most commonly consist of geometric forms, such as solid

Figure 13.1 Illustration of Inca woman carrying an aryballoid jar. Source: Bingham 1930.

bands, rows of diamonds or pendant triangles, concentric diamonds, large expanses of solid color or highly polished buff areas, the "fern motif" on flared-rim jars (likely young maize), and hatching. The result was a labor-intensive, visually distinctive ware of high quality. Apart from rendering the pottery instantly recognizable, the repetitiveness of form and decoration aided duplication by potters performing their labor duties, although regional variants in style and quality can still be readily distinguished. Potters' tendencies to combine elements of Inca pottery with regional styles led to a welter of Inca-related ceramic types throughout the Andes.

Despite its archaeological importance, polychrome pottery manufacture was a minor component of the Inca economy. Although pot-making figured on standard lists of labor duties, it was ranked lower than all activities associated with weaving, feathers, and metals. In the two cases where we have figures for artisans dedicated to specific tasks – Huánuco and Milliraya (see above) – there were ten times as many weavers as potters. While

(a)

(b)   (c)

Plate 13.6   (a) ceramic flared-rim jar (b) ceramic duck-head plate (c) Colonial-era wooden drinking cup; all from Cuzco. Source: reproduced by permission of the American Museum of Natural History.

that difference surely reflects cultural values, it is also true that pots can be cranked out more quickly than tapestry-weave textiles.[3]

Several artisan communities provide evidence for state ceramic production (D'Altroy 2005). At Cajamarca (Peru), an important center along the sierra highway, the Incas transplanted 100 potters from the north coast of Peru. The best-documented workshop in the south is Potrero-Chaquiago, Argentina, where pottery, textiles, and metalworking were carried out in separate sectors of the site (Lorandi 1984; Williams and Lorandi 1986; Williams 1996). Intriguingly, the settlement had a fair amount of locally made, but non-Inca pottery that resembles styles from other regions in the south Andes, probably made by *mitmaqkuna* in the styles of their homelands (Lorandi 1988; Lorandi and Cremonte 1993).

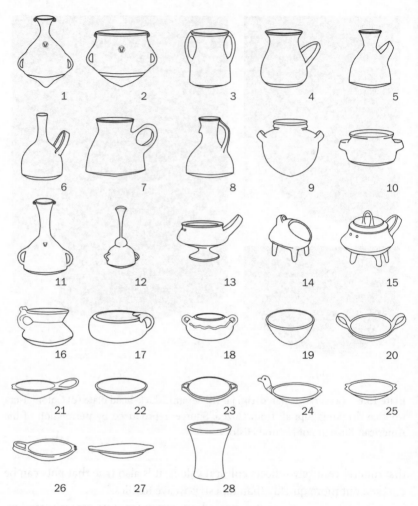

Figure 13.2   Illustration of the twenty-eight different forms of Inca ceramics recovered from Thupa Inka Yupanki's estate at Chinchero. Source: adapted from Rivera 1976.

The Incas also valued pottery made in the styles of some other ethnic groups. Pacajes ceramics, made on the altiplano south of Lake Titicaca, were apparently especially esteemed. Featuring rows of little camelids, the plates were widely distributed in small amounts at Inca sites throughout the southern half of the empire. Similarly, Chimu blackware has been recovered from Inca sites in a number of locations in the north Andes. This style is found among the burials at Machu Picchu, which included pottery made in the styles of at least four different locales. Lucy Salazar (2007) suggests that the people buried there may have been interred with objects from their homelands as a mark of the people annexed by the Incas.

There are very few places in the empire where subjects had access to a large number of state vessels. One such location was the Upper Mantaro valley of Peru, which we know had a privileged status. The region's two largest towns, Hatunmarca and Marca, each housed about 4,500 residents and were probably home to important local lords, whose houses incorporated typical Inca architectural features. Fieldwork at the two towns indicates that their ceramic assemblages each contain one to two million sherds in the polychrome style. Even so, the percentage of Inca pottery never exceeded more than about one-quarter in any residential compound. This pattern suggests that high social status conferred the privilege or, less benignly, the obligation of using state pottery in political and ceremonial activities. High status did not grant elites the right to be sustained at home with goods made entirely in the state style.

Other Things

As described in the introduction to this chapter, artisans of many skills worked for the Inca in materials ranging from wood, to stone, to organics. An extended description of all of those crafts is beyond this text, but among the finest objects that they produced were the large earspools that denoted high status, and musical instruments such as pan pipes and drums. Artisans drafted into service were also responsible for making a wide variety of military supplies, including sandals, armor, weapons, and shields. One class of objects especially worthy of note are the tumblers that were used to serve *chicha*, often in contexts of formalized hospitality. The wooden and ceramic drinking cups are known as *keros* (plate 13.4c), while their gold and silver counterparts are called *aquilla*. Cummins's (2002) study of their design and cultural import, from the Inca to Colonial eras, highlights the importance of objects in social intercourse. A toast with the Inca was not simply a gesture of hospitality, but a statement of social position, obligation, and by implication relations with the ancestors of the land. As described in the next chapter, the Spaniards' abuse of the Inca's cordial of offer of tumblers of *chicha* at their first encounter was grounds for combat, even if the invaders didn't have a clue as to what they were doing. They clearly should have known.

Notes

1 Readers who have seen the first edition of this book may wonder why the title of this chapter was changed from "Artisans and Artistry," which seemed like a pretty reasonable phrase a decade ago. The point of the shift is to highlight the distinctly Andean way of thinking that humans shared the world with many material things in ways that go far beyond technology and display.

2 This quotation comes from the first of three (so far) volumes on the Science of Discworld, in which academics team up with Sir Terry Pratchett to explore the questions of philosophy, biology, and the exact sciences raised by the Discworld series of about forty fantasy novels. I don't know of any other author whose writing so completely beguiles archaeologists, and I assume other scientists, as Pratchett's humor, humanity, and inventiveness combine seamlessly across an endless array of subjects.

3 I thank Melissa Hagstrum for making this point to me.

Chapter Fourteen

Invasion and Aftermath

The invasion of South America that brought down the Inca empire was not launched in a day or even a decade. Over a period of about fifteen years after Vasco Núñez de Balboa first saw the South Sea (Pacific) in 1513, Spanish adventurers had been pushing the limits of European exploration southward from Panama. Among those ambitious men was Francisco Pizarro, who had been on Núñez de Balboa's bloody, not-so-pacific expedition. As so often happened during the tempestuous politics of invasion, Pizarro's allegiance soon shifted, coming to rest with the newly installed governor of Castilla de Oro, Pedro Arias de Ávila (Pedrarias Dávila). On orders from the governor, whose compatriots had long been at odds with Núñez de Balboa, Pizarro arrested his former chief, who was beheaded after a quick trial in 1519. Over the next few years, Pizarro formed his own expeditions, partnering with Diego de Almagro. The company worked its way haltingly into Colombia and down the Ecuadorian coast, showing little profit for the effort. By 1528, however, Bartolomé Ruiz had captured a treasure-laden raft along the Ecuadorian coast that gave promise of a rich land just beyond the Spanish view; his expedition also captured a number of boys who would later serve as interpreters for the first encounters with the Incas. News of Ruiz's success helped Pizarro to obtain a royal concession as governor of the unknown land and to attract financial support and men back in Spain.

Despite the new land's promise, the trying climatic conditions and earlier failures daunted many hardy individuals who had been reared in a society accustomed to challenging times. Back in the home country, the men of recent generations had been tempered in the Reconquista of Spain. Many of the conquistadores in particular hailed from the difficult Extremadura region, and not a few of them were blood kin. Still, it was no accident that several officers of the expedition had participated in the conquest of Mexico, and at least fifty-two of their group had five or more years of experience

The Incas, Second Edition. Terence N. D'Altroy.
© 2015 John Wiley & Sons, Ltd. Published 2015 by John Wiley & Sons, Ltd.

in the New World (Lockhart 1972: 23). In the end, only thirty of the 168 men in the force that Pizarro finally led into the Andes in November of 1532 had just arrived from Spain. Most of the company had already lived through hazards like those they would face in the invasion and were willing to risk health, money, and life in a quest for wealth and that status and security that brought. Those men were as much entrepreneurs as soldiers or adventurers, especially the horsemen who had spent respectable sums to buy their mounts, an investment that would entitle them to double the share of the foot soldiers in any booty they amassed.

In 1531, Pizarro's force made its way to Coaque, on the Ecuadorian coast, which they attacked and occupied. They settled down to wait for reinforcements for several months, but many succumbed to local diseases in the interim. By early 1532, several new boatloads of men had joined the vanguard and the expedition had worked its way southward to Tumbes, on Peru's north coast, which had already been scouted four years earlier. Once again, the Spaniards settled down and began to inspect the surrounding territory. It was only at this time that they began to see concrete evidence of a major civilization – roads, storehouses, and state installations. Again, the Spaniards moved forward with a characteristic mix of caution and bravery, founding a new settlement at San Miguel (now Piura), about 100 km farther south, and planning an expedition into the heartland of the empire whose existence became more apparent with every passing day. By late 1532, Pizarro had finally gathered the resources, men, and boldness to ascend the Andes and meet the Inca prince Atawallpa, who was known to be at Cajamarca, a royal installation along the highway in northern Peru. The knowledge was mutual, of course, for the Spanish pillaging and murder along the coast had been angrily noted in the highlands. In fact, gifts with insulting overtones, such as half-cooked ducks with feathers attached and charred camelid meat, had been sent to the Spaniards. Apparently oblivious to the affront, Pizarro sent gifts in return. As they approached Cajamarca, Atawallpa dispatched his general Rumiñawi at the head of 6,000 men to take custody of and escort the expedition into the center (Cieza 1998: 197–8).

One Account of the Events

As the Spaniards told it, the company finally arrived at Cajamarca on November 15 and entered the plaza in the center of town. While most men took shelter from a hailstorm, Pizarro dispatched Hernando de Soto, fifteen horsemen, and the interpreter Martín to greet the Inca lord at the hot springs outside of town. After first passing through the thousands of soldiers lining the way, the Spaniards approached Atawallpa, who was seated on a small wooden throne, surrounded by his court. Captain de Soto made a brief speech that was translated and then offered the prince a ring as a sign of friendship. Atawallpa did not deign to reply to him but did converse with Hernando Pizarro, once he understood that he was the governor's brother, and invited the Spaniards to dine with him. They declined out of fear of poisoning, but after some hesitation accepted a drink. A fine display of horsemanship by de Soto met with royal approval, but Spanish appeals for Atawallpa to accompany them back to the town fell on deaf ears. Thus ended the first day of contact (Hemming 1970: 32–5; MacQuarrie 2007: 58–68).

Even after de Soto and Hernando Pizarro's encounter with Atawallpa, the Spaniards were undecided about their best course of action.[1] They ranged from feigning friendship and postponing military action for a more propitious moment, to demanding that Atawallpa declare obeisance to the king of Spain, to launching a surprise attack. In the end, they agreed to let Francisco Pizarro judge the best course of action once events were underway. Fortunately for the invaders, Inca settlement planning and architecture provided a wonderful opportunity to conceal their intentions. Access to the main plaza at Cajamarca was restricted to a few passages that could be blocked, and elongated halls that opened onto the plaza had numerous doorways that could permit a rapid charge by walls of horsemen and foot soldiers hidden from view. The Spaniards took advantage of the layout to station artillery, men, and horses inside the buildings for a tortuous overnight wait. For his part, the Inca was making similar plans to affect friendship and then take the Spaniards prisoner. During his captivity, he explained that he had intended to torture and kill a number of them and castrate the remainder for the service of the women's institutions. A happier fate was planned for the horses, which he planned to breed.

Atawallpa was apparently in no hurry to greet the strangers the next day, sleeping in while the Spaniards grew increasingly dismayed. Many took last rites while Pizarro made the rounds to buck up their spirits and urged them to commend their fate to the protection of the Lord. After a long delay, the Inca prince followed his massed soldiers toward the town plaza, on a litter carried by eighty men. He halted just outside town, apparently to make camp for the night, but the Spaniards sent a mission that persuaded him to enter the plaza late in the afternoon of November 16. He was accompanied by some of the highest-ranking lords of the land and several thousand of his personal guard. Garbed in elegant tunics, he was carried on a luxurious litter decorated with parrot feathers and plates of gold and silver. He had his bearers halt in the plaza's center and waited while much of the remaining open space was filled by his entourage. Surprised to find no Spaniards in sight, Atawallpa thought that they had hidden themselves in fear.

But then the Dominican friar Vicente de Valverde approached Atawallpa and began to speak through his interpreter Martín. Following the Spanish legal requirement of the time, he explained how he had been sent to reveal the word of God to the people of the land. In what was surely a garbled version, Atawallpa received translated notice that he was to recognize the legitimate supremacy of the Church, the pope, and the Spanish king. Any failure to do so would result in his destruction, as was only right and proper, and the responsibility of the disaster would rest solely with him (Wright 1992: 65; MacQuarrie 2007: 78–9). Valverde handed a closed breviary to the Inca, who succeeded in opening it only after some effort. After his brief conversation with the priest, Atawallpa cast the book to the ground and rose in his litter to ready his men. At that, Valverde rushed back toward the hidden Spaniards and cried out for them to avenge the affront to the holy word.

Pizarro ordered the signal for the men to charge – firing small cannon and arquebuses into the midst of the crowded square – and the armed Spaniards stormed out to their battle cry, "Santiago." Riding horses, protected by their armor, and carrying superior arms, the Spaniards were almost invulnerable against the massed Andean soldiers. Atawallpa was personally captured by Pizarro, who took a wound while deflecting a Spanish blow intended to fell the Inca. In the two hours of carnage that followed, as many as 7,000 Andeans may have been killed, at the loss of not one Spaniard. Atawallpa was quickly protected by his captors, for they judged that their own safety depended on keeping the ruler alive. As night fell, the Spaniards were in such complete control within Cajamarca that Pizarro invited Atawallpa to dine with him. And that's the way it happened.[2]

Another Account

Or did it? In 1570, the displaced emperor Titu Kusi sent a communiqué to the king of Spain from the new Inca capital in Vilcabamba, petitioning for recognition as co-equals. His account of the encounter at Cajamarca differs markedly from the Spanish version, and is worth reading at length (Titu Cusi 2005: 135–6). He wrote,

Among these Wiraquchas [Spaniards] two were brought by some Yungas [people from the lowlands] before my uncle Ataw Wallpa (who happened to be in Cajamarca) who cordially received them and gave them each to drink, a drink that we drink, from a golden cup. The Spaniard, upon receiving the drink in his hand, spilled it which greatly angered my uncle. And after that, the two Spaniards showed my uncle a letter, or book, or something, saying that this was the qillpa [inscription] of God and the King and my uncle, as he felt offended by the spilling of the chicha, took the letter (or whatever it was) and knocked it to the ground, saying:

I don't know what you have given me. Go on, leave.

And the Spaniards returned to their cohorts, who surely told them of what they had seen and what had came [*sic*] to pass with my uncle Ataw Wallpa.

Many days later, with my uncle Ataw Wallpa at war with his brother Waskar Inqa, over who would be the true king of this land, neither of whom were the legitimate heir as they both had usurped my father of his kingdom (he being quite young at the time) for each of their many uncles and aunts had asked themselves, "why should a boy be king?"[3] ... And being in these disputes as I have said, one against the other though they were brothers on different thrones, there arrived in Cajamarca, the aforesaid town, about forty or fifty Spaniards, it is said, on well-saddled horses. When these events were known by my uncle Ataw Wallpa, who was nearby in a town called Huamachuco hosting the festivities there, he left with his guards not with arms to attack nor harness to defend but with tumis and lassos ...

And when my uncle arrived in Cajamarca with his people, the Spaniards received them in the baths of Conoc, a league and a half from Cajamarca, and so they went with him to Cajamarca. And having arrived, he asked them why they had come and they replied under the mandate of Wiraqucha to tell them how they were to know Him. And my uncle, as he heard what they told them he started and was silent and offered them drink in the aforesaid manner to see whether they would spill the drink in the same way the others had, and so they did, because they didn't drink or listen. And my uncle seeing that they respected little said:

Since you don't respect me I won't respect you either.

And angry, he stood and shouted for the death of the Spaniards and the Spaniards, who were on guard, seized the four entrances to the plazas so that the Indians were surrounded on all sides.

Since the plaza was surrounded and the many Indians inside were like sheep, unable to move and unarmed because they had left their weapons behind, thinking little of the small number of men because they had thought little of the Spaniards; they were carrying only lassos and tumis, as I said before. The Spaniards, infuriated, attacked the center of the plaza where the Inqa's throne stood, as tall as a fortress – what we call an usnu – which they took over and stopped my uncle from mounting. At the foot of the throne they threw him down from his litter and overturning and seizing its contents and the fringe and diadem – which among us is the crown – and having seized everything they attacked him. And as the Indians screamed, with swords they were killed by the horsemen, with muskets, as one who kills sheep, with no resistance given by ten thousand, two hundred who could not escape. And when all were slaughtered, they took my uncle to a prison in the night, where he was held naked, the entire night, with a chain about his neck. The next morning they gave him his clothes and his diadem.

Even if the general outlines are in accord, discrepancies abound between the Spanish and Inca versions of the action. Many of the details are in conflict, among them the number of encounters, the locations of the main actors, and the sequence of events. The minor details aside, the character of the Andean account reflects distinct cultural values and ways of remembering history (figure 14.1). In keeping with the Inca forms of knowing and communicating history, the account reads like the transcription of an oral narrative, rather than a scribe's report. More to the point substantively, the focal point of cultural misunderstanding was not the Inca's blasphemy of the Holy Word, but the Spaniards' affront to the Inca's hospitality. While Titu Kusi wasn't sure what the document in question had been, he was certain that his uncle had treated the interlopers respectfully and they had responded with insults. Moreover, the precise chronology of events was far less important than the conduct of the protagonists, and their behavior in a culturally (in)appropriate manner. In the Andean account, Atawallpa was treated shamefully the first night. Contrary to the Spaniards' assertions, he was not invited to sup with his captors, but was stripped naked and chained. In short, everyone agreed on the outcome, but the legitimacy of actions and the sequence of events was seen through discordant prisms.

A Deity in Captivity

As the Spaniards' passion for gold and silver quickly became obvious, Atawallpa responded by offering an immense quantity of the metals in

Figure 14.1 Atawallpa receiving Pizarro and Valverde, according to Guaman Poma's (1936) Andean viewpoint.

exchange for his freedom. Xérez (1985: 122), Pizarro's secretary, wrote that the Inca promised to have his subjects fill a room about 6.2 × 4.8 m to a white line set at half its height, or about 2.5 m, with gold objects. The room's volume was to be filled twice over with silver objects gathered from the entire empire over the next couple of months. Pizarro agreed to the proposal with alacrity and both sides settled down to wait, while planning their moves for the time when the ransom/tribute had been paid. The Spaniards were willing to let the process drag out for an extended period, while reinforcements could be mobilized from Panama and they could learn more about the political and military situation in the Andes. Atawallpa, in the meantime, was managing the affairs of state from captivity and planning to avenge himself once free from Spanish hands.

As the metallic hoard trickled in, the two sides got to know one another. The Spaniards watched Atawallpa receive visitors and rule his domain, and conversed with him at length about a wide range of subjects concerning the land. For his part, the Inca expressed a certain degree of interest in things Spanish, even learning to play chess. The information that the conquistadores gleaned during the eight months of Atawallpa's captivity led them to correctly believe that they could exploit the divisions that lay between the two Inca factions. Over time they also came to see how to use the resentments harbored by many Inca subjects, who were eager to see the Spaniards as saviors from imperial rule. During this time, Pizarro sent expeditions to Cuzco and coastal Pachacamac. Accompanied by an Inca aristocrat and carried on litters, three men sent to the capital were gone for four long months. Along the road, the soldiers had an interview with the imprisoned Waskhar (figure 14.2), but declined to act on his plea for freedom. They only spent eight days in the capital, but took as full advantage of the visit as they could, seeing the sights and seeking out treasure. The official scribe, Francisco de Xérez wrote down what one of the soldiers, Juan de Zárate, recalled.

> He said that the city of Cuzco is as large as has been described, and that it is located on a hillside near a plain. The streets are very well organized and paved, and in the eight days that they were there they could not see everything. (Translation from Bauer 2004: 109)

Although they found so much gold and silver that they could not begin to transport it, the three Spaniards were accompanied back to Cajamarca by more than 700 porters carrying the treasure they did manage to pillage in just that first visit (Xérez 1985: 149). The other expedition, led by Hernando

Figure 14.2   Overthrown ruler, Waskhar, in custody; from Guaman Poma (1936).

Pizarro, traveled to coastal Pachacamac, where they destroyed the oracular idol who resided there. On the return trip, they persuaded Atawallpa's general Challcochima to accompany them from Hatun Xauxa back to

Cajamarca, which essentially consigned the commander to his death. The success of both expeditions, especially the golden evidence of the empire's wealth brought back from Cuzco, fired the Spaniards' zeal even further.

By late April, 1533, Diego de Almagro, Pizarro's partner, had arrived from Panama with reinforcements and Hernando Pizarro's expedition had reappeared. It seems to have become clear to Atawallpa at that point that the first company of Spaniards was only the vanguard of a much larger invasion and that the prospects of his release were dim. In June and July, the accumulated hoard of gold and silver treasures was melted down and carefully accounted for to ensure that the royal fifth was taken out. Each horseman received about 41 kg of gold – roughly 2.5 million dollars today – and each foot man half that. They received twice that weight of silver, valued at about $75,000 today. Francisco Pizarro took seven times that of the horsemen, but Almagro's new arrivals received only token awards (Hemming 1970: 73). They were not pleased. Neither, apparently, was the king of Spain, since by law the royal hostage was his property. Any ransom collected was owed him in its entirety, not just the royal fifth. When the king found out the circumstances from Hernando Pizarro, he demanded that those who had received shares of the ransom contribute to a large donation to the crown as recompense (Rowe 2006: 7).

By the end of July, the situation in Cajamarca had reached a decision point, since the ransom had been melted down and new action was called for. The Spaniards later testified that they had heard rumors that Atawallpa had ordered Rumiñawi to move on Cajamarca in an effort to free him. Almagro's newcomers took the position that Atawallpa had become a liability whose continued presence exposed the Spaniards to perpetual danger. Conversely, many members of the initial expedition were more loath to kill the Inca. Not only did they see him as their safety card, but a number had grown to appreciate, if not befriend, the captive ruler. Pizarro himself may have preferred to keep the Inca as a hostage while the Spaniards made their way to Cuzco to claim the capital and its remaining riches; he may even have considered packing him off to Spain. In the end, Pizarro may have panicked and given in to the demands to execute the Inca – or he may have simply professed reluctance while planning to replace Atawallpa with a more compliant puppet (Rowe 2006). On Saturday, July 26, 1533 Atawallpa was convicted of treason in a hastily convoked trial. He was garroted forthwith, having been spared burning at the stake only after agreeing to be baptized.

Why did Atawallpa agree to be baptized? The Spaniards possibly felt that he wanted to escape the agony of the flames and some may have thought that he actually had seen the Christian light. A more likely explanation, from an Inca perspective, is that the body needed to remain essentially intact after death to fulfill its journey to a permanent new existence. As suggested in chapter 5, Atawallpa's decision was most likely based on the idea that he could most readily return to his father, the Sun, if his body were entire (minus the internal organs that were to be burned and placed in the belly of the image Punchao) for a year or more. Little did he realize that his corpse would be unceremoniously – from the Inca viewpoint – dumped into a grave, rather than be embalmed as befit a monarch.

On to Cuzco

Atawallpa's passing triggered all manner of response. The Incas in Cajamarca were bereft at the loss of their sovereign and appalled at the small-scale Christian burial that he was accorded – entirely out of keeping with the vast ceremony that he should have enjoyed. On a more personal note, a number of his wives cast about his lodgings, softly calling out for him to reappear until they sadly conceded his death. Crown officials in Panama and King Carlos V himself were outraged that a sovereign should have been so unceremoniously dispatched by social nobodies; Pizarro was later called to account in Spain and forced to defend himself. Among the Andean populations, Waskhar's supporters and numerous ethnic groups were overjoyed at the news, while Atawallpa's partisans were devastated and angered. An especially significant consequence was that the major impediment to Inca attacks on the Spaniards had been removed, so that Quizquiz, Rumiñawi, and other military leaders were free to attempt to rid the land of the invaders (see Hemming 1970: 86–99).

Atawallpa's death also left the Spaniards without a recognized native leader through whom to rule, and the Incas without a sovereign. Pizarro took steps to remedy the situation immediately, by installing one of Waskhar's brothers, named Thupa Wallpa, as a puppet ruler (Sancho 1917).[4] They then set south toward Cuzco, meeting their first significant military resistance upon approaching Hatun Xauxa in the Mantaro valley. The engagement graphically illustrates the divisions that split the Andes. While Atawallpa's army of occupation tried to burn down the town and then put up resistance on the far side of the river, the native Xauxa and Wanka populace, who had sided with Waskhar's cause, celebrated in the center's streets (Sancho 1917). The local people immediately allied themselves with the Spaniards and began to supply them from the royal warehouses, a practice they kept up for two full decades (chapter 13). Hatun Xauxa's strategic location and the support they received there led the Spaniards to choose it as the first Colonial capital of the Andes in 1535.[5] Pizarro bivouacked at the center for a couple of weeks, during which the invaders suffered a serious setback, as Thupa Wallpa succumbed to illness. His death plunged the land into another quagmire of intrigue wholly reminiscent of the Incas' own entangled successions.

Despite his death, the Spaniards pressed southward. Their speed allowed them to surprise and defeat a retreating Inca army stationed at Vilcashuaman, but a tired advance Spanish force was surprised as it neared Cuzco and the Spaniards suffered their first real defeat of the invasion. Five or six soldiers under Soto's command fell in close combat at Vilcaconga, as the surviving Ruiz de Arce described. Fortunately for them, the remaining soldiers lasted the night and, joined overnight by reinforcements, routed the attacking forces the next day. Once Pizarro's principal forces were reunited, they received a report that Quizquiz's warriors were in the act of torching the city. Pizarro immediately dispatched a cavalry brigade, but they were repelled in pitched battle at a point that controlled access to the urban core. Realizing that they could not defend the city, the demoralized force that had just won a war abandoned its defense overnight. Unopposed, Pizarro's men occupied the pivot of the universe on November 15, 1533, a year to the day after marching into the Inca camp at Cajamarca (Hemming 1970: 117).

Cuzco under Co-rule

In the days just preceding their entry into Cuzco, the youthful solution to one of the Spaniards' most vexing problems presented himself in person at Jaquixaguana. Manqo Inka, yet another of Wayna Qhapaq's sons, had escaped the massacre in Cuzco inflicted by Kusi Yupanki on Atawallpa's behalf (chapter 4). The conquistadores' appearance provided him with a chance to lay claim to the throne at the same time that it offered the Spaniards another apparently compliant puppet through whom they could govern. Manqo Inka immediately denounced the Spaniards' great hostage, the general Challcochima. While in captivity, he had been sending messages to his compatriot Quizquiz, apprising him of the Spaniards' vulnerabilities. Enraged, Pizarro had him burned at the stake, while the general called on Wiraqocha, Wanakawri, and Quizquiz to avenge him (Hemming 2012: loc. 1707/14165 [Kindle edn.]).

The force marching into Cuzco thus contained both Inca and Spanish representatives of power. Pizarro quickly set about assigning most of Cuzco's palaces and other buildings to members of his party and the Spaniards undertook their search for booty with a vengeance. They looted the Qorikancha over the strident protests of its priests and generally stripped the imperial capital of its wealth. Only a few of the Spaniards were perceptive enough to lament the destruction (Segovia 1968; Hemming 1970: 134–5). That December, Manqo Inka was formally installed as the Inca ruler, with all of the elaborate ceremonies that attended the coronation of a new monarch. Among the most attentive participants were the embalmed mummies of his ancestors, each crowned and dressed in finery and carried on his own litter (Estete 1985). The festivities – which seemed like little more than extended drunken debauchery to the invaders – lasted for a full month. Pizarro took the opportunity to address the collected aristocracy at one point, repeating the Spanish legalities concerning submission or retribution, after which the Spaniards and new Sapa Inca settled into an uneasy co-rule of the land.

Throughout the next year, the Spaniards met considerable resistance in their efforts to pacify the land. In Ecuador especially, the Inca armies led by Rumiñawi and Quizquiz led a prolonged series of campaigns against the Spaniards. Ultimately, Quizquiz's men rebelled against the continuation of the resistance and killed him, while Rumiñawi was captured and executed by the Spaniards under Benalcázar. At the same time, the Spaniards in Cuzco had renewed their incessant quarrels and Manqo Inka was having difficulty in gaining full support among the remaining Incas. All of these situations had many complications, far too intricate to detail here. An important outcome of these events, however, was the dispatching of Almagro to complete the conquest of the southern Andes, accompanied by another royal brother, Paullu Inka, and the high priest of the Sun, the Willaq Umu.

Over time, Manqo Inka came to realize that his role would never achieve equal status with that of the Spaniards. To the contrary, he would remain a puppet at best. He therefore began to plot a way to escape Spanish supervision and take on the role of leader of the resistance. After one abortive attempt, he managed to escape from Cuzco and began to assemble an army intended to expel the Spaniards, not just from the capital but from the entire land. The resistance came to concrete fruition in 1536, as massive armies

were assembled to lay siege to Cuzco and attack the newly founded Ciudad de Los Reyes (Lima) on the coast. The siege of Cuzco was a lengthy
affair, sustained by somewhere between 200,000 and 400,000 soldiers and
other personnel. Within the desperate capital, there were only a few hundred Spaniards supported by barely more than 1,000 native auxiliaries. The
Incas employed all manner of tactics, including burning the city and flood-
ing the surrounding lands to counter the Spaniards' advantage on horses.
After some time, the Spaniards recognized that they could reduce the direct
attacks by capturing the fortified complex of Saqsawaman above the city.
Led by the young Juan Pizarro, who lost his life in the assault, the Spaniards
drove the Incas out through daring mounted attacks and by scaling the walls
with ladders and winning hand-to-hand combat. In the end, however, the
Spaniards survived the siege because of the demands of the agricultural
cycle. Slowly, but inexorably, the native soldier-farmers disbanded to tend
their fields at home. The next year, another siege was mounted, but it too
failed to take its objective.

On the coast, the attack on Ciudad de Los Reyes in 1536 took the form
of a direct frontal assault. Despite the Incas' overwhelming advantage in
numbers, they suffered from a singular tactical disadvantage. Rather than
oversee battles from a strategic vantage point out of immediate harm's way,
the Inca leadership formed up a vanguard that led their forces into battle.
Recognizing the weakness in such a formation, the Spaniards withdrew into
the city streets. As the Inca commanding officers entered the town, they
were at their most vulnerable, and so were targeted and wiped out. Lead-
erless, the army scattered into the hills in a single night. They left some of
their dead behind, to be discovered just a few years ago along the margins of
the Puruchuco-Huaquerones cemetery (Cock and Goycochea Díaz 2004).
Study of the human remains from a sector of that burial ground found
injuries consistent with firearms and other sixteenth-century European
weapons. The authors infer that the many of the deceased had expired from
the violence that marked the Spanish conquest (Murphy *et al.* 2010: 636).

In retrospect, the early Spanish victories over the Incas can be assigned to
a coincidence of biological, historical, technological, and cultural factors.
Even before the Spaniards took up arms against the Andean peoples, a
wave of smallpox had triggered the deaths of the ruler Wayna Qhapaq
and his designated successor Ninan Kuyuchi. It also took its toll on the
populace, likely rendering a significant portion of it unable to resist.
From the point of view of history, the Spaniards could not have arrived
at a more opportune moment. The victorious Incas in Cajamarca fatally

underestimated the threat posed by the small band of invaders. Later, once Atawallpa had been removed from the picture, perhaps half of the people of the Andes were willing to ally themselves with the Spaniards to save themselves from the bloody retribution that Atawallpa's armies had already visited on many of Waskhar's adherents. These new allies provided thousands of seasoned warriors, along with support personnel and supplies (see Espinoza Soriano 1972).

The conquistadores also had enormous technological advantages in their weapons and armor, but the horses gave them the greatest initial tactical advantage. Native soldiers and battle tactics were simply no match for mounted Spaniards on open terrain and several early engagements amounted to little more than slaughter. The Incas soon learned to dig pits on open fields and restricted many engagements to the kinds of broken terrain that favored their weapons and negated the horses' utility, but those gains simply prolonged the conflict and did not turn the tide in the natives' favor. The Spaniards had another early tactical advantage – their willingness to take the initiative at every opportunity, which ran contrary to the deliberative Inca approach to warfare. Often, their attacks in the face of overwhelming odds helped to break the morale of the native soldiers. Despite the importance of military action at pivotal moments, the longer run foundation of Spanish success lay in their willingness to exploit every advantage that they could, though political intrigue, alliances of convenience, and deception and betrayal as the moment seemed to require (see Rowe 2006).

A number of Andean ideas of order also contributed to the conquistadores' successes. One was the personalized and deified nature of Inca leadership. Initially, with the apparent sovereign held hostage, his subordinates were handicapped in their ability to undertake military initiatives. Once Atawallpa was gone, no leader existed who would be recognized by all and who could marshal a unified resistance. In the end, the practice of mobilizing soldiers seasonally from farmers and herders also meant that it was difficult, if not impossible, to maintain pressure on Spanish enclaves ensconced in Inca installations and the resistance movement stalled. The Incas had no choice but to make a tactical retreat.

An Empire Condensed

The early Inca defeats did not end Andean aspirations for self-rule, but simply sent the empire into the eastern forests or underground. For thirty-six

years after their unsuccessful efforts to throw the Spaniards out of Cuzco and
Lima, the Incas maintained an independent state in the Vilcabamba area,
about 200 km down the Urubamba river from Cuzco (Guillén Guillén 1994;
Lee 2000; Nowack 2006; MacQuarrie 2007: 305–30; Hemming 2012). While
the Incas had established a presence in the region before the Spaniards ever
appeared, the existing settlements were elaborated by Manqo Inka after his
escape from Cuzco, and by his successors. Spanish forays pushed them out
of their initial occupation at Vitcos-Rosaspata, but Vilcabamba provided a
relatively safe haven for the Incas to preserve their liberty and foment plans
for regaining their lost lands (figure 14.3, plate 14.1). Over time, a series of
Inca rulers headed up the shrunken polity: Manqo Inka, Sayri Tupac, Titu
Kusi Yupanki, and Tupac Amaru.

The archaeological remains of Inca Vilcabamba have received increased
attention in recent years. Hiram Bingham's expedition in 1911 actually
found the main Inca royal settlements at Vitcos-Rosaspata (plate 14.2) and
Espíritu Pampa, but he failed to recognize them as such, settling mistakenly
on Machu Picchu as the fabled lost capital of Vilcabamba. It was left to the
explorer Gene Savoy (1970) and later the adventurous architect Vincent
Lee (2000) to rediscover the sites and bring them to the outside world's
attention. Lee's research has been especially fruitful, as he has mapped,
photographed and rendered sketched reconstructions of the settlements

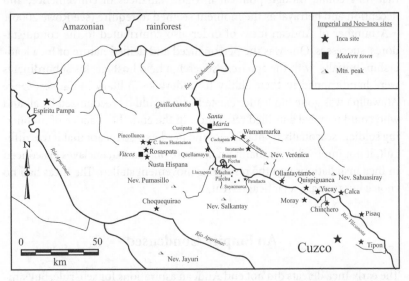

Figure 14.3   Map of Inca sites in the Cuzco heartland and Vilcabamba region.

Plate 14.1 Paved Inca road through the royal coca estates in Amaybamba. Source: reproduced by permission of Darryl Wilkinson.

in some detail (e.g., figure 14.4). His work shows that the settlements were similar to the estates in the Vilcanota/Urubamba drainage. They contained complexes of large rectangular buildings arrayed around spacious plazas,

Plate 14.2   Setting of Vitcos-Rosaspata, the first neo-Inca capital.

laid out on uneven terrain. The constructions received the royal treatment, in their use of ashlar masonry for instance, and in the carving of stone formations both within them and nearby. Among the best-known carvings are those at Ñusta Hispana, which contain all the hallmarks of boulders shaped with smooth planes, channels, and niches, directly associated with channelized springs and watercourses.[6]

With support from some of the highland populace, the Incas under Manqo Inka, Titu Kusi Yupanki, and Thupa Amaru mounted campaigns from their diminished jungle empire. They harassed the Spaniards with forces that emerged from the eastern slopes and punished their Andean collaborators through raids and massacres. Any number of diplomatic

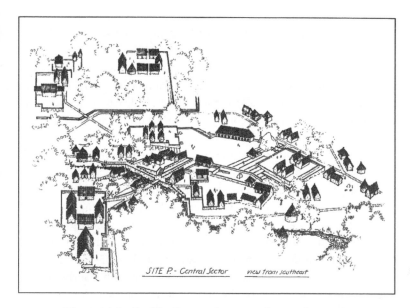

Figure 14.4 Espíritu Pampa city center. Source: Lee 1999.

and military expeditions were sent into the forests, or from Vilcabamba to Cuzco, in an effort to bring the holdouts into the Spanish realm peaceably or otherwise, but to no resolution. As noted earlier in this chapter, Titu Kusi (2005) himself made an effort to work things out, by writing a lengthy missive to the king of Spain, explaining how they ought to co-exist peaceably as rulers of independent realms. Regrettably, he died before any action was taken on his unlikely proposition.

Vilcabamba finally fell in 1572 to an expedition mounted by Viceroy Toledo, for whom the continued existence of a free Inca society had become an insufferable affront to the Crown. When finally taken, the redoubt was almost vacant (Nowack 2006: 61), as the Incas had been unable to keep up much of a resident population. The last ruler, Thupa Amaru, was captured and transported to Cuzco, where he was rapidly convicted of treason and sentenced to death. Numerous Spaniards interceded on his behalf in an effort to save his life, but Toledo was apparently convinced that the only definitive way to break the spine of rebelliousness was to execute the king. Thus, on September 24, 1572, the last of the Inca monarchs was marched into the plaza of his ancestors' majesty and beheaded, bringing an end to the lineage that had descended from the Sun to rule the earth.

The Imposition of Spanish Rule

While the Incas maintained their independence on the eastern side of the Andes, the Spaniards set about killing one another in a series of civil wars that were slowly and erratically supplanted by stable Colonial government. The account of that era is a complicated story in and of itself, but a few key developments can be highlighted here. Francisco Pizarro, architect of Tawantinsuyu's overthrow, did not live long to enjoy his hard-won status as governor of the new land. He soon fell out with his shortchanged and aggrieved partner, Diego de Almagro, the elder. The latter seized Cuzco from Pizarro in 1537 and installed Paullu Inka as a new puppet ruler. The first chapter of this conflict came to an end the next year, with Almagro's death at the hands of Hernando Pizarro, but Almagro's adherents took their vengeance by murdering Francisco Pizarro himself in 1541. The decade of the 1540s continued to be plagued by a series of Spanish insurrections that were ultimately dampened by the arrival of new officials from Spain with the mandate of bringing peace to the troubled land. The last major rebellion was staged by Francisco Hernández Girón in 1553–4, whose defeat came about largely because of the military action of the Wankas allied with the Spanish Crown.

The decapitation of the Inca administrative apparatus resulted in a power vacuum above the level of the regional ethnic group or perhaps even the village. In the face of the Spanish internecine wars, continued Inca resistance, the collapse of the native populace, and the atomized ethnic landscape, it took decades for any semblance of new state order to take effect. The circumstances meant that the incorporation of the Crown's new subjects was a spotty affair, particularly at the village level, but inroads were still made. As the 1540s gave way to later decades, the Spaniards systematically inspected their new holdings. Along with other documents, those records provide some details of life after the loss of Inca dominion and before the Colonial administration really took hold. For Andean peoples civil wars, forced labor, and pestilence wrought devastation on the populace. Within about forty years of the invasion, the population had declined by about 50 percent (Cook 1981). In some coastal valleys, the population ultimately fell to as little as one-twentieth of its size in 1532.

The ways in which Spanish policies rewarded the conquistadores contributed heavily to the devastation. During the earliest years of Colonial rule, native peoples were awarded to individual Spanish soldiers as grants (*encomiendas*) to be exploited. Eighty-eight of the original conquistadores decided to stay in the new land under that umbrella, rather than take their riches back home. More than a few of them treated their vassals as little more than a source of labor to make the new lords rich. The widespread abuse of the native populace, coupled with the theft of their lands, increasingly insupportable tax burdens, death in the mines, and the destruction of the Andean way of life, has understandably given rise to an image of a black time in the former Tawantinsuyu.

Even so, Andeans and Europeans could form alliances as they adjusted to the changing circumstances. Moreover, the Crown and some of the religious institutions took an interest in protecting the well-being of the native population, who turned to the new political structure to resolve disputes among themselves. Many of those disputes arose from multiple claims to prime resources by the colonists installed by the Incas and the local peoples who were trying to reclaim the lands of their ancestors (see, e.g., D'Altroy 1994a). Depending on how it suited their argument, plaintiffs claimed rights based on the pre-Inca situation, awards granted by the Incas, or Spanish legal principles, such as primogeniture. The disputes became so numerous that the Crown authority eventually established the office of native notary and instituted native courts, which held the mandate for resolving local disputes. An intriguing corollary to their practice was the provision that they not keep records, apparently to limit the profusion of paperwork drowning the Colonial authorities (Burns 2010).

Beginning in 1551, the Spanish Crown dispatched a series of viceroys to bring order to the land, which was still riven by civil wars among the last of the conquistadores. Slowly, civil administration was installed and the Spaniards began to take a closer interest in Andean culture. One of the most perceptive of the administrators was Juan Polo Ondegardo, the Magistrate of Cuzco who has been mentioned often in this text. It is Polo who has provided us with much of our knowledge on Inca political organization, economics, religion, and social customs. He also made the startling discovery in 1558 that the descendants of the Inca kings were still worshiping their ancestors' mummies. Horrified, he launched a successful campaign to find the mummies and dispatched them to the coast, while destroying the brother icons of the rulers (table 6.1).

The most sweeping reforms occurred under the administration of Viceroy Toledo, in 1570–2. The most drastic change was the *reducción*, or resettlement, of native peoples out of their traditional communities into new villages near Spanish centers, where they could be supervised more closely for signs of rebellion and lapses from Catholicism. Toledo also drew members of the local societies into the Crown's administrative orbit, by creating native judges who handled low-level cases like property disputes through summary judgments (see above). The indigenous notaries themselves were drawn from the ranks of knowledgeable *khipu kamayuq* (Burns 2010). The idea apparently was to shift certain kinds of native recording into forms that the Spaniards could control, while creating a class of officials whose dual allegiances would help to civilize the Crown's subjects. Many of their tasks were involved with parish affairs, contracts, and wills. With Toledo's reforms and his destruction of the neo-Inca state of Vilcabamba came the end of any semblance of Inca independence in their once proud land.

Wernke's archaeological studies (2010, 2012a, 2012b) in the Colca valley, in Arequipa, Peru, provide insight into how the changes took practical form in one well-populated highland region. An important early imprint was the reconfiguration of social and ritual space and time with the imposition of the new Christian religion. At Malata, a small Inca outpost, the Franciscan order established a new *doctrina* (church district) some time in the 1540s to 1550s, which functioned until the settlement was abandoned during Toledo's reforms. While a church representative was present only intermittently or even at a distance, the changes that were made were few but telling. Most crucially, patterns of movement through the community were reformed, so that the previous center of political and ritual activity – an Inca plaza – was marginalized. The new Christian chapel, which became the touchpoint between the residents and Spanish life, took its place as the focal point of traffic. The restructuring of space at Malata was an incipient example of practices implemented widely in the Spanish holdings in the Americas. In contrast to often agglutinated Andean communities with their meandering pathways, the imposed Spanish settlement plan was a grid focused around a central plaza with its chapel. In the interest of civilizing the populace, household access and spaces were reconfigured to minimize privacy and the immoral or idolatrous practices that they might conceal (Cummins and Rappaport 1998). The goal was nothing less than restructuring people's vision and movement.

The communities' use of land also changed over the years. Many of the terraces and canals so painstakingly constructed over the millennia were abandoned throughout the Andes. Denevan (1987) estimated that fully half of the prehispanic terraces still remained unused toward the end of the twentieth century. Even in the Colca valley, home to some of the most extraordinary terraces in the Americas, widespread abandonment occurred over the first couple of centuries of Colonial rule (Wernke 2010). The population had plummeted, so both demand and the available labor pool decreased in proportion. That situation required that the resettled, remnant communities make hard choices about which irrigation and terracing systems to maintain. Their choices tended to depend on local conditions, so that elevation was important to some people, and distance to the fields important to others. In the area that Wernke studied, over 60 percent of the bench terraces and more than 50 percent of all fields remain unused even today.

The Inca Reborn

Shortly after the discovery and capture of the Inca mummies, a new clandestine movement came to light called the *Taki Onqoy*, or "Dancing Sickness" (Mumford 1998). The Taki Onqoy was a millenarian movement intended to reject all things European and restore the traditional Andean order. In its visible activities, the movement featured ecstatic dancing during which the participants went into trances as if possessed; its leaders also seem to have encouraged the accumulation of weapons as part of an anticipated rebellion. Thus, it was both a response to Catholic efforts to rid the Andes of indigenous religious traditions and an effort to throw off Spanish rule. In an odd twist of confused allegiances, however, the Taki Onqoy was discovered when a participant revealed its existence in the Catholic confessional. The alarmed priest quickly got word to Lima and the Spanish authorities undertook an intensive campaign to find the weapons and call the perceived leaders to account. In the end, the popular uprising never occurred, but its threat fed into careers and conflicts among the Spaniards. The crusading cleric Cristóbal de Albornoz, for example, through whose writings we know of the movement, used its suppression as a platform to advance his career.

As memory of the Incas as living, oppressive rulers began to fade from the popular consciousness, another image of late prehistory as a glorious epoch began to coalesce among Andean peoples, not just the Incas themselves. Over the centuries of Colonial rule, the myth of *Inkarrí* began to take form. He was a syncretic figure who blended the Inca with the *rey* (Spanish king), a man who would return to the Andes to free the native peoples from the bondage into which the Spanish conquest had cast them. Even in modern times, ethnographers have recorded cycles of myths about *Inkarrí* recalling a glorious past that can still be reborn (Urton 1999: 73–5).

The Inca Legacy

Despite the violence, disease, and cultural transformations that Andean peoples experienced during the Colonial era, the legacy of Tawantinsuyu continues to shape the people and cultures of western South America, especially in the Peruvian highlands where many communities still follow traditional ways of life. The most deeply embedded features still lie within the social fabric of local communities and the cultural philosophies that give meaning to relationships among people and between them and the land (Allen 2002; Estermann 2006). Most importantly, life is still defined by links among close kin and an ethic of mutual support. It is not unusual for peasant communities outside the larger towns to be divided into moieties comparable to the upper and lower divisions of ancient times and for young men and women to look for a marriage partner across divisions of local kin groups (e.g., Isbell 1978). Many highland villagers today still rely on cooperative ownership of resources and share the risks and rewards of making an agricultural or pastoral living in the demanding environment (e.g., Flores Ochoa 1978). Similarly, civic tasks, including rebuilding walls, cleaning canals, and maintaining public spaces are still divided up among *ayllu* (Gary Urton, pers. comm. 1997).

The relationship of the people to the land and sky still retains a vibrancy that is expressed in the knowledge, beliefs, and cycles of ceremonies practiced by many communities. Gary Urton (1981), for example, has found that the people of Misminay, not too far from Cuzco, still observe many of the same constellations and celestial passages that formed part of the Inca cosmology in the sixteenth century. Similarly, offerings of coca and *chicha* are often made to Pachamama, the earth mother, throughout the highlands to give thanks for successful harvests (Abercrombie 1998). In Cuzco itself, the celebrations of *Quyllor Rit'i* and *Inti Raymi* have regained a vitality that was dampened in centuries past by the Catholic Church. Some of the celebrations can be attributed to events staged for the tourist trade, but the pilgrimages to high-elevation shrines are clearly not a reinvention of an ancient tradition, but part of a living belief system (Sallnow 1987). Residents of the towns on the high slopes within a day's walk of Cuzco still follow the well-trodden ritual pathways to the summits of Huanacauri, Nevado Sinakara, and nearby peaks to make offerings to the ancient powers that inhabit the landscape. Those events are not taken light-heartedly, even though they feature music and dancing, since the climbs to the summits

Plate 14.3 Pilgrims ascending snow fields in the annual ceremonial trek to the high peaks during the festival of *Quyllor Rit'i*. Source: reproduced by permission of Vicente Revilla.

through permanent snow fields occasionally claim the lives of pilgrims who have lived in the high communities since birth (V. Revilla, pers. comm. 2000; plate 14.3). Many of the ritual calendars have been blended with those of the Catholic Church, of course, but the cycles are still attuned to the ebb and flow of the seasons and stars.

Despite their desire for continuity, a decreasing number of traditional communities hold out as best they can in the face of political strife, modern transport, and communications technology (Abercrombie 1998; Allen 2002). In Peru, the Shining Path and Tupac Amaru insurrections of the 1980s forced many people from their rural homes into the relative safety of more urbanized areas. The attractions of the more modern world have also contributed to the growth of Lima, La Paz, Quito, and, to a lesser extent, Cuzco. That shift has been coupled with increased political action by people long on the outside of national power. As the populations have moved and grown, the archaeological landscape is rapidly disappearing from sight under modern construction. Much of the more portable material legacy of the Andean ancestors has also found its way into private and institutional collections, often illicitly. At the same time, the shrinking but still rich archaeological heritage is rapidly being translated from cultural

Plate 14.4 *Inti Raymi* festival celebrated at Saqsaywaman. Source: reproduced by permission of Johan Reinhard.

patrimony to tourist magnet, marketed internationally in tandem with the spectacular landscape (plate 14.4; Herrera 2013). The Incas' legacy is especially attractive because it combines the beauties of the land with the visually striking archaeological remains found at Cuzco, Machu Picchu, and other sites. Recent growth is a double-edged sword, however, as the degrading effects of tourism will be unsustainable into the future. One of the great challenges facing the Andean nations today is how to harness the economic potential of archaeo-tourism without destroying its very foundations.

In the face of all those transitions, the Incas still retain enormous potency in the self-image of the Peruvian nation. For a time in the 1980s, the national currency was called the *inti*, named after the Sun God of the Incas, and the currency of recent times is still named the *sol*, i.e., the Spanish word for the sun. There are also many referents to the prehispanic past in popular culture. For example, the national soft drink of Peru is a cream soda called Inca Kola and there are many regional variants that draw on ancient names, such as Chavín Cola and Ccori (golden) Cola. References to Inca glory pervade modern politics as well, as even presidential candidates dance to the ancient pipes and drums. No more compelling reminder of the cultural weight of the Incas in modern society can be found than in the protests surrounding the presidential election in Peru in 2000. The election pitted the sitting president against a Peruvian-born but Stanford-trained economist whose personal appearance and cultural vision harked back to the times when the Incas ruled themselves. When a massive rally was staged in Lima to protest the political process, it was called "La Marcha de los Cuatro Suyos" or "The March of the Four Parts." The times may be changing, but the Inca legacy is still alive.

Notes

1   This summary draws heavily from Hemming's (1970: 2012) and MacQuarrie's (2007) excellent narrative histories; for eyewitness accounts, see Sancho 1917; Ruiz de Arce 1933; Mena 1937; Estete 1985; Xérez 1985.
2   Rowe (2006) points out that the official version of events was propounded to show Pizarro in the best light possible, and that there are several reasons to doubt the veracity of aspects of the account.
3   Titu Kusi Yupanki's document was part of an effort to establish his legitimacy as ruler of an Andean domain, and thus put him in a position to establish credentials as an equal for the purpose of creating diplomatic relations with the king of Spain as an equal (Salomon 2005).
4   There is some discord among the early Spanish accounts as to whether Thupa Wallpa had appeared in Cajamarca before or after Atawallpa's execution, and was therefore potentially complicit in his death (Rowe 2006).
5   Within just a few years, they moved the capital to the coastal town of Ciudad de Los Reyes (Lima), apparently owing to a lack of firewood and adequate grazing for their horses.
6   It is hoped that excavations conducted by the National Institute of Culture at Espíritu Pampa and Ñusta Hispana by Brian Bauer will be published soon, providing detailed information on those sites. Current work in the region is complicated, however, by drug trafficking.

References

Abercrombie, Thomas A. (1998). *Pathways of Memory and Power: Ethnography and History among an Andean People.* University of Wisconsin Press, Madison.

Acosta, José de (1986). *Historia natural y moral de las Indias.* Historia 16, Madrid. (Originally written 1590.)

Acuto, Félix A. (2010). Living under the Imperial Thumb. In *Distant Provinces in the Inka Empire: Toward a Deeper Understanding of Inka Imperialism*, edited by Michael Malpass and Sonia Alconini, pp. 109–50. University of Iowa Press, Iowa City.

Adamska, Anna, and Adam Michecsynski (1996). Towards Radiocarbon Chronology of the Inca State. *Andes. Boletín de la Misión Arqueológica Andina* 1: 35–58.

Adelaar, Willem F. H., and Peter C. Muysken (2004). *Languages of the Andes.* Cambridge University Press, Cambridge.

Adorno, Rolena (1986). *Guaman Poma: Writing and Resistance in Colonial Peru.* University of Texas Press, Austin.

Adorno, Rolena (2001). *Guaman Poma and His Illustrated Chronicle from Colonial Peru: From a Century of Scholarship to a New Era of Reading.* Museum Tusculanum Press, University of Copenhagen and the Royal Library, Copenhagen.

Agurto Calvo, Santiago (1980). *Cuzco – Traza urbana de la ciudad Inca.* Proyecto Per 39, UNESCO, Instituto Nacional de Cultura del Perú, Cuzco.

Agurto Calvo, Santiago (1987). *Estudios acerca de la construcción, arquitectura, y planeamiento incas.* Cámara Peruana de la Construcción, Lima.

Aimi, Antonio, and Nicolino De Pasquale (n.d.). Andean Calculators. Online. Available at www.quipus.it (accessed via Google Scholar).

Albarracín-Jordan, Juan, and James E. Mathews (1992). *Asentamientos prehispánicos del Valle de Tiwanaku.* Producciones CIMA, La Paz. Albeck, María. E.

Albarracín-Jordan, Juan, and James E. Mathews (1992–3). Areas agrícolas y densidad de ocupación prehispánica en la Quebrada de Humahuaca. *Avances en Arqueología* 2: 56–77.

Albeck, María E., and M. Cristina Scattolin (1991). Cálculo fotogramétrico de superficies de cultivo en Coctaca y Rodero, Quebrada de Humahuaca. *Avances en Arqueología* 1: 43–58.

The Incas, Second Edition. Terence N. D'Altroy.
© 2015 John Wiley & Sons, Ltd. Published 2015 by John Wiley & Sons, Ltd.

Alberti, Giorgio, and Enrique Mayer, eds. (1974). *Reciprocidad e intercambio en los andes peruanos*. Instituto de Estudios Peruanos, Lima.

Albornoz, Christobal de (1989). Instrucción para descubrir todas las guacas del Piru y sus camayos y haziendas. In *Fábulas y mitos de los Incas*, edited by Henrique Urbano and Pierre Duviols. Crónicas de America 48, pp. 161–98. Historia 16, Madrid. (Originally written 1582.)

Alcina Franch, José (1978). Ingapirca: arquitectura y áreas de asentamiento. *Revista Española de Antropología Americana* 8: 127–46.

Alcina Franch, José, Miguel Rivera, Jesus Galván, María Carmen García Palacios, Mercedes Guinea, Balbina Martínez-Caviró, Luis J. Ramos, and Tito Varela (1976). *Arqueología de Chinchero, 2. Cerámica y otros materiales*. Ministerio de Asuntos Exteriores, Madrid.

Alcock, Susan, Terence N. D'Altroy, Kathleen Morrison, and Carla Sinopoli, eds. (2001). *Empires*. Cambridge University Press, Cambridge.

Alconini, Sonia (2004). The Southeastern Inka Frontier against the Chiriguanos: Structure and Dynamics of the Inka Imperial Borderlands. *Latin American Antiquity* 15: 389–418.

Alconini, Sonia (2008). Dis-embedded Centers and Architecture of Power in the Fringes of the Inka Empire: New Perspectives on Territorial and Hegemonic Strategies of Domination. *Journal of Anthropological Archaeology* 27(1): 63–81.

Alconini, Sonia (2010). Alliances and Local Prestige: Yampara Households and Communal Evolution in the Southeastern Inka Peripheries. In *Distant Provinces in the Inka Empire: Toward a Deeper Understanding of Inka Imperialism*, edited by Michael Malpass and Sonia Alconini, pp. 75–108. University of Iowa Press, Iowa City.

Algaze, Guillermo (2005). *The Uruk World System: The Dynamics of Expansion of Early Mesopotamian Civilization*. 2nd edn. University of Chicago Press, Chicago.

Allen, Catherine (2002). *The Hold Life Has*. 2nd edn. Smithsonian Institution Press, Washington, DC.

Alva, Walter, and Christopher B. Donnan (1994). *Royal Tombs of Sipán*. 2nd edn. Fowler Museum of Cultural History, University of California, Los Angeles.

Ambrosetti, Juan B. (1902). El sepulcro de La Paya últimamente descubierto en los valles Calchaquíes, Provincia de Salta. *Anales del Museo Nacional* 8: 119–48.

Ambrosetti, Juan B. (1907–8). *Exploraciones arqueológicas en la ciudad prehistórica de "La Paya" (Valle Calchaquí, Provincia de Salta)*. 2 vols. Revista de la Universidad de Buenos Aires, Facultad de Filosofía y Letras, vol. 8 (Sección Antropología, 3). M. Biedmaé hijo, Buenos Aires.

Andrien, Kenneth (2008). The Virtual and the Real: The Case of the Mysterious Documents from Naples. *History Compass* 6/5: 1304–24.

Andrushko, Valerie A., Michele R. Buzon, Arminda M. Gibaja, Gordon F. McEwan, Antonio Simonetti, and Robert A. Creaser (2011). Investigating a Child Sacrifice Event from the Inca Heartland. *Journal of Archaeological Science* 38: 323–33.

Andrushko Valerie A., Michele R. Buzon, Antonio Simonetti, and Robert A. Creaser (2009). Strontium Isotope Evidence for Prehistoric Migration at Chokepukio, Valley of Cuzco, Peru. *Latin American Antiquity* 20(1): 57–75.

Andrushko Valerie A., E. C. Torres Pino, and V. Bellifemine (2006). The Burials at Sacsahuaman and Chokepukio: A Bioarchaeological Case Study of Imperialism from the Capital of the Inca Empire. *Ñawpa Pacha* 28: 63–92.

Angles Vargas, Victor (1970). *P'isaq: Metrópoli inka*. Industrial Gráfica, Lima.

Anon. (1934). Relación del sitio del Cuzco y principio de las guerras del Perú hasta la muerte de Diego de Almagro. In *Colección de libros y documentos inéditos para la historia del Perú*, edited by Carlos A. Romero and Horacio H. Urteaga, vol. 2. Sociedad de Bibliófolos Peruanos, Lima.

Arkush, Elizabeth (2011). *Hillforts of the Ancient Andes*. University Press of Florida, Gainesville.

Arriaga, Jesús (1965). *Apuntes de arqueología Cañar*. Universidad de Cuenca, Cuenca, Ecuador.

Ascher, Marcia, and Robert Ascher (1981). *Code of the Quipu*. University of Michigan Press, Ann Arbor.

Ascher, Robert (2002). Inka Writing. In *Narrative Threads: Accounting and Recounting in Andean Khipu*, edited by Jeffrey Quilter and Gary Urton, pp. 103–15. University of Texas Press, Austin.

Atienza, Lope de (1931). Compendio historial del estado de los indios del Perú. In *La religión del imperio de los Incas. Apéndice I*, edited by Jacinto Jijón y Caamaño, vol. 1, pp. 1–235. Escuela Tipográfica Salesiana, Quito. (Originally written 1575?)

Aveni, Anthony F. (2002). *The lines of Nazca*. American Philosophical Society, Philadelphia.

Bandelier, Adoph F. (1910). *The Islands of Titicaca and Coati*. Hispanic Society of America, New York.

Barfield, Thomas J. (2001). The Shadow Empires: Imperial State Formation along the Chinese–Nomad Frontier. In *Empires: Perspectives from Archaeology and History*, edited by Susan Alcock *et al.* pp. 10–41. Cambridge University Press, Cambridge.

Barnes, Monica (2010). John Victor Murra's Provincial Inca Life Project and American Anthropology. *Antiquity* 84(326). Online. Available at www.antiquity.ac.uk /projgall/barnes326/ (accessed December 15, 2013).

Basso, Keith (1988). Speaking with Names: Language and Landscape among the Western Apache. *Cultural Anthropology* 3(2): 99–130.

Bauer, Brian S. (1991). Pacariqtambo and the Mythical Origins of the Inca. *Latin American Antiquity* 2: 7–26.

Bauer, Brian S. (1992). *The Development of the Inca State*. University of Texas Press, Austin.

Bauer, Brian S. (1996). The Legitimization of the Inca State in Myth and Ritual. *American Anthropologist* 98(2): 327–37.

Bauer, Brian S. (1998). *The Sacred Landscape of the Inca: The Cusco Ceque System.* University of Texas Press, Austin.

Bauer, Brian S. (2004). *Ancient Cuzco: Heartland of the Inca.* University of Texas Press, Austin.

Bauer, Brian. S., and R. Alan Covey (2002). Processes of State Formation in the Inca Heartland (Cuzco, Peru). *American Anthropologist* 104: 846–64.

Bauer, Brian. S., and R. Alan Covey (2004). The Development of the Inca State. In Brian Bauer, *Ancient Cuzco: Heartland of the Inca.* pp. 71–90. Austin, University of Texas Press.

Bauer, Brian S., and Antonio Coello Rodríguez (2007). The Hospital of San Andrés (Lima, Peru) and the Search for the Royal Mummies of The Incas. *Fieldiana Anthropology* 39: 1–31.

Bauer, Brian S., and David S. P. Dearborn (1995). *Astronomy and Empire in the Ancient Andes.* University of Texas Press, Austin.

Bauer, Brian S., and Jean-Jacques DeCoster (2007). Introduction: Pedro Sarmiento de Gamboa and *The History of the Incas.* In *The History of the Incas,* by Pedro Sarmiento de Gamboa, translated and edited by Brian S. Bauer and Vania Smith, pp. 1–34. University of Texas Press, Austin.

Bauer, Brian S., and Charles Stanish (1990). *Killke and Killke-Related Pottery from Cuzco, Peru, in the Field Museum of Natural History.* Fieldiana Anthropology, new series 15. Field Museum of Natural History, Chicago

Bauer, Brian S., and Charles Stanish (2001). *Ritual and Pilgrimage in the Ancient Andes: The Islands of the Sun and Moon.* Austin, University of Texas Press.

Bauer, Brian S., Lucas C. Kellett, and Miriam Aráoz Silva (2010). *The Chanka: Archaeological Research in Andahuaylas (Apurimac), Peru.* Monograph 68, Cotsen Institute of Archaeology Press, UCLA, Los Angeles.

Bengtsson, Lisbet (1998a). The Concept of Time/Space in Quechua: Some Considerations. In *Past and Present in Andean Prehistory and Early History,* edited by Sven Ahlgren, Adriana Muñoz, Susana Sjödin, and Per Stenborg. Ethnological Studies 42, pp. 119–27. Gothenburg: Ethnographic Museum.

Bengtsson, Lisbet (1998b). *Prehistoric Stonework in the Peruvian Andes: A Case Study at Ollantaytambo.* Göteborg University, Dept. of Archaeology: Etnografiska museet, Göteborg.

Beorchia Nigris, Antonio (1987). *El enigma de los santuarios indígenas de alta montaña.* Centro de Investigaciones Arqueologicas de Alta Montaña, San Juan, Argentina.

Berberián, Eduardo E., and Rodolfo A. Raffino (1991). *Culturas indígenas de los Andes Meridionales.* Alhambra, Madrid.

Bergh, Susan E. (1993). Death and Renewal in Moche Phallic-Spouted Vessels. *Res: Anthropology and Aesthetics* 24: 78–94.

Berthelot, Jean (1986). The Extraction of Precious Metals at the Time of the Inka. In *Anthropological History of Andean Polities,* edited by John V. Murra, Nathan Wachtel, and Jacques Revel, pp. 69–88. Cambridge University Press, Cambridge.

Bertonio, Ludovico (1956). *Vocabulario de la lengua aymara.* Facscimile edition. La Paz. (Originally written 1612.)

Besom, Thomas (2009). *Of Summits and Sacrifice: An Ethnohistorical Study of Inka Religious Practices.* University of Texas Press, Austin.

Bibar, Gerónimo de (1966). *Crónica y relación copiosa y verdadera de los reynos de Chile,* edited by Irving A. Leonard. Fondo Histórico y Bibliográfico José Toribio Medina, Santiago de Chile. (Originally written 1558.)

Bingham, Hiram (1913). In the Wonderland of Peru. The Work Accomplished by the Peruvian Expedition of 1912, under the Auspices of Yale University and the National Geographic Society. *National Geographic Magazine* 24(4): 387–573.

Bingham, Hiram (1930). *Machu Picchu, a Citadel of the Incas: Report of the Explorations and Excavations made in 1911, 1912 and 1915 under the Auspices of Yale University and the National Geographic Society.* Yale University Press, New Haven.

Boman, Eric (1908). *Antiquités de la région Andine de la République Argentine et du desert d'Atacama.* 2 vols. Imprimerie Nationale, Paris.

Boone, Elizabeth Hill (1994). Beyond Writing. In *Writing without Words: Alternative Literacies in Mesoamerica and the Andes,* edited by Elizabeth Hill Boone and Walter Mignolo, pp. 314–48. Duke University Press, Durham, NC.

Boone, Elizabeth H., and Walter Mignolo, eds. (1994). *Writing without Words: Alternative Literacies in Mesoamerica and the Andes.* Duke University Press, Durham, NC.

Boone, Elizabeth H., and Gary Urton, eds. (2011). *Their Way of Writing: Scripts, Signs, and Pictographies in Pre-Columbian America.* Dumbarton Oaks Research Library and Collection, Washington, DC.

Bouysse-Cassagne, Thérèse (1986). *Urco* and *uma*: Aymara Concepts of Space. In *Anthropological History of Andean Polities,* edited by John V. Murra, Nathan Wachtel, and Jacques Revel, pp. 201–27. Cambridge University Press, Cambridge.

Bram, Joseph (1941). *An Analysis of Inca Militarism.* American Ethnological Society Monograph 4. New York.

Bray, Tamara L. (2003). Inca Pottery as Culinary Equipment: Food, Feasting, and Gender in Imperial State Design. *Latin American Antiquity* 14(1): 1–22.

Bray, Tamara L. (2009). An Archaeological Perspective on the Andean Concept of *Camaquen*: Thinking Through Late Pre-Columbian *Ofrendas* and *Huacas*. *Cambridge Archaeological Journal* 19(3): 357–66.

Bray, Tamara L., Leah D. Minc, María Constanza Ceruti, José Antonio Chávez, Ruddy Perea, and Johan Reinhard (2005). A Compositional Analysis of Pottery Vessels Associated with the Inca Ritual of *Capacocha*. *Journal of Anthropological Archaeology* 24: 82–100.

Brokaw, Galen (2003). The Poetics of *Khipu* Historiography: Felipe Guaman Poma de Ayala's "Nueva corónica" and the "Relación de los quipucamayos." *Latin American Research Review* 8(3): 111–47.

Brokaw, Galen (2010). *A History of the Khipu*. Cambridge University Press, Cambridge.

Browman, David L. (1970). Early Peruvian Peasants: The Culture History of a Central Highlands Valley. Unpublished PhD dissertation, Department of Anthropology. Harvard University, Cambridge, MA.

Brughmans, Tom (2013). Thinking through Networks: A Review of Formal Network Methods in Archaeology. *Journal of Archaeological Method and Theory* 20(4): 623–62.

Brush, Steven B. (1977). *Mountain, Field and Family: The Economy and Human Ecology of an Andean Valley*. University of Pennsylvania Press, Philadelphia.

Burchard, Roderick E. (1974). Coca y trueque de alimentos. In *Reciprocidad e Intercambio en los Andes Peruanos*, edited by Giorgio Alberti and Alberto Meyers, pp. 209–51. Instituto de Estudios Peruanos, Lima.

Burger, Richard L. (1992). *Chavin and the Origins of Andean Civilization*. Thames & Hudson, London.

Burger, Richard L. (2004). Scientific Insights into Daily Life at Machu Picchu. In *Machu Picchu: Unveiling the Mystery of the Incas*, edited by Richard Burger and Lucy C. Salazar, pp. 85–106. Yale University Press, New Haven.

Burger, Richard L., and Lucy C. Salazar, eds. (2004). *Machu Picchu: Unveiling the Mystery of the Incas*. Yale University Press, New Haven.

Burger, Richard L., Craig Morris, and Ramiro Matos Mendieta, eds. (2007). *Variations in the Expression of Inka Power*, Dumbarton Oaks, Washington, DC.

Burns, Kathryn (2010). *Into the Archive: Writing and Power in Colonial Peru*. Duke University Press, Durham, NC.

Cabello Valboa, Miguel (1951). *Miscelánea antártica: una historia del Perú antiguo*. Universidad Nacional Mayor de San Marcos, Instituto de Etnología y Arqueología, Lima.

Calancha, Antonio de la (1974). *Crónica moralizada*, transcribed and edited by Ignacio Prado Pastor. Universidad Nacional Mayor de San Marcos, Lima.

Calderari, Milena (1991). Estilos cerámicos incaicos de La Paya. In *Actas del XI Congreso Nacional de Arqueología Chilena*, vol. 2, pp. 151–64. Museo Nacional de Historia Natural, Sociedad Chilena de Arqueología, Santiago.

Callapiña, Supno, y otros Quipucamayos (1974). *Relación de los Quipucamayos*, edited by Juan José Vega. Biblioteca Universitaria, Lima. (Originally written 1542/1608.)

Casasanto, Daniel, and Lera Boroditsky (2008). Time in the Mind: Using Space to Think about Time. *Cognition* 106: 579–93.

Castillo B., Luis Jaime, and Christopher B. Donnan (1994). La ocupación Moche de San José de Moro, Jequetepeque. In *Moche: propuestas y perspectivas*, edited by Santiago Uceda C. and Elías Mujica B. Travaux de l'Institut Français d'Études Andines 79, Lima.

Castro, Cristóbal de, and Diego de Ortega Morejón (1974). Relación y declaración del modo que este valle de Chincha y sus comarcanos se governaven antes que oviese Ingas y despues q(ue) los vuo hasta q(ue) los Cristianos entraron en esta tierra. *Historia y Cultura* 8: 91–104. (Originally written 1558.)

Cerrón-Palomino, Rodolfo (1976). *Diccionario Quechua Junín-Huanca.* Instituto de Estudios Peruanos, Lima.

Cerrón-Palomino, Rodolfo (1999). Tras las huellas del aimara cuzqueño. *Revista Andina* 33: 137–61.

Cerrón-Palomino, Rodolfo (2000). *Lingüística aimara.* Biblioteca de la Tradición Oral Andina 21. Centro de Estudios Regionales Andinos Bartólome de Las Casas, Cuzco.

Cerrón-Palomino, Rodolfo (2004). El aimara como lengua oficial de los incas. In *Identidad y transformación en el Tawantinsuyu y en los Andes coloniales. Perspectivas arqueológicas y etnohistóricas.* Part 3, edited by Peter Kaulicke, Gary Urton, and Ian Farrington, pp. 9–21. *Boletín de Arqueología PUCP* 8.

Cerrón-Palomino, Rodolfo (2008). *Voces del Ande: ensayos sobre onomástica andina*, Pontificia Universidad Católica del Perú, Lima.

Cerrón-Palomino, Rodolfo (2012). Unraveling the Enigma of the "Particular Language" of the Incas. *Proceedings of the British Academy* 173: 265–94.

Ceruti, María Constanza (1997). *Arqueología de alta montaña.* Salta, Argentina.

Céspedes Paz, Ricardo (1982). La arqueología del area de Pocona. *Cuadernos de Investigación, Serie Arqueología* 1: 89–99.

Chase-Dunn, Christopher, and Thomas D. Hall, eds. (1991). *Core/Periphery Relations in Precapitalist Worlds.* Westview Press, Boulder, CO.

Chepstow-Lusty, Alex, and M. Winfield (2000). Agroforestry by the Inca: Lessons from the Past. *Ambio* 29(6): 322–8.

Christie, Jessica J. (2012). A New Look at Q'enqo as a Model of Inka Visual Representation, Reproduction, and Spatial Structure. *Ethnohistory* 59(3): 597–630.

Cieza de León, Pedro de (1959). *The Incas,* translated by Harriet de Onis; edited with an introduction by Victor Wolfgang von Hagen. University of Oklahoma Press, Norman.

Cieza de León, Pedro de (1967). *El Señorío de los Incas: 2a. parte de la Crónica del Perú.* Instituto de Estudios Peruanos, Lima. (Originally written 1551.)

Cieza de León, Pedro de (1984). *Crónica del Peru: primera parte.* Fondo Editorial de la Pontificia Universidad Católica del Perú: Academia Nacional de la Historia, Lima. (Originally written 1553.)

Cieza de León, Pedro de (1998). *Descubrimiento y conquista del Peru. The discovery and conquest of Peru: chronicles of the New World encounter*, edited and translated by Alexandra Parma Cook and Noble David Cook. Duke University Press, Durham, NC.

Classen, Constance (1993). *Inka Cosmology and the Human Body*, University of Utah Press, Salt Lake City.

Coben, Lawrence S. (2006). Other Cuzcos: Replicated Theaters of Inka Power. In *Archaeology of Performance*, edited by Takeshi Inomata and Lawrence S. Coben, pp. 223–59. Altamira Press, Lanham, MD.

Coben, Lawrence S. (2010). Some Roads do Lead to Incallajta: The Inca Double Road from Vacas. *Ñawpa Pacha* 301: 53–64.

Coben, Lawrence S. (2012). Theaters of Power: Inca Imperial Performance. PhD dissertation, Dept. of Anthropology, University of Pennsylvania, Philadelphia.

Cobo, Bernabé (1979). *History of the Inca Empire: An Account of the Indians' Customs and Their Origin, Together with a Treatise on Inca Legends, History, and Social Institutions*, translated by Roland Hamilton. University of Texas Press, Austin.

Cobo, Bernabé (1990). *Inca Religion and Customs*, edited by Roland Hamilton. University of Texas Press, Austin.

Cock, Guillermo A., and C. E. Goycochea Díaz (2004). Puruchuco y el cementerio Inca de la quebrada de Huaquerones. In *Puruchuco y la sociedad de Lima: un homenaje a Arturo Jiménez Borja*, edited by L. F. Villacorta Ostolaza, L. Vetter Parodi, and C. Ausejo Castillo, pp. 179–97. Concytec, Lima.

Conklin, William J. (2002). A *Khipu* Information String Theory. In *Narrative Threads: Accounting and Recounting in Andean Khipu*, edited by Jeffrey Quilter and Gary Urton, pp. 53–86. University of Texas Press, Austin.

Connell, Samuel V., Chad Gifford, Ana Lucía González, and Maureen Carpenter (2003). Hard Times in Ecuador: Inka Troubles at Pambamarca. www.antiquity.ac .uk/projgall/connell295 (accessed December 9, 2013).

Conrad, Geoffrey W. (1977). Chuquitoy Viejo: An Inca Administrative Center in the Chicama Valley, Peru. *Journal of Field Archaeology* 4(1): 1–18.

Conrad, Geoffrey W., and Arthur Demarest (1984). *Religion and Empire*. Cambridge University Press, Cambridge.

Cook, Noble David (1981). *Demographic Collapse: Indian Peru, 1520–1620*. Cambridge University Press, Cambridge.

Cornejo Guerrero, Miguel A. (2000). An Inka Province: Pachacamac and the Ischma Nation. PhD dissertation, Department of Archaeology and Anthropology. Australian National University, Canberrra.

Costin, Cathy L. (1986). From Chiefdom to Empire State: Ceramic Economy among the Prehispanic Wanka of Highland Peru. Unpublished PhD dissertation, Department of Anthropology, University of California. University Microfilms, Ann Arbor, MI.

Costin, Cathy L. (1993). Textiles, Women, and Political Economy in Late Prehispanic Peru. *Research in Economic Anthropology* 14: 3–28.

Costin, Cathy L. (2001). Production and Exchange of Ceramics. In *Empire and Domestic Economy*, edited by Terence N. D'Altroy *et al.*, pp. 203–34. Kluwer Academic/Plenum Press, New York.

Covey, R. Alan (2006a). Chronology, Succession, and Sovereignty: The Politics of Inka Historiography and Its Modern Interpretation. *Comparative Studies in Society and History* 48(1): 166–99.

Covey, R. Alan (2006b). *How the Incas Built their Heartland*. Ann Arbor, University of Michigan Press.

Cummins, Tom (2000). The Figurine Tradition of Coastal Ecuador: Technological Styles and the Use of Molds. In *Ceramic Production in the Andes: Technology, Organization, and Approaches, MASCA Research Papers in Science and Archaeology*, Supplement to vol. 15, edited by Izumi Shimada, pp. 199–212. University of Pennsylvania Museum of Archaeology and Anthropology, Philadelphia.

Cummins, Tom (2002). *Toasts with the Inca*. University of Michigan Press, Ann Arbor.

Cummins, Tom (2007). Queros, Aquillas, Uncus and Chulpas: The Composition of Inka Artistic Expression and Power. In *Variations in the Expression of Inka Power*, edited by Richard Burger, Craig Morris, and Ramiro Matos Mendieta, pp. 267–311, Dumbarton Oaks, Washington, DC.

Cummins, Tom (2011). *Tocapu*: What Is It, What Does It Do, and Why Is It Not a Knot? In *Their Way of Writing: Scripts, Signs, and Pictographies in Pre-Columbian America*, edited by Elizabeth H. Goone and Gary Urton, pp. 273–313. Dumbarton Oaks Research Library and Collection, Washington, DC.

Cummins, Tom, and Joanne Rappaport (1998). The Reconfiguration of Civic and Sacred Space: Architecture, Image, and Writing in the Colonial Northern Andes. *Latin American Literary Review* 26(52): 174–200.

D'Altroy, Terence N. (1987). Transitions in Power: Centralization of Wanka Political Organization under Inka Rule. *Ethnohistory* 34: 78–102.

D'Altroy, Terence N. (1992). *Provincial Power in the Inka Empire*. Smithsonian Institution, Washington, DC.

D'Altroy, Terence N. (1994a). Factionalism and Political Development in the Central Andes. In *Factional Competition and Political Development in the New World*, edited by Elizabeth Brumfiel and John Fox, pp. 171–87. Cambridge University Press, Cambridge.

D'Altroy, Terence N. (1994b). Public and Private Economy in the Inka Empire. In *The Economic Anthropology of the State*, edited by Elizabeth Brumfiel. Society for Economic Anthropology Monograph 11, pp. 171–222. University Press of America, Lanham, MD.

D'Altroy, Terence N. (2005). Remaking the Social Landscape: Colonization in the Inka Empire. In *The Archaeology of Colonial Encounters*, edited by Gil Stein, pp. 263–95. SAR Press, Albuquerque, NM.

D'Altroy, Terence N. (in press a). Funding the Inka Empire. In *The Inca Empire: A Multidisciplinary Approach to a Holistic Vision*, edited by Izumi Shimada. University of Texas Press, Austin.

D'Altroy, Terence N. (in press b). Killing Mummies: On Inka Epistemology and Imperial Power. In *Death Shall Have No Dominion: The Archaeology of Mortality and Immortality*, edited by Colin Renfrew, Michael Boyd, and Iain Morley. Cambridge University Press, Cambridge.

D'Altroy, Terence N., and Ronald A. Bishop (1990). The Provincial Organization of Inka Ceramic Production. *American Antiquity* 55: 120–38.

D'Altroy, Terence N., and Christine A. Hastorf (1984). The Distribution and Contents of Inca State Storehouses in the Xauxa Region of Peru. *American Antiquity* 49: 334–49.

D'Altroy, Terence N., and Verónica I. Williams (1998). *Final Report: Provisioning the Inka Economy in Kollasuyu*. Grant from the National Science Foundation (SBR-97-07962) to analyze Inka-era ceramics through neutron activation analysis. Washington, DC.

D'Altroy, Terence N., Christine A. Hastorf, and Associates (2001). *Empire and Domestic Economy*. Kluwer Academic/Plenum Press, New York.

D'Altroy, Terence N., Ana María Lorandi, Verónica I. Williams, Christine A. Hastorf, Elizabeth DeMarrais, Milena Calderari, and Melissa Hagstrum (2000). Inka Imperial Rule in the Valle Calchaquí, Argentina. *Journal of Field Archaeology* 27: 1–26.

D'Altroy, Terence N., Verónica Williams, and Ana María Lorandi (2007). The Inkas in the Southlands. In *Variations in the Expression of Inka Power*, edited by Richard Burger, Craig Morris, and Ramiro Matos Mendieta, pp. 88–135. Dumbarton Oaks, Washington, DC.

Daniels, Peter T., and William Bright, eds. (1996). *The World's Writing Systems*. Oxford University Press, New York.

Davies, Nigel (1995). *The Incas*. University Press of Colorado, Boulder.

De Hoyos, María, and Verónica Williams (1994). "Un patrón de asentamiento estatal para propósitos especiales." XI Congreso Nacional de Arqueología Argentina. San Rafael. Mendoza. Mayo de 1994. Actas y Memorias. *Revista del Museo de Historia Natural* 13(1): 196–9.

De la Cadena, Marisol (2010). Indigenous Cosmopolitics in the Andes: Conceptual Reflections beyond "Politics." *Cultural Anthropology* 25(2): 334–70.

de Munter, Koen, and Nicole Note (2009). Cosmopraxis and Contextualising Among the Contemporary Aymara. In N. Note et al. (eds.), *Worldviews and Cultures: Philosophical Reflections from an Intercultural Perspective*, pp. 87–102. Springer, Dordrecht.

Dean, Carolyn (1999). *Inka Bodies and the Body of Christ: Corpus Christi in Colonial Cuzco, Peru*. Duke University Press, Durham, NC.

Dean, Carolyn (2010a). *A Culture of Stone: Inka Perspectives on Rock*. Duke University Press, Durham, NC.

Dean, Carolyn (2010b). The After-life of Inka Rulers: Andean Death before and after Spanish Colonization. *Death and Afterlife in the Early Modern Hispanic World*. *Hispanic Issues Online* 7: 27–54.

Dearborn, David S. P., and Katharina J. Schreiber (1986). Here Comes the Sun: The Cuzco–Machu Picchu Connection. *Archaeoastronomy* 9: 15–37.

Dearborn, David S. P., and Katharina J. Schreiber (1989). Houses of the Rising Sun. In *Time and Calendars in the Inca Empire*, edited by Mariusz S. Ziółkowski and

Robert M. Sadowski, pp. 49–74. British Archaeological Reports, International Series No. 479, Oxford.

Dearborn, David S. P., and Raymond E. White (1983). The Torreón of Machu Picchu as an Observatory. *Archaeoastronomy: Supplement to the Journal for the History of Astronomy* 14(5): 37–49.

Dearborn, David S. P., Katharina J. Schreiber, and Raymond E. White (1987). Intimachay, a December Solstice Observatory. *American Antiquity* 52: 346–52.

Debenedetti, Salvador (1908). *Excursión arqueológica a las ruinas de Kipón (Valle Calchaquí–provincia de Salta)*. Publicaciones de la Sección Antropología 4. Imp. M. Biedma e hijo, Buenos Aires.

Decoster, Jean-Jacques (2008). Casas, Bartolomé de las (1474?–1566). In *Guide to Documentary Sources for Andean Studies, 1530–1900*, edited by Joanne Pillsbury, vol. 1, pp. 127–36. University of Oklahoma Press, Norman.

Deloria, Vine, Jr., (2003). *God Is Red: A Native View of Religion*. 30th anniversary edn. Fulcrum Publishing Company, Golden, CO.

Demarest, Arthur Andrew (1981). *Viracocha: The Nature and Antiquity of the Andean High God*. Harvard University, Peabody Museum of Archaeology and Ethnology, Monograph 6. Cambridge, MA.

DeMarrais, Elizabeth (2012). Quechua's Southern Boundary: The Case of Santiago del Estero, Argentina. In *Archaeology and Language in the Andes: A Cross-disciplinary Exploration of Prehistory*, edited by Paul Heggarty and David Beresford-Jones. pp. 373–406. Proceedings of the British Academy 173. Oxford University Press/British Academy, London.

DeMarrais, Elizabeth, Luis Jaime Castillo, and Timothy Earle (1996). Ideology, Materialization, and Power Strategies. *Current Anthropology* 37(1): 15–86.

Denevan, William (1987). Terrace Abandonment in the Colca Valley. In *Pre-Hispanic Agricultural Fields in the Andean Region*, edited by William M. Denevan, Kent Mathewson, and Gregory W. Knapp, pp. 1–43. BAR International Series 359(1), Oxford.

De Pasquale, Nicolino (n.d.). Decimal Guaman Poma. Online. Available at www.quipus.it/DECIMAL%20POMA.pdf (accessed via Google Scholar).

De Pasquale, Nicolino, and A. Aimi (2003a). Le yupane: gli strumenti di calcolo del mondo andino, in *Perù: tremila anni di capolavori*, edited by A. Aimi, pp. 65–7. Electa, Milan.

De Pasquale, Nicolino, and A. Aimi (2003b). Come funzionano le yupane 1 e 2 di Milano, in *Le culture del Perù da Chavín agli Inca*, edited by A. Aimi, pp. 148–55. Silvana, Cinisello Balsamo.

Diaz, Henry F., and V. Markgraf, eds. (1992). *El Niño: Historical and Paleoclimatic Aspects of the Southern Oscillation*. Cambridge University Press, New York.

Dietler, Michael (2005). The Archaeology of Colonization and the Colonization of Archaeology. In *The Archaeology of Colonial Encounters*, edited by Gil J. Stein, pp. 33–68. School of American Research, Santa Fe.

Diez de Betanzos, Juan (1987). *Suma y narración de los incas.* Transcription and notes by María Carmen Martín del Rubio. Ediciones Atlas, Madrid.

Diez de Betanzos, Juan (1996). *Narrative of the Incas,* edited by Roland Hamilton and Dana Buchanan. University of Texas Press, Austin.

Diez de San Miguel, Garci (1964). *Visita hecha a la Provincia de Chucuito por Garci Diez de San Miguel en el año 1567,* edited by Waldemar Espinoza Soriano. Casa de la Cultura del Perú, Lima.

Difrieri, Horacio (1948). Las ruinas del Potrero de Payogasta (Provincia de Salta, Argentina). In *Actes du XXVIIIe Congrès Internacional des Americanistes:* 599–604. Musée de l'Homme, Paris.

Dillehay, Tom D. (1977). Tawantinsuyu Integration of the Chillon Valley, Peru: A Case of Inca Geo-Political Mastery. *Journal of Field Archaeology* 4(4): 397–405.

Dillehay, Tom D., and Américo Gordon (1988). La actividad prehispánica de los Incas y su influencia en la Araucania. In *La frontera del estado Inca,* edited by Tom D. Dillehay and Patricia J. Netherly. Proceedings of the 45th Congreso Internacional de Americanistas, Bogotá, Colombia, 1985, pp. 215–34. British Archaeological Reports, International Series, no. 442, Oxford.

Dillehay, Tom D., and Patricia Netherly, eds. (1988). *La frontera del estado Inca.* British Archaeological Reports, International Series, 442, Oxford.

Donkin, R. A. (1979). *Agricultural Terracing in the New World.* Viking Fund Publications in Anthropology 56. Wenner-Gren Foundation for Anthropological Research, University of Arizona Press, Tucson.

Donnan, Christopher B. (2004). *Moche Portraits from Ancient Peru.* University of Texas Press, Austin.

Donnan, Christopher B., ed. (1986). *Early Ceremonial Architecture in the Andes.* Dumbarton Oaks, Washington, DC.

Doyle, Michael W. (1986). *Empires.* Cornell University Press, Ithaca, NY.

Durkheim, Emile (1915). *The Elementary Forms of Religious Life.* Allen & Unwin, London.

Duviols, Pierre (1976). "Punchao," Idolo mayor del Coricancha. Historia y typología. *Antropología Andina* 1–2: 156–83.

Duviols, Pierre (1977). Los nombres quechua de Viracocha, supuesto "Dios Creador" de los evangelizadores. *Allpanchis Phuturinqa* 10: 153–64.

Duviols, Pierre (1979a). Datacion, paternité et idéologique de la "Declaración de los Quipucamayos a Vaca de Castro." In *Les cultures ibériques en devenir, essais publiés en homenage à la mémoire de Marcel Bataillon (1895–1977),* pp. 583–91. La Fondation Singer-Polignac, Paris.

Duviols, Pierre (1979b). La dinastía de los Incas: ¿monarquía o diarquía? Argumentos huerísticos a favor de una tesis estructuralista. *Journal de la Société des Americanistes* 64: 67–83.

Duviols, Pierre (1980). La guerra entre el Cuzco y los chanka: ¿Historia o mito? *Revista de la Universidad Complutense* 28(117): 363–72.

Dwyer, Edward B. (1971). The Early Inca Occupation of the Valley of Cuzco, Peru. Unpublished PhD dissertation, Department of Anthropology. University of California, Berkeley.

Earle, Timothy K., and Terence N. D'Altroy (1982). Storage Facilities and State Finance in the Upper Mantaro Valley, Peru. In *Contexts for Prehistoric Exchange*, edited by Jonathan E. Ericson and Timothy K. Earle, pp. 265–90. Academic Press, New York.

Earle, Timothy K., Terence N. D'Altroy, Christine A. Hastorf, Catherine J. Scott, Cathy L. Costin, Glenn S. Russell, and Elsie Sandefur (1987). *Archaeological Field Research in the Upper Mantaro, Peru, 1982–1983: Investigations of Inka Expansion and Exchange*. Institute of Archaeology, University of California, Monograph 28. Los Angeles.

Earls, John, and Gabriela Cervantes (in press). Inka Cosmology in Moray: Astronomy, Agriculture and Pilgrimage. In *The Inca Empire: A Multidisciplinary Approach to a Holistic Vision*, edited by Izumi Shimada. University of Texas Press, Austin.

Eaton, George (1916). *The Collection of Osteological Material from Machu Picchu*. Memoirs of the Connecticut Academy of Arts and Sciences 5. Yale University Press, New Haven.

Engels, Donald W. (1978). *Alexander the Great and the Logistics of the Macedonian Army*. University of California Press, Berkeley and Los Angeles.

Erickson, Clark L. (2006). Intensification, Political Economy, and the Farming Community: In Defense of a Bottom-up Perspective of the Past. In *Agricultural Strategies*, edited by Joyce Marcus and Charles Stanish, pp. 334–63. Cotsen Institute of Archaeology, University of California, Los Angeles.

Espinoza Soriano, Waldemar (1970). Los mitmas yungas de Collique en Cajamarca, siglos XV, XVI, y XVII. *Revista del Museo Nacional* 36: 9–57.

Espinoza Soriano, Waldemar (1972). Los Huancas, aliados de la conquista: Tres informaciones inéditas sobre la participación indígena en la conquista del Perú, 1558–1560–1561. *Anales Científicos de la Universidad de Centro del Perú* 1: 3–407.

Espinoza Soriano, Waldemar (1973). Las colonias de mitmas múltiples en Abancay, siglos XV y XVI. *Revista del Museo Nacional* 39: 225–99.

Espinoza Soriano, Waldemar (1975). Los mitmas huayacuntu en Quito o guarniciones para la represión armada, siglos XV y XVI. *Revista del Museo Nacional* 41: 351–94.

Espinoza Soriano, Waldemar (1976). Los mitmas de Nasca en Ocoña, Vitor y Camaná. *Bulletin de l'Institut Français d'Études Andines* 5(1–2): 85–95.

Espinoza Soriano, Waldemar (1977). Los cuatro suyos del Cuzco. Siglos XV y XVI. *Bulletin de l'Institut Français d'Études Andines* 6(3–4): 109–22.

Espinoza Soriano, Waldemar (1980). Acerca de la historia militar inca. *Allpanchis Phuturinqa* 14(16): 171–86.

Espinoza Soriano, Waldemar (1983). Los mitmas plateros de Ishma en le país de los Ayamarca, siglos XV – XIX. *Boletín de Lima* 30(5): 38 – 52.

Espinoza Soriano, Waldemar (1987a). *Artesanos, transacciones, monedas y formas de pago en el mundo andino. Siglos XV y XVI*. Banco Central de la Reserva del Perú, Lima.

Espinoza Soriano, Waldemar (1987b). Migraciones internas en el Reino Colla: Tejedores, Plumeros, y Alfareros del Estado Imperial Inca. *Chungará* 19: 243 – 89.

Estermann, Josef (2006). *Filosofía andina: estudio intercultural de la sabiduría autóctona andina*. 2nd edn. Abya Yala, Quito.

Estermann, Josef (2009). Andean Philosophy as a Questioning Alterity: An Intercultural Criticism of Western Andro- and Ethnocentrism. In *Worldviews and Cultures: Philosophical Reflections from an Intercultural Perspective*, edited by Nicole Note, Raúl Fornet-Betancout, Josef Estermann, and Diederik Aerts, pp. 129 – 47. Springer, Dordrecht.

Estete, Miguel de (1985). La relación del viaje que hizo el señor Capitán Hernando Pizarro por mandado del señor Gobernador, su hermano, desde el pueblo de Caxamalca a Pachacamac y de allí a Jauja, in *Verdadera relación de la conquista del Perú*, by Francisco de Xérez, edited by Concepción Bravo, pp. 130 – 48. Historia 16, Madrid. (Originally written 1532 – 3.)

Evans-Pritchard, Edward E. (1939). Nuer Time-Reckoning. *Africa: Journal of the International African Institute* 12(2): 189 – 216.

Falcón, Francisco (1946). Representación hecha por el Licenciado Falcón en concilio provincial sobre los daños y molestias que se hacen a los indios. In *Los Pequeños Grandes Libros de Historia Americana*, edited by Francisco A. Loayza. Series 1, vol. 10, pp. 121 – 64. D. Miranda, Lima. (Originally written 1567.)

Faller, Martina (2006). Evidentiality and Epistemic Modality at the Semantics/ Pragmatics Interface. Online at http://web.eecs.umich.edu/~rthomaso/lpw06 /fallerpaper.pdf (accessed December 11, 2013).

Farrington, Ian S. (1983). Prehistoric Intensive Agriculture: Preliminary Notes on River Canalization in the Sacred Valley of the Incas. In *Drained Field Agriculture in Central and South America*, edited by John Darch. British Archaeological Reports, International Series 189, pp. 221 – 35, Oxford.

Farrington, Ian S. (1984). Medidas de tierra en el Valle de Yucay, Cusco. *Gaceta Arqueológica Andina* 11: 10 – 11.

Farrington, Ian S. (1995). The Mummy, Estate, and Palace of Inka Huayna Capac at Quispeguanca. *Tawantinsuyu* 1: 55 – 65.

Farrington, Ian S. (2010). The Houses and "Fortress" of Waskar: Archaeological Perspectives on a Forgotten Building Complex in Inka Cusco. *Journal of Iberian and Latin American Research* 16(2): 87 – 99.

Farrington, Ian S. (2013). *Cusco: Urbanism and Archaeology in the Inka World*. University Press of Florida, Gainesville.

Farrington, Ian S., and Rodolfo Raffino (1996). Moso suyukunapa tariqnin; Nuevos hallazgos en el Tawantinsuyu. Inka news from around the empire. *Tawantinsuyu* 2: 73–7.

Fejos, Paul (1944). *Archaeological Exploration in the Cordillera Vilcabamba, Southeastern Peru*. Viking Fund Publications in Anthropology 3. New York.

Figuencia Pinos, Rolando (1995). *Coyuctor, un recinto sagrado*. Editorial Casa de la Cultura Núcleo del Cañar, Cañar.

Flannery, Kent V., Joyce Marcus, and Robert G. Reynolds (1989). *The Flocks of the Wamani: A Study of Llama Herders on the Punas of Ayacucho, Peru*. Academic Press, San Diego.

Flores Ochoa, Jorge A., ed. (1977). *Pastores de puna = Uywamichiq punarunakuna*, vol. 5. Instituto de Estudios Peruanos, Lima.

Flores Ochoa, Jorge A. (1978). Organization social y complementaridad económica en los Andes centrales. In *Actes de XLII Congrès International des Américanistes*, vol. 4, pp. 9–38, Paris.

Fock, Nils (1961). Inka Imperialism in Northwest Argentina, and Chaco Burial Forms. *Folk* 3: 67–90.

Foucault, Michel (1972). *The Archaeology of Knowledge*, translated by A. M. Sheridan Smith. Pantheon Books, New York.

Franch, José Alcina (1978). Ingapirca: arquitectura y áreas de asentamiento. *Revista española de antropología americana* 8: 127–46

Fresco, Antonio (1984). Excavaciones en Ingapirca (Ecuador): 1978–1982. *Revista española de antropología americana* 14: 85–102

Gade, Daniel W. (1977). Llama, alpaca y vicuña: ficción y realidad. In *Pastores de Puna = uywamichiq punarunakuna*, edited by Jorge Flores Ochoa, pp. 113–20. Instituto de Estudios Peruanos., Lima.

Garcilaso de la Vega, El Inca (1966). *Royal Commentaries of the Incas*, translated with an introduction by Harold V. Livemore. University of Texas Press. Austin. (Originally written 1609.)

Garnsey, Peter, and Richard Saller (1987). *The Roman Empire*. University of California Press, Berkeley.

Gasparini, Graziano, and Luise Margolies (1980). *Inca Architecture*, translated by Patricia J. Lyon. Indiana University Press, Bloomington.

Gell, Alfred (1998). *Art and Agency*. Oxford, Oxford University Press.

Gibaja Oviedo, Arminda (1984). Excavaciones en Ollantaytambo, Cusco. *Gaceta Arqueológica Andina* 3(9): 4–5.

Gibaja Oviedo, Arminda (2000). *Proyecto Maras*. Instituto Nacional de Cultura, Cuzco.

Giovanetti, Marco Antonio (2009). Articulación entre el sistema agrícola, redes de irrigación y áreas de molienda como medida del grado de ocupación Inka en El Shincal y Los Colorados (Prov. de Catamarca). PhD dissertation, Ciencias Naturales, Universidad de La Plata, Argentina.

Glatz, Claudia (2009). Empire as Network: Spheres of Material Interaction in Late Bronze Age Anatolia. *Journal of Anthropological Archaeology* 28: 127–41.

Glave Testino, Luis Miguel, and María Isabel Remy (1983). *Estructura agraria y vida rural en una región andina: Ollantaytambo entre los siglos XVI–XIX*. Centro de Estudios Rurales Andinos "Bartolomé de las Casas," Cuzco.

Glowacki, Mary (2002). The Huaro Archaeological Site Complex: Rethinking the Huari Occupation of Cuzco. In *Andean Archaeology I Variations of Sociopolitical Organization*, edited by William H. Isbell and Helaine Silverman, pp. 267–85. Kluwer Academic, New York.

González, Alberto R. (1979). Pre-Columbian Metallurgy of Northwest Argentina. In *Pre-Columbian Metallurgy of South America*, edited by Elizabeth Benson, pp. 133–202. Dumbarton Oaks, Washington, DC.

González, Alberto R. (1983). Inca Settlement Patterns in a Marginal Province of the Empire: Sociocultural Implications. In *Prehistoric Settlement Patterns: Essays in Honor of Gordon R. Willey*, edited by Evon Z. Vogt and Richard M. Leventhal, pp. 337–60. Harvard University Press, Cambridge, MA.

González, Alberto R., and Pío Pablo Díaz (1992). La Casa Morada. *Estudios de Arqueología* 5: 9–54.

González, Paola, and Tamara Bray, eds. (2008). *Lenguajes visuales de los Inca*, British Archaeological Reports International Series 1848, Oxford.

González Carré, Enrique, Jorge Cosmopolis A., and Jorge Lévano P. (1981). *La ciudad inca de Vilcashuaman*. Universidad Nacional de San Cristóbal de Huamanga, Ayacucho, Perú.

González Corrales, José A. (1984). Arquitectura y cerámica Killke del Cusco. *Revista del Museo e Instituto de Arqueología* 25: 37–46.

González Holguín, Diego (1952). *Vocabulario de la lengua general de todo el Perú, llamada lengua Qquichua o del Inca*. New edn. Imprenta Santa María, Lima. (Originally written 1608.)

Gorbak, Celina, Mirtha Lischetti, and Carmen Paula Munoz (1962). Batallas rituales del Chiaraje y del Tocto de la provincia de Kanas (Cuzco, Peru). *Revista del Museo Nacional* 31: 245–304.

Gosden, Chris (1993). *Social Being and Time*. Blackwell, Oxford.

Gose, Peter (1993). Segmentary State Formation and the Ritual Control of Water under the Incas. *Comparative Studies in Society and History* 35(3): 480–514.

Gose, Peter (1996a). Oracles, Divine Kingship, and Political Representation in the Inka State. *Ethnohistory* 43(1): 1–32.

Gose, Peter (1996b). The Past is Lower Moiety: Diarchy, History, and Divine Kingship in the Inka Empire. *History and Anthropology* 9(4): 383–414.

Gould, Stephen J. (1997). Nonoverlapping Magisteria. *Natural History* 106(2): 16–22.

Grosboll, Sue (1993). " … And He Said in the Time of the Ynga, They Paid Tribute and Served the Ynga." In *Provincial Inca: Archaeological and Ethnohistorical Assessment of the Impact of the Inca State*, edited by M. Malpass, pp. 44–76. University of Iowa Press, Iowa.

Guaman Poma de Ayala, Felipe (1936). *Bueva corónica y buen gobierno*. Travaux et mémoires de l'Institut d'Ethnologie 22. Paris.

Guaman Poma de Ayala, Felipe (1980). *El primer nueva corónica y buen gobierno*, edited by John V. Murra, Rolena Adorno, and Jorge Urioste. Siglo Veintiuno, México, DF.

Guaman Poma de Ayala, Felipe (2006). *The First New Chronicle and Good Government* (abridged), selected, translated, and annotated by David Frye. Hackett Books, Indianapolis.

Guillén Guillén, Edmundo (1994). *La guerra de la reconquista inka*. R. A. Ediciones, Lima.

Gyarmati, János, and András Varga (1999). *The Chacaras of War: An Inka State in the Cochabamba Valley, Bolivia*. Museum of Ethnography, Budapest.

Haas, Jonathan, and Winifred Creamer (2006). Crucible of Andean Civilization. The Peruvian Coast from 3000 to 1800 BC. *Current Anthropology* 46(5): 745–75.

Haggard, J. Villasana, and Malcolm D. McLean (1941). *Handbook for Translators of Spanish Historical Documents*. Semco Color Press, Oklahoma City.

Hamilton, Roland (1990). Introduction: Father Cobo and the Incas. In *Inca Religions and Customs*, translated and edited by Roland Hamilton, pp. xi–xx. University of Texas Press, Austin.

Hamilton, Roland (1996). Introduction. In *Narrative of the Incas*, edited by Roland Hamilton and Dana Buchanan, pp. ix–xiv. University of Texas Press, Austin.

Hardman, Martha, ed. (1986). *The Aymara Language in its Social and Cultural Context*. University Press of Florida, Gainesville.

Harris, William V. (1979). *War and Imperialism in Republican Rome, 327–70 BC*. Clarendon Press, Oxford.

Harrison, Regina (2002). Pérez Bocanegra's Ritual *formulario*: *Khipu* Knots and Confession. In *Narrative Threads: Accounting and Recounting in Andean Khipu*, edited by Jeffrey Quilter and Gary Urton, pp. 266–90. University of Texas Press, Austin.

Hassig, Ross (1985). *Trade, Tribute, and Transportation: The Sixteenth-Century Political Economy of the Valley of Mexico*. University of Oklahoma Press, Norman.

Hastorf, Christine A. (1990). The Effect of the Inka State on Sausa Agricultural Production and Crop Consumption. *American Antiquity* 55: 262–90.

Hastorf, Christine A. (1993). *Agriculture and the Onset of Political Inequality before the Inka*. Cambridge University Press, Cambridge.

Hastorf, Christine A., and Michael DeNiro (1985). Reconstruction of Prehistoric Plant Production and Cooking Practices by a New Isotopic Method. *Nature* 315: 489–91.

Haun, Susan J., and Guillermo A. Cock Carrasco (2010). A Bioarchaeological Approach to the Search for *Mitmaqkuna*. In *Distant Provinces in the Inka Empire: Toward a Deeper Understanding of Inka Imperialism*, edited by Michael Malpass and Sonia Alconini, pp. 193–220. University of Iowa Press, Iowa City.

Hayashida, F. (1999). Style, Technology, and State Production: Inka Pottery Manufacture in the Leche Valley, Peru. *Latin American Antiquity* 10: 337–52.

Heffernan, Kenneth J. (1989). Limatambo in Late Prehistory: Landscape Archaeology and Documentary Images of Inca Presence in the Periphery of Cuzco. Unpublished PhD dissertation, Department of Anthropology, Australian National University, Canberra.

Heffernan, Kenneth J. (1996). *Limatambo: Archaeology, History, and the Regional Societies of Inca Cusco.* British Archaeological Reports International Series 644. Tempus Reparatum, Oxford.

Heggarty, Paul (2008). Linguistics for Archaeologists: A Case-study in the Andes. *Cambridge Archaeological Journal* 18(1): 35–56.

Heggarty, P., and D. G. Beresford-Jones, eds. (2012). *Archaeology and Language in the Andes.* Proceedings of the British Academy 173, Oxford University Press, Oxford.

Helmer, Marie (1955–6). "La visitación de los Yndios Chupachos". Inka et encomendero 1549. *Travaux de l'Institut Français d'Études Andines* 5: 3–50. (Originally written 1549.)

Hemming, John (1970). *The Conquest of the Incas.* Macmillan, London.

Hemming, John (2012). *The Conquest of the Incas* (Kindle edition, revised and updated). Macmillan, London

Herrera, Alexander (2013). Heritage Tourism, Identity, and Development in Peru. *International Journal of Historical Archaeology* 17: 275–95.

Herrera y Tordesillas, Antonio de (1952). *Historia general de los hechos de los Castellanos en las Islas y Tierra Firme del Mar Océano,* vol. 10. Década Quinta, Madrid.

Heyerdahl, Thor, Daniel H. Sandweiss, and Alfredo Narváez (1995). *Pyramids of Túcume: The Quest for Peru's Forgotten City.* Thames & Hudson, New York.

Hollowell, Lee (1987). *Study of Precision Cutting and Fitting of Stone in Pre-historic Andean Walls and Re-assessment of the Fortaleza at Ollantaytambo, Peru.* National Geographic Society, report no. 2832. Washington, DC.

Hornberger, Esteban, and Nancy H. Hornberger (1983). *Diccionario tri-lingüe, quechua de Cusco: quechua, English, castellano.* 2nd edn. Qoya Raymi, La Paz.

Hosler, Diane, Heather Lechtman, and Olaf Holm (1990). *Axe-Monies and Their Relatives.* Studies in Pre-Columbian Art and Archaeology 30. Dumbarton Oaks, Washington, DC.

Houston, Stephen D., ed. (2004). *The First Writing: Script Invention as History and Process.* Cambridge University Press, Cambridge.

Howard, Rosaleen (2002). Spinning a Yarn: Landscape, Memory, and Discourse Structure in Quechua Narratives. In *Narrative Threads: Accounting and Recounting in Andean Khipu,* edited by Jeffrey Quilter and Gary Urton, pp. 26–49. University of Texas Press, Austin.

Howe, Ellen, and Ulrich Petersen (1994). Silver and Lead in the Late Prehistory of the Mantaro Valley, Peru. In *Archaeometry of Pre-Columbian Sites and Artifacts: Proceedings of a Symposium organized by the UCLA Institute of Archaeology and* the *Getty Conservation Institute*, edited by D. A. Scott and P. Meyers, pp. 183–98. Getty Conservation Institute, Malibu, CA.

Hunt, Robert C. (1988). Size and Structure of Authority in Canal Irrigation Systems. *Journal of Anthropological Research* 44(4): 335–55.

Hyland, Sabine (2003). *The Jesuit and the Incas*. University of Michigan Press, Ann Arbor.

Hyland, Sabine (2007). *The Quito Manuscript: An Inca History Preserved by Fernando de Montesinos*. Yale University Publications in Anthropology 88. Peabody Museum of Natural History, New Haven, CT.

Hyland, Sabine (2011). *Gods of the Andes: An Early Jesuit Account of Inca Religion and Andean Christianity*. Latin American Originals 6. Pennsylvania State University Press, University Park.

Hyslop, John (1984). *The Inka Road System*. Academic Press, New York.

Hyslop, John (1985). *Inkawasi: The New Cuzco*. British Archaeological Reports, International Series 234, Oxford.

Hyslop, John (1990). *Inka Settlement Planning*. University of Texas Press, Austin.

Hyslop, John (1993). Factors Influencing the Transmission and Distribution of Inka Cultural Materials throughout Tawantinsuyu. In *Latin American Horizons*, edited by Don S. Rice, pp. 337–56. Dumbarton Oaks, Washington, DC.

Idrovo Urigüen, Jaime (1984). Prospection archeologique de la vallée de Cuenca – Ecuador. PhD dissertation, Université de Paris I, Panthéon-Sorbonne, Paris.

Idrovo Urigüen, Jaime (1988). Tomebamba: primera fase de conquista incaica en los Andes septentrionales: los Cañaris y la conquista incasica del austro ecuatoriano. In *La frontera del estado inca*, edited by Tom D. Dillehay and Patricia J. Netherly. Proceedings of the 45th Congreso Internacional de Americanistas, Bogotá, Colombia, 1985, pp. 87–104. British Archaeological Reports, International Series 442, Oxford.

Instituto Nacional de Cultura (1999). *Plano topográfico, plano de delimitación Parque Arqueológico de Tipón*. Instituto Nacional de Cultura, Cuzco.

Isbell, Billie Jean (1978). *To Defend Ourselves: Ecology and Ritual in an Andean Village*. Institute of Latin American Studies, University of Texas, Austin.

Isbell, William, and Alexei Vranich (2004). Experiencing the Cities of Wari and Tiwanaku. In *Andean Archaeology*, edited by Helaine Silverman, pp. 167–82. Blackwell, Oxford.

Janusek, John W. (2008). *Ancient Tiwanaku*. Cambridge University Press, Cambridge.

Jenkins, David (2001). A Network Analysis of Inka Roads, Administrative Centers, and Storage Facilities. *Ethnohistory* 48(4): 655–87.

Jennings, Justin (2010). *Globalizations and the Ancient World*. Cambridge University Press, Cambridge.

Jennings, Justin, and Brenda J. Bowser, eds. (2009). *Drink, Power, and Society in the Andes*. University Press of Florida, Gainesville.

Jijón y Caamaño, Jacinto (1919). *La religión del imperio de los incas.* Tipografía y encuadernación salesianas, Quito, Ecuador.

Jijón y Caamaño, Jacinto, and Carlos Manuel Larrea (1918). *Un cementerio incásico en Quito y notas acerca de la Incas en el Ecuador.* Imprenta de la Universidad Central, Quito.

Julien, Catherine J. (1982). Inca Decimal Administration in the Lake Titicaca Region. In *The Inca and Aztec States 1400–1800: Anthropology and History,* edited by George A. Collier, Renato I. Rosaldo, and John D. Wirth, pp. 119–51. Academic Press, New York.

Julien, Catherine J. (1983). *Hatunqolla: A View of Inca Rule from the Lake Titicaca Region.* Publications in Anthropology 15. University of California Press, Berkeley.

Julien, Catherine J. (1988). How Inca Decimal Administration Worked. *Ethnohistory* 35: 257–79.

Julien, Catherine J. (1993). Finding a Fit: Archaeology and Ethnohistory of the Incas. In *Provincial Inca: Archaeological and Ethnohistorical Assessment of the Impact of the Inca State,* edited by Michael Malpass, pp. 177–233. University of Iowa Press, Iowa City.

Julien, Catherine J. (1999). History and Art in Translation: The *Paños* and other Objects Collected by Francisco de Toledo. *Colonial Latin American Review* 8(1): 61–89.

Julien, Catherine J. (2000). *Reading Inca History.* University of Iowa Press, Iowa City.

Julien, Catherine J. (2004 [1987–9]). Las tumbas de Sacsahuaman y el estilo Cuzco-Inca. *Ñawpa Pacha* 25/27: 1–125.

Julien, Catherine J. (2008). On the Beginning of the Late Horizon. *Ñawpa Pacha* 29: 163–77.

Kadwell, Miranda, Matilde Fernandez, Helen F. Stanley, Ricardo Baldi, Jane C. Wheeler, Raul Rosadio, and Michael W. Bruford (2011). Genetic Analysis Reveals the Wild Ancestors of the Llama and the Alpaca. *Proceedings of the Royal Society of London, Bulletin* 268: 2575–84.

Kellett, Lucas (2010). Chanka Settlement Ecology: Hilltop Sites, Land Use and Warfare in Late Prehispanic Andahuaylas, Peru. PhD dissertation. University of New Mexico.

Kendall, Ann (1976). Descripción e inventario de las formas arquitectónicas inca. Patrones de distribución e inferencias cronológicas. *Revista del Museo Nacional* 42: 13–96.

Kendall, Ann (1985). *Aspects of Inca Architecture – Description, Function, and Chronology.* 2 vols. British Archaeological Reports International Series 242, Oxford.

Kendall, Ann (1994). *Proyecto Arqueológico Cusichaca, Cusco. Investigaciones arqueológicas y de rehabilitación agrícola,* vol. 1. Southern Peru Copper Corporation, Lima.

Kendall, Ann (1996). An Archaeological Perspective for Late Intermediate Period Inca Development in the Cuzco Region. *Structure, Knowledge, and Representation in the Andes* 24(1/2): 121–56.

Kendall, Ann, Rob Early, and Bill Sillar (1992). Report on Archaeological Field Season Investigating Early Inca Architecture at Juchuy Coscco (Q'aqya Qhawana) and Warq'ana, Province of Calca, Dept. of Cuzco, Peru. In *Ancient America: Contributions to New World Archaeology*, edited by Nicholas J. Saunders, pp. 189–255. Oxbow Books, Oxford.

King Kendall, A. and Nancy H. Hornberger (2006). Quechua as a Lingua Franca. *Annual Review of Applied Linguistics* 26: 177–94.

Kirchhoff, Paul (1949). The Social and Political Organization of the Andean Peoples. In *Handbook of South American Indians*, vol. 5, edited by Julian Steward. Bureau of American Ethnology Bulletin 143: 293–311, US Government Printing Office, Washington, DC.

Kolata, Alan L. (1993). *The Tiwanaku: Portrait of an Andean Civilization*. Blackwell, Cambridge, MA.

Kosiba, Steven B. (2010). Becoming Inka: The Transformation of Political Place and Practice during Inka State Formation (Cusco, Peru). PhD dissertation, Dept. of Anthropology, University of Chicago.

Kosiba, Steven B., and Andrew M. Bauer (2013). Mapping the Political Landscape: Toward a GIS Analysis of Environmental and Social Difference. *Journal of Archaeological Method and Theory* 20: 61–101.

Kosok, Paul (1965). *Life, Land, and Water in Ancient Peru*. Long Island University Press, New York.

Kremkau, Scott (2010). Late Horizon Imperial Landscapes in the Jequetepeque Valley, Peru. PhD dissertation, Dept. of Anthropology, Columbia University, New York.

Kroeber, Alfred L. (1930). *Archaeological Exploration in Peru, Part II: The Northern Coast*. Field Museum of Natural History, Anthropology Memoirs 2. Chicago.

La Lone, Darrell E. (1994). An Andean World-System: Production Transformations under the Inka Empire. In *The Economic Anthropology of the State*, edited by Elizabeth Brumfiel. Society for Economic Anthropology Monograph 11, pp. 17–41. University Press of America, Lanham, MD.

La Lone, Mary B. (1985). Indian Land Tenure in Southern Cuzco: From Inca to Colonial Patterns. PhD dissertation, Department of Anthropology, UCLA. University Microfilms, Ann Arbor, MI.

La Lone, Mary B., and Darrell E. La Lone (1987). The Inka State in the Southern Highlands: State Administrative and Production Enclaves. *Ethnohistory* 34: 47–62.

Lane, Kevin (2009). Engineered Highlands: The Social Organization of Water in the Ancient North-Central Andes (AD 1000–1480). *World Archaeology* 41(1) special issue: *The Archaeology of Water*: 169–90.

Las Casas, Bartolomé de (1967). *Apologética historia sumaria*, vol. 2, edited by Edmundo O'Gorman. Universidad Nacional Autónoma de México, Instituto de Investigaciones Históricas, Mexico City. (Originally written 1550s.)

Latour, Bruno (1993). *We Have Never Been Modern*, translated by Catherine Porter. Harvester Wheatsheaf, New York and London.

Lattimore, Owen (1988). *Inner Asian Frontiers of China*. Oxford University Press, Oxford

Laurencich-Minelli, Laura (1998). Una contribución a la etnohistoria del Perú. El documento "Historia et Rudimenta Linguae Piruanorum". *Tawantinsuyu* 5: 103–12.

Laurencich-Minelli, Laura (2007). *Exsul Immeritus Blas Valera Populo Suo e Historia et Rudimenta Linguae Piranorum: Indios, gesuiti, e spagnoli in due documenti segret i sul Perù' del secolo*. CLUEB, Bologna.

Lechtman, Heather (1984). Andean Value Systems and the Development of Prehistoric Metallurgy. *Technology and Culture* 25: 1–36.

Lee, Vincent R. (1990). *The Building of Sacsayhuaman, and Other Papers*. Sixpac Manco Publications, Wilson, WY.

Lee, Vincent R. (1999). *Vilcabamba*. Sixpac Manco Publications, Wilson, WY.

Lee, Vincent R. (2000). *Forgotten Vilcabamba*. Sixpac Manco Publications, Wilson, WY.

Lee, Vincent R. (2010). Choquequirao to Machu Picchu at the Speed of Light: Visual Signaling among the Incas. *Ñawpa Pacha* 30(1): 1–24.

Legnani, Nicole D. (2005). Introduction. In *Titu Cusi: A Sixteenth-Century Account of the Conquest*, translated by Nicole D. Legnani, pp. 1–72. Harvard University Press, Cambridge, MA.

Levillier, Roberto, ed. (1940). *Don Francisco de Toledo, supremo organizador del Perú: Su vida, su obra [1515–1582]*, 3 vols. Espasa-Calpe, Buenos Aires.

Levin, Erik (2006). A Reanalysis of the Aymara Verb Using Prototypes. *Coyote Papers* 13, 1–13. Special Volume Dedicated to the Indigenous Languages of the Americas. web source: http://coyotepapers.sbs.arizona.edu/CPXIII/levin.pdf (accessed December 10, 2013).

LeVine, Terry Y. (1985). Inka Administration in the Central Highlands: A Comparative Study. PhD dissertation, Institute of Archaeology, University of California, Los Angeles. University Microfilms, Ann Arbor, MI.

LeVine, Terry Y. (1987). Inka Labor Service at the Regional Level: The Functional Reality. *Ethnohistory* 34: 14–46.

LeVine, Terry Y., ed. (1992). *Storage Systems in the Inka Empire*. University of Oklahoma Press, Norman.

Locke, Leland L. (1923). *The Ancient Quipu or Peruvian Knot Record*. The American Museum of Natural History, New York.

Lockhart, James (1972). *The Men of Cajamarca*. University of Texas Press, Austin.

Lorandi, Ana María (1984). Soñocamayoc: Los olleros del Inka en los centros manufactureros del Tucumán. *Revista del Museo de la Plata, Sección Antropología* 7(62): 303–27.

Lorandi, Ana María (1988). Los Diaguitas y el Tawantinsuyu: Una hipótesis de conflicto. In *La Frontera del Estado Inca*, edited by Tom D. Dillehay and Patricia J. Netherly. Proceedings of the 45th Congreso Internacional de Americanistas, Bogotá, Colombia, 1985, pp. 235–59. British Archaeological Reports, International Series, no. 442, Oxford.

Lorandi, Ana María, and Roxana Boixadós (1987–8). Etnohistoria de los valles calchaquíes en los siglos XVI y XVII. *Runa* 17–18: 263–420.

Lorandi, Ana María, and Beatriz Cremonte (1993). Evidencias en torno a los *mitmaqkuna* incaicos en el noroeste argentino. In *Actas del XII Congreso Nacional de Arqueología Chilena* 1: 245–56.

Lounsbury, Floyd G. (1986). Some Aspects of the Inka Kinship System. In *Anthropological History of Andean Polities*, edited by John V. Murra, Nathan Wachtel, and Jacques Revel, pp. 121–36. Cambridge University Press, Cambridge.

Lucas, Gavin (2005). *The Archaeology of Time*. Routledge, New York.

Luteyn, James L., and Steven P. Churchill (2000). Vegetation of the Tropical Andes. In *Imperfect Balance: Pre-Columbian Human Ecosystems*, edited by David Lentz, pp. 281–310. Columbia University Press, New York.

Luttwak, Edward N. (1976). *The Grand Strategy of the Roman Empire from the First Century AD to the Third*. Johns Hopkins University Press, Baltimore.

MacCormack, Sabine (1991). *Religion in the Andes: Vision and Imagination in Early Colonial Peru*. Princeton University Press, Princeton, NJ.

Mackey, Carol (2002). The Continuing *Khipu* Traditions: Principles and Practices. In *Narrative Threads: Accounting and Recounting in Andean Khipu*, edited by Jeffrey Quilter and Gary Urton, pp. 320–47. University of Texas Press, Austin.

Mackey, Carol (2010). The Socioeconomic and Ideological Transformation of Farfán under Inka Rule. In *Distant Provinces in the Inka Empire: Toward a Deeper Understanding of Inka Imperialism*, edited by Michael Malpass and Sonia Alconini, pp. 222–59. University of Iowa Press, Iowa City.

Mackey, Carol, Hugo Pereyra, Carlos Radicati, Humberto Rodriguez, and Oscar Valverde, eds. (1990). *Quipu y yupana: Colección de escritos*. Consejo Nacional de Cienca y Techologia, Lima.

MacLean, Margaret G. (1986). Sacred Land, Sacred Water: Inca Landscape Planning in the Cuzco Area. PhD dissertation, Department of Anthropology, University of California, Berkeley. University Microfilms, Ann Arbor, MI.

MacQuarrie, Kim (2007). *The Last Days of the Incas*. Simon & Schuster, New York.

Maffie, James (2005). Ethnoepistemology. *Internet Encyclopedia of Philosophy*. Online, available at www.iep.utm.edu/ethno-ep/ (accessed December 13, 2013).

Makowski, Krzystof, and Milena Vega Centeno A. (2004). Estilos regionales en la costa central en el horizonte tardío: Una aproximación desde el valle del Lurín. *Bulletin de l'Institut Français d'Études Andines* 33(3): 681–714.

Malotki, Ekkehart (1983). *Hopi Time: A Linguistic Analysis of the Temporal Concepts in the Hopi Language*. Walter de Gruyter, Berlin.

Malpass, Michael, ed. (1993). *Provincial Inca: Archaeological and Ethnohistorical Assessment of the Impact of the Inca State*. University of Iowa Press, Iowa City.

Malpass, Michael, and Sonia Alconini, eds. (2010). *Distant Provinces in the Inka Empire: Toward a Deeper Understanding of Inka Imperialism*. University of Iowa Press, Iowa City.

Mann, Michael (1986). *The Sources of Social Power*. Cambridge University Press, Cambridge.

Mannheim, Bruce (1988). "Time, not the Syllables, Must be Counted": Quechua Parallelism, Word Meaning and Cultural Analysis. *Michigan Discussions in Anthropology*, 13(1): 239–81.

Mannheim, Bruce (1991). *The Language of the Inka since the European Invasion*. University of Texas Press, Austin.

Mannheim, Bruce, and Krista Van Vleet (1998). The Dialogics of Southern Quechua Narrative. *American Anthropologist* 100(2): 326–46.

Manzo, Ángel, Philippe Delcourt, and Daniel Gutiérrez Osinaga (2011). *La red vial prehispánica en el sur de Bolivia*. Yahuar, La Plata, Argentina.

Mar, Ricardo, and J. Alejandro Betrán-Caballero (in press). El conjunto arqueológico de Saqsawaman (Cusco). Una aproximación a su arquitectura. *Revista Española de Antropología Americana*.

Marcus, Joyce, and Jorge E. Silva S. (1988). The Chillón Valley "Coca Lands": Archaeological Background and Ecological Context. In *Conflicts over Coca Fields in Sixteenth-Century Peru*, Memoirs of the Museum of Anthropology 21, edited by María Rostworowski de Diez Canseco, pp. 1–32. University of Michigan, Ann Arbor.

Masuda, Shozo, Izumi Shimada, and Craig Morris, eds. (1985). *Andean Ecology and Civilization*. University of Tokyo Press, Tokyo.

Matienzo, Juan de (1967). *Gobierno del Perú*, edited by Guillermo Lohmann Villena. Travaux de l'Institut Français d'Études Andines 11, Lima. (Originally written 1567.)

Matos Mendieta, Ramiro (1994). *Pumpu: Centro Administrativo Inka de la Puna de Junín*. Editorial Horizonte, Lima.

Mazzotti, José Antonio (2008). Garcilaso de la Vega (1539–1616). In *Guide to Documentary Sources for Andean Studies, 1530–1900*, edited by Joanne Pillsbury, vol. 2, pp. 239–41. University of Oklahoma Press, Norman.

McEwan, Colin, and María Isabel Silva (1989). Que fueron a hacer los Incas en la costa central del Ecuador? *Proceedings of the 46th International Congress of Americanists*, pp. 163–85. British Archaeological Reports International Series 503, Oxford.

McEwan, Colin, and Maarten van de Guchte (1992). Ancestral Time and Sacred Space in Inca State Ritual. In *The Ancient Americas: Art from Sacred Landscapes*, edited by Richard F. Townsend, pp. 359–73. The Art Institute of Chicago, Chicago.

McEwan, Gordon F. (2006). *The Incas: New Perspectives*. ABC-CLIO, Santa Barbara, CA.

McEwan, Gordon F., and Arminda Gibaja O. (n.d.). New Radiocarbon Data for Dating the Beginning of the Inca Imperial Expansion. Unpublished ms.

McTaggart, J. M. Ellis (1908). The Unreality of Time. *Mind: A Quarterly Review of Psychology and Philosophy*, new series 68(4): 457–74.

Means, Philip A. (1928). Biblioteca Andina. *Transactions of the Connecticut Academy of Arts and Sciences* 29: 271–525.

Mellor, David H. (1998). *Real Time II*. Routledge, New York.

Mena, Cristóbal de (El Anónimo Sevillano) (1937). La conquista del Perú. In *Las relaciones primitivas de la conquista del Perú, Cuadernos de historia*, edited by Raúl Porras Barrenechea. Los cronistas de la conquista 1, vol. 2, pp. 79–101. Les Presses Modernes, Paris. (Originally written 1534.)

Menzel, Dorothy (1959). The Inca Conquest of the South Coast of Peru. *Southwestern Journal of Anthropology* 15: 125–42.

Miller, George R. (2003). Food for the Dead, Tools for the Afterlife: Zooarchaeology at Machu Picchu. In *The 1912 Yale Peruvian Scientific Expedition Collections from Machu Picchu: Human and Animal Remains*, edited by Richard L. Burger and Lucy C. Salazar, pp. 1–63. Yale University Publications in Anthropology 85. Peabody Museum of Natural History, New Haven.

Miller, George R., and Anne L. Gill (1990). Zooarchaeology at Pirincay, a Formative Period Site in Highland Ecuador. *Journal of Field Archaeology* 17(1): 49–68.

Miracle, Andrew W., and Juan de Dios Yapita Moya (1981). Time and Space in Aymara. In *The Aymara Language in Its Social and Cultural Context*, edited by M. J. Hardman, pp. 33–56. University Press of Florida, Gainesville.

Mitchell, William P. (1976). Irrigation and Community in the Central Peruvian Highlands. *American Anthropologist* 78(1): 25–44.

Mitchell, William P. (1980). Local Ecology and the State: Implications of Contemporary Quechua Land Use for the Inca Sequence of Agricultural Work. In *Beyond the Myths of Culture: Essays in Cultural Materialism*, edited by Eric B. Ross, pp. 139–54. Academic Press, New York.

Mitchell, William P., and David Guillet, eds. (1994). *Irrigation at High Altitudes: The Social Organization of Water Control Systems in the Andes*. American Anthropological Association, Washington, DC.

Molina, Cristóbal de (el Cuzqueño) (1988). Relación de la fábulas y ritos de la Incas. In *Fábulas y ritos de los Incas*, edited by Henrique Urbano and Pierre Duviols, pp. 47–134. Historia 16, Madrid. (Originally written 1575.)

Molina, Cristóbal de (el Cuzqueño) (2011). *Account of the Fables and Rites of the Incas*, translated and edited by Brian S. Bauer, Vania Smith-Oka, and Gabriel E. Cantarutti. University of Texas Press, Austin. (Originally written 1575.)

Montesinos, Fernando (1920). *Memorias antiguas historiales del Perú*, translated and edited by Philip Ainsworth Means. Hakluyt Society, London,

Moore, Jerry D., and Carol J. Mackey (2008). The Chimú Empire. In *Handbook of South American Archaeology*, edited by Helaine Silverman and William H. Isbell, pp. 783–807. Springer, New York.

Moore, Sally F. (1958). *Power and Property in Inca Peru*. Greenwood Press, Westport, CT.

Morris, Craig (1967). Storage in Tawantinsuyu. PhD dissertation, Department of Anthropology, University of Chicago. University Microfilms, Ann Arbor, MI.

Morris, Craig (1972). State Settlements in Tawantinsuyu: A Strategy of Compulsory Urbanism. In *Contemporary Archaeology*, edited by Mark P. Leone, pp. 393–401. Southern Illinois University Press, Carbondale.

Morris, Craig (1982). The Infrastructure of Inka Control in the Peruvian Central Highlands. In *The Inca and Aztec States, 1400–1800: Anthropology and History*, edited by George A. Collier, Renato I. Rosaldo, and John D. Wirth, pp. 153–71. Academic Press, New York.

Morris, Craig (1988). Mas allá de las fronteras de Chincha. In *La Frontera del Estado Inca*, edited by Tom D. Dillehay and Patricia J. Netherly. Proceedings of the 45th Congreso Internacional de Americanistas, Bogotá, Colombia, 1985, pp. 131–40. British Archaeological Reports, International Series 442, Oxford.

Morris, Craig (1990). Arquitectura y estructura del espacio en Huánuco Pampa. *Cuadernos Instituto Nacional de Antropología* 12: 27–45.

Morris, Craig (1991). Signs of Division, Symbols of Unity: Art in the Inka Empire. In *Circa 1492: Art in the Age of Exploration*, edited by Jay A. Levenson, pp. 521–8. National Gallery of Art and Yale University Press, Washington, DC, and New Haven, CT.

Morris, Craig (1995). Symbols to Power: Styles and Media in the Inka State. In *Style, Society, and Person: Archaeological and Ethnological Perspectives*, edited by Christopher Carr and Jill E. Neitzel, pp. 419–33. Plenum Press, New York.

Morris, Craig (1998). Inka Strategies of Incorporation and Governance. In *Archaic States*, edited by Gary M. Feinman and Joyce Marcus, pp. 293–309. School of American Research Press, Santa Fe.

Morris, Craig (2007). Andean Ethnohistory and the Agenda for Inka Archaeology. In *Variations in the Expression of Inka Power*, edited by Richard Burger, Craig Morris, and Ramiro Matos Mendieta, pp. 1–10, Dumbarton Oaks, Washington, DC.

Morris, Craig, and Donald E. Thompson (1985). *Huánuco Pampa: An Inca City and Its Hinterland*. Thames & Hudson, London.

Morris, Craig, and Ariana von Hagen (2011). *The Incas: Lords of the Four Quarters*. Thames & Hudson, New York.

Morris, Craig, R. Alan Covey, and Pat Stein (2011). *The Huánuco Pampa Archaeological Project*, vol. 1: *The Plaza and Palace Complex*. American Museum of Natural History Anthropological Papers 96. New York.

Moseley, Michael E. (1975). *The Maritime Foundations of Andean Civilization*. Cummings Publishing Company, Menlo Park, CA.

Moseley, Michael E. (1983). The Good Old Days Were Better: Agrarian Collapse and Tectonics. *American Anthropologist* 85: 773–99.

Moseley, Michael Edward, and Alana Cordy-Collins, eds. (1990). *The Northern Dynasties: Kingship and Statecraft in Chimor: A Symposium at Dumbarton Oaks, 12th and 13th October 1985*. Dumbarton Oaks Research Library and Collection, Washington, DC.

Moseley, Michael E., D. Wagner, and James B. Richardson III (1992). Space Shuttle Imagery of Recent Catastrophic Climate Change along the Arid Andean Coast. In *Paleoshorelines and Prehistory: An Investigation of Method*, edited by L. L. Johnson, pp. 215–35. CRC Press, Boca Raton, LA.

Mosko, Mark S. (1992). Motherless Sons: "Divine Kings" and "Partible Persons" in Melanesia and Polynesia. *Man*, new series 27(4): 697–717.

Mould de Pease, Mariana (2001). Un día en la vida peruana de Machu Picchu: Avance de historia intercultural. *Revista complutense de historia de América* 27: 257–79.

Mulvany de Peñaloza, Eleanora (1986). Nuevas evidencias de la ocupación incaica en el valle de Lerma. *Runa* 16: 59–84.

Mulvany de Peñaloza, Eleanora, and Silvia Soria (1998). Sitios y caminos en los bosques serranos de los Andes meridionales. *Tawantinsuyu* 5: 120–6.

Mumford, Jeremy (1998). The Taki Onqoy and the Andean Nation: Sources and Interpretations. *Latin American Research Review* 33(1): 150–65.

Munn, Nancy D. (1992). The Cultural Anthropology of Time: A Critical Essay. *Annual Review of Anthropology* 21: 93–123.

Murphy, Melissa S., Catherine Gaither, Elena Goycochea, John W. Verano, and Guillermo Cock (2010). Violence and Weapon-Related Trauma at Puruchuco-Huaquerones, Peru. *American Journal of Physical Anthropology* 142: 636–49.

Murra, John V. (1958). On Inca Political Structure. *Proceedings of the Annual Spring Meeting of the American Ethnological Society*, pp. 30–41. University of Washington, Seattle.

Murra, John V. (1962). Cloth and Its Functions in the Inca State. *American Anthropologist* 64: 710–28.

Murra, John V. (1968). An Aymara Kingdom in 1567. *Ethnohistory* 15: 115–51.

Murra, John V. (1972). El "control vertical" de un máximo de pisos ecológicos en la economía de las sociedades andinas. In *Visita de la provincia de León de Huánuco en 1562, Iñigo Ortiz de Zúñiga, Visitador*, edited by John V. Murra, vol. 2, pp. 427–76. Universidad Nacional Hermilio Valdizán, Huánuco, Peru.

Murra, John V. (1975). *Formaciones económicas y políticas del mundo andino*. Instituto de Estudios Peruanos, Lima.

Murra, John V. (1978). Los olleros del Inka: Hacia una historia y arqueología del Qollasuyu. In *Historia, problema, y promesa: Homenaje a Jorge Basadre*, edited by F. Miro Quesada, Franklin Pease G. Y., and Daniel Sobrevilla, pp. 415–23. Pontificia Universidad Católica del Perú, Lima.

Murra, John V. (1980a). Derechos a las tierras en el Tawantinsuyu. *Revista de la Universidad Complutense* 28(117): 273–87.

Murra, John V. (1980b). *The Economic Organization of the Inka State*. JAI Press, Greenwich, CT. (Doctoral dissertation originally written 1956.)

Murra, John V. (1982). The *Mit'a* Obligations of Ethnic Groups to the Inka State. In *The Inca and Aztec States, 1400–1800; Anthropology and History*, edited by G. Collier, R. Rosaldo, and J. Wirth, pp. 237–62. Academic Press, New York.

Murra, John V. (1986). The Expansion of the Inka State: Armies, War, and Rebellions. In *Anthropological History of Andean Polities*, edited by John V. Murra, Nathan Wachtel, and Jacques Revel, pp. 49–58. Cambridge University Press, Cambridge.

Murúa, Fray Martín de (1986). *Historia general del Perú.*, edited by Manuel Ballesteros. Historia 16, Madrid. (Originally written *c.* 1605.)

Nair, Stella (2007). Witnessing the Invisibility of Inca Architecture in Colonial Peru. *Buildings & Landscapes: Journal of the Vernacular Architecture Forum* 14: 50–65.

Netherly, Patricia J. (1978). Local Level Lords on the North Coast of Peru. PhD dissertation, Department of Anthropology, Cornell University. University Microfilms, Ann Arbor, MI.

Netherly, Patricia J. (1984). The Management of Late Andean Irrigation Systems on the North Coast of Peru. *American Antiquity* 49(2): 227–54.

Nielsen, Axel (1996). Demografía y cambio social en Quebrada de Humahuaca (Jujuy, Argentina) 700–1535 d.C. *Relaciones de la Sociedad Argentina de Antropología* 21: 307–85.

Niles, Susan A. (1980). Pumamarca,: A Late Intermediate Period site near Ollantaytambo. *Ñawpa Pacha* 18: 49–62.

Niles, Susan A. (1987). *Callachaca: Style and Status in an Inca Community*. University of Iowa Press, Iowa City.

Niles, Susan A. (1999). *The Shape of Inca History: Narrative and Architecture in an Andean Empire*. University of Iowa Press, Iowa City.

Niles, Susan A. (in press). Considering Inca Royal Estates: Architecture, Economy, History. In *The Inca Empire: A Multidisciplinary Approach to a Holistic Vision*. ed. Izumi Shimada. University of Texas Press, Austin.

Note, Nicole, Raúl Fornet-Betancourt, Josef Estermann, and Diederik Aerts (2009). *Worldviews and Cultures: Philosophical Reflections from an Intercultural Perspective*, Springer, Dordrecht.

Nowack, Kerstin (2006). Las mercedes que pedía para su salida. The Vilcabamba Inca and the Spanish State 1539–1572. In *New World, First Nations: Native Peoples of Mesoamerica and the Andes under Colonial Rule*, edited by David Cahill and Blanca Tovías, pp. 57–91. Sussex Academic Press, Portland, OR.

Núñez, Lautaro (1986). The Evolution of a Valley: Population and Resources of Tarapacá over a Millennium. In *Anthropological History of Andean Polities*, edited by John V. Murra, Nathan Wachtel, and Jacques Revel, pp. 23–34. Cambridge University Press, Cambridge.

Núñez, Rafael E. (2011). No Innate Number Line in the Human Brain. *Journal of Cross-Cultural Psychology* 42(4): 651–68.

Núñez, Rafael E., and Eve Sweetser (2006). With the Future Behind Them: Convergent Evidence from Aymara Language and Gesture in the Crosslinguistic Comparison of Spatial Construals of Time. *Cognitive Science* 30: 401–50.

Orlove, Benjamin S., John C. H. Chiang, and Mark A. Cane (2002). Ethnoclimatology in the Andes: A Cross-Disciplinary Study Uncovers a Scientific Basis for the Scheme Andean Potato Farmers Traditionally Use to Predict the Coming Rains. *American Scientist* 90(5): 428–35.

Ortiz de Zúñiga, Iñigo (1967). *Visita de la Provincia de León de Huánuco en 1562, Iñigo Ortiz de Zúñiga, visitador*, edited by John V. Murra, vol. 1. Universidad Nacional Hermilio Valdizán, Huánuco, Perú. (Originally written 1562.)

Ortiz de Zúñiga, Iñigo (1972). *Visita de la Provincia de León de Huánuco en 1562, Iñigo Ortiz de Zúñiga, visitador*, edited by John V. Murra, vol. 2. Universidad Nacional Hermilio Valdizán, Huánuco, Perú. (Originally written 1562.)

Ortloff, Charles R., and Alan Kolata (1989). Hydraulic Analysis of Tiwanaku Aqueduct Structures at Lukurmata and Pajchiri, Bolivia. *Journal of Archaeological Science* 16: 513–35.

Oviedo y Valdés, Gonzalo Fernández de (1992). *Historia general y natural de la Indias*. Biblioteca de Autores Españoles (continuación), vols. 117–21. Ediciones Atlas, Madrid. (Originally written 1535–45.)

Owen, Bruce (2001). The Economy of Metal and Shell Wealth Goods. In *Empire and Domestic Economy*, edited by Terence N. D'Altroy *et al.*, pp. 265–95. Kluwer Academic/Plenum Press, New York.

Owen, Bruce D., and Marilyn A. Norconk (1987). Appendix I: Analysis of the Human Burials, 1977–1983 Field Seasons: Demographic Profiles and Burial Practices. In *Archaeological Field Research in the Upper Mantaro, Peru, 1982–1983*, edited by Timothy K. Earle *et al.*, pp. 107–23. Institute of Archaeology Monograph 28, University of California, Los Angeles.

Pachacuti Yamqui Salcamaygua, Joan de Santa Cruz (1993). *Relación de antigüedades deste Reyno del Piru*. Estudio etnohistórico y lingüístico de Pierre Duviols y César Itier. Institut Français d'Études Andines, Centro de Estudios Regionales Andinos "Bartolomé de Las Casas," Cuzco. (Originally written 1613.)

Pacheco Farfán, Juvenal (1994). *Filosofía inka y su projección al futuro*. Universidad Nacional de San Antonio Abad del Cusco, Cuzco.

Paredes, Mónica (2003). Prácticas funerarias incaicas en Sacsayhuamán: enterramientos ceremoniales y complejo funerario. *Boletín de Arquqología PUCP* 7: 79–111.

Parsons, Jeffrey R., and Charles M. Hastings (1988). The Late Intermediate Period. In *Peruvian Prehistory*, edited by Richard W. Keatinge, pp. 190–229. Cambridge University Press, Cambridge

Parsons, Jeffrey R., Charles M. Hastings, and Ramiro Matos Mendieta (1998). Rebuilding the State in Highlands Peru: Herder–Cultivator Interaction during the Late Intermediate Period in the Tarama–Chinchaycocha Region. *Latin American Antiquity* 8(4): 317–41.

Parsons, Jeffrey R., Charles M. Hastings, and Ramiro Matos Mendieta (2000). *Prehispanic Settlement Patterns in the Upper Mantaro and Tarma Drainages, Junín, Peru*. University of Michigan, Museum of Anthropology, Memoirs 34. Ann Arbor.

Parsons, Jeffrey R., Charles M. Hastings, and Ramiro Matos Mendieta, eds. (2013). *Prehispanic Settlement Patterns in the Upper Mantaro and Tarma Drainages, Junín, Peru*. Vol. 2. *The Wanka Region*. University of Michigan, Museum of Anthropology Monograph Series. Ann Arbor.

Pärssinen, Martti (1992). *Tawantinsuyu: The Inca State and Its Political Organization*. Societas Historica Finlandiae, Helsinki.

Pärssinen, Martti (in press). *Collasuyu* of the Inka State. In *The Inca Empire: A Multidisciplinary Approach to a Holistic Vision*, Izumi Shimada, ed. University of Texas Press, Austin.

Pärssinen, Martti, and Jukka Kiviharju (2004). *Textos andinos*. Instituto Iberoamericano de Finlandia: Departamento de Filología, Universidad Complutense de Madrid, Madrid.

Pärssinen, Martti, and Ari Siiriäinen (1997). Inca-Style Ceramics and Their Chronological Relationship to the Inca Expansion in the Southern Lake Titicaca Area (Bolivia). *Latin American Antiquity* 8: 255–71.

Pasztory, Esther (2010). *Inka Cubism: Reflections on Andean Art*. Online. Available at www.columbia.edu/~ep9/Inka-Cubism.pdf (accessed December 13, 2013).

Pease G. Y., Franklin (1973). *El Dios creador andino*. Mosca Azul Editores, Lima.

Pease G. Y., Franklin (1982). The Formation of Tawantinsuyu: Mechanisms of Colonization and Relationship with Ethnic Groups. In *The Inca and Aztec States, 1400–1800: Anthropology and History*, edited by George A. Collier, Renato I. Rosaldo, and John D. Wirth, pp. 173–98. Academic Press, New York.

Pease G. Y., Franklin (1995). *Las Crónicas y los Andes*. Pontificia Universidad Católica del Perú, Lima.

Pease G. Y., Franklin (2008a). Chronicles of the Andes in the Sixteenth and Seventeenth Centuries. In *Guide to Documentary Sources for Andean Studies, 1530–1900*, edited by Joanne Pillsbury, vol. 1, pp. 11–22. University of Oklahoma Press, Norman.

Pease G. Y., Franklin (2008b). Sarmiento de Gamboa, Pedro (1535–92?). In *Guide to Documentary Sources for Andean Studies, 1530–1900*, edited by Joanne Pillsbury, vol. 3, pp. 752–6. University of Oklahoma Press, Norman.

Pillsbury, Joanne, ed. (2001). *Moche Art and Archaeology in Ancient Peru*. National Gallery of Art, Washington, DC.

Pillsbury, Joanne, ed. (2008). *Guide to Documentary Sources for Andean Studies, 1530–1900*, 3 vols. University of Oklahoma Press, Norman.

Pizarro, Hernando (1959). Carta a Oidores de Santo Domingo, Panama. In *La historia general y natural de la Indias [1550], by Gonzalo Fernández de Oviedo y Valdés*. Biblioteca de Autores Españoles (continuación), vol. 121, pp. 84–90. Ediciones Atlas, Madrid. (Originally written 1533.)

Pizarro, Pedro (1986). *Relación del descubrimiento y conquista de los reinos del Perú*. 2 edn., edited by Guillermo Lohmann Villena. Pontificia Universidad Católica del Perú, Fondo Editorial, Lima. (Originally written 1571.)

Planella, María Teresa, and Rubén Stehberg (1994). Etnohistoria y arqueología en el estudio de la fortaleza indigena de Cerro Grande de la Compañía. *Revista Chungará* 26(1): 65–78.

Planella, Maria Teresa, Rubén Stehberg, Blanca Tagle, Hans Niemeyer, and Carmen del Río (1991). La fortaleza indígena del Cerro Grande de la Compañía (Valle del Cachapoal) y su relación con el proceso expansivo meridional incaico. In *Actas del XII Congreso Nacional de Arqueología Chilena*, pp. 403–21, Temuco, Chile.

Platt, Tristan (2002). Without Deceit or Lies: Variable *Chinu* Readings during a Sixteenth-Century Tribute-Restitution Trial. In *Narrative Threads: Accounting and Recounting in Andean Khipu*, edited by Jeffrey Quilter and Gary Urton, pp. 225–65. University of Texas Press, Austin.

Plaza Schuller, Fernando (1976). *La incursión inca en el septentrión andino ecuatoriano*. Serie Arqueología 2. Instituto Otavaleño de Antropología, Otavalo, Ecuador.

Plaza Schuller, Fernando (1980). *El Complejo de fortalezas de Pambamarca*. Serie Arqueología 3. Instituto Otavaleño de Antropología, Otavalo.

Polo de Ondegardo, Juan (1916). Relación de los fundamentos acerca del notable daño que resulta de no guardar a los indios sus fueros. In *Colección de libros y documentos referentes a la historia del Perú*, edited by Horacio H. Urteaga, vol. 3, pp. 45–188. Sanmartí, Lima. (Originally written 1571.)

Polo de Ondegardo, Juan (1917). La Relación del linaje de los Incas y cómo extendieron ellos sus conquistas. In *Colección de libros y documentos referentes a la historia del Perú*, edited by Horacio H. Urteaga, vol. 4, pp. 45–94. Sanmartí, Lima. (Originally written 1567.)

Polo de Ondegardo, Juan (1940a). Información hecha en el Cuzco por orden del Virrey Toledo, con respuestas al mismo interrogatorio utilizado en las cuatro informaciones anteriores. Añádese un auto del año 1563 del Conde de Nieva, en el cual otorga ese Virrey investidura a un cacique en la misma forma en que antes la daban los incas a los curacas. In *Don Francisco de Toledo, Supremo Organizador del Peru: su vida, su obra [1515–1582]*, edited by Roberto Levillier, vol. 2, pp. 65–98. Espasa-Calpe, Buenos Aires. (Originally written 1571.)

Polo de Ondegardo, Juan (1940b). Informe del Licenciado Juan Polo de Ondegardo al Licenciado Briviesca de Muñatones sobre la perpetuidad de las encomiendas en el Perú. *Revista Histórica* 13: 128–96. (Originally written 1561.)

Polo de Ondegardo, Juan (1965a). On the Errors and Superstitions of the Indians, Taken from the Treatise and Investigation done by Licentiate Polo. In *Information concerning the Religion and Government of the Incas*, translated by A. Brunel, John Murra, and Sidney Muirden, pp. 1–53. Human Relations Area Files, New Haven, CT.

Polo de Ondegardo, Juan (1965b). A Report on the Basic Principles Explaining the Serious Harm which Follows when the Traditional Rights of the Indians are not Respected. In *Information Concerning the Religion and Government of the Incas*, translated by A. Brunel, John Murra, and Sidney Muirden, pp. 53–196. Human Relations Area Files, New Haven, CT.

Polo de Ondegardo, Juan (1965c). Instruction against the Ceremonies and Rites that the Indians Practice in Conformance with the Stage of their Infidelity. In *Information Concerning the Religion and Government of the Incas*, translated by A. Brunel, John Murra, and Sidney Muirden, pp. 196–208. Human Relations Area Files, New Haven, CT.

Polo de Ondegardo, Juan (1965d). Superstitions of the Indians, taken from the Second Provincial Council of Lima. In *Information Concerning the Religion and Government of the Incas*, translated by A. Brunel, John Murra, and Sidney Muirden, Appendix B, pp. 209–11. Human Relations Area Files, New Haven, CT. (Originally written 1567.)

Ponsonby, Arthur (1928). *Falsehood in War-Time*. Dutton and Company, New York.

Pratchett, Terry, and Stephen Baxter (2012). *The Long Earth*. HarperCollins, New York.

Pratchett, Terry, Ian Stewart, and Jack Cohen (1999). *The Science of Discworld*. Ebury Press, London.

Protzen, Jean-Pierre (1982). Inca Quarrying and Stonecutting. *Ñawpa Pacha* 21: 183–219.

Protzen, Jean-Pierre (1986). Inca Stonemasonry. *Scientific American* 254: 94–105.

Protzen, Jean-Pierre (1993). *Inca Architecture and Construction at Ollantaytambo*. Oxford University Press, Oxford.

Protzen, Jean-Pierre, and Stella Nair (2013). *The Stones of Tiahuanaco: A Study of Architecture and Construction*. Cotsen Institute of Archaeology Press, University of California, Los Angeles.

Pulgar Vidal , Javier (1987). *Geografía del Perú*. 9th edn. Editorial Inca, Lima.

Quilter, Jeffrey, and Luis Jaime Castillo B., eds. (2010). *New Perspectives on Moche Political Organization*. Dumbarton Oaks, Washington, DC.

Quilter, Jeffrey, and Gary Urton, eds. (2002). *Narrative Threads: Accounting and Recounting in Andean Khipu*. University of Texas Press, Austin.

Quirita, R. A. (2002). *Conjunto arqueológico de Moray*. Instituto Nacional de Cultura, Cuzco.

Radicati di Primeglio, Carlos (1976). *El sistema contable de los incas: yupana y quipu*. Librería Studium, Lima.

Radicati di Primeglio, Carlos (1990). Tableros de escaques en el antiguo Perú. In *Quipu y Yupana, Colección de Escritos*, edited by Carol Mackey *et al.*, pp. 219–34. Consejo Nacional de Cienca y Techologia, Lima.

Raffino, Rodolfo (1983). *Los Inkas del Kollasuyu*. 2nd edn. Ramos Americana Editora, La Plata, Argentina.

Raffino, Rodolfo (1993). *Inka. Arqueología, historia, y urbanismo del altiplano andino*. Corregidor, Buenos Aires.

Ramírez, Susan E. (1982). Retainers of the Lords or Merchants: A Case of Mistaken Identity? In *El Hombre y su ambiente en los Andes centrales*, edited by Luis Millones and Hiroyasu Tomoeda. Senri Ethnological Studies 10, pp. 123–36. National Museum of Ethnology, Osaka.

Ramírez, Susan E. (1990). The Inca Conquest of the North Coast: A Historian's View. In *The Northern Dynasties: Kingship and Statecraft in Chimor*, edited by Michael E. Moseley and Alana Cordy-Collins, pp. 507–37. Dumbarton Oaks, Washington, DC.

Ramírez, Susan E. (2005). *To Feed and Be Fed: The Cosmological Bases of Authority and Identity in the Andes*. Stanford University Press, Stanford, CA.

Ramos Gavilán, Alonso (1976). *Historia de Nuestra Senora de Copacabana*. 2nd edn. Academia Boliviana de la Historia, La Paz. (Originally written 1621.)

Rappaport, Roy A. (1971). The Sacred in Human Evolution. *Annual Review of Ecology and Systematics* 2: 23–44.

Rappaport, Roy A. (1999). *Ritual and Religion in the Making of Humanity*. Cambridge University Press, Cambridge.

Rawls, Joseph (1979). An Analysis of Prehispanic Andean Warfare. PhD dissertation, Department of Anthropology, University of California, Los Angeles. University Microfilms, Ann Arbor, MI.

Raimondi, Antonio, and José Balta (1874). *El Perú*. Imprenta del Estado, Lima.

Regal Matienzo, Alberto (1936). *Los caminos del Inca en el antiguo Perú*. Sanmartí, Lima.

Regal Matienzo, Alberto (1972). *Los puentes del Inca en el antiguo Perú*. Imprenta Gráfica Industrial, Lima, DC.

Regalado de Hurtado, Liliana (2008). Titu Cusi Yupanqui, Diego de Castro (*c.* 1535–1571). In *Guide to Documentary Sources for Andean Studies, 1530–1900*, edited by Joanne Pillsbury, vol. 3, pp. 662–6. University of Oklahoma Press, Norman.

Reinhard, Johan (1985). Sacred Mountains: An Ethno-Archaeological Study of High Andean Ruins. *Mountain Research and Development* 5(4): 299–317.

Reinhard, Johan (1993). Llullaillaco: An Investigation of the World's Highest Archaeological Site. *Latin American Indian Literatures Journal* 9(1): 31–65.

Reinhard, Johan (2005). *The Ice Maiden: Inca Mummies, Mountain Gods, and Sacred Sites in the Andes*. National Geographic Society, Washington, DC.

Reinhard, Johan (2007). *Machu Picchu: Exploring an Ancient Sacred Center*. 4th rev. edn. Cotsen Institute of Archaeology, University of California, Los Angeles.

Reinhard, Johan, and Stephen Alvarez (1996). Peru's Ice Maidens: Unwrapping the Secrets. *National Geographic* 189(6): 62–81.

Reinhard, Johan, and M. Constanza Ceruti (2005). Sacred Mountains, Ceremonial Sites, and Human Sacrifice among the Incas. *Archaeoastronomy* 19: 1–43.

Reinhard, Johan, and M. Constanza Ceruti (2010). *Inca Rituals and Sacred Mountains: A Study of the World's Highest Archaeological Sites*. Cotsen Institute of Archaeology Press, University of California, Los Angeles.

Relaciones Geográficas de Indias (RGI) (1965). Biblioteca de Autores Españoles (continuación), vols. 183–5. Ediciones Atlas, Madrid. (Originally written 1557–86.)

Renard-Casevitz, F. M., Thierry Saignes, and A. C. Taylor (1986). *L'Inca, l'Espagnol, et les sauvages*. Éditions Recherche sur les Civilisations, Synthèse 21, Paris.

Rivera, Miguel (1976). La cerámica inca de Chinchero. In *Arqueología de Chinchero 2. Cerámica y otros materiales*, edited by José Alcina Franch *et al.* Memorias de la Misión Científica Española en Hispanoamerica, vol. 3, pp. 27–90. Ministerio de Asuntos Exteriores, Madrid.

Roman y Zamora, Jerónimo (1897). *Repúblicas de Indias, idolatrías y gobierno en México y Perú antes de la conquista*, vols. 1–2. Colección de Libros Raros o Curiosos que Tratan de América 14–15. V. Suárez, Madrid.

Rossen, Jack, María Teresa Planella, and Rubén Stehberg (2010). Archaeobotany of Cerro del Inga, Chile, at the Southern Inka Frontier. In *Distant Provinces in the Inka Empire: Toward a Deeper Understanding of Inka Imperialism*, edited by Michael Malpass and Sonia Alconini, pp. 14–43. University of Iowa Press, Iowa.

Rostworowski de Diez Canseco, María (1960a). *Pesos y medidas en el Perú pre-hispánico*. Imprenta Minerva, Lima.

Rostworowski de Diez Canseco, María (1960b). Succession, Coöption to Kingship, and Royal Incest among the Inca. *Southwestern Journal of Anthropology* 16: 417–26.

Rostworowski de Diez Canseco, María (1962). Nuevos datos sobre tenencia de tierras reales en el incario. *Revista del Museo Nacional* 31: 130–59.

Rostworowski de Diez Canseco, María (1963). Dos manuscritos inéditos con datos sobre Manco II, tierras personales de los Incas y mitimaes. *Nueva Corónica* 1: 223–39.

Rostworowski de Diez Canseco, María (1966). Las tierras reales y su mano de obra en el Tahuantinsuyu. In *XXXVI Congreso Internacional de Americanistas, Spain 1964*, vol. 2, pp. 31–4, Seville.

Rostworowski de Diez Canseco, María (1970). El repartimiento de doña Beatriz Coya, en el valle de Yucay. *Historia y Cultura* 4: 153–268.

510 *References*

Rostworowski de Diez Canseco, María (1977). *Etnía y Sociedad Costa Peruana prehispánica*. Instituto de Estudios Peruanos, Lima.

Rostworowski de Diez Canseco, María (1983). *Estructuras andinas del poder*. Instituto de Estudios Peruanos, Lima.

Rostworowski de Diez Canseco, María (1989). *Costa peruana prehispánica*. Instituto de Estudios Andinos, Lima.

Rostworowski de Diez Canseco, María (1990). *Conflicts over Coca Fields in Sixteenth-Century Peru*. Memoirs of the Museum of Anthropology 21. University of Michigan, Ann Arbor.

Rostworowski de Diez Canseco, María (1999). *History of the Inca Realm*, translated by Harry B. Iceland. Cambridge University Press, Cambridge.

Rowe, Ann P. (1978). Technical Features of Inca Tapestry Tunics. *Textile Museum Journal* 17: 5–28.

Rowe, Ann P. (1997). Inca Weaving and Costume. *Textile Museum Journal* 34–5: 5–54.

Rowe, John H. (1944). *An Introduction to the Archaeology of Cuzco*. Peabody Museum of American Archaeology and Ethnology Papers 27, no. 2. Cambridge, MA.

Rowe, John H. (1946). Inca Culture at the Time of the Spanish Conquest. In *Handbook of South American Indians*, edited by Julian Steward. Bulletin 143, vol. 2, pp. 183–330. Bureau of American Ethnology, Washington, DC.

Rowe, John H. (1948). The Kingdom of Chimor. *Acta Americana* 6: 26–59.

Rowe, John H. (1958). The Age Grades of the Inca Census. In *Miscellanea Paul Rivet Octogenario Dicata II. XXXI Congreso Internacional de Americanistas*, pp. 499–522. Universidad Nacional Autónoma de México, Mexico.

Rowe, John H. (1960). The Origins of Creator Worship among the Incas. In *Culture in History*, edited by Stanley Diamond, pp. 408–29. Columbia University Press, New York.

Rowe, John H. (1967). What Kind of a Settlement Was Inca Cuzco? *Ñawpa Pacha* 5: 59–77.

Rowe, John H. (1979a). An Account of the Shrines of Ancient Cuzco. *Ñawpa Pacha* 17: 2–80.

Rowe, John H. (1979b). Foreword. In *History of the Inca Empire by Bernabé Cobo*, edited by Roland Hamilton, pp. ix–xi. University of Texas Press, Austin.

Rowe, John H. (1979c). Standardization in Inca Tapestry Tunics. In *The Junius B. Bird Pre-Columbian Textile Conference*, edited by Ann P. Rowe, Elizabeth P. Benson, and Anne-Louise Schaffer, pp. 239–64. The Textile Museum, Dumbarton Oaks, Washington, DC.

Rowe, John H. (1982). Inca Policies and Institutions Relating to the Cultural Unification of the Empire. In *The Inca and Aztec States, 1400–1800: Anthropology and History*, edited by George A. Collier, Renato I. Rosaldo, and John D. Wirth, pp. 93–118. Academic Press, New York.

Rowe, John H. (1985a). La constitución inca del Cuzco. *Histórica* 9(1): 35–73.

Rowe, John H. (1985b). Probanza de los Incas nietos de conquistadores. *Histórica* 9(2): 193–245.

Rowe, John H. (1990a). Foreword. In *Inca Religion and Customs*, edited by Roland Hamilton, pp. vii–ix. University of Texas Press, Austin.

Rowe, John H. (1990b). Machu Picchu a la luz de documentos de siglo XVI. *Histórica* 14(1): 139–54.

Rowe, John H. (1991). Los monumentos perdidos de la plaza mayor del Cuzco incaico. *Saqsawaman* 3: 81–109.

Rowe, John H. (1997). Las tierras reales de los incas. In *Arqueología, Antropología, e Historia en los Andes*, edited by Rafael Varón Gabai and Javier Flores Espinoza, pp. 277–87. Instituto de Estudios Peruanos, Lima.

Rowe, John H. (2006). The Inca Civil War and the Establishment of Spanish Power in Peru. *Ñawpa Pacha* 28: 1–9.

Rowe, John H. (2008). A Question of Time: Juan de Betanzos and the *Narrative of the Incas*, translated by Catherine Julien. *Ñawpa Pacha* 29: 155–62.

Ruiz de Arce, Juan (1933). Relación de servicios en Indias. *Boletín de la Real Academia de Historia* 102: 327–84. (Originally written c. 1545.)

Russell, Glenn S. (1988). The Effect of Inka Administrative Policy on the Domestic Economy of the Wanka, Peru: The Production and Use of Stone Tools. PhD dissertation, Department of Anthropology. University of California, Los Angeles.

Rydén, Stig (1947). *Archaeological Researches in the Highlands of Bolivia*. Elanders Boktryckeri Aktiebolag, Göteborg.

Sadowski, Robert M. (1989). The Sky above the Incas: An Abridged Astronomical Calendar for the Sixteenth Century. In *Time and Calendars in the Inca Empire*, edited by Mariusz S. Ziółkowski and Robert M. Sadowski, pp. 75–106. British Archaeological Reports, International Series 479, Oxford.

Sahlins, Marshall David (1981). *Historical Metaphors and Mythical Realities: Structure in the Early History of the Sandwich Islands Kingdom*, vol. 1. University of Michigan Press, Ann Arbor.

Said, Edward W. (1978). *Orientalism*. Vintage Books, New York.

Saignes, Thierry (1985). *Los Andes orientales: historia de un olvido*. Instituto Francés de Estudios Andinos and Centro de Estudios de la Realidad Económica y Social, Cochabamba, Bolivia.

Salazar, Lucy C. (2004). Machu Picchu: Mysterious Royal Estate in the Cloud Forest. In *Machu Picchu: Unveiling the Mystery of the Incas*, edited by Richard Burger and Lucy C. Salazar, pp. 20–47. Yale University Press, New Haven.

Salazar, Lucy C. (2007). Machu Picchu's Silent Majority: A Consideration of the Inka Cemeteries. In *Variations in the Expression of Power in the Inka Empire*, edited by Richard Burger, Craig Morris, and Ramiro Matos Mendieta, pp. 165–84. Dumbarton Oaks, Washington, DC.

Salazar, Lucy C., and Richard S. Burger (2004). Lifestyles of the Rich and Famous: Luxury and Daily Life in the Households of Machu Picchu's Elite. In *Palaces of the*

Ancient New World, edited by Susan T. Evans and Joanne Pillsbury, pp. 325–57. Washington, DC, Dumbarton Oaks.

Sallnow, Michael J. (1987). *Pilgrims of the Andes: Regional Cults in Cusco*. Smithsonian Institution Press, Washington, DC.

Salomon, Frank (1986). *Native Lords of Quito in the Age of the Incas*. Cambridge University Press, Cambridge.

Salomon, Frank (1987). A North Andean Status Trader Complex under Inca Rule. *Ethnohistory* 34(1): 63–77.

Salomon, Frank (1991). Introduction. In *The Huarochirí Manuscript: A Testament of Ancient and Colonial Andean Religion*, edited by Frank L. Salomon and Jorge Urioste. University of Texas Press, Austin.

Salomon, Frank (1995). "The Beautiful Grandparents": Andean Ancestor Shrines and Mortuary Ritual as Seen Through Colonial Records. In *Tombs for the Living: Andean Mortuary Practices*, edited by Tom D. Dillehay, pp. 315–53. Dumbarton Oaks Research Library and Collection, Washington, D.C.

Salomon, Frank (2004). *The Cord-Keepers*. Duke University Press, Durham, NC.

Salomon, Frank (2005). Preface. In *Titu Cusi: A Sixteenth-Century Account of the Conquest*, translated by Nicole Delia Legnani, pp. v–vi. Harvard University, Cambridge, MA.

Salomon, Frank L., and Sabine Hyland (2010). Guest Editors' Introduction to *Ethnohistory* 57 (1), special issue *Graphic Pluralism*: 1–9.

Salomon, Frank L., and Mercedes Niño-Murcia (2011). *The Lettered Mountain: A Peruvian Village's Way with Writing*. Duke University Press, Durham, NC.

Salomon, Frank L., and Jorge Urioste, eds. (1991). *The Huarochirí Manuscript: A Testament of Ancient and Colonial Andean Religion (Often attributed to Francisco de Ávila)*. University of Texas Press, Austin.

Salvatore, Ricardo D. (2003). Local versus Imperial Knowledge: Reflections on Hiram Bingham and the Yale Peruvian Expedition. *Nepantla: Views from the South* 4(1): 67–80.

Sámano-Xérez (1937). *Relación*, edited by Raúl Porras Barrenechea. Cuadernos de Historia del Perú, Paris.

Sancho de la Hoz, Pedro (1917). Relación. In *[1532–1533] Colección de Libros y Documentos Referentes a la Historia del Perú*, edited by Horacio H. Urteaga, vol. 5, pp. 122–202. Sanmartí, Lima. (Originally written 1532–3.)

Sandefur, Elsie (2001). Animal Husbandry and Consumption. In *Empire and Domestic Economy*, edited by Terence N. D'Altroy *et al.*, pp. 179–202. Kluwer Academic/Plenum Press, New York

Santillán, Hernando de (1968). *Relación del orígen, descendencia, política y gobierno de los incas*. Biblioteca de Autores Españoles (continuación), vol. 209, pp. 97–149. Ediciones Atlas, Madrid. (Originally written 1563.)

Santo Tomás, Fray Domingo de (1951). *Lexicón, o vocabulario de la lengua general del Perú*. Facsimile edition by Raúl Porras Barranechea, Lima. (Originally written 1560.)

Sarmiento de Gamboa, Pedro (2007). *The History of the Incas*, translated and edited by Brian S. Bauer and Vania Smith. University of Texas Press, Austin. (Originally written 1572.)

Savoy, Gene (1970). *Antisuyo: the Search for the Lost Cities of the Amazon*. Simon & Schuster, New York.

Schaedel, Richard P. (1978). Early State of the Incas. In *The Early State*, edited by Henri M. Claessen and Peter Skalnik, pp. 289–320. Mouton, The Hague.

Schjellerup, Inge (1997). *Incas and Spaniards in the Conquest of the Chachapoyas: Archaeological and Ethnohistorical Research in the North-Eastern Andes of Peru*. Gothenberg University, Dept. of Archaeology Series B. Gothenberg Archaeological Theses 7. Gothenberg.

Schobinger, Juan (1995). *Anconcagua. Un enterratoria incaico a 5.300 metros de altura*. Inca Editorial, Mendoza, Argentina.

Schobinger, Juan, *et al.*, eds. (1966). *La "momia" del Cerro el Toro*. Suppelement to *Anales de Arqueología y Etnología* 21. Mendoza, Argentina.

Schreiber, Katharina J. (1992). *Wari Imperialism in Middle Horizon Peru*. Museum of Anthropology, University of Michigan, Ann Arbor.

Schreiber, Katharina J. (2001). The Wari Empire of Middle Horizon Peru: The Epistemological Challenge of Documenting an Empire without Documentary Evidence. In *Empires*, edited by Susan E. Alcock, Terence N. D'Altroy, Kathleen D. Morrison, and Carla M. Sinopoli, pp. 70–92. Cambridge University Press, Cambridge.

Segovia, Bartolomé de (1968). Relación de muchas cosas acaecidas en el Peru … In *Crónicas peruanas de interés indígena* [often attributed to Cristóbal de Molina (el Almagrista)]. Biblioteca de Autores Españoles 209. Ediciones Atlas, Madrid. (Originally written 1553.)

Selder, Dennis W. S. (2007). Toward a Sound Methodology for Comparative Rhetoric with Aymara as a Case Study. PhD dissertation, Dept. of English, University of Arizona, Tucson.

Seltzer, Geoffrey O., and Christine A. Hastorf (1990). Climatic Change and Its Effect on Prehispanic Agriculture in the Central Peruvian Andes. *Journal of Field Archaeology* 17: 397–414.

Shady Solís, Ruth (2006). America's First City? The Case of Late Archaic Caral. In *Andean Archaeology III*, edited by William H. Isbell and Helaine Silverman, pp. 28–66. Springer, New York.

Shady Solís, Ruth (2008). *Caral: la primera civilización de América*. Universidad de San Martín de Porres, Lima.

Shady Solís, Ruth, Jonathan Haas, and Winifred Creamer (2001). Dating Caral, a Preceramic Site in the Supe Valley on the Central Coast of Peru. *Science* 292: 723–6.

Sherbondy, Jeanette E. (1992). Water Ideology in Inca Ethnogenesis. In *Andean Cosmologies through Time*, edited by Robert V. H. Dover, Katharine E. Seibold, and John H. McDowell, pp. 46–66. Indiana University Press, Bloomington.

Sherbondy, Jeanette E. (1994). Water and Power: The Role of Irrigation Districts in the Transition from Inca to Spanish Cuzco. In *Irrigation at High Altitudes: The Social Organization of Water Control Systems in the Andes*, edited by William P. Mitchell and David Guillet. Society for Latin American Anthropology Publication Series 12, pp. 69–97. American Anthropological Association, Washington, DC.

Shimada, Izumi (1994). *Pampa Grande and the Mochica Culture*. University of Texas Press, Austin.

Shimada, Izumi, ed. (in press). *The Inca Empire: A Multidisciplinary Approach to a Holistic Vision*. University of Texas Press, Austin.

Shinoda, Ken-Ichi (in press). Tracing the Origin of Inka People through Ancient DNA Analysis. In Izumi Shimada, ed. *The Inca Empire: A Multidisciplinary Approach to a Holistic Vision*. University of Texas Press, Austin.

Shinoda, Ken-ichi, Noboru Adachi, Sonia Guillen, and Izumi Shimada (2006). Mitochondrial DNA Analysis of Ancient Peruvian Highlanders. *American Journal of Physical Anthropology* 131(1): 98–107. Online at http://onlinelibrary. wiley.com/doi/10.1002/ajpa.20408/abstract (accessed December 10, 2013).

Sillar, Bill (2009). The Social Agency of Things? Animism and Materiality in the Andes. *Cambridge Archaeological Journal* 19: 367–77.

Silva, Shanaka de, and Jorge Alzueta (2000). The Socioeconomic Consequences of the A.D. 1600 Eruption of Huaynaputina, Southern Peru. *Geological Society of America Special Paper* 345: 15–24.

Silverblatt, Irene (1987). *Moon, Sun, Witches: Gender Ideologies and Class in Inca and Colonial Peru*. Princeton University Press, Princeton.

Silverman, Helaine, and Donald Proulx (2002). *The Nasca*. Blackwell, Malden, MA.

Sinopoli, Carla M. (1994). The Archaeology of Empires. *Annual Review of Anthropology* 23: 159–80.

Smith, Michael (2012). *The Aztecs*. 3rd edn. Wiley-Blackwell, Oxford.

Smith, Monica (2005). Networks, Territories, and the Cartography of Ancient States. *Annals of the Association of American Geographers* 95(4): 832–49.

Snead, James (1992). Imperial Infrastructure and the Inka State Storage System. In *Inka Storage Systems*, edited by Terry Y. LeVine, pp. 62–106. University of Oklahoma Press. Norman.

Spencer, Herbert (1974). *The Evolution of Society: Selections from Herbert Spencer's Principles of Sociology*, edited and with an introduction by Robert L. Carneiro. University of Chicago Press, Chicago.

Spurling, Geoffrey E. (1982). Inka Militarism. Unpublished manuscript.

Spurling, Geoffrey E. (1992). The Organization of Craft Production in the Inka State: The Potters and Weavers of Milliraya. PhD dissertation, Department of Anthropology, Cornell University. University Microfilms, Ann Arbor, MI.

Squier, George E. (1877). *Peru: Incidents of Travel and Exploration in the Land of the Incas*. Macmillan, London.

Stanish, Charles (1997). Nonmarket Imperialism in the Prehispanic Americas: The Inka Occupation of the Titicaca Basin. *Latin American Antiquity* 8: 195–216.

Stark, Louisa R. (1969). The Lexical Structure of Quechua Body Parts *Anthropological Linguistics* 11(1): 1–15.

Stehberg, Rubén (1976). *La fortaleza de Chena y su relación con la ocupación incaica de Chile Central.* Museo Nacional de Historia Natural, publicación ocasional 23. Santiago, Chile.

Strathern, Marilyn (1988). *The Gender of the Gift: Problems with Women and Problems with Society in Melanesia.* University of Califomia Press, Berkeley.

Strube Erdmann, León (1963). *Vialidad Imperial de los Incas.* Serie Histórica 33. Instituto de Estudios Americanistas, Facultad de Filosofía y Humanidades, Universidad Nacional de Córdoba, Córdoba, Argentina.

Swanson, Stephanie (2008–9). Repatriating Cultural Property: The Dispute between Yale and Peru over the Treasures of Machu Picchu. *San Diego International Law Journal* 10: 469–94.

Szemiñski, Jan (2008). Montesinos, Fernando de (*c.* 1600–1651). In *Guide to Documentary Sources for Andean Studies, 1530–1900,* edited by Joanne Pillsbury, vol. 3, pp. 429–32. University of Oklahoma Press, Norman.

Taussig, Michael (1993). *Mimesis and Alterity: A Particular History of the Senses.* Routledge, New York.

Taylor, Gérald (1974). *Camay, camac et camasca* dans le manuscript Quechua de Huarochirí. *Journal de la Société des Américanistes* 63: 231–44.

Thomas, R. Brooke (1973). *Human Adaptation to a High Andean Energy Flow System.* Department of Anthropology, Pennsylvania State University, Occasional Papers in Anthropology 7. University Park.

Thompson, Donald E. (1967). Investigaciones arqueológicas en las aldeas chupachu de Ichu y Auquimarka. In *Visita de la Provincia de León de Huánuco en 1562: Iñigo Ortiz de Zúñiga, visitador,* edited by John V. Murra, vol. 1, pp. 357–62. Universidad Nacional Hermilio Valdizán, Huánuco, Peru

Thompson, Donald E., and John V. Murra (1966). The Inca Bridges in the Huánuco Region. *American Antiquity* 31(5): 632–9.

Thompson, L. G., E. Mosley-Thompson, J. F. Bolzana, and B. R. Koci (1985). 1500-Year Record of Tropical Precipitation in Ice Cores from the Quelccaya Ice Cap, Peru. *Science* 229: 971–3.

Titu Cusi Yupanqui (2005). *Titu Cusi: A Sixteenth-Century Account of the Conquest,* introduction, Spanish modernization, England translation and notes by Nicole Delia Legnani. Harvard University Press, Cambridge, MA. (Originally written 1570.)

Toledo, Francisco de, (1940). Información hecha por orden de Don Francisco de Toledo en su visita de las Provincias del Perú, en la que declaran indios ancianos sobre el derecho de los cicaciques y sobre el gobierno que tenían aquellos pueblos antes que los Incas los conquistasen. In *Don Francisco de Toledo, Supremo Organizador del Peru: su Vida, su Obra [1515–1582],* edited by Roberto Levillier, vol. 2, pp. 14–37. Espasa-Calpe, Buenos Aires. (Originally written 1570.)

Tomka, Steven A. (1987). Resource Ownership and Utilization Patterns among the Yanque-Collaguas as Manifested in the *Visita de Yanque-Collaguas*, 1591. *Andean Perspective Newsletter* 5: 15–24.

Torero, Alfredo (2002). *Idiomas de los Andes: lingüística e historia.* Travaux de l'Institut Français d'Études Andines 162. Instituto Francés de Estudios Andinos, Horizonte, Lima.

Trawick, Paul (2001). The Moral Economy of Water: Equity and Antiquity in the Andean Commons. *American Anthropologist* 103(2): 361–79.

Trimborn, Hermann (1925). Straftat und Sühne in Alt-Peru. *Zeitschrift für Ethnologie* 57: 194–240.

Trimborn, Hermann (1937). Der Rechtsbruch in den Hochkuturen Amerikas. *Zeitschrift für vergleichende Rechtswissenschaft* 51: 8–129.

Truhan, Deborah L. (1997). Demografía y etnicidad: Los Cañaris del Corregimiento de Cuenca, siglos XVI–XVII. Presentation at the 49th International Congress of Americanists, Quito.

Trujillo, Diego de, (1985). *Relación del descubrimiento del reino del Peru*, in *Verdadera relación de la conquista del Perú*, by Francisco de Xérez, edited by Concepción Bravo, pp. 191–206. Historia 16, Madrid. (Originally written 1571.)

Turner, Bethany L., George D. Kamenov, John D. Kingston, George J. Armelagos (2009). Insights into Immigration and Social Class at Machu Picchu, Peru, Based on Oxygen, Strontium, and Lead Isotopic Analysis. *Journal of Archaeological Science* 36: 317–32.

Tylor, Edward B. (1958). *Primitive Culture*. Harper, New York.

Uhle, Max (1903). *Pachacamac – Report of the William Pepper, MD, LLD, Peruvian Expedition of 1896*. Department of Archaeology, University of Pennsylvania, Philadelphia.

Uhle, Max (1909). La esfero de influencias del país de los incas. *Revista Histórica* 4: 5–40.

Uhle, Max (1917). Fortalezas incaicas: Incallacta – Machupichu. *Revista Chilena de Historia y Geografía* 21: 154–70.

Uhle, Max (1923). *Las ruinas de Tombebamba*. Imprenta Julio Sáenz Rebolledo, Quito.

Urton, Gary (1981). *At the Crossroads of the Earth and the Sky: An Andean Cosmology*. University of Texas Press, Austin.

Urton, Gary (1990). *The History of a Myth: Pacariqtambo and the Origin of the Inkas*. University of Texas Press, Austin.

Urton, Gary (1993). Contesting the Past in the Peruvian Andes. In *Mémoire de la tradition*, edited by Aurore Becquelin and Antoinette Molinié with assistance of Danièle Dehouve, pp. 107–44. Nanterre, Société d'ethnologie.

Urton, Gary (1997). *The Social Life of Numbers*. University of Texas Press, Austin.

Urton, Gary (1998). From Knots to Narratives: Reconstructing the Art of Historical Record-Keeping in the Andes from Spanish Transcriptions of Inka *Khipus*. *Ethnohistory* 45(3): 409–38.

Urton, Gary (1999). *Inca Myths*. University of Texas Press, Austin.

Urton, Gary (2001). A Calendrical and Demographic Tomb Text from Northern Peru. *Latin American Antiquity* 12: 127–47.

Urton, Gary (2003). *Signs of the Inka Khipu.* University of Texas Press, Austin.

Urton, Gary (2010). Recording Measure(ment)s in the Inka *khipu.* In *The Archaeology of Measurement,* edited by Iain Morley and Colin Renfrew, pp. 54–68. Cambridge University Press, Cambridge.

Valcárcel, Luis E. (1934–5). Sajsawaman redescubierto. 3 parts. *Revista del Museo Nacional* 3(1–2): 3–36.

Valdivia, Pedro de (1960). *Carta al Emperador Carlos V.* Biblioteca de Autores Españoles (continuación), vol. 131, pp. 3–74. Ediciones Atlas, Madrid.

Valencia Zegarra, Alfredo, and Arminda Gibaja Oviedo (1992). *Machu Picchu: La investigación y conservación del monumento arqueológico después de Hiram Bingham.* Municipalidad de Qosqo, Cuzco.

Valera, Blas (1945). La historia de los Incas. In *Las costumbres antiqugas de los Incas,* edited by Francisco de Loyaza. Pequeños Grandes Libros de Historia Americana, series 1, vol. 8, Lima. (Originally written *c.* 1585–90.)

Van Creveld, Martin L. (1977). *Supplying War: Logistics from Wallenstein to Patton.* 1st paperback edn. Cambridge University Press, New York.

Van de Guchte, Maarten J. D. (1990). "Carving the World": Inca Monumental Sculpture and Landscape. PhD dissertation, Department of Anthropology, University of Illinois at Urbana-Champaign. University Microfilms, Ann Arbor, MI.

Van de Guchte, Maarten J. D. (1996). Sculpture and the Concept of the Double among the Inca Kings. *RES: Anthropology and Aesthetics* 29/30, *The Pre-Columbian*: 256–68.

Van de Guchte, Maarten J. D. (1999). The Inca Cognition of Landscape: Archaeology, Ethnohistory, and the Aesthetic of Alterity. In *Archaeologies of Landscape: Contemporary Perspectives,* edited by Wendy Ashmore and A. Bernard Knapp, pp. 149–68. Blackwell, Malden, MA.

Vega, Andrés de (1965). La descripción que se hizo en la Provincia de Xauxa por la instrucción de Su Majestad que a la dicha provincia se invió de molde [1582]. In *Relaciones geográficas de Indias, Biblioteca de autores españoles* 183, pp. 166–75. Ediciones Atlas, Madrid.

Verano, John W. (2003). Human Skeletal Remains from Machu Picchu. A Reexamination of the Yale Peabody Museum's Collections. In *The 1912 Yale Peruvian Scientific Expedition Collections from Machu Picchu: Human and Animal Remains,* edited by Richard L. Burger and Lucy C. Salazar, pp. 65–117. Yale University Publications in Anthropology 85, Peabody Museum of Anthropology, New Haven, CT.

Verosub, Kenneth. L., and Jake Lippman (2008). Global Impacts of the 1600 Eruption of Peru's Huaynaputina Volcano. *Eos* 89: 15: 141–8.

Vilímek, Vit, J. Zvelebil, J. Klimeš, Z. Patzelt, F. Astete, V. Kachlík, and F. Hartvich (2007). Geomorphological Research of Large-scale Slope Instability at Machu Picchu, Peru. *Geomorphology* 89(3): 241–57.

Villanueva Urteaga, Horacio (1971). Documentos sobre Yucay, siglo XVI. *Revista del Archivo Histórico de Cuzco* 13: 1–148.

Wachtel, Nathan (1977). *The Vision of the Vanquished*, translated by Ben Reynolds and Sian Reynolds. Barnes & Noble, New York.

Wachtel, Nathan (1982). The Mitimas of the Cochabamba Valley: The Colonization Policy of Huayna Capac. In *The Inca and Aztec States 1400–1800: Anthropology and History*, edited by George A. Collier, Renato I. Rosaldo, and John D. Wirth, pp. 199–235. Academic Press, New York.

Wallerstein, Immanuel (1974). *The Modern World-System I*. Academic Press, New York.

Wedin, Åke (1965). *El sistema decimal en el imperio incáico. Estudio sobre estructura política, división territorial y población*. Instituto Ibero-Americano, Gothenburg, and Insula, Madrid.

Wernke, Steven (2010). A Reduced Landscape: Toward a Multi-Causal Understanding of Historic Period Agricultural Deintensification in Highland Peru. *Journal of Latin American Geography* 9(3): 51–83.

Wernke, Steven (2012a). *Negotiated Settlements: Andean Communities and Landscapes under Inka and Spanish Colonialism*. University Press of Florida, Gainesville.

Wernke, Steven (2012b). Spatial Network Analysis of a Terminal Prehispanic and Early Colonial Settlement in Highland Peru. *Journal of Archaeological Science* 39(4): 1111–22.

West, Terry L. (1981). Llama Caravans of the Andes. *Natural History* 90(12): 62–73.

Wicander, Reed, and James S. Monroe (1989). *Historical Geology: Evolution of the Earth and Life through Time*. West Publishing Co., St. Paul, MN.

Wilkinson, Darryl (2013). Politics, Instrastructure and Non-human Subjects: The Inka Occupation of the Amaybamba Cloud Forests. PhD dissertation, Dept. of Anthropology, Columbia University, New York.

Williams, Verónica I. (1996). La ocupación inka en la región central de Catamarca (República Argentina). PhD dissertation, Facultad de Ciencias Naturales. La Plata, Universidad Nacional de La Plata.

Williams, Verónica I., and Ana María Lorandi (1986). *Evidencias funcionales de un establecimiento incaico en el noroeste argentino*. Comechingonia, Córdoba.

Wilson, Andrew, Timothy Taylor, Constanza Ceruti, Johan Reinhard, José Antonio Chávez, Vaughan Grimes, Wolfram Meier-Augenstein, Larry Cartmell, Ben Stern, Michael Richards, Michael Worobey, Ian Barnes, and Thomas Gilbert (2007). Stable Isotope and DNA Evidence for Ritual Sequences in Inca Child Sacrifice. *Proceedings of the National Academy of Sciences* 104(42): 16456–61.

Windley, B. F. (1995). *The Evolving Continents*. 3rd edn. Wiley, New York.

Wright, Kenneth R., and Valencia Zegarra, Alfredo (2000). *Machu Picchu: A Civil Engineering Marvel*. American Society of Civil Engineers, Reston, VA.

Wright, Kenneth R., Gordon Francis McEwan, and Ruth M. Wright (2006). *Tipón: Water Engineering Masterpiece of the Inca Empire*. American Society of Civil Engineers, Reston, VA.

Wright, Kenneth R., Ruth M. Wright, Alfredo Valencia Zegarra, and Gordon Francis McEwan (2011). *Moray: Inca Engineering Mystery*. American Society of Civil Engineers, Reston, VA.

Wright, Ruth M., and Alfredo Valencia Zegarra (2001). *The Machu Picchu Guidebook: A Self-Guided Tour*. Johnson Books, Boulder, CO.

Xérez, Francisco de (1985). *Verdadera relación de la conquista del Perú y provincia del Cuzco llamada la Nueva Castilla*, edited by Concepción Bravo. Historia 16, Madrid. (Originally written 1534.)

Zárate, Augustín de (1862). *Historia del descubrimiento y conquista de la Provincia del Perú*. Biblioteca de Autores Españoles (continuación), vol. 26, pp. 459–574. Ediciones Atlas, Madrid. (Originally written 1555.)

Ziółkowski, Mariusz S. (1996). *La guerra de los Wawqi: los objetivos y los mecanismos de la rivalidad dentro de la élite inka, siglos XV–XVI*. Ediciones Abya-Yala, Quito, Ecuador.

Ziółkowski, Mariusz S., and Robert M. Sadowski, eds. (1989). *Time and Calendars in the Inca Empire*. British Archaeological Reports, International Series 479, Oxford.

Zuidema, R. Tom (1964). *The Ceque System of Cuzco*, translated by Eva M. Hooykaas. International Archives of Ethnography, Supplement to vol. 50. E. J. Brill, Leiden, Netherlands.

Zuidema, R. Tom (1977). The Inca Kinship System: A New Theoretical View. In *Andean Kinship and Marriage*, edited by Ralph Bolton and Enrique Mayer, pp. 240–81. American Anthropological Association Special Publication 7, Washington, DC.

Zuidema, R. Tom (1982). Myth and History in Ancient Peru. In *The Logic of Culture*, edited by I. Rossi, pp. 150–75. Bergin, South Hadley, MA.

Zuidema, R. Tom (1983). Hierarchy and Space in Incaic Social Organization. *Ethnohistory* 30: 49–75.

Zuidema, R. Tom (2010). *El calendario inca: tiempo y espacio en la organización ritual del Cuzco: la idea del pasado*. Fondo Editorial de la Pontificia Universidad Católica del Perú, Lima.

Zuidema, R. Tom, and D. Poole (1982). Los límites de los cuatro suyus incaicos en el Cuzco. *Bulletin de l'Institut Français d'Études Andines* 11(1–2): 83–9.

Glossary of Foreign Terms

This glossary contains most of the non-English terms used in the text, with the preferred definition for this book listed first. Because translations and meanings of the terms vary, a range of definitions is provided, but this glossary should not be taken as an exhaustive survey. Specific quoted definitions, attributed in brackets, are derived from Cerrón-Palomino 1976 [CP]; González Holguín 1952 [1608] [DGH]; Urioste's glossary-index in Guaman Poma 1980: 1075–108 [GP]; Haggard and McLean 1941 [HM]; Hornberger and Hornberger 1983 [HH]; Hyslop 1990: 333–4 [JH]; Murra 1980b [1956]: 191–4 [JVM]; and Santo Tomás 1951 [ST]. Cerrón-Palomino's dictionary refers to the modern Quechua of the Junín region, while the Hornbergers' dictionary is based on the modern Quechua from the Cuzco region. Languages are Arawak (Ar), Aymara (Ay), Quechua (Q), and Spanish (S). Words in square brackets in the text are this author's insertions.

allawqa (Q; also *allauco* [CP: p. 26]) right.

altiplano (S) high-elevation plain in Bolivia and far northwestern Argentina.

Ananwanka (Q) upper (moiety) division of *Wanka* ethnic group; southernmost of three political divisions of Inca province of *Wanka Wamaní*, populated principally by *Wanka* and *Xauxa* ethnic groups.

Antisuyu (Q; also *Andesuyo*) northeastern part of Inca empire, generally corresponding to warm lowlands.

apu (Q, also sp. *apo*) "great lord or superior judge" [GP: p. 1076].

aqlla (Q; plural *aqllakuna*) "woman chosen for state and religious service" [JH: p. 333]; "hidden" [GP: p. 1076].

awasqa (Q) rough cloth; "common, thick cloth" [GP: p. 1077].

The Incas, Second Edition. Terence N. D'Altroy.
© 2015 John Wiley & Sons, Ltd. Published 2015 by John Wiley & Sons, Ltd.

ayllu (Q) localized descent group, varying in inclusiveness, frequently sub-divided into moieties, lineages, or both; "division, genealogy, lineage, or kinship" [GP: p. 1078, after DGH: p. 39]; "kinsman, family relation" [CP: p. 33]; generally, any group of things or beings.

Aymara (called *Haquru* by its speakers) one of three principal Andean languages, spoken primarily from far southern Peru through Bolivian altiplano.

bulto (S): mummy-bundle, icon made of hair and nail clippings, or a stone icon standing in for those things.

cacique (Ar) leader, a term frequently applied by Spaniards to anyone in a position of indigenous authority.

cacique principal (Ar–S) paramount leader of sociopolitical unit.

camaquen (Q): vitality; *camac*: a being or thing that confers vitality; *camay*: the capacity to confer vitality.

ceja de la montaña (S) upper forested area on eastern slopes of Andes.

ceja de selva (S) upper fringe of the jungle.

ch'arki (Q) freeze-dried (jerked) meat.

chala (Q) coastal environmental zone.

chaski (Q) "postal messenger" [GP: p. 1079].

chicha (Ar) "a fermented beverage, generally of maize, originally a Caribbean word" [JH: p. 333]; in Quechua *aqha, aswa* [GP: p. 1079].

Chinchaysuyu (Q) northwestern part of Inca empire, generally correspond-ing to the Peruvian and Ecuadorian highlands and coast.

chinu (A) mnemonic knot-register, known as *khipu* in Quechua.

chullpa (Q) above-ground tomb.

chunka kamayuq (Q) official at head of 10-household census unit.

chuño (Q) freeze-dried potatoes.

Cuntisuyu (Q; also sp. *Condesuyo, Kuntisuyu*) southwestern part of Inca empire, generally corresponding to the southernmost Peruvian highlands, and the south Peruvian and northern Chilean coast.

encomienda (S) early Spanish grant of the labor service of native peoples to Spanish recipient.

etnía (S) Spanish term referring to named ethnic group, corresponding unevenly to self-identified prehispanic groups.

hanon (Q) upper half or moiety of dual units characterizing Inca sociopolitical organization.

hanega (S) a dry measure approximating 1.60 bushels [HM: p. 76], 56.6 liters, or 43.6 kg for shelled maize.

hanegada measure of land corresponding to 0.64 ha or 1.59 acre (HM: p. 77).

hatun (Q) big.

hatun runa (Q) "adult, married male" [GP: p. 1081]; "Male peasant" [DGH: p. 154]. "An adult male, married and enumerated in the Inca census. Literally 'big man'" [JVM: p. 192].

hunu (Q) unit of 10,000; often used to refer to census or sociopolitical unit ostensibly consisting of 10,000 households.

hunu kuraka (Q) official at head of 10,000-household census unit.

hurin (Q) lower half or moiety of dual units characterizing Inca sociopolitical organization.

ichuq (Q; also sp. *ichoca* [CP: p. 56], *lloq'e* [HH: p. 386]) left.

indios (S) generally, the indigenous commoner population.

janca (Q) the highest elevation environmental zone, without permanent human occupation, characterized by glaciers and sparse biota.

kallanka (Q) "a long hall, often with a gabled roof" [JH: p. 333].

kancha (Q) "an enclosure; several rooms placed around a patio, generally within a rectangular perimeter wall" [JH: p. 333].

khipu (Q; also sp. *quipu*) "cords with knots used [as a mnemonic device] in Inka accounting" [GP: p. 1086]; "knot, ancient Andean recording system" [HH: p. 89]; from "*Qquipuni*. To count by [use of] knots" [DGH: p. 309].

khipu kamayuq (Q) official responsible for keeping records on knotted strings.

Kollasuyu (Q; [HH: p. 188], also sp. *Collasuyo, Qollasuyu*) southeastern part of Inca empire.

kuraka (Q; also sp. *curaca, kuraqka* [JVM: p. 192]) native elite; "local ethnic authority" [GP: p. 1085]; "representative of the local god" [HH: p. 84].

libra (S) a measure of weight equal to about 0.46 kg, for Peru and Mexico (HM: p. 79).

llaqta (Q; also sp. *llacta* [DGH: p. 207]) "town" [GP: p. 1087]; "'Pueblo' [DGH: p. 207]. A town, a nucleated settlement" [JVM: p. 192]; "town, city, fatherland, nation, country, community" [HH: p. 111].

mallki (Q): mummy; planted thing, sprout ready for planting, any fruit-bearing tree, sapling [ST: p. 314; DGH: p. 224].

marca (Q; also sp. *malka* [CP: p. 85]) "people [town], population" [CP: p. 85].

mascaypacha (Q) woven textile fringe worn as insignia of emperor's office.

mit'a (Q) "A period, one's turn ... Prestations to one's ethnic group, one's lord and to the Inca state" [JVM: p. 192]; "period [season]; that which returns cyclically, and the turn in which to undertake something [task]" [GP: p. 1090].

mit'ayuq (Q) individual serving rotational labor service to the Inca state [Spurling 1992 118, n. 177].

mitmaq (Q; pl. *mitmaqkuna*) "a settler from some other place; an Inka state colonist" [JH: p. 333]; "from *mit'iy* to send; sent by one's ethnic group of origin to attend to outside interests" [GP: p. 1090].

montaña (S) upper, humid, forested environmental zone on eastern side of the Andes; source of fruit and wild biota.

orejón (S) long-ear; Inca nobility, distinguished by large earspools.

pacha (A, Q): space–time; "time, ground, place" [DGH: p. 268].

pachaka (Q; [GP: p. 1090], also sp. *pachak* [HH: p. 151]) unit of 100; often used to refer to census or sociopolitical unit ostensibly consisting of 100 households.

pachaka kuraka (Q) official at head of 100-household census unit.

panaqa (Q) royal dynastic descent group, or *ayllu*, founded by each ruler.

páramo (S) high rolling grassland of Ecuador and far northern Peru.

pichkachunka (Q, also sp. *pisqachunka* [GP: p. 1090]) unit of 50; often used to refer to census or sociopolitical unit ostensibly consisting of 50 households.

pichkachunka kamayuq (Q) official at head of 50-household census unit.

pichkapachaka (Q) unit of 500; often used to refer to census or sociopolitical unit ostensibly consisting of 500 households.

pichkapachaka kuraka (Q) official at head of 500-household census unit.

pichkawaranqa (Q) unit of 5,000; often used to refer to census or sociopolitical unit ostensibly consisting of 5,000 households.

pichkawaranqa kuraka (Q) official at head of 5,000-household census unit.

pirka (Q) rustic or fieldstone masonry.

pueblo (S) town, people.

puna (Q) high-elevation environmental zone, generally characterized by rolling grasslands; natural habitat of camelids and principal zone for herding.

pururaucas (Q) ["Hidden Thieves"] idols venerated by Incas as stones risen as warriors to aid defense of Cuzco against Chanka attack.

qhapaq ñan (Q; also sp. *capac ñan*) powerful road, i.e., imperial Inca highway [see GP: p. 1096].

qollana (Q) excellent; one of three divisions, *qollana – payan – kayaw*, found in Cuzco area sociopolitical organization.

qollqa (Q; also sp. *colca, qullqa* [GP: p. 1095], *qolqa* [HH: p. 187]) storehouse.

qompi (Q; also sp. *cumbi, qumpi* [GP: p. 1095]) fine cloth.

qoya (Q) queen, principal wife of ruler.

Quechua (Q) dominant language group in central Andean highlands; also, ethnic group that inhabited the northwest side of Lake Titicaca at the time of the Inca expansion.

quechua (Q; also sp. *qheshwa, qheswa* [HH: p. 109]) temperate, mid-elevation environmental zone, found on eastern and western slopes of Andes, as well as in intermontane valleys; principal highland zone for maize-complex crops.

relación (S) account, report.

runakhipu (Q) state officials responsible for census-taking.

runasimi (Q) human speech, i.e., Quechua.

saya (Q) a sociopolitical subdivision; "the upper or lower, the right or left moiety, in Andean dual organization" [JVM: p. 193].

selva alta (S) upper jungle.

selva baja (S) lower jungle.

señorío (S) a polity ruled by a native lord.

suni (Q) moderately high-elevation environmental zone, above *quechua* and below *puna*; principal highland zone for tuber-complex crops.

suyu (Q) "territory, region" [HH: p. 242].

suyuyoc apu (Q) lord of a great political unit, sometimes specifically meaning half of the empire; *suyuyuq* "administration of a subdivision" [GP: p. 1101].

tampu (Q, also sp. *tanpu* [GP: p. 1101]) "Inka state lodging on the road system" [JH: p. 333].

Tawantinsuyu "the Inka empire; land of the four (*tawa*) parts or provinces (*suyu*)" [JH: p. 333].

tokoyrikoq (Q) independent Inca inspector who visited the provinces; "He Who Sees All" [Rowe 1946 264].

tokrikoq (Q; also sp. *toricoq* [JH: p. 333], *t'oqrikuq* [JVM: p. 193]) Inca provincial governor.

tumi (Q) ceremonial knife with a crescent-shaped head often used in sacrifices.

tupu (Q) "a measure of any kind, a league" [DHG: p. 347]; "agricultural measure" [CP: p. 1102]; "general measure" [CP: p. 136]; "measure (volume), measure of land" [HH: p. 253]. Not to be confused with an alternative meaning of *tupu* – "fastening pin" [HH: p. 253].

usnu (Q, also sp. *ushnu* [JH: p. 334]) platform mound in a ceremonial complex or a drain into which libations were poured; "a centrally located ritual complex consisting of a drain with a stone, basin, and platform within Inka settlements" [JH: p. 334]; "ceremonial or administrative construction" [GP: p. 1103]; "a niche, usually in a wall, used for placing idols or other venerated or sacred objects" [HH: p. 274].

wak'a (Q; also sp. *huaca*, *waqa* [JH: p. 334]) shrine, sacred place, object, or power; "tutelary divinity, at the local level" [GP: p. 1104].

wamani (Q) "Incaic administrative district" [GP: p. 1104]; also, mountain peak spirit.

waranqa (Q) unit of 1,000; often used to refer to census or sociopolitical unit ostensibly consisting of 1,000 households.

waranqa kuraka (Q) official at head of 1,000-household census unit.

wawqi (Q): brother or brother-image, of human or other being, most often mentioned in context of Inca rulers.

yana (Q; pl. *yanakuna*) "a servant, a young man in service [DGH: p. 363], from *yanapa*, reciprocal services given without accounts being kept" [JVM: p. 194].

yunga (Q) low-elevation environmental zone, above the coastal plain on the west and the jungle on the east; principal zone for coca and fruits.

yupana (Q): counting-device, generally a board with receptacles for counters.

zeqʼe (Q; also sp. *ceque*, *zeque*) "a radial line or path; a radial system of forty-one lines in Cuzco that integrated Inka kinship, cosmology, and calendrics" [JH: p. 334].

zinchi (Q; plural *zinchikuna*) valiant man, native elite or warlord, generally applied to pre-Inca era.

Index

Page numbers in *italic* refer to figures and plates.

Abancay valley 117 (n. 8), 374–5, *375*, 404
Aconcagua, Mount 35, 283
Acosta, José de 20, 23, 135, 159, 161, 249
administration 174, 354–6
    Spanish 468–71
afterbirth 135
afterlife 184, 306–8
agriculture *see* farming
Agurto Calvo, Santiago 203
Albornoz, Cristóbal de 22, 249, 264, 418, 471
Allen, Catherine 41, 43, 126, 141, 167 (n. 6), 171 (n. 7), 243
Almagro, Diego de (the elder) 341–2, 449, 458, 461, 468
alpaca *see* camelids
Amaru Thupa Inka 195, 213, 276
Amarukancha *200*, 206–7, *207*
amauta (poet-historian) 7, 31 (n. 3), 124, 300, 304
Amaybamba 215, 244, 371, 374, 407, 465
Ambrosetti, Juan de 28, 308, 429
Anachumbi 99
Anawarki 276
ancestor worship 17, 42, 70, 71–2, 125, 128, 135, 136–7, 144, 176, 177, 192, 214, 243, 247–9, 277, 288, 341, 384, 405, 406, 420, 431, 447, 469
    see also mummies
Andahuaylas 69, 75, 94–5

Andes, environment 35–42
animacy *see* vitality
Anta 92
Antisuyu 102, 118 (n. 8), 176, 263, 353
    road 368
    shrines 266, 269–70, *434*
apu
    lord 175, 179, 291–2
    mountain being 42, 309
    see also tirakuna
Apurimac river 80, 202, 252, 347, 371–2, *372*
aqllakuna (Chosen Women) 206, 236, 255, 301, *302*, 308, 366, 379, 397, 429
Arapa 385, 404
Araucanians 103, 333, 390
archaeology, Inca 27–32
architecture 17, 78, 273
    colonies 377
    Cuzco 5, 29, 198–214 *passim*
    estates 162, 214–46 *passim*
    imperial 14, 83, 443
    military 326, 327, 331, 349
    monumental, ritual 14, 47, 48, 81
    of performance 364
    of power 364
    pre-imperial 81–3, 295
    provincial 364–6, 382, 383, 388, 398
    shrines 274, 280, *365*
    stone working 308, 420, 431–6
    storehouses 414

---

aristocracy 80, 108, 176, 181, 187–9, 192, 198, 290
 Chan Chan 54
 education 151, 300
 estates, residences 88 (n. 4), 213–46, 354, 374, 383, 394, 407
 internal conflicts 21, 93, 115, 178, 196
 law and crime 359
 oral and written accounts 7, 19, 87, 174, 190
 rites of passage 303, 427
 and Spaniards 461
 see also elites, *orejones, panaqa*
Arriaga, José de 23, 249
artisans 51, 54, 155, 198, 238, 354, 374, 382, 385, 394–5, 418–48
Ascher, Marcia and Robert 152, 157–8, 166, 173 (n. 53)
ashlar masonry *207*, 209, 221, *223*, 233, 234, 308, 379, 388, 420, 432–3, *433*, 434, 466
astronomy 140, 154, 243, 257–62, 405–6
Atawallpa 6
 Atoq's skull 349
 brother icon 186
 comet 261
 court 179, 181, 451, *455*
 dynastic war against Waskhar 107–13, 387
 encounter with Spaniards 1, 2, 5, 179, 181, 450–1
 genealogy and succession *193–4*, 196
 imprisonment and execution 181–3, 451–9
 military campaigns 105, 333–5, 342–3, 338, 339
 Pachacamac (destruction of idol) 279
 personal guard 338
 ransom 1, 134, 186, 438, 454–8
 wife 19
Atienza, Lope de 344
Atoq 109–10, 341, 349
Aveni, Anthony 268
Ávila, Francisco de 23, 286
Awkaypata 183, *200*, 204–10 *passim, 206*, 260, 340, *367*, 431

Awki Thupa Inka 104
Awki Toma 347
Ayar Awka *71*, 71, 73, 78
Ayar Kachi *71*, 71–2
Ayar Uchu *71*, 71–2
Ayarmaca 74–5, 81, 266
Ayaviri people 97, 373, 384, 416
ayllu (kin group) 32–3
 domestic activities 316–17
 farming 311–12
 grouping of related things 65 (n. 1)
 kin group 42, 72, 146, 155
 marriage 86, 304
 modern 472
 non-royal Inca *ayllu* 188, 208, 214, 263, 270, 309
 peasant communities 294, 314
 provincial system 355–6, 430
 see also Hatun ayllu, panaqa, Qhapaq ayllu
Aymara (people, region) 46, 117 (nn. 5, 8), 169 (n. 21), 264
Aymara language 23, 58–61, *61*, 66 (n. 6), 85, 126, 131, 133
 chinu (*khipu* knot-record) 149, 159
 measurement 162
 nobility (terminology) 291–3
 space–time 139–43, 170 (n. 26)
Azángaro 101, 369, 410

Bandelier, Adolph 28, 78, 280
Barfield, Thomas J. 13
battle tactics 344–8
Bauer, Brian S.
 calendars 257–8, 260
 Cuzco region archaeology 30, 82–3, 207, 245 (n. 2), 264–72
 human sacrifice 279
 Inca origins 73–4
 shrines 264–72
Bertonio, Fray 23, 162, 291–2
Betanzos, Juan Diez de 19–20, 23, 142
 calendar 258–9
 Cuzco 77, 204
 dynastic war 107, 112
 emperor 178–9, 183–4, 186

imperial formation and expansion 93,
    98, 100–4, 117 (n. 8)
origin narratives 72
Punchao (statue of the Sun) 254
Queen 191
storage system 410
time frames 66 (nn. 7, 9)
Bibar, Gerónimo de 23
Bingham, Hiram 28, 78, 224–39,
    245 (n. 7), 464
birth 136, 299–300
Brazamoros 105
bridges 110, 205, 221, 350 (n. 5), 354,
    370–2, *371–2*, 381
brother-image (*wawqi*) 134–5,
    169 (n. 17), 184, 186, 276, 310
bureaucracy 174, 351
Burger, Richard *38*
burials 49, 51, 279, 284, 306–7, 308, 459
    Machu Picchu 236–9, 447
    Saqsawaman, Chokepukio 307
    see also Puruchuco-Huaquerones,
        qhapaq ucha

Cabello Valboa, Miguel de 22
    chronology 22, 62–4, 69
    death of Wayna Qhapaq 108
    images 135
    military campaigns 98, 105, 347
    royal estates 218
    Waskhar and Atawallpa 108–13, 334
Cajamarca
    camelids 409
    ceramics 445
    dynastic war 111
    imperial expansion 97, 98, 99, 104, 327,
        333
    military conduct 343
    provincial center 362
    Spanish invasion 1, 113, 134, 179, 209,
        261, 335, 338–9, 450–9
    storage 430–1
Calancha, Antonio de la 151, 159
calendars 121, 138–9, 140–1, 154, 255,
    257–61, 264, 268, 288, 405, 473
Callachaca 213, 266

camac, camaquen, camay see vitality
camelids 39–40, 41, 42, 44, 103, 125, 145,
    183, 184, 205, 209, 278, 283, 303,
    344, 408, 409, 415, 427, 446
    alpaca 33, 40, 44–5, 52, 239, 284, 408,
        409, 429, 439
    camelid meat 239, 314, 317, 450; *ch'arki*
        (freeze-dried) 45
    guanaco 40, 44
    llama 33, *40*, 40, 44, 45, 52, 74, 125, 163,
        247, 252, 256, 262, 263, 276, 283,
        284, 288, 303, 315, 340, 344, 370,
        405, 408–9, 427, 429, 438, 439
    vicuña 40, 44, 45, 429
    see also herding, logistics, textiles
Campo de Pucará 411
canals 30, 37, 38, 44, 54, 75, 80, 82, 200,
    204, 205, 213, 214, 220, 221, 232,
    268, 274, 313–19, 381, 404, 407, 414,
    416, 435, 441, 470, 472
    see also fountains, irrigation
Canas 75, 102, 386
Canche 75, 102, 386
canon
    architecture 273, 382
    knowledge 87, 120–1, 129, 133
    objects 421
Caquia Xaquixaguana 94, 186, 215,
    219–20
    see also Juchuy Cuzco
Caranqui 105, 333, 338, 347
Castro, Cristóbal de 404, 406
Cayambe 324, 327, 337
cemeteries *see* burials
census
    flocks 408
    human 144, 147, 152, 154, 295, 353,
        356–8, 380, 396, 398
ceramics
    community production 319
    distribution of imperial Inca style 388,
        442–3
    mortuary goods 238, 307, 419, 443, 447
    mountaintop shrines 283, 286
    pre-imperial (Killke) style 80

ceramics (*continued*)
  state production 421, 430, 441–7, *444,*
    445, 446
ceremonies 247–89 *passim*
  ceremonial cycle 262–3
  farming 405–6
  marriage 303–4
  militarism 340–1
  rites of passage 301–3
Cerro Azul 100
Cerro Sechín 50
Chachapoyas
  dynastic war 111
  emperor's personal guard 337
  people 104, 105, 111, 150, 208, 325,
    337–8, 356, 373–4, 397
  rebellions 325
  region *357,* 389, 399
Challcochima 112–13, 334, 414–15, 457,
    460–1
Chan Chan 54
Chanka wars 69–70, 93–5
Chankas 62, 76, 97–8, 117 (nn. 5, 6, 8),
    264, 332
  archaeology 94–5
Charkas 103, 116 (n. 3), 337, 362, 365,
    408
chaski see messengers
chaupi (center) 42
Chaupi Ñamca 287
Chavez, Ballón 268
Chavín de Huantar 50, *60–1,* 249
chicha (*aqha,* maize beer) 54, 301, 303,
    316, 317, 320, 349, 379, 401, 404,
    438, 453
  aqllakuna 302
  and the dead 134, 185
  encounter with Spaniards 453
  offerings 205, 254, 263, 306, 405–6, 472
Chichas 103, 337, 386
Chilque 208
Chimor 54, 98, 114, 290, 423
Chimu 54
  ceramics 446
  labor service 238, 395
  language (Muchik) 293

military service 339
moon worship 255
provincial rule 54, 381–2
social hierarchy 319, 323, 360
Chincha
  ethnic group 175, 339, 382–3
  valley 66 (n. 9), 97–8, 100, 116 (n. 3),
    323, 383, 404, 406
Chinchaysuyu *3,* 155
  Cuzco *200,* 256
  provinces 102, 353
  Quechua *60*
  shrines 264, 265, 269–71, *270–1*
Chinchero 29, 79, 216, 240, 443, *446*
Chiriguanos (Guaraníes) 103, 106
Choquepukio 81–2, 95, 284
Choquequirau 226–7, *227*
Christianity, Christians 13, 249, 250, 340,
    438
  burial 459
  perspective, thought 18, 22, 24, 25, 123,
    125, 139, 141, 167 (n. 6),
    169 (nn. 15, 21), 249, 253, 288,
    459
  relics 125
  space 470
Christie, Jessica 145
chronology 27–8, *48,* 62–5
Chucuito 101, 103, 116 (n. 3), 362, 385,
    398, 408
Chunchos 101
Chupachu (Chupachos) 337, 398–400,
    430, 440
Chuquiabo (La Paz) 103, 362, 440,
    441
Chuquisaca 103
Cieza de León, Pedro 5, 19
  colonists 428
  comets 261
  diarchy 189–90
  dynastic war 109–11
  fortifications 331
  Inca history 7
  Pachakuti's ascension 94
  provincial rule, infrastructure 5, 361,
    371–2, 384

religion 249
Saqsawaman 211
storehouses 410
Yawar Waqaq 76
Ciudad de Los Reyes (Lima) 321, 335, 462
Classen, Constance 126
classes, social 290–4, 304, 349, 360, 420
    see also aristocracy, elites, peasant
        communities
climate 36–8
cloth, clothing *see* textiles
Coaque 450
Coaquiri 101
coastal provinces, provincial rule 253–5
Cobo, Bernabé 26
    census 354
    ceremonies 261, 263, 277–9, 405, 406
    clothing 428
    crime 359–60
    deities 256–7
    estates 214–15
    human origins 250
    installation of ruler 183
    land allocation 392
    military vestments 345
    mines 439
    mummies, brother-images 134, 183,
        186
    past, Inca sense of 63, 141
    resettlement 373
    shrines 260, 263–77
    social relations 290–320 *passim*
    tribute obligations 396
coca 38, 40, 42, 43, 118 (n. 8), 340, 343,
    400, 440
    estates, lands 231, 240, 243–4, 323,
        356, 371, 373, 364, 376, 381, 382,
        389, 394, 403, 404, 407, *465*
    exchange 130, 164, 304, 315–16, 320
    offerings 128, 263, 276, 283, 284, 288,
        294, 404, 472
Cochabamba 103, 104, 115, 343, 373, 374,
    384, 401–2, *402*, 411
Cochaguilla 111
Coctaca-Rodero *403*, 403
Colca valley *34*, 286, 313, 470–1

colonists (*mitmaqkuna*) 27, 85, 100, 338,
    373–7
    administration 356, 354, 386
    canal engineering 381, 404
    census 353
    decimal hierarchy 387
    ceramics 430, 445
    Colonial era disputes 469
    conduct, resistance and punishment
        359
    Cuzco 198, 374
    estates 220, 244
    frontiers 105, 327, 390
    inducements 428
    labor status 397
    military 325, 373
    mining 389
    native lords 407–8
    religious installations 384
    state farms 401–4
    weaving 430
    see also resettlement policy
comets 261
community 30–1, 293–5, 312–20,
    392–3, 470
Conde Mayta 75
conquistadores *see* Spaniards
Copacabana 243, 279, 280, *281*, 374,
    384–5
Coquimbo 102
Cora Cora *200*, 207–8
core and periphery 9, 13
Cortaderas 329–30
Cortés, Hernán 2
cosmos 124–5, 131, 201, 213, 230, 248,
    273, 280, 286, 418
    cosmopraxis 123
    origins 250–1
Costin, Cathy 423
Cotapachi 363, 401, 411
Covey, Alan 30, 80, 82, 83
Coyuctor 274, 436
crafts *see* ceramics, metallurgy, textiles,
    stone working
creation 2, 3, 73, 140, 169 (n. 15), 250–1,
    277

Creator God *see* Wiraqocha
crime 359–60
Cuntisuyu 3, 102, 118, 155
   Cuzco 176, *200*, 263
   provinces 176
   shrines 267, *269*, 270, *271*
currency 383, 474
Cusi Atachi 108
Cusi Yupanki 6, 110, 113, 196, 341, 460
Cusicancha 265, 276
Cusipampa 110–11
Cuzco 198–214, *199–200*
   archaeology 22–3
   architecture, plan 5, 198–213
   ceremonies 4–5
   Chanka wars 93–4
   core 198–201
   court 7
   divisions 77
   dynastic war resolution 112–13
   "El Cuzco" 77
   founding 72–3
   greater Cuzco 213–14
   major architecture 205–8, *207*
   meaning of name 76–8
   "New Cuzcos" 100, 132, 331, 365, 377, 384
   plazas 204–5, *206*
   politics 174–97
   pre-imperial (Killke) era 79–80
   reconstruction in imperial era 79
   setting and urban plan 201–4
   shrine network (*wak'a, zeq'e*) 26, 263–77
   siege 461–2
   Spanish capture, rule 19, 20–2, 459–61, 466–9
   Spanish first impressions 4
   spatial positioning 11–12
   temples 208–10, *209*
   see also Lower Cuzco, Upper Cuzco
Cuzco region (imperial heartland)
   pre-imperial (Killke) era 80–4, *81*

data/information recording 15, 54, 92, 131, 143, 146–61, 172 (n. 46), 470

Dean, Carolyn 136, 434
Dearborn, David S. P. 257–60, 261
death 306–8; *see also* burials
death penalty 354, 359
decimal administration 354–6, *355*
deities (gods) 51, 52, 72, 85, 87, 93, 115, 128, 131, 165, 168 (n. 13), 277, 287, 392, 404
   Inca pantheon 251–7
   see also ceremonies, Inti, Inti-Illapa, Mama-Quilla, Mamacocha, Pachacamac, sacrifices, vitality, Wiraqocha
DNA analysis 31, 156
   animal 44
   human 85, 90 (n. 16), 237–8, 286, 376
Duviols, Pierre 94, 253

earthquakes 34, 35, 44, 432
   ceremonies to counter 277
   Cuzco 79, 201
   deity (Pachacamac) 309
   Machu Picchu 236, 239
eclipses 261
economy 392–448
Einstein, Albert 119, 120, 166 (n. 1)
El Niño *see* ENSO
El Quinche 327
elites (subject) 293
   administrative responsibilities 351–6 *passim*
   burial 306–8
   military roles 322, 334, 336
   native lords (*kuraka*) 290, 293, 295, 300
   obligations, perquisites 311–12, 314, 316, 317, 319–20
   terms for nobility 291–2
   see also aristocracy, *panaqa*
emperor *see* ruler
empires, models of 9–14
ENSO (El Niño Southern Oscillation) 37, 44
environmental zones 38–42
epistemology 121, 123, 132–3
Espinoza Soriano, Waldemar 176, 373, 422

Espíritu Pampa 228, 464, *464, 467*
estates 23, 27, 29, 43, 75, 79, 83, 94, 116,
    136, 159, 162, 179, 185, 201, 213,
    307, 326, 354, 356, 362, 371, 374,
    380, 384, 422, 430, 433, 434–5, 440,
    443
  aristocratic grants 387, 407–8
  Vilcanota/Urubamba valley 214–46
Estete, Miguel de 18, 181, 370
ethnic groups (*etnías*) 6, 43, 54–6, *55, 56,*
    147, 379
  archaeological identification 299, 307,
    375–7
  ayllu 65 (n.1)
  Cuzco, Cuzco region 63, 74, 80–1, 177,
    208, 374
  emperors' wives 191
  government 176–7, 351, 353, 468
  marriage 46
  military organization 325, 334,
    336–40, 345
  resettlement 280, 315, 374–5, 379–80,
    384, 387, 390, 401
  social standing 293, 295, 356
  special labor service 397, 422
exchange
  of gifts 42, 86, 144, 243, 316, 321, 349,
    351, 356, 427, 428, 441
  of goods 315–16, 317, 318, 320, 381,
    393, 394, 421
  of labor 130, 315–16
  monetary 164, 419
  see also trade

Falcón, Francisco 20, 23, 155, 386
falcon
  brother image of ruler 135, 186
  Cuzco 78, 89–90 (n. 13)
family 177–204, 266
farming 33–4, 37–44, 311–14
  ceremonies 405–6
  Cuzco 213
  gender roles 309
  labor service 398, 399–400
  state and Sun farms 401–5
Farrington, Ian S. 162, 245 (n. 1)

Fejos, Paul 28
fishing 36
foragers 47–8
forestry 394–5
fortresses, fortifications 4, 93–4, 97, 100,
    102–6, 110, 321, 322, 324–32,
    328–9, 411
fountains 200, 205, 235, *434, 435,* 438
  see also canals, irrigation
Fresco, Antonio *55,* 388
frontiers 103–6, 225, 274, 321–31, 348,
    341, 363, 373–7, 381, 388–91

García, Alejo 106
Garcilaso de la Vega, El Inca 6
  ancestry 6, 91, 250
  census 357–8
  children 300
  cosmic order 125, 167 (n. 6)
  Cuzco 200, 206–8 *passim*
  farming and herding 311–12, 314, 392,
    405
  imperial expansion 25, 76
  influence 24–5, 174
  khipu 151–2, 157
  measurement 163, 311
  messengers 370
  mummies, icons 169 (n. 18), 185–7
  religion 250
  royal honorifics 179
  signals 231
  social relations 290, 299–300
  sources 25, 116 (n. 2)
garrisons 97, 100, 102, 103, 106, 321,
    324–32
Gasparini, Graziano 364
gender 126
  census 144, 153
  complementarity 292–3, 308–10
  identity markers 307, 420, 439
  punishment for crime 359–60
  roles 290–320 *passim*
  tasks 43, 429
genealogy 5, *71,* 136, 188–97, *190, 193,*
    194
geography 33–42

geology 35–6
Gibaja Oviedo, Arminda 29, 90
gifts *see* exchange of gifts
gods *see* deities
gold 100, 103, 145, 151, 211, 320, 359,
    363, 387, 397, 415, 442
  Atawallpa's ransom 1, 31 (n. 1), 20,
    454–8
  metallurgy 50, 436–9
  mining 36, 41, 115, 155, 374, 389, 394,
    396, 399–400, 439–41
  objects 72, 73, 74, 93, 98, 108, 134–6,
    164, 181–4 *passim*, 205, 220,
    252–4, 276, 278–9, 283, 308, 345,
    349, 405, 419, 425, 427–8, 447,
    452, 453
  shrines 265–7
  sweat of the Sun 255, 431, 436
  see also Inti
Golden Enclosure *see* Qorikancha
González Holguín, Diego 131, 291–2
Gose, Peter 190, 322
government 174–97
governors 100, 102, 108, 110, 301, 304,
    (*tokrikoq*) 353, 354, 359, 362, 410,
    430
  Spanish 449, 451, 468
grants of land 407–8
Grosboll, Sue 381
Guaman Poma de Ayala, Felipe
  aqllakuna 302
  arithmetic calculations 160
    yupana 8, 161
  Atawallpa receiving Pizarro *455*
  calendar 258–9
  chronicle, illustrations 25–6, 159, 181,
    250, 424, 426
  cycles of creation 2
  early expansions 91, 116 (n. 3),
    117 (n. 5)
  emperors *71*
  herding 315
  Huánuco Pampa 377
  khipu kamayuq 8
  military song 345
  mummy *130*

poetry 304–5
pre-imperial era 75, 76
provincial centers 238, 361
Queens *180*
social hierarchy *177*
stages of life 295–9, *298*
storehouses 412, *413*
Thupa Inka Yupanki, brothers'
    murders 195–6
Waskhar as prisoner *457*
Wayna Qhapaq 108, *346*
Guaraníes (Chiriguanos) 72, 76
Guarco 100, 324, 350 (n. 3), 384
Guasco, imperial expansion 102

Hanan Cuzco *see* Upper Cuzco
Harrison, Regina 142
Hastorf, Christine 317
Hatun ayllu 178, 188, 196
Hatun Xauxa 111–12
  bridges *371*
  ceramics 443
  household economy 423
  military 327, 335, 360
  provincial center 162, 294, 295, 319,
    362, 363, 441
  Spaniards 350 (nn. 4, 5), 414–15, 457,
    459–60
  state farms 403
  storehouses 414–15
Hatunkancha *200*, 206, *207*
Hatunmarca 294, 447
Hatunqolla *3*, 101, 362, 365, 385
Heffernan, Kenneth J. 30, 81, 283
herding 33, *40*, 40, 41, 44–5, 298, *298*,
    314–15
  state herds 408–9
Hernández Girón, Francisco 468
High Priest of the Sun (*willaq umu*) 187,
    341, 461
Howard, Rosaleen 168 (n. 12)
Huanacauri 273
  peak 61, 72, 202, 267, 303, 472
  stone icon (original ancestor) 72,
    272–3, 276, 277, 278, 341
Huancayo Alto 382

Huánuco Pampa 245, 337, 362, 365, 369, *369*, 377–81, *378*, *380*, 401
   aqllakuna, aqllawasi 301, 379
   architecture 162, 327, 343, 366, 377–81
   ceramics 304, 379
   labor assignments 400, 422, 430, 440, 443, 444
   "new Cuzco" 365, 377
   storehouses 379, 412, 414
Huánuco Project 29
Huánuco region 217, 315, 337, 389, 398, 441
Huarochirí Manuscript 286–8
Huatanay river *200*, 202, 387, 391 (n. 7)
Huaynaputina 35
human physiology 45–6
human sacrifice 50, 51, 247, 261, 276, 349
   installation, death of ruler 183–4
   itu and *qhapaq ucha* ceremonies 277–9
   mountaintop shrines 281–6, 376
   provincial shrines 279, 308
   see also offerings and sacrifices
Humboldt Current 36
Hurin Cuzco see Lower Cuzco
Hyslop, John
   ceramics 443
   measurement 163
   provincial centers 325, 362, 368
   road system 3, 12, 32, 366–72 *passim*, 381
   tampu (provincial installations) 32, 361

ideology 247–89
idols 134, 135, 176, 184, 185, 220, 249, 254, 265–6, 276, 279, 288, 341, 431, 439
Idrovo Urigüen, Jaime 388
Inca
   ethnic group 55 ("Cuzco"), 176–7
   meaning 68, 88 (n. 1)
Inca Ocllo 254
Incas by Privilege 177, *177*, 293, 356, 412
infrastructure 361–72
Ingapirca 274, 388
inheritance 27, 47, 218, 290, 311
   split inheritance 115–16, 117, 188, 218

Inka Roq'a (brother of Pachakuti) 89 (n. 8)
Inka Roq'a (sixth ruler) 6, 75–6, 89 (n. 10), 117 (nn. 5, 8), 135, 186, 197 (n. 1), 215
Inka Urqon 92–4, 117 (n. 5), *194*, 195, 197
Inka Yupanki *see* Pachakuti Inka Yupanki
Inkallajta 328–9, *328*, *330*, 436
Inkarrí 471
Inkawasi 100, 327, 331, 362, 365, 384
inspectors
   Inca 358, 412
   Spanish 26
Inti (Sun deity) 61, 252, 253–5, 256, 340
   farms and farming 404
   forms 253–4
   herds 255
   offerings 254
   storehouses 255
   temples 255, *see also* Qorikancha
   see also gold, Punchao
Inti Raymi ceremony 249, 258, 262, 266, 472, *474*
Inti-Illapa (Thunder deity) 252, 253, 254, 255–6, 276, 309
   icon 134
irrigation 34, 37, 38, 39, 41, 43, 44, 50, 80, 82, 89 (n. 7), 214, 242, 313–14, 381, 394, 395, 404, 406, 430, 471
   water allocation 313, 314
Isla la Plata 283
Isla Puná 99
itu ceremony 277

Juchuy Cuzco 83, 88 (n. 88), *217*, 217, 219
judges 358, 470
Julien, Catherine 66 (nn. 7, 9), 380, 398

kamayuq (master) 293, 418
   see also khipu kamayuq
Kañari 76, 78–80, 119, 219, 220, 259
kancha 45, 221, *222*, 366
Kendall, Ann 83, 84, 220

khipu (knot-records) 2, 17, 23, 31, 64,
149–61, *150*, *151*, 170–3 *passim*,
322, 412
census 357–8
destruction 2
information recorded 154–6
living beings 138
messengers 370
motion 131
writing 156–8
khipu kamayuq 7, 8, 104, 117 (n. 5), 124,
278, 300, 335, 415, 470, *413*
Killke era *see* pre-imperial era
kin groups *see ayllu*, *panaqa*
king *see* ruler
Kiswarkancha 208, 210
knot-records *see khipu*
knowledge, basis 121–4
Kollasuyu *3*, 102, 176, 352
Cuzco 176, *200*, 263
fortifications 327, 329–30
provincial rule 105, 353, 385–7
shrines 267, *269*, 269, *271*
Kónoj 1
Kosiba, Steven 30, 82, 223
Kunturkancha 208
kuraka see elites
Kusipata *200*, 204–5, 206

La Centinela 383
La Lone, Darrell 395
labor 199–201
capture, control 86, 87
community and household 42–4, 293,
305, 309, 311, 315–20
exchange 42–4, 130, 312, 315–16
values 55
labor service/tax 147, *150*, 164, 174, 323,
351, 354, 364, 365, 370, 379, 392,
393, 394, 410, 415
agricultural 238, 401–5
effects on households 415–17, 422–3
labor tax system overview 395–401
military 322, 336–9
pre-Inca 80
Spanish 468–9

see also ceramics, farming, herding,
mines and mining, textiles
Lake Titicaca
agriculture 313, 395
architecture 223, 308
body of water 41
ceramics 84, 286, 364, 421, 446
deities 252
imperial expansion 76, 95
languages 58, *60*, *61*, 61, 85
Inca origins 84, 85, 238, 250–1
provincial rule 369, 384–5
region 46, 65
shrines 28, 52, 253, 255, 279
societies 13, 57, 76, 92, 101, 102, 114,
176, 237, 238, 316, 325, 327, 340,
397, 407
land use, traditional 42–5
languages 58–62
Las Casas, Bartolomé de 21–2
Lee, Vincent *222*, 231, 432, 464, *467*
LeVine, Terry Y. 362, 398
Lima 321, 335, 339, 347–8, 462, 473, 475
Spanish Royal Court 415
Lima La Vieja 383
Limatambo 30, 98
llama *see* camelids
Lloq'e Yupanki 6, 74–5, 186, 188, 189
Llullaillaco 283, 284–6, *285*
logistics 343–4
Lower Cuzco (*Hurin Cuzco*)
Cuzco, layout *200*, 203
kin groups (*panaqa*) 72, 75, *177*, 112,
176, 178, 191, 196, 214, 270
origins of 188–9
Lunahuaná 99
Lupaqa 57, 323, 364
burials 308
military service 337
provincial rule 384, 407–8, 430
rebellion 101
Wiraqocha Inka 93, 95

Machu Picchu 28, 29
archaeology 79
burials 307, 376

ceramics 447
fortifications 326
royal estate 214, 215, 220, 224–40, 407
stones *127, 435*, 435
Torreón 260–1
Vilcabamba 226–8, 464
see also Bingham, Hiram
Mackey, Carol 382
MacLean, Margaret G. 233, 326
maize 50, 148, 415
  accounting 161
  calendar, ceremonial cycle 258–9, 262, 427
  cosmography 273
  Cuzco region 81
  diet 238–9, 294, 316–17
  divination 340
  environment 38–9, 40, 57, 317, 320, 394, 404
  sacred gardens 209, 213, 280, 405, 438
  shrines 267
  supplies, storage 343, 414
  see also chicha, estates, farming, offerings and sacrifices
mallki 136, 184
  see also mummy
Mama Chukuy Juypa 108
Mama Ipakura/Kura 71
Mama Kawa 75
Mama Kuka 74
Mama Oqllu 71–2
Mama Qori Willpay 75
Mama-Quilla (Mother Moon) 252, 255
Mama Rawa 71
Mama Waku 71, 73
Mamacocha (Mother of the Lakes) 252, 256, 309
mamakuna (mothers, women's order) 179, 206, 255, 301, 423. 429
  burials 307
  shrines 265
Mamancik (Our Mother) 179
Manqo Inka 460
  Cuzco 113, 201, 335, 345, 461
  festival to the Sun 249, 262–3
  High Priest 341

investiture 249, 461
military campaigns 201, 224, 335, 345, 466
Ollantaytambo 224
personal guard 338
Vilcabamba (neo-Inca state) 254, 464
Manqo Qhapaq (founding ancestor) 6, *71*, 74, 87, 180, 289
kin group (*panaqa*) 188, 189, 270
origin narratives 70–3
shrines 267
stone image, brother-image 137, 186, 341, 419
succession *190*
Temple of the Sun 210
Mapuche 183, 286, 390
Maras 29, 72, 80, 241
Marca 447
Margolies, Luise *212*, 364
Matagua 72–3
Matienzo, Juan de 23
Maukallaqta 74, 89 (n. 7)
Mayca Yupanki 112
Mayta Qhapaq 6, 75, 267
Mayta Yupanki 6, 186
measurement 161–4
men
  clothes 429
  domestic activities 316–17
  gender relations 308–10
  icons for sacrifice 427
  marriage 303–6
  military service 336–40
  punishment for crime 359–60
  rites of passage 301, 303
  stages of life 296–7, *298*
Mena, Cristóbal de 18–19, 335, 338, 349
Menzel, Dorothy 29
messengers (*chaski*) 151, 295, *298*, 370
metallurgy 50, 238, 309, 386, 403, 421, 436–9
  see also gold, silver
military 321–50
  armies, formation of 334–40
  in battle, tactics 344–8

military (*continued*)
  on campaign 341–4
  organization 332–4
  ritual 340–1
  strategy 322–5
  triumphs and reward 348–9
Milliraya 364, 374, 385, 429–30, 444
Minchançaman 54, 98
mines and mining 36, 359, 439–42
  see also gold
mit'a (labor service) *see* labor service/tax
Mitchell, William 43, 405
mitmaqkuna see colonists, resettlement
  policy
Moche *49*, 51–2, 395, 421, 437
models
  mimetic miniatures (*enqa*) 145, 436
  physical (architecture, Cuzco, terrain)
    132, 145, 198, 344, 436
Mojos 101
Molina, Cristóbal de 22, 141–2, 143–4,
    210, 248, 249, 253, 254, 263, 278–9,
    289 (n. 5), 355, 406
Montesinos, Fernando 22, 172 (n. 44),
    340–1
Moon *see* Mama-Quilla
Moore, Sally F. 360, 391 (n. 3), 398
Moquegua *61–2*, 323
Moray 29, 241–3, *242*
Morris, Craig 29
  Huánuco Project 29
  provincial centers 205, 245 (n. 5),
    307–8, 363–4, 379
  storage, storehouses 364, 410, 414
motion 129–31
mountaintop shrines 281–6, 376
Muelle, Jorge 28, 78
mullu (spondylus products) 276, 383
mummies (*mallki*) 3, 10, 129, 186, 272
  appearance 187
  burials, cemeteries 137, 184, 276, 307
  creation 135
  discovery and destruction 20, 113,
    117 (n. 6), 125, 143, 184, 194, 196,
    197 (n. 1), 215–16, 219, 220, 249,
    469, 471

marriage 192
mountaintop shrines 284–6
rulers: roles, powers, treatment 4, 134,
    136, 176, 185–7, 205, 247, 288,
    461
  worship 17, 117 (n. 6), *130*, 209, 214
  see also ancestor worship, estates,
    panaqa
Murra, John V. 16
  agriculture 163
  cloth 424
  Huánuco Project 29
  Inca economy 45, 393, 395, 408, 415,
    416, 417 (n. 3), 424
  military 337, 338
  politics 360
Murúa, Fray Martín de 22, 159, 163, 300,
    341
  cloth 427
  illustrations 181
  khipu 150–1, 155
  labor 396–7
myths, mytho-history 32, 52
  early reigns 74–6
  origin narratives 69–74, 248, 250–1,
    280, 309

Naples documents 159
Nasca lines 52
neo-Inca state 226, 254, 463–7
Nevado Ampato 293–6
Niles, Susan 213
Niñachumbi 99
Ninan Cuyuchi 107, *193*, *194*
ñusta (princess) 179

offerings and sacrifices 38, 42, 100, 112,
    144, 165, 243, 248, 249, 253–65
    passim, 270, 299–304 *passim*, 312,
    406, 443, 472
  camelids 247, 276, 405, 408, 409, 427
  ceremonial calendar 258–9
  emperor 183–5
  militarism 340–1
  shrines 265–7
  textiles 427–8, 429

see also chicha, coca, human sacrifice, Inti, mountaintop shrines

officials 125, 162, 174, 179, 187–8, 300, 304, 314, 351, 353, 358, 366, 373, 401, 429
  decimal 293, 354–6, 380
  labor service 394–401 *passim*, 422, 430
  punishment for dereliction, crime 359–60
  Spanish 20, 459, 468, 470
  weaving 297

Ollantaytambo 29, 30, 78, 79, 117 (n. 8), 214, 215, *217*, 217, 220–4, *222*, *223*, 226, 244, 326, 407, 412, 432, 433

oracles 93, 112, 128, 249, 252, 256, 279, 384, 419

oral literature 304–5

orejones ("big-ears," Inca aristocrats) 106, 181, 291–2
  emperor 181
  military service 106, 110, 337–8, 347, 350 (n. 2)
  rites of passage 303

origin narratives 42, 47, 52, 65 (n. 1), 68, 70–4, 84, 90 (n. 15), 128, 132, 136, 137, 145, 202, 228, 249, 250–1, 272, 286, 287–8, 309, 431

Ortega Morejón, Diego de 404, 406

Otavalo people 105

Owen, Bruce 442

Pacajes, ceramics 446

Pacariqtambo 72, 89 (n. 7), 208, 228, 272, 309

Pacariqtambo Quipucamayos 89 (n. 10), 104, 116 (n. 3), 117 (n. 5)

pacarisqa (origin place) 249

pacha 131–2, 138
  see also space–time

Pachacamac 27, 251, 255
  burials 308, 376
  Earth Maker deity 256, 279, 309
  oracle 249, 252, 279, 308
  Spaniards 456–7

Pachacuti Yamqui Salcamayhua, Joan de Santa Cruz 77, 94, 136, 165, 192, 250, 253

pachakuti (turning over of space–time) 2, 69, 143–4

Pachakuti Inka Yupanki 2, 5
  ascension 69, 143, 195
  brother-image 134, 186, 265
  Chankas 69–70, 93–5
  Cuzco, design 79, 198–213 *passim*, 410
  death 66 (n. 10), 183–4
  death house *see* Patallacta, Q'enqo
  estates 215, 216, 220–40
  founder of empire 23, 175
  genealogy 6, 188–9, *193*, *194*
  government, reforms 175, 188, 192
  imperial expansion 95–104
  kin group (*Hatun ayllu, iñaqa panaca*) 188, 196, 270
  military 332–3
  mummy 134, 184, 186
  names 6, 69
  narratives favoring 19–23 *passim*
  other Pachakutis 25
  resettlement 373
  shrines 265–6, 274–7 *passim*
  Sun cult 253–4

Pachamama (Earth Mother) 252, 256, 309, 472

palla 179

Palpa Ocllo 254

Pambamarca 327, *329*, 330, 363

panaqa (royal kin groups) 136
  Atawallpa's ransom 438
  ceremonies 263
  estates 214–45 *passim*, 354
  formation 177–8, 188–91, 195
  political role 187–8, 192, 196
  residences in Cuzco 203, 208, 213
  shrines 214, 265–72 *passim*

Pantillijlla 82

Paracas Peninsula 50

Pardo, Luis 28

Paria 103, 116 (n. 3), 362, 401

Paria Caca 287

Pärssinen, Martti 95, *96*, 116 (n. 4), 172

Paruro 30, 74, 80–1
Pasto people/region 105, 333, 388, 390
Patallacta
    death house of Pachakuti 134, 184, 186, 274, *275*, 276, 405
    royal estate 214, 215, 231, 238, 274
Paucartambo 244, 391 (n. 8), 407
Paullu 186, 215
Paullu Inka 113, 272, 341, 461, 468
peasant communities 293–5
Pinta 106
Pisac 214, 215, *217*, 217, 220, *221*, 307, 407
Pisco 97, 383
Pizarro, Francisco 1, 2, 20, 240, 409, 449–79 *passim*, *455*
    death 20, 468
Pizarro, Gonzalo 186, 220
Pizarro, Hernando 18, 279, 414, 468
Pizarro, Juan 462
Pizarro, Pedro 4–5, 17, 19, 182–3, 185, 219, 335, 411, 418–19, 425
Plaza Schuller, Fernando 327
Pleiades 37, 140, 233, 252, 256–7, 260–1
poetry, prayer, invocation 121, 124, 154, 165, 248, 253, 300, 304–5
politics 174–97, 360
Polo Ondegardo, Juan 20, 26, 469
    calendar 258–9
    census 354
    economy 393–4
    estate grants 407
    gifts 429
    imperial succession 89 (n. 8)
    labor service 339–40
    magistrate of Cuzco 20, 204–5, 264, 469
    mining 397, 440, 441
    mummies, brother-images 117 (n. 6), 134, 135, 184, 186–7, 220, 469
    punishment for crime 360
    religion, ritual 249, 256–7, 264, 277, 340
    road system 371
    state and Sun farms 401, 404
    storage 414, 415

warfare 327
zeq'e system 264, 289 (n. 5)
potatoes
    chuño (freeze-dried) 45
    diet 316–17
    environment 37, 39, 40, 41, 57
    storage 409, 414, 415
    see also farming
Potrero-Chaquiago 445
pottery *see* ceramics
Pratchett, Sir Terry 418, 448 (n. 2)
pre-imperial era (Killke)
    Cuzco region 80–4
    Inca society 84–8
Probanza de Qhapaq Ayllu 23
Protzen, Jean-Pierre 224, 432
provincial centers 162, *302*, 307, 325, 343, 361–6, 401, 422, 442–3
provincial system 351–91
Puerta de La Paya 28, 308, 429
Pukamarka 208, 210, 256
Pulgar Vidal, Javier 38
Puma Orqo 72, 74
Pumamarca 83
Pumpu 111, 327, 343, 362, 417 (n. 2)
Punchao 134, 136, 187, 209, 252, 253–4, 437, 459
Puquina language 58, 60, 61, 66 (n. 6), 77, 78, 85, 90 (n. 13), 159
Puruchuco-Huaquerones 137, 348, 462
pururaucas 93, 276, 273

Qari (Lupaqa lord) 93
Qasana 135, *200*, 207
Q'enqo 184, 274, *275*, *365*, 436
Qhapaq Raymi 258, 259, 262, 303
Qhapaq ayllu 23, 178, 188, 196, 218, 270
qhapaq ucha ceremony 74, 205, 266, 277–9, 283–4, 340
Qhapaq Wari 195
Qhapaq Yupanki (brother of Pachakuti) 89 (n. 8), 97–8, 332
Qhapaq Yupanki (fifth ruler) 6, *71*, 75, 89 (n. 8), 117 (n. 5), 118 (n. 8), 186, 188–9, 267

Qolla 57, 76, 299, 323, 364
  imperial expansion 93, 95, 97
  masons 223, 384, 397
  rebellion and resettlement 101–2, 208,
    325, 375
  suyu name (Qollasuyu) 176
Qorikancha (Golden Enclosure/Temple
  of the Sun) 80, 136, 145, 187,
  209–10, *209*, 253, 432, 427
  looting 461
  shrines 265–7, 272, 276
qoya see Queen
Quechua language 29, 58–62, *60*
  lingua franca 58, *60*, 334
Quechuas 76
Queen (*qoya*) 17, 155, 176, 179, *180*, 185,
  191–4, *193–4*, 247, 310
  ceremonial role in agriculture 405
  estates, holdings 218
  narratives 304–5
  role in successions 191–4, 310
Queen Mother 310
Queen's Festival 259, 263
Quillacinga 106, 124, 338
quinoa 39, 266, 267, 317, 394, 414, 415,
  434
Quinoapuquio 266, 276
Quipucamayos de Vaca de Castro 23,
  89 (n. 10), 91, 116
Quiquijana 75
Quispiguanca 216, 240–1
Quito 99, 325, 327, 335, 337, 347
  dynastic war 108–11 *passim*,
    109
  provincial rule 362, 365, 387, 407
  road system 162, 361, 367, 370
  Wayna Qhapaq 107, 169 (n. 18)
Quizo Yupanki 347–8
Quizquiz 111–13, 334, 335, 342, 409,
  459–61
Quyllor Rit'i 472–3, *473*

Raimondi, Antonio 27, 226, 366
Ramírez, Susan 77
Rappaport, Roy 122, 288

Reinhard, Johan 230, *282*, 282–4, *439*,
  474
Relaciones Geográficas de Indias (*RGI*) 26
religion 247–89
  see also ancestor worship, deities,
    offerings and sacrifices, shrines,
    temples
resettlement policy 373–7, 380–1, 382,
  384, 386, 387
  see also colonists (*mitmaqkuna*)
rites of passage 301–3, 424, 427
roads 3, 5, 10, 11–12, 14, 27, 110, 124,
  272, 329, 381, 382, 385, 386, 399,
  410, 450, *465*
  army on the road 341–3
  building, maintenance 124, 398–9, 407
  Cuzco 200, 204, 263, *367*, *368*
  distance measures 162–3
  infrastructure 366–72
  logistics 324, 325, 343–4
  Machu Picchu 225, *225*, 231
  rituals, shrines 272, 278, 280
  "roads of life" 295–9
  Wari 54
Roman y Zamora, Jerónimo 408
Rostworowski de Diez Canseco, María
  16, 189, 194–5, 291–2, 293, 320,
  397
Rowe, John 16, 25, 28, 78, 332, 370, 428,
  475 (n. 2)
  archaeology 78, 80
  census 320, 358
  chronology 62–3, 66 (nn. 7, 9)
  estates 217, 225–6
  ethnic groups 55
  imperial expansion 91–118 *passim*
  kin groups (*panaqa*) 188
  measurement 162–4
  myths 251
  religion 254, 258–9, 340
  shrines 268, 276
  stages of life 295–7
royalty *see* aristocracy, *panaqa*, Queen,
  ruler
Rucanas 117–18 (n. 8), 179, 339, 397
Ruiz, Bartolomé 449

Ruiz de Arce, Juan 18, 110, 182, 202–3, 343, 350 (n. 5), 460
ruler (emperor, king)
  appearance and deportment 179, 181–2, 427
  ascension 178, 183
  brother-image (*wawqi*) 134–6
  bulto (icon) 135, 184
  death 183–4
  estates, properties 214–45, 354, 440
  farming ceremony 405
  honorifics, titles 6, 77, 178–9
  marriage 191–4, 427
  military role 105, 115, 333
  palaces, other housing 205–8, 366
  personal guard 337–8
  political role 187–91
  role after death 185
  Sapa Inca (Unique Lord) 3, 5, 178–87
  sanctity 183
  "son of the Sun" 2, 94, 179, 197, 437
  Spanish co-rule 460–1
  succession 194–7
  see also government, *panaqa*, politics
Rumiñawi 113, 450, 458, 459, 461
Russell, Glenn 318–19

sacrifices see offerings and sacrifices; see also human sacrifice
Sadowski, Robert M. 257
Salazar, Lucy 238, 447
Salomon, Frank 65 (n. 1), 126, 136, 158–60 *passim*, 172 (n. 48), 287, 387
Samaipata 103, 274, 389, 436, 440
Sancho, Pedro 18–19
  Cuzco 4, 202–3, 213
  mummies 135–6, 185
  Saqsawaman 211
  storehouses 411
Sandefur, Elsie 317
Saño 62
Santo Tomás, Domingo de 23, 291–2
Sapa Inca 178–87
  see also ruler

Saqsawaman 28, 77, 79, 85, 210–13, *210, 212*
  building of 204
  excavations 28, 307
  fortifications 203, 327, 411
  shrines 255–6, 273, 274
  Spanish capture 341, 462
  stone working 432–3, *433*
Sarmiento, Pedro de 21
  brother-images, mummies 135, 186
  chronicle 21–2, 63
  Cuzco 203
  imperial expansion 92–118 *passim*
  Inca genealogy 71–2
  military executions 332
  narratives of early reigns 71–88 *passim*
  origin narratives 250–1
saya (provincial divisions) 353
Schaedel, Richard 87
science (and religion) 122–3, 167 (n. 1)
Segovia, Bartolomé de 22, 262–3
señorios 55, 291, 323
Serra, Mancio 253
sex, sexuality
  and kinship 126–9
  and numbers 148
  sexual relations, human 19, 52, 169 (n. 19), 300, 340, 359–60, 391 (n. 4)
  sexual relations, non-human 13, 124, 126
Sherbondy, Jeanette 214, 268
Shippee-Johnson photo expedition 31, *34, 199, 206,* 241
shrines (*waka*) 72, 74, 93, 231, 232, 248
  accounts 26
  Cuzco 207–14 *passim*, 260
  mountains 35, 281–6, 386–7, 472–3, *473*
  offerings, sacrifices 183, 253, 277–9, 281–6 *passim*, 306
  provinces 22, 279–81
  Spaniards 249
  zeqe system 263–77

silver 145, 151, 155, 359, 415
  Atawallpa's ransom 1, 31 (n. 1), 20, 454–8
  metallurgy 50, 436–9, 440–2
  mines and mining 36, 396, 399–400
  objects 74, 109, 182–5 *passim*, 205, 211, 278–9, 283–5 *passim*, 308, 318, 345, 349, 419, 425, 427, 428, 447, 452
  tears of the moon 255, 431, 436
  see also Mama-Quilla
Silverblatt, Irene 309
Siquillapucara 324
social order 358–60
social relations 290–320
Soto, Hernando de 343, 450–1, 460
space–time (*pacha*) 69, 131–2, 139–44, 164, 168 (n. 11)
Spaniards
  Colonial rule 468–71
  conquistadores 1, 5, 68, 94, 107, 114, 181, 203, 249, 307, 343, 419, 438, 449–50, 456, 463, 468–9
  Cuzco: co-rule and resistance 460–3, 467
  internal conflicts 468
  invasion 1–5, 449–60
  neo-Inca state, relations 463–7
  see also Christianity, languages, Pizarro, F., H., J., and P., time frames, Toledo, written sources
Spanish language orthography 62
spondylus shell 49, 115, 145, 205, 279, 283, 284, 348, 363, 364, 387, 425, *439*
Spurling, Geoffrey E. 430
Squier, Ephraim George 27, 78, 280
stages of life 295–304, *298*
Stone of Sayhuite 273–4, *273*, 436
stone working 431–6
storage, storehouses 202, 220, 241, 255, 308, 313, 317, 425, 427, 443
  state storage facilities 5, 179, 213, 324, 325, 343, 361–3, 364, 379, 382, 390, 401–5 *passim*, 409–15, *412*, *413*, 430, 450

storehouse (*qollqa*, Pleiades) constellation 252
Sun *see* Inti
Susurpuquio 266, 274
suyu 3, 175–6, 203, *368*

Taki Onqoy (Dancing Sickness) 22, 143–4, 471
Tambo Colorado 362, *383*
tampu see provincial centers
Tarapacá 103, 441
Tarqo Waman 89 (n. 8), *190*
Tawantinsuyu 1, 3, 3, 3, 6, 7, 9, 34, 44, 57, 132, 175–6, 468, 472
taxation, response to 416
Temple of the Sun *see* Qorikancha
temples, Cuzco 208–10
  see also Qorikancha (Temple of the Sun)
terracing 30, 40, 78, 80, 82, 287, 381, 394, *403*, 403, 431
  carved stones 145
  Colca valley *34*, 34, 313, 470–1
  Cuzco and environs 198, 200, 202, 204–6 *passim*, *206*, 208, 211, 212, 213
  estates 162, 219, 220–36 *passim*, *221*, *242*, 326
  shrines 266, 267, 274, 276, 280
  Wari 395
textiles 17, 45, 50, 52, 86, 131, 136, 148, 149, 276, 284, 319, 343, 348, 364, 376, 382, 385, 393, 401, 420, 421–6, 443
  arithmetic 148, 160, 310
  awasqa (common cloth) 425, 427
  cloth 3, 5, 45, 134, 155, 166, 181, 183, 211, 236, 278, 284, 299, 301, 316, 317, 318, 340, 347, 356, 359, 383, 393, 397, 398, 415, 418, 421, 423, 427–8, 440
  clothing 42, 98, 111, 113, 136, 179, 181–4 *passim*, 187, 211, 263, 272, 283, 284, 299, 301, 306, 314, 318, 343, 345, 347, 359, 374, 408, 410, 411, 428–9, 439, 442, 454

textiles (*continued*)
  qompi (fine, tapestry weave) 83, 340,
    359, 425, *426*, 427, 428, 429, 443,
    445
  weaving 30, 131, 236, 295, 300–1,
    308–9, 316–18, 379, 399, 409,
    421, 422–3, 429–31, 445
Thomas, Brooke 46
Thompson, Donald 29
Throne of the Inca 212, *212*, 265, 273
Thunder *see* Inti-Illapa
Thupa Amaru 21, 254, 456, 467
Thupa Inka Yupanki 5, 6
  ascension 195–6
  brother-image 186
  death 66 (n. 10), 195
  decimal administration 354
  estates, holdings 208, 216–19, 374,
    384, 440, 443
  frontiers 389
  imperial expansion 94–104, *96*,
    116–18 (nn. 4, 5, 8)
  infrastructure 361
  kin group (*panaqa*: Qhapaq ayllu) 21,
    23, 155, 178, 188, 196, 197
  marriage 179, 192, 196
  military command 333, 335
  mummy (burnt) 113, 186, 247
  Pachacamac 279
  personal guard 337, 350 (n. 1)
  Saqsawaman 204, 210
  shrines 270, 276
  storehouses 412, *413*
  succession crisis 195–6
  voyage to Pacific 99
Thupa Wallpa 459–60
Tiahuanaco 52–4, 385
  agriculture 395
  architecture 223, 280
  colonies 379, 395
  creation myths 251
  Creator God 251
  decline 280
  Gateway of the Sun 52, *53*, 254
  provincial rule (Inca) 362
  statuary 140, 251

Ticlio 40
time *see* space–time
time frames 62–5
Tipón 29, 79, 215, 220
tirakuna (sacred places) 41
Tired Stone (Collaconcho) 87, 213, 265,
    274
Titu Kusi Yupanki 24, 31, (n. 2), 452–4,
    464, 466–7
Tocoripuquiu 267, 274
Toledo, Viceroy Francisco de 18, 181
  neo-Inca state 226, 254, 467
  reforms 26, 469–70
  religion 249
  written accounts 20–1, 24, 203
Torreón 232–4, *233–4*, 260–1
trade, traders 315, 318, 320
Tucumán 104–5, 386, 390
Túcume 283, 382–3
Tullumayo river 77, *200*, 203, 433
Tumbes 113, 182, 450
Tumipampa *3*
  descendant kin group of Wayna
    Qhapaq 387
  dynastic war between Waskhar and
    Atawallpa 108–10, *109*, 332–3
  imperial capital 27, 41, 105, 107, 135,
    198, 241, 352, 361, 387–8
  military base 105–6, 347
  provincial rule 343, 361–2, 365
Tunanmarca 324

Uhle, Max 27–8, 78
UNESCO 29, 203, 239, 246 (n. 11)
Ungará 100, 331
Upper Cuzco (*Hanan Cuzco*)
  Cuzco, layout *200*, 203
  kin groups (*panaqa*) 72, 75, 108, 176,
    177, 178, 195, 196, 214, 270
  origins of 188–9
Upper Mantaro valley 105
  agricultural productivity 57, 317
  bridges *371*, 371
  ceramics 447
  garrisons 339
  grants of land 407

household economy 317–19
imperial expansion 324, 335
metallurgy 442
military service 337
mortuary practices 308
settlement patterns 294
state farms 403
storage 411, 414–15
Urton, Gary
   khipu (knot-records) 149–60, *149, 150,*
     170–3
   measurement 162–3
   Quechua cosmology 472
   Quechua numbers 131, 147–9, 299
   violation of principles of order
     168 (n. 10)
Urubamba (town) *129*
Urubamba river, valley 27, 28, 43,
   117 (n. 8), 162, 202, 214–21 *passim,*
   224, 228, 230–1, 240, 246 (n. 9), 326,
   389, 407, *412,* 412, 464, 465
Urus, *uru* (worm) 13, 397
Uturunku Achachi 101–2

Vaca de Castro Cavellero, Cristobal 23,
   361
Valcárcel, Luis 28, 78, 80, 211, 307
Valdivia (Chile) 390
Valdivia, Pedro de 23
Valencia Zagarra, Alfredo 29, 90, 235
Valera, Blas 20, 22, 25, 91, 117 (n. 5), 151,
   157, 159, 359–60
Valverde, Vicente de 452, *455*
Van de Guchte, Maarten 268, 274
Verano, John 237–8
Vilcabamba 18, 21, 24, 226–7, 231, 254,
   371, 407, 436, 452, 464–7, *464,*
   466–7
Vilcanota (regional deity) 252
Vilcanota river, valley 75, 80, 82, 83, 131,
   202, 214–15, *217,* 219, 230,
   246 (n. 9), 326, 465
Vilcaswaman *3,* 326
vitality 124, 125–6, 132–8, 142, 145, 156,
   164, 165, 178, 249, 273, 420, 421
   camac (beings that confer vitality) 125

camaquen (vitality) 125–6, 132, 134,
   145, 148
Camay (month) 258
camay (power to confer vitality)
   137–8, 145, 156
volcano 35, 284

wak'a see shrines
Wallerstein, Immanuel 10
Wallpaya 218
Waman Achachi 104
wamani *see apu*
Wamanmarka 244
Wanka Awki 110–12
Wankas 57, 338, 468
warfare 50, 56–7, 87–8, 111, 114, 321–50
Wari 9, 52–4, 65 (n. 5), 74, 85, 150, 369,
   373, 395, 410
Waskhar 6
   ascension 192–3
   behavior 196
   capture and death 107, *194,* 456, *457*
   dynastic war against Atawallpa 2,
     107–13, 143, 192
   estates, palaces 116, 206–8, 216–19,
     276, 380
   imperial expansion *96,* 110–11
   kin group 2, 21, 196–7, 341
   marriage 191
   mother 192–3
   names 6, 77
   personal guard 337–8
   Spanish invaders 107
Wat'a 82
wawqi see brother-image
Wayna Qhapaq 5, 6
   ascension 115, 195–6
   brother-images, icons 134, 135, 169
   death (and comet) 66 (n. 10), 135, 261,
     151–4, 462
   estates 116, 216, 218–19, 240–4, 276,
     430
   High Priest 187
   imperial expansion 98, 99, 104–7, 327,
     333, 342, 366
   marriage 191

Wayna Qhapaq (*continued*)
    mummy 135–6, 185–6, 192,
        197 (n. 1), 272
    names 6, 77
    palaces in Cuzco 201, 207
    panaqa 197
    personal guard 192, 337–9
    resettlement policy 374, 422, 430
    shrines 265, 276
    state farms 384, 402
    succession 107, 115
    Tumipampa 196, 387
    warfare *346*, 347
    weavers 374, 430
weapons
    Andean/Inca 183, 261, 322, 334, 336,
        343–9, 381, 399–400, 405,
        420–1, 447, 454, 471
    Spanish 462–3
Wernke, Steven 470–1
Wiener, Charles 27, 78, 280
Wiraqocha (Creator God) 252
    creation narratives 72, 169 (n. 15),
        250–3, 280
    gender 128, 309
    glosses 133–4, 168 (n. 13), 289 (n. 1)
    militarism 340–1
    poetry 165
    sacrifices and prayers to 183, 278, 461
    temples 210, 404
    vitality 133
Wiraqocha Inka 6
    Chanka wars 93–4
    conquests 23, 76, 87, 92–3,
        116–17 (nn. 3, 4, 5), 323
    estates, holdings 208, 214–17, 219–20
    kin group (*panaqa*) 188–9, 266, *434*
    mummy and icon 186, 220
    narratives concerning 23
    succession crises 5, 69, 76, 92–4,
        193–4, 195
    Sun cult 253

women
    birth and childcare 299–300
    burials 306–7, 308, 424, 428
    clothes 419, 427–9, 442
    descent 309
    estates, holdings 218
    human sacrifice 308
    icons for sacrifice 427
    labor roles 43, 148, 309, 312, 316–17,
        320, 399–400, 409, 423, 440
    Machu Picchu 236–7
    marriage 304, 376, 472
    military campaigns 335, 342, 344
    mourning 306
    mummies 187
    political power 191–4
    portage 344, 350 (nn. 4, 5)
    punishment for crime 359–60
    rape, capture 322, 349, 359
    rites of passage 301–3
    royalty 91–3
    stages of life 295–9, *298*
    textiles, weaving 409, 421–3, 429
    widows, divorcees 306, 358
    see also aqllakuna, gender, *mamakuna*,
        ñusta, palla, Queen
worldview 123
Wright, Ken 235, 241, 243
written sources 17–27
    inspections, church, court records
        26–7
    native ancestry 23–6
    Spanish chronicles 19–23, 26

Xauxa 105, 317, 324
Xérez, Francisco de 18–19, 261, 430, 456

Yacha 337, 398
Yamque Yupanki 98, 100. 102
yanakuna (lifelong servants) 356, 397,
    401, 408
Yanamarca valley 112, 334

Yasca 106, 341

Yawar Waqaq 6, *71*, 76, 214

Yucay 29, 79, 216, 218–19, 240–1, 339, 430

yupana (counting board) *8*, 160–1

Yupanque, Doña Angelina (Cuxirimay Ocllo) 19–20

Zárate, Augustín de 23, 342, 409, 456

zeqè system 207, 263–77

Zinchi Roq'a 6, 72, 74, 186, 267

Ziółkowski, Mariusz S. 195, 257, 261

Zuidema, R. Tom 189–91, 260, 268, 289 (n. 3)

Zuries 103